Barnstead New Hampshire Vital Records 1887-2000

❦

Richard P. Roberts

HERITAGE BOOKS
2009

HERITAGE BOOKS
AN IMPRINT OF HERITAGE BOOKS, INC.

Books, CDs, and more—Worldwide

For our listing of thousands of titles see our website at
www.HeritageBooks.com

Published 2009 by
HERITAGE BOOKS, INC.
Publishing Division
100 Railroad Ave. #104
Westminster, Maryland 21157

Copyright © 2001 Richard P. Roberts

All rights reserved. No part of this book may be reproduced or transmitted in any form or by any means, electronic or mechanical, including photocopying, recording or by any information storage and retrieval system without written permission from the author, except for the inclusion of brief quotations in a review.

International Standard Book Numbers
Paperbound: 978-0-7884-1991-1
Clothbound: 978-0-7884-8219-9

CONTENTS

Introduction	1
Births	4
Marriages	155
Brides' Names	317
Deaths	354

INTRODUCTION

Early vital records of many New Hampshire towns can be located either through the State's Vital Records Department or on microfilms made available through LDS Family History Centers. Some, however, have been lost or are inaccessible for various reasons. A valuable, but time-consuming, source of information for events occurring after 1886 is the vital statistics which are provided in a section of the Annual Town Reports of many New Hampshire towns. Many of these town reports have been collected at the New Hampshire State Library in Concord, as well as more local repositories.

The amount of information published in these Annual Town Reports varies tremendously over time. Early records are far more detailed and comprehensive. Recent records are rather cursory, but issues of confidentiality and sensitivity to the privacy of those residents still living offsets the lack of information of genealogical value.

While the information provided is often very helpful, one must remember that it is not fool-proof or universally accurate, nor is it the primary source or the actual vital record itself. The fact that much of the data is self-reported suggests that it is reliable. However, errors in transcription, spelling (particularly with respect to French-Canadian and European families), and printing often are obvious. In addition, there may be, for example, two children listed as the third child of a particular couple, or the mother's maiden name, age or place of birth differs or is inconsistent from one entry to another. It is also important to note that a birth, marriage or death may have been reported in another town although the subject resided in Barnstead, or the entry may not have been made in the first place.

Despite these shortcomings, the information contained in the Annual Town Reports can be a valuable tool for the genealogist. Marriage and death records from the late 1800's often identify parents who were married nearly a century before. Finally, those families that have remained in Barnstead or adjacent towns for several generations can be traced and connected to the present.

Births - To the extent the information is available, the entries in the list of births are given as follows: child's name; date of birth; place of birth (Barnstead, unless otherwise indicated); the number of children in the family; father's name, place of birth, age and occupation; and the mother's maiden name, age and place of birth. The residence of the parents is sometimes given when it is shown as other than Barnstead. As noted above, the amount of information in earlier records is substantially greater than in more recent years. The births for the year 1995 were not published.

At times, the given names of many children are missing from the early reports. In this case, the sex of the child is given and they are listed chronologically at the beginning of the surname heading. On occasion, the child's name can be determined from marriage or death records, as well as secondary sources. These names are shown in brackets where available.

Marriages - To the extent the information is available, the entries in the list of marriages follow this format: groom's name; groom's residence; bride's name; brides residence; date of marriage; place of marriage (Barnstead, unless otherwise indicated, although no place of marriage is given in recent years); H, signifying husband's information, and W, signifying wife's information, each in the following order - age, occupation, number of the marriage (if other than first), father's name, father's place of birth, father's occupation, mother's

BIRTHS

ACKERMAN,
son, b. 9/5/1887; fourth; Peter P. Ackerman (farmer, 33, Alexandria) and Ida B. Berry (31, Concord)
daughter, b. 12/6/1887; first; Arthur Ackerman (farmer, 25, Alexandria) and Clara E. Berry (27, Barnstead)
daughter, b. 4/29/1899; fourth; Arthur Ackerman (farmer) and Clara Berry

ADAMS,
Aimee Elizabeth, b. 10/29/1975 in Concord; James Henry Adams (NH) and Kristine Barbara Jenisck (NH)
Stephanie Marie, b. 12/1/1988 in Concord; Michael Christian Adams and Sharon Marie Briggs

AIKENS,
Percy G., b. 5/21/1890; sixth; David L. Aikens (carpenter, Barnstead) and [Annie Shaw] (Concord) (1892)

ALDEN,
John Cross, b. 12/20/1924; first; Arthur Wheeler Alden (Westwood, MA) and Marguerite Chesley Hill (Lynn, MA)

ALLARD,
Bert Edward, Jr., b. 5/28/1975 in Rochester; Bert Edward Allard (MA) and Cynthia May Brown (MA)

ALLEN,
Christopher Michael, b. 11/21/1990 in Manchester; Keith Evan Allen and Janet Ruth Allen
Gwenn Michelle, b. 5/31/1973 in Concord; Wayne Edward Allen (MA) and Susan Jane Quinn (MA); residence - Ctr. Barnstead

ALLEY,
daughter, b. 7/26/1888; third; Richard Alley (shoemaker, Lynn, MA) and Angie Nichols (Lynn, MA)
son, b. 11/4/1889; fourth; Richard E. Alley (shoemaker, Lynn, MA) and Angie Nichols (Dixmont, ME)
son [Robert], b. 12/5/1891; fifth; Richard E. Alley (shoemaker, Lynn, MA) and Angie Nichols (Dixmont, ME)
son, b. 11/26/1894; sixth; Richard Alley (shoemaker, 35) and Angie Nichols (30, Dixmont, ME)

child, b. 6/6/1897; seventh; Richard Alley (shoemaker, Lynn, MA)
and Angie Nichols (Lynn, MA)
son, b. 11/30/1899; seventh; Richard E. Alley (shoemaker,
Philadelphia, PA) and Angie Nichols (Lynn, MA)
son, b. 1/25/1902; ninth; Richard E. Alley (shoemaker, 42, Lynn,
MA) and Angie Nichols (38, Dixmont, ME)

ALLISON,
Lora Anne, b. 8/19/1983 in Concord; Gene William Allison and
Suzanne Claire Catelli
Sara Beth, b. 7/27/1979 in Concord; Gene William Allison and
Suzanne Claire Catelli

AMELL,
Marvin H., b. 1/2/1958 in Laconia; Darrel L. Amell and Lois E.
Sansouci

AMES,
Marjorie Esther, b. 2/26/1935 in Wolfeboro; first; Irving M. Ames
(farmer) and Harriet Richardson

ANDERSON,
Lennas H., b. 12/28/1922; second; August N. Anderson (farmer,
Sweden) and Edith Anderson (Sweden)

ANDY,
Jacob Kingsbury, b. 12/8/1972 in Concord; Gary Andy (PA) and
Mary Etta Kingsbury (CT)

ANTONUCCI,
Hayley Johanna, b. 1/3/2000 in Concord; Anthony Antonucci and
Kniertje Antonucci

ARCHAMBAULT,
Dakota Elizabeth, b. 3/12/1999 in Concord; Brad Archambault and
Kelly Archambault

ARCHIBALD,
Hannah Tegan, b. 4/12/1994 in Concord; Peter Ellis Archibald, Jr.
and Liisa Reiman

Madison Grey, b. 10/12/1996 in Concord; Peter Ellis Archibald, Jr. and Liisa Reiman

ARMSTRONG,
son [Darrell], b. 9/25/1905; second; James Armstrong (shoemaker, 27, Portsmouth) and Alma Shackford (26, Barnstead)
Jane C., b. 1/6/1948 in Center Barnstead; John C. Armstrong and Lucille K. MacDonald (1954)
Margaret, b. 5/12/1901; first; James Armstrong (shoemaker, 23, Portsmouth) and Elma Shackford (22, Barnstead)
Tom, b. 7/27/1910; third; James W. Armstrong (morocco worker, 32, Portsmouth) and Elma Shackford (31, Barnstead)

ASHLEY,
Arnold Maxfield, b. 10/14/1927; second; I. Adelbert Ashley (Rumney) and Alice Maxfield (Barnstead)
Ryan Scott, b. 12/26/1992 in Concord; Brad Scott Ashley and Sherry Ann Giddis

ATKINS,
Aaron Jack, b. 1/15/1988 in Derry; Alvin Ronald Atkins and Patricia Ann Towle
Arielle Lauren, b. 8/21/1991 in Derry; Alvin Ronald Atkins and Patricia Ann Atkins
Austin Ryan, b. 2/3/1990 in Derry; Alvin Ronald Atkins and Patricia Ann Towle

ATWELL,
Carol J., b. 12/29/1930; second; Ralph B. Atwell (farmer) and Louise Wilhelm

AUDET,
Adam Henry, b. 5/15/1989 in Concord; Henry Joseph Audet and Margaret Ann Walters
Connor Graeme, b. 5/21/1997 in Concord; Todd C. Audet and Kelly-Jo A. Moore

AVERY,
daughter, b. 3/18/1889; fourth; John Avery (farmer, Strafford) and Mary Avery (New Durham)

Minnie A., b. 6/23/1887; second; John Avery (farmer, 44, Barnstead) and Mary A. Avery (36, Milton) (1893)

AYERS,
daughter, b. 9/6/1893; first; Charles Ayers (salesman, 27, Barnstead) and Nellie Jenkins (25, Barnstead); residence – Pittsfield

BAAS,
Janet Elizabeth, b. 7/8/1987 in Concord; John Charles Baas, III and Janet Coughlin

BABB,
Harold, b. 1/13/1894; second; William Babb (shoemaker, 29, Barnstead) and Mildred Nichols (27, Lynn, MA)

BAGLEY,
Nicholas Allen, b. 9/24/1989 in Concord; James Bryan Bagley and Katherine McGill

BAILEY,
Brittany Anne Rowles, b. 10/22/1991 in Exeter; Peter James John Bailey and Kathleen Mary Brown
Chelsea Jane, b. 10/29/1980 in Concord; Gordon Allan Bailey and Debra Jane Scamman
Tyler Gordon, b. 9/17/1982 in Concord; Gordon Allan Bailey and Debra Jane Scamman

BAIRD,
Andrew John, b. 11/3/1972 in Concord; James Clyde Baird (AL) and Roberta Klenck (NJ)

BAKER,
daughter, b. 12/25/1914; first; Edward I. Baker (farmer, 27, NY) and Hazel E. Bess (26, NY)

BANKS,
Linda Mary, b. 1/19/1946 in Concord; third; Earl A. Banks (plumber) and Florence B. Taylor

BARKER,
Katherine H., b. 11/27/1955 in Rochester; John H. Barker (lineman) and Eileen E. Rasch

BARRETT,
stillborn son, b. 5/5/1913; first; Daniel L. Barrett (barber, 39, Antrim) and Addie M. Downs (28, Belmont)
Briana Rose, b. 7/1/1999 in Concord; Steven Barrett and Amy Barrett

BARTELS,
Allison Mae, b. 7/15/1993 in Rochester; Wellington Phillips Bartels, IV and Jennifer Rita Guay
Elizabeth Sarah, b. 7/18/1989 in Concord; Wellington Phillips Bartels, IV and Jennifer Rita Guay

BARTON [see O'Barton],
son, b. 11/25/1901; seventh; Ezra Barton (farmer, 32, Plattsburgh, NY) and Virginia Dupuires (27, Hooksett)
son, b. 2/22/1904; first; Edward O. Barton (laborer, 26, Canada) and Jennie Dailey (18, Gilmanton)

BASHA,
John Robert, b. 7/23/1917; first; John Lewis Basha (farmer, Goffstown) and Emma G. Lavoie (Westville)

BEAN,
daughter, b. 12/21/1901; third; Leslie E. Bean (merchant, 31, Canada) and Clara Carbee (33, Canada)

BEANE,
Susan, b. 2/18/1954 in Milton, MA; Harry L. Beane (asst. manager) and Margaret J. Dixon

BEBO,
son [Nelson F.], b. 5/27/1909; first; Felix Bebo (laborer, 31, Montreal, Canada) and Harriett Gray (17, Chichester)
Jerry Frank, b. 5/12/1933; first; Nelson Bebo (clerk) and Dorothy Wilson

BECK,
Judith Anne Marie, b. 5/24/1997 in Concord; William H. Beck and Jennifer A. Schultz

BEIJER,
Gabrielle Simone, b. 8/23/1998 in Concord; Alexander Beijer and Diane Beijer

BELL,
Ruth Q., b. 3/30/1907; fifth; George W. Bell (farmer, 30, Pleasant Valley, NY) and Alice M. Littlefield (29, Winchester, MA)
Warren V., b. 3/30/1907; fourth; George W. Bell (farmer, 30, Pleasant Valley, NY) and Alice M. Littlefield (29, Winchester, MA)

BELVILLE,
Gerald C., b. 8/9/1960 in Rochester; fifth; George W. Belville (equipment operator, Mansfield, MA) and Alison E. Arns (No. Attleboro, MA)

BENNETT,
Alex Michael, b. 3/18/1997 in Concord; Michael S. Bennett and Debra L. Provencal
Caitlin Elizabeth, b. 9/13/1987 in Concord; Robert Royce Bennett and Katherine Catozella
Cheryl E., b. 4/15/1966 in Concord; fifth; Roland A. Bennett (Portsmouth) and Barbara A. Fox (New London, CT)
Courtney Alyssa, b. 9/1/1993 in Concord; Michael Scott Bennett and Debra Lynn Provencal

BERCHMER,
Raymond, b. 2/8/1918; first; William H. Berchmer (weaver, Germany) and Mertta Sanborn (Chichester)

BERGERON,
Bryce Herve, b. 6/9/1999 in Concord; Herve Bergeron and Brenda Bergeron
James Alfred Osgood, Jr., b. 5/16/1997 in Concord; James Alfred Bergeron and Cheryl Z. Erff
Joseph William Norman, b. 8/6/1929; seventh; Emile Bergeron (Canada) and Marie C. Larouche (Canada)

Noel Amarisa, b. 2/27/2000 in Concord; James Bergeron and
   Cheryl Bergeron

BERRY,
daughter [Ina P.], b. 9/30/1888; first; Stephen Berry (farmer,
   Barnstead) and Emma ----- (Strafford)
daughter, b. 1/14/1891; first; Fred Berry (farmer, Barnstead) (1892)
child [Lorraine Blanche], b. 7/19/1939; fifth; Arthur Berry (cutter)
   and Bessie Gray
Christon Einar, b. 2/11/1980 in Concord; James Nathan Berry and
   Carole Ann Johnson
Daniel Frank, Jr., b. 6/17/1971 in Laconia; Daniel Frank Berry (NH)
   and Barbara Lee Heath (NH)
Evelyn Blanche, b. 1/3/1943; second; John M. Berry (lumberman)
   and Shirley M. Otis
Jodi Lee, b. 2/18/1975 in Laconia; Daniel Frank Berry (NH) and
   Barbara Lee Heath (NH)
Michael Wallace, b. 2/11/1980 in Concord; James Nathan Berry
   and Carole Ann Johnson

BERUBEE,
Rodney John, b. 12/1/1980 in Concord; Douglas Berubee and
   Patricia June Smith

BICKFORD,
daughter, b. 1/14/1895; Albert A. Bickford (farmer, Newton) and
   Ella F. Peabody (Lowell, MA)
Belynda R., b. 2/28/1967 in Concord; fourth; Richard O. Bickford
   (machinist, Barnstead) and Hulda A. Hast (Springfield, MA)
Carrie L., b. 11/24/1965 in Concord; second; Richard O. Bickford
   (Barnstead) and Hulde A. Hast (Springfield, MA)
Marilyn Jean, b. 6/14/1940 in Pittsfield; first; Herbert S. Bickford
   (carpenter) and Lillian M. Smith
Richard Oliver, b. 10/19/1939; second; Clarence H. Bickford
   (carpenter) and Vera Hill

BILY,
Dorothy E., b. 5/6/1935; second; Joseph Bily (mechanic) and Ruth
   Vermand

BIXBY,
son, b. 11/12/1886; fifth; William H. Bixby (shoemaker, Manchester) and Marrith ----- (Strafford) (1888)

BLACK,
son [Richard], b. 12/4/1914; second; Herbert F. Black (farmer, 19, Boston, MA) and Marguerite Emerson (18, Barnstead)
Harlan P., b. 4/9/1916; third; Herbert F. Black (farmer, Boston, MA) and Marguerite Emerson (Barnstead)
James Norman, b. 7/6/1940 in Pittsfield; Norman E. Black (laborer) and Lewanie A. Brousseau
Norman E., b. 3/20/1918; third; Herbert F. Black (farmer, Boston, MA) and Marguerite Emerson (Barnstead)

BLACKEY,
Jonathan William, b. 2/2/1988 in Concord; Dennis Sammy Blackey and Donna Marie Komisarek
Michelle Anne, b. 4/20/1986 in Concord; Dennis Sammy Blackey and Donna Marie Komisarek

BLAISDELL,
John Samuel, b. 9/13/1973 in Concord; Willard John Blaisdell (NH) and Linda Lee Greenfield (NH)

BLAMBACH,
George, b. 8/7/1914; second; Paul Blambach (weaver, 43, Germany) and Addie Spalulingu (25, Germany)

BOMASTER,
Daniel Keegan, b. 12/2/1998 in Rochester; Robert Bomaster and Paula Bomaster

BOOTH,
Catherine Kelley, b. 1/25/1988 in Rochester; Jonathan Gregory Booth and Nancy Jean Kolodzinski

BORDEAU [see Boudreau],
daughter, b. 12/25/1907; first; Lester Bordeau (woodman, 34, Canada) and Lillian Florie (18, Pittsfield)

BORGMAN,
Aaron Michael, b. 12/11/1987 in Concord; Gary Michael Borgman and Susan Mary Trotter
Nathan Zimri, b. 2/11/1986 in Nashua; Gary Michael Borgman and Susan Mary Trotter

BORREGO-NARVAEZ,
Jose Armando, Jr., b. 3/10/1990 in Manchester; Jose Armando Borrego-Narvaez, Sr. and Pamela Jean Dicey

BOSTON,
Brandi Lyn, b. 2/19/1990 in Hanover; Robert Alan Boston and Mary Ann Woods
Melissa Ann, b. 7/26/1971 in Concord; Stuart Lee Boston (ME) and Harriet Ann Young (NH)
Robert A., b. 4/12/1965 in Concord; second; Stuart L. Boston (Kittery, ME) and Harriet A. Young (Strafford); residence - Ctr. Barnstead
Stuart L., Jr., b. 5/15/1963 in Concord; first; Stuart L. Boston, Sr. (Kittery, ME) and Harriet A. Young (Strafford); residence - Ctr. Barnstead

BOUDEREAU [see Boudreau],
son [Arthur], b. 7/6/1908; third; Albert Boudereau (laborer, 20, Canada) and Clara Oshier (20, Pittsfield)

BOUDREAU [see Bordeau, Boudereau],
son, b. 8/15/1909; second; Albert Boudreau (laborer, 21, Canada) and Carrie Oshier (21, Suncook)
Alva D., b. 11/27/1909; second; Lister Boudreau (laborer, 39, Canada) and Lillian Frowley (20, Lakeport)

BOURGEOIS,
Stephanie Lynn, b. 10/3/1980 in Concord; Denis Henry Bourgeois and Lynn S. Yianakopolos

BOUSQUET,
Jeffrey Judson, Jr., b. 9/9/1994 in Concord; Jeffrey Judson Bousquet and Staci Lynn Clark
Melanie Jayne, b. 12/11/1977 in Concord; Dennis Wales Bousquet (NH) and Brenda-Lee Pratt (NH); residence - Ctr. Barnstead

Paul Judson, Jr., b. 10/24/1968 in Concord; Paul Judson Bousquet, Sr. (NH) and Anita Linda Clement (ME)

BOUTSIANIS,
Nicholas Paul, b. 7/13/1990 in Concord; Richard Joseph Boutsianis and Wendy Jean Attanasio

BOVA,
Jessica Marie, b. 9/10/1992 in Concord; Bruce Kendall Bova and Jeannie Marie Moody

BOWEN,
Denys Tolo, b. 6/19/1998 in Concord; David Bowen and Rosario Bowen
Paul W., b. 10/25/1967 in Concord; fifth; Burton M. Bowen (construction, Rochester) and Geraldine F. Corson (Ctr. Barnstead)
Tammy L., b. 10/19/1963 in Concord; fourth; Burton M. Bowen (Rochester) and Geraldine F. Corson (Ctr. Barnstead); residence - Ctr. Barnstead

BOYD,
Amy Kathleen, b. 11/2/1970 in Concord; Rodney Thomas Boyd (NY) and Brenda Joyce Riel (NH)
Doris Adelaide, b. 2/15/1949; first; Randolph Leslie Boyd, Jr. (fisherman) and Emma Jane Gray
Grace Elizabeth, b. 12/5/1919; first; William Boyd (teacher, Norwich, CT) and Grace Elizabeth Berry (Barnstead)
Mary Louise, b. 9/13/1926; third; William Boyd (Manchester) and Grace E. Berry (Barnstead)
Randolph L., Jr., b. 5/5/1953 in Concord; third; Randolph L. Boyd (unemployed) and Emma J. Gray
Ruth Elaine, b. 5/3/1951 in Pittsfield; second; Randolph L. Boyd (woodsman) and Emma J. Gray
William, Jr., b. 2/3/1921; second; William Boyd (teacher, Norwich, CT) and Grace Elizabeth Berry (Barnstead)

BRADY,
son [Albert S.], b. 12/6/1901; fourth; John F. Brady (salesman, 39, Lawrence, MA) and Alice Davis (27, Lynn, MA)

BRASSAW,
Ricky A., b. 7/14/1962 in Concord; third; Wallace G. Brassaw (Hillsboro) and Mary A. Sullivan (Farmington); residence - Ctr. Barnstead

BRENNAN,
Danielle Twila, b. 3/21/1996 in Concord; Richard Sheffield Brennan and Diana Strobel
Stephanie Anne, b. 11/26/1999 in Concord; Robert Brennan and Patricia Brennan

BRETON,
Taryn Ann, b. 8/7/2000 in Concord; Normand Breton and Janet Breton

BREWSTER,
John M., b. 9/16/1892; second; Mark W. Brewster (farmer, Barnstead) and Annie E. Merrill (Barnstead)
John Merrill, Jr., b. 6/29/1935 in Pittsfield; first; John M. Brewster (farmer) and L. Gladys Call
Verna Harriet, b. 8/1/1939; second; John M. Brewster (farmer) and L. Gladys Call

BRICKNER,
Alex Michael, b. 6/27/1998 in Concord; Adam Brickner and Heather Brickner

BRIGHAM,
Joshua Dean, b. 10/30/1985 in Concord; Donald Roland Brigham and Sarah Louise Heath

BROADBENT [see Broadbout],
Robert J., b. 1/25/1921; fifth; Hiram J. Broadbent (farmer, Madison, WI) and Hazel M. Stephens (Chatam, ON)
Thomas S., b. 1/2/1924; sixth; Hiram J. Broadbent (Middleton, WI) and Hazel Stephen (Chatham, ON)

BROADBOUT [see Broadbent],
James T., b. 12/5/1917; fourth; Hiram J. Broadbout (farmer, Middleton) and Harvel Stephen (Canada)

BRONNENBERG,
Jacob Prosper, b. 9/21/1983 in Concord; Jackie Ray Bronnenberg and Mary Margaret Fontaine
Michael Philip, b. 4/16/1986 in Concord; Jackie Ray Bronnenberg and Mary Margaret Fontaine

BROOKS,
Marissa Elaine, b. 9/4/1992 in Concord; Wayne Phillips Brooks and Phyllis Elaine Leithead
Matthew Philip, b. 12/7/1989 in Concord; Wayne Phillips Brooks and Phyllis Elaine Leithead
Shirley Ellen, b. 8/28/1947; fourth; Glen P. Brooks (mill roller) and Della E. Crowninshield
Tyler William, b. 8/9/1994 in Concord; Wayne Phillips Brooks and Phyllis Elaine Leithead

BROWN,
child, b. 8/2/1900; William Brown (shoemaker, Barrington) and Ella Hall (Epsom)
daughter, b. 2/4/1904; second; Willie B. Brown (shoemaker, 35, Barrington) and Ella Hall (38, Epsom)
child, b. 6/26/1921; first; Scott Parsons (farmer) and Ethel Brown (Farmington)
Alison Mackenzie, b. 7/16/2000 in Concord; Michael Brown and Mychelle Brown
Angela Courtney, b. 7/29/1982 in Concord; Randolph Bradford Brown and Judy Alice Flanders
Clayton R., b. 7/16/1964 in Concord; first; Roland E. T. Brown (Rochester) and Madgeline E. Gerlack (Jamaica, VT); residence - Ctr. Barnstead
Clifton R., b. 8/23/1967 in Concord; second; Roland E. Brown (inner sole tacker, Rochester) and Madgeline E. Gerlack (Jamaica, VT)
Craig Richard, b. 11/15/1970 in Concord; Roland Everett Brown (NH) and Madgeline Elizabeth Gerlack (VT)
David M., Jr., b. 2/6/1963 in Concord; first; David M. Brown (Concord) and Cecelia C. Gerlack (Epping); residence - Ctr. Barnstead
Dolores Achrista, b. 4/25/1928; third; Joseph C. Brown (Portsmouth) and Achrista E. Sear (TX)

Howard Ivory, b. 7/19/1937; first; Forrest Brown (tractor driver) and Rebekah Swain

Jesse Alexander, b. 12/26/1992 in New London; Randy John Brown and Pamela Jeanne Rock

Lillian Edith, b. 6/10/1917; fifth; John A. Brown (farmer, Alton) and Alice Tebbetts (Brunswick, ME)

Marla May, b. 7/27/1989 in Concord; Russell Donald Brown and Marla May Estabrook

Michael Philip, b. 5/1/1971 in Concord; Carleton Philip Brown (NH) and Johnette Gladys Glover (NH)

Michelle Lynn, b. 11/28/1971 in Concord; Roland Everett Brown (VT) and Madgeline E. Gerlack (NH)

Ralph Charles, b. 6/15/1952 in Wolfeboro; first; Ralph A. Brown (bridge const.) and Vera B. Wheet

Randolph B., b. 5/17/1959 in Concord; Wesley F. Brown and Martha E. Tasker

Randy J., b. 11/12/1956 in Wolfeboro; Ralph H. Brown (bridgeman) and Vera B. Wheet

Raymond R., b. 2/12/1954 in Wolfeboro; Ralph A. Brown (bridgeman) and Vera B. Wheet

Richard A., b. 7/17/1965 in Concord; second; David M. Brown, Jr. (Concord) and Cecelia C. Gerlack (Epping)

Rodney W., b. 6/25/1967 in Concord; third; David M. Brown (woodsman, Concord) and Cecelia C. Gerlack (Epping)

Russell D., b. 5/27/1962 in Wolfeboro; fourth; Ralph A. Brown (Arlington, MA) and Vera B. Wheet (Barnstead); residence - Ctr. Barnstead

Sahara Jordan, b. 9/2/1994 in New London; Randy John Brown and Pamela Jeanne Rock

Shannon Lindsey, b. 3/13/1984 in Concord; Randolph Bradford Brown and Judy Alice Flanders

Shirley Louise, b. 2/4/1939 in Concord; first; Wilbur J. Garland (woodsman) and Lillian Edith Brown

Stephanie Tyler, b. 7/9/1987 in Concord; Russell Donald Brown and Marla May Estabrook

Steven, b. 7/14/1972 in Concord; Carleton Philip Brown (NH) and Johnette Gladys Glover (NH)

Tyler Michael, b. 11/30/1998 in Concord; Michael Brown and Mychelle Brown

Zachary Kenneth, b. 5/16/1987 in Concord; Robert Anthony Brown and Theresa Mary Laderbush

BRUMFIELD,
Kirsten Marie, b. 1/28/1999 in Concord; Gary Brumfield and Paula Brumfield
Trevor John, b. 7/14/1996 in Concord; Gary Wayne Brumfield and Paula Jane St. Jean

BUCHNER,
Helda, b. 5/21/1919; second; William Buchner (weaver, Germany) and Rittie Sanborn (Chichester)

BUCKMAN,
Matthew David, b. 5/6/1982 in Barnstead; George S. Buckman III and Kathleen L. Dunleavy

BUGIEDA,
Nicholas John, b. 10/2/1991 in Concord; Anthony Edward Bugieda and Terese Suzanne McCarthy

BUNKER,
son [Roland E.], b. 12/13/1890; first; John M. Bunker (farmer, Barnstead) and Amy Bunker (Portland, ME)
Debra Ann, b. 1/27/1951 in Concord; first; Roland E. Bunker (mechanic) and Charlotte E. Cate
Doris A., b. 5/20/1908; third; Joseph S. Bunker (farmer, 39, Barnstead) and Nellie Aikens (35, Concord)
Everett, b. 8/31/1893; third; Lewis Bunker (shoemaker, 25, Barnstead) and Alice Perkins (29, Wells, ME)
Haley Amelia, b. 2/17/1991 in New London; William Emery Bunker and Ann Marie Cammarata
Leon, b. 12/4/1894; second; Joseph Bunker (shoemaker, 26, Barnstead) and Nellie Aikin (21, Barnstead)
Lewis W., b. 3/5/1868; Ammon R. Bunker (farmer) and Hannah B. Webster (1942)
Robert John, b. 5/19/1923; second; Roland E. Bunker (Barnstead) and Ruth A. Evans (Barnstead)
Roland E., b. 2/8/1922; first; Roland E. Bunker (loom fixer, Barnstead) and Ruth A. Evans (Barnstead)
William E., b. 6/1/1954 in Concord; Roland E. Bunker, Jr. (mechanic) and Charlotte E. Cate

BURKHARDT,
Lauren Mae, b. 3/23/1994 in Rochester; Melvin Walter Burkhardt, Jr. and Katherine Louise Foote

BURLEY,
Brooke Kathleen, b. 8/29/1996 in Concord; Richard Oscar Burley and Amy Beth Bousquet

BURNAD,
son [Kenneth Emerson], b. 4/21/1913; first; Herbert Burnad (saw mill, 35) and Marguerite Emerson (17, Barnstead)

BURNELL,
Gerald Arthur, b. 10/26/1947; second; Frederick A. Burnell (store keeper) and Frances G. Heywood
Judith Ann, b. 9/25/1940; first; Frederick R. Burnell (shoe shop) and G. Francis Heywood

BURNETTE,
Sarah Katherine, b. 9/8/1985 in Concord; Reginald Lee Burnette and Joan Myrtie Hillsgrove

BURROUGHS,
daughter, b. 9/28/1891; eighth; George F. Burroughs (shoemaker, Barnstead) and Cedelia A. Gowen (Barnstead)
daughter, b. 11/16/1893; ninth; George F. Burroughs (shoemaker, 46, Barnstead) and Adelia Gowen (Berwick, ME)

BYERS,
Logan Charles, b. 6/3/1998 in Concord; Steven Byers and Melissa Byers
Marjorie Gayle, b. 4/16/1968 in Concord; Steven Charles Byers (MA) and Marjorie Pearl French (NH)
Natasha Marie, b. 10/31/1996 in Concord; Steven Israel Byers and Melissa Marie Byers
Steven Israel, b. 3/23/1969 in Concord; Steven Charles Byers (MA) and Marjorie Pearl French (NH)
Wesley Steven, b. 6/19/1980 in Concord; Steven Charles Byers and Patricia Marie Richardson

CALDERONE,
Christine Gale, b. 5/25/1985 in Concord; Gary Michael Calderone and Debra Gale Carmel
James Michael, b. 11/20/1987 in Concord; Gary Michael Calderone and Debra Gale Carmel

CALDWELL,
Lisa Marie, b. 10/5/1974 in Concord; Bruce Edward Caldwell (NH) and Carolyn Frances Hillsgrove (NH)
Samantha Ann, b. 5/8/1991 in Concord; William Davis Caldwell and Deborah Ann Piaseczny
Tyler Davis, b. 9/14/1993 in Concord; William Davis Caldwell and Deborah Ann Piaseczny

CALL,
Lois Bessie, b. 7/6/1901; first; Horace C. Call (laborer, 23, Concord) and Bessie A. Downs (18, Barnstead)

CALLAHAN,
Kevin Thomas, b. 12/12/1975 in Concord; Michael John Callahan (MA) and Teresa Ann Waskiewicz (MA)

CAMERON,
Robert W., b. 2/28/1954 in Concord; Donald E. Cameron (weaver) and Alice A. Evans
William Edward, b. 8/21/1947 in Wolfeboro; first; Daniel R. Cameron (store clerk) and Mabel I. Cate

CANFIELD,
Dorothy P., b. 4/12/1917; first; Archie M. Canfield (weaver, Guildhall, VT) and Clara D. Mears (Pittsfield)
Gilbert Archie, b. 9/18/1932; third; Archie M. Canfield (weaver) and Clara D. Meara
Mark D., b. 11/6/1956 in Concord; Gilbert A. Canfield (truck driver) and Irma L. Pugh
Reta B., b. 2/25/1918; second; Archie M. Camfield (sic) (weaver, Lunenburg, VT) and Clara D. Mears (Pittsfield)

CARDINAL,
Ernest Joseph, b. 8/28/1942 in Concord; first; Ernest E. Cardinal (US Army) and Alice Marion Weeks

John Henry, b. 11/26/1944 in Concord; second; Ernest Cardinal (mechanic, US Army) and Alice M. Weeks

CAREY,
daughter, b. 5/8/1894; second; Thomas Carey (shoemaker, Exeter) and Euphema Parshley (Barnstead); residence – Bradford, MA

CARMAN,
Mary Grace, b. 11/20/1980 in Laconia; Donald Vincent Carman and Regina Ann Kach

CARPENTER,
James Tyler, b. 6/7/1983 in Concord; Glen Stanley Carpenter and Jane Meredith
Nicholas Glen, b. 8/17/1980 in Barnstead; Glen Stanley Carpenter and Jane Meredith
Rachel Ann, b. 2/12/1989 in Concord; William Thurstan Carpenter and Kathleen Elizabeth Walker
Samuel Emmett, b. 9/15/1993 in Barnstead; Glen Stanley Carpenter and Jane Meredith
Sarah Jane, b. 10/9/1991 in Concord; William Thurston Carpenter and Kathleen Elizabeth Walker

CARR,
son [George S.], b. 1/30/1893; fourth; Sylvester Carr (farmer, Pawtucket, RI) and Martha Greenleaf (Pittsfield)
child, b. 3/22/1933; fifth; George S. Carr (auto dealer) and Ella May Powell
Christopher John, b. 11/24/1980 in Concord; Richard John Carr and Ann Cecile Huleski
Donald Leonard, b. 12/11/1926; second; George S. Carr (Barnstead) and E. May Powell (Barnstead)
Earl Leonard, b. 6/8/1933; first; Fred M. Carr (laborer) and Vida T. Littlefield
Evelyn May, b. 12/7/1929; third; George S. Carr (Barnstead) and E. May Powell (Barnstead)
Fred M., b. 2/16/1935 in Pittsfield; second; Fred M. Carr (farmer) and Vida T. Littlefield
John K., b. 2/8/1958 in Concord; Kenneth G. Carr and Dorothy A. Cotton

Kenneth George, b. 4/6/1931; fourth; George S. Carr (auto
   salesman) and May Powell
Kimberly Anne, b. 12/16/1983 in Concord; Richard John Carr and
   Anne Cecile Hulecki
Nancy A., b. 9/16/1959 in Concord; Kenneth G. Carr and Dorothy A.
   Cotton
Robert Berry, b. 8/17/1920; first; Raymond L. Carr (mechanic,
   Grafton) and E. Louise Berry (Barnstead)
Warren Russel, b. 8/18/1936; third; Fred M. Carr (farmer) and Vida
   T. Littlefield

CARSON [see Corson],
son, b. 5/5/1902; first; Harry Carson (farmer, 26, Pittsfield) and
   Stella F. Carr (16, Barnstead)
daughter [Maud T.], b. 4/24/1908; fifth; Harry O. Carson (farmer,
   32, Pittsfield) and Stella Carr (21, Epsom)
daughter [Flora I.], b. 11/8/1911; eighth; Harry O. Carson (farmer,
   35, Pittsfield) and Stella F. Carr (25, Epsom)
Autumn Starr, b. 11/26/1982 in Barnstead; Stephen Gary Carson
   and Sharron Ann Silver
Bertha D., b. 6/26/1909; sixth; Harry O. Carson (farmer, 33,
   Pittsfield) and Stella Carr (23, Epsom)
Florence O., b. 12/6/1903; Harry O. Carson (farmer, 27, Pittsfield)
   and Stella Carr (17, Epsom)
Harry M., b. 5/19/1910; seventh; Harry O. Carson (farmer, 34,
   Pittsfield) and Stella F. Carr (24, Epsom)
Kathleen J., b. 8/8/1959 in Concord; Floyd J. Carson and Patricia
   R. Kimball
Stephen G., b. 7/14/1955 in Wolfeboro; Floyd J. Carson (laborer)
   and Patricia R. Kimball

CARTER,
Jenny Leigh, b. 10/22/1992 in Concord; David Bernard Carter and
   Kathy Jean Bussiere
Keith David, b. 6/3/1988 in Concord; David Bernard Carter and
   Kathy Jean Bussiere
Lisa Elizabeth, b. 10/10/1985 in Concord; William Ruston Carter
   and Kim Anne Hawkins

CARUSO,
Christopher Robert, b. 5/31/1985 in Concord; Robert Christopher Caruso and Laura Ann Chagnon

CASHMAN,
son, b. 5/23/1953 in Concord; second; Leonard Cashman (inspector) and Dorothy M. Clancy

CATE,
son [Harold], b. 9/21/1906; first; William S. Cate (steam mill em., 31, Alton) and Sadie F. Gray (20, Barnstead); residence – Pittsfield
Derek Levi, b. 6/17/1984 in Concord; Douglas James Cate, Sr. and Janet Ann Pecoraro
Mabel Idella, b. 10/17/1915; second; William S. Cate (farmer, Alton) and Sadie Francis Gray (Barnstead)

CATRON,
Amanda Jean, b. 7/23/1982 in Rochester; Michael George Catron and Patricia Lee Ward

CHADWICK,
Kevin Tyler, b. 11/2/1992 in Rochester; Arnold Herbert Chadwick and Donna Marie Huckins

CHAGNON,
Daniel Vincent, b. 3/11/1974 in Concord; Terry Martin Chagnon (NH) and Margaret Ann Tilton (NH)
Delphis Mark, b. 8/21/1932; fourth; Nelson L. Chagnon (farmer) and Pearl Purtell
Gordon Keith, b. 2/10/1939 in Wolfeboro; second; Maurice L. Chagnon (cotton mill) and Doris A. Kenison
Kristi Lee, b. 5/22/1978 in Concord; Donald Louis Chagnon, Jr. (NH) and Barbara Lee Theriault (MA)
Nathaniel Allen, b. 10/9/1992 in Concord; Andre Marcel Chagnon and Catherine Lee Wheeler
Robert W., b. 11/15/1967 in Concord; second; Richard A. Chagnon (Suncook leathers, Pittsfield) and Bonnie L. Graeme (Concord)
Ronald Edward, b. 5/7/1936; first; Maurice L. Chagnon (mill worker) and Doris A. Kenison

Twyla Nicole, b. 4/20/1985 in Concord; Bennett Jon Chagnon and Pamela Jean Sherman

CHAMBERLAIN,
daughter, b. 7/26/1890; third; Charles Chamberlain (fish merchant, Boston, MA) and Bertha Emerson (Barnstead)
Gertrude L., b. 7/15/1873; H. M. Chamberlain and Anna L. Pickering (1938)
Lance T., b. 4/28/1961 in Laconia; Ernest R. Chamberlain (Alton) and Beverly A. Brothers (Natick, MA); residence - Ctr. Barnstead
Meloney L., b. 9/25/1958 in Laconia; Ernest R. Chamberlain and Beverly A. Brothers
Michael A., b. 9/6/1959 in Laconia; Ernest R. Chamberlain and Beverly A. Brothers
Scott K., b. 5/16/1962 in Wolfeboro; fourth; Ernest R. Chamberlain (Alton) and Beverly A. Brothers (Natick, MA); residence - Ctr. Barnstead
Wilfred, b. 8/4/1900; Louis Chamberlain (farmer) and Adeline Bolduc (1942)

CHAMBERS,
Keith Robert, b. 10/14/1952 in Concord; third; Nathan E. Chambers (mechanic) and Waneta F. Carter
Mary Lou, b. 7/23/1951 in Concord; second; Nathan E. Chambers (mechanic) and Waneta F. Carter

CHANDLER,
Kathleen O., b. 9/2/1919; third; Chester W. Chandler (farmer, Rockland, MA) and Olive E. Maier (Gloucester, MA)

CHAPPELLE,
Nicholaus John, b. 2/26/1980 in Concord; John Edward Chappelle, Jr. and Dorothy Ann Riel
Tyler Ernest, b. 3/17/1983 in Concord; John Edward Chappelle and Dorothy Ann Riel

CHASE,
Steven Aaron, b. 12/26/1980 in Concord; Robert Steven Chase and Charlene Molly Parry

CHATTEN,
Jeremy Pennington, b. 10/21/1988 in Concord; Clarence Bowen Chatten and Gale Marie Freeman

CHEENEY,
son, b. 6/8/1896; Elmer C. Cheeney (station agent, Dunstable, MA) and Grace Butterfield

CHESLEY,
son, b. 1/22/1892; first; Herbert L. Chesley (farmer, Barnstead) and Annie E. Ayers (Barnstead)

CHROMIAK-MUNROE,
Zachary John, b. 2/15/1980 in Concord; Gary Wayne Munroe and Nadine Ann Chromiak

CHURCHILL,
Amy Lynn, b. 4/30/1986 in Concord; Dale Scott Churchill and Patricia Marie Wabegijek
Joshua Daniel, b. 12/1/1984 in Portsmouth; Dale Scott Churchill and Patricia Marie Wabegijik

CLARK,
daughter, b. 10/27/1889; second; Jonathan Clark (shoemaker, Barnstead) and Ida Clark (Barnstead)
son, b. 3/2/1892; fourth; Adalbert E. Clark (farmer, NB) and Elizabeth McKentley (NB)
son [Sewell J.], b. 12/19/1892; third; Jonathan Clark (farmer, Barnstead) and Ida Hanson (Barnstead)
son, b. 5/12/1893; sixth; Adelbert Clark (teamster, 33, NB) and Elizabeth McKennelly (26, NB)
child [Ella Frances], b. 4/30/1895; Jonathan Clark (farmer, Barnstead) and Ida Hanson (Barnstead)
son, b. 4/26/1896; Frank Clark (farmer, Barnstead) and Ethel Bodge (Barnstead)
son [Theodore H.], b. 10/27/1908; seventh; Jonathan Clark (farmer, 60, Barnstead) and Ada M. Hanson (44, Barnstead)
Amelia Rose, b. 9/4/1990 in Concord; Timothy Tileston Clark and Melissa Ann Carbee
Autumn Cheyenne, b. 10/15/1992 in Concord; Timothy Tileston Clark and Melissa Ann Carbee

David Jonathan, b. 12/7/1926; first; Eugene F. Clark (Barnstead) and Marion E. Howe (Shrewsbury, MA)

Eunice Ida, b. 2/22/1919; first; Guy E. Clark (farmer, Barnstead) and Dora MacKenzie (E. Boston, MA)

Harold, b. 6/13/1897; first; H. E. Clark (merchant, Barnstead) and Lillian Tasker (Barnstead)

Howard Avery, b. 1/3/1944; second; Albert H. Clark (laborer) and Vera M. Roberts

Jason Errol, b. 4/30/1981 in Rochester; Danny Errol Clark and Lily Edith Troughton

Jean A., b. 8/16/1933; second; Eugene F. Clark (garage prop.) and Marguerite Barton

Jeremy John, b. 8/10/1978 in Concord; Danny Errol Clark (NH) and Lily Edith Troughton (CT); residence - Ctr. Barnstead

Jonathan, b. 5/30/1905; sixth; Jonathan Clark (farmer, 57, Barnstead) and Ida Hanson (40, Barnstead)

Kyle Robert, b. 1/20/1986 in Concord; Richard Everett Clark and Darla Sue Keene

Lester J., b. 11/19/1878; Cyrus Clark and Cora E. Nutter (1938)

Patrick James, b. 11/30/1979 in Rochester; Danny Errol Clark and Lily Edith Troughton

Teresa Kelly, b. 8/9/1977 in Concord; Ralph Ronald Clark (NH) and Shirley Ann Rowell (WY); residence - Ctr. Barnstead

Tina Marie, b. 12/26/1978 in Concord; Ralph Ronald Clark (NH) and Shirley Ann Rowell (WY)

Virginia Carolyn, b. 5/10/1929; second; Eugene F. Clark (Barnstead) and Marion E. Ham (Shrewsbury, MA)

Walter L., b. 8/11/1896; Robert L. Clark (farmer, NB) and Hattie Belle Otis (Gilmanton)

CLEAR,
Rachel Marion, b. 4/5/1983 in Nashua; Edward Joseph Clear and Deborah Jeanne Barton

CLEMENT,
Ann Marie, b. 1/31/1979 in Concord; George Edward Clement III and Theresa Ann Jennings

Betty A., b. 7/8/1964 in Laconia; fourth; George E. Clement (Dover) and Barbara L. Clark (Pittsfield); residence - Ctr. Barnstead

Christine Louise, b. 2/27/1968 in Laconia; George Edward Clement (NH) and Barbara Leona Clark (NH)

Jasmine Marie, b. 3/22/1999 in Concord; Michael Clement and Angela Clement

Jennifer Barbara, b. 11/4/1973 in Concord; George Edward Clement, Jr. (NH) and Barbara Leona Clark (NH)

Mark E., b. 2/10/1966 in Laconia; fifth; George E. Clement (Dover) and Barbara L. Clark (Pittsfield); residence - Ctr. Barnstead

Michael George, b. 5/27/1975 in Concord; George Edward Clement III (NH) and Theresa Ann Jannings (MA)

Virginia Faith, b. 2/11/1972 in Dover; George Edward Clement (NH) and Barbara Leona Clark (NH); residence - Ctr. Barnstead

CLEMENTS,
Ashley Marie, b. 1/14/1990 in Concord; David Lee Clements and Lisa Ann Varney

CLEMONS,
Andrew David, b. 8/2/1990 in Concord; David Niles Clemons and Judith Ann Bongiovanni

Erica Nicole, b. 11/23/1992 in Concord; David Niles Clemons and Judith Ann Bongiovanni

CLEVELAND,
Norma Jane, b. 6/11/1925; thirteenth; George E. Cleveland (Hyde Park, NY) and Delia Demers (Canada)

CLOUGH,
Dorothy G., b. 3/4/1916; fifth; Harry G. Clough (machinist, Lynn, MA) and Edith Flagg (Conway, MA)

Frances, b. 12/29/1913; fourth; Harry G. Clough (farmer, 31, Lynn, MA) and Edith E. Clough (38, Conway, MA)

Leonard Walter, b. 9/5/1942 in Pittsfield; first; Walter L. Clough (weaver) and Elsie M. Hill

CLOUTIER,
Miranda Ashley, b. 3/18/1999 in Portsmouth; Anthony Cloutier and Denise Cloutier

COFFIN,
son, b. 6/1/1907; fourth; Silas A. Coffin (farmer, 32, Freeport, ME) and Seling J. Sapiese (27, W. Strazlo, NY)

daughter, b. 1/6/1910; fifth; Silas A. Coffin (farmer, 34, Freeport, ME) and Salina LePiere (29, West Shasee, NY)

COLBATH,
son, b. 11/15/1901; first; Ernest Colbath (clerk, 23, Barnstead) and Stella M. Foss (21, Strafford)

COLBY,
Olivia Anya-Tuttle, b. 9/4/1998 in Concord; Blair Colby and Trasea Colby

COLLINS,
Beverly Joyce, b. 7/27/1932; second; Blinn S. Collins (laborer) and Ruth E. Mason
Florence, b. 1/16/1899; first; Frank O. Collins (26, Malden, MA) and Elizabeth Ferris (25, Boston, MA); residence – Boston, MA
Heidi L., b. 10/28/1965 in Concord; second; Richard K. Collins (Concord) and Sandra A. Davis (Pittsfield); residence - Ctr. Barnstead
Jason Kenneth, b. 10/29/1971 in Concord; Ralph Kenneth Collins (NH) and Elizabeth Madeline Rogers (NH); residence - Ctr. Barnstead
Joseph Martin, b. 12/6/1970 in Concord; Ralph Kenneth Collins (NH) and Elizabeth Madeleine Rogers (NH); residence - Ctr. Barnstead
Martin Ralph, b. 2/28/1935 in Pittsfield; first; Ralph M. Collins (wood heel worker) and Flora I. Corson
Ralph Kenneth, b. 1/6/1945 in Concord; third; Ralph M. Collins (lathe operator) and Flora I. Carson

COME,
daughter, b. 12/11/1905; fifth; Charles Come (laborer, 26, Pittsfield) and Angie Sampson (26, Canada)

COMEAU,
Dennis James, b. 5/23/1987 in Concord; Fred Lewis Comeau and Susan Marie Thoroughgood
Fred Lewis, Jr., b. 11/27/1984 in Concord; Fred Lewis Comeau and Susan Marie Thoroughgood
Susan Chastiti, b. 1/15/1990 in Concord; Fred Lewis Comeau and Susan Marie Thoroughgood

CONSTANT,
Felix Henry, b. 11/18/1916; fourth; Nestor Constant (morocco, Canada) and Albertina Plourde (Canada)
Jennifer Lynn, b. 5/9/1978 in Concord; Guy Arthur Constant (NH) and Dorothy Ann Drouin (MA); residence - Ctr. Barnstead
Nicole Ann, b. 6/5/1973 in Concord; Guy Arthur Constant (NH) and Dorothy Ann Drouin (MA)
Stacie Jean, b. 11/9/1976 in Concord; Guy Arthur Constant (NH) and Dorothy Ann Drouin (MA)

COOGAN,
John Macklin, b. 5/5/1983 in Concord; Thomas Dennis Coogan, Jr. and Sandra Lee Litz

COOK,
son [Herbert], b. 6/5/1893; first; Watt P. Cook (farmer, 19, Milton) and Cynthia F. Caverley (18, Strafford)
daughter, b. 10/10/1904; third; Nat P. Cook (farmer, 31, Milton) and Cynthia F. Caverly (29, Strafford)
child, b. 5/11/1917; third; Herbert Cook (farmer, Barnstead) and Anna B. Dalby (New York, NY)
Earl Leland, b. 6/20/1921; second; Cecil L. Cook (brakeman, Boston, MA) and Margaret Cook (Saugus, MA)
Ernest P., b. 4/1/1915; first; Herbert Cook (farmer, Barnstead) and Anna R. Dalby (New York, NY)
Harold E., b. 4/1/1915; second; Herbert Cook (farmer, Barnstead) and Anna R. Dalby (New York, NY)
Herbert, Jr., b. 8/18/1920; fourth; Herbert Cook (farmer, Barnstead) and Anna Dally (New York, NY)
Hussey I., b. 10/16/1908; fourth; Nat P. Cook (farmer, 36, Milton) and Cynthia M. Cook (34, Strafford)
Nat Parker, b. 7/2/1922; first; George W. Cook (farmer, Milton) and Lillian B. Cook (Barnstead)
Rosa Ellen, b. 7/1/1918; first; Cecil Leland Cook (shoemaker, Boston, MA) and Magrete Cook (Saugus, MA)
Silvia V., b. 2/13/1895; Natt P. Cook (farmer, Milton) and Cynthia F. Caverley (Rochester)

COOPER,
Erik Thomas, b. 1/15/2000 in Concord; Todd Cooper and Heather Cooper

COPP,
son, b. 4/2/1891; third; John Copp (farmer, Farmington) and Hattie J. Hutchinson (Brunswick, ME)

CORLISS,
stillborn son, b. 12/18/1905; second; Charles Corliss (engineer, 25, Topsham, VT) and Helen G. Tilton (24, Chichester)
daughter, b. 8/22/1911; fourth; Charles Corliss (engineer, 31, Topsham, VT) and Helen G. Tilton (29, Chichester)
Charles Albert, b. 10/24/1946 in Pittsfield; first; Stanley L. Corliss (stitcher) and Helen E. Ambrose
Charles Chester, b. 8/28/1915; fifth; Charles Samuel Corliss (weaver, Topsham, VT) and Helen Tilton (Chichester)
Earle S., b. 6/12/1908; second; Charles S. Corlis (sic) (engineer, 27, Topsham, VT) and Helen Tilton (26, Pittsfield)
Edward C., b. 2/21/1918; sixth; Charles S. Corliss (machinist, Topsham, VT) and Helen G. Tilton (Chichester)
Evelyn Ruth, b. 11/14/1931; first; Earl S. Corliss (laborer) and Mildred Hill
Janice Marie, b. 10/25/1935; Earl S. Corliss (watchman) and Mildred Hill
Kalvin Stanley, b. 1/12/2000 in Concord; Eric Corliss and Sherri Corliss
Richard Gary, b. 7/16/1949 in Pittsfield; third; Stanley Lenwood Corliss (shoe shop) and Helen Elizabeth Ambrose
Robert Lee, b. 11/10/1947 in Pittsfield; second; Stanley L. Corliss (shoe shop) and Helen E. Ambrose
Thomas, b. 9/21/1951 in Concord; fourth; Stanley L. Corliss (carpenter's helper) and Helen E. Ambrose
Wendy Genella, b. 7/13/1976 in Concord; Richard Gary Corliss (NH) and Mary Genella Barton (NH)

CORSON [see Carson],
daughter [Thelma], b. 2/5/1905; third; Harry O. Corson (farmer, 28, Pittsfield) and Stella Carr (18, Epsom)
daughter [Sybel Madeline], b. 3/4/1907; third; Harry O. Corson (farmer, 31, Pittsfield) and Stella Carr (20, Epsom)
child, b. 2/11/1937; sixth; Floyd O. Corson (farmer) and Helen Durkin
Alfred Burton, b. 2/10/1939; seventh; Floyd Corson (laborer) and Helen Durkin

Cheryl A., b. 3/11/1954 in Concord; Raymond D. Corson (US Army) and Evelyn M. Drake

Clyde D., b. 9/16/1962 in Concord; fourth; Clyde E. Corson (Wolfeboro) and Barbara J. French (Gilmanton); residence - Ctr. Barnstead

Clyde Edgar, Jr., b. 10/17/1936; fourth; Clyde E. Corson (laborer) and Esther E. Swain

Emily Elizabeth, b. 2/24/1933; first; Clyde E. Corson (laborer) and Esther Swain

Geraldine Florence, b. 7/7/1934; second; Clyde E. Corson (laborer) and Esther Swain

Melissa J., b. 7/7/1960 in Concord; second; Clyde E. Corson (supervisor, Wolfeboro) and Barbara J. French (Gilmanton)

Michael J., b. 12/14/1963 in Concord; fifth; Clyde E. Corson (Wolfeboro) and Barbara J. French (Gilmanton); residence - Ctr. Barnstead

Priscilla G., b. 9/21/1961 in Concord; Clyde E. Corson, Jr. (Wolfeboro) and Barbara J. French (Gilmanton)

Stella Florence, b. 12/4/1934; fifth; Floyd O. Corson (laborer) and Helen Durkin

Sylvia Ann, b. 9/11/1935; third; Clyde E. Corson (laborer) and Esther Swain

COSTANZO,
Erica Linay, b. 6/28/1988 in Concord; Steven Costanzo and Rosemary Hawk

COTTON,
Marjorie May, b. 5/19/1936; first; George R. Cotton (shoe stitcher) and Marjorie H. Hallett

Sandra Jean, b. 3/1/1940; fourth; Joseph H. Cotton (farmer) and Ruth E. Hallett

COULTER,
William Ernest, Jr., b. 6/9/1982 in Concord; William Ernest Coulter and Laurie Ellen Grass

COURTNEY,
Garry Holbrook, b. 1/30/1993 in Concord; Garry Francis Courtney and Wendy Victoria Holbrook

Victoria Naomi, b. 7/2/1991 in Concord; Gary Francis Courtney and Wendy Victoria Holbrook

COVINGTON,
Taylor Elizabeth, b. 4/3/1985 in Concord; Robert Michael Covington and Denise Miscavige

COX,
Roy Henry, Jr., b. 11/25/1974 in Concord; Roy Henry Cox (NH) and Susan Ruth Scott (NH)

CRAWFORD,
Bailey Ann, b. 6/14/1997 in Concord; Todd H. Crawford, Jr. and Kelly L. Akerley
Joshua Joe, b. 2/16/1990 in Concord; David John Crawford and Barbara Marie Francis

CROSBY,
Bria Jean, b. 12/4/1997 in Concord; Dean N. Crosby and Valerie M. MacEachen

CROSS,
Lindsay Elizabeth, b. 7/23/1987 in Concord; John Franklin Cross and Sandra Jean St. Denis

CROSSETT,
Thomas Ernest, b. 6/7/1942 in Pittsfield; second; Wilbur W. Crossett (defense work) and Arline M. Boyd
Wilbur, b. 6/10/1918; second; Ernest W. Crossett (weaver, Newport) and Mildred Dow (Barnstead)
William W., b. 11/25/1916; first; Ernest William Crossett (weaver, Newport) and Mildred Dow (Barnstead)
William Wilbur, b. 6/11/1940; first; W. Wilbur Crossett (bookkeeper) and Arline M. Boyd

CROW,
child, b. 9/12/1988 in Concord; Edward Evans Crow and Barbara Ann Bader
Jenna Marie, b. 9/10/1990 in Concord; Edward Evans Crow and Barbara Ann Bader

CULLEN,
Gwen Laraine, b. 11/17/1979 in Rochester; James Bruce Cullen and Anne Pauline Swift

CURRIER,
Fred Eric, V, b. 5/10/1988 in Rochester; Fred Eric Currier, IV and Theresa Peters

CURTIS,
daughter [Katherine C.], b. 1/27/1905; first; Asa A. Curtis (farmer, 25, Milton) and Jennie M. Foss (20, Barnstead)
Albion A., b. 4/14/1906; second; Asa A. Curtis (farmer, 27, Milton) and Jennie M. Foss (21, Barnstead)
Beverly Irene, b. 7/22/1944 in Pittsfield; second; Maurice F. Curtis (US Army) and Evelyn M. Picard
Ethel J., b. 4/12/1913; third; Asa Curtis (farmer, 33, Milton) and Jennie M. Foss (31, Barnstead)
Hattie J., b. 3/15/1916; fourth; Asa A. Curtis (farmer, Milton) and Jennie Foss (Barnstead)
Mary, b. 4/3/1916; fourth; Fred Curtis (farmer, Farmington) and Carrie Howard (Farmington)
Maurice F., b. 4/21/1920; fifth; Asa A. Curtis (farmer, Milton) and Jennie M. Foss (Barnstead)

CUTTER,
son [Harry], b. 8/20/1912; fourth; Frank R. Cutter (laborer, 32, Brighton, MA) and Lucelle Varney (26, Strafford)

DAHLQUIST,
son [Theodore G.], b. 6/22/1912; first; Theodore S. Dahlquist (bookkeeper, 18, Boston, MA) and Marion S. Clapp (17, Auburndale, MA); residence – Quincy, MA

DAIGLE,
child, b. 10/7/1975 in Manchester; Richard Roland Daigle (NH) and Nancy Theresa Mahoney (NH)

DALPHOND,
John Charles, b. 9/3/1946 in Pittsfield; first; Charles E. Dalphond (teamster) and Anna E. Downs

DAME,
Daniel Conrad, b. 11/10/1971 in Concord; Philip Lovering Dame (MA) and Carolyn Ann Gustafson (NH)
Elaine Marcia, b. 11/7/1947 in Concord; first; Herman P. Dame (shoe worker) and Edna Mertle Banks
Mary A., b. 7/17/1956 in Concord; Herman P. Dame (pressman) and Edna M. Banks
Maureen Eleanor, b. 5/16/1950 in Pittsfield; second; Herman P. Dame (maintenance man) and Edna M. Banks

DANIELS,
Robert Lawrence, b. 10/21/1982 in Wolfeboro; Robert Wilbur Daniels and Mary Esther DeVore

DANIS,
Henry J., b. 3/2/1966 in Concord; first; Joseph H. Danis (Pittsfield) and Caroline A. Gerbert (Concord)
Patrick F., b. 3/17/1967 in Concord; second; Joseph H. Danis (grocery store, Pittsfield) and Caroline A. Gerbert (Concord)

DAROSKA,
Benjamin, Jr., b. 12/22/1950 in Concord; first; Benjamin Daroska, Sr. (logger) and Eleanor D. Leavitt
Gloria L., b. 1/28/1955 in Concord; Benjamin Daroska, Sr. (mill operator) and Eleanor D. Leavitt
Norman L., b. 8/21/1959 in Concord; Benjamin Daroska and Eleanor D. Leavitt
Phyllis A., b. 4/16/1957 in Concord; Benjamin Daroska (self-employed) and Eleanor D. Leavitt

DARRELL,
Rosalie Elizabeth, b. 9/8/1990 in Ctr. Barnstead; Douglas Richard Darrell and Gail Oakes

DAVIDSON,
Caitlin Leigh, b. 11/29/1987 in Dover; Dana Kent Davidson and Cindy Leigh Case

DAVIES-BROWN,
Gareth Michael, b. 1/21/1998 in Concord; Michael Brown and Fiona Davies-Brown

DAVIS,
son, b. 1/4/1890; first; Charles B. Davis (shoemaker, Nashua) and
  Amy G. Eaton (Barnstead)
daughter, b. 2/19/1892; second; Charles B. Davis (shoemaker) and
  Amy G. Eaton (Barnstead)
daughter, b. 10/15/1896; Charles B. Davis (farmer) and Amy Eaton
  (Barnstead)
son [Percy], b. 8/4/1898; Charles B. Davis (shoemaker, Barrington)
  and Amy Eaton (Barnstead)
son [Percy], b. 10/30/1898; Clarence N. Davis (section hand,
  Barnstead) and Mamie Manson (Portsmouth)
daughter, b. 1/15/1914; eighth; Clarence N. Davis (morocco
  finisher, 38, Barnstead) and Mary J. Manson (37, Portsmouth)
Alan K., b. 1/12/1955 in Concord; Ernest A. Davis (meter reader)
  and Virginia C. Kelley
Bruce A., b. 6/23/1957 in Concord; Norman B. Davis (laborer) and
  Judith A. Burnell
Colby Alan, b. 7/8/1974 in Concord; Alan Kelley Davis (NH) and
  Linda Alice Schwall (NY)
Ernest Albert, b. 10/6/1923; first; Albert C. Davis (Auburn) and
  Helen E. Brown (Farmington)
Holly Jean, b. 12/2/1950 in Pittsfield; first; Ernest A. Davis (public
  service emp.) and Virginia C. Kelley
Lois Ann, b. 12/20/1931; first; Chester Davis (carpenter) and Laura
  Pitman
Lucille Edna, b. 2/27/1927; third; Albert C. Davis (Auburn) and
  Helen E. Brown (Farmington)
Lucy J., b. 8/27/1888; Joseph A. Davis and Susan Pendergast
  (1952)
Madeline F., b. 7/29/1904; sixth; Charles B. Davis (shoemaker, 37,
  Barrington) and Amy G. Eaton (36, Pittsfield)
Marguerite Helen, b. 10/20/1925; second; Albert C. Davis (Auburn)
  and Helen E. Brown (Farmington)
Megan Lynne, b. 4/25/1980 in Concord; Alan Kelley Davis and
  Linda Alice Schwall
Neil Robinson, b. 10/15/1990 in Manchester; Glenn Michael Davis
  and Cynthia Dellinger
Nelson H., b. 9/2/1911; first; Clarence N. Davis (section hand,
  Barnstead) and Mary J. Manson (Portsmouth)
Paul Howard, b. 4/13/1946 in Concord; fourth; Howard E. Davis
  (farmer) and Ardith G. Shea

Shelby Wellington, b. 9/18/1982 in Concord; Alan Kelley Davis and
    Linda A. Schwall

DAY,
Jason Julius, b. 11/28/1977 in Concord; Warren Levon Day (NH)
    and Judith May Garland (NH); residence - Ctr. Barnstead
Krystle Jennifer, b. 3/10/1981 in Concord; Warren Levon Day and
    Judith May Garland

DEBOLD,
Hannah Smith, b. 5/20/1994 in Concord; Richard Wayne Debold
    and Faith Ann Weldon
Tynan Hall, b. 4/4/1990 in Concord; Richard Wayne Debold and
    Faith Ann Weldon

DEBOW,
David Scott, b. 4/9/1984 in Concord; Ronald David Debow and Tina
    Marie Phillips

DEGLER,
Abigail Elizabeth, b. 11/11/2000 in Concord; David Degler and
    Jocelyn Degler

DELLNER,
Alexis Marie, b. 11/4/2000 in Concord; David Dellner and Lorra
    Dellner
Tia Lee, b. 4/22/1999 in Concord; David Dellner and Lorra Dellner

DEMELLO,
Sara Nichole, b. 5/4/1999 in Concord; Charles Demello and
    Shannon Demello

DEMERS,
Curtis Richard, b. 11/2/1999 in Concord; Richard Demers and
    Correen Demers
Jason Charles, b. 7/28/1992 in Concord; Charles Ronald Demers
    and Tracy Lee Earley
Jessica Lynn, b. 4/26/1990 in Concord; Charles Ronald Demers and
    Tracy Lee Earley
Lucas Brian, b. 11/2/1999 in Concord; Richard Demers and Correen
    Demers

DENNETT,
child, b. 11/15/1890; eighth; Oliver A. Dennett (farmer, Barnstead) and Fanny Hopsom (Lebanon) (see Elsie May)
Elsie May, b. 11/13/1890; Oliver A. Dennett (farmer) and Fraunt Hopson (1942) (see child above)
John Alexander, b. 3/23/1878; Oliver A. Dennett (farmer) and Fraunt Hopson (1942)
Louis B., b. 2/12/1893; ninth; Oliver A. Dennett (farmer, 57, Barnstead) and Fanny E. Hopson (43, Norwich, VT) (1894)

DENNEY,
daughter, b. 7/4/1894; ninth; Clara A. Denney (30, Center Harbor)

DENNIS,
Edward Frederick, b. 11/17/1930; ninth; Gerald W. Dennis (lumberman) and Lilly M. Cooper

DENTON,
Nicholas Price Taylour, b. 2/16/1991 in Manchester; Stuart Price Denton and Sylvia K. Klesse

DERBY,
daughter [Frances Isabelle], b. 3/26/1913; first; Charles L. Derby (carpenter, 28, VT) and Sylvia V. Cook (18, Barnstead)
daughter [Verlie], b. 8/7/1915; second; Charles L. Derby (carpenter, Montpelier, VT) and Sylvia A. Cook (Barnstead)
child, b. 5/10/1918; third; Charles L. Derby (laborer, Montpelier, VT) and Sylvia V. Cook (Barnstead)
Mead V., b. 6/22/1920; fifth; Charles L. Derbey (sic) (laborer, Montpelier, VT) and Sylvia Vivian Cook (Barnstead)
Mertle L., b. 6/22/1920; fourth; Charles L. Derbey (sic) (laborer, Montpelier, VT) and Sylvia Vivian Cook (Barnstead)

DEVOID,
Hazel M., b. 7/7/1925; first; Clarence Devoid (New Haven, VT) and Della J. Paige (Loudon)

DOCKHAM,
daughter [Angela], b. 12/24/1890; O. A. Dockham (blacksmith, Gilmanton) and Mary E. Dockham (Gilmanton)
child, b. 4/2/1892; fourth; Orrin Dockham (blacksmith)

DODGE,
Marion Elizabeth, b. 12/5/1930; first; Walter Swett Dodge (clerk) and Cora E. Clough

DOHERTY,
Aimee Rose, b. 5/21/1984 in Concord; Michael Patrick Doherty and Susan Beth Chesler
Heather Kathleen, b. 10/26/1986 in Concord; Michael Patrick Doherty and Susan Beth Chesler
Patrick Timothy, b. 2/15/1982 in Concord; Michael Patrick Doherty and Susan Beth Chesler

DOIRON,
Clifford Robert, b. 9/6/1996 in Manchester; Clifford Neil Doiron and Michelle Teresa Moreau

DONAHOE,
Megan Elise, b. 7/2/1983 in Concord; Patrick Gerrard Donahoe and Deborah Elaine Conrad

DONATO,
stillborn daughter, b. 8/28/1916; fifth; Angelo Donato (weaver, Italy) and Zena Siras (Italy)

DONNELLY,
Tyler Richard, b. 9/7/1989 in Concord; Kenneth William Donnelly and Michelle Lee Stewart

DONOVAN,
Darlynda S., b. 7/18/1953 in Concord; first; J. H. Donovan, Jr. (woodsman) and Bernice A. Charbono
Jack S., b. 3/27/1957 in Concord; John H. Donovan (logging) and Bernice A. Charboro
Katie Lynn, b. 12/9/1990 in Concord; Keith J. Donovan and Susan Lee Mortell
Keith J., b. 3/18/1960 in Concord; fourth; John H. Donovan (self-employed, Manchester) and Bernice A. Charbond (Lebanon)
Randal J., b. 12/30/1954 in Concord; John H. Donovan (logging) and Bernice A. Charboro

DORE,
Dylan Parker, b. 8/21/1992 in Concord; Deane Alan Dore and Kellie Blair Sweezey

DORN,
Anthony Ryan, b. 5/13/1994 in Manchester; Douglas Michael Dorn and Tracy Michelle Dorn

DORNNIS,
daughter, b. 4/13/1901; fourth; Onid Dornnis (farmer, 26, Canada) and Anna Paro (26, Canada)

DOUGHTY,
Dana L., b. 1/12/1967 in Concord; second; Dale F. Doughty (school principal, Portland, ME) and Barbara A. King (Bristol, CT)
Kathleen Elaine, b. 1/23/1969 in Concord; Dale Freeman Doughty (ME) and Barbara Ann King (CT)

DOW,
son [William H.], b. 8/17/1892; first; George W. Dow (farmer, Barnstead) and Edith M. Shackford (Barnstead)
son [John H.], b. 8/30/1901; fourth; Wilbur Dow (farmer, Barnstead) and Edith Shackford
daughter [Zelma K.], b. 12/17/1902; fifth; George W. Dow (farmer, Barnstead) and Edith Shackford (Barnstead)
Linda Irene, b. 3/20/1949; third; Alvah Hayes Dow (woodsman) and Barbara Mary Gray
Margaret Ina, b. 3/7/1948; second; Alvah H. Dow (woodsman) and Barbara M. Gray
Mary Edith, b. 3/10/1896; George W. Dow (farmer, Barnstead) and Edith M. Shackford (Barnstead)
Mildred, b. 10/26/1897; third; George W. Dow (farmer, 30, Barnstead) and Edith M. Shackford (26, Barnstead) (1907)
Reginald G., b. 5/2/1954 in Rochester; Alvah H. Dow (lobsterman) and Barbara M. Gray

DOWNING,
Jason Paul, b. 1/21/1980 in Wolfeboro; Gregory E. Downing and Pauline E. Price

DOWNS,
son [Arthur L.], b. 8/23/1888; sixth; Herbert O. Downs (farmer, Barnstead) and Clystia McKeen
son [Archer L.], b. 8/23/1888; seventh; Herbert O. Downs (farmer, Barnstead) and Clystia McKeen
son, b. 6/18/1890; ninth; Herbert O. Downs (farmer, Barnstead) and Clystia McKun (Farmington)
Cecil F., b. 11/24/1886; Herbert O. Downs and Calista M. Downs (1952)
D. A. [son], b. 8/19/1914; first; Archur L. Downs (morocco finisher, 26, Barnstead) and Edith L. Gordon (30, Haverhill, MA)
Fred Welch, b. 12/26/1916; third; Arthur L. Downes (sic) (morocco, Barnstead) and Maud Gladys Welch (Tunbridge, VT)
Herbert, b. 1/15/1915; second; Arthur L. Downs (morocco, Barnstead) and Maud G. Welch (Tunbridge, VT)
Unie C., b. 3/18/1913; first; Arthur L. Downs (morocco worker, 24, Barnstead) and Maud Welch (16, Tunbridge, VT)

DRAKE,
son [Howard], b. 12/17/1894; first; Edwin B. Drake (lumber dealer) and Georgia Emerson (Barnstead)
son [Harvey W.], b. 2/13/1902; third; Edwin B. Drake (lumberman, 39, Pittsfield) and Georgie D. Emerson (31, Barnstead)
Norman H., b. 9/14/1931; first; Harvey W. Drake (mill operator) and Annie J. Prince

DRESCHER,
Thomas Charles, b. 7/11/1984 in Concord; Robert W. Drescher and Susan Meredith
Sally Eleanor, b. 9/14/1987 in Concord; Robert William Drescher and Susan Meredith

DREW,
Calyn Elizabeth, b. 9/4/1997 in Concord; John L. Drew, Jr. and Bethany A. Winterle
Cameron John-Douglas, b. 1/8/2000 in Lebanon; John Drew and Bethany Drew

DRISCOLL,
Cody James, b. 4/17/1994 in Concord; Richard James Driscoll and Paula Ann Nickerson

David Andrew, b. 10/21/1973 in Concord; Richard James Driscoll (MA) and Margaret Louise Vaughn (MA)
Jesse Allen, b. 6/12/1996 in Concord; Richard James Driscoll and Paula Ann Nickerson
Korie Jo, b. 10/12/2000 in Concord; David Driscoll and Jennifer Driscoll

DROLET,
Jordan Leigh, b. 5/16/1991 in Concord; Robert Lionel Drolet and Susan Marie Komisarek
Robert Rene, b. 11/5/1932; fourth; Fernando J. Drolet (storekeeper) and Anette Nerbonne
Therese Priscilla, b. 5/19/1929; third; Fernando J. Drolet (Canada) and Annette Nelbourne (Allenstown)
Travis Lionel, b. 8/15/1989 in Concord; Robert Lionel Drolet and Susan Marie Komisarek

DROUIN,
Brandon Allan, b. 3/14/1989 in Concord; John Fitzgerald Drouin and Martha Beverly White
Jonathan Ashley, b. 5/22/1985 in Concord; John Fitzgerald Drouin and Martha Beverly White
Melissa Yvonne, b. 6/9/1987 in Concord; John Fitzgerald Drouin and Martha Elizabeth White

DUDLEY,
Christopher Robin, b. 10/19/1999 in Barnstead; Michael Dudley and Robin Dudley

DUDMAN,
Allyson Gayle, b. 4/28/1988 in Laconia; Gary Steven Dudman and Karen Buckley
Cory Scott, b. 3/15/1990 in Concord; Gary Steven Dudman and Karen Buckley

DUGAN,
Timothy Robert, b. 5/8/1978 in Concord; George Arnold Dugan (ME) and Donna Jean Hamblett (NH)

DUHAIME,
Dale Armand, b. 5/25/1991 in Concord; Daniel Armand Duhaime and Gail Marie Chagnon
Diane L., b. 11/21/1961 in Concord; Maurice A. Duhaime (Manchester) and Lea S. Grioux (Wauregan, CT)
Ryan Daniel, b. 8/29/1986 in Concord; Daniel Armand Duhaime and Gail Marie Chagnon

DUMONT,
Robert J., Jr., b. 11/22/1958 in Concord; Robert J. Dumont, Sr. and Judith D. Locke

DUNBAR,
Joel Michael, b. 3/9/1987 in Laconia; Raleigh Edward Dunbar and Donna Lee Blajda
Tucker Nathaniel, b. 8/25/1990 in Laconia; Raleigh Edward Dunbar, Jr. and Donna Lee Blajda

DUQUETTE,
Jennifer Lee, b. 3/31/1977 in Concord; Michael Wendell Duquette (NH) and Mary Lee Stackman (NH)

DURKEE,
Christina Anne, b. 6/30/1978 in Concord; Kevin Donald Durkee (NH) and Marjorie Anne Hillsgrove (NH)

DUSTIN,
Thomas R., b. 3/27/1957 in Concord; Robert E. Dustin (student, UNH) and Priscilla J. Parsons

EASTMAN,
Carolyn Joyce, b. 12/23/1935 in Wolfeboro; Ralph W. Eastman (garage owner) and Beatrice V. Carpenter
Charles Carroll, b. 8/15/1970 in Concord; Paul Russell Eastman (MA) and Jean Frances Abbott (NH); residence - Ctr. Barnstead
Cody Zachary, b. 6/23/1992 in Concord; Michael Paul Eastman and Amy Rose Emerson
Derek Leighton, b. 10/21/1978 in Concord; Ricky Leighton Eastman (NH) and Susan Denise Genest (NH)

Judith L., b. 5/19/1956 in Concord; James I. Eastman (carpenter) and Frances J. Banks

Marjorie Jean, b. 12/17/1946 in Concord; first; James I. Eastman (shoe worker) and Francis J. Banks

Michael P., b. 8/1/1961 in Concord; Paul R. Eastman (Boston, MA) and Jean F. Abbott (Wolfeboro); residence - So. Barnstead

Nicole Marie, b. 8/1/1981 in Concord; Ricky Leighton Eastman and Susan Denise Jenest

Penny J., b. 11/6/1964 in Concord; second; Paul R. Eastman (Boston, MA) and Jean F. Abbott (Wolfeboro); residence - Ctr. Barnstead

Robert J., b. 1/14/1953 in Concord; second; James I. Eastman (carpenter) and Frances J. Banks

ECKERT,

Brian John, b. 10/14/1981 in Dover; John Francis Eckert and Janet Elise Smith

EDGE,

Aspen Elizabeth, b. 4/30/1990 in Concord; John Thomas Edge and Karyn Elizabeth Bennett

Bryce Kathryn, b. 12/30/1992 in Wolfeboro; John Thomas Edge and Karyn Elizabeth Bennett

EKSTROM,

Jamie Lyn, b. 2/11/1981 in Concord; Robert Elton Ekstrom and Melanie Jean Tasker

ELKINS,

John Harry, b. 9/19/1927; second; John H. Elkins (Pittsfield) and Sybil Corson (Barnstead)

ELLIS,

Alexa Kate Taylor, b. 3/10/1986 in Hanover; Robert Buckingham Ellis and Teresa Louise Taylor

Colin Taylor, b. 3/10/1986 in Hanover; Robert Buckingham Ellis and Teresa Louise Taylor

Sophie Anna Taylor, b. 5/11/1988 in Concord; Robert Buckingham Ellis and Teresa Louise Taylor

ELLISON,
Raymond, b. 9/23/1922; sixth; Walter Ellison (lumberman, Nottingham) and Alta Glover (Nottingham)

EMERSON,
daughter [Marguerite A.], b. 8/2/1896; Ansel Emerson (blacksmith, Barnstead) and Alice Page (Gilmanton)
son [Earl L.], b. 11/5/1901; second; Albert Emerson (laborer, Barnstead) and Georgia Brown (Northwood)
daughter [Ellen Lydia], b. 9/24/1902; fourth; Ansel Emerson (blacksmith, 42, Barnstead) and Alice Page (33, Gilmanton I.W.)
daughter [Bessie F.], b. 7/2/1903; second; Augustus F. Emerson (farmer, 36, Dover) and Georgie Brown (23, Farmington)
daughter, b. 9/25/1903; third; Albert Emerson (laborer, Barnstead) and Georgie Brown
son [Harold B.], b. 3/25/1906; fourth; Albert F. Emerson (laborer, 31, Barnstead) and Georgia B. Brown (29, Northwood)
son [Oscar], b. 12/25/1906; third; Carlton E. Emerson (farmer, 24, Barnstead) and Lula E. Wilkins (23, Whitefield)
son [William], b. 1/9/1907; first; Henry W. Emerson (farmer, 18, Barnstead) and Lena M. Hillsgrove (18, Barnstead)
son [Ralph A.], b. 7/10/1909; fifth; Albert Emerson (blacksmith, 35, Barnstead) and Georgia Brown (32, Northwood)
daughter [Ruth], b. 6/25/1912; first; John O. Emerson (farmer, 28, Barnstead) and Minnie B. Wells (29, Alton)
son [Woodrow W.], b. 8/31/1912; sixth; Albert F. Emerson (blacksmith, 38, Barnstead) and Georgie B. Brown (32, Northwood)
daughter, b. 5/26/1914; fourth; Arthur C. Emerson (farmer, 28, Barnstead) and Essel Clough (28, Chichester)
child, b. 11/26/1918; fourth; Arthur C. Emerson (farmer, Barnstead) and Essel M. Clough (Pittsfield)
child, b. 3/22/1939 in Concord; fifth; Albert L. Emerson (truck driver) and Madeline Jenkins
Albert L., b. 10/12/1904; first; Carlton E. Emerson (farmer, 22, Barnstead) and Lulu E. Wilkins (20, Whitefield)
Camela Louise, b. 1/4/1948 in Pittsfield; third; Ralph A. Emerson (farmer) and Ruth E. Emerson
Carroll Walter, b. 7/18/1935; third; Albert L. Emerson (laborer) and Madeline A. Jenkins

Ellena Louise, b. 8/22/1937; first; Harold B. Emerson (laborer) and Margaret L. Davis

Ernest H., b. 2/17/1900; Albert F. Emerson (RR employee, Barnstead) and George Brown (Northwood)

Ethan Locke, b. 6/3/2000 in Concord; Roger Emerson and Margaret Emerson

Florence L., b. 8/15/1911; second; Arthur C. Emerson (farmer, 26, Barnstead) and Essiel E. Clough (25, Pittsfield)

Frances E., b. 12/13/1907; fourth; Ansel Emerson (blacksmith, 38, Barnstead) and Alice J. Page (38, Gilmanton)

Glendle Delena, b. 2/6/1930; first; Albert L. Emerson (laborer) and Madeline A. Jenkins

Harold Arthur, b. 7/20/1944; in Rochester; third; Harold B. Emerson (teamster) and Madeline Sargent

Harold Bernard, Jr., b. 6/25/1939; second; Harold B. Emerson (lumberman) and Margaret Davis

Juliana Locke, b. 8/8/1994 in Concord; Roger Burke Emerson and Margaret Jean Locke

Keith Maurice, b. 11/23/1943; Woodrow Emerson (truck driver) and Althea B. Kenison

Linda Lee, b. 3/11/1946 in Wolfeboro; second; Woodrow W. Emerson (shoe cutter) and Altha B. Kenison

Loretta Ellen, b. 12/14/1936; second; Ralph A. Emerson (laborer) and Ruth E. Emerson

Lula E., b. 10/10/1905; second; Carlton E. Emerson (farmer, 23, Barnstead) and Lula E. Wilkins (21, Whitefield)

Marjorie N., b. 4/7/1921; sixth; Arthur C. Emerson (farmer, Barnstead) and Essie Clough (Pittsfield)

Muriel Ruth, b. 8/4/1933; first; Ruth E. Emerson

Paulette Madeline, b. 9/29/1946 in Concord; seventh; Albert L. Emerson (lumberman) and Madeline A. Jenkins

Pauline Lue, b. 8/1/1932; second; Albert L. Emerson (laborer) and Madeline A. Jenkins

Ray, b. 8/18/1894; first; Llewellyn Emerson (shoemaker, Barnstead) and Mary Jenkins (Barnstead)

Raymond Clinton, b. 10/16/1975 in Concord; Raymond Clinton Emerson (NH) and Helen Louise Kulp (VA)

Sheila Vienna, b. 8/29/1937 in Ctr. Barnstead; fourth; Albert L. Emerson (laborer) and Madeline A. Jenkins

Shirley Mae, b. 6/21/1941; first; Harold B. Emerson (truck driving) and Madeline P. Sargent

Tanya Leigh, b. 11/13/1977 in Concord; Raymond Clinton Emerson (NH) and Helen Louise Kulp (VA); residence - Ctr. Barnstead

Tyler Keith, b. 1/10/1993 in Concord; Keith Maurice Emerson, Jr. and Deanna Jean Poirier

Velma Eldora, b. 3/23/1941; sixth; Albert L. Emerson (laborer) and Madeline A. Jenkins

Wilbur A., b. 3/21/1913; third; Arthur E. Emerson (farmer, 27, Barnstead) and Essiel A. Clough (26, Pittsfield)

EMERY,

Albert Chester, b. 2/3/1923; first; Alden C. Emery (Essex, VT) and Jennie L. Wallingford (Lebanon, ME)

Nathan Charles, b. 1/27/1927; third; Alden C. Emery (Chester) and Jennie Wallingford (Lebanon, ME)

Ralph Charles, b. 7/6/1925; second; Elden C. Emery (Chester) and Jennice L. Wallingford (Gilmanton)

EMORY,

Jessica Ashley, b. 4/6/1990 in Concord; Robert Lewis Emory and Frances Ursula Bluger

ERFF,

Jaime Lynn, b. 5/2/1989 in Concord; Scott Michael Erff and Deborah Ann Caruso

ERWIN,

Verna Patricia, b. 4/15/1937; first; Richard H. Erwin (school teacher) and Margaret I. Marston

EVANS,

son [Clarence], b. 8/11/1893; first; Austin Evans (laborer, Northwood) and Myra Munsey (Barnstead)

daughter [Ruth A.], b. 7/22/1901; third; Austin Evans (RR employee, 35, Strafford) and Myra Munsey (32, Barnstead)

Alice Audrey, b. 10/25/1929; first; Arva Evans (Barnstead) and Gladys Brown (Wolfeboro)

Arva, b. 9/26/1904; fourth; Austin Evans (RR employee, 39, Strafford) and Myra M. Munsey (36, Barnstead)

Florence, b. 2/14/1897; second; Austin Evans (RR employee, Strafford) and Myra Munsey (Barnstead)

EVERETT,
Rashaun O'Neal, b. 8/21/2000 in Concord; Joseph Everett and Catherine Everett

FAIR,
Christopher John, b. 12/4/1973 in Concord; Robert Campbell Fair (NY) and Lynne Teresa Cusumano (NY)
Corey Nathan, b. 10/4/1989 in Concord; Timmie Robert Fair and Deborah Lynn Clement
Karla Lee, b. 4/21/1980 in Laconia; Lawrence Ernest Fair, Sr. and Dorothy Marie Vien
Kattie Marie, b. 7/31/1980 in Laconia; Ronnie Kent Fair and Mary Frances Chase
Lance Robert, b. 5/12/1986 in Concord; Timmie Robert Fair and Deborah Lynn Clement
Lawrence Ernest, Jr., b. 4/21/1980 in Laconia; Lawrence Ernest Fair, Sr. and Dorothy Marie Vien
Timmie George, b. 5/3/1983 in Concord; Timmie Robert Fair and Deborah Lynn Clement

FAMIGLIETTI,
Matthew Neal, b. 8/31/1991 in Concord; Michael Joseph Famiglietti and Carolyn Elaine Downs

FARIA,
Matthew Edward, b. 11/14/1984 in Concord; Leonard Martin Faria and Mary Anne Terenzoni

FARNHAM,
Haley Mae, b. 10/4/1993 in Concord; Donald Burton Farnham and Dawn Mae Bergeron
Nathan Graham, b. 6/19/1997 in Concord; Donald B. Farnham and Dawn M. Bergeron

FARNSWORTH,
Dana Francis, II, b. 6/25/1972 in Concord; Dana Francis Farnsworth, II (CA) and Sandra Faye Kenison (ME)

FEENY,
Jeffrey Alan, b. 4/22/1989 in Concord; William Robert Feeny and Nancy Ann Turner

FEGLEY,
Carly Ann, b. 8/29/1990 in Concord; James Edward Fegley and Barbara Ann Psarudakis
Nicholas Robert, b. 11/14/1988 in Concord; James Edward Fegley and Barbara Ann Psarudakis

FELDMAN,
Gail Madge, b. 1/20/1947 in Concord; third; Arthur E. Feldman (lawyer) and Abbigail T. Estes

FIFE,
Alexander Orville, b. 3/9/1998 in Concord; Malcolm Fife and Antoinetta Barbato
Michael Angelo, b. 7/11/1996 in Concord; Malcolm Harold Fife and Antoinetta Marie Barbato

FINETHY,
Kaitlyn Laura, b. 6/26/2000 in Concord; David Finethy and Debra Finethy

FINNIGAN,
Margaret Esther, b. 10/4/1942; first; Jack F. Finnigan (clergyman) and Ruth A. Stubbs

FIRMAN,
Benjamin William, b. 7/1/1992 in Manchester; Kenneth John Firman and Tami-Jill Perrins

FIS[C]HER,
Floyd Erwin, Jr., b. 7/23/1933; second; Floyd E. Fischer (laborer) and Imogene Miller
Richard Lawrence, b. 8/28/1935; third; Floyd E. Fisher (laborer) and Imogene Miller

FLAD,
John A., b. 12/16/1966 in Concord; fourth; William G. Flad (Concord) and Patricia E. Higgins (Concord)

FLETCHER,
daughter, b. 7/14/1888; first; Fred P. Fletcher (farmer, New Durham) and Nellie M. Jones (Alton)

Ida L., b. 3/1/1908; first; Frank L. Fletcher (farmer, 27, Claremont) and Edith M. Ackerman (25, Barnstead)

FLOYD,
Christopher West, Jr., b. 1/21/1978 in Derry; Christopher West Floyd (NH) and Lisa Ann Bukoski (MA); residence - Ctr. Barnstead
Nicholas Ralph, b. 2/27/1979 in Derry; Christopher West Floyd and Lisa Ann Bukoski

FLYNN,
Jacob Riley, b. 10/20/2000 in Concord; Michael Flynn and Sara Flynn

FOLLANSBEE,
Calvin Albert, Jr., b. 4/17/1991 in Concord; Calvin Albert Follansbee and Leslie Jean Boudreau

FONTAINE,
Maggie Ray, b. 10/3/2000 in Rochester; Scott Fontaine and Amy Fontaine

FOOTE,
Michael Armand, Jr., b. 2/24/1994 in Concord; Michael Armand Foote and Ann Marie Bamford

FORD,
Damien Christopher, b. 9/9/1989 in Concord; Thomas Archie Ford and Debbie Lynn Pagan
David Thomas, b. 6/10/1985 in Concord; Thomas Archie Ford and Debbie Lynn Pagan

FORTIER,
Sarah Elizabeth, b. 10/7/1984 in Concord; Richard George Fortier, Sr. and Diane Catherine Meuse

FORTIN,
Melissa Lynn, b. 3/1/1992 in Laconia; Raymond Joseph Fortin and Lynn Marie Messier

FOSS,
child [George G.], b. 12/12/1890; third; Albion N. Foss (farmer, Barnstead) and Josie Foss (Belmont)
son, b. 9/24/1893; second; Haven B. Foss (farmer, 37, Strafford) and Hattie C. Varney (22, Farmington)
son, b. 2/4/1898; Haven B. Foss (farmer, Strafford) and Hattie C. Varney (Farmington)
daughter, b. 3/28/1902; first; Oliver M. Foss (farmer, 38, Strafford) and Abbie L. Avery (34, Barnstead)
son [Warren], b. 5/29/1904; second; Frank G. Foss (mail carrier, 40, Strafford) and Bessie G. Hall (32, Strafford)
son, b. 7/11/1906; third; Oliver M. Foss (teamster, 39, Strafford) and Abbie L. Avery (37, Barnstead)
daughter, b. 12/12/1906; third; Frank G. Foss (mail carrier, 42, Strafford) and Bessie G. Hall (34, Strafford)
son, b. 5/10/1922; fourth; William B. Foss (laborer, Strafford) and Grace B. Drake (Barnstead)
child, b. 5/18/1924; second; James Henry Foss (Haverhill, MA) and Nina Higgins (Fasley, VT)
Alice F., b. 5/19/1881; Charles A. Foss and Emma F. Young (1954)
Brianne Marie, b. 5/15/1981 in Concord; David Langdon Foss and Dawn Marie Bedell
David L., b. 9/13/1956 in Concord; Lindy E. Foss (stitcher) and Bettie A. Kenney
Derek Langdon, b. 10/9/1979 in Concord; David Langdon Foss and Dawn Marie Bedell
Eleanor Sanborn, b. 11/1/1920; second; Fred Foss (farmer, Barnstead) and Velna E. Foss (Loudon)
Hattie E., b. 3/15/1892; first; Haven B. Foss (farmer, Strafford) and Hattie E. Varney (Farmington)
Jason Aloise, b. 5/15/1980 in Concord; Dan Hale Foss and Cynthia Lee Ayer
Laura Gail, b. 7/22/1975 in Concord; Robert Arthur Foss (NH) and Christine D. Anderson (NH)
Lindy Eugene, b. 1/19/1928; sixth; William B. Foss (Strafford) and Grace Drake (Barnstead)
Lois Marion, b. 10/30/1922; second; John H. Foss (RR watchman, Haverhill, MA) and Nina M. Higgins (Fairlee, VT)
Mildred, b. 8/3/1915; first; William B. Foss (laborer, Strafford) and Grace Drake (Barnstead)

Norman Ordway, b. 6/26/1919; first; Fred Foss (farmer, Barnstead) and Velna Emma Ordway (Loudon)

Robert S., b. 1/4/1925; fifth; William B. Foss (Strafford) and Grace Drake (Barnstead)

Russell John, b. 3/22/1978 in Concord; Robert Arthur Foss (NH) and Christine Diane Anderson (NH)

Ruth, b. 8/29/1918; third; William B. Foss (lumberman, Strafford) and Grace Drake (Barnstead)

Wilbur Roscoe, b. 11/6/1916; second; William B. Foss (carpenter, Strafford) and Grace Drake (Barnstead)

FOSTER,

daughter, b. 1/27/1885; first; William P. Foster (millwright) and ----- (Chichester) (1888)

Dorothy M., b. 6/4/1926; first; Kenneth R. Foster (Berwick, ME) and Margaret Barton (Pittsfield)

FOURNIER,

son, b. 9/22/1890; first; Alphonzo Fournier (farmer, Canada) and Abbie Jones (Barnstead)

FOWLER,

George Timothy, b. 3/15/1923; fifth; Jesse Fowler (laborer) and Mary E. Pleasant

FRAME,

Marion E., b. 3/25/1908; second; Frederick P. Frame (mail agent, 37, Lynn, MA) and Myra A. Jenkins (27, Barnstead)

Norman F., b. 3/25/1908; first; Frederick P. Frame (mail agent, 37, Lynn, MA) and Myra A. Jenkins (27, Barnstead)

FRAMENT,

Lauren Elma, b. 7/4/1991 in Concord; William Robert Frament and Robin Jean Gwinn

Zachary William, b. 1/17/1998 in Concord; William Frament and Robin Frament

FRANGIONE,

Anthony Donald, b. 2/12/1993 in Dover; Thomas Arthur Frangione and Katherine Irma Conway

FRASER,
M. Taylor, II, b. 6/29/1985 in Concord; Mark Taylor Fraser and
 Linda Joyce Boisvert
Robyn Lee, b. 8/5/1982 in Concord; Mark Taylor Fraser and Linda
 Joyce Boisvert

FRASIER,
son, b. 9/6/1952 in Concord; fifth; Warren G. Frasier (self
 employed) and Verona Taylor
Jonathan W., b. 7/5/1955 in Concord; Warren G. Fraser (sic)
 (hoisting engineer) and Verona Taylor
Warren Gerald, 2nd, b. 3/22/1950 in Concord; third; Warren G.
 Frasier (engineer) and Verona Taylor

FRENCH,
Jasonn John, b. 5/15/1972 in Concord; John David French (NH)
 and Gail Ann Raymond (NH)
John David, b. 2/6/1929; third; Herbert E. French (Benton) and
 Marie R. Sumner (Boston, MA)
Ralph S., b. 7/9/1915; first; Herbert C. French (farmer, Barnstead)
 and Marie Sumer (Boston, MA)

FRIZZELL,
Elliot Ray, b. 7/18/2000 in Concord; Richard Frizzell and Pamela
 Frizzell

FROST,
Maurice A., Jr., b. 2/17/1967 in Concord; first; Maurice A. Frost
 (mechanic, Pittsfield) and Jean L. McClary (Pittsfield)

FRYE,
Diana L., b. 9/1/1955 in Concord; Walter H. Frye (woodsman) and
 Minnie E. Wycoff

FUESSTINER,
Samuel, b. 7/4/1918; first; Samuel Fuesstiner, Jr. (farrier, Russia)
 and Almira J. Mera (Chichester)

GADOMSKI,
Samuel Andrew, b. 4/18/1991 in Concord; Robert Steven Gadomski
 and Gayle Ellen Pocock

GAGE,
Mariah Janel, b. 4/7/1991 in Concord; Wayne Everett Gage and Debra Jean Mandigo
Tyler Austin, b. 2/22/1996 in Concord; Wayne Everett Gage and Debra Jean Mandigo

GAGNE,
Gloria Jean, b. 7/7/1943 in Pittsfield; second; David J. Gagne (cutter) and Beulah G. Gray
Lynda Lee, b. 1/3/1942 in Wolfeboro; first; David Joseph Gagne (cutter-perforator) and Beulah Gertrude Gray

GAGNON,
Derek Stephen, b. 3/5/1999 in Concord; Norman Gagnon and Rhonda Gagnon
Hannah Pearl, b. 9/18/1998 in Concord; William Gagnon and Lisa Gagnon
Lynn Anne, b. 7/7/1987 in Manchester; Mark Thomas Gagnon and Doreen Ann Landry
Mark Thomas, II, b. 3/26/1990 in Manchester; Mark Thomas Gagnon and Doreen Ann Landry
Norman Leon, b. 9/3/1947 in Concord; second; Roland L. Gagnon (mill worker) and Frances E. Davis

GALLAGHER,
Melissa Marie, b. 11/16/1984 in Concord; Scott Walter Gallagher and Sandra Marie Corlin
Shaun Christopher, b. 5/17/1987 in Concord; Scott Walter Gallagher, Sr. and Sandra Marie Gallagher

GANNON,
Dylan James, b. 1/3/1994 in Manchester; Michael Sean Gannon and Jennifer Carlie Walkins
Ryan Michael, b. 7/20/1992 in Manchester; Michael Sean Gannon and Jennifer Carlie Walkins

GARCIA,
Collin Robert, b. 8/8/1993 in Dover; Robert Christopher Garcia and Regina Marie Collins

GARDNER,
Ines M., b. 3/7/1888; Julius Gardner and Olive L. Knowles (1951)
Paul A., b. 11/21/1959 in Concord; Kenneth A. Gardner and Sandra E. Curtis

GARLAND,
son [Frank], b. 6/25/1891; second; Oscar J. Garland (farmer, Barnstead) and Eliza McVean (PEI)
Barbara Mae, b. 11/7/1916; first; Frank R. Garland (clerk, Barnstead) and Nellie T. Fisher (Craftsbury, VT)
Esther L., b. 5/7/1899; third; Melvin H. Garland (farmer, 46, Barnstead) and Nellie J. Green (44, Loudon) (1910)
Gary R., b. 1/6/1953; Wilbur J. Garland (lumberman) and Lillian E. Brown
Judith May, b. 3/30/1945 in Pittsfield; second; Wilbur J. Garland (farmer) and Lillian E. Brown
Mary Elizabeth, b. 3/18/1920; first; Wilbur J. Garland (farmer, Barnstead) and Hattie M. Cohan (Pembroke)
Norman Wilbur, b. 4/2/1947 in Concord; third; Wilbur John Garland (lumbering and farmer) and Lillian Brown
Robert M., b. 4/2/1922; second; Wilbur J. Garland (farmer, Barnstead) and Hattie M. Cofran (Pembroke)
Ronald Frank, b. 3/31/1948; fourth; Wilbur J. Garland (lumbering) and Lillian E. Brown
Wilbur J., b. 4/8/1888; first; Oscar J. Garland (farmer, 26, Barnstead) and Eliza McVean (30, PEI) (1912)

GARNETT,
Darien Richard, b. 6/25/1993 in New London; Lawrence Alan Garnett and Patricia Jean Bridge
Peter Barton, b., 1/29/1988 in Concord; Lawrence Alan Garnett and Patricia Bridge

GARONE,
Laura Ashley, b. 8/11/1983 in Laconia; Thomas Harry Garone and Debra Lee Golden

GASKELL,
Bessie Elizabeth, b. 8/8/1923; third; Harry C. Gaskell (Ellsworth, ME) and Etta May Smith (Gilmanton)

Harry Carl, b. 5/24/1921; first; Harry C. Gaskell (farmer, Ellsworth, ME) and Etta M. Smith (Gilmanton)

John L., b. 7/6/1922; second; Harry C. Gaskell (farmer, Ellsworth, ME) and Ella Smith (Gilmanton)

GATES,
Solomon Jacob, b. 7/19/1981 in Concord; Robert Kenneth Gates and Carol Louise Tiede

GAUDREAU,
Kerry Quinn, b. 6/12/1992 in Concord; Robert Eldon Gaudreau and Sheila Ann Wood

GAULT,
Edith June, b. 5/20/1923; first; Roland W. Gault (Bridgewater, VT) and Zelma K. Dow (Barnstead)

Ida Caroline, b. 4/21/1927; second; Roland W. Gault (Bridgewater) and Zelma Dow (Barnstead)

GAUTHIER,
Julie Ann, b. 11/22/1971 in Concord; Ronald Arthur Gauthier (AL) and Virginia Fay Fauver (MA)

GAY,
Christopher Wesley, b. 9/22/1980 in Portsmouth; Barry Elliott Gay and Martha S. Beacham

GEDDES,
Andrew Thomas, b. 11/30/1992 in Laconia; David Walter Geddes, Jr. and Diane Lee Gray

GENEST,
Colleen L., b. 8/12/1967 in Concord; third; Roger E. Genest (lineman, Pittsfield) and Maxine J. Reed (Barnstead)

Elizabeth Madeline, b. 5/3/1924; first; Henry Genest (Pittsfield) and Bertha E. Stone (New York, NY)

Josie Lynne, b. 3/13/1999 in Concord; Randolph Genest and Jessica Genest

Karen Lynn, b. 1/27/1964 in Concord; second; Roger E. Genest (Pittsfield) and Maxine J. Reed (Barnstead)

Lisa J., b. 1/14/1961 in Concord; Roger E. Genest (Pittsfield) and Maxine J. Reed (Barnstead)

GENTILE,
Ashley Jean, b. 10/7/1987 in Concord; Angelo Augustus Gentile and Jean Susan Sokolowsky
Christopher Augustus, b. 10/29/1990 in Concord; Angelo Augustus Gentile and Jean Susan Sokolowsky

GERLACK,
Arthur L., b. 8/14/1955 in Concord; Henry C. Gerlack, Jr. (woodsman) and Lorraine B. Berry
Barbara M., b. 8/17/1958 in Concord; Henry C. Gerlack and Lorraine B. Berry
Russell A., b. 2/7/1959 in Concord; Alfred F. Gerlack and Patricia L. Cate

GIAQUINTA,
Donald Anthony, b. 9/20/1987 in Concord; Joseph Anthony Giaquinta and Karen Ruth Newcomb

GIBBONS,
Kevin Paul, b. 8/13/1985 in Concord; Paul Kevin Gibbons and Robin Lee Riel
Sean Patrick, b. 5/5/1988 in Concord; Paul Kevin Gibbons and Robin Riel

GILBERT,
son, b. 2/15/1895; Christopher Gilbert (laborer, NB) and Mattie Gilbert (NB)
Joshua Mark, b. 4/28/2000 in Portsmouth; Jon Gilbert and Joyce Gilbert

GILMAN,
Mary Louise, b. 3/31/1939 in Nashua; first; Victor E. Gilman (farmer) and Olga G. Littlefield

GINGRAS,
Keith, b. 4/14/1993 in Lebanon; Scott Gingras and Wendy D. Ricker

GINTER,
Adrienne Rae, b. 7/7/1980 in Laconia; Eric Ginter and Jeri Ann Van Doren
Lindsay Anne, b. 7/2/1982 in Laconia; Eric Ginter and Jeri Anne Van Doren

GIRARD,
Cory Paul, b. 7/28/1991 in Concord; David Marc Girard and Kristine Marie Berwick
Rebecca Lynn, b. 7/22/1996 in Concord; Christopher Jean Girard and Heide Ann Dupont

GLANCY,
Cynthia Annette, b. 8/18/1987 in Manchester; Benjamin Francis Glancy and Cynthia Annette Dicey

GLASS,
William Louis, b. 5/31/1979 in Manchester; Richard Louis Glass and Pamela Anne Bullivant

GLINES,
Kathleen, b. 6/18/1914; first; Joseph A. Glines (station agent, 43, MA) and Valeria May Fickett (25, ME)

GOLDBERG,
Crystal Marie, b. 8/31/2000 in Concord; Michael Goldberg and Dana Goldberg

GOLDEN,
Alfred Kenneth, b. 8/11/1928; eleventh; John E. Golden (Plattsburg, NY) and N. Blanche Locke (Pittsfield)
Carter Richard Barrett, b. 10/5/1992 in Concord; Quinn Richard Golden and Vivian Lee Prichard
Daniel Philbrick, b. 2/21/1937; seventeenth; John E. Golden (shoe shop) and Blanche Locke
David Edward, b. 1/28/1923; seventh; John E. Golden (Plattsburg, NY) and Nellie Blanche Locke (Pittsfield)
Frances May, b. 11/13/1930; twelfth; John E. Golden (wood heel worker) and Blanche Lock
Garry, b. 2/11/1932; thirteenth; John E. Golden (wood heel worker) and Blanche Locke

Hannah Elaine Gladys, b. 10/5/1992 in Concord; Quinn Richard
Golden and Vivian Lee Prichard
Jean Rose, b. 6/23/1935; sixteenth; John E. Golden (shoe worker)
and Blanche N. Locke
Joan Francena, b. 9/14/1933; fifteenth; John E. Golden (laborer)
and Blanche Locke
John Franklin, b. 9/14/1933; fourteenth; John E. Golden (laborer)
and Blanche Locke
Kenneth Linwood, b. 1/30/1980 in Concord; Scott Linwood Golden
and Joyce Mae Smith
Leona, b. 2/1/1924; eighth; John E. Golden (Plattsburg, NY) and
Nellie Blanch Lock (Pittsfield)
Margaret E., b. 9/6/1921; sixth; John E. Golden (watchman,
Plattsburg, NY) and Nellie Blanch Locke (Pittsfield)
Paul Anthony, b. 10/8/1918; fourth; John E. Golden (RR watchman,
Plattsburg, NY) and Blanche Locke (Pittsfield)
Quinn R., b. 11/26/1960 in Concord; second; Richard L. Golden
(mechanic, Sanford, ME) and Judith M. Strickland (Boston,
MA)
Rebecca Rae Judith, b. 7/19/1988 in Concord; Quinn Richard
Golden and Vivian Lee Prichard
Richard Michael, b. 2/9/1927; tenth; John E. Golden (Plattsburg,
NY) and N. Blanche Locke (Pittsfield)
Robert Francis, b. 2/19/1920; fifth; John E. Golden (watchman,
Plattsburg, NY) and Nellie Blanche Locke (Pittsfield)
Ruth Blanche, b. 4/27/1925; ninth; John E. Golden (Plattsburg, NY)
and Blanche Locke (Pittsfield)
Samantha Donna Kathleen, b. 8/8/1990 in Concord; Quinn Richard
Golden and Vivian Lee Prichard
Scott L., b. 6/10/1957 in Wolfeboro; Richard L. Golden (mechanic)
and Judith M. Strickland
Shanda E., b. 11/16/1962 in Concord; third; Richard L. Golden
(Sanford, ME) and Judith M. Strickland (Boston, MA);
residence - Ctr. Barnstead
William Henry, b. 7/28/1917; third; John E. Golden (watchman,
Plattsburg, NY) and Nellie Blanch Locke (Pittsfield)

GOLDTHWAITE,
Dana Ann, b. 6/15/1969 in Concord; David Alan Goldthwaite (CT)
and Janet Irene Pope (OK)

David Alan, b. 3/8/1971 in Haverhill, MA; David A. Goldthwaite (CT) and Janet I. Pope (OK); residence - Ctr. Barnstead

GOODWIN,
Belinda Rae, b. 7/19/1972 in Epsom Circle; Cressy Goodwin (NH) and Jeanne Elizabeth Pike (NH); residence - Ctr. Barnstead
Ethan L., b. 10/21/1966 in Peterborough; first; Gressy Goodwin (Concord) and Jeanne E. Pike (Littleton); residence - Ctr. Barnstead
Heather Jeanne, b. 1/9/1969 in Peterborough; Cressy Goodwin (NH) and Jeanne Elizabeth Pike (NH)
Margaret J., b. 2/24/1954 in Newton, MA; Delmar L. Goodwin (teacher) and Hortense Lovejoy
Sadie June, b. 6/24/1929; fifth; Clifton Goodwin (Gilmanton) and Ethel Dame (New Durham)
Severin Leighton, b. 1/11/1975 in Concord; Cressy Goodwin (NH) and Jeanne Elizabeth Pike (NH)

GOSSE,
Ann Louise, b. 12/21/1949 in Concord; second; Arthur Malcolm Gosse (service attendant) and Mary Louise Donovan
James Thomas, b. 3/15/1960 in Concord; fourth; Arthur M. Gosse (shop foreman, Arlington, MA) and Mary L. Donovan (Malden, MA)
Karen M., b. 9/20/1954 in Concord; Arthur M. Gosse (foreman) and Mary L. Donovan
Robert A., b. 1/25/1964 in Concord; fifth; Arthur M. Gosse (Arlington, MA) and Mary L. Donovan (Malden, MA); residence - Ctr. Barnstead
Seth Thomas, b. 12/17/1994 in Concord; Thomas Arthur Gosse and Allison Jean Burritt
Spencer Aaron, b. 6/14/1997 in Concord; Thomas Arthur Gosse and Allison J. Burritt
Tania Eileen, b. 4/17/1972 in Concord; William Arthur Gosse (NH) and Candice Eileen Hoyt (NH)
William Arthur, b. 11/5/1947 in Concord; first; Arthur M. Gosse (store clerk) and Mary L. Donovan

GOSSELIN,
Stephanie Anne, b. 9/15/1991 in Concord; Andrew Edward Gosselin and Christine Lee Francey

GRACIE,
Curtis Ingram, b. 3/25/1942 in Wolfeboro; first; Louis Ingram Gracie (machinist) and Doris Mae Jukes

GRADY,
Patrick Trevor, b. 6/26/1999 in Concord; Joseph Grady and Joanne Grady
Shane Raymond, b. 6/26/1999 in Concord; Joseph Grady and Joanne Grady

GRAFTON,
Derek Christopher, b. 9/20/1987 in Wolfeboro; David Christopher Grafton and Deborah Lynn Ventola

GRAHAM,
Angela Marie, b. 8/10/1990 in Concord; Alan Douglas Graham and Dina Marie Zimbone
Gordon Michael, b. 5/6/1950 in Concord; first; Gordon H. Graham (commercial pilot) and Irene Rama

GRAVES,
Madeline Ann, b. 12/17/1996 in Concord; Michael Lynn Graves and Deborah Elaine Byrnes

GRAY,
son [William C.], b. 2/2/1888; second; Orris D. Gray (shoemaker, Barnstead) and Harriet A. Hannaford (Carlisle, MA)
son [Fred W.], b. 6/6/1897; sixth; Herbert Gray (farmer, Barnstead)
son [George, Jr.], b. 3/18/1898; George Gray (farmer, Barnstead) and Emma Jane Cole (Barnstead)
son [Myron Earl], b. 9/30/1898; Herbert A. Gray (farmer, Barnstead) and Myrtle S. Cate (Allenstown)
son [Edward A.], b. 5/31/1902; first; Albert B. Gray (farmer, 21, Strafford) and Bessie J. Brown (20, Durham)
daughter [Emma J.], b. 5/2/1905; second; Albert B. Gray (farmer, 24, Strafford) and Bessie J. Brown (23, Durham)
daughter [Hazel M.], b. 10/30/1906; eighth; Herbert Gray (laborer, 42, Barnstead) and Myrtie S. Cate (35, Allenstown)
daughter [Violet], b. 5/17/1909; fourth; Albert Gray (farmer, 28, Strafford) and Bessie J. Brown (27, Durham)

son [Cohin L.], b. 10/16/1912; fifth; Albert B. Gray (laborer, 32, Strafford) and Bessie H. Brown (30, Durham)

child [Frank Clarence], b. 5/9/1920; second; William C. Gray (farmer, Barnstead) and Ruth Davis (Auburn)

Beatrice Mary, b. 2/8/1923; second; Myron E. Gray (Barnstead) and Hattie V. Prince (Rochester)

Bessie E., b. 3/23/1907; third; Albert B. Gray (laborer, 26, Barnstead) and Bessie J. Brown (25)

Beulah Gertrude, b. 8/1/1921; first; Myron E. Gray (fireman, Barnstead) and Viola H. Prince (Rochester)

Blanche Lillian, b. 8/15/1925; fourth; William C. Gray (Barnstead) and Ruth Davis (Auburn)

Brenda Joyce, b. 1/14/1947 in Pittsfield; first; Barbara M. Gray

Carol A., b. 8/8/1955 in Concord; Frank C. Gray (laborer) and Angie M. Bartlett

Dennis Brian, b. 4/28/1971 in Concord; Dennis Robert Gray (NH) and Andrea Lee Coburn (NH)

Dennis Robert, b. 3/26/1947 in Concord; first; Robert L. Gray (machinist) and Shirley H. McIntosh

Donald Nelson, b. 2/13/1937; seventh; William C. Gray (farmer) and Ruth Davis

Dorothy Ruth, b. 7/13/1922; third; William C. Gray (farmer, Barnstead) and Ruth Davis (Auburn)

Emma Jane, b. 10/24/1931; fourth; Violet M. Gray

Grace Evelyn, b. 3/13/1923; first; Bessie O. Gray (Barnstead)

Henry Frank, b. 9/17/1932; third; Edward A. Gray (weaver) and Ada Laro

Laura Anna, b. 4/22/1927; fifth; William C. Gray (Barnstead) and Ruth Davis (Auburn)

Linda J., b. 7/23/1961 in Concord; Walter A. Gray (Barnstead) and Jean G. Locke (Pittsfield)

Louise Helen, b. 12/23/1917; first; William C. Gray (farmer, Barnstead) and Ruth Davis (Auburn)

Margaret Ina, b. 5/15/1923; sixth; Albert B. Gray (Strafford) and Bessie J. Brown (Durham)

Marion Edna, b. 8/5/1924; first; Albert Wallingford and Violet May Gray (Barnstead)

Mary Madeline, b. 1/17/1927; first; Edward A. Gray (Barnstead) and Ada M. Laro (Pittsfield)

Milisia Suzanne, b. 1/12/1982 in Concord; Robert Loring Gray and Carla Lee Burbank

Ralph Howard, b. 3/20/1930; sixth; William C. Gray (farmer) and Ruth Davis
Richard Malcom, b. 9/12/1926; third; Leslie M. Gray (Barnstead) and Virginia E. Chagnon (E. Charleston, VT)
Robert A., Jr., b. 11/21/1957; Robert A. Gray, Sr. (mason worker) and Eleanor L. McKenzie
Robert Anthony, b. 7/2/1939; first; Grace E. Gray
Robert Lee, b. 7/29/1930; third; John Frank Gray (mechanic) and Edith Langmaid
Robert Loring, Jr., b. 11/26/1983 in Concord; Robert Loring Gray and Carla Lee Burbank
Steven E., b. 7/1/1966 in Concord; fourth; Walter A. Gray (Barnstead) and Jean G. Locke (Concord)
Timothy James, b. 8/12/1977 in Concord; William Frank Gray (NH) and Carol Ann Poulius (MA)
Velna V., b. 11/6/1921; first; Leslie M. Gray (weaver, Barnstead) and Virginia E. Shorey (Charlestown)
Walter Albert, b. 7/8/1929; second; Edward A. Gray (Barnstead) and Ada M. Laro (Pittsfield)
Wanda Anne, b. 12/4/1969 in Laconia; Edwin Albert Gray (MA) and Margaret Louise Newell (ME); residence - Ctr. Barnstead
Wayne S., b. 7/14/1959 in Concord; George H. Gray and Mary E. Beede

GREEN-BARBER,
Lindsay Nicole, b. 11/2/1983 in Franklin; Mitchell John Barber and Lisa Joan Green

GREENE,
Ernest G., b. 8/5/1878; Orrin P. Greene and Ellen A. Paige (1952)
Justin Daniel, b. 9/18/1999 in Laconia; Daniel Greene and Carole Dodge-Greene

GREENFIELD,
Charles H., b. 7/21/1912; first; Oswald J. Greenfield (plumber, 31, Boston, MA) and Mary F. Clapp (32, Norfolk, MA)

GREGOIRE,
Jacqueline Ellen, b. 5/6/1971 in Concord; David Arthur Gregoire (NH) and Noelle Rose Boucher (NH)

Jeffrey Arthur, b. 5/6/1971 in Concord; David Arthur Gregoire (NH) and Noelle Rose Boucher (NH)
Jennifer Sue, b. 5/6/1971 in Concord; David Arthur Gregoire (NH) and Noelle Rose Boucher (NH)

GRENERT,
Abbie Elizabeth, b. 12/19/1976 in Manchester; Mark Walter Grenert (MA) and Susan Jean Fudala (NH)

GRIFFIN,
Thelma M., b. 11/14/1922; first; Charles E. Griffin (weaver, Boston, MA) and Clara E. Alm (Pittsfield)

GROLEAU,
Keith James, b. 4/5/1985 in Concord; James Philip Groleau and Devere Darlene Hurst
Stephanie DeVere, b. 1/17/1984 in Concord; James Philip Groleau and DeVere Darlene Hurst

GUERCIONI,
Vern Alfred, b. 9/15/1944 in Pittsfield; second; Frank A. Guercioni (mechanic) and Opal M. Stevens

GUPTILL,
Jessica Lynn, b. 11/1/1991 in Concord; Kerry Frank Guptill and Susan Marie Socha

GUSTAFSON,
Christine R., b. 4/30/1967 in Hanover; first; Frank R. Gustafson (truck driver, Malden, MA) and Betty A. Weare (Rochester)

GUTERMANN,
June Ellen, b. 6/22/1940 in Concord; first; William T. Gutermann (storekeeper) and Lillian B. E. Evans

HADLEY,
Jack Donald, b. 9/28/1929; first; Vaughn E. Hadley (Concord) and Irene Pouliot (Lawrence, MA)

HAINES,
Eva May, b. 5/7/1901; first; Lewis Haines (brakeman, 24, Concord) and Gertie L. Leavitt (Suncook)

HALL,
daughter, b. 9/16/1890; second; George L. Hall (farmer, Barnstead) and Mary E. Holmes (Barnstead)
child, b. 8/9/1920; third; George F. Hall (farmer, Barnstead) and Ruth H. Baker (Troy)
Corey Wayne, b. 9/2/1971 in Concord; Wayne Russell Hall (NH) and Lucile Mae Heino (NH)
Gordon Kenneth, b. 3/13/1919; first; Harold C. Hall (laborer, Gilmanton) and Flora H. Parsons (Gilmanton)
Heidi Mae, b. 8/22/1969 in Concord; Wayne Russell Hall (NH) and Lucile Mae Heino (NH)
Ruth Elizabeth, b. 12/13/1918; second; George F. Hall (farmer, Barnstead) and Ruth Helen Baker (Troy, NH)

HALLGREN,
Corey Dale, b. 5/30/1982 in Concord; Dale Robert Hallgren and Lee Ellen Gillis

HAM,
daughter, b. 8/11/1916; fifth; Charles Llewellyn Ham (board sawyer, Strafford) and Cora May Drew (Dover)
child, b. 3/25/1938 in Wolfeboro; first; Charles L. Ham (farmer) and Elizabeth Pedigo

HAMMOND,
Nicholas Alan, b. 10/29/1991 in Manchester; David Edward Hammond and Karen Ella Wing

HAMPTON,
Kristina Lee, b. 1/15/1980 in Concord; Brian Lee Hampton and Daiva Jane Simanskis

HANLEY,
Patrick Paul, b. 8/14/1981 in Concord; John William Hanley and Michelle AnnMarie Beaudette

HANNAFORD,
Owen Nicholas, b. 11/8/2000 in Concord; Dana Hannaford and Jessica Hannaford

HANSCOM,
Megan Nicole, b. 5/12/1994 in Concord; Alan Gregory Hanscom and Lisa Gay Fogg
Naomi Rose, b. 11/17/1989 in Concord; Gary John Hanscom and Corrine Michelle Crawford

HANSON,
son, b. 8/3/1889; fifth; Levi Hanson (farmer, Barnstead) and ----- (Barnstead)
daughter [Vina H.], b. 6/1/1904; fourth; Sidney Hanson (farmer, 28, Barnstead) and Lura M. Nutter (22, Gilmanton)
daughter, b. 3/28/1906; first; Alvin G. Hanson (blacksmith, 37, Barnstead) and Ellen M. Carbee (27, Canada)
daughter, b. 7/8/1909; sixth; Sidney Hanson (farmer, 31, Barnstead) and Lura M. Nutter (26, Gilmanton)
Abbie D., b. 5/8/1913; eighth; Sidney E. Hanson (farmer, 36, Barnstead) and Lura M. Nutter (31, Gilmanton)
Carl, b. 3/26/1928; first; Vina G. Hanson (Barnstead)
Carl N., b. 6/28/1906; fifth; Sidney E. Hanson (farmer, 29, Barnstead) and Lura M. Nutter (24, Gilmanton)
Catherine Mary, b. 12/24/1973 in Wolfeboro; Robert David Hanson (NH) and Roberta Ann Plastridge (MA); residence - Ctr. Barnstead
Edward C., b. 8/14/1911; seventh; Sidney E. Hanson (farmer, 33, Barnstead) and Lura M. Nutter (28, Gilmanton)
Eleanor Mary, b. 4/27/1925 in Wolfeboro; second; Carl N. Hanson (farmer) and Sarah E. Nutter
Leonard D., b. 8/3/1953 in Rochester; Lloyd G. Hanson (marker) and Natalie L. Wyatt
Leslie Carroll, b. 11/6/1932; first; Carl N. Hanson (farmer) and Sarah E. Nutter
Lloyd George, b. 9/17/1919; second; George G. Hanson (farmer, Barnstead) and Alice M. Pickernell (Dorchester, MA)
Lloyd George, Jr., b. 2/3/1947 in Rochester; third; Lloyd G. Hanson (teamster) and Natalie L. Wyatt
Lorraine, b. 6/26/1924; third; George G. Hanson (Barnstead) and Alice Pickernell (Dorchester, MA)

Marjorie E., b. 5/19/1915; ninth; Sidney E. Hanson (farmer, Barnstead) and Lura M. Nutter (Gilmanton)

Millicent K., b. 7/25/1918; second; Alvin G. Hanson (wheelwright, Barnstead) and Ellen Carbee (Canada)

Phyllis Marjorie, b. 8/30/1929; fourth; George G. Hanson (Barnstead) and Alice Pickernell (Dorchester, MA)

Willard L., b. 1/10/1918; first; George G. Hanson (farmer, Barnstead) and Alice M. Pickernell (Dorchester, MA)

HARDY,
Barbara A., b. 12/28/1960 in Concord; Frank A. Hardy (Wilton, ME) and Marilyn R. Whitehead (New York, NY)

HARNOLD,
Alfred G., b. 11/14/1916; first; Frederick C. Harnold (weaver, England) and Ella May Powell (Barnstead)

HARRIMAN,
Francis R., b. 8/27/1896; stillborn; I. E. Harriman (shoemaker, ME) and Grace Sellman (Lyman, MA)

HARRINGTON,
John Joseph, b. 2/7/1977 in Laconia; Rodney Eldridge Harrington (ME) and Clara Jean Thornton (NH)

HARTSHORN,
Kristi Leigh, b. 5/21/1978 in Concord; Edward Leigh Hartshorn (MA) and Ellen Mary Munato (MA); residence - Ctr. Barnstead

HATCH,
Tarsha Lynn, b. 5/14/1986 in Concord; Richard Joseph Hatch and Lisa Ann Cowdrey

HATHAWAY,
Andrew John, b. 2/5/1983 in Concord; Michael Joseph Hathaway and Diane Elizabeth Fraser

Jaclyn Marie, b. 4/28/1985 in Concord; Michael Joseph Hathaway and Diane Elizabeth Fraser

HAWKINS,
Amy Beth, b. 5/7/1983 in Concord; Carl Rolland Hawkins and Debra Lisa Wessley

HAYES,
Arnold Warren, Jr., b. 7/2/1974 in Concord; Arnold Warren Hayes (NH) and Shirley Mae Vien (MA); residence - Ctr. Barnstead
Constance M., b. 1/5/1954 in Concord; Warren Arnold Hayes (lumberman) and Virginia L. Wyatt
Deborah S., b. 7/28/1961 in Laconia; William C. Hayes (Attleboro, MA) and Sylvia J. French (Gilmanton)
Devon Louise, b. 1/13/1994 in Lebanon; Michael John Hayes and Patricia Jane Kenney
Mychelle Lynn, b. 3/22/1971 in Concord; Arnold Warren Hayes (NH) and Shirley Mae Vien (NH); residence - Ctr. Barnstead
Vicki Lee, b. 3/2/1951; fourth; Warren A. Hayes (lumberman) and Virginia L. Wyatt

HAYWOOD [see Heywood],
daughter, b. 10/15/1899; third; Fred L. Haywood (farmer, Barnstead) and Grace A. Knowles

HEBERT,
Aaron Mitchell, b. 10/2/1975 in Concord; Alfred Antonio Hebert, Jr. (ME) and Anita Marie Gaugler (ME)
Eric Michael, b. 10/27/1972 in Concord; Michael Alan Hebert (ME) and Holly Frances Faulkner (ME)

HEDERMAN,
Michael Raymond, b. 4/28/1996 in Concord; James Newton Hederman and Joan Elizabeth St. Onge

HERNDON,
Diana Rose, b. 5/19/1946 in Concord; first; Alton J. Herndon (REA public service) and Alma R. Hayward
Jane Elizabeth, b. 1/15/1979 in Concord; Eric Clinton Herndon and Sarah Ann Geraghty
John C., b. 4/25/1955 in Concord; Alton J. Herndon (lineman) and Alma R. Hywood
Mary, b. 8/1/1975 in Concord; Eric Clinton Herndon (SC) and Sarah Ann Geraghty (NY)

HEYWOOD [see Haywood],
son [Warren Harold], b. 11/4/1889; first; Fred Heywood (shoemaker, Barnstead) and Grace Knowles (Concord)
daughter, b. 7/31/1896; Fred L. Heywood (farmer, Barnstead) and Grace A. Knowles
Alma R., b. 1/26/1927; fourth; Warren H. Heywood (Barnstead) and Rose A. Leduc (Pittsfield)
Evelyn, b. 2/16/1921; second; Warren H. Heywood (weaver, Barnstead) and Rosalma LeDuc (Pittsfield)
Lincoln W., b. 12/14/1923; third; Warren H. Heywood (Barnstead) and Rose A. Leduc (Pittsfield)
Nancy A., b. 7/18/1933; fifth; W. Harold Heywood (poultry raiser) and Rose A. Leduc

HIDDEN,
Gren A., b. 8/11/1963 in Concord; second; Edwin W. Hidden (Laconia) and Nancy E. Thomas (Everett, MA)

HIGGENS [see Higgins],
Charles Porter, b. 5/28/1924; first; William A. Higgens (Bradford, VT) and Olive M. Crollis (sic) (Suncook)

HIGGINS [see Higgens],
child, b. 12/28/1920; first; John Smith and Mary N. Higgins (Fairly, VT)
child, b. 10/19/1928; second; William Higgins (Bradford, VT) and Olive M. Corliss (Suncook)
Grace Annette, b. 6/19/1939; fourth; William A. Higgins (laborer) and Olive M. Corliss
Ray William, b. 8/19/1931; third; William Albert Higgins (fireman) and Olive Corliss

HILL,
son, b. 5/28/1892; second; Joseph E. Hill (carpenter, Strafford) and Flora E. Webber (Strafford)
son, b. 5/10/1893; first; Sylvester J. Hill (farmer, 25, New Durham) and Effie J. Hill (27, Barnstead)
son, b. 9/5/1895; Sylvester J. Hill (farmer, New Durham) and Effie Wentworth (Barnstead)
son [Earl], b. 10/2/1899; third; Sylvester J. Hill (farmer, 32, New Durham) and Effie J. Wentworth (35, Barnstead)

Elsie R., b. 12/25/1908; second; William Hill (laborer, 21, Strafford) and Marguerite Gray (19, Barnstead)

Madeline, b. 12/18/1917; fifth; James W. Hill (sawyer, Strafford) and Margaret Gray (Barnstead)

Mary L., b. 1/20/1964 in Concord; first; Levi D. Hill (Bartlett) and Mary K. Price (Westminster, VT)

HILLIS,
Samantha Marie, b. 10/20/1993 in Concord; Michael Kenneth Hillis and Karen Louise Soczewinski

HILLSGROVE,
daughter [Lena M.], b. 9/28/1888; eighth; Joseph M. Hillsgrove (shoemaker, Portsmouth) and Lydia Webster (Strafford)

son, b. 7/16/1893; first; George E. Hillsgrove (laborer, 24, Danbury) and Grace A. Pickering (21, Barnstead)

stillborn daughter, b. 11/30/1903; fourth; George E. Hillsgrove (farmer, 34, Danbury) and Grace A. Pickering (31, Barnstead) (1904)

daughter, b. 12/17/1911; sixth; George E. Hillsgrove (farmer, 41, Danbury) and Grace A. Pickering (38, Barnstead)

son [Robert H.], b. 4/5/1913; seventh; George E. Hillsgrove (farmer, 43, Danbury) and Grace A. Pickering (41, Barnstead)

son [W. Merl], b. 2/6/1914; second; Walter J. Hillsgrove (farmer, 34, Wilmot) and Myrtie Day (28, Northwood)

son [Casper Ewell], b. 6/23/1915; third; Walter J. Hillsgrove (farmer, Wilmot) and Myrtie Day (Northwood)

son, b. 12/7/1915; eighth; George E. Hillsgrove (farmer, Danbury) and Grace A. Pickering (Barnstead)

Amy Elizabeth, b. 6/10/1977 in Concord; Thomas Bruce Hillsgrove (NH) and Roseanna Eva Perkins (NH)

Barbara May, b. 5/20/1939 in Wolfeboro; first; Casper E. Hillsgrove (farmer) and Doris K. Bixby

Bruce E., b. 10/1/1965 in Rochester; third; Richard A. Hillsgrove (Wolfeboro) and Virginia M. Polhamus (Stafford, VA)

Carter James, b. 1/5/1998 in Concord; Todd Hillsgrove and Heidi Hillsgrove

Clinton J., b. 8/28/1895; second; George E. Hillsgrove (shoemaker, 26, Danbury) and Grace Pickering (23, Barnstead) (1903)

Frank S., b. 6/11/1908; fifth; George E. Hillsgrove (farmer, 38, Danbury) and Grace A. Pickering (36, Barnstead)

George Casper, b. 6/23/1944 in Wolfeboro; third; Casper E. Hillsgrove (truck driver) and Doris Katherine Bixby

Irene Doris, b. 8/7/1940 in Wolfeboro; second; Casper E. Hillsgrove (farmer) and Doris K. Bixby

Joan M., b. 8/16/1956 in Wolfeboro; Casper E. Hillsgrove (farmer) and Doris K. Bixby

Leon E., b. 6/7/1900; third; George E. Hillsgrove (laborer, 31, Danbury) and Grace Pickering (28, Barnstead) (1903)

Norman Walter, b. 7/14/1943 in Concord; first; Fred N. Hillsgrove (farmer) and Ella E. Goodwin

Ola E., b. 8/12/1908; first; Walter J. Hillsgrove (farmer, 28, Wilmot) and Myrtie O. Day (22, Northwood) (1909)

Patricia Louise, b. 6/4/1934; first; Walter Merl Hillsgrove (laborer) and Louise E. Pike

Rachel Fay, b. 8/14/1947 in Wolfeboro; fourth; Casper E. Hillsgrove (lumberman) and Katherine D. Bixby

Raymond W., b. 3/31/1958 in Wolfeboro; Casper E. Hillsgrove and Doris K. Bixby

Richard Allen, b. 4/21/1940 in Wolfeboro; third; Walter M. Hillsgrove (farmer) and Louise E. Pike

Ricky A., b. 4/4/1967 in Rochester; fourth; Richard A. Hillsgrove (equip. operator, Wolfeboro) and Viola M. Polhamus (Stafford, VA)

Robert Merle, b. 9/25/1936; second; Walter M. Hillsgrove (farmer) and Louise Pike

Tali Mark, b. 5/9/1968 in Rochester; Richard Allen Hillsgrove (NH) and Viola M. Polhamus (VA)

Thomas Bruce, Jr., b. 4/5/1974 in Concord; Thomas Bruce Hillsgrove (NH) and Roseanna Eva Perkins (NH)

Wayne H., b. 8/4/1955 in Wolfeboro; Joseph H. Hillsgrove (saw mill) and Lois F. Partridge

HINGSTON,
Alexa Nicole, b. 5/5/1994 in Concord; Mark Richard Hingston and Leslie Delores Hingston

Ryan Joseph, b. 4/30/1991 in Concord; Mark Richard Hingston and Leslie Dolores O'Meara

HOBSON,
Emily Dodge, b. 4/23/1991 in Concord; Christopher Lee Hobson and Mary Cynthia Dodge

Jessalyn Blakeslee, b. 7/31/1989 in Concord; Christopher Lee Hobson and Mary Cynthia Dodge

HODGDON,
Chelsea Jean, b. 9/11/1989 in Wolfeboro; Maurice Clyde Hodgdon and Judith Frances Dunleavey
Paul Golda, b. 4/11/1997 in Laconia; Philip B. Hodgdon and Sharen R. Goldberg
Thomas L., b. 5/11/1956 in Pittsfield; Carroll Hodgdon (lumberman) and Naomi R. Joy

HOGENCAMP,
Anelda Lolila, b. 10/30/1937; second; John L. Hogencamp (laborer) and Florence L. Newcomb

HOLMES,
son, b. 9/18/1894; first; Frank J. Holmes (teamster, 28, Barnstead) and Hattie McKennelly (34, NB)
daughter, b. 8/29/1906; third; Frank J. Holmes (farmer, 39, Barnstead) and Hattie McKinley (35, NB)
Glen Oliver, b. 3/15/1940; second; William E. Holmes (farmer) and Marjorie E. Hanson

HOLT,
Everett G., b. 8/9/1902; third; Nathaniel Holt (farmer, 43, Lynn, MA) and Flora Greenleaf (41, Northwood)

HOOPER,
Jeffrey Franklin, b. 12/27/1969 in Concord; George Thomas Hooper (NH) and Janet Lynne Rudy (IN)

HORAN,
David John, b. 4/10/1968 in Dover; John Sydney Horan (NH) and Maureen Patricia Ayer (NH); residence - Strafford
Marilee, b. 7/31/1969 in Dover; John Sydney Horan (NH) and Maureen Patricia Ayer (NH); residence - Strafford
Maurice T., b. 12/19/1964 in Dover; second; John S. Horan (Strafford) and Maureen P. Ayer (Dover); residence - Strafford

HORTON,
Daniel P., b. 3/12/1954 in Laconia; John A. Horton (engineer) and
   Dorothy I. Olson
Everett Gunner, b. 7/8/1944 in Pittsfield; third; John A. Horton
   (industrial engineer) and Dorothy O. Olson
Ruth Ingrid, b. 7/8/1944 in Pittsfield; second; John A. Horton
   (industrial engineer) and Dorothy O. Olson
Timothy, b. 7/6/1955 in Laconia; John A. Horton (salesman) and
   Dorothy S. Olson

HOUGH,
Joshua Ethan, b. 5/16/1991 in Concord; Joseph Nelson Hough, Jr.
   and Nancy Louise Ellis

HOWARD,
Abigail Lillian, b. 6/30/1980 in Concord; Timothy Richard Howard
   and Susan Michelle Rath
Kristin Marie, b. 11/4/1982 in Barnstead; Timothy Richard Howard
   and Susan Michelle Rath
Rebekah Lynn, b. 6/29/1981 in Ctr. Barnstead; Timothy Richard
   Howard and Susan Michelle Rath
Shelby Taylor, b. 3/18/1992 in Concord; John Alden Howard and
   Lisa Ann Rossuck

HOWE,
Darwin F., b. 12/16/1908; first; Edgar G. Howe (carpenter, 37,
   Newport) and Cora F. Davis (27, Barnstead)
Thomas Grant, b. 11/4/1936; second; Elmer H. Howe (weaver) and
   Frances Chase

HOYT,
Harry, b. 8/2/1886 in North Barnstead; Alonzo Hoyt and Gertrude
   Hoyt (1951)
Kayley Lorraine, b. 12/16/1999 in Concord; Randolph Hoyt and
   Michele Hoyt
Kelsey Fay, b. 1/14/1998 in Concord; Randolph Hoyt and Michele
   Hoyt

HROMIS,
Julianna Rose, b. 6/6/1998 in Concord; Vladimir Hromis and
   Marianne David

HUBBELL,
Stephanie Lynn, b. 10/14/1974 in Concord; Thaddeus David Hubbell (MA) and Linda Sue Davis (NH)

HUCKABY,
Eugenia Honor, b. 7/17/1976 in Barnstead; Harold O. Huckaby (NC) and Cynthia Alice Tripp (MA)
Solange Khan, b. 3/29/1973 in Ctr. Barnstead; Harold Owen Huckaby (NC) and Cynthia Alice Tripp (MA); residence - Ctr. Barnstead

HUGGINS,
Brian Joseph, b. 6/2/1982 in Concord; Michael Huggins and Paula Marie Labrecque
Joshua, b. 7/27/1980 in Concord; Michael Huggins and Paula Marie Labrecque
Michael Edward, b. 8/20/1974 in Concord; Michael Huggins (NH) and Paula Marie LaBrecque (NH)
Paul Matthew, b. 1/7/1978 in Concord; Michael Huggins (NH) and Paula Marie LaBrecque (NH); residence - Ctr. Barnstead
Sarah Louise, b. 12/25/1983 in Concord; Michael Huggins and Paula Marie Labrecque

HUGHES,
Benjamin Donald, b. 9/8/2000 in Concord; Donald Hughes and Carolyn Hughes
Meaghan Leigh, b. 6/7/1990 in Manchester; Dennie William Hughes and Rhonda Kim Carter
Nicholas Harold, b. 3/10/1997 in Concord; Donald D. Hughes and Carolyn Cutler

HUNSBERGER,
Derrike Cole, b. 12/16/1998 in Concord; Jeffrey Hunsberger and Kimberly Hunsberger

HUNT,
Barbara A., b. 9/30/1890; John S. Hunt (shoemaker, Lynn, MA) and Emma A. Marsh (Barnstead) (1895)
Heather Jane, b. 2/7/1997 in Concord; Robert D. Hunt and Patricia Broadrick

HUNTON,
Alexander Scott, b. 7/3/1994 in Lebanon; George William Hunton and Linda May Pease
Benjamin Eric, b. 7/3/1994 in Lebanon; George William Hunton and Linda May Pease
Emily Catherine, b. 1/22/1992 in Concord; George William Hunton and Linda May Pease

HUNTOON,
daughter, b. 9/3/1888; first; Charles Huntoon (shoemaker, Peabody, MA) and Nellie ----- (Stoneham, MA)

HURD,
son [Winfield], b. 10/7/1899; first; Luther B. Hurd (laborer, 32, Conway) and Edith E. Townsend (26, Plaistow)
Nathaline, b. 3/23/1907; fifth; Ray Hurd (B&M fireman, 30, Springfield, VT) and Mabel Brown (25, Manchester)

HYSLOP,
Gerald Brian, II, b. 2/5/1979 in Rochester; Gerald Brian Hyslop and Ruth Elaine Boyd

IADONISI,
Emily Gayle, b. 12/22/1979 in Laconia; Dominic Gregory Iadonisi and Linda Marie Bott

JACKSON,
Jazmine Azariah, b. 1/31/2000 in Boston, MA; Jerome Jackson and Joyce Jackson

JACOBS,
daughter, b. 3/1/1892; Covan Jacobs (shoemaker, Barnstead) and Lettie Hillsgrove
son, b. 9/3/1899; fifth; Coran M. Jacobs (farmer, 32, Barnstead) and Lettie Hillsgrove (28)
daughter [Lura B.], b. 12/20/1901; sixth; Coran Jacobs (farmer, 35, Barnstead) and Lettie Hillsgrove (31, Danbury)
Mial, b. 8/4/1893; second; Coran Jacobs (shoemaker, 27, Barnstead) and Lettie Hillsgrove (23, Danbury)

JACQUES,
J. Richard, b. 8/22/1986 in Concord; J. Richard Jacques and Melanie Loretta Mankiewicz

JAWORSKI,
Alan E., b. 7/27/1962 in Laconia; second; Edward M. Jaworski (Concord) and Althea J. French (Gilmanton); residence - Ctr. Barnstead

JEANSON,
Alexandra Severine, b. 8/11/1997 in Concord; Gregory W. Jeanson and Janet L. Winterle

JENISCH,
son [Frederick K.], b. 10/30/1911; second; Alois Jenisch (weaver, 29, Austria) and Mathilda Packle (26, Austria)
daughter, b. 11/10/1913; third; Alvis Jenisch (weaver, 32, Austria) and Mathilde Pachl (29, Austria)
child, b. 7/1/1941 in Concord; first; William H. Jenisch (textile worker) and Mary Louise Park
Alfred F., b. 6/17/1921; seventh; Alvis Janisch (sic) (weaver, Austria) and Matilda Pohl (Austria)
Alois, b. 1/31/1917; fifth; Alois Jenisch (weaver, Austria) and Matiller Pashel (Austria)
Douglas Henry, b. 5/24/1942 in Concord; third; William Henry Jenisch (textile worker) and Marion Louise Park
Felix, b. 9/25/1919; sixth; Alivs Jenisch (weaver, Austria) and Matilda Pachl (Austria)
Helen Aenlia, b. 5/3/1919; second; Frank Jenisch (weaver, Austria) and Matilda Sclennis (Hoboken, NJ)
Kristine Barbara, b. 11/10/1950 in Pittsfield; second; Richard R. Jenisch (clerk) and Barbara E. Turner
Raymond Louis, b. 6/12/1926; third; Frank Jenisch (Austria) and Matilda Schunf (Hoboken, NJ)
Richard, b. 4/8/1915; fourth; Alsio Jenisch (weaver, Austria) and Matilda Pochil (Austria)
Richard Alexander, b. 1/31/1947 in Pittsfield; first; Richard Jenisch (artistic web co.) and Barbara E. Turner
William H., b. 5/14/1910; first; Alois Jeisch (sic) (weaver, 28, Austria) and Mathilda Pachl (25, Austria)

William Park, b. 5/24/1942 in Concord; second; William Henry Jenisch (textile worker) and Marion Louise Park

JENKINS,
son [Ernest C.], b. 8/14/1888; second; Joseph E. Jenkins (farmer, Barnstead) and Clara ----- (Loudon)
daughter, b. 8/3/1890; first; Willie A. Jenkins (farmer, Barnstead) and Madge A. Foss (Barnstead)
son [Carroll E.], b. 10/22/1891; third; Erskine Jenkins (shoemaker, Barnstead) and Clara Carter (Loudon)
daughter, b. 12/22/1891; second; William A. Jenkins (brakeman, Barnstead) and Madge A. Foss (Barnstead)
son, b. 2/1/1894; third; William A. Jenkins (RR employee, 27, Barnstead) and Margaret A. Foss (31, Barnstead)
son, b. 4/7/1895; Edgar Jenkins (merchant, Barnstead) and Grace Willey (Barnstead)
child [Nina H.], b. 12/30/1900; John J. Jenkins (farmer, Barnstead) and Edith Maxfield (Barnstead)
stillborn daughter, b. 4/29/1903; second; Harry L. Jenkins (merchant, 28, Barnstead) and Ora M. Tower (27, Boston, MA)
son [Raymond], b. 9/5/1904; third; Harry L. Jenkins (merchant, 29, Barnstead) and Ora M. Tower (28, Boston, MA)
son [Kenneth], b. 11/9/1905; fourth; Harry L. Jenkins (merchant, 31, Barnstead) and Ora M. Tower (30, Boston, MA)
daughter [Madeline A.], b. 12/10/1905; second; Charles Jenkins (shoemaker, 36, Barnstead) and Lilla Foss (32, Barnstead)
daughter, b. 10/17/1908; fifth; Harry L. Jenkins (merchant, 34, Barnstead) and Ora M. Tower (32, Boston, MA)
child, b. 2/2/1925; second; John J. Jenkins (Barnstead) and Marion Clapp (Auburndale, MA)
child, b. 2/2/1925; third; John J. Jenkins (Barnstead) and Marion Clapp (Auburndale, MA)
Donald Warren, b. 3/2/1928; fifth; John J. Jenkins (Barnstead) and Marion S. Clapp (Auburndale, MA)
Doris A., b. 8/1/1902; first; Charles W. Jenkins (shoemaker, 33, Barnstead) and Lilla Foss (29, Gilmanton)
Doris C., b. 11/21/1911; second; Ernest C. Jenkins (stoker, 23, Barnstead) and Bertha Brown (25, Gilmanton)
Earle M., b. 1/4/1899; second; John J. Jenkins (farmer, 26, Barnstead) and Edith Maxfield (20, Lynn, MA)

Edith M., b. 2/27/1926; fourth; John J. Jenkins (Barnstead) and
  Marion S. Clapp (Auburndale, MA)
Leon M., b. 6/7/1901; first; Harry Jenkins (merchant, 26, Barnstead)
  and Ora M. Tower (25, Boston, MA)
Merton B., b. 3/20/1907; first; Ernest C. Jenkins (morocco worker,
  18, Barnstead) and Bertha Brown (20, Gilmanton)
Merton Brown, Jr., b. 9/21/1931; second; Merton B. Jenkins
  (shipping clerk) and Bertha L. Pierce
Russell F., b. 3/17/1912; third; Charles W. Jenkins (shoemaker, 43,
  Barnstead) and Lilla Foss (39, Gilmanton)
Urban, b. 7/9/1902; fourth; Joseph E. Jenkins (shoemaker, 42,
  Barnstead) and Clara A. Carter (42, Loudon)

JOHNSON,
daughter, b. 7/1/1901; first; Harry Johnson (shoemaker, 27,
  Rochester) and Ora Munsey (23, Barnstead)
daughter, b. 5/16/1914; third; Michael C. Johnson (section foreman,
  29, N. Derby, VT) and Augustine Bowchard (26, Pittsfield)
Helen M., b. 2/14/1922; first; Walter F. Johnson (teamster,
  Pittsfield) and Ella McAllen (Lynn, MA)
Kristian Thane, b. 9/30/1969 in Wolfeboro; Peter Thoralf Johnson
  (MA) and Sarah Margo Matthewman (MA)
Olive Gail, b. 3/9/1934; fourth; Chester A. Johnson (farmer) and
  Elinor V. Leavitt
Tamara Kaci, b. 6/3/1983 in Wolfeboro; Peter Thoralf Johnson and
  Sarah Margo Matthewman
Tonda Melissa, b. 8/13/1973 in Wolfeboro; Peter Thoralf Johnson
  (MA) and Sarah Melissa Matthewman (MA)

JOHNSTON,
Jaclyn Heather, b. 12/22/1993 in Concord; Kevin Scott Johnston
  and Nancy Marie Johnston

JONES,
Brianna Celia, b. 10/22/1994 in New London; Joseph Stephen
  Jones and Maureen Renee Martineau
Bryan Joseph, b. 10/22/1994 in New London; Joseph Stephen
  Jones and Maureen Renee Martineau
John S., b. 3/26/1965 in Concord; third; Francis D. Jones (Suffern,
  NY) and Diane R. Johnson (New Rochelle, NY)

KAIME,
Amy Francis, b. 8/1/1901; first; Samuel F. Kaime (farmer, 24, Barnstead) and Libbie E. Smith (29, NS)

KALLGREN,
Abby, b. 1/23/1990 in Concord; James Phillip Kallgren and Sally Nelson
Emily, b. 1/24/1994 in Concord; James Phillip Kallgren and Sally Nelson

KASHULINES,
Daniel Martin, b. 2/5/1998 in Concord; David Kashulines and Dianna Kashulines
Donald David, b. 6/14/1994 in Concord; David Martin Kashulines and Dianna Whitney

KEATING,
Justin Patrick, b. 2/20/1974 in Concord; Brian Richard Keating (NH) and Sylvia Elizabeth Kimball (NH)

KEEFE,
Eric Edward, b. 7/5/1973 in Derry; Edward Emmett Keefe (MA) and Jean Isabel Giurieo (MA); residence - Ctr. Barnstead

KEENE,
daughter, b. 12/29/1954 in Concord; Richard M. Keene (weaver) and Roberta Cotton
son, b. 12/29/1954 in Concord; Richard M. Keene (weaver) and Roberta Cotton
Brian L., b. 10/16/1956 in Concord; Marshall G. Keene (laborer) and Leone M. Perkins
Cheryl L., b. 10/29/1959 in Rochester; Marshall G. Keene and Leone M. Perkins
Darla S., b. 7/2/1956 in Concord; Richard M. Keene (designer) and Roberta Cotton
Kevin M., b. 3/30/1955 in Concord; Marshall G. Keene (laborer) and Leone M. Perkins
Kevin Marshall, Jr., b. 2/21/1985 in Concord; Kevin Marshall Keene and Katrina Marie Miller
Richard M., II, b. 3/20/1961 in Concord; Richard M. Keene, Sr. (Worcester, MA) and Roberta Cotton (Woburn, MA)

Sheila M., b. 8/19/1953 in Wolfeboro; first; Marshall G. Keene (laborer) and Leone M. Perkins

Wyatt Adin, b. 12/7/1992 in Concord; Richard Merlin Keene, II and Martha Theresa Yelle

KELLEY,

son [John], b. 2/13/1896; second; Joseph Kelley (teamster, NY) and Myra Kelley (Rumney) (1897)

daughter, b. 9/25/1902; fourth; Joseph Kelley (teamster, 43) and Myra Colburn (36, Dorchester, MA)

Daniel John, b. 4/21/1972 in Concord; Paul Edwin Kelley (MA) and Elizabeth Ann Winn (MA); residence - Ctr. Barnstead

David James, b. 3/11/1969 in Concord; Edward Rodney Kelley (NH) and Ilse Madeline Frey (NY)

Edward R., b. 5/6/1930; fourth; Charlie H. Kelley (mechanic) and Bessie O. Gray

Fred, b. 7/9/1893; first; Joseph Kelley (shoemaker, NY) and Myra Kelley (Rumney)

Kathryn A., b. 7/14/1953 in Concord; Edward R. Kelley (mason tender) and Ilse M. Frey

Linda Sue, b. 1/6/1956 in Concord; Edward R. Kelley (mason) and Ilse M. Frye

Marisa Ann, b. 4/24/1978 in Concord; Richard Allan Kelley (NH) and Elizabeth Whitehouse (NH)

Melody Margaret, b. 10/29/1999 in Concord; David Kelley and Kathy Kelley

Michael S., b. 3/7/1966 in Concord; fifth; Edward R. Kelly (sic) (Ctr. Barnstead) and Ilse M. Frey (New York City, NY); residence - Ctr. Barnstead

Richard Allen, b. 9/7/1951 in Concord; first; Edward R. Kelley (laborer) and Ilse M. Frey

Rosemary J., b. 9/21/1958 in Concord; Edward R. Kelley and Ilse M. Frey

Tabitha Macie Clare, b. 8/11/1999 in Concord; Michael Kelley and Hollie Kelley

Tara Jean, b. 2/10/1975 in Concord; Richard Allan Kelley (NH) and Elizabeth Whitehouse (NH)

Thelma M., b. 2/28/1925; third; Charles H. Kelley (Northwood) and Bessie Gray (Barnstead)

Velna M., b. 2/28/1925; second; Charles H. Kelley (Northwood) and Bessie Gray (Barnstead)

KELSON,
William Harold, b. 4/24/1974 in Manchester; Carlisle William Kelson (MA) and Ellen Mary Strapla (NH); residence - E. Barnstead

KENDALL,
Alexandria Christine, b. 10/4/1997 in Concord; Daniel W. Kendall and Arlene C. Tilton
Curtis Andrew, b. 2/24/2000 in Concord; Mark Kendall and Virginia Kendall
Elizabeth Marie, b. 12/22/1992 in Concord; Richard Alan Kendall and Cheryl Elizabeth Begg

KENISCH [see Kinsch, Knirsch],
Grenke V., b. 12/6/1922; first; Konard Kenisch (weaver, Austria) and Emma Penka (Austria)
Henry, b. 7/17/1917; third; Kanrade Kenisch (weaver, Austria) and Mathilda Balch (Austria)
Reinhold B., b. 12/22/1925; second; Konard Kenisch (Austria) and Emma Penka (Austria)
Ruth H., b. 9/29/1918; fourth; Konard Kenisch (weaver, Austria) and Mathilda Balch (Austria)

KENISON,
Doris, b. 3/15/1897; first; Herbert Kenison (farmer, Barnstead) and Blanche Tuttle (Barnstead)
Ethan Thomas, b. 8/15/1996 in Rochester; Terry Lee Kenison and Dale Donna Twitchell
Herbert C., b. 9/2/1874; first; Owen M. Kenison (shoe worker) and Lydia A. Clark (1938)

KENISTON,
Althea B., b. 6/6/1918; third; Fred R. Kenison (sic) (farmer, Sweden) and Gladys Brady (Barnstead)
Doris, b. 2/12/1917; second; Fred R. Keniston (farmer, Sweden) and Gladys Brady (Barnstead)
Harry Herbert, b. 7/2/1915; first; Fred R. Keniston (farmer, Sweden) and Gladys Brady (Barnstead)

KENNEALLY,
Thomas Joseph, Jr., b. 10/11/1925; third; Thomas J. Kenneally (Ireland) and Edith Medrieos (Cambridge, MA)

KENNEDY,
Hope Rosemarie, b. 1/29/1991 in Concord; Lena Agnes Kennedy
James Brian, b. 1/7/1980 in Concord; Thomas Francis Kennedy, Jr. and Nancy Elizabeth Boyd
Justin Dale, b. 6/12/1989 in Concord; Gerald Edward Kennedy and Linda Corson
Michael David, b. 1/7/1980 in Concord; Thomas Francis Kennedy, Jr. and Nancy Elizabeth Boyd
Shayne Thomas, b. 6/11/1992 in Concord; Gerald Edward Kennedy and Linda Joy Corson

KENNELLY,
Christen Elizabeth, b. 6/1/1984 in Dover; Kevin Alan Kennelly and Sherrill Ann Rucker

KIBBE,
Justin Wallace, b. 9/28/1977 in Concord; Robert Charles Kibbe (MD) and Julia Carolyn Leslie (NJ); residence - Ctr. Barnstead
Mary Allerton, b. 8/28/1979 in Ctr. Barnstead; Robert Charles Kibbe and Julia Carolyn Leslie
Ned Robert, b. 1/6/1975 in Concord; Robert C. Kebbe (sic) (MD) and Julia C. Leslie (NJ)

KIBBE-LADD,
Shonas Maize, b. 8/16/1978 in Barnstead; Jonathan Levi Ladd (NH) and Shellie Jean Kibbee (NH); residence - Barnstead Parade

KIDDER,
Craig James, b. 4/10/1987 in Concord; James Wilbur Kidder and Bonnie Dupuis
Dana James, b. 12/27/1973 in Concord; James Wilbur Kidder (NH) and Patricia Ann Ford (NH)
James W., b. 10/14/1953 in Laconia; first; Wilbur A. Kidder (mechanic) and Rachel E. Osborne
Jennifer J., b. 8/28/1985 in Concord; James Wilbur Kidder and Bonnie Lou Dupuis

John Henry, b. 8/24/1930; seventh; Harold E. Kidder (R.P.O. clerk) and Bernice E. Carswell
Kenneth Charles, b. 1/12/1934; eighth; Harold E. Kidder (RR mail clerk) and Bernice E. Carswell
Lloyd D., b. 11/21/1921; fourth; Harold E. Kidder (Ry. mail clerk, Goffstown) and Bernice E. Caswell (Manchester)
Mary R., b. 12/13/1955 in Concord; Wilbur A. Kidder (mechanic) and Rachel E. Osborne
Michael David, b. 6/12/1978 in Concord; James Wilbur Kidder (NH) and Patricia Ann Ford (NH)
Virginia May, b. 6/4/1924; fourth; Harold E. Kidder (Manchester) and Bernice E. Caswell (Manchester)

KILEY,
Kimberly Leigh, b. 11/15/1985 in Concord; Michael Jon Kiley and Rita Janet Doucette
Ryan Michael, b. 5/14/1987 in Concord; Michael John Kiley and Rita Janet Doucette

KILTY,
Meghan Elizabeth, b. 9/8/1986 in Concord; John Joseph Kilty, Jr. and Ann Mary Dmohowksi

KIMBALL,
Alex Edward, b. 7/14/1987 in Concord; Edward Curtis Kimball and Lori Newell
Becky Ann, b. 9/14/1971 in Franklin; Russell Harrison Kimball (NH) and Joan Mary Genest (NH)
Beth Marie, b. 9/14/1971 in Franklin; Russell Harrison Kimball (NH) and Joan Mary Genest (NH)
Edward Curtis, II, b. 10/19/1951; second; Edward C. Kimball (truck driver) and Rita B. Canfield
Kenneth Russell, b. 7/3/1975 in Franklin; Russell H. Kimball (NH) and Joan Mary Genest (NH)
Sylvia Elizabeth, b. 12/6/1946; first; Edward C. Kimball (poultry man) and Rita B. Canfield
Wendy L., b. 12/14/1964 in Laconia; first; Russell H. Kimball (Pittsfield) and Joan M. Genest (Pittsfield)

KING,
Edna May, b. 1/13/1945 in Pittsfield; first; John C. King (US Army) and Julia A. McNulty
Marcia Elaine, b. 8/31/1933; second; Guerdon E. King (laborer) and Lucille Williams

KINNEY,
Kristen Elizabeth, b. 12/18/1975 in Concord; Roger Bruce Kinney (OH) and Helen Jean Hart (MO)

KINSCH [see Kenisch, Knirsch],
daughter [Helda], b. 2/29/1912; second; Konrad Kinsch (weaver, 28, Austria) and Mathilda Pachl (24, Austria)

KIRK,
Aaron William, b. 2/17/1977 in Concord; Peter MacDonald Kirk (NS) and Alicia Jane Ellingson (NH); residence - Ctr. Barnstead

KNIGHT,
Meredith Ann, b. 1/22/1992 in Concord; Burton Wilder Knight, II and Harriet Ann Meredith

KNIRSCH [see Kenisch, Kinsch],
son [Earl Frederick], b. 7/23/1909; first; Konrad Knirsch (weaver, 27, Moravia, Austria) and Mathilda Belyel (22, Moravia, Austria)
Heidi Jo., b. 7/24/1975 in Concord; Robert Konrad Knirsch (NH) and Joanne May Senior (NH)
Krystal Lorraine, b. 1/18/1979 in Concord; Robert K. Knirsch and Joanne May Senior
Robert K., b. 6/19/1953 in Concord; first; Reinhold B. Knirsch (weaver) and Ruth L. Finnegan

KNOWLES,
George R., b. 10/2/1916; first; Russell H. Knowles (farmer, Nashua) and Agnes Thompson (Barnstead)
Katherine Laura Louise, b. 1/19/1994 in Nashua; Joseph Louis Knowles and Robin Sue Littlefield
Kevin Joseph, b. 1/19/1994 in Nashua; Joseph Louis Knowles and Robin Sue Littlefield

KNOWLTON,
Elizabeth Anne, b. 11/8/1979 in Rochester; David Lee Knowlton and Anne Elizabeth Fitzpatrick
Rachel Marie, b. 11/7/1984 in Concord; David Lee Knowlton and Lisa Marie Transue

KORDIC,
Paul Antony, b. 9/13/1997 in Concord; Craig Arthur Kordic and Darlene Marie Kouri

KRAFT-LUND,
Arianne, b. 9/24/1980 in Concord; Peer Lund and Sharon Ann Kraft

KRAMER,
Daniel O'Brien, b. 9/26/1989 in Concord; Daniel Kramer and Mary Ellen O'Brien
Madison O'Brien, b. 1/29/1992 in Concord; Daniel Kramer and Mary Ellen O'Brien
Timothy O'Brien, b. 3/27/1988 in Concord; Daniel Kramer and Mary Ellen O'Brien

KRAUSE,
child, b. 8/14/1957 in Concord; George R. Krause (Sur. & M.D. Rep.) and Emelyn F. Ayer
Danielle Kristen, b. 12/19/1982 in Concord; George Russell Krause II and Roxann Mae Tasker
Jonathan A., b. 4/7/1956 in Concord; George R. Krause (farmer) and Emelyn F. Ayer
Tiffany Marie, b. 3/12/1981 in Concord; George Russell Krause II and Roxann Mae Tasker

LABRECQUE,
Ann M., b. 3/13/1963 in Rochester; tenth; Albert R. Labrecque (Rochester) and Pauline M. Salice (Rochester); residence - Ctr. Barnstead
Arthur G., b. 6/14/1954 in Concord; Roland V. LaBrecque (laborer) and Alice M. Pitman
Carol A. M., b. 1/17/1962 in Rochester; ninth; Albert R. Labrecque (Rochester) and Pauline M. Salice (Rochester); residence - Ctr. Barnstead

David A., b. 5/31/1959 in Concord; Roland V. LaBrecque and Alice M. Pitman
Dennis Joseph, Jr., b. 5/4/1977 in Laconia; Dennis Joseph LaBrecque (NH) and Dorothy Ann Smith (CT)
Donald Leon, Jr., b. 3/18/1978 in Concord; Donald Leon Labrecque (NH) and Carolyn Ann Courley (FL)
Joseph M., b. 2/13/1962 in Rochester; sixth; Roland V. Labrecque (Rochester) and Alice M. Pitman (Ctr. Barnstead); residence - Ctr. Barnstead
Joshua Adam, b. 5/9/1984 in Rochester; David Albert LaBrecque and Wendy Ann Potter
Karen M., b. 9/2/1956 in Concord; Roland V. LaBrecque and Alice M. Pitman
Kevin R., b. 6/4/1966 in Rochester; seventh; Roland V. LaBrecque (Rochester) and Alice M. Pitman (Ctr. Barnstead); residence - Ctr. Barnstead
Laurena M., b. 1/29/1953 in Concord; first; Roland V. LaBrecque (laborer) and Alice M. Pitman
Matthew Robert, b. 12/17/1980 in Concord; Donald Leon Labrecque and Carolyn Ann Cunley
Michael R., b. 3/25/1964 in Concord; eleventh; Albert R. Labrecque (Rochester) and Pauline M. Salice (Rochester); residence - Ctr. Barnstead
Michelle Marie, b. 7/24/1969 in Concord; Albert Robert Labrecque (NH) and Pauline Marie Solice (NH)
Roland V., Jr., b. 8/24/1957 in Concord; Roland V. LaBrecque (shaver) and Alice M. Pitman

LACHANCE,
Brittany Marie, b. 2/5/1996 in Concord; Michael R. LaChance II and Kathleen Margaret Knowles
Rachael Lynn, b. 5/7/1998 in Concord; Michael LaChance and Kathleen LaChance

LADIEU,
Aspen Taylor, b. 8/3/1997 in Concord; Sage Jason Ladieu and Tamson L. Whitehouse

LAMBERT,
Maxwell Wayne, b. 11/8/2000 in Manchester; Billy Lambert and Melinda Lambert

LAMSON,
John Sanford, b. 7/23/1992 in Concord; Lee John Lamson and Robin Sanford
Scott Thomas, b. 11/2/1990 in Concord; Lee John Lamson and Robin Sanford

LANDRY,
Candace Taylor, b. 6/30/1993 in Manchester; Thomas Arthur Landry and Daylan Rachel Hickey

LANE,
Stephanie Gayle, b. 7/14/1990 in Concord; Stacy Curtis Lane and Gayle Byers

LANGENDORFER,
Tyler Ian Paul, b. 5/16/1984 in Concord; Dwight Paul Langendorfer and Linda Lee Greenfield

LANGEVIN,
Nicholas Joseph, b. 11/13/1999 in Concord; Ronald Langevin and Angela Langevin

LANK [see Lauk],
Amie Sue, b. 10/16/1987 in Concord; Clinton Lloyd Lank and Susan Desjardins
Cody Lloyd, b. 10/9/1996 in Concord; Clinton Lloyd Lank and Susan Marie Desjardins
Dorothy Lucille, b. 5/9/1940 in Laconia; seventh; Clinton L. Lank (carpenter) and Ruth O. Butman
Howard Robert, Jr., b. 1/4/1978 in Concord; Howard Robert Lank (NH) and Duska Joy Murphy (ME); residence - Ctr. Barnstead
John Howard, b. 4/10/1985 in Concord; Clinton L. Lank and Suzan Marie Desjardins
Joshua James, b. 6/9/1972 in Concord; Stephen David Lank (NH) and Margie Ann Morse (NH)
Katrina Lee, b. 11/26/1974 in Concord; Howard Robert Lank (NH) and Duska Joy Murphy (ME)
Kim J., b. 9/10/1959 in Concord; Clinton L. Lank and Carolyn R. Locke
Lori Lynn, b. 5/4/1968 in Concord; Clinton Lloyd Lank (RI) and Carolyn Rose Locke (NH)

Richard, b. 9/15/1934; fifth; Clinton L. Lank (laborer) and Ruth O. Butman

Ronald J., b. 7/10/1962 in Concord; fourth; Clinton L. Lank (Providence, RI) and Carolyn R. Locke (Ctr. Barnstead); residence - Ctr. Barnstead

Rory D., b. 10/10/1965 in Concord; fifth; Clinton Lloyd Lank (Providence, RI) and Carolyn R. Locke (Ctr. Barnstead); residence - Ctr. Barnstead

Stephen David, b. 6/2/1943 in Wolfeboro; eighth; Clinton L. Lank (lumberman) and Ruth O. Butman

Susan D., b. 6/19/1955 in Rochester; Clinton L. Lank, Jr. (lineman) and Carolyn R. Locke

LAPOINTE,
Shirley Lois, b. 2/3/1935; first; Leopold G. Lapointe (laborer) and Dorothy G. Welch

LAROCHE,
Allison Katherine, b. 8/18/1993 in Concord; Eric Stephen Laroche and Christine Elizabeth Williams

LATORELLA,
Matthew Robert, b. 1/12/1993 in Concord; Robert Louis Latorella, Jr. and Lynne Marie Sickau

LAUDANI,
Mark James, b. 6/27/1999 in New London; Mark Laudani and Shelby Laudani

LAUK [see Lank],
Elinor Nancy, b. 11/12/1938 in Laconia; sixth; Clinton L. Lauk (carpenter) and Ruth Olive Butman

LAVERTY,
Brenna Marie, b. 5/29/1993 in Concord; Christopher James Laverty and Kristin Anne Cofsky

Keenan Christopher, b. 8/16/1989 in Concord; Christopher James Laverty and Kristin Anne Cofsky

William Patrick, b. 4/9/1991 in Concord; Christopher James Laverty and Kristin Anne Cofsky

LAW,
stillborn son, b. 11/15/1902; first; Daniel Law (farmer, 42, England) and Annie Lawson (35)
Daniel F., b. 5/23/1905; second; Daniel L. Law (florist, 48, Leicester, England) and Annie D. Lawson (38, Ulsaker, Norway)

LEACH,
Thelma V., b. 11/7/1901; first; Harry L. Leach (merchant, 22, Bucksport, ME) and Adelaide Jenkins (19, Barnstead)

LEARY,
John Joseph, III, b. 8/24/1979 in Concord; John Joseph Leary, Jr. and Jean Marie McGrail

LEAVITT,
Tricia Anne, b. 8/1/1986 in Portsmouth; Jeffrey Scott Leavitt and Brenda Lee Gagnon

LEBLANC,
Corey Daniel, b. 1/7/1991 in Concord; Steven Edward LeBlanc and Judith Maureen Price
Steven Herve, b. 2/8/1988 in Concord; Steven Edward LeBlanc and Judith Maureen Price

LEDUC,
Arthur Reginald, b. 12/10/1928; first; Edward H. LeDuc (Pittsfield) and Eldora E. Chagnon (Isle Pond, VT)

LEE,
Jami Krista, b. 6/15/1979 in Concord; Michael Robert Lee and Roberta Elben Aversa
Shawn Michael, b. 11/11/1977 in Concord; Michael Robert Lee (NH) and Roberta Ellen Aversa (FL)

LEIGHTON,
son [Earl D.], b. 7/23/1893; first; Charles I. Leighton (shoemaker, 25, Farmington) and Addie A. Dow (25, Barnstead); residence – Farmington

LEMAY,
Corey Ray, b. 7/23/1993 in Manchester; Arthur Armand Lemay and Lisa Sue Brown

LEMIEUX,
Maria Elizabeth, b. 11/20/1998 in Barnstead; Robert Lemieux and Heidrun Lemieux

LENT,
Jonathan Keith, b. 7/31/1984 in Concord; Russell Eugene Lent, Jr. and Cheryl Anne Gamache

LEONARD,
Kristin Elisabeth, b. 3/28/1986 in Concord; John Patrick Leonard and Marcia Lyn Richard

LESSARD,
Andrew Brian, b. 1/25/1981 in Concord; Patrick Alan Lessard and Dorothy Jean Levesque

LEVESQUE,
Jean-Rock, b. 8/19/1991 in Concord; Jean-Pierre Levesque and Ellen Marie Hayes

LEVINE,
Joshua Adam, b. 1/19/1977 in Concord; Daniel Jay Levine (NY) and Diana Gartner (NY)

LEWIS,
Rebekah Kathryn, b. 4/25/1977 in Concord; Barry Bigelow Lewis (VT) and Deborah Roberts (ME); residence - Ctr. Barnstead
Xyelle Overton Gabriella McKean, b. 5/27/1994 in Laconia; Greg Mathewson Lewis and Karen Lee Schacht McKean Lewis

LICHTY,
Bethany Leah, b. 10/29/1978 in Concord; John Bellows Lichty (MA) and Bonnie Ruth White (MA)
Linda S., b. 11/7/1966 in Kittery, ME; fourth; John E. Lichty (IA) and Lois Bellows (RI); residence - Ctr. Barnstead

LILLY,
Kate Mercer, b. 6/28/1981 in Concord; Alfred Smysor Lilly III and
   Cynthia Mary Mercer
Meghan Dorothy, b. 8/24/1979 in Concord; Alfred Smysor Lilly III
   and Cynthia Mary Mercer

LINDQUIST,
Carrin Marie, b. 2/19/1979 in Concord; Paul William Lindquist and
   Janice Ruth Holloway

LITTLEFIELD,
son, b. 8/14/1910; second; George F. Littlefield (farmer, 29, ME)
   and Susie Lyon (29, NS)
son [Wilmer L.], b. 1/10/1912; third; George F. Littlefield (farmer,
   30, ME) and Susie Lyon (30, NS)
Edith F., b. 6/11/1920; first; Stilson W. Littlefield (teamster,
   Woburn, MA) and Agnes L. Holmes (Roxbury, MA)
Fred W., b. 9/7/1918; first; Chester Littlefield (shoemaker, Woburn,
   MA) and Margeret Williams (New York, NY)
Hattie Louise, b. 7/16/1885; George W. Littlefield (farmer) and
   Lillian A. Pike (1942)
Olga F., b. 8/28/1910; fourth; Orin Littlefield (farmer, 51, Albany)
   and Laura P. Botting (40, Ox Bow, ME)
Susie E., b. 5/24/1908; first; George F. Littlefield (farmer, 26, ME)
   and Susie E. Lyon (26, Famouth, NS)
Vila Theresa, b. 8/13/1915; fourth; George F. Littlefield (farmer,
   ME) and Susie E. Tyon (NS)

LIZOTTE,
Michelle Brittany, b. 12/17/1992 in Laconia; Thomas Joseph Lizotte
   and Patricia Joan Dodier

LOAN,
Connor Edward McKee, b. 12/29/1998 in Concord; Michael Loan
   and Betty Loan
Michael Warwick, III, b. 12/24/1991 in Concord; Michael Warwick
   Loan, Jr. and Betty Jo McKee

LOCKE,
daughter [Edna R.], b. 2/17/1907; first; Wayland B. Locke (teamster, 27, Barnstead) and Bertha F. Emerson (25, Barnstead)
Amber Beth, b. 6/22/1980 in Concord; Richard Malcolm Locke and Carol Nina Smith
Arlene Janet, b. 6/10/1938; eighth; Elias Wesley Locke (teamster) and Violet May Gray
Bruce Paul, b. 1/9/1973 in Concord; Robert Sterling Locke (NH) and Sylvia Arlene Dudley (NH)
Carolyn Rose, b. 4/22/1936; seventh; E. Wesley Locke (teamster) and Violet M. Gray
Christina Mae, b. 11/8/1999 in Concord; Bruce Locke and Stacie Locke
Christopher Elias, b. 3/3/1969 in Rochester; Elias E. Locke (NH) and Linda Carol Brooks (MA)
Clayton Wallace, b. 12/1/1952 in Rochester; fourth; Ernest E. Locke (engineer) and Rachel Y. Belville
Crystal Lee, b. 9/10/1983 in Concord; James Nutter Locke II and Tara Lee Deinhardt
Denise Joi, b. 8/20/1981 in Concord; Harvey Roy Locke, Jr. and Katherine Margaret Corcoran
Dennis Mark, b. 4/16/1948 in Concord; fourth; Wallace W. Locke (teamster) and Winifred M. Pollard
Douglas Walter, b. 7/11/1951; third; Ernest E. Locke (lineman) and Rachel Y. Belville
Ernest Eugene, b. 7/31/1924; sixth; Elias Wesley Locke (Haverhill, MA) and Elsie M. Garrick (Jamaica Plains, MA)
Flora May, b. 9/4/1918; third; Elias Wesley Locke (farmer, Haverhill, MA) and Elsie May Garrick (Jamaica Plain)
George M., II, b. 10/5/1966 in Wolfeboro; fourth; John M. Locke (Rochester) and Evelyn M. Tasker (Strafford)
Harvey Roy, b. 12/4/1922; fifth; Elias W. Locke (farmer, Haverhill, MA) and Elsie M. Garick (Jamaica Plain)
Harvey Roy, Jr., b. 5/8/1946 in Concord; second; Harvey R. Locke (taxidermist) and Althea E. Perkins
Harvey Roy, III, b. 10/5/1980 in Concord; Harvey Roy Locke, Jr. and Katherine M. Corcoran
J. Sterling, b. 7/16/1898; George E. Locke (lumber dealer, Barnstead) and Mabel F. Kelley (Gilmanton)

Jamie Lee, b. 9/7/1984 in Concord; James Nutter Locke II and Tary Lee Deinhardt

Jenica Ann, b. 8/30/1999 in Concord; John Locke and Sherri Locke

Jennifer Lynne, b. 1/19/1971 in Concord; Ernest Eugene Locke, Jr. (NH) and Brenda Lee Pratt (NH); residence - Ctr. Barnstead

Jeremy Thomas, b. 3/22/1969 in Concord; Thomas George Locke (NH) and Joanne Dee Meunier (NY)

Jessica Amy, b. 11/25/1977 in Wolfeboro; Richard Malcolm Locke (NH) and Carol Nina Smith (NY)

Judith Dora, b. 8/25/1941; first; Harvey R. Locke (corporal) and Althea E. Perkins

Kathleen F., b. 8/14/1910; fourth; George E. Locke (farmer, 37, Barnstead) and Mabel F. Kelley (32, Gilmanton)

Kent Drew, b. 4/17/1909; third; George E. Locke (farmer, 36, Barnstead) and Mabel F. Kelley (31, Gilmanton) (1910)

Kent Drew, Jr., b. 9/10/1936; first; Kent Drew Locke (farmer) and Margaret Johnson

Kerry Wesley, b. 8/13/1951 in Wolfeboro; first; Wesley E. Locke (lineman) and Mary E. Garland

Leona Dorothy, b. 5/4/1935; sixth; E. Wesley Locke (laborer) and Violet M. Gray

Margret J., b. 11/2/1963 in Concord; second; James N. Locke (Wolfeboro) and Natalie J. Price (Wolfeboro)

Marguerite, b. 6/12/1900; George E. Locke (lumber dealer, Barnstead) and Mabel F. Kelley (Gilmanton)

Marjorie, b. 6/12/1900; George E. Locke (lumber dealer, Barnstead) and Mabel F. Kelley (Gilmanton)

Mary K., b. 10/29/1911; fifth; George E. Locke (farmer, 39, Barnstead) and Mabel F. Kelley (34, Gilmanton) (1912)

Nathan J., b. 1/1/1958 in Concord; John M. Locke and Evelyn M. Tasker

Patricia Ann, b. 3/16/1942; eighth; Elias Westley Locke (laborer) and Violet M. Gray

Philip Alan, b. 5/4/1971 in Concord; Robert Sterling Locke (NH) and Sylvia Arlene Dudley (NH)

Samantha Jean, b. 8/19/1996 in Concord; Bruce Paul Locke and Stacie Ann Locke

Sara A., b. 4/6/1967 in Concord; first; Thomas G. Locke (teacher, Wolfeboro) and Joanne D. Meunier (Mineola, NY)

Sarah Kerr, b. 1/22/1987 in Concord; Clayton Wallace Locke and Thelma Marie Kerr

Shayla Lee, b. 11/6/1996 in Concord; John Alan Locke, Jr. and
 Sherri Lee Locke
Tammy Lynn, b. 10/30/1971 in Rochester; Elias E. Locke (MA) and
 Linda C. Brooks (NH)
Wallace Gary, b. 2/7/1947 in Pittsfield; third; Wallace W. Locke
 (teamster) and Winifred N. Pollard
Wallace W., b. 12/21/1920; fourth; Elias Willey Locke (farmer,
 Haverhill, MA) and Elsie Gerrick (Jamaica Plain, MA)
Wilfred Lee, b. 9/1/1944 in Wolfeboro; eleventh; Elias W. Locke
 (farmer) and Violet M. Gray
William Rexford, b. 12/30/1937; second; Charles W. Locke
 (laborer) and Anna M. Walker
Zachary, b. 4/24/1988 in Concord; Clayton Wallace Locke and
 Thelma Marie Kerr

LODESTEIN-RIEL,
Colter Jon, b. 1/21/1982 in Barnstead; Kevin Jon Riel and Andrea
 Kay Lodestein

LONTZ,
Megan, b. 3/8/1970 in Portsmouth; Phillip Townsend Lontz (MO)
 and Barbara Elizabeth Sullivan (MO); residence - Northwood

LOUGEE,
son [Harold S.], b. 7/28/1901; first; Leslie G. Lougee (farmer, 35,
 Barnstead) and Emma Whitehouse (29, Canada)
stillborn son, b. 12/22/1906; second; Leslie G. Lougee (farmer, 40,
 Barnstead) and Emma Whitehouse (35, Canada)

LUCIUS,
Robert Howard, Jr., b. 11/6/1948 in Pittsfield; second; Robert H.
 Lucius (box shop employee) and Flora Zecha

LYNCH,
Andrew, b. 10/24/1945 in Malden, MA; fourth; John J. Lynch
 (salesman) and Rita Marie Hagerty

LYNN,
Frederick Jason, b. 12/29/1977 in Wolfeboro; Frederick John Lynn
 (NJ) and Darlene Ann Benson (NH); residence - Ctr. Barnstead

Kristen Beth, b. 4/28/1975 in Wolfeboro; Frederick J. Lynn (NJ) and Darlene Ann Benson (NH)

MACKINNON,
Ewen Ian Stewart, III, b. 12/9/1992 in Concord; E. I. S. MacKinnon, II and Ottilie Alane Harling

MACNEIL,
Diana E., b. 5/30/1966 in Concord; fourth; Donald J. Macneil (Stoneham, MA) and Verna H. Brewster (Barnstead)
Douglas J., b. 8/5/1964 in Manchester; third; Donald J. MacNeil (Stoneham, MA) and Verna H. Brewster (Barnstead)

MACPHERSON [see McPherson],
child, b. 3/13/1937; ninth; Albert MacPherson (farmer) and Edna McDuffee
Bryant N., b. 7/21/1959 in Concord; Norman F. MacPherson and Prudence A. L. Giroux
Donald Edwin, b. 1/24/1930; sixth; Albert MacPherson (farmer) and Edna May McDuffee
Marjorie Edna, b. 8/21/1928; fifth; Albert MacPherson (Roxbury, MA) and Edna M. McDuffee (Barnstead)
Mildred May, b. 9/6/1923; second; Albert MacPherson (Roxbury, MA) and Edna May McDuffee (Barnstead)
Norman, b. 2/15/1932; seventh; Albert MacPherson (farmer) and Edna McDuffee
Russell M., b. 3/1/1956 in Kittery, ME; Norman F. MacPherson (USN) and Prudence A. Giroux
Troy A., b. 7/24/1961 in Concord; Norman F. MacPherson (Barnstead) and Prudence A. Grioux (Manchester)

MAHANES,
Michael Carter, b. 6/25/1992 in Concord; Maxwell Reed Mahanes and Kathy Em Smith

MANDIGO,
Rhoda Lucille, b. 4/12/1944; fourth; Harland F. Mandigo (farmer) and Della Iva Rowe
Warren Robert, b. 6/26/1946; fifth; Harland F. Mandigo (laborer) and Della I. Rowe

MANNING,
daughter, b. 6/19/1909; second; Robert C. Manning (farmer, 23, Canada) and Offidella C. Seaver (23)

MARIATT [see Marlatt],
Pamela A., b. 4/21/1963 in Concord; fourth; Ray G. Mariatt (Orange, NJ) and Lilly V. Carlson (Quincy, MA); residence - Ctr. Barnstead

MARION,
Christina Marie, b. 1/22/1990 in Concord; Robert John Marion and Carol Jane Hartvigsen
Lauren Elizabeth, b. 4/20/1991 in Concord; Robert John Marion and Carol Jane Hartvigsen

MARLATT [see Mariatt],
Gregory S., b. 12/14/1957 in Concord; Ray G. Marlatt (asst. admin.) and Lilly V. Carlson

MARSAL,
James, b. 4/3/1931; third; Charles H. Marsal (farmer) and Bessie S. Camina
Ruth, b. 1/23/1935; fourth; Charles Marsal (farmer) and Bessie Slanina
Susanne H., b. 2/17/1957 in Concord; Thomas Marsal (laborer) and Virginia S. Holmes

MARSH,
Ardena H., b. 1/7/1905; second; William A. Marsh (farmer, 29, Barnstead) and Emma Holmes (22, Strafford)
Gerald W., b. 11/19/1909; fourth; Wilfred A. Marsh (shoemaker, 33, Barnstead) and Emma Holmes (27, Strafford)
Lillian F., b. 1/15/1911; fifth; Wilfred A. Marsh (farmer, 35, Barnstead) and Emma Holmes (28, Strafford)

MARTENS,
Candy Sue, b. 3/23/1973 in Concord; Ralph Andrew Martens (ME) and Gloria Lynne Hebert (ME); residence - Ctr. Barnstead
Daryl Allan, b. 7/15/1971 in Concord; Ralph Andrew Martens (ME) and Gloria Lynne Hebert (ME)

MARTIN,
Doris Alice, b. 12/8/1975 in Concord; Ronald Edward Martin (NH) and Linda Ruth Barton (NH)
Gregory Jon, b. 1/28/1989 in Concord; Jonathan Wayne Martin and Maryanne Helen Gardner
Jillian Theresa, b. 11/8/1985 in Concord; Jonathan Wayne Martin and Maryanne Helen Gardner
Kimberly Anne, b. 5/6/1994 in Concord; Jonathan Wayne Martin and Maryanne Helen Gardner
Rhonda M., b. 9/24/1965 in Concord; second; Ronald E. Martin (Wolfeboro) and Loretta A. Brown (Concord); residence - Ctr. Barnstead
Ricky W., b. 8/2/1968 in Laconia; Percy C. Martin (ME) and Helen J. Mayberry (CT)
Tracey L., b. 7/5/1967 in Concord; third; Ronald E. Martin (mechanic, Wolfeboro) and Loretta A. Brown (Concord)

MARTINEAU,
Donna M., b. 1/2/1963 in Concord; second; Marcel F. Martineau (Manchester) and Patricia C. Giroux (Hooksett); residence - Ctr. Barnstead

MARTINEZ,
Joseph William, b. 2/18/1987 in Laconia; Carlos Luis Martinez and Janet Mary Butterfield

MASON,
Andrew Raymond, b. 5/1/1990 in Rochester; Raymond Allsop Mason, Jr. and Elizabeth Toureille
James Leslie, b. 9/1/1948 in Rochester; second; Maurice J. Mason (woodsman) and Alva C. Hall
Lindsey Lee, b. 9/18/1984 in Rochester; Raymond Alsop Mason, Jr. and Elizabeth Anne Toureille

MASSEY,
Jessica Rachel, b. 3/17/1997 in Concord; Philip E. Massey and Jennifer L. Mayville
Lindsey Megan, b. 3/14/1999 in Concord; Philip Massey and Jennifer Massey

MAXFIELD,
daughter, b. 7/17/1889; first; Frank A. Maxfield (shoemaker, Loudon) and Emma E. Winkley (Pittsfield)
daughter, b. 12/25/1889; second; Austin C. Maxfield (farmer, Pittsfield) and Sletea G. Hooper (Berwick, ME)
son, b. 11/27/1890; second; Frank A. Maxfield (shoemaker, Loudon) and Emma E. Winkley (Pittsfield)
daughter [Amy T.], b. 11/4/1891; Austin C. Maxfield (farmer, Pittsfield) and Stella G. Hooper (Berwick, ME)
daughter, b. 3/24/1892; third; Frank A. Maxfield (shoemaker, Loudon) and Emma E. Winkley (Pittsfield)
daughter, b. 11/25/1894; first; Austin C. Maxfield (farmer, 30, Pittsfield) and Maggie Dickey (19, NB)
daughter, b. 5/20/1902; sixth; Austin C. Maxfield (farmer, 38, Barnstead) and Maggie Dickey (27, St. Johns, NB)
son [John], b. 3/23/1904; fourth; Austin C. Maxfield (farmer, 39, Pittsfield) and Maggie Dickey (29, Chipman, NB)
daughter, b. 1/9/1908; fifth; Austin C. Maxfield (farmer, 42, Pittsfield) and Magie Dickey (33, NB)
Janel Marie, b. 8/14/1974 in Concord; John Austin Maxfield (NH) and Debra Ellen Eastman (NY)

MAXWELL,
Barbara May, b. 2/20/1929; second; Warren E. Maxwell and Violet M. Gray (Barnstead)
Reginald W., b. 2/26/1930; third; Warren E. Maxwell (laborer) and Violet M. Gray

MAY,
Hannah Marie, b. 12/6/2000 in Concord; Jamie May and Darcy May

MAYO,
daughter, b. 7/13/1904; first; Everett C. Mayo (clerk, 23, Boston, MA) and Jeanette A. Gilbsie (22, Boston, MA); residence – Boston, MA

McCARTNEY,
Riley Matthew, b. 4/19/2000 in Manchester; Kevin McCartney and Dawn McCartney
Shane Patrick, b. 8/16/1996 in Manchester; Kevin Shamus McCartney and Dawn Mae Phillips

McCLINTOCK,
Lance William, b. 12/11/1981 in Concord; Scott William McClintock and Debra Lee Colby

McCONNELL,
stillborn son, b. 6/6/1906; William A. McConnell (brakeman RR, 25, Montreal, Canada) and Annie Obertin (24, Canada); residence – Manchester
Gary Lee, b. 9/4/1952 in Concord; third; Lawrence R. McConnell (shoe worker) and Ellen L. Fellows
Stephen Ray, b. 6/27/1949 in Pittsfield; second; Lawrence Ray McConnell (woodsman) and Ellen Lillian Fellows

McCORMACK,
Christopher David, b. 8/30/1992 in Concord; David Anthony McCormack and Donna Marie Ehrhardt
Mark Anthony, b. 7/5/1994 in Concord; David Anthony McCormack and Donna Marie Ehrhardt
Sharon Lee, b. 1/20/1948 in Concord; first; Bernard P. McCormack (shoe maker) and Marjorie A. Atwell

McCORMICK,
Ralph Warren, b. 3/4/1950 in Pittsfield; second; Bernard P. McCormick (shoe worker) and Marjorie A. Atwell

McCREADY,
Crystal Marie, b. 1/27/1987 in Manchester; Alan McCready and Ronda Dee Gagne
Kristen Elaine, b. 8/11/1976 in Concord; Alan Reed McCready (RI) and Janice Elaine Mankiewicz (MA)

McDONALD,
son, b. 5/1/1908; first; Frank McDonald (farmer, 23, Haverhill, MA) and Florence Pearl (22, West Boxford, MA)
Sarah Elizabeth, b. 12/23/1980 in Rochester; Wayne Travis McDonald and Marie Terese Metta

McDUFFEE,
son [Frank S.], b. 8/31/1888; first; David L. McDuffee (farmer, Alton) and Mary E. Bessir (Foxcroft, ME)

daughter, b. 12/18/1890; second; David L. McDuffee (farmer, Alton) and Mary E. Bessee (Foxcroft, ME)

daughter [Bessie Wellington], b. 5/8/1894; third; David L. McDuffee (farmer, 44, Alton) and Mary E. Bessee (39, Barnstead)

daughter [Edna May], b. 9/5/1895; David L. McDuffee (farmer, Alton) and Mary E. Bessee (Foxcroft, ME)

McGINNIS,

Benjamin Edward, b. 2/4/1993 in Concord; Donald Edward McGinnis and Gail Gonsalves

Kathryn Mary, b. 4/28/1997 in Concord; Donald E. McGinnis and Gail Gonsalves

Matthew John, b. 12/23/1994 in Concord; Donald Edward McGinnis and Gail Gonsalves

McGONAGLE,

Madeline Mary, b. 2/16/1996 in Concord; Matthew John McGonagle and Amy Papaioanou

McKECHNIE,

Kaitlin Patrice, b. 7/19/1989 in Manchester; Robert John McKechnie and Sharon Patrice McGrath

McKEEVER,

Joseph Edward, V, b. 8/24/1991 in Manchester; Joseph Edward McKeever, IV and Cherie Davia Kostreva

McKENZIE,

Jeffrey T., b. 5/25/1965 in Concord; second; Kenneth R. McKenzie, Jr. (Pittsfield) and Sandra J. Cotton (Barnstead); residence - Barnstead Parade

Kolby Kaitlyn, b. 6/14/1998 in Concord; Russell McKenzie and Nicole McKenzie

McKILLOP,

Devin Christopher, b. 7/22/1997 in Concord; Christopher B. McKillop and Janet A. Nadeau

McKINNEY,

Amelia Erin, b. 4/24/1974 in Concord; Todd Wilson McKinney (OH) and Margaret Ellen Callahan (CT)

Amy Elizabeth, b. 6/10/1977 in Concord; Todd Wilson McKinney (OH) and Margaret Ellen Callahan (CT); residence - Ctr. Barnstead

MCLEAN,
Aaron Augustus, b. 8/10/1999 in Concord; Timothy Mclean and Debra Mclean

McPHERSON [see MacPherson],
Ailen Lillian, b. 7/16/1926; fourth; Albert McPherson (Roxbury, MA) and Edna May McDuffee (Barnstead)
Albert, b. 4/26/1922; first; Albert McPherson (farmer, Roxbury, MA) and Edna M. McDuffee (Barnstead)
Reta Joan, b. 7/10/1933; eighth; Albert McPherson (farmer) and Edna M. McDuffee
Ruth Alma, b. 6/28/1938; ninth; Albert McPherson (farmer) and Edna May McDuffee
Shirley Emma, b. 2/2/1925; third; Albert McPherson (Roxbury, MA) and Edna McDuffee (Barnstead)

MELE,
Joshua Robert, b. 1/13/1993 in Concord; Bruce John Mele, Sr. and Jennifer Lawrence Pickering

MELVIN,
Adam Tucker, b. 4/27/1983 in Concord; Donald Walter Melvin and Joan Louise Tucker

MEREDITH,
Harriet A., b. 8/25/1954 in Concord; William H. Meredith (US Coast Guard) and Mildred A. Ballard

MERRILL,
Diane F., b. 9/28/1966 in Concord; first; Stuart B. Merrill (Lexington, MA) and Grace A. Higgins (Barnstead)
Frances Louise, b. 8/24/1927; third; Clarence Merrill (Pembroke) and Rebecca Harriman
Gail L., b. 10/7/1954 in Kittery, ME; Douglas S. Merrill (US Army) and Nancy A. Heywood

MERRITT,
Amy Lyn, b. 2/4/1976 in Concord; Dexter Reed Merritt (MA) and Susan Linda McCarthy (MA)

MESERVE,
stillborn child, b. 4/26/1888; first; Albert F. Meserve (shoemaker, Pittsfield) and Annie ----- (Boston)
Arthur Percy, b. 3/17/1933; eighth; Frank C. Meserve (auto salesman) and Marguerite Emerson

MICHAUD,
Cody Joseph, b. 12/8/2000 in Concord; Mitchell Michaud and Sonia Michaud
Erin Rose, b. 9/12/2000 in Concord; Randell Michaud and Julie Michaud

MICHIE,
William P., Jr., b. 12/14/1906; first; William P. Michie (electrician, 30, Lancaster, MA) and Myrtie E. Jenkins (25, Barnstead); residence – Manchester

MIDDLETON,
Lindsay Katherine, b. 12/27/1996 in Laconia; Dana Jerome Middleton and Pamela Jean Middleton

MIKOLYSKI,
Lois Marie, b. 11/2/1978 in Concord; John Wayne Mikolyski (NH) and Merrilee Smith (NH)

MIKULA,
Manny Michael, b. 2/6/1968 in Concord; Manny Mikula (NH) and Barbara Jean Graeme (NH)

MILLER,
Eric Joseph, b. 9/30/1975 in Manchester; Robert Allen Miller (NY) and Cynthia Ann White (NH)
Megan Ann, b. 7/16/1985 in Concord; Thomas Joseph Miller and Deborah Ann Cove

MILLS,
Ashley Maria, b. 8/19/1992 in Concord; Salvatore Rocco Mills and
    Cynthia Martine Wright
John Lowell, Jr., b. 5/23/1929; first; John Lowell Mills (Henniker)
    and Dora E. Lougee (Portsmouth)

MINER,
Jason Edward, b. 8/23/1979 in Concord; Edward Leo Miner and
    Colleen Rose Conway
Jillian Roberta, b. 4/22/1980 in Concord; David Ashley Miner and
    Julie Lynn Luckett
John Pitman, b. 12/14/1986 in Concord; David Ashley Miner and
    Julie Lynn Luckert
Peter James, Jr., b. 3/19/1985 in Concord; Peter James Miner and
    Tammy Lynn Huckins
Wade Edward, b. 7/11/1986 in Concord; Dennis Alan Miner and
    Susan Kathrine Hart

MITCHELL,
Albert Carl, b. 4/9/1969 in Concord; Herbert Gale Mitchell (NH) and
    Freda Mae Nutter (NH)
Jillian Zee, b. 12/13/1976 in Concord; Joseph James Mitchell (NH)
    and Judith Alice Riel (NH)

MONTGOMERY,
Mark Alan, b. 11/11/1993 in Concord; Rickie Glenn Montgomery
    and Karen Marie Labrecque
Rickie Glenn, II, b. 3/25/1992 in Lebanon; Rickie Glenn
    Montgomery and Karen Marie Labrecque
Rosina May Pitman, b. 6/15/1996 in Concord; Rickie Glenn
    Montgomery and Karen Marie LaBrecque

MOORE,
Alfred Edwin, b. 11/6/1915; first; John H. Moore (weaver,
    Barnstead) and Lettie Harriman (Lynn, MA)
John H., b. 10/19/1891; first; Frank H. Moore (clerk, 32, Loudon)
    and Sarah F. Hillsgrove (22, Wilmot) (1906)

MORGAN,
Edna, b. 2/12/1901; fourth; J. Hollis Morgan (section foreman, 23,
    Bow) and Mary J. Cate (22, Hooksett)

MORRIS,
Jacob David, b. 12/21/1992 in Concord; David Edward Morris and Robin Lynn Stock

MORRISON,
Grace H., b. 8/22/1887; first; Charles H. Morrison (farmer, 30, Barnstead) and Helen M. Colbath (24, Barnstead) (1905)

MORSE,
Adam Lee, b. 4/3/1990 in Manchester; Kevin M. Morse and Lynne Carol Gauron
Tracey Ann, b. 11/4/1971 in Concord; George Haley Morse (NS) and Carole Marie Brown (MA); residence - Ctr. Barnstead

MOTT,
Keri Elizabeth, b. 8/4/1987 in Hanover; Kevin Wayne Mott and Mary Ann Arnold

MOULTON,
Amber Lynn, b. 5/28/1991 in Laconia; Scott Carl Moulton and Linda Ellen Watts
Holly Elizabeth, b. 2/18/1989 in Laconia; Scott Carl Moulton and Linda Ellen Watts
Jordan Scott, b. 5/28/1991 in Laconia; Scott Carl Moulton and Linda Ellen Watts

MOUNTAIN,
Katie Macknight, b. 7/1/1980 in Concord; H. David Mountain and Karen Macknight
Ryan David, b. 12/6/1985 in Concord; Henry David Mountain and Karen MacKnight

MOUSSEAU,
Danielle Leigh, b. 11/12/1990 in Concord; Joel Stone Mousseau and Deborah Ann Bergeron
Jay Cote, b. 12/27/1994 in Concord; Joel Stone Mousseau and Deborah Ann Bergeron
Jordan Stone, b. 4/10/1988 in Concord; Joel Stone Mousseau and Deborah Ann Bergeron

MULCAHY,
Christopher Anthony, b. 4/3/1993 in Exeter; Shawn Adrian Mulcahy and Stacy Luann Shaw
Elizabeth Paula, b. 5/14/1988 in Dover; Robert Emmett Mulcahy, III and Bonnie Ratcliffe
Miranda Ann, b. 8/25/1994 in Exeter; Shawn Adrian Mulcahy and Stacy Luann Shaw
Shawn, b. 11/16/1959 in Manchester; first; Robert E. Mulcahy (foreman, Somerville, MA) and Dorothy A. Doran (Somerville, MA)

MUNROE,
Erin Casey, b. 10/5/1993 in Concord; Dale Kenneth Munroe and Lori Jean Gray
Marcus Scott, b. 3/24/1992 in Concord; Dale Kenneth Munroe and Lori Jean Gray

MUNSEY,
child, b. 10/16/1893; fourth; George Munsey (shoemaker, Barnstead) and Kate Weld (Lynn, MA)
Muriel Marilyn, b. 9/28/1926; first; Linwood B. Munsey (Lynn, MA) and Cecil M. Prince (Milton)

MURCHISON,
Kellie Lynne, b. 9/9/1977 in Laconia; Dale Edward Murchison (ME) and Lucie Elisabeth Blomme (Netherlands); residence - Ctr. Barnstead

MURPHY,
Samantha Kae, b. 1/24/1991 in Concord; Calvin Earl Murphy, Jr. and Lorraine Lynn Marcoux
Thomas James, b. 11/4/1977 in Concord; James Thomas Murphy (NY) and Gail Nancy Lank (NH); residence - Ctr. Barnstead

MURRAY,
Joseph P., b. 7/21/1939; third; John Paul Murray (carpenter) and Jeanne Avis Davis

MURZIN,
Naomi Dawn, b. 6/28/1999 in Concord; Donald Murzin and Rebecca Murzin

MYERS,
Elwood Gene, b. 3/1/1945 in Pittsfield; third; William H. Myers (mechanical engineer) and Priscilla E. Wells

MYRE,
David J., b. 9/11/1962 in Concord; second; Paul H. Myre, Jr. (Pawtucket, RI) and Patricia I. Maddress (Pawtucket, RI); residence - Ctr. Barnstead

Kevin P., b. 8/5/1966 in Concord; third; Paul H. Myre (Pawtucket, RI) and Patricia I. Maddress (Pawtucket, RI); residence - Barnstead Parade

Steven P., b. 7/24/1960 in Concord; first; Paul H. Myre, Jr. (weaver, Pawtucket, RI) and Patricia I. Maddress (Pawtucket, RI)

NADEAU,
Darrell Dunton, b. 12/5/1975 in Concord; Harvey Roland Nadeau (MA) and Barbara Grace Dunton (MA)

NATION [see Notion],
Alfred Edmund, Jr., b. 6/20/1946 in Concord; first; Alfred E. Nation (shoe worker) and Barbara L. Hallett

Dawn Noel, b. 9/3/1949 in Pittsfield; second; Alfred Edmond Nation (US Army) and Barbara Louise Hallett

NEISTER,
Scott Edward, b. 11/13/1971 in Stoneham, MA; Sanford Edward Neister (MA) and Ursula Susan Crawford (VA)

NELSON,
Erik Owen, b. 11/23/1990 in Concord; John Scott Nelson and Gail Webster

Katheryn Bea, b. 12/28/1994 in Concord; John Scott Nelson and Gail Marie Webster

Shaina Beth, b. 1/16/1990 in Concord; John Peter Nelson and Tasha Terry Chagnon

Tara Evangeline, b. 6/1/1982 in Concord; Jerry Nelson and Linda MacKnight

Todd Everett, b. 5/16/1971 in Concord; Jerry Nelson (NH) and Judith Alice Riel (NH)

NEWELL,
Xavier Ray, b. 2/9/2000 in Concord; William Newell and Cassandre Newell

NICHOLS,
daughter, b. 3/24/1911; third; Frank J. Nichols (laborer, 32, Kennebunk, ME) and Georgia Towne (34, NS)

NIGHELLI,
Lisandra Felicia, b. 11/16/1983 in Concord; Benjamin R. Nighelli and Jeston Marie Doughty

NILSSON,
Dameon Wayne, b. 11/2/2000 in Concord; Todd Nilsson and Nicole Nilsson

NOBLE,
Joshua Steven, b. 9/7/1999 in Concord; William Noble and Crystal Noble

NORMANDIN,
Alexandra Lee, b. 3/10/1997 in Concord; Thomas J. Normandin and Kristina L. Conti
Christopher Thomas, b. 6/11/2000 in Concord; Thomas Normandin and Kristina Conti-Normandin

NOTION [see Nation],
Michelle Louise, b. 4/3/1970 in Concord; Alfred Edmund Notion (NH) and Cynthia Coleman Wallace (VA)

NUTTER,
daughter, b. 11/13/1897; first; R. L. Nutter (Barnstead) and Addie Powell (Barnstead)
son, b. 2/9/1909; second; Frank C. Nutter (farmer, 28, Barnstead) and Iva P. Berry (20, Barnstead)
child, b. 4/23/1951 in Concord; sixth; Malcolm H. Nutter (lumberman) and Grace E. Gray
Frank C., b. 6/28/1881; second; Frank S. Nutter (farmer, 26, Barnstead) and Sarah E. Caswell (26, Barnstead) (1905)
Freda Mae, b. 11/18/1948 in Concord; fifth; Malcolm H. Nutter (woodsman) and Grace Gray

Joseph C., b. 7/21/1918; fourth; Frank C. Nutter (farmer, Barnstead) and Iva Berry (Barnstead)

Marilyn Grace, b. 11/17/1946 in Concord; fourth; Malcolm H. Nutter (laborer) and Grace E. Gray

Robert Carroll, b. 10/31/1916; third; Frank Carroll Nutter (farmer, Barnstead) and Iva P. Berry (Barnstead)

Sarah E., b. 11/18/1905; first; Frank C. Nutter (farmer, 24, Barnstead) and Iva Pearl Berry (17, Barnstead)

Violet Elaine, b. 5/27/1943; third; Malcolm H. Nutter (woodsman) and Grace Gray

NYEGARD,
Paula Jean, b. 6/23/1988 in Concord; Donald Eugene Nyegard and Cheryl Ann Farretta

O'BARTIN [see Barton, O'Barton],
Arthur, b. 3/12/1907; tenth; Ezra O'Bartin (farmer, 37, Plattsburgh, NY) and Virginia Duprus (32, Hooksett)

David G., b. 3/18/1907; third; Edward O'Bartin (laborer, 29, Canada) and Jennie B. Daly (22, Gilmanton)

O'BARTON [see Barton, O'Bartin],
daughter [Rosa], b. 1/4/1909; eleventh; Ezra O'Barton (farmer, 39, NY) and Virginia Duprus (34, Hooksett)

O'BRIEN,
Ashley Anne, b. 6/8/1988 in Concord; Mark James O'Brien and Shirley Ann O'Brien

Denise N., b. 12/7/1969 in Wolfeboro; James Edward O'Brien (MA) and Alice Catherine Blackmer (MA); residence - Ctr. Barnstead

O'GARA,
Patrick Sean, b. 4/9/1999 in Manchester; John O'Gara and Colleen O'Gara

O'MEARA,
Corey Stephen, b. 2/27/1984 in Concord; Stephen H. O'Meara and Dary Ann Deinhardt

Kelly Ann, b. 7/8/1982 in Concord; Stephen Hugh O'Meara and Dary Ann Deinhardt

O'NEIL,
Alyssa Marie, b. 11/8/1979 in Concord; Dennis O'Neil and Linda Kay Sawyer
Joshua Sawyer, b. 4/11/1988 in Laconia; Dennis O'Neil and Linda Kay Sawyer

O'SHEA,
Adam James, b. 10/29/1976 in Concord; Christen Gerald O'Shea (ME) and Kathleen Joyce Shea (MA)

OLMSTED,
Bradley James, b. 4/13/1992 in Rochester; Ronald Allen Olmsted and Tracy Ellen Saulnier

OLSON,
Jonathan Christopher, b. 1/30/1994 in Concord; Ronald John Olson and Brenda Elizabeth Lee

ORDWAY,
Courtney Marie, b. 4/14/1986 in Concord; Keith Michael Ordway and Lynn Esther Donnelly

OTIS,
daughter [Nellie B.], b. 12/29/1893; first; Arthur Otis (farmer, 25, Strafford) and Etta Hanson (21, Barnstead)
son [Ernest], b. 12/3/1906; fourth; Arthur D. Otis (farmer, 38, Strafford) and Etta Hanson (33, Barnstead)
Donald E., b. 10/15/1921; fourth; Lewis L. Otis (garage owner, Barnstead) and Gladys Brady (Barnstead)
Earlma Jane, b. 6/28/1927; sixth; Lewis L. Otis (Barnstead) and Gladys Brady (Barnstead)
Shirley May, b. 7/27/1923; fifth; Lewis L. Otis (Barnstead) and Gladys Brady (Barnstead)

OZELIUS,
Ethan Carl, b. 12/29/1992 in Concord; John Edwin Ozelius and Lori Anna Parent
Peter Anton, b. 10/30/1990 in Concord; John Edwin Ozelius and Lori Anna Parent

PACHE,
Jacob Ross, b. 9/29/1998 in Concord; Franci Pache and A. Heather Pache

PACKER,
Jason Cole, b. 11/5/1986 in Concord; George William Packer, Jr. and Sharon Faye Gillenwater

PAGE,
son, b. 10/23/1891; fifth; William Page (farmer, Danvers, MA)
daughter, b. 11/1/1892; eighth; William Page (teamster, Woburn, MA) and Katherine Kearns (Canada)
Cassi Jean, b. 2/9/1988 in Concord; Jesse Howard Page and Susan Marie Smith
Clark Archie, b. 5/24/1984 in Concord; Clark Dwight Page and Patricia Jean Moore
Emma A., b. 5/22/1900; Walter Page (farmer, Gilmanton) and Alice Foss (Barnstead)
Jeremiah Leonard, b. 5/31/1986 in Concord; Jesse Howard Page and Susan Marie Smith
Willard R., b. 12/12/1908; second; Walter Page (farmer, 34, Gilmanton) and Alice Foss (27, Barnstead)

PALMER,
son [Lawrence], b. 2/10/1891; fifth; Frank E. Palmer (carpenter, Barnstead) and Ida J. Shackford (Barnstead)
daughter, b. 5/4/1906; first; Arthur G. Palmer (carpenter, 25, Barnstead) and Mildred Aikin (19, Barnstead)
Elmer, b. 7/21/1893; sixth; Charles E. Palmer (carpenter, Barnstead) and Sarah Carr (Loudon) (1894)
Elwin, b. 7/21/1893; fifth; Charles E. Palmer (carpenter, Barnstead) and Sarah Carr (Loudon) (1894)

PAQUIN,
Wyatt Lionel, b. 10/16/2000 in Laconia; Steven Paquin and Lauraine Paquin

PARELIUS,
Caleb Alan, b. 12/22/2000 in Concord; Walter Parelius and April Parelius

PARENT,
Phillip Jonathan, b. 9/18/1952 in Concord; second; William H.
  Parent (credit reporter) and Emma T. Fasciano
Theodore Harrison, b. 5/23/1950 in Concord; first; William H.
  Parent (credit investigator) and Emma T. Fasciano

PARSHLEY,
daughter, b. 6/23/1909; third; Levi C. Parshley (teamster, 30,
  Barnstead) and Fannie A. Adams (26, Fitchburg, MA)
son [Frank], b. 6/30/1910; fourth; Levi C. Parshley (teamster, 32,
  Barnstead) and Fannie A. Adams (28, Fitchburg, MA)
son [Earl], b. 10/20/1912; fifth; Levi C. Parshley (teamster, 34,
  Barnstead) and Fannie A. Adams (30, Fitchburg, MA)
Cora M., b. 1/14/1906; second; Levi C. Parshley (teamster, 28,
  Barnstead) and Fannie A. Adams (23, Fitchburg, MA)
W. D. [son], b. 10/27/1914; fourth; William D. Parshley (farmer, 27,
  Pittsfield) and Eugenie J. Serville (24, Laconia)

PARSONS,
son [Scott D.], b. 4/22/1888; first; Charles A. Parsons (farmer,
  Lawrence, MA) and Electa S. Ricker (Lee, ME)
son [Ralph A.], b. 8/4/1890; second; Charles A. Parsons (farmer,
  Lawrence, MA) and Electa A. Ricker (Lee, ME) (1891)
son, b. 3/4/1892; tenth; Charles R. Parsons (stage driver, Salmon
  Falls) and Carrie Kelley (NY)
son, b. 3/4/1892; eleventh; Charles R. Parsons (stage driver,
  Salmon Falls) and Carrie Kelley (NY)
son, b. 4/13/1900; Charles A. Parsons (farmer, Lawrence, MA) and
  Electa S. Ricker (Lee, ME)
Irene Elizabeth, b. 11/18/1932; second; Scott D. Parsons (farmer)
  and Sadie F. Hoyt
Linda Mary, b. 11/19/1947 in Concord; second; Charles A. Parsons
  (laborer) and Elizabeth Pearl Coombs

PATTERSON,
Paige Frances, b. 1/30/1998 in Concord; Steven Patterson and
  Catherine Patterson

PEABODY,
son, b. 8/20/1888; second; Walter A. Peabody (shoemaker, Boston,
  MA) and Lulu B. Aikins (Barnstead)

PEACOCK,
Matthew George, b. 8/21/1983 in Concord; Ralph Dean Peacock and Cheryl Ann Peterson
Stephen Michael, b. 11/17/1980 in Concord; Ralph Deane Peacock and Cheryl Ann Peterson

PEALE,
Andrew Innes, b. 11/8/1986 in Concord; James Innes Peale and Carol McIntyre
Caitlin Sumner, b. 6/8/1984 in Concord; James Innes Peale and Carol McIntyre

PEARCE,
Corrine May, b. 5/26/1990 in Concord; David Gordon Pearce and Jane Elizabeth Gross

PEASE,
Corrinne Rochelle, b. 7/18/2000 in Concord; Benjamin Pease and Kristi Pease

PEIRCE [see Pierce],
Harold Dixon, b. 4/11/1938; fourth; Kenneth L. Peirce (farmer) and Esther Helena Dixon

PELLETIER,
Matthew Joseph, b. 2/8/1996 in Concord; Shawn David Pelletier and Tammy Lynn Cox

PELTON,
Kathryn L., b. 10/1/1961 in Concord; Bruce I. Pelton (New York, NY) and Margaret L. Surdy (Bronxville, NY)

PENNEY,
Joshua Matthew, b. 11/17/1987 in Wolfeboro; Richard Douglas Penney and Paula Sue Smith
Tyler Daniel, b. 8/3/1992 in Wolfeboro; Richard Douglas Penney and Paula Sue Smith

PERKINS,
Althea Edna, b. 5/16/1923; first; David M. Perkins (Strafford) and Dora Edna Foss (Strafford)

Doraine Mae, b. 4/12/1935 in Wolfeboro; fifth; David M. Perkins
(garage owner) and Dora F. Foss
Gloria Jean, b. 3/11/1949 in Concord; first; William Carroll Perkins
(linesman) and Gloria Hazel Wade
Kelci Alexandria, b. 6/17/1997 in Concord; Robert A. Perkins, Jr.
and Nicki J. Saltmarsh
Laura Catherine, b. 4/15/1990 in Concord; William Anthony
Perkins, Jr. and Margaret Ann Concannon
Leone Mabel, b. 5/16/1931; fourth; David M. Perkins (garage
owner) and Dora F. Foss
Maynard Harry, b. 7/12/1926; second; David M. Perkins (Strafford)
and Dora Foss (Strafford)
Osborn Murray, b. 9/24/1904; second; Osborn M. Perkins (clerk, 32,
Providence, RI) and Gertrude Osborn (26, Sherbrooke, PQ)
Philip O., b. 3/10/1906; third; Osborn M. Perkins (clerk, 33,
Providence, RI) and Gertrude E. Osborn (28, Sherbrooke, PQ)
Wanda S., b. 4/11/1954 in Rochester; Maynard H. Perkins
(lineman) and Dorothy E. Belville
William A., b. 6/2/1955 in Concord; William C. Perkins (lineman)
and Gloria H. Wade
William Anthony, II, b. 7/17/1992 in Concord; William Anthony
Perkins, Jr. and Margaret Ann Concannon
William Carroll, b. 10/16/1928; third; David M. Perkins (Strafford)
and Dora E. Foss (Strafford)

PETHIC,
Erika L., b. 12/18/1967 in Concord; second; Wayne T. Pethic
(salesman, Meredith) and Ann E. Riel (Concord)

PHILBRICK,
Scott L., b. 3/27/1961 in Concord; Gary L. Philbrick (Pittsfield) and
Dorothy L. Lank (Laconia); residence - Barnstead Parade
Tanya Lee, b. 2/8/1974 in Rochester; Eugene Holden Philbrick (NH)
and Wanda Sue Perkins (NH); residence - Ctr. Barnstead

PHILLIPS,
Debra J., b. 11/16/1953 in Wolfeboro; first; Shirley N. Phillips
(laborer) and Lona J. Sullivan
Donna J., b. 11/4/1954 in Rochester; Shirley N. Phillips (plumber)
and Lona J. Sullivan

Muriel V., b. 1/16/1965 in Concord; third; Ceiland A. Phillips (Colebrook) and Kathleen Holly (Verdun, PQ)
Pamela S., b. 6/1/1960 in Concord; first; Shirley N. Phillips (plumbing mechanic, Colebrook) and Wendy P. Smith (Boston, MA)
Patrick M., b. 4/2/1964 in Concord; second; Ceiland A. Phillips (Colebrook) and Kathleen Holly (Verdun, CT)
Simone, b. 8/14/1992 in Wolfeboro; Jonathan Paul Phillips and Robin Denise Barrier
Stephen R., b. 5/3/1961 in W. Stewartstown; Ceiland A. Phillips (Colebrook) and Thelma V. Lyons (Colebrook)
Wade R., b. 3/25/1960 in W. Stewartstown; third; Ceiland A. Phillips (laborer, Colebrook) and Thelma V. Lyons (Colebrook)

PIASECZNY,
Courtney Sylvia, b. 9/10/1993 in Concord; Steven Roger Piaseczny and Debra Jean Locke
Jacob Steven, b. 2/17/1997 in Concord; Steven R. Piaseczny and Debra J. Locke
Jacquelyn Theresa, b. 12/30/1987 in Hanover; James Daniel Piaseczny and Kara Leigh Hast

PICARD,
Jennifer Marie, b. 7/5/1989 in Concord; Michael Richard Picard and Therese Laurette Goudreau

PICKARD,
Dale A., b. 12/28/1956 in Concord; Robert A. Pickard (lineman) and Carol K. Cookson

PICKERING,
daughter [Elizabeth May], b. 7/3/1893; second; Tobias B. Pickering (farmer, 51, Barnstead) and Ada R. Evans (38, Barnstead)
daughter, b. 9/23/1893; Albert C. Pickering (laborer, Barnstead) and Nettie Gray (Strafford) (1895)
son [Ralph], b. 11/5/1897; third; Albert C. Pickering (laborer, Barnstead) and Nettie Gray (Strafford)
daughter, b. 3/13/1912; second; Fred C. Pickering (bartender, 49, Barnstead) and Fannie Chadwick (36, Farmington); residence – Concord

PICKETT,
Carl Frederick, b. 1/26/1988 in Concord; Frederick Worthington
 Pickett and Sandra Jean Boisvert
Nathan Alan, b. 11/14/1990 in Concord; Fredrick Worthington
 Pickett and Sandra Jean Boisvert
Sarah Jean, b. 2/12/1985 in Concord; Fredrick W. Pickett and
 Sandra Jean Boisvert

PIERCE [see Peirce],
Donald Edward, b. 11/27/1939; sixth; Kenneth L. Pierce (farmer)
 and Esther H. Dixon
Donald F., b. 1/6/1937; fourth; Kenneth L. Pierce (farmer) and
 Esther Dixon
Shirley J., b. 5/20/1935; third; Kenneth L. Pierce (farmer) and
 Esther Dixon
Wilbert Maurice, b. 11/9/1940; seventh; Kenneth L. Pierce (laborer)
 and Esther H. Dixon

PINARD,
Jennifer L., b. 5/30/1958 in Concord; Roger A. Pinard and Dorothy
 J. Ross
Pamela J., b. 7/18/1953 in Concord; Roger A. Pinard (chemist) and
 Dorothy J. Ross
Rebecca G., b. 7/19/1956 in Concord; Roger A. Pinard (chemist)
 and Dorothy J. Ross

PINKHAM,
Alan W., b. 8/22/1953 in Concord; John H. Pinkham (mail carrier)
 and Ethel L. McAllister
Ashley Marie, b. 11/2/1987 in Rochester; Alan Winthrop Pinkham
 and Diane Virginia Hunter
Mary E., b. 11/8/1956 in Concord; John H. Pinkham (mail carrier)
 and Ethel L. McAllister
Philip Jackson, b. 8/18/1949 in Concord; fourth; John Herbert
 Pinkham (manager) and Ethel Lillian McAllister
Sara Ann, b. 7/17/1978 in Concord; Phillip Jackson Pinkham (NH)
 and Sally Ann Sutton (NH); residence - Ctr. Barnstead

PINTO,
Gage Anthony, b. 12/31/1995 in Lebanon; Robert Pinto and
 Christine Louise Clement

PITMAN,
son, b. 2/15/1889; first; Charles Pitman (cutter, Barnstead) and Nettie Stevens (Manchester)
son [Fred T.], b. 8/24/1901; second; Oscar Pitman (farmer, Barnstead) and Rena Spooner (Barre, VT)
daughter, b. 5/18/1905; third; Albert G. Pitman (farmer, 34, Alexandria) and Nellie F. Clough (37, Belmont)
daughter, b. 10/3/1907; fourth; Albert G. Pitman (farmer, 37, Alexandria) and Nellie F. Clough (39, Belmont)
son [Robert], b. 10/17/1907; fourth; Edward Pitman (farmer, 28) and Anny DeMerrett (28, Barnstead)
daughter, b. 5/26/1908; fourth; Oscar Pitman (farmer, 43, Barnstead) and Lurena Spooner (29, Barre, VT)
Alice May, b. 11/26/1932; sixth; Fred T. Pitman (farmer) and Harriet M. Laurence
Arthur William, b. 10/4/1930; fifth; Fred F. Pitman (farmer) and Harriet M. Lawrence
Beatrice Ellen, b. 2/9/1929; fourth; Fred T. Pitman (Barnstead) and Harriet Lawrence (Leominster, MA)
Doris Louise, b. 6/10/1926; first; Fred T. Pitman (Barnstead) and Harriett M. Lawrence (Leominster, MA)
Elizabeth M., b. 12/8/1922; fifth; Oscar E. Pitman (farmer, Barnstead) and Lurena B. Spooner (Huntington, VT)
Fred Austin, b. 12/11/1927; second; Fred T. Pitman (Barnstead) and Harriet M. Lawrence (Leominster, MA)
Fred Thomas, Jr., b. 9/18/1923; first; Fred Thomas Pitman (Barnstead) and Ann T. Lindquist (Deerfield)
George A., b. 3/16/1909; first; Albert G. Pitman (farmer, 38, Alexandria) and Nellie F. Clough (40, Belmont)
George F., b. 9/26/1903; third; Oscar E. Pitman (farmer, 38, Barnstead) and Serena Spooner (24, Huntington, VT)
Kenneth George, b. 5/28/1942 in Pittsfield; first; George Albert Pitman (saw mill operator) and Alma Louisa Lakeman
Roger Carlton, b. 6/11/1946 in Concord; third; George A. Pitman (saw mill operator) and Alma L. Lakeman
Ruth Agnes, b. 12/11/1927; third; Fred T. Pitman (Barnstead) and Harriet M. Lawrence (Leominster, MA)
Viola P., b. 8/6/1900; Oscar Pitman (farmer, Barnstead) and Rena Spooner (Barre, VT)

PLAISTED,
son [Leon A.], b. 10/13/1893; second; George Plaisted (express messenger)
Madeline, b. 9/10/1895; George G. Plaisted (ex. messenger, Meredith) and Emma B. Hunt

PLANTE,
Kaela Elizabeth, b. 4/16/1991 in Concord; Kenneth William Plante and Pamela Jean Sargent

PLUMER,
Natasha, b. 9/24/1971 in Concord; Charles Thomas Plumer (CA) and Peggy Lu Jolly (VT)

POCOCK,
Kimberley Anne, b. 10/18/1981 in Concord; Leslie Erle Pocock and Anne Patricia Nadeau

POMROY,
Velerie Ann, b. 1/12/1970 in Rochester; Birlem Bailey Pomroy (NH) and Jane Elizabeth Snook (MA); residence - Ctr. Barnstead

POOLE,
Jordan Daniel, b. 4/20/1992 in Concord; Daniel J. Poole and Bethany Ann Winterle

POPPEMA,
Marie M. L., b. 4/10/1953 in Rochester; second; Donald R. Poppema (forester) and Rachel M. Pomerleau

PORTER,
Paige Brooke, b. 4/13/1987 in Concord; Peter Brooks Porter and Linda Gail Davis

POST,
Norman, b. 5/1/1912; first; Chester Post (laborer, 27, Rockland, ME) and Winnie B. Littlefield (20, Ashland, ME)

POTHIER,
Cindy Lian, b. 4/5/1988 in Concord; Joseph Francis Pothier and Donna Marie Castine

POTTER,
Joan B., b. 8/3/1962 in Concord; first; Robert L. Potter (Gilmanton) and Nancy J. Sanborn (Laconia); residence - Ctr. Barnstead

POULIN,
Bryce Scott Robert, b. 9/28/1998 in Laconia; Scott Poulin and Sonya Poulin
Kevin Robert, b. 10/9/1989 in Manchester; Robert Aime Poulin and Phyliss Maria St. Onge

POWELL,
Ella May, b. 5/12/1896; Sylvester Powell (painter, Concord) and Etta C. Powell (Barnstead)

POWERS,
Austin Roger, b. 9/10/1990 in Concord; Timothy Allen Powers and Diana Tobias

PRATT,
Timothy C., b. 8/2/1961 in Concord; Conrad M. Pratt (Granville, MA) and Mary S. Pelky (Rutland, VT); residence - Ctr. Barnstead

PRESCOTT,
Allan Gordon, b. 5/5/1951 in Concord; first; Gordon H. Prescott (carpenter) and Mary E. Wheet
Frances Luanna, b. 9/29/1928; fourth; Harold Prescott (Barnstead) and Caroline Eastman (Chelsea, MA)
Gary Harold, b. 9/5/1952 in Concord; second; Gordon H. Prescott (carpenter) and Mary E. Wheet
Gordon Harry, b. 10/5/1926; third; Harold F. Prescott (Barnstead) and Caroline Eastman (Chelsea, MA)
Harold J., b. 9/4/1896; Frank A. Prescott (farmer, Alton) and Susanna M. Hurd (Barnstead)
Jan Marie, b. 1/24/1954 in Concord; Gordon H. Prescott (carpenter) and Mary E. Wheet
Lauren Rose, b. 6/7/1992 in Concord; Alan Gordon Prescott and Roseann Greenwood
Lynn R., b. 9/17/1955 in Concord; Gordon H. Prescott (carpenter) and Mary E. Wheet

Megan Marie, b. 7/2/1998 in Concord; Alan Prescott and Rose
Prescott
Muriel Bertha, b. 3/16/1932; fifth; Harold F. Prescott (farmer) and
Caroline H. Eastman
Scott H., b. 12/19/1959 in Concord; Gordon H. Prescott and Mary
E. Wheet
Sherley Caroline, b. 11/9/1924; second; Harold F. Prescott
(Barnstead) and Caroline Eastman (Chelsea, MA)
Virginia A., b. 11/10/1922; first; Harold F. Prescott (farmer,
Barnstead) and Caroline Eastman (Chelsea, MA)

PRESTON,
Tyler Kevin, b. 5/1/1999 in Concord; Marvin Preston and Lynn
Preston

PRINCE,
Charles Herbert, b. 9/2/1929; first; Charles R. Prince (Milton) and
Dorothy I. Davis (Northwood)
George Henry, b. 8/14/1931; second; Charles R. Prince (laborer)
and Dorothy I. Davis

PROCTOR,
daughter, b. 9/20/1897; first; Irvill T. Proctor (farmer, Alton) and
Lillian C. Bennett (Alton)

PROULX,
Elizabeth Gabrielle, b. 7/12/1982 in Derry; Robert Peter Proulx and
Mary Elizabeth Demers
Jonathan Robert, b. 9/5/1984 in Manchester; Robert Peter Proulx
and Mary Elizabeth Demers

PROVENCAL,
Carol J., b. 10/3/1967 in Concord; second; Frank J. Provencal
(construction, Laconia) and Jane A. Witham (Gloucester, MA)
Christine A., b. 8/28/1963 in Laconia; first; Frank J. Provencal
(Laconia) and Jane A. Witham (Gloucester, MA)

PSZONOWSKY,
Jacob Dennett, b. 4/16/1975 in Concord; Roger Dennett
Pszonowsky (RI) and Violet Nadine Bateman (HI)

Michele Linn, b. 1/28/1969 in Concord; Michael George
    Pszonowsky (RI) and Gloria Jean Hathaway (RI)
Peter Joseph, b. 9/30/1972 in Concord; Michael George
    Pszonowsky (RI) and Gloria Jean Hathaway (RI)

PUBLICOVER,
Kenneth George, Jr., b. 3/28/1974 in Concord; Kenneth George
    Publicover (NH) and Pamela Leona Ayer (NH)

PYNE,
Melinda Sue, b. 10/8/1977 in Concord; Robert Scott Pyne (MA) and
    Mary Ellen Vangiell (NH)

RADCLIFFE,
Robert Bryant, b. 1/11/1969 in Plymouth; George Ernest Radcliffe
    (NH) and Elaine Gwen Radcliffe (NH)
Shawn Walter, b. 3/19/1971 in Plymouth; George Ernest Radcliffe
    (NH) and Elaine Gwen Newton (NH)

RAND,
Ruth Rena, b. 9/12/1941 in Wolfeboro; first; Dona C. Rand
    (machine operator) and Shirley M. Otis

RANDALL,
Krystal Marie, b. 8/20/1992 in Concord; William James Randall and
    Katherine Marie Stubbs
Travis James, b. 2/3/1994 in Concord; William James Randall and
    Katherine Marie Stubbs

READY,
Jeremiah Joseph, b. 4/8/1981 in Concord; Joseph Michael Ready
    and Kathy Mae Clark

REDMAN,
Douglas Arthur, b. 4/1/1994 in Laconia; Douglas Arthur Redman
    and Suzette Marie Cadieux

REED,
Ethan Robert, b. 6/18/1999 in Ctr. Barnstead; Harry Reed and
    Jennifer Reed

Heather Marie, b. 8/27/1969 in Concord; Terry Archie Reed (NH) and Sharyn Dorinda Drolet (NH)
Jennifer Marie, b. 5/18/1968 in Concord; Ronald Neal Reed (NH) and Patricia Lorraine Riley (NH)
Karrie Ann, b. 10/25/1974 in Concord; Terry Archie Reed (NH) and Sharyn Davinda Drolet (NH)
Katelyn Elizabeth, b. 6/26/1997 in Ctr. Barnstead; Harry E. Reed and Jennifer R. Blount
Maxine Jane, b. 7/19/1941; first; Warren G. Reed (clothing factory) and Dorothy P. Canfield
Ronald N., Jr., b. 4/13/1966 in Rochester; first; Ronald N. Reed (Newport) and Patricia L. Riley (Concord); residence - Barnstead Parade
Staci Lyn, b. 1/21/1976 in Concord; Terry Archie Reed (NH) and Sharyn Darinda Drolet (NH)
Terry Archie, b. 6/21/1947 in Pittsfield; second; Warren Reed (truck driver) and Dorothy Canfield

REGNIER,
Leona M., b. 3/18/1903; first; George E. Regnier (dynamo engineer, 24, Manchester) and Calista E. Bunker (24, Gilmanton); residence – Manchester

REIDY,
Doris Louise, b. 6/30/1919; second; Michael J. Reidy (shoemaker, Manchester) and Evelyn L. Davis (Barnstead)

REYNOLDS,
Karen Gayle, b. 9/19/1951 in Concord; first; Robert L. Reynolds, Jr. (farmer) and Phyllis A. Carlton

RHODES,
Hannah Emily, b. 11/13/1998 in Laconia; Andrew Rhodes and Brook Rhodes

RICARD,
Elizabeth Jane, b. 10/18/1989 in Manchester; Scott Henry Ricard and Nancy Ann Walsh
Kevin James, b. 9/1/1993 in Concord; Scott Henry Ricard and Nancy Ann Walsh

Trevor Scott, b. 10/8/1991 in Concord; Scott Henry Ricard and Nancy Ann Walsh

RICHARDS,
Aidan Michael Thomas, b. 10/24/1998 in Portsmouth; Keith Richards and Cara Richards

RICHARDSON,
daughter [Mary A.], b. 7/1/1891; Walter Richardson (merchant, Boston, MA) and Hattie Brown (Barrington) (1896)
son, b. 12/5/1896; Walter Richardson (merchant, Boston, MA) and Hattie Brown (Barrington)
Arthur Carroll, b. 1/5/1949 in Pittsfield; fifth; Carroll F. Richardson (wood chopper) and Virginia D. Campbell
Elizabeth, b. 8/30/1902; fourth; Walter Richardson (merchant, 42, Boston, MA) and Hattie B. Brown (37, Barrington)
Ernest Russell, b. 5/15/1945 in Concord; first; Russell P. Richardson (farmer) and Martha Welch
Harriet, b. 1/2/1910; fifth; Walter Richardson (merchant, 49, Boston, MA) and Hattie B. Brown (45, Barrington)
Jeremy Russell, b. 4/12/1978 in Dover; Christopher M. Richardson (PA) and Phyllis Mary Chaplin (NH); residence - Ctr. Barnstead

RICHEY,
Megan Lee, b. 4/9/1981 in Concord; Robert Haynes Richey and D'Arcy Annette Fontaine

RICKER,
Jack Kenneth, b. 12/1/1989 in Exeter; Walter Earl Ricker and Kim Julia Lyden

RIEL,
Aaron Victor, b. 2/2/1984 in Concord; Peter Alan Riel and Priscilla Margaret Rollins
Ann Elizabeth, b. 3/9/1946 in Concord; second; Arthur D. Riel (farmer) and Mary Elizabeth Clark
Chelsey Patricia, b. 7/27/1996 in Concord; Michael David Riel and Kimberley Anne Grant
Christian Travers, b. 11/24/1972 in Concord; Daniel Paul Riel (NH) and Judith Ann Richardson (MA)

James A., b. 2/13/1963 in Concord; second; Arnold J. Riel
(Concord) and Patricia D. Nyhan (Concord); residence - Ctr.
Barnstead
Jesse Daniel, b. 12/5/1983 in Concord; Timothy Michael Riel and
Rosemary Jean Kelley
Jonathan Donald, b. 3/4/1974 in Concord; Donald Cleon Riel, Jr.
(NH) and Diane Lee Pyne (MA)
Kevin W., b. 5/1/1967 in Concord; first; George W. Riel (student,
Pittsfield) and Cynthia A. Paige (Concord)
Michael D., b. 11/18/1964 in Concord; third; Arnold J. Riel
(Concord) and Patricia D. Nyhan (Concord); residence - Ctr.
Barnstead
Nathan Alexander, b. 5/18/1979 in Concord; Peter Alan Riel and
Priscilla Margaret Rollins
Robin Lee, b. 11/29/1960 in Manchester; first; Arnold J. Riel (asst.
hydro-operator, Concord) and Patricia D. Nyhan (Concord)
Sabrina Gayle, b. 5/28/1980 in Concord; Timothy Michael Riel and
Rosemary Jean Kelley
Tammy M., b. 4/10/1958 in Concord; Leonard E. Riel and Ruth J.
Lank
Travis George, b. 12/26/1994 in Concord; Kevin Warren Riel and
Deborah Ann Sweet
Virginia Albertine, b. 2/25/1886; Victor Riel and Vitaline Bilodeau
(1938)

RIENDEAU,
Ashley Lynn, b. 9/4/1988 in Concord; Michael Rene Riendeau and
Ann Marie Giguere

RIGOR DA EVA,
Arthur H., III, b. 8/7/1959 in Concord; Arthur H. Rigor da Eva, Sr.
and Mary R. Cannon
Donna M., b. 1/14/1961 in Concord; Arthur H. Rigor da Eva
(Boston, MA) and Mary R. Gannon (Cleveland, OH); residence
- Ctr. Barnstead
Laura, b. 3/14/1964 in Concord; sixth; Arthur H. Rigor da Eva
(Brookline, MA) and Mary R. Gannon (Cleveland, OH);
residence - Ctr. Barnstead
Michael, b. 5/6/1962 in Concord; fifth; Arthur H. Rigor da Eva, Jr.
(Boston, MA) and Mary R. Cannon (Cleveland, OH); residence
- Ctr. Barnstead

RILEY,
Mark J., b. 3/17/1961 in Rochester; Warren E. Riley (Medford, MA) and Charlotte L. Baldwin (Quincy, MA); residence - Ctr. Barnstead

Michael E., b. 2/1/1965 in Rochester; fifth; Warren K. Riley (Medford, MA) and Charlotte L. Baldwin (Quincy, MA); residence - Ctr. Barnstead

RINES,
Keith C., b. 7/23/1968 in Concord; George H. Rines (NH) and Priscilla M. Cotton (NH)

Kelley C., b. 7/23/1968 in Concord; George H. Rines (NH) and Priscilla M. Cotton (NH)

Nadine C., b. 12/6/1964 in Concord; first; George H. Rines (Wolfeboro) and Priscilla M. Cotton (Pittsfield)

ROBB,
Eric Lichty, b. 8/28/1980 in Plattsburgh, NY (1981)

ROBERGE,
Rachel Ayla, b. 1/13/1993 in Manchester; Roger Wilford Roberge and Cheryl Anne Fauteaux

ROBERTS,
Addie E., b. 9/8/1880; Charles Roberts and Ella A. Nutter (1952)

Alysha Marie, b. 12/11/1987 in Concord; Jonathan Whitney Roberts and Lynne Marie Staley

Benjamin Thomas, b. 7/24/1989 in Dover; Paul Thomas Roberts and Katherine Mireault

Krystal Andrea, b. 8/20/1984 in Concord; Ernest George Roberts and Kristine Sue Heil

Shawn Ernest, b. 8/4/1981 in Concord; Ernest George Roberts and Kristine Sue Neil

ROBICHAUD,
Kaleigh Marie, b. 8/15/1988 in Manchester; Jay Robert Robichaud and Joanne Marie Vezina

ROBIE,
Martha Elizabeth, b. 3/2/1989 in Concord; Dwight Alan Robie and Deborah Anne Jordan

ROBINSON,
Denise Mary, b. 7/5/1983 in Concord; Dennis Allen Robinson and Helen Louise Hubbard
Eric Burton, b. 7/7/1979 in Concord; Gregory Luther Robinson and Paula Ann Inman
Erik Paul, b. 7/3/1980 in Concord; Dennis Allen Robinson and Helen Louise Hubbard
Kelli Ann, b. 9/17/1982 in Concord; Gregory Luther Robinson and Paula Ann Inman

ROCKWELL,
Priscilla, b. 6/18/1926; third; John Alfred Rockwell (Town Plos, NS) and Lena F. Neall (Lynn, MA)

ROGERS,
Benjamin Winslow, b. 8/12/1991 in Concord; Douglas Ronald Rogers and Lori Rita Martin
Christopher Scott, b. 11/17/1970 in Wolfeboro; Larry Albert Rogers (NH) and Bernadette Mary Reuter (NJ)
Joseph Douglas, b. 4/26/1993 in Concord; Douglas Ronald Rogers and Lori Rita Martin

ROJEK,
Cody James, b. 3/3/1990 in Laconia; Russell Greg Rojek and Lisa Marie Desautelle

ROKES,
Christine Marie, b. 6/19/1978 in Concord; Frederick Ralph Rokes (NY) and Emily Mary George (MA); residence - Ctr. Barnstead

ROLLINS,
Leeann Belle, b. 6/9/1994 in Concord; Leon Selden Rollins and Alicia Renee Mahon
Patti A., b. 1/27/1964 in Laconia; fourth; Selden B. Rollins (Gilmanton I.W.) and Belle J. Parker (Detroit, MI); residence - Ctr. Barnstead
Peter A., b. 1/27/1964 in Laconia; third; Selden B. Rollins (Gilmanton I.W.) and Belle J. Parker (Detroit, MI); residence - Ctr. Barnstead
Terry J., b. 7/3/1956 in Rochester; Selden B. Rollins (tacker) and Belle J. Parker

ROOP,
son, b. 6/22/1897; third; C. G. Roop (clergyman, PA) and Mazie Roop
son, b. 6/28/1898; C. G. Roop (clergyman, PA) and Mazie Spencer (PA)
son, b. 6/28/1898; C. G. Roop (clergyman, PA) and Mazie Spencer (PA)

ROSADO,
Zachary Elias, b. 12/16/1992 in Wolfeboro; Gerald Rosado and Michelle Marie Smith

ROSEMOND,
Brittany Lee, b. 2/1/1990 in Concord; Stephen James Rosemond and Bonnie Rose Cliff

ROSENQUIST [see Rosinquist],
Eline M., b. 9/29/1953 in Wolfeboro; second; Bror A. Rosenquist (retired) and Annie L. Pettersen

ROSINQUIST [see Rosenquist],
Bror Axel, b. 6/27/1951 in Concord; first; Bror A. E. Rosinquist (retired) and Annie L. Pettersen

ROSS,
daughter, b. 1/27/1904; first; Frank I. Ross (shoemaker, 24, Ossipee) and Hildred Merryfield (17, Manchester); residence - Derry

ROTT,
Nicole Alveda, b. 9/13/1994 in Concord; Nicholas Christopher Rott and Linda Gertrude Houle

ROY,
Kenny A., b. 12/8/1967 in Concord; second; Lennis A. Roy (buffer, Rochester) and Diane M. Schmalke (Minneapolis, MN)

RUGGIERI,
Gina Marie, b. 11/20/2000 in Concord; Daniel Ruggieri and Christine Ruggieri

RUNNALS,
Pauline Marion, b. 9/7/1903; first; Paul M. Runnals (laborer, 28, New Durham) and Blanche B. White (18, New Durham)

RUSSELL,
Aaron James, b. 7/9/1993 in Barnstead; James Edward Russell and Jean Maria Geer
Josephine M., b. 9/23/1911; second; Arthur Russell (laborer, 34, Canada) and Catherine Conley (24, Ireland)
Paul Robert, Jr., b. 5/4/1983 in Lawrence, MA; Paul Robert Russell and Elizabeth June Hanley
Wesley Paul, b. 8/29/1977 in Rochester; Bruce Russell (MA) and Dawnna Russell (MA)

RUTHERFORD,
Collen J., b. 5/20/1957 in Concord; Ivan D. Rutherford (office manager) and Patricia M. Duguay

RYAN,
Nathaniel Matthew, b. 1/25/1985 in Manchester; Timothy Matthew Ryan and Mary Elizabeth Buxton

RYDELL,
Jacob Steven, b. 6/26/1996 in Concord; Steven James Rydell and Valerie Patricia Brown

RYDER,
Kenneth A., b. 1/3/1915; first; Warren A. Ryder (weaver, Salem, MA) and Alma M. Heywood (Barnstead)
Malia May, b. 1/3/1919 in Pittsfield; second; Warren A. Ryder (weaver, Salem, MA) and Alma M. Heywood (Barnstead)

RZPECKI,
Krista Leigh, b. 4/16/1975 in Dover; Stanley J. Rzpecki (RI) and Maureen J. Baldwin (RI)

ST. GEORGE,
Mark D., b. 5/17/1960 in Concord; first; David St. George (clerk, Pittsfield) and Edith E. Yeaton (Barnstead)

SACKETT,
daughter [Lois], b. 8/7/1888; third; George Sackett (shoemaker, Barnstead) and Alice Huckins (Alton)
daughter, b. 5/31/1903; first; Ernest Sackett (21, Lynn, MA) and Mabel Wheeler (21, Pittsfield); residence – Lynn, MA

SAINSBURY,
Adam Charles, b. 11/11/1982 in Concord; Charles F. Sainsbury and Sandra Jean Maddock

SALEY,
Earl Davis, III, b. 11/9/1983 in Concord; Earl Davis Saley, Jr. and Ellen Margaret Giovannucci
Timothy Edwin, b. 7/29/1982 in Concord; Edwin Norman Saley and Roseanna Eva Perkins

SAMSON,
Jared James, b. 1/26/1993 in Portsmouth; Kevin James Samson and Valerie Jeanne Johnson

SANDERS,
child, b. 5/28/1923; fourth; William B. Sanders (Madbury) and Lena M. Hamilton (Somersworth)

SANDIN,
Douglas Eric, b. 11/18/1994 in Concord; Douglas Eugene Sandin and Victoria Marie Laroche
Kathleen Nicole, b. 3/19/1991 in Concord; Douglas Eugene Sandin and Victoria Marie Laroche

SARGENT,
Deidra Lynn, b. 10/13/1987 in Concord; Mark Christopher Sargent and Darlene Rita Hebert
Kathy Ellen, b. 9/12/1950 in Concord; fourth; John M. Sargent (White Mt. Power co.) and Ruth A. Hussey
Pamela J., b. 12/18/1964 in Concord; second; Roy A. Sargent (Epsom) and Janice M. Corliss (Barnstead); residence - Barnstead Parade
Peter Geoffrey, b. 6/18/1947 in Concord; third; John M. Sargent (grocer) and Ruth A. Hussey

Richard Wayne, Jr., b. 4/16/1982 in Rochester; Richard Wayne
Sargent and Roberta Pauline Keefe

Roy A., b. 6/13/1957 in Concord; Roy A. Sargent (laborer) and
Janice M. Corliss

Ryann Elizabeth, b. 6/22/1990 in Concord; Mark Christopher
Sargent and Darlene Rita Hebert

SAWYER,

Judith Ann, b. 3/14/1968 in Concord; Kenneth George Sawyer (NH)
and Joan Sylvia Danis (NH)

Karen Leigh, b. 4/12/1990 in Concord; Tom Alan Sawyer and
Penny Jane Clattenburg

Tom Allen, b. 2/6/1965 in Concord; fourth; Kenneth G. Sawyer, Sr.
(Epsom) and Joan S. Dainis (Pittsfield); residence - Ctr.
Barnstead

SCAHILL,

Timothy Michael, b. 9/10/1996 in Concord; Michael Thomas Scahill
and Teresa Louise Flanders

SCHNOUDT,

Louissa E., b. 3/1/1915; first; Fritz Schnoudt (weaver, Germany)
and Teresa Jenisch (Austria)

SCHULTZ,

Michael Joseph, b. 3/25/1993 in Rochester; Larry Joseph Schultz
and Amy Lee Dansereau

SCHWAB,

Brittanie Anne, b. 11/22/1992 in Concord; Dennis Michael Schwab
and Robin Renee Morse

SEARLE,

Louise F., b. 3/20/1909; first; Charles M. Searle (farmer, 30, Bath)
and Bessie F. Fletcher (19, Manchester)

SEARLES,

Travis John, b. 11/4/1987 in Concord; James Joseph Searles and
Nancy Rachel Brodeur

SEVERANCE,
Justin Adam, b. 7/2/1977 in Concord; Bruce Walter Severance (VT) and Debra Jean Evans (VT); residence - Ctr. Barnstead

SEVIGNY,
Joseph Oma, b. 2/28/1918; first; Frank Sevigny (shoemaker, Somersworth) and Aurora Carrigan (Somersworth)

SHAMPNEY,
Jeffrey Lee, b. 11/7/1978 in Concord; John Robert Shampney, Jr. (NH) and Katherine Diane Smith (NH)
Lisa Marie, b. 4/15/1976 in Concord; John Robert Shampney, Jr. (NH) and Katherine Diane Smith (NH)

SHEA,
Ryan Laflamme, b. 8/15/1981 in Concord; Robert Gerard Shea and Elaine Marie Laflamme

SHONYO,
Charlie D., b. 1/4/1908; fourth; Mark Shonyo (farmer, 57, Canada) and Flora Raymond (38, Manchester)

SILVA,
Kassi Marie, b. 5/2/1992 in Concord; Christopher Michael Silva and Rebecca Kathleen Dunne

SIMONEAU,
Kaela Marie, b. 3/12/1997 in Barnstead; Richard G. Simoneau and Margaret M. Burke
Kari Ann, b. 4/2/1999 in Barnstead; Richard Simoneau and Margaret Simoneau

SIMPSON,
Jessica Mary, b. 2/26/1998 in Concord; John Simpson and Lori Simpson
Mark R., b. 4/29/1967 in Concord; second; Robert S. Simpson (US Army, Beverly, MA) and Brigitte U. Fink (Berchtesgaden, Germany)
Scott S., b. 4/22/1966 in Concord; second; Robert S. Simpson (Beverly, MA) and Brigitte U. Fink (Germany); residence - Ctr. Barnstead

SINCLAIR,
Nathan Zachariah, b. 10/5/1999 in Concord; Craig Sinclair and Tenny Sinclair

SKABO,
Taylor Ryan, b. 1/16/2000 in Derry; Jason Skabo and Vanessa Skabo

SKIDMORE,
Emily Mae, b. 6/12/1999 in Concord; Frank Skidmore and Raeann Skidmore

SKINNER,
Hope Bonnie, b. 5/4/1998 in Laconia; John Skinner and Tracy Skinner

SKOBY,
Michael Garran, b. 7/1/1987 in Concord; Stephen Victor Skoby and Catherine Robin Skoby

SMALL,
daughter, b. 6/9/1891; Frederick L. Small (clergyman, VT) and Ella J. Lancaster (Northwood)

SMART,
child, b. 3/16/1939 in Wolfeboro; third; Fred T. Smart (salesman) and Lyra A. Davis

SMITH,
son, b. 10/10/1891; first; Albert W. Smith (blacksmith)
daughter, b. 2/2/1907; second; George F. Smith (RR employee, 28, Auburn) and Emma Brown (20, Candia)
Bertha F., b. 6/28/1907; second; Benjamin F. Smith (deceased, 56, Sandwich) and Lida J. Wilde (37, South Acton, MA)
Cary Bruce, b. 2/14/1968 in Concord; R. Bruce Smith (MA) and Joanne Murriel Robins (NH)
Chance Shannon, b. 6/6/1998 in Concord; Chance Smith and Wendy Smith
Charles, b. 7/2/1910; fifth; Arthur W. Smith (42, Alton) and Eva A. Weeks (31, Gilmanton) (1913)

Daniel James, b. 9/7/1985 in Concord; James Edward Smith and Lisa Marie Bungay

Dorothea R., b. 10/5/1957 in Concord; Joseph M. Smith (laborer) and Shirley P. Gerlack

Elizabeth R., b. 8/21/1963 in Rochester; thirteenth; William R. Smith (Harrisville, RI) and Mildred R. Noonan (Boston, MA); residence - Ctr. Barnstead

Emily Jane, b. 5/5/1982 in Concord; James Edward Smith and Leslie Claire Brown

Frederick Roland, b. 8/16/1968 in Rochester; William Ross Smith (RI) and Mildred Rita Noonan (MA)

Heather Elizabeth, b. 2/12/1984 in Concord; Harry Hendrick Smith and Nancy Jean Hill

Holly Anne, b. 2/14/1996 in Concord; Michael David Smith and Ramona Theresa Martin

Jennifer Lynn, b. 7/12/1981 in Concord; Harry Hendrick Smith and Nancy Jean Hill

Katherine D., b. 10/1/1956 in Laconia; Joseph M. Smith (truck driver) and Shirley P. Gerlack

Kayley Michele, b. 6/2/1988 in Concord; Timothy Van Smith and Cynthia Helen Therrien

Larry Ricky, b. 10/13/1975 in Concord; Louis Richard Smith (MA) and Mary Lou Stoddard (VA)

Leonard Harold, b. 8/19/1924; first; Harold A. Smith (Barnstead) and Ella Clark (Barnstead)

Louis Richard, Jr., b. 11/3/1973 in Concord; Louis Richard Smith (MA) and Mary Lou Stoddard (VA)

Megan Christine, b. 4/18/1999 in Concord; Thomas Smith and Melissa Smith

Michael R., b. 6/24/1962 in Rochester; eleventh; William R. Smith (Harrisville, RI) and Mildred R. Noonan (Boston, MA); residence - Ctr. Barnstead

Michelle Lynn, b. 12/9/1972 in Concord; Jack David Smith (FL) and Mary Jean Beauchine (NH)

Michelle M., b. 7/19/1965 in Concord; second; Paul S. Smith (Eldridge, MI) and Arlene J. Locke (Ctr. Barnstead)

Noah David, b. 2/14/1999 in Laconia; David Smith and Kristie Smith

Paul R., b. 11/14/1960 in Rochester; eleventh; William R. Smith (rope maker, Harrisville, RI) and Mildred R. Noonan (Boston, MA)

Reginald A., b. 6/5/1959 in Concord; Joseph M. Smith and Shirley P. Gerlack

Robin M., b. 6/15/1954 in Wolfeboro; Gilbert H. Smith (shoe worker) and Emily E. Corson

Samuel R., b. 2/21/1965 in Rochester; thirteenth; William R. Smith (Harrisville, RI) and Mildred R. Noonan (Boston, MA); residence - Ctr. Barnstead

Taylor Rae, b. 11/21/1991 in Concord; Shawn Michael Smith and Donna Virginia McCready

Valerie Marie, b. 7/8/1971 in Concord; Joseph Melvin Smith (NH) and Shirley Pansy Gerlack (VT)

William Ross, IV, b. 10/10/1983 in Concord; William Ross Smith, Jr. and Penny Sue Nyberg

SNEDEKER,
Keith A., b. 8/7/1967 in Concord; second; John C. Snedeker III (loader, Rochester) and Julie A. Gagne (Dover)

SNELL,
Katelyn Priscilla, b. 3/15/1990 in Concord; David Raymond Snell and Julie Beth Allen

SOBLE,
Daina, b. 4/26/1969 in Concord; Eugene Maurice Soble (MA) and Ilona Aira Reinberge (Latvia)

SOUCY,
Justin Gene, b. 7/13/1996 in Laconia; Steven Paul Soucy and Tanya Lee Soucy

Rebecca Lynn, b. 6/13/1998 in Laconia; Steven Soucy and Tanya Soucy

SOULIA,
Kathleen Elizabeth, b. 11/3/1950 in Pittsfield; third; John L. Soulia (steam fitter) and Helen A. Lyons

Priscilla Eileen, b. 5/16/1948 in Pittsfield; second; John L. Soulia (steam fitter) and Helen A. Lyons

SPEIDEL,
Nicole Elizabeth, b. 6/21/1990 in Rochester; Mark Edward Speidel and Diana Leigh Towle

SPERDUTO,
Talia Boutwell, b. 9/28/1998 in Concord; Daniel Sperduto and Ann Sperduto

STAPLETON,
Benjamin John, b. 1/5/1979 in Concord; Timothy John Stapleton and Sandra Jean Drolet

STARKEY,
Amanda Paige, b. 5/6/1984 in Concord; John McMahon Starkey and Susan Lynn Paige
Patrick McMahon, b. 1/5/1982 in Concord; John McMahon Starkey and Susan Lynn Paige

STAVROPOULOS,
James Lane, b. 8/23/1978 in Rochester; James Stavropoulos (MA) and Ann Marie Lane (MA); residence - Ctr. Barnstead

STENBERG,
Erik Forbes, b. 9/10/1986 in Concord; Douglas Forbes Stenberg and Kristen Ruth Hennessy

STEVENS,
son, b. 2/15/1896; Edgar N. Stevens (surveyor, Middleton) and Annie M. Cleveland (NB)
Susan J., b. 12/9/1965 in Concord; second; William D. Stevens (Concord) and Maralyn J. Bickford (Pittsfield); residence - Ctr. Barnstead
Thurlow B., b. 8/30/1906; first; Timothy B. Stevens (salesman, 21, Bedford) and Gertrude H. Sawyer (22, Manchester); residence – Manchester

STEWART,
Holly Lynn, b. 9/21/1993 in Concord; Phillip Neil Steward (sic), Jr. and Cynthia Lee Button

STOCK,
Barbara Jane, b. 9/6/1941; seventh; Arthur H. Stock (RR employee) and Martha C. Henry
Carol Audrey, b. 7/6/1934; fifth; Arthur H. Stock (fireman) and Martha C. Henry

Hamilton Henry, b. 2/5/1939; sixth; Arthur H. Stock (fireman) and
   Martha C. Henry
Norman James, b. 8/14/1943; eighth; Arthur H. Stock (engineer)
   and Martha C. Henry
Robert Perry, b. 5/22/1929; fourth; Arthur Stock (Reading, MA) and
   Martha Henry (Manchester)
Robin E., b. 10/1/1959 in Wolfeboro; Robert P. Stock and Annie L.
   Pettersen

STOCKMAN,
Amanda Lee, b. 6/7/1983 in Concord; Michael Lee Stockman and
   Pamela Jean Benson
Garrick Leo, b. 7/18/1950 in Pittsfield; fourth; Everett L. Stockman
   (shoe worker) and Marion E. Gray
Gregg Alan, b. 6/27/1979 in Concord; Michael Lee Stockman and
   Pamela Jean Benson
Jacky L., b. 5/14/1954 in Rochester; Everett L. Stockman (shoe
   shop) and Marion E. Gray
Joseph Edward, b. 12/22/1987 in Concord; Garrick Lee Stockman
   and Lynn Marie Boudreau
Larry Lee, b. 8/9/1942; first; Everett L. Stockman (shoe shop) and
   Marion E. Gray
Mary Lee, b. 3/11/1949 in Pittsfield; third; Everett Lee Stockman
   (shoe shop) and Marion Edna Gray
Michael L., b. 12/28/1956 in Wolfeboro; Everett L. Stockman (shoe
   worker) and Marion E. Gray
Richard Allen, b. 6/8/1970 in Concord; Larry Lee Stockman (NH)
   and Patricia Ann Daley (NH)
Ronald Lee, b. 8/11/1945 in Pittsfield; second; Everett L. Stockman
   (US Army) and Marion E. Gray
Ryan Lee, b. 6/23/1975 in Concord; Ronald Lee Stockman (NH)
   and Donna Ilene Locke (NH)

STOHLBERG,
Anthony Gunnar, b. 9/21/1993 in Concord; Paul Gunnar Stohlberg
   and Christine Ann Bonoli
Carl Thorin, b. 4/12/1996 in Ctr. Barnstead; Paul Gunnar Stohlberg
   and Christine Ann Bonoli

STOKES,
Marion B., b. 11/21/1905; second; Fred W. Stokes (farmer, 35, Gorham, ME) and Lizzie J. Jasper (26, Brook Vil., Cape Breton)

STONNER,
Tovah Josie, b. 10/17/2000 in Concord; Jason Stonner and Cheryl Stonner

STOREY,
Hannah Beth, b. 5/8/1981 in Concord; Charles Sidney Storey and Theresa Lynn Potter
Joshua Charles, b. 6/2/1979 in Concord; Charles Sidney Storey and Theresa Lynn Potter
Seth Adam, b. 10/6/1977 in Concord; Charles Sidney Storey (MA) and Theresa Lynn Potter (NH)

STOVER,
Robert Perry, b. 6/20/1946 in Winthrop, MA; Robert H. Stover (apprentice carpenter) and Elizabeth M. Stevenson

STOWELL,
Melissa Arlene, b. 10/9/1999 in Concord; Andrew Stowell and Judith Stowell

STRAW,
son [Cecil Thomas], b. 9/26/1909; first; Alba C. Straw (farmer, 47, Barnstead) and Celia M. Tibbetts (27, New Durham)
Mina May, b. 4/6/1941 in Pittsfield; first; Cecil T. Straw (laborer) and Lois M. Foss

STRESE,
Emily Elizabeth, b. 12/11/1990 in Manchester; Robin Lee Strese and Cheryl Ann Roberts
Kristin Michelle, b. 6/4/1987 in Manchester; Robin Lee Strese and Cheryl Ann Roberts

STRICKLAND,
Elizabeth Braxmar, b. 1/26/1985 in Concord; Robert Bronson Strickland and Sharon Braxmar Briscoe

Karen Lee, b. 1/14/1969 in Rochester; Robert B. Strickland (MA)
and Shirley D. Whiteher (NH)
Molly Sexton, b. 2/23/1981 in Concord; Robert Bronson Strickland
and Sharon Braxmar Briscoe
Susan Deborah, b. 8/31/1970 in Rochester; Robert Bronson
Strickland (MA) and Shirley Deborah Witcher (NH)

STRONG,
Alexis Rachel, b. 8/5/1994 in Concord; James Arthur Strong and
Dianne Lynn Moore
Ezra Roy, b. 3/19/1996 in New London; Nathan Ballard Strong and
Shawna Kay Benge

SULLIVAN,
Dawn Marie, b. 11/9/1969 in Wolfeboro; Thomas Warren Sullivan,
Jr. (NH) and Virginia Ann Doten (MA); residence - Ctr.
Barnstead
Katelyn Rose, b. 2/25/1987 in Stoneham, MA; Francis Timothy
Sullivan and Janet Marie Nadworny
Maureen Lois, b. 5/17/1936; sixth; Thomas Sullivan (shoe worker)
and Gladys Wilkes
Savannah Mirisola, b. 10/8/1987 in Hanover; Timothy George
Sullivan and Susan Claire Mirisola
Thomas E., b. 3/11/1965 in Rochester; second; Thomas W.
Sullivan, Jr. (Farmington) and Virginia A. Doten (Lynn, MA);
residence - Ctr. Barnstead
Thomas Warren, b. 6/14/1935; fifth; Thomas Sullivan (shoe worker)
and Gladys Wilkes

SUPRY,
Daniel James, b. 5/20/1984 in Concord; Daniel Patrick Supry and
Linda Beatrice Kenney

SUSI,
Jonathan Paul, b. 3/16/1988 in Concord; Kevin William Susi and
Karen Elaine Driscoll
Nicole Marie, b. 7/3/1989 in Concord; Kevin William Susi and
Karen Elaine Driscoll

SWAIN,
Esta Elizabeth, b. 4/21/1918; second; Henry B. Swain (teamster, Northwood) and Florence M. Gray (Barnstead)
Etta May, b. 11/24/1925; fifth; Henry B. Swain (Northwood) and Florence Gray (Barnstead)
Fremont Henry, b. 1/3/1928; sixth; Henry B. Swain (Northwood) and Florence M. Gray (Barnstead)
Lida Jane, b. 2/10/1931; seventh; Henry B. Swain (marker) and Florence M. Gray
Rebekah, b. 6/9/1915; first; Henry B. Swain (farmer, Northwood) and Florence M. Gray (Barnstead)

SWEENEY,
Kathleen Margaret, b. 10/27/1978 in Portsmouth; John Vincent Sweeney, Jr. (MA) and Mary Ann Bisbee (MA)
Kelley Marie, b. 10/27/1978 in Portsmouth; John Vincent Sweeney, Jr. (MA) and Mary Ann Bisbee (MA)

SWEET,
Jesse Maurice, b. 10/22/1981 in Concord; Mark Herbert Sweet and Pamela Diana Shepard
Joshua Arthur, b. 11/1/1982 in Concord; Mark Herbert Sweet and Pamela Diana Shepard
Rachel Jaclyn, b. 2/20/2000 in Concord; Michael Sweet and Stacey Sweet

SYLVAIN,
Aaron Michael, b. 7/29/1980 in Concord; Sidney Antonio Sylvain and Elaine Ruth Kelsea
Debrah Fate, b. 5/8/1949; fourth; Antonio Joseph Sylvain (woodsman) and Ethel Lougee Emerson
Gilbert M., b. 9/18/1954 in Rochester; Antonio J. Sylvain (laborer) and Ethel L. Emerson
Jacqueline Ethel, b. 11/12/1944; first; Antonio J. Sylvain (farmer) and Ethel L. Emerson
Judith Grace, b. 7/28/1950; fifth; Antonio J. Sylvain (woodsman) and Ethel L. Emerson
Luke Antonia, b. 5/10/1977 in Concord; Sidney Antonio Sylvain (NH) and Elaine Ruth Kelsea (NH); residence - Ctr. Barnstead
Paul B., b. 11/23/1955 in Rochester; Antonio J. Sylvain (woodsman) and Ethel L. Emerson

Sidney Antonio, b. 4/4/1947 in Pittsfield; third; Antonio Sylvain (teamster) and Ethel Emerson

TABLER,
Sean Logan, b. 5/17/1985 in Concord; Robert William Tabler and Wendy Jean Hodgkins

TARBOX,
Ashley Lynn, b. 10/28/1983 in Concord; Clarence Earl Tarbox and Audrey Lee Aubertin
Frances Irene, b. 4/9/1944 in Concord; fourth; Fred O. Tarbox (shoe shop) and Eleanor P. Chellis
Frieda Jean, b. 7/22/1945 in Concord; fifth; Fred O. Tarbox (wood chopper) and Eleanor P. Chellis

TASKER,
son [Arthur W.], b. 7/28/1891; first; Andrew B. Tasker (shoemaker, Strafford) and Jane George (Barnstead); residence – Pittsfield
son [Malcolm], b. 5/23/1903; second; Arthur W. Tasker (laborer, 20, Center Barnstead) and Alice M. Seward (19, Alton)
son, b. 10/12/1904; third; Arthur Tasker (mill operator, 22, Barnstead) and Alice Sewards (21, Barnstead)
daughter, b. 2/13/1906; fourth; Arthur W. Tasker (sawyer, 23, Barnstead) and Alice M. Seward (22, Alton)
son [Arthur L.], b. 4/19/1910; first; Arthur W. Tasker (mill operator, 19, Pittsfield) and Helen L. Merrill (19, Haverhill, MA)
son [Leighton E.], b. 5/5/1911; second; Arthur W. Tasker (mill operator, 20, Pittsfield) and Helen L. Leighton (20, Haverhill, MA)
child, b. 9/6/1924; sixth; Arthur W. Tasker (Barnstead) and Helen Merrill (Barnstead)
Adam George, b. 3/27/1978 in Concord; Philip George Tasker (NH) and Ivy Rose Troughton (CT)
Arthur William, II, b. 1/21/1949 in Waltham, MA; Leighton Enos Tasker (US Army) and Beulah Marjorie Jesseman
Eliza Kate Somers, b. 11/5/1983 in Concord; Edward Arthur Tasker and Linda Jane Somers
Emma Jane Somers, b. 7/5/1985 in Concord; Edward Arthur Tasker and Linda Jane Somers
Lance Michael, b. 11/13/1980 in Concord; Michael Francis Tasker and Nancy Ann Wilson

Lenard George, b. 8/24/1919; fourth; Arthur W. Tasker (weaver, Pittsfield) and Helen M. Merrill (Haverhill, MA)

Melanie J., b. 6/4/1955 in Concord; Milton S. Tasker (mechanic) and Nancy R. Cotton

Michael F., b. 7/29/1954 in Concord; Francis H. Tasker (farming) and Evelyn R. Corliss

Paul Elijah, b. 6/10/1922; fifth; Arthur W. Tasker (weaver, Barnstead) and Helen Merrel (Haverhill, MA)

Paul Elijah, Jr., b. 1/8/1977 in Concord; Paul Elijah Tasker (NH) and Paulette Madeline Emerson (NH)

Paul Elijah, III, b. 6/30/1996 in Concord; Paul Elijah Tasker and Sherry Ann Giddis

Philip George, b. 2/21/1952 in Concord; second; Leonard G. Tasker (tacker) and Jessie F. Hickey

Richard Emery, b. 8/16/1946 in Pittsfield; first; Paul E. Tasker (conservation officer) and Barbara E. Robinson

Rickie Alan, b. 3/9/1952 in Concord; first; Milton S. Tasker (mechanic) and Nancy R. Cotton

Roscoe W., Jr., b. 11/10/1957 in Concord; Roscoe W. Tasker, Sr. (farmer) and Janet A. Tuttle

Roxann M., b. 11/14/1953 in Wolfeboro; first; Roscoe W. Tasker (farmer) and Janet A. Tuttle

Sarah Elizabeth, b. 8/12/1998 in Concord; Paul Tasker and Sherry Tasker

TAYLOR-ELLIS,
Cassidy Buckingham, b. 9/29/1984 in Concord; Robert Buckingham Ellis and Teresa Louise Taylor

TEDCASTLE,
Brian Dale, b. 6/27/1973 in Concord; Douglas Coe Tedcastle (NY) and Elaine Marcia Dame (NH)

THIBODEAU,
Breanna Morgan, b. 5/26/1998 in Concord; Todd Thibodeau and Jane Thibodeau

THOMPSON,
daughter, b. 2/18/1889; first; Silas Thompson (farmer, Barnstead) and Josie Babb (Barnstead)

daughter [Arline M.], b. 7/30/1895; Silas Thompson (farmer, Barnstead) and Josie Babb (Barnstead)
son [Millard H.], b. 1/25/1898; Silas L. Thompson (farmer, Gilmanton) and Josephene Babb (Barnstead)
child, b. 2/15/1926; first; Ina M. Thompson (Epping)
Carol Lynn, b. 6/22/1948 in Pittsfield; second; Vernol M. Thompson (shoe worker) and Louise Fischer
Thomas Millard, b. 8/29/1946 in Pittsfield; first; Vernol M. Thompson (interior decorator) and Louise Fischer
Vernol M., b. 11/26/1918; first; Millard H. Thompson (laborer, Barnstead) and Caroline Hogencamp (Philadelphia, PA)

THOROUGHGOOD,
Kenneth L., b. 10/27/1958 in Concord; Ralph H. Thoroughgood and Phyllis A. Young
Richard J., b. 8/18/1957 in Concord; Ralph H. Thoroughgood (buffer) and Phyllis A. Young
Susan M., b. 12/1/1960 in Concord; third; Ralph H. Thoroughgood (washer, Alton) and Phyllis A. Young (Barnstead)

THYNG,
son [John C.], b. 10/12/1888; second; Charles E. Thyng (farmer, Alton) and Nora Fletcher (Dover) (1890)
daughter [Elizabeth A.], b. 8/27/1895; Charles E. Thyng (farmer, Alton) and Ora A. Fletcher (Dover)
Charles William, b. 6/3/1919; second; James E. Thyng (farmer, Barnstead) and Marrietta Burke (Ireland)
Dorothy, b. 2/19/1914; first; John C. Thyng (farmer, 25, Barnstead) and Grace A. Downs (23, Barnstead)
Herbert J., b. 4/9/1915; second; John C. Thyng (farmer, Barnstead) and Grace A. Dorons (Barnstead)
Walter, b. 11/25/1916; third; John C. Thyng (farmer, Barnstead) and Grace Downes (Barnstead)

TIEDE,
Alan R., b. 12/16/1951; second; Ernest E. Tiede (mechanic) and Carol A. Stock
Brett H., b. 3/12/1959 in Concord; Ernest E. Tiede and Carol A. Stock
Brian David, b. 2/2/1981 in Barnstead; Kurt Frederick Tiede and Terry Jean Rollins

Carol L., b. 12/30/1956 in Concord; Ernst E. Tiede (mechanic) and Carol A. Stock

Cory Alan, b. 8/1/1981 in Concord; Ernst Emil Herman Tiede, Jr. and Laurel Troughton

David E., b. 5/8/1960 in Concord; seventh; Ernst E. H. Tiede (night foreman, E. Dedham, MA) and Carol A. Stock (Center Barnstead)

Erin Nancy, b. 8/16/1981 in Concord; Alan Russell Tiede and Lynn Meloni Pethic

Gary R., b. 1/6/1953; Ernst E. Tiede (mechanic) and Carol A. Stock

Jamie Beth, b. 3/7/1981 in Concord; Robert Arthur Tiede and Priscilla Beth Kirby

Jared Alad, b. 6/13/1986 in Concord; Alan Russell Tiede and Lynn Meloni Pethic

Jennifer Ruth, b. 5/10/1975 in Concord; Ernst E. Tiede, Jr. (MA) and Laurel Troughton (CT)

Kara Lyn, b. 2/2/1984 in Concord; Alan Russell Tiede and Lynn Meloni Pethic

Kevin Frederick, b. 9/26/1979 in Concord; Kurt Frederick Tiede and Terry Jean Rollins

Kurt F., b. 5/4/1954; Ernst E. Tiede (mechanic) and Carol A. Stock

Michael Scott, b. 8/5/1983 in Concord; Kurt Frederick Tiede and Terry Jean Rollins

Robert A., b. 12/10/1952; Ernst E. Tiede (mechanic) and Carol A. Stock

Shanna Carol, b. 4/9/1978 in Concord; Ernst Emil Tiede, Jr. (MA) and Laurel Troughton (CT)

TILTON,

Grace R., b. 7/7/1904; first; Frank S. Tilton (29, Pittsfield) and Nettie J. Reynolds (23, Boston, MA)

Margaret Ann, b. 2/24/1951 in Concord; first; George E. Tilton (weaver) and Lillian V. Hill

TODD,

James Edwin, b. 9/2/1935 in Concord; first; Richard Todd (laborer) and Dorothy Moncrieff

TOPHAM,

Alexandra Marie, b. 11/5/1991 in Concord; Jonathan Hayes Topham and Sara Ann Locke

Justin Leigh, b. 10/8/1999 in Concord; James Topham and Laurie Topham
Noah James, b. 10/8/1999 in Concord; James Topham and Laurie Topham

TOTHILL,
Daniel Jevington, b. 1/4/1989 in Concord; David Newall Tothill and Nancy Marie Metras
Katherine Ann, b. 9/10/1985 in Hanover; David Newall Tothill and Nancy Marie Metras

TOUTAIN,
Abigail Marie, b. 2/1/1991 in Concord; Timothy Michael Toutain and Elaine Leslie Patten

TOWLE,
son, b. 6/3/1900; William Towle (merchant, Northwood) and Gertrude Evans (Strafford)
Jacob Michael, b. 3/5/1997 in Concord; Michael P. Towle and Joanne S. St. Hilaire
Mikayla Elizabeth, b. 9/29/2000 in Concord; Michael Towle and Joanne Towle

TRASK,
stillborn son, b. 1/10/1910; third; Alvin Trask (RR employee, 43, Mt. Vernon, ME) and Nellie E. Foss (30, Strafford)

TREADWELL,
Michelle Evelyn, b. 10/16/1981 in Concord; Gordon Ben Treadwell and Cynthia Louise Brown
Nicole Marie, b. 12/25/1998 in Concord; Joel Decato and Michelle Treadwell

TREFRY,
Gerald Michael, b. 5/19/1988 in Concord; Michael Joseph Trefry and Karen Ann Albee

TREMBLAY,
Lauretta Rae, b. 5/14/1993 in Concord; Leo Paul Tremblay and Amy Louise Griffin

TROTTER,
Ian Johnson, b. 5/7/1984 in Concord; Gary Hugh Trotter and Patricia Frances Johnson
Sarah Beth, b. 5/12/1983 in Concord; Gary Hugh Trotter and Patricia Frances Johnson

TRUDEL,
Leo Louis, b. 10/14/1984 in Concord; Leo Louis Trudel and Julie-Ann Wojcik

TRUETT,
Kimberly Anne, b. 6/11/1990 in Concord; Kenneth David Truett and Shelli Elizabeth Kearsley

TSIVOGION,
Helena, b. 9/4/1914; first; Constantine Tsivogion (merchant, 35, Stoneham, MA) and Lucinda Stern (20, Boston, MA); residence – Stoneham, MA

TUDOR,
Margaret Gail, b. 10/8/1952 in Concord; fourth; Andrew Tudor (painter) and Charlotte V. Tabor
Thurston Harry, b. 1/22/1951 in Concord; third; Andrew Tudor (painter) and Charlotte V. Taber

TURCOT,
Norman, b. 10/14/1912; fourth; Oliver Turcot (laborer, 50, Canada) and Georgie Dubay (34, NB)

TURCOTTE,
son, b. 12/1/1935; Homer Turcotte (laborer) and Leona Marcou

TURMELLE,
Cuita M., b. 6/3/1924; second; Alfred A. Turmelle (Rochester) and Lula May Foss (Strafford)

TUTTLE,
son, b. 5/14/1891; first; Owen H. Tuttle (farmer, Barnstead) and Nettie E. Foss (Strafford)
Agnes May, b. 4/22/1931; second; Merlon A. Tuttle (farmer) and Ida M. Thompson

Arthur Gordon, b. 3/25/1934; second; George S. Tuttle (weaver) and Lillian Tuttle

Bertha E., b. 1/1/1912; fourth; Charles Tuttle (farmer, 35, Barnstead) and Annie H. Norris (36, Sweden)

Dana Michael, b. 9/19/1973 in Concord; Norman Morin Tuttle (NH) and Mary Ellen Tuttle (NH)

Elsie, b. 12/13/1907; second; Charles Tuttle (farmer, 31, Barnstead) and Anna Morin (32, Sweden)

George S., b. 10/18/1909; third; Charles F. Tuttle (farmer, 33, Barnstead) and Annie H. Morin (32, Sweden)

Janet Alice, b. 11/15/1932; first; George S. Tuttle (weaver) and Lillian Buzzell

Matthew Norman, b. 8/2/1991 in Concord; Peter Gordon Tuttle and Heather Marie Giddis

Norman E., b. 10/13/1965 in Concord; first; Norman N. Tuttle (Barnstead) and Mary E. Howe (Pittsfield)

Norman Norin, b. 7/9/1939; third; George S. Tuttle (weaver) and Lillian G. Buzzell (1941)

Peter Gordon, b. 10/24/1968 in Concord; Norman Norin Tuttle (NH) and Mary-Ellen Howe (NH)

TWOMBL[E]Y,
son, b. 9/29/1889; second; Albert H. Twombley (shoemaker, Barnstead) and Addie E. Brown (Strafford)

Arthur G., b. 10/21/1892; fifth; Charles H. Twombly (shoemaker, Barnstead) and Elizabeth Briggs (Kittery, ME)

ULMER,
Aaron Joseph, b. 9/8/1989 in Concord; Fred Laverne Ulmer and Deborah Jeannette Butler

UNDERHILL,
Clayton R., b. 5/1/1912; first; Frank Underhill (clerk, 31, Canaan) and Inez E. Parshley (31, Barnstead)

Florence A., b. 6/9/1905; second; Arlen R. Underhill (farmer, 35, Orange) and Anna B. Blake (33, Manchester)

Raymond E., b. 9/10/1909; third; Lancelott G. Underhill (laborer, 33, Orange) and Agusta Welch (32, Lyme)

VACHON,
Emily E., b. 5/29/1997 in Concord; David R. Vachon and Stacey G. Stevens
Kyler William, b. 5/25/1996 in Concord; David Richard Vachon and Stacey Gail Stevens

VALENTI,
Justin Leighton, b. 8/15/1990 in Concord; Michael Valenti and Susan Anne Leighton

VARNEY,
John Berry, b. 12/6/1923; first; John C. Varney (Barnstead) and Ruth Berry (Middleboro, MA)
John C., b. 10/18/1894; first; John H. Varney (farmer, 44, Milton) and Ida Chesley (37, Barnstead)
Lisa Ann, b. 8/18/1971 in Wolfeboro; Maurice Earl Varney (NH) and Joanne Ruth Stanley (ME)
Lynn Marie, b., 4/26/1976 in Wolfeboro; Maurice Earl Varney (NH) and Joanne Ruth Stanley (ME)

VARNUM,
Brett Edward, b. 7/26/1975 in Winchester, MA; Edward Henry Varnum (MA) and Jennifer Lynn Johnson (England)

VAZQUEZ,
Ginnessa Lynn, b. 1/9/1990 in Concord; Richard Edgardo Vazquez and Lynn Boynton

VENNE,
Carmen B., b. 4/22/1955 in Concord; Les C. Venne (lumber business) and Georgette T. Clermont
Paul Leo, b. 9/8/1950 in Lowell, MA; Leo C. Venne (lumber sawyer) and Georgette T. Clermont

VENO,
Sandra Lee, b. 8/26/1945 in Concord; second; Gerald A. Veno (truck driver) and Barbara R. Finlayson

VERNAL,
Gregory Thomas, b. 4/14/1993 in Concord; Steven Edward Vernal and Diana Lynn Petschauer

VERVILLE,
Jeremy Michael, b. 12/8/1988 in Concord; Ronald Norman Verville and Rachel Ann Jarest
Nicole Rachel, b. 1/21/1986 in Concord; Ronald Norman Verville and Rachel Ann Jarest

VICK,
Tyler Arthur, b. 12/3/1989 in Laconia; Scott Arthur Vick and Jessica Lynn Burley

VIEN,
Jocelyn Brooke, b. 8/12/1997 in Concord; Randolph A. Vien and Michelyn E. Vien

VILLAMER,
daughter, b. 3/20/1915; second; Louis Sophus Villamer (upholsterer, Sweden) and Nellie Hanscom (Sweden)

VOGEL,
Shawn Michael, b. 11/10/1989 in Concord; John Thomas Vogel and Karen Breault

WAKEFIELD,
Frank C., b. 11/29/1920; first; Clyde Wakefield (weaver, Rochester) and Ida M. Davis (Epsom)
Lorna May, b. 9/5/1922; second; Clyde F. Wakefield (weaver, Rochester) and Ida May Davis (Epsom)

WALDRON,
son, b. 9/10/1888; fifth; Samuel Waldron (shoemaker)

WALKER,
Seth Allen, b. 6/3/1977 in Concord; James Walter Walker (NH) and Debra Marlene Keene (NY)

WARD,
Elaine Cynthia, b. 1/11/1945 in Pittsfield; first; Arnold P. Ward (clerk) and Elizabeth Jenisch

WARREN,
Florence M., b. 11/13/1894; first; John H. Warren (shoemaker, 33, Chichester) and Florence M. Shackford (20, Barnstead)

WASHINGTON,
Gayle Elisabeth, b. 4/23/1982 in Concord; Lamar Washington and Kin Ann Kehres

WATERS,
Shirley Ann, b. 10/6/1936; first; Edwin L. Waters (motorcycle officer) and Anne E. Tilton

WATSON,
Amanda Jo, b. 7/19/1978 in Concord; Curtis Douglas Watson (MA) and Phyllis Arlene Sargent (ME); residence - Ctr. Barnstead
Cynthia L., b. 2/22/1951 in Concord; third; Howard C. Watson (engineer) and Audry B. Evans
Heather Lynn, b. 6/20/1988 in Concord; Curtis Douglas Watson and Linda Sue Kelley

WEBBER,
Nicholas Robert, b. 11/5/1980 in Concord; Stephen Paul Webber and Patricia M. Henshaw

WEBSTER,
R. A. [son], b. 1/23/1914; first; Allen G. Webster (machinist, 30, Grafton) and Pearl C. Ketchum (18, NY)

WEEKS,
Alfred Herbert, b. 12/17/1928; fourth; Henry P. Weeks (Gilmanton) and Myrtie S. Hanson (Barnstead)
Alice Marion, b. 2/9/1920; first; Henry P. Weeks (farmer, Gilmanton) and Myrtie Hanson (Barnstead)
Calvin Henry, b. 11/1/1927; third; Henry Weeks (Alton) and Myrtie Hanson (Barnstead)
Christopher M., b. 6/7/1952 in Concord; first; Calvin H. Weeks (farmer) and Alice E. Therrien
Edna Persis, b. 4/9/1921; second; Henry P. Weeks (farmer, Gilmanton) and Myrtle E. Hanson (Barnstead)
Kami Marie, b. 1/28/1983 in Concord; Peter Howard Weeks and Randy Rae Edinger

Peter H., b. 6/20/1953 in Concord; Calvin H. Weeks (farmer) and
Alice E. Therrien
Richard A., b. 9/26/1958 in Concord; Calvin H. Weeks and Alice E.
Therrien
Terry A., b. 5/10/1957 in Concord; Calvin H. Weeks (farmer) and
Alice E. Therrien

WELCH,
daughter [Dorothy G.], b. 4/18/1911; third; Frank W. Welch (farmer,
27, Pittsfield) and Sadie E. Morrison (24, Ctr. Sandwich)
son [Earlon], b. 11/3/1914; fifth; Frank W. Welsh (sic) (farmer, 29,
Pittsfield) and Sadie Morrison (29, Sandwich)
Charles, b. 7/18/1913; fourth; Frank Welch (farmer, 29, Barnstead)
and Sadie Morrison (25, Sandwich)
Francis J., b. 6/17/1907; first; Frank W. Welch (farmer, 22,
Pittsfield) and Sadie E. Morrison (21, Center Sandwich)
Fred, b. 2/18/1909; second; Frank W. Welch (farmer, 23, Pittsfield)
and Sadie Morrison (22, Sandwich)
Howard Daniel, b. 10/1/1934; second; Fred T. Welch (farmer) and
Rena E. Wells
Mary Louise, b. 11/25/1951 in Pittsfield; second; Charles H. Welch
(shoe worker) and Florence A. Potter
Raymond William, b. 1/7/1931; first; Fred T. Welch (farmer) and
Rena E. Wells
Rebecca Lynn, b. 2/10/1970 in Concord; Ronald Charles Welch
(NH) and Virginia Louise Norberg (ME)
Susan May, b. 11/13/1949 in Concord; first; Charles Ham Welch
farmer) and Florence Adeline Potter

WELDON,
Ruby Joyce, b. 3/24/1986 in Concord; Brenda Lyn Towle

WELLS,
son, b. 5/17/1909; third; Edgar S. Wells (superintendent, 28,
London, England) and Gertrude O'Disscol (26, Boston, MA)
Adam Wade, b. 6/11/1972 in Concord; Oscar Allen Wells, Sr. (NH)
and Della May Gerlack (NH)
Alfred Joseph, b. 1/10/1916; seventh; Edgar Stanley Wells (mill
supt., England) and Gertrude O'Driscoll (Boston, MA)
Dakota Flint, b. 8/17/1996 in Concord; Gary Flint Wells and Darlene
Marie Clay

Damien Bruce, b. 8/3/1999 in Concord; Gary Wells and Darlene Clay-Wells

Edgar S., Jr., b. 3/27/1908; second; Edgar S. Wells (superintendent, 27, London, England) and Gertrude O'Disscol (25, Boston, MA)

Evelyn, b. 8/24/1914; sixth; Edgar S. Wells (superintendent, 33, London, England) and Gertrude O'Driscoll (33, Boston, MA)

Frank, b. 6/14/1911; stillborn; fourth; Stanley Wells (foreman, 30, England) and Gertrude O'Driscoll (30, Boston, MA)

Frederick, b. 4/30/1913; fifth; Edgar S. Wells (superintendent, 32, England) and Gertrude O'Driscoll (32, Boston, MA)

Julie A., b. 12/20/1965 in Concord; first; Oscar A. Wells (Rochester) and Della M. Gerlack (Antrim); residence - Ctr. Barnstead

Oscar A., Jr., b. 12/24/1966 in Concord; second; Oscar A. Wells, Sr. (Rochester) and Della M. Gerlack (Antrim); residence - Ctr. Barnstead

WESTGATE,

Steven Thomas, Jr., b. 10/16/1991 in Concord; Steven Thomas Westgate and Kimberly Jane Story

WHEAT [see Wheet],

Margaret Hulda, b. 10/29/1926; third; Rexford E. Wheat (Groton) and Bessie McDuffee (Barnstead)

WHEELER,

daughter, b. 8/29/1890; second; Frank W. Wheeler (mason, Bedford, ME) and Evelyn F. Clark (Barnstead) (1891)

son [Louis M.], b. 8/7/1894; seventh; Loren A. Wheeler (RR conductor, Loudon) and ----- Griffin (Loudon)

son, b. 12/8/1895; Loren Wheeler (RR conductor, Loudon) and Abbie Griffin (Loudon)

Jeffrey Don, b. 11/18/1993 in Concord; Larry Don Wheeler and Madeline Ann O'Rourke

Marjorie E., b. 4/10/1921; first; George S. Carr (auto dealer) and Marion E. Wheeler (Barnstead)

Patrick Kenneth, b. 7/19/1988 in Manchester; Warren Russell Wheeler and Maura Martin

WHEET [see Wheat],
child [Mary E.], b. 12/2/1928; fifth; Rexford E. Wheet (Groton) and Bessie McDuffee (Barnstead)
David Josiah, b. 8/28/1931; sixth; Rexford E. Wheet (farmer) and Bessie McDuffee
Irene Ava, b. 1/2/1933; seventh; Rexford E. Wheet (farmer) and Bessie W. McDuffee
Lee Edna, b. 11/26/1935; Rexford E. Wheet (farmer) and Bessie W. McDuffee
Misle Rexford, b. 1/11/1924; first; Rexford E. Wheet (Groton) and Bessie M. McDuffee (Barnstead)
Phyllis Abbie, b. 4/2/1925; second; Rexford Elwin Wheet (Groton) and Bessie M. McDuffee (Barnstead)
Vera Bessie, b. 12/1/1927; fourth; Rexford E. Wheet (Groton) and Bessie W. McDuffee (Barnstead)

WHELPLEY,
William W., b. 3/6/1921; sixth; William W. Whelpley (Waltham, MA) and Lulu Geisendeor (Wilmington, DE)
Williemina, b. 3/6/1921; fifth; William W. Whelpley (Waltham, MA) and Lulu Geisendeor (Wilmington, DE)

WHIPPLE,
son [Earl], b. 8/18/1896; George H. Whipple (farmer)

WHITE,
Amanda Lynn Allen, b. 11/5/1981 in Concord; Brian Arey White and Vera Lucette Wessely
Cameron Stephen, b. 9/6/2000 in Lebanon; Stephen White and Jennifer White
Carly Jill, b. 9/6/2000 in Lebanon; Stephen White and Jennifer White
Kellie Marie, b. 1/20/1988 in Concord; Brian Arey White and Evelyn Hilt
Kristie Mae, b. 1/20/1988 in Concord; Brian Arey White and Evelyn Hilt
Matthew David, b. 6/24/1974 in Rochester; James W. White (MA) and Nancy C. Alton (MA); residence - Ctr. Barnstead

WHITEHOUSE,
Edna B., b. 6/30/1917; third; Alfred S. Whitehouse (farmer, Canada) and Olive B. St. John (New Haven, VT)
Elsie G., b. 6/30/1917; fourth; Alfred S. Whitehouse (farmer, Canada) and Olive B. St. John (New Haven, VT)
George Arland, b. 9/30/1910; second; Alfred S. Whitehouse (farmer, 29, Canada) and Olive St. John (28, New Haven, VT)
Lucy G., b. 7/5/1909; first; Alfred S. Whitehouse (farmer, 28, Canada) and Olive B. St. John (27, New Haven, VT)
Mabel C., b. 8/20/1918; sixth; Alfred S. Whitehouse (farmer, Canada) and Olive St. John (VT)
Marion, b. 8/20/1918; fifth; Alfred S. Whitehouse (farmer, Canada) and Olive St. John (VT)

WHITNEY,
Elliott W., Jr., b. 12/12/1918; third; Elliott W. Whitney (merchant, Brooklyn, NY) and Elizabeth S. Dates (Passaic, NJ)
Marjorie, b. 12/5/1911; first; Elliott W. Whitney (merchant, 33, Brooklyn, NY) and Elizabeth Dates (31, Passaic, NJ)
R. S. [son], b. 10/27/1914; second; Elliott W. Whitney (merchant, 36, Brooklyn) and Elizabeth Dates (34, Passaic, NJ)

WHITTINGTON,
Lynn Marie, b. 12/18/1971 in Concord; Glen Dale Whittington (NH) and Ruth Elaine Boyd (AR)

WILD,
daughter, b. 6/19/1887; sixth; William Wild (shoemaker, 44, Boston, MA) and Emma ----- (44, Bath)

WILE [see Wils],
son, b. 2/26/1909; second; Lawrance E. Wile (laborer, 22, Bridgewater, NS) and Mary E. Linscott (22, Pittsfield)
Rupert F., b. 7/3/1910; third; Lawrence E. Wile (morocco worker, 23, NS) and Mary E. Linscott (23, Pittsfield)

WILKES,
George L., Jr., b. 4/28/1907; second; George T. Wilkes (farmer, 40, Thompson, MA) and Eutha Coman (25, Thompson, MA)
Gladys T., b. 1/13/1905; George T. Wilkes (farmer, 41, Thompson, CT) and Bertha E. Wilkes (23, Thompson, CT)

WILLEY,
Donald Marshall, b. 8/9/1927; third; Marshall J. Willey (Meredith) and Laura Gould (Orange)

WILS [see Wile],
Harold E., b. 1/20/1907; first; Lawrence E. Wils (carriage painter, 21, Bridgewater, NS) and Mary E. Linscott (20, Pittsfield)

WILSON,
Amity Grace, b. 1/8/2000 in Concord; Michael Wilson and Carla Wilson
Brittany Lynn, b. 6/9/1986 in Concord; Martin Oliver Wilson and Arlene Jo Douglass
Paige Allyson, b. 11/6/1994 in Concord; Martin Oliver Wilson and Arlene Jo Douglass
Timothy Amos, b. 4/10/1998 in Concord; Michael Wilson and Carla Wilson

WIMSATT,
Augustin James, b. 7/8/1990 in Ctr. Barnstead; Michael James Wimsatt and Chiara Grazia Dolcino

WINKLEY,
daughter, b. 8/22/1910; second; Herman P. Winkley (farmer, 36, Strafford) and Winifred E. Chesley (31, Barnstead)
Lewis C., b. 5/15/1909; first; Herman P. Winkley (farmer, 35, Strafford) and Winifred E. Chesley (30, Barnstead)
William, b. 8/3/1916; third; Herman P. Winkley (farmer, Strafford) and Winnifred Chesley (Barnstead)

WINSLOW,
daughter, b. 2/27/1907; eighth; Edgar L. Winslow (farmer, 57, Casco, ME) and Tillie A. Winslow (39, Raymond, ME)

WINSOR,
David R., b. 9/17/1955 in Concord; Kenneth C. Winsor (mink rancher) and Barbara E. MacMillan

WITTENBERG,
David William, b. 4/29/1977 in Concord; Thomas William Wittenberg (NY) and Doreen Ann Doucette (NH)

Kevin William, b. 10/3/1978 in Concord; Thomas William Wittenberg (NY) and Doree Ann Doucette (NH)

WOLCOTT,
Benjamin Carey, b. 11/12/1986 in Concord; Jonathan Giles Wolcott and Margery Kay Klucik

WOODARD,
son, b. 9/2/1901; George M. Woodard (teamster, 26, Franklin) and Susie M. Wiggin (23, Laconia)
daughter, b.3/12/1905; fifth; George M. Woodard (mill operator, 30, Franklin) and Susie M. Wiggin (26, Laconia)

WOODBURY,
daughter, b. 12/12/1894; David A. Woodbury (blacksmith, Bangor, NY) and Ella F. Emery (Manchester) (1895)

WOODWARD,
Keren L., b. 8/20/1963 in Concord; third; William Woodward (Concord) and Barbara J. Stock (Ctr. Barnstead); residence - Ctr. Barnstead

WORKMAN,
Bryce McCracken, b. 11/15/1997 in Manchester; Todd M. Workman and Sylvie L. Couture
Corey Robert, b. 8/11/1988 in Concord; Robert Hal Workman and Melodie Jean Seddon

YEATON,
Barbara Lee, b. 10/4/1943; third; Earl M. Yeaton (lumber worker) and Phyllis L. McIntosh
Douglas William, b. 7/4/1940; second; Earle M. Yeaton (truck driver) and Phyllis L. McIntosh
Edith Ethel, b. 11/16/1938; first; Earle M. Yeaton (truckman) and Phyllis L. McIntosh

YIANAKOPOLOS,
Jennifer Marie, b. 11/17/1981 in Manchester; David Andrew Yianakopolos and Nancy Marie Sherman

YODER,
Daniel S., b. 7/31/1962 in Wolfeboro; first; Charles R. Yoder (Elkhart, IN) and Ardith A. Knox (Ctr. Ossipee); residence - Ctr. Barnstead
Sue A., b. 3/3/1964 in Wolfeboro; second; Charles R. Yoder (Elkhart, IN) and Ardith A. Knox (Wolfeboro); residence - Ctr. Barnstead

YOUNG,
son, b. 3/12/1893; second; Percy C. Young (farmer, 19, Belmont) and Clara B. Hillsgrove (18, Wilmot)
Adam Lee, b. 7/30/1974 in Concord; Forrest Benjamin Young (NH) and Jacquelyn Sharon Lee (NH); residence - Ctr. Barnstead
Beatrice Elizabeth, b. 7/25/1924; second; William H. Young (Dover) and Irene Davis (Bedford)
Bethany Nicole, b. 7/8/1986 in Concord; Christopher John Young and Roxanne Lee Tibbetts
Forrest Benjamin, b. 3/23/1946; fourth; Benjamin N. Young (farmer) and Edna P. Lakeman
Lindsey Marie, b. 7/8/1986 in Concord; Christopher John Young and Roxanne Lee Tibbetts
Lydia Margaret, b. 9/1/1924; second; James H. Young (Laconia) and Edith Wyley (Dover)
Noah Victor, b. 10/23/1998 in New London; Adam Young and Jennifer Young
Percy J., b. 12/14/1922; first; James H. Young (farmer, Laconia) and Edith M. Wyley (Dover)
Phyllis Alma, b. 1/10/1937; first; Benjamin N. Young (farmer) and Edna P. Lakeman
Robert, b. 8/6/1947 in Concord; fifth; Benjamin Young (laborer) and Edna P. Lakeman
William H., b. 4/8/1922; first; William H. Young (teamster, Northwood) and Irene E. Davis (Bedford)

ZANES,
stillborn son, b. 8/26/1891; third; Noah M. Zanes (farmer, Pembroke) and Nellie E. Blake (Gilmanton)

ZARLI,
Dianna Grace, b. 10/1/1985 in Rochester; Martin Michael Zarli and Ann Elizabeth Petrozzi

Laura Ann, b. 9/14/1984 in Rochester; Martin Michael Zarli and Ann Elizabeth Petrozzi

ZINN,
son [Walter], b. 8/26/1907; second; Robert Zinn (weaver, 24, Barmen, Germany) and Agnes Wiegandt (25, Barmen, Germany)
Agnes, b. 6/25/1909; third; Robert Zinn (weaver, 27, Barmen, Germany) and Agnes Wigandt (27, Barmen, Germany)
George H., b. 6/18/1933; first; Erwin Zinn (laborer) and Violet Gray

ZWAHLEN,
John, b. 9/27/1932; third; Hans Zwahlen (farmer) and Santina Floria

MARRIAGES

ABBOTT,
John E. of Ctr. Barnstead m. Diana M. **Degan** of Ctr. Barnstead 4/25/1987

John E., Jr. of Ctr. Barnstead m. Stacey A. **Gagne** of Ctr. Barnstead 9/16/2000

John Emerson of Wakefield m. Theresa Irene **Bousquet** of Ctr. Barnstead 5/3/1974 in Union; H - b. 7/10/1948 in MA, s/o Ralph Emerson Abbott (ME) and Helen L. Grace (NH); W - b. 5/22/1950 in NH, d/o Raymond E. Couch (NH) and Marguerite Beauchaise (VT)

Joshua O. of Barnstead m. Tara L. **Antonelli** of Barnstead 11/7/2000

Richard G. of Concord m. Leona D. **Daneault** of Barnstead 7/28/1961 in Chichester; H - 34, const., b. NH, s/o William H. Abbott (NH) and Sarah C. Smith (NH); W - 26, at home, b. NH, d/o Elias W. Locke (NH) and Violet M. Gray (NH)

ACKERMAN,
Peter P. of Barnstead m. Carrie M. **Larabee** of Bath, ME 3/11/1903 in Dover; H – 49, teamster, 2nd, b. Alexandria, s/o Peter T. Ackerman (farmer, Strafford) and Emily J. Berry (domestic, Strafford); W – 37, housework, 2nd, b. Bath, ME, d/o John Larabee (ship builder) and Ernestine Moses (dress maker, Bath, ME)

Royal L. of Barnstead m. Maud S. **Huston** of Derry 10/18/1903 in Milton; H – 23, farmer, b. Barnstead, s/o Peter P. Ackerman (teamster, Alexandria) and Ida B. Berry (domestic, Concord); W – 16, housework, b. Derry, d/o Benjamin Huston (steam mill, Derry) and Clara A. Robinson (domestic, Londonderry)

ADAMS,
James Henry of NH m. Kristine Barbara **Jenisch** of NH 10/4/1969 in Pittsfield; H - 19, b. NH, s/o Bruce Earl Adams (NH) and Beatrice Eleanor Stone (MA); W - 19, b. NH, d/o Richard R. Jenisch (NH) and Barbara E. Turner (MA)

Michael C. of Ctr. Barnstead m. Sharon M. **Briggs** of Ctr. Barnstead 6/11/1988 in Bedford

ADJUTANT,
Dennis W. of East Wolfeboro m. Alice H. C. **Grau** of Ctr. Barnstead 6/26/1965 in Wolfeboro; H - 19, carpenter, b. NH, s/o Norman Adjutant (NH) and Edith Champagne (NH); W - 25, nurse, b. Boston, MA, d/o Henry Grau (Germany) and Ellen M. Christensen (MA)

AGUILAR,
Carlos Edward of Barnstead m. Cricket Lee **Plante** of Barnstead 9/17/1994 in Merrimack

AIKENS,
Edwin J. of Barnstead m. Mary **McKennelley** of Barnstead --/--/1895 in Pittsfield; H – 20, shoemaker, b. Barnstead, s/o David L. Aikens (carpenter, Barnstead) and Annie Shaw (housewife, Concord); W – 22, stitcher, b. NB, d/o Charles W. McKennelley (miller, NB) and Lou's A. McKennelley (housewife, NB)

AIKINS,
George L. of Barnstead m. Augusta G. **Nutter** of Barnstead 12/25/1890 in Pittsfield; H – 21, mechanic, b. Barnstead, s/o Abbie S. Drew (housework); W – 19, b. Dover

ALBEE,
G. Paige of Ctr. Barnstead m. Jairetta E. **Springfield** of Ctr. Barnstead 1/1/1977; H - b. 5/1/1927 in WI, s/o Curtis Albee (NH) and Emma Paige (NH); W - b. 3/31/1920 in NH, d/o Lyman E. Main (ME) and Maude Lockhart (NH)
G. Paige of Barnstead m. Rose A. **St. Louis** 4/21/1979

ALDEN,
Arthur W. m. Margaret C. **Hill** 9/29/1923; H – 34, s/o Charles L. Alden and Bessie L. Wheeler; W – 31, d/o Herbert M. Hill and Abbie M. Cross

ALDRICH,
Paul Richard of ME m. Jane **Fraser** of Barnstead 12/23/1967 in Pittsfield; H - 26, teacher, b. MI, s/o John B. Aldrich, Sr. (NY)

and Margaret M. Holland (NY); W - 21, dental assistant, b. MA, d/o Warren G. Fraser (MA) and Verona Taylor (AL)

ALEXANDER,
Paul Stephen of Beverly, MA m. Denise M. **Brown** of Peabody, MA 8/24/1991

ALLARD,
Robert Wallie of Barnstead m. Constance Marie **Hayes** of Barnstead 1/19/1981 in Rochester

ALLEN,
David Ormes of St. Paul, MN m. Ethel Webb **McConaghy** of Ctr. Barnstead 6/15/1990
Michael R. of Concord m. Lori **Allen-Serell** of Barnstead 6/12/1999 in Concord

ALMEIDA,
Steven Leo of Ctr. Barnstead m. Suzanne Jean **Hanchett** of Ctr. Barnstead 12/24/1990 in Ctr. Barnstead

AMES,
Harold m. Jane **Czerwienska** 11/26/1936 in Manchester; H – 26, s/o Earl W. Ames and Edna Kelley; W – 18, d/o Botesaw Czerwienska and Cecilia -----
Irving M. m. Harriet **Richardson** 6/24/1933; H – 27, s/o H. Thurlow Ames and Ida Irving; W – 23, d/o Walter Richardson and Hattie Brown

ANDERSON,
Clarence E. of Barnstead m. Carole A. **Ponusky** of Boston, MA 2/15/1964 in Pittsfield; H - 27, auto mech., b. Portland, ME, s/o Frank S. Anderson (ME) and Kathleen A. Smith (ME); W - 22, tel. oper., b. Athol, MA, d/o Walter W. Ponusky (WV) and Pauline L. Lapenas (MA)
William G. of Barnstead m. Janina M. **Manning** of Barnstead 10/17/1998

ANDREWS,
Leonard E. of Barnstead m. Edith J. **Erwin** of Barnstead 4/19/1964 in Chichester; H - 57, retired, b. Waltham, MA, s/o Thomas G. Andrews (ME) and Harriet E. Brown (MA); W - 58, retired, b. MA, d/o John S. Thompson (MA) and Josephine K. Bryson (MA)

ANTONUCCI,
Anthony S. of Barnstead m. Kniertje A. **Rog** of Barnstead 8/22/1998

ARCHIBALD,
Peter Ellis, Jr. of Ctr. Barnstead m. Liisa **Reimann** of Ctr. Barnstead 1/1/1994 in Durham

ARMER,
James H. of Barnstead m. Paula M. **Broxy** of Barnstead 5/9/1985
James H. of Ctr. Barnstead m. Elizabeth M. **Kyllonen** of Ctr. Barnstead 9/8/1989 in Ctr. Barnstead

ARMSTRONG,
James W. of Portsmouth m. Alma I. **Shackford** of Barnstead 7/2/1898; H – 20, shoemaker, b. Portsmouth, s/o James Armstrong (brewer, Portsmouth) and Annie Dempsey; W – 19, shoe stitcher, b, Barnstead, d/o William H. Shackford (hotel keeper, Barnstead) and Augusta M. Shackford (housekeeper, Barnstead)

ARNETT,
Gregory Arlen of Barnstead m. Mary **Lord** of Barnstead 12/26/1990 in Ctr. Barnstead

ARTESI,
John S. of Barnstead m. Velvet L. **LeRoux** of Barnstead 10/24/1993

ASHCROFT,
Mitchell D. of Concord m. Christine M. **DiPerri** of Barnstead 5/17/1986 in Pittsfield

ASHLEY,
Brad Scott of Barnstead m. Sherry Ann **Giddis** of Pittsfield 8/24/1991 in Pittsfield

George M. of Farmington, CT m. Debra A. **Bunker** of Barnstead 5/28/1976 in Chichester; H - b. 9/9/1952 in Washington, DC, s/o George M. Ashley (NH) and Glendle Emerson (NH); W - b. 1/27/1951 in NH, d/o Roland E. Bunker (NH) and Charlotte Cate (NH)

George M., III of Pittsfield m. Glendle D. **Emerson** of Barnstead 6/24/1951; H – 20, Navy Yard, b. NH, s/o George M. Ashley, Jr. (NH) and Alice M. Humphreys (Canada); W – 21, student, b. NH, d/o Albert L. Emerson (NH) and Madeline Jenkins (NH)

Jack E. of Barnstead m. Velma E. **Emerson** of Barnstead 9/24/1966; H - 27, painter, b. Pittsfield, s/o George M. Ashley (NH) and Alice Humphries (Canada); W - 25, inspector, b. Barnstead, d/o Albert L. Emerson (NH) and Madeline Jenkins (NH)

ATTON,
Arthur of Charlestown, MA m. Patricia N. **Connelly** of Charlestown, MA 8/16/1959; H - 35, s/o Clarence Atton and Mildred Christie; W - 29, d/o Martin Murphy and Nora Early

AUBERTIN [see Barton, O'Barton],
Donald Everett of Ctr. Barnstead m. Muriel T. **Gagne** of Bedford 4/20/1990 in Bedford

Ezra, Jr. m. Doris Louise **Forbes** 8/17/1931 in Pittsfield; H – 26, s/o Ezra Aubertin and Virginia Dupuis; W – 20, d/o Louis Augustus Forbes and Anna Paine

AVERSA,
Michael S. of Barnstead m. Charna L. **Smith** of New Durham 9/14/1985 in Rochester

AVERY,
Daniel H. of Barnstead m. Sallie L. **Avery** of Strafford 3/31/1888 in Strafford; H – 38, farmer, b. Barnstead, s/o Samuel Avery (farmer, Barnstead) and Lucinda Avery (Barnstead); W – 22, b. Strafford, d/o John W. Avery (farmer, Strafford) and Hannah Avery (Strafford)

AYERS,

Charles F. of Barnstead m. Nellie M. **Jenkins** of Barnstead 6/1/1890 in New Durham; H – 22, clerk, b. Barnstead, s/o George W. Ayers (farmer, Barnstead) and Mary Ayers (Barnstead); W – 21, stitcher, b. Barnstead, d/o George W. Jenkins (farmer, Barnstead) and Victoria Jenkins (Barnstead)

Lyman J. of Barnstead m. Clara J. **Winkley** of Barnstead 8/15/1918; H – 44, b. Barnstead, s/o George W. Ayers and Mary J. Jenkins; W – 53, b. Barnstead, d/o Thomas S. Straw and Louise A. Hill

BAAS,

John C., III of Barnstead m. Karen H. **Hunt** of Barnstead 2/18/1995

BARDWELL,

Thomas Stevens of Ctr. Barnstead m. Angela Marie **Zotto** of Ctr. Barnstead 5/18/1991 in Concord

BARNARD,

William A., Jr. m. Florence **Fox** 4/6/1933 in Chichester; H – 27, s/o William A. Barnard and Edith P. Atwood; W – 28, d/o Harry O. Corson and Stella F. Carr

BARNES,

John Squarey of New York, NY m. Frances Conwell **Gillespie** of New York, NY 7/20/1948; H – 36, insurance, b. Troy, NY, s/o John A. Barnes and Jean C. Squarey; W – 34, secretary, b. Bradenton, FL, d/o Horace C. Gillespie and May H. Henderson

BARNET,

Paul A. of Ctr. Barnstead m. Amy L. **Dansereau** of Ctr. Barnstead 10/9/2000

BARRETT,

Daniel L. of Barnstead m. Addie M. **Downs** of Barnstead 4/22/1905; H – 31, farmer, 2nd, b. Antrim, s/o C. A. Barrett (Lancaster) and B. A. Butler (housewife, Antrim); W – 20, housework, b. Barnstead, d/o W. H. Downs (farmer, Loudon) and Mary Randall (New Durham)

BARRIERE,
Laurian of Manchester m. Christine J. **Linehan** of Barnstead 7/28/1979

BARRY,
John J. of MA m. Marjorie E. **Smith** of MA 7/17/1965 in Pittsfield; H - 37, USAF, b. Mamaroneck, NY, s/o Frederick H. Barry (MA) and Pauline C. Icy (NY); W - 41, house keeper, b. MA, d/o Richard L. Robicheau (Canada) and Dasie M. Lincoln (MA)

BARTLETT,
J. O. D. of Deerfield m. Clara **Roberts** of Barnstead 12/26/1889 in Gilmanton; H – 70, minister, 2nd, s/o John Bartlett and Elizabeth Bartlett; W – 65, 2nd, d/o Samuel Pickering and Polly Pickering

BARTON [see Aubertin, O'Barton],
David E. m. Laura **Whithan** 2/10/1926 in Northwood; H – 20, s/o Edward O. Barton and Jennie Dailey; W – 18, d/o Luther Whithan and Martha Pender
Kevin Albert of Pittsfield m. Sandra Jean **Soles** of Barnstead 5/18/1991 in Pittsfield

BEAUDRY,
Gene Edward of Ctr. Barnstead m. Terese Lee **Clifford** of Ctr. Barnstead 1/20/1990 in Gilmanton

BEAUPRE,
Douglas Herve of San Diego, CA m. Stacey Ellen **Smith** of San Diego, CA 7/4/1992

BEBO,
Nelson F. m. Dorothy E. **Wilson** 11/21/1932 in Gilmanton; H – 23, s/o John F. Bebo and Harriet E. Gray; W – 21, d/o Clarence W. Wilson and Ada E. Chadborne
Philix of Barnstead m. Harriett E. **Gray** of Barnstead 3/29/1909 in Pittsfield; H – 31, saw mill, b. Montreal, PQ, s/o Joe Bebo (laborer, Montreal, PQ) and Mary Green (housewife, Montreal, PQ); W – 17, housework, b. Chichester, d/o Orris D. Gray

(farmer, Barnstead) and Harriett Hannaford (housewife, Carlisle, MA)

BECK,
William H. of Barnstead m. Jennifer Anne **Poirier** of Barnstead 11/12/1994

BEESMER,
Richard R. of Barnstead m. Beverly F. **Adams** of Barnstead 2/9/1982

BEETZ,
Robert P. of Ctr. Barnstead m. Manon T. **Hallee** of Ctr. Barnstead 10/22/1994 in Manchester

BEIJER,
Alexander F. of Ctr. Barnstead m. Diane M. **Jordan** of Nashua 5/25/1997 in Concord

BELL,
Eric S. of Barnstead m. Jessica L. **Blackey** of Barnstead 9/12/1998

BENNET,
Michael Scott of Barnstead m. Debra L. **Provencal** of Pittsfield 8/23/1986 in Pittsfield

BENSON,
Ronald K. of Barnstead m. Shirley M. **Gray** of Barnstead 11/26/1977; H - b. 8/29/1919 in ME, s/o Robert Drew (ME) and Alzada Littlefield (MA); W - b. 11/15/1924 in NH, d/o Howard W. McIntosh (NH) and Edith Sargeant (NH)

BERCHNER,
William H. of Barnstead m. Meretta **Sanborn** of Chichester 8/25/1917; H – 24, b. Bremen, Germany, s/o William Berchner and Bertha Zina; W – 19, b. Chichester, d/o Edwin Sanborn and Bertha Cole

BERGERIN,
Donald A. of Suncook m. Stella F. **Carson** of Barnstead 9/1/1956 in Pittsfield; H - 23, laborer, b. NH, s/o Antonio Bergerin (NH) and Alice Renard (NH); W - 21, tel. operator, b. NH, d/o Floyd O. Corson (sic) (NH) and Helen Durkin (Ireland)

BERGERON,
Herve R. of Barnstead m. Brenda M. **Courchene** of Barnstead 8/29/1998 in Loudon
James A. Osgood of Barnstead m. Cheryl Zannah **Erff** of Barnstead 10/13/1996

BERGEVIN,
Ernest A. of Suncook m. Pamela J. **Watson** of Alton 8/25/1974 in Alton; H - b. 4/8/1935 in NH, s/o William J. Bergevin (NH) and Gladys Nason (NH); W - b. 9/3/1950 in ME, d/o William Watson (MA) and Gloria Riley (Deane) (ME)

BERRY,
John of Barnstead m. Alphonsine **Frenette** of Barnstead 2/11/1906 in Pittsfield; H – 23, laborer, b. PEI, s/o Frank Berry (PEI) and Mary White (PEI); W – 21, weaver, b. Canada, d/o Prudent Frenette (laborer, Canada) and Hortaline Marcotte (housewife, Canada)
John Melvin m. Shirley Mae **Otis** 6/7/1942; H – 24, s/o Nelson M. Berry and Mabel Fay Canney; W – 19, d/o Lewis L. Otis and Gladys Brady
Kenneth A. of Strafford m. Charlotte M. **Tudor** of Ctr. Barnstead 7/3/1964 in Pittsfield; H - 24, student, b. Rochester, s/o Alberton H. Berry (NH) and Marjorie E. Wilkinson (NH); W - 19, student, b. Weymouth, MA, d/o Andrew Tudor (MA) and Charlotte V. Taber (MA)
S. J. of Barnstead m. Emma A. **Webster** of Barnstead 7/17/1887; H – 32, farmer, 2nd, b. Barnstead, s/o Stephen B. Berry (farmer, Strafford) and Eliza Berry (Strafford); W – 23, dressmaker, b. Danbury, d/o Joseph Webster (shoemaker, Springfield) and Sarah Webster (Strafford)

BERUBEE,
Douglas of Barnstead m. Patricia J. **Smith** of Barnstead 7/1/1978; H - b. 5/25/1958 in MA, s/o Rodney A. Berubee (MA) and Shirley D. French (MA); W - b. 2/1/1960 in CA, d/o Ronald H. Smith (CA) and June P. Kinum (MO)

BICCHIERI,
Joseph W. of Barnstead m. Adrith L. **Bedore** of Tilton 8/23/1997 in Belmont

BICKFORD,
Alfred L. of Ctr. Barnstead m. Carla A. **Tillinghast** of Ctr. Barnstead 11/25/1995 in Ctr. Barnstead

George A. of NH m. Edna N. **Banks** of NH 12/31/1970 in Ctr. Barnstead; H - b. 2/10/1920 in NH, s/o Arthur R. Bickford (NH) and Ida M. Brewster (NH); W - b. 2/16/1920 in Canada, d/o Elbourn N. Banks (Canada) and Mary J. Musgrave (Canada)

Herbert S. of Ctr. Barnstead m. Edna R. **Perry** of Ctr. Barnstead 9/7/1962 in Chichester; H - 55, carpenter, b. NH, s/o Arthur R. Bickford (NH) and Ida M. Brewster (NH); W - 55, postmaster, b. NH, d/o Wayland B. Locke (NH) and Bertha F. Emerson (NH)

Howard James of Barnstead m. Sarah Louise **Brigham** of Barnstead 4/27/1990

Richard O. of Barnstead m. Hulda Ann **Hast** of Pittsfield 2/10/1961 in Pittsfield; H - 21, machinist, b. NH, s/o Clarence H. Bickford (NH) and Vera Hill (NH); W - 19, beautician, b. MA, d/o Augustus T. Hast (NH) and Clara B. Johnson (MA)

BISHOP,
Jerry L. of Zion, IL m. Jenipher S. **Plumer** of Barnstead 9/17/1989 in Portsmouth

BITTUES,
Armo Alexander of Montreal, PQ m. Alice Maud **O'Brien** of Barnstead 6/3/1916; H – 40, manager, b. Augusta, ME, s/o Armo Alexander Bittues and Maud Ransom; W – 27, b. NB, d/o Frederick T. O'Brien and Mary Lloyd

BLACK,
Harland P. of Barnstead m. Ruth E. **Schaffer** of Barnstead 9/24/1945 in Alton; H – 29, s/o Herbert Black and Margaret Emerson; W – 40, d/o William Leavitt and Margaret McCarney

Herbert F. of Barnstead m. Marguerite A. **Emerson** of Barnstead 6/24/1914; H – 19, laborer, b. Boston, MA, s/o Frederick Black (cocoa sifter, Boston, MA) and Annie Petterson (ME); W – 18, domestic, b. Barnstead, d/o Ansel Emerson (farmer, Barnstead) and Alice Paige (housewife, Gilmanton)

Norman Emerson m. L. Aldea **Brousseau** 5/11/1940 in Lakeport; H – 22, s/o Herbert Black and Marguerite Emerson; W – 34, d/o Joseph A. Brousseau and Desauge Audet

William Osburn m. Ethel M. **Pitman** 6/7/1925 in Pittsfield; H – 29, s/o Alexander M. Black and Nettie O. -----; W – 24, d/o Oscar E. Pitman and Laurena B. Spooner

BLAISDELL,
Joseph P. of Barnstead m. Myra A. **Rowe** of Pittsfield 8/10/1898 in Pittsfield; H – 74, shoemaker, 3rd, b. Campton, s/o Nathaniel Blaisdell and Annie Blaisdell; W – 34, shoe stitcher, 2nd, b. Gilmanton, d/o Charles Bunker and Mary E. Bunker (housekeeper)

BLAKE,
George F. of Barnstead m. Olive **Hall** of Barnstead 1/12/1900 in Gilmanton; H – 51, carpenter, b. Barnstead, s/o John Blake (Epsom) and Mary J. Blake (housekeeper, Gilford); W – 47, housework, 2nd, b. Barnstead, d/o John J. Merrill (farmer, Barnstead)

BLANCHARD,
John E. of Barnstead m. Marie E. **Seavey** of Pittsfield 10/12/1892; H – 29, merchant, b. Barnstead, s/o Cyrus W. (merchant, Windham) and Lovey (Barnstead); W – 25, dressmaker, 2nd, b. Philadelphia, d/o L. M. Halfman (musician, Philadelphia)

BLANCHETTE,
Gene R. of Barnstead m. Valerie S. **Anderson** of Gilmanton I.W. 2/14/1976 in Gilmanton I.W.; H - b. 9/9/1951 in NH, s/o Roland Blanchette (NH) and Leatrice Drosia (NH); W - b. 2/13/1954 in

MA, d/o Howard E. Anderson (MA) and Dorothy M. Spaulding (MA)

BLUTT,
Stephen Richard of Barnstead m. Christina Marie **Spataro** of Barnstead 8/1/1992 in Pittsfield

BOOCOCK,
John of Dover m. Myra S. **George** of Barnstead 5/20/1894 in Northwood; H – 38, barber, 2nd, b. NJ, s/o Joseph Boocock and Mary Cornick; W – 28, stitcher, b. Barnstead, d/o C. S. George (farmer, Barnstead) and Almyra Waldron

BOSTON,
Robert Alan of Ctr. Barnstead m. Mary Ann **Woods** of Auburn 2/17/1990 in Pittsfield
Stuart L. of Gloucester, MA m. Harriet A. **Young** of Barnstead 1/5/1961; H - 25, Army, b. ME, s/o Elijah Boston (ME) and Effie Shields (MA); W - 19, typist, b. NH, d/o Benjamin Young (NH) and Edna Lakeman (NH)

BOUDREAU [see Bourdreau],
Nester of Barnstead m. Lilian M. **Florie** of Barnstead 11/24/1906 in Hooksett; H – 33, farmer, b. Canada, s/o Clophos Boudreau (farmer, Canada) and Adelle Houle (Canada); W – 18, b. Pittsfield, d/o George Florie and Nellie Larow
William A. of Milford, MA m. Sandra Lee **Veno** of Ctr. Barnstead 9/26/1964 in Pittsfield; H - 18, machinist, b. Milford, s/o William F. Boudreau (Milford, MA) and Ruth B. Williams (Milford, MA); W - 19, telephone co., b. Concord, d/o Gerald A. Veno (ME) and Barbara A. Finlayson (MA)

BOUDREAULT,
Albert of Barnstead m. Clara **Auger** of Barnstead 8/15/1904 in Pittsfield; H – 17, laborer, b. Canada, s/o John Boudreault (carpenter, Canada) and Mattie Marcoux (housekeeper, Canada); W – 17, factory, b. Pittsfield, d/o Joseph Auger (farmer, Worcester, MA) and Phebe Bishop (factory, Canada)

BOURASSA,
Andrew Gerard of Barnstead m. Pamela J. **Martin** of Barnstead 5/2/1992 in Pittsfield
Steven H. of Ctr. Barnstead m. Susan E. **Mitrano** of Ctr. Barnstead 4/2/1994 in Nashua

BOURDREAU [see Boudreau],
Nestor m. Lumma **Duhamme** 7/16/1932 in Hooksett; H – 61, s/o Chopos Bourdreau and Adelle Houle; W – 58, d/o Joseph Gamelin and Melina Larosee

BOUSQUET,
Alfred J. of Barnstead m. Ruth J. **Lank** of Barnstead 9/2/1950 in Pittsfield; H – 22, shoe shop, b. Richford, VT, s/o Tancrede A. Bosquet (VT) and Olive Buzzel (VT); W – 20, shoe shop, b. Providence, RI, d/o Clinton L. Lank (Canada) and Ruth O. Bartman (RI)
Jeffrey J. of Barnstead m. Staci L. **Clark** of Barnstead 3/26/1994 in Pittsfield
John A. of Pittsfield m. Betty J. **Bickford** of Ctr. Barnstead 10/26/1963 in ME; H - 19, b. Pittsfield, s/o Tancrede A. Bousquet (VT) and Olive Buzzell (VT); W - 16, b. No. Conway, d/o Lawrence Bickford (Madison) and Florence Kittredge (Glen)
Paul Judson of Pittsfield m. Anita Linda **Clement** of Ctr. Barnstead 9/15/1968 in Ctr. Barnstead; H - 22, b. NH, s/o Tancerd A. Bousquet (VT) and Olive Buzzell (VT); W - 17, b. NH, d/o George E. Clement (NH) and Kathleene P. Katec (ME)
Paul Judson, Jr. of Barnstead m. Tammy Jean **Ross** of Barnstead 7/5/1992
Peter Judson of Ctr. Barnstead m. Rebecca Jeannine **Sherman** of Ctr. Barnstead 8/7/1992 in Epsom

BOWEN,
Burton M. of Brooklyn, NY m. Geraldine F. **Corson** of Barnstead 11/28/1961 in Pittsfield; H - 26, bartender, b. NH, s/o Myron Bowen and Lena Johnson (ME); W - 27, shoe shop, b. NH, d/o Clyde E. Corson, Sr. (NH) and Esther Swain (NH)
Dale M. of Barnstead m. Patricia A. **Scott** of Loudon 3/15/1985 in Concord

BOYD,
Allan R. of Ctr. Barnstead m. Lauri A. **Roberts** of Ctr. Barnstead 2/14/1982

Howard M. m. Freda A. **Gilman** 11/18/1933 in Pittsfield; H – 21, s/o Melvin S. Boyd and Jennie E. Graham; W – 23, d/o Fred S. Gilman and Etta Belle Coffin

Randolph Leslie, Jr. of Seabrook m. Emma Jane **Gray** of Barnstead 7/13/1948; H – 21, fisherman, b. Seabrook, s/o Randolph L. Boyd and Doris A. Dockam; W – 16, housework, b. Barnstead, d/o Violet M. Gray

Richard P. of Pittsfield m. Elinor N. **Lank** of Barnstead 7/2/1960 in Pittsfield; H - 23, technician, b. Pittsfield, s/o Clyde S. Boyd (NH) and Anne Michalchuk (NH); W - 21, receptionist, b. Laconia, d/o Clinton Lank, Sr. (Canada) and Ruth O. Butman (RI)

Rodney T., Jr. of Barnstead m. Brenda J. **Riel** of Barnstead 7/31/1959 in Chichester; H - 21, s/o Rodney W. Boyd and Edna H. Raynor; W - 17, d/o Warren J. Riel and Rita Chabut

BRADY,
Kim D. of Gilmanton I.W. m. Eliza B. **Johnson** of Gilmanton I.W. 6/15/1981 in Rye

Robert M. of MA m. Diane M. **Welch** of MA 6/11/1999

BRAND,
Thomas E. of MA m. Jennifer L. **Conrad** of Barnstead 7/18/1998 in Wolfeboro

BRANNIGAN,
Eugene of NJ m. Bonita G. **Southard** of MA 8/12/1969; H - 22, b. NJ, s/o Thomas J. Brannigan (PA) and Elizabeth Yurasek (PA); W - 23, b. MA, d/o Reginald Southard and Edna King (NH)

BRASSAW,
Ricky Allen of Barnstead m. Tara F. **Milne** of Barnstead 6/4/1994 in Pittsfield

BRASSE,
Peter A. of Strafford m. Ruth E. **Whittington** of Ctr. Barnstead 5/19/1972 in Farmington; H - b. 7/21/1931 in NY, s/o George Brasse (Denmark) and Imelda Boudreau (Canada); W - b. 5/3/1951 in NH, d/o Randolph L. Boyd, Sr. (NH) and Emma J. Gray (NH)

BRENNAN,
Richard Sheffield of Barnstead m. Diana **Golubinski** of Barnstead 9/29/1990 in Concord

BREWSTER,
John M. of Ctr. Barnstead m. Lorraine Y. **Bisson** of Concord 8/7/1954 in Concord; H - 19, salesman, b. NH, s/o John M. Brewster (NH) and L. Gladys Coll (NH); W - 21, typist, b. NH, d/o Edwin A. Bisson (NH) and Jeanette Y. Rivet (NH)
John Merrill m. Lura Gladys **Call** 12/17/1923 in Pittsfield; H – 31, s/o Mark W. Brewster and Annie E. Merrill; W – 21, d/o Clyde C. Call and Ellen Berry Young

BRIDGE,
John W. of Rochester m. Abbie J. **Pitman** of Barnstead 6/29/1916 in Rochester; H – 29, clerk, b. Lawrence, MA, s/o J. W. Bridge and Beatrice S. Gage; W – 19, at home, b. Barnstead, d/o Albert Pitman and Nellie Clough

BRIGGS,
Russell M. of Ctr. Barnstead m. Sandra J. **Pierce** of Ctr. Barnstead 7/27/1996

BROCK,
Burley Barton m. Doris Esther **Brock** 6/6/1939 in Concord; H – 44, s/o Irving C. Brock and Caroline Dowst; W – 35, d/o William A. Chapman and Catherine E. Lidstone

BRONNENBERG,
Jackie R. of Barnstead m. Mary M. **Fontaine** of Penacook 10/24/1981 in Penacook

BROOKS,

Fred of Barnstead m. Lena **Barron** of Barnstead 9/19/1903 in Pittsfield; H – 28, laborer, b. Canada, s/o Peter Brooks (teamster) and Rose Degger (domestic); W – 22, factory, b. Canada, d/o Frank Barron (teamster)

Glenn P. of Ctr. Barnstead m. Edna A. **Lund** of So. Barre, MA 10/30/1954 in Ctr. Barnstead; H - 39, lumber, b. VT, s/o George E. Brooks (VT) and Mamie I. Bourn (VT); W - 36, mill hand, b. MA, d/o Edwin H. Bullard (MA) and Florence A. Edson (MA)

Wayne P. of Ctr. Barnstead m. Phyllis E. **Leithead** of Ctr. Barnstead 10/8/1988 in Exeter

BROWN,

Allan P. of CT m. Gail Ruth **Carter** of MD 8/6/1994

Bradbury P. of Barnstead m. Margaret O. **Connell** of Pittsfield 1/2/1890; H – 18, expressman, b. Pittsfield, s/o H. L. Brown (expressman, Pittsfield) and Mary P. Brown (housework, Pittsfield); W – 18, clerk, b. Nashua, d/o D. O. Connell (laborer, Ireland) and Mary C. Connell (housework, Nashua)

David M. of Ctr. Barnstead m. Cecelia C. **Gerlack** of Ctr. Barnstead 7/28/1962 in Chichester; H - 20, laborer, b. NH, s/o Willie Brown (VT) and Dorothy Fraser; W - 18, at home, b. NH, d/o Henry Gerlack (NJ) and Dorinda Come (VT)

Floyd J. of Ctr. Barnstead m. Shirley M. **Durham** of Laconia 9/11/1954 in Laconia; H - 21, lumber jack, b. NH, s/o John P. Brown (NH) and Mabel Prescott (NH); W - 18, stitcher, b. NH, d/o Leon W. Durham (NH) and Vina M. Dupont (NH)

Forrest P. m. Rebekah M. **Swain** 4/11/1937 in Northwood; H – 26, s/o Ivorie Brown and Gertrude Pender; W – 21, d/o Henry Swain and Florence Gray

Gordon J. of Alton m. Jeri-Anne **Higgins** of Ctr. Barnstead 8/24/1995 in Alton

Kent Lewis of Ctr. Barnstead m. Antonia Maria **Sterken** of Ctr. Barnstead 12/17/1994 in Chichester

Michael Philip of Ctr. Barnstead m. Mychelle Lynn **Hayes** of Barnstead 4/16/1994 in Pittsfield

Philip W. m. Marjorie E. **Crossett** 10/27/1939; H – 26, s/o Aubrey F. Brown and Mabel L. Pratt; W – 20, d/o Ernest W. Crossett and Mildred D. Dow

Ralph A. of Barnstead m. Vera B. **Wheet** of Barnstead 10/6/1951; H – 19, highway dept., b. MA, s/o Charles R. Brown (MA) and Evelyn M. Watson (MA); W – 23, Blue Cross, b. NH, d/o Rexford E. Wheet (NH) and Bessie W. McDuffee (NH)

Roland E. of Ctr. Barnstead m. Madgeline E. **Gerlack** of Ctr. Barnstead 4/14/1962 in Chichester; H - 20, shoe shop, b. NH, s/o Richard E. Brown (NH) and Florence W. Wells (NH); W - 20, shoe shop, b. VT, d/o Henry A. Gerlack (NJ) and Dorinda I. Come (VT)

Roland E. of Northwood m. Madgeline E. **Brown** of Barnstead 7/4/1969 in Northwood; H - 28, b. NH, s/o Richard Brown (NH) and Florence E. Wells (NH); W - 28, b. VT, d/o Henry A. Gerlack (NJ) and Dorinda Come (VT)

Russell D. of Ctr. Barnstead m. Marla M. **Hillsgrove** of Ctr. Barnstead 6/27/1986 in Ctr. Barnstead

Willie W. of Ctr. Barnstead m. Kristen L. **Winch** of Manchester 6/25/1988 in Manchester

BRUNK,
Michael D. of Barnstead m. Cynthia J. **Martin** of Gilmanton 7/12/1980 in Concord

BRYANT,
Harry E. of Andover, MA m. Margaret A. **Lane** of Chelsea, MA 9/2/1961; H - 34, mech. tec., b. MA, s/o Charles A. Bryant (MA) and Anna Heinge (MA); W - 20, at home, b. MA, d/o Joseph A. Desjadon (MA) and Margaret T. Scanlon (MA)

BUCKMAN,
George S., III of Barnstead m. Kathleen L. **Dunleavy** of Meredith 4/11/1981 in Meredith

BUIEL,
Richard S. of Ctr. Barnstead m. Cathryn M. **Johnson** of Ctr. Barnstead 9/20/1980

BUNKER,
Daniel of Barnstead m. Florence L. **Hillard** of Loudon 8/26/1907 in Pittsfield; H – 34, farmer, s/o Daniel Bunker (deceased, Barnstead) and Hannah Tilton (housekeeper, Barnstead); W –

26, housekeeper, b. Loudon, d/o Hiram Hillard (deceased, Loudon) and Jane Hillard (housekeeper)

George M. of Barnstead m. Addie F. **Aikins** of Barnstead 4/5/1888; H – 20, shoemaker, b. Gilmanton, s/o Sidney P. Bunker (mechanic, Gilmanton) and Jen. M. Batchelder (Gilmanton); W – 18, b. Barnstead, d/o David L. Aikins (carpenter, Barnstead) and Annie Aikins (Concord)

George M. of Barnstead m. Addie F. **Young** of Barnstead 10/12/1889; H – 22, shoemaker, b. Gilmanton, s/o S. P. Bunker (mechanic) and Jennie M. Batchelder; W – 19, 2nd, b. Barnstead, d/o David L. Aikins (mechanic, Barnstead) and Annie Aikins (Concord)

Joseph S. of Barnstead m. Nellie M. **Aikens** of Barnstead 7/3/1892; H – 23, shoemaker, b. Barnstead, s/o Hannah (stitcher); W – 19, stitcher, b. Barnstead, d/o David L. (carpenter, Barnstead) and Annie (Concord)

Lewis W. of Barnstead m. Alice L. **Chesley** of Barnstead 10/22/1892; H – 24, shoemaker, b. Barnstead, s/o Ammon R. (farmer, Barnstead) and Hannah B. (VT); W – 28, housekeeper, 3rd, b. Wells, ME, d/o Charles F. (fisherman, Gloucester) and Mary J. (North Berwick)

Robert John of Barnstead m. Eunice Edwina **Dickinson** of Loudon 6/28/1947; H – 24, Scott & Williams, b. Barnstead, s/o Roland E. Bunker and Ruth Evans; W – 32, domestic, b. New Hartford, CT, d/o Frederick Minery and Margaret Kimberly

Roland E. of Barnstead m. Mary Elmerta **Tilton** of Pembroke 4/28/1917 in Manchester; H – 26, b. Barnstead, s/o John M. Bunker and Mary A. Ellsworth; W – 29, b. Deerfield, d/o George C. Tilton and Hattie E. Call

Roland E. of Barnstead m. Ruth A. **Evans** of Barnstead 7/31/1920 in Manchester; H – 29, b. Barnstead, s/o John M. Bunker; W – 19, b. Barnstead, d/o Austin H. Evans

Roland E., Jr. of Barnstead m. Charlotte **Cate** of Concord 7/29/1945 in Epsom; H – 23, s/o Roland Bunker and Ruth Evans; W – 20, d/o William Cate and Lura French

BURKE,

Andrew S. of Ayer, MA m. Dana M. **Davis** of Barnstead 9/30/1989

William Albert of Barnstead m. Susan Janet **Houle** of Barnstead 11/23/1977 in Keene; H - b. 8/27/1948 in MA, s/o Albert R.

Burke (MA) and Una B. Huklander (NH); W - b. 12/4/1951 in MA, d/o Alfred T. Houle (Canada) and Jeannette Loiselle (MA)

BURKHALTER,
Joe Rayne of Houston, TX m. Sally A. **Riel** of Ctr. Barnstead 6/27/1970 in Ctr. Barnstead; H - b. 3/24/1939 in TX, s/o John C. Burkhalter (TX) and Bertha Payne (TX); W - b. 1/21/1942 in NH, d/o Maurice Riel (NH) and Birgetta Skarp (NH)

BURLEIGH,
Eugene Fred of Barnstead m. Maude Kent **Robinson** of Concord 12/15/1921 in Concord; H – 27, b. E. Andover, s/o Fred Burleigh and Alice -----; W – 25, b. Bow, d/o Frederick Robinson and Belle Morgan

BURLEY,
Richard O. of Pittsfield m. Amy B. **Bousquet** of Ctr. Barnstead 8/19/1995 in Ctr. Barnstead

BURNELL,
Fred Arthur m. Grace Frances **Heywood** 3/4/1939 in Chichester; H – 23, s/o Adlor Burnell and Florence Hodgdon; W – 20, d/o Harold Heywood and Rose E. Leduc

BUTTAFUOCO,
James of Arlington, MA m. Allison M. **Yelle** of Ctr. Barnstead 10/28/1989 in Concord

BUTTERFIELD,
William Albert of Ctr. Barnstead m. Kathleen Ann **Potito** of Ctr. Barnstead 8/28/1994

BUTTERWORTH,
William M. of Barnstead m. Sonya Ann **Longval** of Barnstead 7/4/1993

BYERS,
Patrick Timothy of Ctr. Barnstead m. Dorothy Ann **Langevin** of Chichester 10/19/1991 in Manchester

Steven C. of Barnstead m. Marjorie P. **French** of Barnstead 1/21/1967; H - 19, mill work, b. Chelsea, MA, s/o Berton J. Byers (TN) and Agnes M. Duffey (NH); W - 17, home, b. Gilmanton, d/o Ivo R. French (NH) and Althea F. Fulton (NH)

Steven C. of Barnstead m. Patricia M. **Richardson** of Barnstead 8/7/1977 in Wolfeboro; H - b. 8/20/1947 in MA, s/o Burton J. Byers (TN) and Marion Briggs (MA); W - b. 12/4/1956 in MA, d/o James W. Richardson (MA) and Ruth M. Whoriskey (MA)

Steven C. of Ctr. Barnstead m. Jane A. **Dorsey** of Ctr. Barnstead 4/5/1997 in Gilford

Steven I. of Barnstead m. Melissa M. **Thompson** of Barnstead 8/27/1994 in Manchester

CALDER,
John W. of Ctr. Barnstead m. Patricia B. **Kremser** of Germany 4/26/1994 in Chichester

CALDWELL,
William D. of Barnstead m. Deborah A. **Piaseczny** of Pittsfield 9/10/1988 in Pittsfield

CALL,
Horace C. of Barnstead m. Bessie A. **Downes** of Barnstead 11/2/1899; H – 22, laborer, b. Concord, s/o Horace Call and Emma S. Call; W – 17, housework, b. Barnstead, d/o Herbert O. Downes (farmer, Barnstead) and Calista M. Downes (housewife, Barrington)

Will H., Jr. m. Hazel Miriam **Wood** 11/21/1941; H – 22, s/o Will H. Call and Mabel Pennington; W – 18, d/o Ernest W. Wood and Emily F. Turner

CAMERON,
Daniel R. of Pittsfield m. Mabel Idella **Cate** of Barnstead 11/9/1946; H – 18, s/o Edward J. Cameron and Gladys M. Richardson; W – 31, d/o William S. Cate and Sadie F. Gray

Daniel R. of Ctr. Barnstead m. Elizabeth S. **Kidder** of Pittsfield 7/20/1974 in Pittsfield; H - b. 3/30/1928 in NH, s/o Edward J. Cameron (MA) and Gladys M. Richardson (NH); W - b. 4/16/1935 in NH, d/o John W. Smart (NH) and Florence A. Arlin (NH)

Donald E. m. Beatrice Mary **Gray** 3/8/1941 in Antrim; H – 21, s/o Edward J. Cameron and Gladys M. Richardson; W – 18, d/o Myron E. Gray and Viola H. Prince

Donald E. of Barnstead m. Alice A. **Evans** of Barnstead 3/10/1950 in Chichester; W – 30, labor, b. NH, s/o Edward J. Cameron (NH) and Gladys M. Richardson (MA); W – 20, fancy stitcher, b. NH, d/o Arva Evans (NH) and Gladys M. Brown (NH)

CAMPBELL,

Clyde Foster of Barnstead m. Helen Mary **Huckins** of Epsom 1/1/1968 in Epsom; H - 74, retired, b. VT, s/o John A. Campbell (Scotland) and Minnie E. Collier (VT); W – 64, housewife, b. Walpole, d/o James F. Brown (Epsom) and Mary S. Chesley (Chichester)

Donald C. of Rochester m. Mariana J. **Hanson** of Barnstead 12/19/1964 in Pittsfield; H – 25, man. trainee, b. Hiram, ME, s/o Dave C. Campbell (ME) and Virginia M. Durgin (ME); W - 19, beautician, b. Rochester, d/o Richard H. Hanson (NH) and Natalie L. Wyatt (NH)

CARPENTER,

Glenn S. of Barnstead m. Jane **Meredith** of Barnstead 5/21/1978 in Ctr. Barnstead; H - b. 8/31/1951 in IL, s/o Glenn W. Carpenter (IL) and Lorraine Jordan (IL); W - b. 6/2/1954 in MA, d/o Robert K. Meredith (TX) and Mary M. Martin (MS)

William T. of Barnstead m. Kathleen E. **Walker** of Barnstead 6/20/1987

CARR,

Archie B. of Barnstead m. Marguerite **Cram** of Pittsfield 7/6/1913 in Pittsfield; H – 25, farmer, b. Pittsfield, s/o Sylvester W. Carr (farmer, Pautuckett) and Martha Perkins (housewife, Pittsfield); W – 18, box maker, b. Pittsfield, d/o Harry E. Cram (harness maker) and Mary Tucker (domestic, Pittsfield)

Fred of Barnstead m. Marjorie **Holmes** of Barnstead 1/2/1953 in Chichester; H - 42, lineman, b. NH, s/o Archie Carr (NH) and Marguerite Cram (NH); W - 37, shoe worker, b. NH, d/o Sidney Hanson (NH) and Lura Nutter (NH)

Fred M. m. Vida **Littlefield** 1/1/1933 in Pittsfield; H – 22, s/o Archie B. Carr and Marguerite Cram; W – 17, d/o George F. Littlefield and Susie E. Lyon

George S. of Barnstead m. Katherine C. **Frennette** of Pittsfield 11/30/1952 in Chichester; H – 59, tannery, b. NH, s/o Sylvester W. Carr (RI) and Martha Perkins (NH); W – 47, telephone oper., b. NH, d/o Asa Curtis (NH) and Jennie Foss (NH)

John Kenneth of Barnstead m. Pamela Catherine **Kirby** of Barnstead 9/15/1990

Robert B. of Barnstead m. Ellamarie N. **Axinger** of Marshfield, MA 10/27/1951; H – 31, well driller, b. NH, s/o Raymond Carr (NH) and Edith L. Berry (NH); W – 33, school teacher, b. MA, d/o Oliver L. Nourse (MA) and Anna Monkerud (Norway)

CARSON,

Charles Louis m. Ruth Margaret **Farrell** 8/14/1942 in Chichester; H – 20, s/o Charles B. Carson and Eva B. Morgan; W – 18, d/o Christopher J. Farrell and Amelia A. Baker

Floyd J. of Ctr. Barnstead m. Patricia R. **Kimball** of Alton Bay 6/19/1954 in Chichester; H - 24, construction, b. MI, s/o Floyd O. Carson (NH) and Helen Durkin (Ireland); W - 19, clerk, b. NH, d/o Chester A. Kimball (NH) and Helen A. Emerson (NH)

CARSWELL,

William H. m. Irene V. **Bennett** 10/19/1932; H – 33, s/o Luther E. Carswell and Jennie Eva Titus; W – 24, d/o Ira B. Bennett and Lulu B. Flint

CARTER,

Benjamin Joshua of Ctr. Barnstead m. Tamika Laura **Perkins** of Concord 8/10/1996 in Concord

Marc Donald of Barnstead m. Tracy Lynn **Kimborowicz** of Barnstead 3/27/1993 in Salem

Mark A. of Ctr. Barnstead m. Nicole M. **Hastings** of Epsom 8/12/1995 in Loudon

Scott A. of Ctr. Barnstead m. Susan J. **Belleville** of Ctr. Barnstead 3/28/1997 in Barnstead

CARUSO,
Robert C. of Barnstead m. Laura A. **Chagnon** of Loudon 4/23/1983 in Loudon

CASWELL,
Samuel D. of Barnstead m. Laura E. **Ricker** of Lee 3/12/1891; H – 45, farmer, 2nd, b. Barnstead, s/o Enoch and Judith; W – 28, housekeeper

CATE,
Willie of Barnstead m. Sadie F. **Gray** of Barnstead 12/24/1904 in Alton; H – 34, farmer, b. Alton, s/o Joseph Cate (So. Berwick, ME) and Mary Hurd (housework, New Durham); W – 19, housework, b. Barnstead, d/o Orris D. Gray (farmer) and Harriet Hannaford (housework)

CHAGNON,
David Wayne of Ctr. Barnstead m. Sheryl Ann **Davis** of Ctr. Barnstead 5/26/1990 in Pittsfield

Jerry Martin of Pittsfield m. Margaret Ann **Tilton** of Barnstead 3/7/1970 in Chichester; H - b. 11/10/1945 in NH, s/o Nelson Lyle Chagnon (VT) and Pearl May Purtell (Canada); W - b. 2/24/1951 in NH, d/o George E. Tilton (NH) and Lillian Hill (NH)

Leon Oscar of Pittsfield m. Dorothy Loretta **Drouin** of Ctr. Barnstead 8/18/1990 in Pittsfield

Maurice L. m. Doris A. **Kenison** 6/21/1935; H – 18, s/o Arthur Chagnon and Carey Bishop; W – 18, d/o Fred Kenison and Gladys Brady

Norman D. m. Edith J. **Toutloff** 8/4/1958 in Chichester

CHAMBERLAIN,
George C. of Barnstead m. Lilla F. **Ranger** of Nottingham 10/17/1887 in Pittsfield; H – 21, farmer, b. Loudon, s/o M. Chamberlain (farmer, Boston, MA) and Anna Chamberlain (housework, Alton); W – 18, housework, b. Nottingham, d/o Frank Ranger (shoemaker) and Lizzie Ranger (housework, Nottingham)

CHAPMAN,
David A. of Ctr. Barnstead m. Carol I. **Jacques** of Ctr. Barnstead 7/31/1999 in Ctr. Barnstead

CHAPPELLE,
John E. of Ctr. Barnstead m. Shirley M. **Corrow** of Ctr. Barnstead 2/14/1997 in Concord
John E., Jr. of Ctr. Barnstead m. Dorothy A. **Riel** of Pittsfield 11/22/1975 in Pittsfield; H - b. 12/27/1951 in MA, s/o John E. Chappelle (MA) and Florence Pastena (MA); W - b. 9/10/1957 in NH, d/o Ernest R. Riel (NH) and Edith F. Kenneally (NH)

CHARETTE,
Paul J. of Fall River, MA m. Cheryl-Ann **Caldwell** of Barnstead 8/15/1981

CHASE,
Jackson E. of Barnstead m. Grace Kathryn **Green** of Barnstead 10/8/1916 in Pittsfield; H – 30, clerk, b. Bangor, ME, s/o Elbridge Gerry Chase and Lillian D. Collins; W – 21, b. Lynn, MA, d/o William Henry Green and Annie L. Hutchins
Lester Henry m. Rose Opland **Phelps** 5/16/1925 in Pittsfield; H – 21, s/o Daniel Chase and Addie Falls; W – 18, d/o Edward Philps (sic) and Rose Phelps
Ricky L. of Pittsfield m. Mary Beth **Sherman** of Barnstead 10/16/1999 in Chichester

CHESLEY,
Charles W. of Barnstead m. Jennie M. **White** of Barnstead 6/21/1897; H – 33, shoemaker, 2nd, b. Australia, s/o Albert Chesley and Mahala Young (Barnstead); W – 33, shoe stitcher, b. Quebec, d/o Anthony White (farmer, Quebec) and Jennie H. White (housewife, Quebec)
Herbert L. of Barnstead m. Annie E. **Ayers** of Barnstead 12/13/1891; H – 38, farmer, 2nd, b. Barnstead, s/o Orrin F. (shoemaker, Barnstead) and Lydia A. (housekeeper, Barnstead); W – 25, teacher, b. Barnstead, d/o Samuel T. (farmer, Barnstead) and Clara J. (housekeeper, Wayland, MA)
Orrin F. of Barnstead m. Lydia A. **Locke** of Barnstead 3/2/1853 in Pittsfield; H – 18, cooper, b. Barnstead, s/o Jefferson Chesley

(farmer, Barnstead) and Irene Hussey (housework, Acton, ME); W – 17, housework, b. Barnstead, d/o Sampson B. Locke (farmer, Barnstead) and Esther Nutter (housework, Barnstead) (1902)

CHRISTIANSEN,
Kevin Lee of Ctr. Barnstead m. Denise Germaine **Bouley** of Ctr. Barnstead 10/2/1994 in Chichester

CHRISTOPHER,
Elmwood of Lynn, MA m. Ida J. **Leavitt** of Barnstead 7/5/1888 in Pittsfield; H – 25, shoemaker, b. England; W – 19, operator, b. Chichester, d/o George M. Leavitt and Rachel Leavitt

CHURCHILL,
Ralph K. of Ctr. Barnstead m. Mona E. **Wolcott** of Ctr. Barnstead 12/16/1989 in Ctr. Barnstead

CIMON,
Peter N. of Barnstead m. Ivy R. **Tasker** of Barnstead 3/15/1997 in Chichester

CLARK,
Charles A. W. of Barnstead m. Libbertie W. **Pickering** 4/3/1906 in Farmington; H – 64, farmer, 3rd, divorced, b. Barnstead. So William Clark (Barnstead) and Olive B. Munsey (Barnstead); W – 64, housework, 4th, widow, b. Farmington, d/o Samuel Ham (Farmington) and Jane Jenness (Wolfeboro)
Dennis E. m. Catherine E. **Neal** 5/23/1958 in Chichester
Eugene F. m. Marguerite **Barton** 11/29/1933; H – 28, s/o Jonathan Clark and Ida M. Hanson; W – 26, d/o George A. Barton and Flora B. Roberts
Eugene Fremont m. Marion Elizabeth **Ham** 5/23/1925 in Pittsfield; H – 19, s/o Jonathan Clark and Ida A. Hanson; W – 15, d/o Henry Ham and Gertrude Davis
Frank H. of Barnstead m. Ethel G. **Bodge** of Barnstead 3/20/1895; H – 31, shoemaker, b. Barnstead, s/o Charles J. Clark and Mary A. Snell (Barnstead); W – 21, stitcher, b. Barnstead, d/o Jeremiah Bodge (Barnstead) and Helen M. Bodge (housewife, Alton)

Herbert E. of Barnstead m. Lillian E. **Tasker** of Barnstead 11/27/1895 in Gilmanton; H – 28, merchant, b. Barnstead, s/o John A. Clark (merchant, Barnstead) and Lucy A. Thompson (housewife, Barrington); W – 22, stitcher, b. Barnstead, d/o Albert F. Tasker (postmaster, Strafford) and Georgia A. Tasker (housewife, Pittsfield)

Isaac H. of Barnstead m. Ann L. **Sanders** of Barnstead 6/30/1896 in Pittsfield; H – 62, farmer, 2nd, b. Barnstead, s/o Isaac Clark and Rebecca Hovey; W – 58, housekeeper, 2nd, b. Barnstead, d/o Ezra S. Pendergast and Ann M. Ham

Robert L. of Barnstead m. Nettie **Otis** of Barnstead 3/14/1895 in Gilmanton; H – 22, laborer, b. NB, s/o John Clark and Rachel I. Clark (housewife); W – 24, housework, b. Gilmanton, d/o Harrison Otis (farmer) and Nancy Merrill (housewife, Barnstead)

Robert T. of Brunswick, ME m. Jody L. **Emerson** of Barnstead 8/22/1992

Sewell J. of Barnstead m. Ella H. **Davis** of Barnstead 12/25/1922; H – 30, b. Barnstead, s/o Jonathan Clark and Ida M. Hanson; W – 32, b. Portsmouth, d/o John Davis and Amelia E. Gordon

Sewell J. of Barnstead m. Marie S. **French** of Barnstead 10/15/1960 in Chichester; H - 68, farm, 2nd, widower, b. NH, s/o Jonathan Clark (NH) and Ida N. Hanson (NH); W - 66, at home, 2nd, widow, b. MA, d/o Howard W. Sumner (MA) and Hannah Joyce (Scotland)

Solomon of Barnstead m. Annie **Jones** of Barnstead 6/6/1888; H – 71, shoemaker, 2nd, b. Barnstead, s/o Solomon Clark (carpenter, Barnstead) and Sally Clark (Barnstead); W – 50, b. Wiscasset, ME, d/o Peter Jones (sailor, Wiscasset, ME) and Abigail Jones (Wiscasset, ME)

CLEMENT,

George E., III of Barnstead m. Theresa A. **Jennings** of Ctr. Barnstead 7/6/1974; H - b. 8/16/1954 in NH, s/o George E. Clement (NH) and Kathleen Cates; W - b. 1/18/1955 in MA, d/o Gerald L. Jennings (MI) and Marie C. Rossi (MA)

George E., III of Ctr. Barnstead m. Jeanne T. **Gray** of Pittsfield 11/14/1986 in Barrington

CLEMENTS,
David L. of Pittsfield m. Lisa A. **Varney** of Ctr. Barnstead 10/22/1988 in Chichester
Michael P. of Ctr. Barnstead m. Cheryl L. **Bowen** of Ctr. Barnstead 8/16/1980 in Chichester

CLOUGH,
Charles H. m. Frances J. **Welch** 11/4/1928 in Sandwich; H – 22, s/o Harry G. Clough and Edith Flagg; W – 21, d/o Frank W. Welch and Sadie Morrison
George T. of Barnstead m. Dora A. **Coffin** of Alton 4/10/1894 in Bow; H – 59, farmer, 3rd, b. Belmont, s/o Isaiah Clough and Nancy Clough; W – 42, 3rd, b. Alton, d/o Henry Young and Sarah Young
Leonard W. of Barnstead m. Sandra J. **Rothwell** of Pittsfield 11/30/1963 in Pittsfield; H - 21, student, b. Pittsfield, s/o Walter L. Clough (MA) and Elsie M. Hill (NH); W - 16, at home, b. Pittsfield, d/o Robert L. Rothwell (NH) and Ourice A. Langevin (NH)
Walter L. m. Elsie M. **Hill** 2/22/1932 in Chichester; H – 22, s/o Harry G. Clough and Edith E. Flagg; W – 23, d/o James W. Hill and Margaret Gray

CLOUTIER,
Laurent A. of Barnstead m. Diane M. **Belanger** of Barnstead 7/5/1985 in Nashua

COBB,
Warren James m. Nellie Ruth **Little** 9/16/1925; H – 38, s/o Henry John Cobb and Mary Frances Herbert; W – 30, d/o Harry E. Little and Bertha Stella Crosby

COFFEREN,
Arthur F., Jr. of Barnstead m. Deborah L. **Carson** of Barnstead 10/8/1987 in Northwood

COLBATH,
Ernest of Barnstead m. Stella M. **Foss** of Strafford 12/31/1900 in Strafford; H – 23, shoemaker, b. Barnstead, s/o J. H. Colbath (Barnstead) and Nellie H. Colbath (housekeeper, Barnstead);

W – 21, stenographer, b. Strafford, d/o B. M. Foss (farmer, Strafford) and Sarah E. Foss (housewife, Rochester)

Frank J. of Barnstead m. Florence L. **Jenkins** of Barnstead 5/31/1905 in Manchester; H – 29, RR employee, b. Barnstead, s/o James H. Colbath (Barnstead) and Ellen M. Nutter (housewife, Barnstead); W – 27, housework, b. Barnstead, d/o Charles F. Jenkins (farmer, Barnstead) and Mary Jenkins (Barnstead)

George F. of Barnstead m. Estella G. **Foss** of Gilmanton 4/17/1895 in Gilmanton; H – 43, shoemaker, b. Nottingham, s/o E. C. Colbath (shoemaker, Alton) and Lucinda F. Colbath (housewife, Augusta, ME); W – 24, housework, b. Danvers, MA, d/o John Foss and Ella Lougee (housewife, Alton)

COLLINS,

Joseph Martin of Barnstead m. Deborah Sue **Burley** of Pittsfield 7/6/1991 in Pittsfield

Ralph K. of Barnstead m. Elizabeth M. **Rogers** of Pittsfield 4/8/1967 in Pittsfield; H - 22, printer, b. Concord, s/o Ralph M. Collins (Canada) and Flora I. Corson (NH); W - 19, office work, b. Pittsfield, d/o Joseph C. Rogers (NH) and Madeline M. Huckins (NH)

Ralph M. m. Flora I. **Corson** 3/26/1931; H – 29, s/o Martin W. Collins and Grace B. Hall; W – 20, d/o Harry O. Corson and Stella B. Carr

Richard K. of Barnstead m. Sandra A. **Davis** of Pittsfield 7/18/1959 in Pittsfield; H - 20, s/o Ralph M. Collins and Flora S. Corson; W - 18, d/o Stephen A. Davis and Alice V. Dickey

COMEAU,

Fred L. of Epsom m. Susan M. **Thoroughgood** of Ctr. Barnstead 2/3/1983

CONANT,

Frank A. of E. Pepperell m. Barbara A. **Hunt** of Barnstead 11/25/1914; H – 55, carpenter, 2nd, b. Boston, MA, s/o Frederick Conant and Rachel Rogers; W – 24, teacher, b. Barnstead, d/o John S. Hunt (farmer, Barnstead) and Emma A. Marsh (Barnstead)

CONGDON,
William P. of Barnstead m. Sandra A. **Morgan** of Barnstead 3/17/1981 in Laconia

CONLEY,
James E. of Barnstead m. Carol A. **Morasse** of Barnstead 1/18/1981 in Chichester

CONNOLLY,
Carl Bartlett of Warren m. May Pierce **Huntress** of Barnstead 11/21/1899 in Suncook; H – 25, RR employee, b. Manchester, s/o Charles P. Connolly (teacher) and Sarah B. Connolly (teacher, Warner); W – 29, stitcher, b. Dover, d/o Henry O. Huntress (Barnstead) and Julia A. Huntress (housekeeper)

CONNORS,
Stephen A. of Ctr. Barnstead m. LeeAnne M. **Varney** of Billerica, MA 9/16/1989 in Gilford

CONRAD,
Gregory S. of Barnstead m. Kelly J. **Towle** of Pittsfield 6/24/2000 in Pittsfield
Harold, III of Barnstead m. Susan L. **Towle** of Pittsfield 7/1/1967 in Chichester; H - 20, student, b. CT, s/o Harold Conrad, Jr. (PA) and Helena Davis (MA); W - 19, typist, b. Pittsfield, d/o Herman A. Towle, Jr. (NH) and Norma L. Frenette (NH)

COOK,
Hervey A. of Barnstead m. Mary E. **Penley** of Farmington 9/14/1951 in Farmington; H – 42, woodsman, b. NH, s/o Natt P. Cook (NH) and Cynthia Caverly (NH); W – 22, shoe shop, b. NH, d/o Chester O. Drew (NH) and Laura Cushin (NH)

CORLISS,
Earl S. m. Mildred **Hill** 7/2/1931 in Chichester; H – 23, s/o Charles S. Corliss and Helen Tilton; W – 18, d/o James Hill and Margaret Hill
Eric R. of Barnstead m. Sherri L. **Reynolds** of Barnstead 9/28/1997
Raymond of Barnstead m. Evelyn **Drake** of Barnstead 6/30/1953; H - 22, US Army, b. NH, s/o Jessie Corson (NH) and Barbara

McKay (NH); W - 20, quiller, b. NH, d/o Harvey Drake (NH) and Annie Prince (NH)

CORRIVEAU,
Edward C. of Concord m. Linda F. **Perry** of Ctr. Barnstead 3/18/1989 in Concord

Troy T. of Ctr. Barnstead m. Heather M. **Patterson** of Ctr. Barnstead 7/5/1997

CORSON,
Clyde C., Jr. m. Barbara J. **French** 6/21/1958

Clyde E. m. Esther E. **Swain** 8/29/1932; H – 24, s/o Miss Gertrude Carr; W – 14, d/o Henry B. Swain and Florence M. Gray

Harry M. m. Gladys E. **Reil** 1/22/1933; H – 23, s/o Harry O. Corson and Stella F. Carr; W - 23

William H. of Ctr. Barnstead m. Susan L. **Thurston** of Ctr. Barnstead 6/10/1995 in Laconia

COSTA,
Steven D. of Ctr. Barnstead m. Patricia I. **Jensen** of Ctr. Barnstead 4/26/1997 in Epsom

COTTON,
John G. of NH m. Clara Jane **Sargent** of NH 8/11/1972; H - b. 11/23/1933 in MA, s/o John L. Cotton (MA) and Dorothy Buckle (MA); W - b. 10/30/1940 in NH, d/o Nathan P. Smith (VT) and Mary Stone (MA)

John G. of Barnstead m. Patricia N. **Riel** of Ctr. Barnstead 9/5/1980 in Ctr. Barnstead

John Patrick of Pepperell, MA m. Joanne L. **Bond** of Barnstead 10/16/1971 in Pittsfield; H - b. 5/2/1952 in NH, s/o John Henry Cotton (MA) and Edwina M. McCarthy (MA); W - b. 2/16/1951 in MA, d/o Richard Henry Bond (MA) and Phyllis MacIntosh (MA)

Joseph H., Jr. of Barnstead m. Virginia **Cummings** of Loudon 6/2/1956 in Loudon; H - 28, trucking, b. MA, s/o Joseph H. Cotton (MA) and Ruth Hallett (MA); W - 25, sorter, b. NH, d/o George W. Cummings (MA) and Rena J. Wiggin (NH)

COWDREY,
John H., Jr. of Barnstead m. Tina M. **Hopkins** of Barnstead 10/8/1989 in Chichester

COYMAN,
Terrence J., Jr. of Ctr. Barnstead m. April L. **deSouza** of Tilton 6/15/1991 in Sanbornton

CROSSETT,
Ernest William of Barnstead m. Mildred **Dow** of Barnstead 9/16/1916 in Bellows Falls, VT; H – 24, weaver, b. Newport, s/o William Crossett and Agnes -----; W – 18, at home, b. Barnstead, d/o George W. Dow and Edith M. Shackford
William Wilbur m. Arline Marjorie **Boyd** 10/17/1937 in Pittsfield; H – 20, s/o Ernest W. Crossett and Mildred Dow; W – 21, d/o William S. Boyd and Angie L. Nelson

CROTEAU,
Peter J. of Barnstead m. Sandra J. **Stapleton** of Barnstead 9/8/1984

CUNNINGHAM,
Thomas of Ctr. Barnstead m. Patricia A. **Clark** of MA 9/21/1996

CURLEY,
Walter W. of Brookhaven, NY m. Marie T. **Sullivan** of Barnstead 11/9/1963 in Alton; H – 40, librarian, b. Boston, MA, s/o Walter C. Curley (Boston, MA) and Lillian E. Berg (Cambridge, MA); W - 31, librarian, b. Lynn, MA

CURRIER,
John W. of Concord m. Mildred E. **Harlow** of Barnstead 1/26/1921 in Nashua; H – 54, b. Enfield, s/o John C. Currier and Mary C. Hazelton; W – 62, b. Barnstead, d/o Oliver G. Caswell and Wealthy A. Clark

CURTIN,
Michael J. of Strafford m. Florence M. **Clark** of Boston, MA 7/5/1952; H – 63, retired engineer, b. Ireland, s/o William

Curtin (Ireland) and Mary Collins (Ireland); W – 41, coil worker, b. NH, d/o John Clark (MA) and Sarah Therrien (MA)

CURTIS,
Asa A. of Farmington m. Jennie M. **Foss** of N. Barnstead 4/6/1904 in N. Barnstead; H – 25, lumberman, 2nd, b. Milton, s/o Moses P. Curtis (shoemaker, Milton) and Juliette Cook (housekeeper, Milton); W – 20, teacher, b. Barnstead, d/o Albion N. Foss (farmer, Gilmanton) and Josie M. Clough (housekeeper)

DAHLQUIST,
Theodore G. m. Milda P. **Pugh** 5/18/1935 in Manchester; H – 22, s/o Theodore S. Dahlquist and Marion S. Clapp; W – 23, d/o Charles Pugh and Amelia Rockwood

DALHAUS,
Richard W. of Penacook m. Pamela J. **Riel** of Ctr. Barnstead 1/21/1967 in Ctr. Barnstead; H - 23, student, b. IL, s/o Edward W. Dalhaus (IL) and Martha F. Werner (MI); W - 22, teacher, b. Pittsfield, d/o Maurice E. Riel (NH) and Birgetia M. Skarp (NH)

DALL,
Gary P. of Barnstead m. Amy E. **Blair** of Barnstead 9/25/1999 in Ctr. Barnstead

DALPE,
Dean A. of Barnstead m. Barbara A. **Herzog** of Barnstead 12/11/1993

DAME,
Herman Perley of Barnstead m. Edna Myrtle **Banks** of Barnstead 12/5/1946; H – 36, s/o Perley C. Dame and Eva M. Straw; W – 26, d/o Elbourn N. Banks and Mary J. Musgrave

DANAHER,
Michael D. of Barnstead m. Karen I. **Ossoff** of Barnstead 10/24/1981

DANEAULT,
Andre J. of Suncook m. Leona D. **Locke** of Ctr. Barnstead 5/3/1952 in Pittsfield; H – 26, shoe worker, b. NH, s/o Desere Daneault (Canada) and Josephine Houle (NH); W – 17, home, b. NH, d/o Desere Daneault (Canada) and Josephine Houle (NH)

DARLING,
Philip S. of Exeter m. Patricia M. **Johnson** of Barnstead 3/19/1982 in Ctr. Barnstead

DAVIS,
Albert C. of Barnstead m. Helen E. **Brown** of Barnstead 3/22/1922 in Manchester; H – 21, b. Alton, s/o Daniel C. Davis and Annie Cate; W – 17, b. Farmington, d/o John A. Brown and Alice Tibbetts

Burt N. of Barnstead m. Annie **Miller** of Barnstead 4/6/1890 in Hooksett; H – 19, shoemaker, b. Lynn, MA, s/o Albert Davis (shoemaker, Barnstead) and Lizzie N. Davis (NY); W – 17, b. Springfield, MA, d/o John Miller and Laura Miller

Charles B. of Epping m. Amy G. **Eaton** of Barnstead 1/5/1889; H – 21, shoemaker, b. Barrington, s/o Charles W. Davis (Barrington) and Mary A. Davis (Nottingham); W – 20, shoe stitcher, b. Pittsfield, d/o John C. Eaton (Pittsfield) and Abbie F. Eaton (Barnstead)

Clarence N. of Barnstead m. Mary J. **Manson** of Portsmouth 12/21/1895; H – 20, RR employee, b. Barnstead, s/o Albert Davis (shoemaker, Barnstead) and Elizabeth Neville (New York, NY); W – 19, dressmaker, b. Portsmouth, d/o Martha A. Johnson (dressmaker, Portsmouth)

Coran K. of Barnstead m. Annie F. **Tuttle** of Barnstead 10/27/1894; H – 24, teacher, b. Barnstead, s/o John K. Davis (farmer, Alton) and Abigail D. Walker (Barnstead); W – 21, housekeeper, b. Barnstead, d/o James C. Tuttle (farmer, Barnstead) and Alice J. Hill (Strafford)

Ernest Albert of Barnstead m. Virginia Charlotte **Kelley** of Pittsfield 4/27/1946 in Concord; H – 22, s/o Albert C. Davis and Helen E. Brown; W – 24, d/o Jerome A. Kelley and Charlotte S. Ellis

Howard Everett m. Ardith Grace **Derosier** 10/2/1943 in Pittsfield; H – 38, s/o Daniel C. Davis and Anna D. Cate; W – 27, d/o John H. Shea and Maude B. Hall

Jose L. of Barnstead m. Georgia Mae **Griffin** of Gilmanton 6/9/1897 in Laconia; H – 27, farmer, b. Rochester, s/o Lewis B. Davis and Josie Howard; W – 23, teacher, b. Gilmanton, d/o J. T. Griffin (Gilmanton) and Mary O. Brown (Candia)

Leroy A. m. Freedith **Churchill** 10/27/1930 in Washburn, ME; H – 46, s/o Benjamin W. Davis and Wilhelmina A. Foss; W – 23, d/o Neathel G. Churchill and Lucy J. Corliss

Paul Howard of Barnstead m. Maryann M. **Jessop** of Barnstead 6/27/1982 in Pembroke

Percy A. m. Emma J. **Gray** 9/24/1924; H – 25, s/o Clarence N. Davis and May J. Manson; W – 19, d/o Albert B. Gray and Bessie O. Brown

William Charles m. Erlma Jane **Otis** 11/11/1944; H – 20, s/o E. Henry Davis and Louise D. Deselle; W – 17, d/o Lewis L. Otis and Gladys W. Brady

DAWSON,

Richard Thomas, Jr. of Ctr. Barnstead m. Lisa Marie **Knowlton** of Ctr. Barnstead 6/29/1996 in Epsom

Robert W. of Gilmanton m. Lee E. **Wheet** of Barnstead 5/12/1962 in Gilmanton; H - 28, farming, b. NH, s/o Joseph C. Dawson (MA) and Mary C. Fantom (MA); W - 26, at home, b. NH, d/o Rexford E. Wheet (NH) and Bessie W. McDuffee (NH)

DEBOLD,

Richard W. of Concord m. Faith A. **Weldon** of Ctr. Barnstead 5/29/1988 in Jackson

DECROW,

Delbert S. of Barnstead m. Carrie A. **Murray** of Lynn, MA 10/26/1912 in Lynn, MA; H – 61, RR employ, b. Marsfield, MA, s/o Luther Decrow and Hannah Sherman; W – 50, dressmaker, b. Lebanon, CT, d/o Albert Harvey and Mary Foote

DEEGAN,

Thomas John of Ctr. Barnstead m. Eleanor Margret **Mahar** of Canada 1/11/1971 in Ctr. Barnstead; H - b. 12/29/1949 in MA, s/o John Deegan (MA) and Elizabeth Cadwell (MA); W - b. 11/25/1944 in MA, d/o Ralph C. Mahar (MA) and Margaret Macklin (MA)

DELOIS,
Jeffrey J. of Ctr. Barnstead m. Norma L. **Rose** of Ctr. Barnstead 5/28/2000 in Manchester

DELOLLIS,
Joseph B. of Ctr. Barnstead m. Sally Ann **Barnett** of Ctr. Barnstead 4/18/1976 in Pembroke; H - b. 5/12/1942 in MA, s/o Blase Delollis (MA) and Marie Monte (MA); W - b. 10/5/1954 in NH, d/o Robert Barnett (NH) and Arlene Hoyt (NH)

DEMPSEY,
Chadd James of Wolfeboro m. Renee Lynn **Oberg** of Barnstead 7/30/1994 in Ctr. Barnstead

DENNETT,
Linn M. of Barnstead m. Grace M. **Ward** of Concord 10/7/1911 in Concord; H – 25, farmer, b. Barnstead, s/o Oliver M. Dennett (farmer, Barnstead) and Francis E. Hopson (housewife, West Lebanon); W – 24, case liner, b. Concord, d/o Joseph F. Ward (teamster, Cape Cod, MA) and Ruth A. McDonald (housewife, Sydney, CB)

DENTON,
Stuart P. of Barnstead m. Sylvia **Klesse** of Barnstead 8/27/1988 in Center Harbor

DERBY,
Francis C. of Somerville, MA m. Ada P. B. **Cornell** of Barnstead 10/8/1912 in Laconia; H – 26, clerk, b. Somerville, MA, s/o George H. Derby (retired, Leominster, MA) and Mary A. Langer (housewife, Somerville, MA); W – 24, domestic, b. Canada, d/o Dexter Manning (engineer, Boston, MA) and Alice Quebec (housekeeper, Canada)

DEROSIA,
Joseph E. m. Elsie C. **Heath** 5/14/1933; H – 26, s/o Walter A. Derosia and Virginia M. Gilbert; W – 18, d/o Bert Heath and Margaret G. Moorehouse

DEYETTE,
Ronald A. of Ctr. Barnstead m. Joan E. **Katz** of Ctr. Barnstead 9/14/1991 in Ctr. Barnstead

DIAS,
Alden of Barnstead m. Lillian —— of Barnstead 4/15/1889; H – 36, mechanic, 2nd, b. Montpelier, VT, s/o John Dias (Montpelier, VT) and Sarah Dias (Montpelier, VT); W – 25, b. Barnstead, d/o Jethro N. Locke (Barnstead) (1890) (see following entry)

Aldin of Barnstead m. Lillian M. **Locke** of Barnstead 1/27/1889 in Farmington; H – 36, carpenter, 2nd, b. Montpelier, VT, s/o John Dias (Charlestown, MA) and Sarah E. Dias (VT); W – 25, shoe stitcher, b. Barnstead, d/o Jethro N. Locke (Barnstead) and Electa A. Locke (Barnstead) (see preceding entry)

DICEY,
Harold of Barnstead m. Anna V. **Jones** of Alton 10/21/1912 in Farmington; H – 24, farmer, b. Farmington, s/o George R. Dicey and Nellie F. Prescott (Alton); W – 19, domestic, b. Alton, d/o James M. Jones (farmer, Alton) and Emma J. Glidden (housewife, Alton)

DICKERMAN,
Irving M. of Ctr. Barnstead m. Helena M. **Edgerly** of Concord 5/3/1983 in Chichester

Lester D. of Barnstead m. Donna Marie **Pervere** of Pittsfield 5/21/1977 in Pittsfield; H - b. 8/25/1958 in MA, s/o Irving Dickerman (MA) and Irene Carreaux (MA); W - b. 9/18/1958 in NH, d/o Arthur Pervere (NH) and Annie Portigue (VT)

DICKEY,
Charles B. of Barnstead m. Lizzie E. **Brodie** of Pittsfield 11/28/1900; H – 27, agent, b. Medway, MA, s/o George W. Dickey and Catherine Dickey (Chelsea, MA); W – 17, housekeeper, b. Dover, d/o Ephraim Brodie and Bridget Brodie (Scotland)

DICKINSON,
Charles A., Jr. of Cambridge, MA m. Lynda S. **Azar** of Barnstead 6/30/1979

Gary E. of Barnstead m. Amy S. **Biddle** of Barnstead 6/29/1998

DILLON,
John Mathew of NH m. Whanitta P. **Dudley** of NH 10/7/1972; H - b. 5/24/1939 in NY, s/o James W. Dillon (NY) and Mae Manlley (NY); W - b. 9/26/1941 in VT, d/o Everett Parry (VT) and Gladys French (OH)

DODGE,
Walter S. m. Cora B. **Clough** 5/27/1930 in Alton; H – 22, s/o Eben G. Dodge and Sarah R. Swett; W – 18, d/o Harry G. Clough and Edith E. Flagg

DOELZ,
Adolf of Barnstead m. Auguste **Blachsl** of Barnstead 10/7/1905; H – 27, weaver, b. Germany, s/o Richard Doelz (weaver, Germany) and Wilhelmine Roecker (Germany); W – 25, weaver, b. Austria, d/o Augustein Blachsl (weaver, Austria) and Maria Jarvish (Austria)

DONOVAN,
Keith J. of Ctr. Barnstead m. Susan L. **Mortell** of Laconia 6/11/1988 in Meredith

DORE,
Rawland Edwin m. Virginia May **Kidder** 9/25/1943 in Alton; H – 21, s/o Leon Dore and Doris V. Hale; W – 19, d/o Harold E. Kidder and Bernice E. Carswell

DOTSON,
William Marvin of Cambridge, MA m. Charlotte **Marsal** of Barnstead 10/18/1947; H – 23, mechanic, b. Holyoke, MA, s/o William Dotson and Emma Schmidt; W – 24, factory, b. Chicago, IL, d/o Charles Marsal and Bessie Slanina

DOUCETTE,
Donald David of Chichester m. Sylvia Ann **Corson** of Barnstead 6/26/1954 in Pittsfield; H - 21, shoe shop, b. NH, s/o Arthur Doucette (NH) and Ora V. Martell (NH); W - 18, shoe shop, b. NH, d/o Clyde Edgar Corson (NH) and Ester E. Swain (NH)

Paul E., Jr. of Ctr. Barnstead m. Tania E. **Gosse** of Ctr. Barnstead 8/8/1992

Paul E., Jr. of Ctr. Barnstead m. Victoria A. **Ricker** of Ctr. Barnstead 5/13/2000

DOW,

George W. of Barnstead m. Edith M. **Shackford** of Barnstead 11/27/1890; H – 22, farmer, b. Barnstead, s/o John Dow (farmer, Barnstead) and Mary J. Dow (Alton); W – 18, b. Barnstead, d/o Horatio H. Shackford (shoemaker, Barnstead) and Mary A. Shackford (Barnstead)

John H. m. Beatrice M. **Cleveland** 7/7/1930 in Chichester; H – 28, s/o George W. Dow and Edith M. Shackford; W – 20, d/o George E. Cleveland and Delia F. Demers

DOWNING,

Henry C. of Calais, ME m. Iva **Webber** of Barnstead 8/11/1908 in New Durham; H – 45, salesman, 2nd, b. Middleton, s/o Samuel H. Downing and Eliza Whitehouse; W – 27, housekeeper, 2nd, b. Gilmanton, d/o Charles Weeks (farmer, Alton) and Alice Berry (housewife, Danvers, MA)

DOWNS,

Archer L. of Barnstead m. Edith L. **Gorden** of Lawrence 12/25/1913 in Gilmanton; H – 25, finisher, b. Barnstead, s/o Herbert O. Downs (farmer, Barnstead) and Calesta M. McKean (housewife, Farmington); W – 29, teacher, b. Haverhill, d/o John Gordon (Ginan) and Ada L. Strouach (housewife, Cornnallis)

Arthur L. of Barnstead m. Maud E. **Welch** of Barnstead 8/10/1912 in Gilmanton; H – 23, morocco finisher, b. Barnstead, s/o Herbert O. Downs (farmer, Barnstead) and Calista M. McKean (housewife, Farmington); W – 15, domestic, b. Tunbridge, VT, d/o Fred Welch (doctor, Barnstead) and Annie L. Lyman (housekeeper, Tunbridge, VT)

Herbert L. of Barnstead m. Celia R. **Lougee** of Gilmanton Iron Works 9/10/1904 in Gilmanton Iron Works; H – 31, laborer, b. Barnstead, s/o Herbert O. Downs (farmer, Barnstead) and Calista McKeen (housekeeper, Strafford); W – 18, housework, b. Gilmanton, d/o Reuben P. Lougee (trader, Gilmanton) and Ella Place (Gilmanton)

DRAKE,
Edwin B. of Barnstead m. Carrie E. **Harmon** of Barnstead
12/28/1891 in Pittsfield; H – 28, sawyer, b. Pittsfield, s/o
Walter B. (lumber dealer, Center Harbor) and Sarah J.
(housekeeper, Pittsfield); W – 18, carton maker, b.
Portsmouth, d/o William M. (clergyman, New Castle) and
Fronia L. (housekeeper, Manchester)

Edwin B. of Barnstead m. Georgia D. **Emerson** of Barnstead
6/30/1894 in Pittsfield; H – 31, lumber dealer, 2nd, b. Pittsfield,
s/o Walter B. Drake (Center Harbor) and Sarah J. Drake
(Pittsfield); W – 24, stitcher, b. Barnstead, d/o David M.
Emerson (Pittsfield) and Elizabeth F. Emerson (Northwood)

Harvey W. m. Annie J. **Prince** 6/17/1926; H – 24, s/o Edwin B.
Drake and Georgia Emerson; W – 29, d/o George H. Prince
and Mary E. Moore

DRESCHER,
Robert W. of Barnstead m. Annie M. **Wiggins** of Barnstead
9/23/1978; H - b. 12/14/1949 in NY, s/o Richard W. Drescher
(NY) and Eleanor Kuntz (NY); W - b. 9/9/1951 in NH, d/o
Edward J. Wiggins (NH) and Virginia Hersey (ME)

Robert W. of Barnstead m. Susan **Meredith** of Barnstead 4/4/1981

DREW,
Brian Everette of Ctr. Barnstead m. Pamela Jean **Doub** of Ctr.
Barnstead 9/15/1990 in Epsom

David of Barnstead m. Sarah E. **Hall** of Stoneham, MA 11/18/1887
in Reading, MA; H – 57, farmer, 2nd, b. Barnstead, s/o Aaron
Drew (farmer, Barrington) and Elizabeth Drew (VT); W – 47,
school teacher, b. Barnstead, d/o Joseph Hall (farmer,
Barnstead) and Betsey Hall (Alton)

John L., Jr. of Barnstead m. Bethany A. **Poole** of Barnstead
8/22/1999

DRISCOLL,
David A. of Barnstead m. Jennifer R. **Tiede** of Barnstead
11/21/1998 in Concord

Harry P. of Randolph, MA m. Joan **Parsons** of Barnstead
10/29/1955 in Pittsfield; H - 22, carpenter, b. MA, s/o Harold B.
Driscoll (MA) and Beatrice A. Payne (MA); W - 21, nurse, b.

MA, d/o Douglas S. Parsons (MA) and Margaret F. Belanger (MA)

Richard J., Jr. of Barnstead m. Paula **Nickerson** of Pittsfield 6/20/1987 in Alton

DROLET,
Robert L. of Barnstead m. Susan M. **Komisarek** of Barnstead 1/5/1985 in Suncook

DROUIN,
John F. of Barnstead m. Martha B. **White** of Barnstead 7/2/1983 in Pittsfield

Serge Yvan of Ctr. Barnstead m. Andrea Jeanette **Stanley** of Ctr. Barnstead 9/9/1993 in Bow

DUANE,
Richard D., Jr. of Barnstead m. Carole J. **Ham** of Barnstead 10/16/1982 in Boscawen

DUBOIS,
Paul R. of Ctr. Barnstead m. Julieann **O'Neill** of Ctr. Barnstead 11/9/1996

DUCEY,
Richard James of Ctr. Barnstead m. Pamela Jean **Stockman** of Ctr. Barnstead 10/12/1991 in Ctr. Barnstead

DUFORD,
Robert of Boscawen m. Elaine C. **Gelinas** of Barnstead 4/12/1975 in Weirs Beach; H - b. 8/14/1947 in NH, s/o Rodolph Duford (NH) and Rollande Ayotte (NH); W - b. 7/1/1951 in NH, d/o Robert Gelinas (NH) and Lillian Whitney (MA)

DUHAIME,
Daniel A. of Barnstead m. Gail M. **Chagnon** of Barnstead 6/29/1985 in Pittsfield

DUMONT,
Robert J. m. Judith D. **Locke** 6/27/1958 in Pittsfield

DUPONT,
David G. of San Diego, CA m. Jane Marie **Veroneau** of San Diego, CA 6/21/1986 in Ctr. Barnstead
Robert D. of Barnstead m. Lori-Anne **Phillips** of Manchester 11/27/1981 in Goffstown

DUSTIN,
Robert E. of Pittsfield m. Priscilla J. **Parsons** of Barnstead 9/15/1956 in Pittsfield; H - 19, student, b. NH, s/o Thomas B. Dustin (MA) and Thelma Knudson (IL); W - 19, at home, b. MA, d/o Douglas S. Parsons (MA) and Margaret F. Belanger (MA)

EASTMAN,
James Irving of Barnstead m. Frances Jeannette **Banks** of Barnstead 3/15/1946; H – 21, s/o Charles E. Eastman and Cora M. Nuttall; W – 18, d/o Elbourn N. Banks and Mary J. Musgrave
Michael Paul of Barnstead m. Amy Rose **Emerson** of Barnstead 12/9/1985 in Chichester
Ralph W. m. Beatrice V. **Carpenter** 11/12/1932 in Rochester; H – 26, s/o Hiram B. Eastman and Caroline Schuermann; W – 25, d/o Elbridge Carpenter and Maud Stevens
Ralph W. of Barnstead m. Elsie **Rines** of Alton 10/20/1959 in Pittsfield; H - 53, s/o Hiram B. Eastman and Caroline Schuman; W - 44, d/o Nelson Londo and Mildred Carson
Ralph W. of Ctr. Barnstead m. Ruth F. **Richey** of Rochester 6/24/1967 in Pittsfield; H - 60, carpenter, b. MA, s/o Hiram Eastman (ME) and Caroline Schuman (MA); W - 52, tel. operator, b. MA, d/o Loyd Crosby (Canada) and Edith Feeney (MA)
Ralph Waldo m. Thelma Stevens **Dame** 11/7/1943 in Belmont; H – 37, s/o Hiram Eastman and Caroline Schuman; W – 25, d/o Harry Daine and Carrie Puffinburger
Robert W. m. Gladys M. **Crosby** 2/15/1931 in Newmarket; H – 21, s/o H. B. Eastman and Caroline Shuerman; W – 21, d/o Lloyd Crosby and Carrie Curry
Roger L. of Ctr. Barnstead m. Karen J. **Hannaford** of Ctr. Barnstead 7/8/1995

EATON,
Lewis F. of Barnstead m. Mary E. **Green** of Barnstead 9/11/1907; H – 34, carpenter, b. Pittsfield, s/o George A. Eaton (deceased, Pittsfield) and Millie A. Merserve (Deerfield); W – 25, housework, b. St. John, NB, d/o Andrew T. Green (St. John, NB) and Mary E. Seward (Evon Harbor, NB)

ECKERT,
John F. of Minot, ND m. Janet E. **Eckert** of Ctr. Barnstead 12/23/1989 in Ctr. Barnstead

ECKHARDT,
Ralph F. of Barnstead m. Marilyn L. **Keefe** of Rochester 8/25/1962 in Rochester; H - 28, asst. mgr., b. MA, s/o George H. Eckhardt (MA) and Frieda E. Knaus (MA); W – 20, receptionist, b. NH, d/o Aubrey G. Keefe (NH) and Florence M. Coull (NY)
Ralph Frank of Barnstead m. Agnes Jean **Elkins** of Pittsfield 9/17/1971 in Chichester; H - b. 1/17/1934 in MA, s/o George H. Eckhardt (MA) and Frieda E. Knaus (MA); W - b. 1/17/1930 in IN, d/o Alton Herndon (TN) and Agnes L. Galbreath (IN)

EDGE,
Charles K. of Barnstead m. Angela R. **Harrington** of Barnstead 9/26/1998 in Pittsfield

EHRSTEIN,
Barry N. of Braintree, MA m. Viola M. **Slaney** of Malden, MA 5/7/1964 in Pittsfield; H - 23, machinist, b. Quincy, MA, s/o Gerald G. Ehrstein (Rochester) and Marion C. Frazer (Quincy, MA); W - 20, secretary, b. Chelsea, MA, d/o Clarence A. Slaney (Chelsea, MA) and Grace M. Sargent (Chelsea, MA)

ELDRIDGE,
John Owen m. Sylbie Elizabeth **Little** 9/16/1925; H – 33, s/o John C. Eldridge and Emma Blake; W – 28, d/o William L. Little and Sarah F. Parker

ELKINS,
John Hollis m. Sybel Madeline **Corson** 8/19/1925; H – 20, s/o Walter Elkins and Mary Tucker; W – 18, d/o Harry O. Corson and Stella F. Carr

ELLIOTT,
Charles L. of Pittsfield m. Judith L. **Karsch** of Barnstead 3/18/1978; H - b. 3/22/1954 in NH, s/o Earl Elliott (NH) and Marion Harper (CT); W - b. 10/16/1954 in MA, d/o Otto Karsch (Germany) and Roberta Boss (RI)

Eugene W. of Alton m. Patricia A. **Tarbox** of Ctr. Barnstead 6/17/1972 in Pittsfield; H - b. 1/8/1928 in NH, s/o Walter E. Elliott (NH) and Ella F. Gilman (NH); W - b. 2/5/1943 in NH, d/o Fred O. Tarbox (NH) and Eleanor P. Chellis (NH)

ELLIS,
Robert B. of Barnstead m. Teresa L. **Taylor** of Barnstead 8/20/1983

EMERSON,
Albert F. of Barnstead m. Georgia B. **Brown** of Northwood 3/2/1898; H – 23, teamster, b. Barnstead, s/o Frank Emerson (blacksmith, Barnstead) and Electa Emerson (Barnstead); W – 29, housework, b. Northwood, d/o Henry Brown (farmer, Northwood) and ----- Brown (Pittsfield)

Albert L. m. Madeline A. **Jenkins** 8/24/1929; H – 24, s/o Carlton E. Emerson and Lula Wilkins; W – 23, d/o Charles W. Jenkins and Lilla D. Foss

Arthur C. of Barnstead m. Essel **Clough** of Chichester 4/5/1908 in Pittsfield; H – 22, farmer, b. Barnstead, s/o S. E. Emerson (farmer, Barnstead) and Eldora Lougee (housewife); W – 22, housekeeper, b. Pittsfield, d/o Frank Clough (shoemaker, Wolfeboro) and Adele A. Marston (housewife)

Carleton E. m. Sarah A. **Manson** 6/16/1928; H – 45, s/o Simeon E. Emerson and Eldora M. Lougee; W – 43, d/o Calvin W. Cummings and Emmagene P. Brown

Carleton E. m. Florence **Newcomb** 5/6/1940 in Hubbardston, MA; H – 57, s/o Simeon E. Emerson and Eldora M. Lougee; W – 61, d/o Charles Sweatland and Beula Hurlburt

Carlton E. of Barnstead m. Lulu E. **Wilkins** of Farmington 3/30/1904 in Farmington; H – 21, farmer, b. Barnstead, s/o

Simeon E. Emerson (farmer, Barnstead) and Eldora M. Lougee (housekeeper, Alton); W – 20, teacher, b. Whitefield, d/o John H. Wilkins (clergyman, Stockfort, England) and Linnie F. Quimby (Whitefield)

Charles of Barnstead m. Adela **Brown** of Laconia 4/19/1893 in Laconia; H – 33, shoemaker, b. Barnstead, s/o Timothy Emerson (blacksmith, Barnstead) and Sarah E. Foster (Barnstead); W – 32, b. Sanbornton, d/o David Brown (farmer, Sanbornton) and Hannah Fox

Daniel E., Jr. of Barnstead m. Ruth L. **Hutchins** of Barnstead 10/13/2000 in Concord

Elmer J. of Barnstead m. Josie **Clark** of Barnstead 7/26/1909 in Pittsfield; H – 39, farmer, b. Barnstead, s/o Jefferson Emerson (farmer, Barnstead) and Vianna Cilley (housewife, Bath); W – 40, housekeeper, b. Deerfield, d/o Daniel D. Clark (shoemaker, Dover) and Sarah J. Meserve (housewife, Barnstead)

Harold B. m. Alma M. **Berry** 7/17/1929; H – 23, s/o Albert F. Emerson and Georgie B. Brown; W – 20, d/o John Berry and Alphonson Berry

Harold B. m. Margaret L. **Davis** 2/21/1937; H – 22, s/o Fred Emerson and Esther Brailey; W – 16, d/o E. Henry Davis and Louise Desille

Harold Brown m. Madeline **Sargent** 4/30/1940; H – 34, s/o Albert F. Emerson and Georgia B. Brown; W – 18, d/o Roy Sargent and Selma Moody

Harry m. Nellie Mira **Brewster** 6/27/1923 in Pittsfield; H – 44, s/o George H. Emerson and Mary E. Pickering; W – 28, d/o Mark W. Brewster and Annie M. Merrill

Henry W. of Barnstead m. Lena M. **Hillsgrove** of Barnstead 6/6/1906 in Pittsfield; H – 18, morocco factory employee, b. Barnstead, s/o Herman H. Emerson (farmer, Barnstead) and Ada L. Kenney (housewife, Lynn, MA); W – 17, b. Barnstead, d/o Joseph M. Hillsgrove (Portsmouth) and Lydia M. Webster (housework, Strafford)

Herbert O. of Barnstead m. Effie **Nutter** of Barnstead 11/19/1890 in Pittsfield; H – 27, shoemaker, b. Pittsfield, s/o David M. Emerson (shoemaker, Pittsfield) and Isabel F. Emerson (stitcher, Northwood); W – 28, stitcher, b. Barnstead, d/o John L. Nutter (farmer, Barnstead) and Hannah W. Nutter

James C. of Barnstead m. Annie R. **Haines** of Barnstead 11/8/1893; H – 27, clergyman, b. Barnstead, s/o Jefferson

Emerson (farmer, Barnstead); W – 21, housekeeper, b. Barnstead, d/o Eben Hanson (farmer, Barnstead) and Jennie Hodgdon (housewife, Barnstead)

John O. of Barnstead m. Minnie B. **Wells** of Alton 12/25/1910 in Gilmanton Iron Works; H – 26, farmer, b. Barnstead, s/o Simeon E. Emerson (farmer, Barnstead) and Edora M. Lougee (housewife, Alton); W – 28, housework, b. Alton, d/o Horace Wells (Woburn, MA) and Ida Hill (housework, Alton)

Keith M. of Ctr. Barnstead m. Kathleen M. **Minery** of Pittsfield 1/1/1970 in Pittsfield; H - b. 11/23/1943 in NH, s/o Woodrow W. Emerson (NH) and Altha Kennison (NH); W - b. 6/5/1949 in NH, d/o James W. Minery (CT) and Mary Magob (CT)

Llewellyn H. of Barnstead m. Grace D. **Jenkins** of Barnstead 12/25/1888; H – 22, shoemaker, b. Barnstead, s/o Charles F. Emerson (Barnstead) and Emily J. Emerson (Barnstead); W – 18, stitcher, b. Barnstead, d/o John H. Jenkins (Barnstead) and Elvira R. Jenkins (Ashburnham)

Llewellyn H. of Barnstead m. Mary A. **Jenkins** of Barnstead 12/16/1893 in Pittsfield; H – 28, shoemaker, 2nd, b. Barnstead, s/o Charles F. Emerson (farmer, Barnstead) and Emily J. Hall (housewife, Barnstead); W – 32, stitcher, b. Barnstead, d/o John H. Jenkins (RR employee, Barnstead) and Elvira Marble (housewife, Ashburnham, MA)

Ralph A. m. Ruth **Emerson** 7/19/1936; H – 26, s/o Albert F. Emerson and Georgi Brown; W – 24, d/o John O. Emerson and Minnie B. Wells

Roger Burke of Barnstead m. Margaret Jean **Locke** of Barnstead 10/4/1991 in Gilmanton I.W.

Roland C., Jr. of Pittsfield m. Dolores Ann **Miner** of Barnstead 8/20/1970 in Gilmanton; H - b. 4/1/1952 in NH, s/o Roland Emerson (NH) and Phyllis Twombly (NH); W - b. 10/1/1954 in NH, d/o Harold Miner (NH) and Marjorie Wade (NH)

Wilbur A. m. Beatrice A. **Fraedrich** 2/27/1941 in Fort Myers, FL; H – 27, s/o Arthur Emerson and Essie Clough; W – 28, d/o Henry J. Fraedrich

Woodrow W. m. Altha **Kenison** 10/30/1936; H – 24, s/o Albert F. Emerson and Georgi Brown; W – 18, d/o Fred Kenison and Gladys Brady

ENGLE,
Tracy R. of Boston, MA m. Carlotta M. **Huse** of Barnstead 6/28/1911; H – 23, salesman, b. Jackson, PA, s/o Sanford J. Engle (doctor, Vestal, NY) and Ella M. McWade (musician, Union, NY); W – 22, school teacher, b. Pittsfield, d/o George W. Huse (hotel prop., Manchester) and Adeline Montgomery (housekeeper, Strafford)

EVANS,
Arva m. Gladys M. **Brown** 8/8/1926 in Wolfeboro; H – 21, s/o Austin H. Evans and Myra M. Munsey; W – 19, d/o John A. Brown and Alice Tebbets

Austin H. of Strafford m. Myria M. **Munsey** of Barnstead 1/8/1889; H – 23, shoemaker, b. Strafford, s/o Enoch Evans (Strafford) and H. L. Evans (Strafford); W – 19, housekeeper, b. Barnstead, d/o Henry J. Munsey (Barnstead) and Anna M. Munsey (Barnstead)

John Joseph of Ctr. Barnstead m. Patricia L. **Reid** of Ctr. Barnstead 5/31/1974 in Pittsfield; H - b. 5/20/1942 in NH, s/o Emmeline Evans (NH); W - b. 4/7/1948 in NH, d/o Warren E. Riley (MA) and Charlotte L. Baldwin (MA)

EVERETT,
Joseph E. of Barnstead m. Catherine M. **Hanson** of Barnstead 5/16/1998

FAIR,
Lawrence E., Jr. of Barnstead m. Donna M. **Watts** of Pittsfield 9/29/1979

Timmie R. of Barnstead m. Nancy Lee **Laplante** of Pittsfield 9/7/1979 in Pittsfield

Timmie Robert of Barnstead m. Deborah Lynn **Clement** of Barnstead 3/19/1982 in Ctr. Barnstead

FARNHAM,
Donald Burton of Ctr. Barnstead m. Dawn Mae **Bergeron** of Ctr. Barnstead 5/5/1990 in Pittsfield

FARNSWORTH,
Dana Francis of Concord m. Sandra Faye **Kenison** of Barnstead 10/2/1971; H - b. 4/17/1948 in CA, s/o Francis Farnsworth (VT) and Elizabeth Wilson (ME); W - b. 2/3/1953 in ME, d/o Robert Kenison (ME) and Evelyn Sargent (ME)

FEINN,
Maurice H. of Barnstead m. Ruth L. **Bond** of Barnstead 7/16/1983

FERNALD,
Charles W. of Barnstead m. Lillian P. **Wright** of Sebago, ME 4/3/1920; H – 40, b. Somersworth, s/o Isaac Fernald and Carrie -----; W – 18, b. Sebago, ME, d/o Eugene E. Wright and Annie Sanborn

FIFE,
Stephen Allen of Pittsfield m. Melanie Jean **Tasker** of Pittsfield 6/8/1974; H - b. 10/28/1953 in NH, s/o Clifford A. Fife (NH) and Alice E. Moses (MA); W - b. 6/4/1955 in NH, d/o Milton S. Tasker (NH) and Nancy R. Cotton (MA)

FINLAYSON,
Donald R. m. Virginia **Oelcher** 3/21/1933 in Salem; H – 24, s/o Willard Finlayson and Emily Dole; W – 24, d/o Bernard Oelcher and Florence Keeler

FISHER,
Thomas P. of Ctr. Barnstead m. Frances M. **Martin** of Ctr. Barnstead 5/4/1968 in Ctr. Barnstead; H - 40, b. NH, s/o Thomas P. Fisher (MA) and Ellen Dalton (MA); W - 33, b. NH, d/o Fred R. Wells (NH) and Dorothea Lucia (MA)

FITZMORRIS,
Bernard P. of Loudon m. Linda Lee **Emerson** of Ctr. Barnstead 10/16/1965 in Ctr. Barnstead; H - 22, mill worker, b. Berlin, s/o Philip A. Fitzmorris (NH) and Juliet E. Landry (NH); W - 19, beautician, b. Wolfeboro, d/o Woodrow W. Emerson (NH) and Altha B. Kenison (NH)

FITZPATRICK,
Ronald S., Jr. of Ctr. Barnstead m. Norma J. **Carlson** of Ctr. Barnstead 7/22/1989 in Ctr. Barnstead

FLANDERS,
Alan Joseph of Pittsfield m. Tammy Marie **Riel** of Barnstead 12/10/1976 in Pittsfield; H - b. 1/30/1952 in NH, s/o George E. Flanders (NH) and Marilyn T. Davis (NH); W - b. 4/10/1958 in NH, d/o Leonard E. Riel (NH) and Ruth J. Lank (RI)
Henry J. of Barnstead m. Vera L. **White** of Barnstead 3/25/1995

FLETCHER,
Fred P. of Barnstead m. Ella R. **Jones** of Barnstead 10/20/1890; H – 29, farmer, 2nd, b. New Durham, s/o James A. Fletcher (shoemaker, Dracut, MA) and Elizabeth P. Fletcher (New Durham); W – 25, b. Barnstead, d/o James Jones (farmer, Strafford) and Nancy Jones (Barnstead)
James of Lynn, MA m. Eleanor Rae **Lynch** of Barnstead 4/26/1947; H – 39, baker, b. Clyde Banks, Scotland, s/o James Hossack and Jeanie Forrest; W – 35, shoeworker, b. Lynn, MA, d/o Willard R. Finlayson and Emily P. Dole

FLEURY,
Ronald G. of Ctr. Barnstead m. Alison P. **Bickford** of Ctr. Barnstead 6/24/2000 in Bedford

FLORENCE,
David J. of Barnstead m. Leanne B. **Fortunata** of Barnstead 8/23/1998 in Gilford

FOLLANSBEE,
Calvin A. of Ctr. Barnstead m. Leslie Jean **Boudreau** of Pittsfield 12/1/1990 in Pittsfield

FOLSOM,
Richard B. of Barnstead m. Joan E. **Scalese** of Barnstead 9/19/1987 in Concord

FOOTE,
James O. of Ctr. Barnstead m. Renie A. **Hebert** of Londonderry 9/23/1989 in Hudson
Michael Armand of Ctr. Barnstead m. Ann Marie **Bamford** of Ctr. Barnstead 9/26/1992 in Manchester

FORBES,
Lewis Augustus, Jr. m. Elizabeth Emma **Fletcher** 10/12/1932 in Concord; H – 23, s/o Lewis A. Forbes and Anna T. Fletcher; W – 20, d/o Edgar J. Fletcher and Minerva B. Laws

FORD,
Michael T. of Ctr. Barnstead m. Diane E. **Engel** of Ctr. Barnstead 9/4/1982 in Ctr. Barnstead

FORST,
Barry John of Barnstead m. Bette Anne **Labrecque** of Barnstead 5/29/1993 in Concord

FORSYTH,
George S. of Barnstead m. Judith L. **Eastman** of Barnstead 6/30/1984
Ralph Gordon of Gilmanton I.W. m. Leslie Ann **Brown** of Ctr. Barnstead 5/18/1974 in Gilmanton I.W.; H - b. 6/21/1942 in NH, s/o Harry G. Forsyth (Canada) and Evelyn Rollins (NH); W - b. 10/13/1946 in MA, d/o Charles Brown (NY) and Elizabeth Godfrey (MA)
Richard W. of Barnstead m. Arlene E. **Martel** of Barnstead 8/28/1999

FORSYTHE,
James Edward of Ctr. Barnstead m. Huguette L. **Pinet** of MA 9/14/1996

FORTADO,
Stephen M. of Barnstead m. Janice M. **Kenney** of Nashua 7/7/1979 in Concord

FORTIER,
David Laurent of Laconia m. Susan Marie **Cunniff** of Barnstead 1/14/1978 in Pittsfield; H - b. 3/16/1952 in ME, s/o Gerard Fortier (Canada) and Thelma Roussan (ME); W - b. 5/31/1958 in MA, d/o Robert Cunniff (MA) and Concetta Farrara (MA)

FORTIN,
Raymond J. of Ctr. Barnstead m. Lynn M. **Messier** of Ctr. Barnstead 5/19/1990 in Newton

FOSS,
Dan H. of Pittsfield m. Cynthia L. **Ayer** of Barnstead 2/7/1975; H - b. 12/20/1952 in NH, s/o John Foss (NH) and Rita Doucette (NH); W - b. 1/30/1957 in NH, d/o Charles Ayer (NH) and Barbara Clark (NH)

David L. of Barnstead m. Dawn M. **Bedell** of Pittsfield 12/24/1977; H - b. 9/13/1956 in NH, s/o Lindy E. Foss (NH) and Betty Kenny (NH); W - b. 12/28/1959 in NH, d/o Gary L. Bedell (NH) and Doris Cameron (NH)

Donald Clyde of Farmington m. Maureen L. **Sullivan** of Ctr. Barnstead 7/31/1954 in Farmington; H - 18, lumber, b. NH, s/o Woodrow Foss (NH) and Earline M. Terrill (NH); W - 18, home, b. NH, d/o Thomas W. Sullivan (NH) and Gladys T. Wilkes (NH)

Fred of Barnstead m. Velna Emma **Ordway** of Pittsfield 9/11/1918 in Pittsfield; H – 31, b. Barnstead, s/o Rufus S. Foss and Mary E. Tasker; W – 34, b. Loudon, d/o Horace Ordway and A. Augusta Sanborn

George G. of Barnstead m. Hattie A. **Terry** of Alton 8/31/1913 in New Durham; H – 22, farmer, b. Barnstead, s/o Albion N. Foss (farmer, Gilmanton) and Josie M. Clough (housewife, Belmont); W – 25, stenographer, b. Roanoke, d/o Samuel W. Terry (farmer, Roanoke) and Willie A. Brental (Floyde)

Haven B. of Barnstead m. Hattie C. **Varney** of Farmington 3/9/1891; H – 35, farmer, b. Strafford, s/o George L. (farmer, Strafford) and Elizabeth (housekeeper, Barnstead); W – 20, housekeeper, b. Farmington, d/o John F. (farmer, Farmington) and Emeline C. (housekeeper, Farmington)

John H. of Barnstead m. Estella M. **Mayhew** of Barnstead 1/9/1911; H – 49, RR employ, b. Haverhill, MA, s/o John Foss (farmer,

Alton) and Emily A. Watson (housewife, Alton); W – 38, housekeeper, b. Manchester, d/o Charles Farmer (Lowell, MA) and Jennie Blaisdell (housekeeper, Candia)

John H. of Barnstead m. Lucinda **Patten** of Gilmanton 3/18/1913 in Gilmanton; H – 52, railroad, 4th, b. Haverhill, s/o John Foss (farmer, Alton) and Emily A. Watson (housewife, Alton); W – 53, housekeeper, 3rd, b. West Fairlee, d/o Daniel Ballard (Brookfield) and Clarissa Batchelder (Grantham)

John Henry of Gilmanton m. Nina M. **Higgins** of Barnstead 11/12/1921 in Gilmanton; H – 60, b. Haverhill, MA, s/o John Foss and Emily A. Watson; W – 22, b. Farley, VT, d/o Frank Higgins and Sadie Porter

Lindy E. of Barnstead m. Bettie A. **Kenney** of Loudon 12/3/1955 in Pittsfield; H - 27, lumberman, b. NH, s/o William Foss (NH) and Grace Drake (NH); W - 17, student, b. NH, d/o Charles L. Kenney (NH) and Viola I. Bailey (NH)

Lindy E. of Barnstead m. Margaret L. **Chapman** of Concord 12/8/1967 in Concord; H - 39, milkman, b. NH, s/o William Foss (NH) and Grace Drake (NH); W - 35, secretary, b. NH, d/o Charles M. Coburn (MA) and Mildred E. Ansley (MA)

Richard Colby m. Ada Belle **Wakefield** 7/17/1943; H – 17, s/o Frank W. Foss and Florence A. Foss; W – 20, d/o Myron Wakefield and Josephine Davis

Russell J. of Barnstead m. Alicia E. **Russell** of Barnstead 12/11/1999 in Allenstown

William B. of Pittsfield m. Grace **Drake** of Barnstead 11/6/1914; H – 22, laborer, b. Strafford, s/o Fred L. Foss (shoemaker, Strafford) and Ada Caverly (housewife, Strafford); W – 18, domestic, b. Barnstead, d/o Edwin B. Drake (lumberman, Pittsfield) and Georgia D. Drake (housewife, Barnstead)

FOURNIER,
Edgar G. of Ctr. Barnstead m. Patricia F. **Hanscom** of Ctr. Barnstead 9/16/1989 in Pittsfield

FRAME,
Frederick P. of Barnstead m. Mirie A. **Jenkins** of Barnstead 6/18/1906 in Gilmanton; H – 36, postal clerk, b. Lynn, MA, s/o Henry L. France (sic) (shoemaker, Halifax) and Ellen M. Alley (housewife, Lynn, MA); W – 26, housekeeper, b. Barnstead,

d/o John H. Jenkins (farmer, Barnstead) and Elvira R. Wilkes (housewife, Ashburnham)

FRANSWAY,
John D. of Ctr. Barnstead m. Deborah A. **Chown** of Ctr. Barnstead 1/24/2000 in Northwood

FRASER,
Mark T. of Barnstead m. Linda J. **Albrecht** of Barnstead 2/20/1982

FREEHLING,
Joseph M. of Lynn, MA m. Cynthia A. **Gustafson** of Saugus, MA 9/8/1984

FRENCH,
Herbert C. of Barnstead m. Marie P. **Sumner** of Barnstead 10/4/1910; H – 20, farmer, b. Benton, s/o Lewis E. French (merchant, Warren) and Anna G. Little (housewife, Warren); W – 16, housework, b. Boston, MA, d/o Howard Sumner (Boston)

John D. of Barnstead m. Pauline F. **Bassett** of Barnstead 5/24/1952; H – 23, farming, b. NH, s/o Herbert C. French (NH) and Marie Sumner (MA); W – 23, clothing worker, b. MA, d/o Edward Fay (MA) and Dolly Clanton (NH)

John David, II of Barnstead m. Gail Ann **Raymond** of Epsom 2/26/1973 in Chichester; H - b. 1/24/1953 in NH, s/o John David French (NH) and Pauline Jeannette Fay (NH); W - b. 1/28/1955 in NH, d/o Paul L. Raymond (NH) and Lorraine M. Dennis (NH)

Walter E. of Everett, MA m. Ruby M. **Nichols** of Barnstead 8/9/1892 in Everett, MA; H – dentist; W – 17, stitcher, b. Lynn, MA, d/o George A. (foreman, Dixmont, ME) and Nancy L. (forewoman, Dixmont, ME)

Walter of White River Jct., VT m. Priscilla W. **Myers** of Barnstead 8/4/1950 in Hartford, VT; H – 40, research lab., V.A.C., b. Colebrook, s/o Asa L. French (Northfield, VT) and Jessie Williams (Colebrook); W – 30, housewife, b. Concord, d/o Walter B. Wells (Concord) and Sophronia Yeaton (Concord)

FREY,
Eric C. of Ctr. Barnstead m. Eva A. **Fortier** of W. Epping 6/11/1966 in Raymond; H - 32, furniture, b. New York City, s/o Leo Frey (Germany) and Josephine Dufeler (Germany); W - 22, shoe shop, b. Amesbury, MA, d/o Thomas Fortier (NH) and Evelyn Bishop (MA)

FROST,
Maurice A. of Barnstead m. Jean L. **McClary** of Gilmanton 11/19/1966 in Chichester; H - 19, mechanic, b. Pittsfield, s/o Arthur L. Frost (NH) and Betty J. Frenette (NH); W - 19, manager, b. Pittsfield, d/o George F. A. McClary (NH) and Lura M. Bunker (NH)
Theodore W., III of Concord m. Vickie J. **Ashton** of Ctr. Barnstead 11/16/1989 in Concord

FUNG,
Pak Kuen of Dallas, TX m. Karen Lynn **Genest** of Barnstead 6/19/1993 in Concord

FURGERSON,
Arthur W. of Charlestown, MA m. Abbie **Richards** of Barnstead 6/15/1887; H – 24, b. Charlestown, MA, s/o J. W. Furgerson (mason) and Hannah Furgerson (Cornish); W – 21, housework, b. Whiting, ME, d/o Stephen Richards (farmer, Whiting, ME) and Elizabeth Richards (Potter Place)

FUST,
William H. m. William H. **Just** (sic) 7/20/1924 in Center Harbor; H – 69, s/o Frank C. Just and Fridessia Miller; W – 69, d/o James L. Foss and Eliza J. Blake

GADOMSKI,
Robert S. of Ctr. Barnstead m. Carole A. **Ernest** of Ctr. Barnstead 7/26/1996 in Alton

GAFFNEY,
John F. of MA m. Cathy S. **Pichette** of MA 2/13/1999

GAGNE,
David Joseph m. Beulah Gertrude **Gray** 6/29/1940 in Wolfeboro; H – 24, s/o Alfred Gagne and Nathalie Pauquette; W – 18, d/o Myron E. Gray and Viola Prince

GAGNON,
William D. of Jaffrey m. Lisa J. **Genest** of Barnstead 2/18/1995 in Concord

GANNON,
Shawn Gregory of Ctr. Barnstead m. Cheryl Jean **Montague** of Ctr. Barnstead 8/31/1991 in Litchfield

GARDINER,
Craig T. of Huntington, NY m. Jacquelyn P. **Ritchie** of Huntington, NY 10/7/1995

GARDNER,
Kenneth A. of Taunton, MA m. Sandra E. **Curtis** of Barnstead 2/28/1959 in Pittsfield; H – 23, s/o Kenneth F. Gardner and Margaret B. McCall; W - 16, d/o Morris F. Curtis and Evelyn M. Packard

GARLAND,
Charles Leroy of Ctr. Barnstead m. Dorinda Louise **Martin** of Ctr. Barnstead 1/1/1994 in Wolfeboro
Edward C. of Barnstead m. Lizzie B. **Munsey** of Pittsfield 3/2/1912 in Pittsfield; H – 27, shoemaker, b. Bangor, ME, s/o Edward Mulligan (teamster, Boston, MA); W – 18, shoemaker, b. Pittsfield, d/o Lyman Munsey (mason, Pittsfield) and Ida Butman (housewife, Pittsfield)
Gary R. of Ctr. Barnstead m. Tracy L. **Canfield** of Pittsfield 3/14/1980 in Chichester
Robert Minot m. Lillian Smart **Carson** 4/10/1942; H – 20, s/o Wilbur J. Garland and Hattie M. Cofran; W – 25, d/o David L. Carson and Iva Towle
Wilbur J. of Barnstead m. Hattie M. **Coffan** of Lowell, MA 5/16/1917 in Concord; H – 29, b. Barnstead, s/o Oscar J. Garland and Eliza V. McVean; W – 19, b. Pembroke, d/o Edward A. Coffan and Nellie E. Hartford

Wilbur J. of Barnstead m. Lillian E. **Brown** of Barnstead 1/1/1945 in Chichester; H – 56, s/o Oscar J. Garland and Eliza V. McVean; W – 29, d/o John A. Brown and Alice M. Tibbetts

GASKELL,
Harry C. of Barnstead m. Etta M. **Smith** of Gilmanton 8/13/1918 in Concord; H – 25, b. ME, s/o Clinton D. Gaskell and Millie Flyer; W – 20, b. Gilmanton, d/o Warren Smith and Annie -----

GATES,
Robert Kenneth of Pittsfield m. Carol Louise **Tiede** of Barnstead 10/7/1978; H – b. 8/16/1955 in NH, s/o Sidney C. Gates (MA) and Patricia Perkins (NH); W – b. 12/30/1956 in NH, d/o Ernst E. Tiede (MA) and Carol A. Stock (NH)

GAULT,
Roland W. of Barnstead m. Zelma K. **Dow** of Barnstead 10/10/1922 in Pittsfield; H – 18, b. Bridgewater, VT, s/o John Gault and Mellie Battis; W – 19, b. Barnstead, d/o George W. Dow and Edith Shackford
Rowland W. m. Florence I. **Emerson** 1/21/1931 in Chichester; H – 26, s/o John Gault and Nellie Battis; W – 20, d/o Arthur C. Emerson and Elsie Clough

GEHRIG,
August of Manchester m. Clover V. **Devino** of Barnstead 2/18/1922 in Manchester; H – 29, b. Milford, PA, s/o Ernest H. Gehrig and Anna Peters; W – 28, b. Pittsfield, d/o George O. Devino and Hattie M. Foss

GELINAS,
William M. of Barnstead m. Gladys **Carney** of Barnstead 9/19/1998 in Portsmouth

GENEST,
Henry m. Bertha E. **Stone** 11/8/1923 in Pittsfield; H – 22, s/o Fred Genest and Mary Doucette; W – 18, d/o Charles E. Stone and Mary J. Ellis
John E. of Pittsfield m. Ann C. **Ohlson** of Barnstead 2/20/1960 in Pittsfield; H - 21, clerical, b. Pittsfield, s/o Edward A. Genest

(NH) and Phyllis E. Boyd (NH); W - 16, at home, b. Roxbury,
MA, d/o Bertil I. Ohlson (MA) and Charlotte Pinkham (MA)
Roger E. of Pittsfield m. Maxine J. **Reed** of Barnstead 2/5/1960; H -
18, shoe worker, b. Pittsfield, s/o Edward R. Genest (NH) and
Theda A. Leavitt (NH); W - 18, bookkeeper, b. Barnstead, d/o
Warren G. Reed (NH) and Dorothy P. Canfield (NH)

GERLACK,
Alfred F. of Barnstead m. Patricia L. **Cate** of Barnstead 6/29/1957
in Chichester; H - 19, shoe shop, b. MA, s/o Henry A. Gerlack
(NJ) and Dorinda Come (VT); W - 18, shoe shop, b. NH, d/o
Albert Cate (NH) and Margaret Desham (NH)
Arthur L. of Ctr. Barnstead m. Patricia A. **Levasseur** of Barnstead
6/28/1974 in Chichester; H - b. 8/14/1955 in NH, s/o Henry C.
Gerlack, Jr. (VT) and Lorraine Berry (NH); W - b. 8/24/1954 in
ME, d/o Conrad Levasseur (ME) and Juliette E. Fournier (ME)
Clarence G. of Ctr. Barnstead m. Doris C. **Joy** of Pittsfield
12/22/1962 in Chichester; H - 22, shoe shop, b. MA, s/o Henry
Gerlack and Dorinda Come; W - 18, at home, b. NH, d/o
Calvin C. Joy (NH) and Gladys E. Fifield (NH)
Frank R. of Barnstead m. Eunice J. **Hillsgrove** of Pittsfield
3/8/1965 in Chichester; H - 17, shoe shop, b. Peterborough,
s/o Henry A. Gerlack (NJ) and Dorinda I. Come (VT); W - 18,
elec. work, b. Concord, d/o Fred N. Hillsgrove (NH) and Ella E.
Goodwin (NH)
Henry Charles of Ctr. Barnstead m. Lorraine Blanche **Berry** of Ctr.
Barnstead 3/12/1955 in Chichester; H - 20, surveying, b. VT,
s/o Henry A. Gerlack (NJ) and Dorinda Come (VT); W - 15, at
home, b. NH, d/o Arthur L. Berry (NH) and Bessie O. Gray
(NH)
Rolla D. of Ctr. Barnstead m. Patricia A. **Vernal** of Alton 6/5/1965 in
Alton; H - 19, shoe worker, b. Manchester, s/o Henry A.
Gerlack (NJ) and Dorinda I. Come (VT); W - 20, shoe worker,
b. Laconia, d/o Eugene A. Vernal (NH) and Caroline G.
Marden (NH)

GIBBONS,
Paul K. of Ctr. Barnstead m. Robin L. **Riel** of Ctr. Barnstead
6/4/1983 in Alton

GILMAN,
Gary E. of Barnstead m. Velma L. **Bartlett** of Franklin 3/3/1979 in Franklin

Leonard G., Jr. of Pittsfield m. Linda L. **Jennings** of Barnstead 10/19/1974; H - b. 6/25/1954 in NH, s/o Leonard G. Gilman, Sr. (NH) and Norma H. Clark (NH); W - b. 10/19/1957 in MA, d/o Gerald L. Jennings (MI) and Marie C. Rossi (MA)

William E. of Barnstead m. Debbie A. **Nilges** of Barnstead 12/21/1985

GIRARD,
David M. of Ctr. Barnstead m. Kristine **Berwick** of Ctr. Barnstead 8/19/1989 in Concord

GLASHOW,
David J. of Barnstead m. Susan G. **Delaney** of Barnstead 6/21/1981 in Eaton

GLIDDEN,
Albert E. of Pittsfield m. Mary L. **Duquette** of Barnstead 7/2/1983

Herbert of Barnstead m. Catherine **Harris** of Boston, MA 6/10/1900 in Pittsfield; H – 48, farmer, 2nd, b. Sandwich, s/o Daniel F. Glidden and Adeline E. Glidden; W – 32, housework, 2nd, b. Cambridge, MA

Robert L. of Ctr. Barnstead m. Gail L. **Podmore** of Ctr. Barnstead 10/11/1998 in Moultonboro

GLINES,
Jonathan A. of Danbury m. Jodi L. **Berry** of Barnstead 8/1/1998 in Somersworth

Joseph A. of Winchester, MA m. Annie M. **Knowles** of Barnstead 12/7/1897; H – 26, ticket agent, 2nd, b. N. Scituate, MA, s/o A. R. Glines (W. Rumney) and Mercy Brown (N. Scituate, MA); W – 26, housekeeper, b. Northwood, d/o J. H. Knowles (farmer) and Sarah F. Bickford

Joseph A. of Barnstead m. Valeria M. **Fickett** of Concord 6/2/1912 in Concord; H – 40, station agent, b. No. Scituate, MA, s/o Alvin R. Glines (shoemaker, Rumney) and Mercy E. Brown (housekeeper, N. Scituate, MA); W – 22, teacher, b. Portland,

ME, d/o George E. Fickett (electrician, Deering, ME) and Rose H. Butler (housekeeper, Scarboro, ME)

GOLDEN,

James E. m. Ruth H. **Ross** 1/14/1932 in Nashua; H – 19, s/o John E. Golden and Nellie B. Locke; W – 18, d/o Frank Ross and Flossie Welch

John E. of Barnstead m. Blanche N. **Locke** of Pittsfield 10/25/1910; H – 25, shoe oper., b. Plattsburg, NY, s/o John Golden (Plattsburg, NY) and Marguerite Thornton (housework, Plattsburg, NY); W – 17, shoemaker, b. Pittsfield, d/o John W. Locke (shoemaker, Barnstead) and Maud P. Green (shoemaker, Pittsfield)

Paul Anthony of Barnstead m. Leona Christine **Parker** of Gilmanton 5/28/1946; H – 27, s/o John E. Golden and Blanche N. Locke; W – 20, d/o Leon D. Parker and Bella MacLeod

Richard L. of Barnstead m. Lucille E. **Aubertin** of Barnstead 6/10/1977 in Ctr. Barnstead; H - b. 4/22/1934 in ME, s/o Linwood Golden (NH) and Elizabeth Gray (Canada); W - b. 10/16/1938 in MA, d/o Lawrence Gwinn (MA) and Lois Clogston (MA)

Richard L. of Barnstead m. Elizabeth A. **Sargent** of Barnstead 5/17/1985 in Chichester

Robert F. m. Lena Rita **Richards** 5/10/1941 in Keene; H – 21, s/o John E. Golden and Nellie B. Locke; W – 23, d/o Louis G. Richards and Ida M. Farmer

Scott L. of Barnstead m. Joyce M. **Smith** of Barnstead 4/29/1978; H - b. 6/10/1957 in NH, s/o Richard L. Golden (ME) and Judith Strickland; W - b. 9/8/1959 in NH, d/o George L. Smith (NH) and Ellen M. Davis (NH)

Scott L. of Barnstead m. Anita M. **Brock** of Pittsfield 9/14/1984

William m. Marion **Wyatt** 5/19/1940 in Lebanon, ME; H – 22, s/o John Golden and Blanche Locke; W – 20, d/o Ralph Wyatt and Ellen Thompson

GOLOTTO,

Robert M. of Barnstead m. Norma V. **Bianchi** of Barnstead 7/21/1979 in Chester

GOODWIN,
Harold S. m. Dorothy May **Hildreth** 10/25/1930 in Manchester; H – 22, s/o Clifton Goodwin and Ethel Dane; W – 18, d/o Hiram T. Hildreth and Cora E. Chanette

Ray F. of Ctr. Barnstead m. Nilda A. **Perkins** of Pittsfield 8/24/1963 in Northwood; H - 67, retired, b. Northwood, s/o Walter N. Goodwin (Concord) and Inez A. Fuller (Bow); W - 63, at home, b. Somerville, NH, d/o William E. Anderson (NS) and Nellie M. Carpenter (Gilmanton)

Ray Fuller m. Irene Elizabeth **Hersey** 3/30/1941 in Manchester; H – 56, s/o Walter N. Goodwin and Inez A. Fuller; W – 56, d/o George W. Huse and Addie M. Montgomery

GORALSKI,
Stephen T. of Pittsfield m. Wendy L. **Leavitt** of Barnstead 8/11/1984 in Chichester

GORMAN,
George L., Jr. of Pittsfield m. Linda S. **Hubbell** of Barnstead 2/24/1989

GOSSE,
Harvey Willis of Barnstead m. Mary Ellen **Rogers** of Loudon 9/30/1949; H – 31, fish culturist, b. Arlington, MA, s/o Moses Gosse and Lavinia Waterman; W – 31, reg. nurse, b. Jamaica Plain, MA, d/o William J. Rogers and Agnes F. Graham

Robert Alan of Ctr. Barnstead m. Christie Anna **Campbell** of Ctr. Barnstead 9/12/1992 in Dover

Thomas Arthur of Barnstead m. Allison Jean **Burritt** of Barnstead 10/6/1990 in Pittsfield

William A. of Ctr. Barnstead m. Candice E. **Hoyt** of Weare 8/12/1967 in Concord; H - 19, parts clerk, b. NH, s/o Arthur M. Gosse (MA) and Mary L. Donavan (MA); W - 17, secretary, b. NH, d/o Carl E. Hoyt, Sr. (NH) and Margaret M. Fox (NH)

William A. of Ctr. Barnstead m. Donna K. **Enright** of Ctr. Barnstead 12/31/1989 in Ctr. Barnstead

GOTTLIEB,
Sheldon L. of Strafford m. Jeanne M. **Chatham** of Ctr. Barnstead 1/9/1982 in Exeter

GOULD,
Daniel A. of Barnstead m. Augusta I. **Shackford** of Barnstead 7/4/1901 in Gilmanton Iron Works; H – 50, sawyer, 2nd, b. So. Hiram, ME, s/o Daniel Gould (millwright, So. Hiram, ME) and Deborah Gould (Durham); W – 50, housekeeper, 2nd, b. Barnstead, d/o Nathaniel Smart (carpenter) and Marette Smart (Westmoreland)

GOURLEY,
Chester m. Marjorie E. **Michie** 7/13/1929; H – 21, s/o Herbert Gourley and Charlotte Brauer; W – 21, d/o William P. Michie and Myrtie E. Jenkins

GRATTAGE,
Wanton A. of Penacook m. Laura A. **Gray** of Barnstead 7/3/1955; H - 32, tannery, b. VT, s/o William Grattage (RI) and Clara Lamont (VT); W - 28, shoe shop, b. NH, d/o William Gray (NH) and Ruth Davis (NH)

GRAY,
Albert B. of Loudon m. Bessie J. **Brown** of Barnstead 9/3/1899 in Loudon; H – 19, farmer, b. Strafford, s/o George A. Gray (farmer, Barnstead) and Frances H. Gray (housewife, Pittsfield); W – 18, housework, b. Durham, d/o Charles E. Brown (farmer, Loudon) and Emma F. Brown (housewife, Portsmouth)
Clifford F. m. Edna Irene **Riel** 1/24/1931 in Pittsfield; H – 28, s/o Fred L. Gray and Anna F. Clough; W – 19, d/o William V. Riel and Albertina Currier
Dennis Robert of Barnstead m. Andrea Lee **Pomerleau** of Chichester 10/25/1969 in Chichester; H - 22, b. NH, s/o Robert L. Gray (NH) and Shirley McIntosh (NH); W - 19, b. NH, d/o Andrew Coburn (NH) and Carmel Emerson (NH)
Edward A. m. Ada Mae **Laro** 6/15/1925 in Pittsfield; H – 23, s/o Albert B. Gray and Bessie Brown; W – 22, d/o Frank L. Laro and May Frenette
Edwin A. of Ctr. Barnstead m. Margaret L. **Herbert** of Ctr. Barnstead 2/13/1972 in Ctr. Barnstead; H - b., 11/21/1913 in MA, s/o Albert Gray (MA) and Sadie Hatstat (MA); W - b.

7/5/1928 in ME, d/o Linwood Newell, Sr. (ME) and Laura Cole (ME)

Frank Clarence of Barnstead m. Augie Mae **Bartlett** of Northwood 12/18/1948; H – 28, trucking, b. Barnstead, s/o William C. Gray and Ruth Davis; W – 25, laundry worker, b. Nottingham, d/o William E. Bartlett and Alice G. Garland

Frank W. of Alton m. Maud E. **Shackford** of Barnstead 11/24/1894; H – 24, shoemaker, b. New Durham, s/o William A. Gray (blacksmith, Alexandria) and Sarah F. Gray; W – 19, stitcher, b. Lynn, MA, d/o Horatio H. Shackford (shoemaker, Barnstead) and Mary A. Holmes (Barnstead)

George H. of Barnstead m. Mary E. **Beede** of Pittsfield 10/22/1956 in Pittsfield; H - 23, lineman, b. NH, s/o Erwin Zinn and Violet M. Gray (NH); W - 19, secretary, b. NH, d/o Ralph C. Beede (NH) and Bessie M. Wilkins (NH)

Leslie M. of Barnstead m. Virginia E. **Shonyo** of Barnstead 10/26/1919 in Pittsfield; H – 23, b. Barnstead, s/o Oveis D. Gray and Hattie Hannaford; W – 18, b. Island Pond, VT, d/o Mark Shonyo and Flora Raymond

Myron Earl of Barnstead m. Hattie Viola **Prince** of Barnstead 11/1/1920 in Pittsfield; H – 22, b. Barnstead, s/o Herbert A. Gray and Myrtie S. Cate; W – 16, b. Rochester, d/o George H. Prince and Mary E. -----

Richard Malcolm of Barnstead m. Nancy Marie **Boland** of Penacook 8/14/1948; H – 21, factory, b. Barnstead, s/o Leslie M. Gray and Virginia E. Sponyo; W – 20, secretary, b. Norwood, MA, d/o Joseph I. Boland and Anne L. Murphy

Robert A. of Barnstead m. Eleanor L. **MacKenzie** of Barnstead 5/16/1957 in Chichester; H - 17, shoe shop, b. NH, s/o Grace E. Gray (NH); W - 26, shoe shop, b. VT, d/o Leonard Compo (VT) and Dorinda I. Come (VT)

Steven E. of Barnstead m. Jennifer L. **Constant** of Barnstead 4/17/1999 in Chichester

William C. of Barnstead m. Ruth **Davis** of Barnstead 2/22/1917; H – 29, b. Barnstead, s/o Orres D. Gray and Harriet A. Hanford; W – 19, b. Candia, d/o Danie C. Davis and Anna D. Cate

William Frank of Barnstead m. Carol Ann **Parelius** of Barnstead 8/21/1976 in Ctr. Barnstead; H - b. 5/20/1950 in NH, s/o Frank C. Gray (NH) and Angie Bartlett (NH); W - b. 12/5/1957 in MA, d/o Walter N. Parelius (MA) and Ruth Heinstrom (MA)

GREEN,

Elwin G. of Epsom m. Ruth E. **Cramp** of Ctr. Barnstead 3/1/1957 in Farmington; H - 42, lumberman, b. VT, s/o George H. Green (VT) and Annie D. Bean (VT); W - 45, shoeworker, b. ME, d/o Donald E. McEacheon (PEI) and Sarah G. McIntyre (ME)

Wesley W. m. Mildred **Fothergill** 9/20/1930 in Pittsfield; H – 20, s/o Harry C. Green and Bertha L. Pentell; W – 19, d/o John Fothergill and Elizabeth Riley

GREENE,

Clarence Elmer of Moultonborough m. Grace Aurilla **Pitman** of Barnstead 4/30/1915 in North Barnstead; H – 26, salesman, b. Moultonborough, s/o Nathan Green (sic) (farmer, Moultonborough) and Roxana Plummer (housework, Thornton); W – 23, teacher, b. Barnstead, d/o Albert G. Pitman (blacksmith) and Nellie F. Clough (housework)

Daniel J. of Barnstead m. Carole J. **Dodge** of Barnstead 2/19/1999 in Laconia

GREENLEAF,

Milton of Barnstead m. May E. **Hillsgrove** of Barnstead 3/21/1905 in Pittsfield; H – 46, shoemaker, 2nd, b. Northwood, s/o George W. Greenleaf (shoemaker, Northwood) and Mary J. Winslow (shoemaker, Deerfield); W – 42, housewife, 2nd, b. East Boston, d/o John Jarvis (mail carrier, England) and Almira Stowe (housewife, PEI)

GRIFFIN,

Charles E. m. Clara E. **Alm** 4/21/1923 in Manchester; H – 30, s/o Ewin Griffin and Matte Quimby; W – 22, d/o John Alm and Anna Norin

James J. of Barnstead m. Margaret H. **Webster** of Barnstead 4/28/1990 in Hudson

GRIMES,

Steven P. of Essex, MA m. Juddy H. **McCarron** of Ludlow, MA 5/3/1997

GROLEAU,
James P. of Gilmanton m. Devere D. **Hurst** of Barnstead 6/30/1979 in Laconia

GROSS,
Dennis B. of Concord m. Shanah Lynn **Foster** of Ctr. Barnstead 9/9/1989 in Chichester

GUILBERT,
Brian P. of Ctr. Barnstead m. Cindy J. **Morren** of Derry 12/19/1988 in Derry
Scott R. of Ctr. Barnstead m. Cheryl J. **Troegel** of Ctr. Barnstead 10/21/1989 in Hudson

GUINARD,
Scott M. of Hancock m. Gretchen A. **Johnson** of Barnstead 4/20/1985 in Peterborough

GULLAGE,
J. Russell m. Elizabeth B. Stone **Gennest** 11/19/1926 in Pittsfield; H – 25, s/o Joseph Gullage and Helen Russell; W – 20, d/o Charles E. Stone and Mary J. Stone

GUO,
Fan of Ctr. Barnstead m. Kelly A. **McWilliams** of Ctr. Barnstead 7/25/1999 in Webster

GUSTAFSON,
Michael Eric of Barnstead m. Patty Ellen **Berg** of Barnstead 3/24/1990 in Gilmanton I.W.

GUSTIN,
Walter S. of Thetford, VT m. Florence H. **George** of Barnstead 9/14/1898; H – 24, physician, b. Strafford, VT, s/o Walter Gustin and Nancy Quimby (housekeeper, Lyndon, VT); W – 23, teacher, b. Barnstead, d/o Jonathan Clark (farmer, Barnstead) and Alice George (dressmaker, Barnstead)

HACKETT,
Patrick Charles of Barnstead m. Lucille A. **Gaudreault** of Manchester 5/21/1976 in Manchester; H - b. 8/22/1952 in ME, s/o Michael Hackett (NY) and Rena Blanchette (ME); W - b. 2/27/1955 in NH, d/o Aime Gaudreault (NH) and Rosa Roy (NH)

HALL,
David E. of Barnstead m. Joan A. **Foss** of Barnstead 10/15/1983
George F. of Barnstead m. Beth H. **Baker** of Troy 3/31/1915 in Troy; H – 29, teacher, b. Barnstead, s/o George L. Hall (farmer, Barnstead) and Mary E. Holmes (housewife, Barnstead); W – 21, housework, b. Troy, d/o Elliot K. Baker (teamster, Troy) and Junie E. Hale (housewife, Royalston, MA)

HAM,
Charles L. of Barnstead m. Cora M. **Drew** of Strafford 12/16/1902 in Manchester; H – 21, farmer, b. No. Strafford, s/o Charles E. Ham (farmer, Milton) and Ellen A. Kenney (housekeeper, Barnstead); W – 21, housework, b. Dover, d/o Albert R. Drew (farmer, Strafford) and Abbie J. Tilton (housekeeper, Pittsfield)

HAMMOND,
David Edward, Jr. of Ctr. Barnstead m. Karen Ella **Leblanc** of Ctr. Barnstead 4/20/1992

HANSON,
Alvin G. of Barnstead m. Mary E. **O'Rourke** of Barnstead 1/1/1892; H – 23, carriage maker, b. Barnstead, s/o Levi H. (farmer, Barnstead) and Abbie (Barnstead); W – 22, b. Boston, MA, d/o Edward and Margaret
Carl N. m. Sarah E. **Nutter** 7/10/1930; H – 24, s/o Sidney E. Hanson and Lena M. Nutter; W – 24, d/o Carroll Nutter and Iva Berry
Leonard D. of Ctr. Barnstead m. Terri Lee **Wolfgang** of Somersworth 4/9/1975 in Rochester; H - b. 8/3/1953 in NH, s/o Lloyd Hanson (NH) and Natalie Wyatt (NH); W - b. 2/23/1958 in MO, d/o John Wolfgang (PA) and Sandra Shafer (MS)

Lloyd G. of Barnstead m. Natalie L. **Hanson** of Milton 12/7/1945 in Farmington; H – 26, s/o George G. Hanson and Alice M. Pickernell; W – 22, d/o Ralph Wyatt and Ellen Thompson

Lloyd George, Jr. of Ctr. Barnstead m. Elaine Lee **Ingalls** of Hillsboro 3/14/1970 in Hillsboro; H - b. 2/3/1947 in NH, s/o Lloyd G. Hanson, Sr. (NH) and Natalie Wyatt (NH); W - b. 5/25/1951 in NH, d/o George Ingalls (NH) and Mary Day (NH)

Ronald D. of Barnstead m. Jean M. **Genest** of Pittsfield 11/19/1961 in Pittsfield; H - 18, clerk, b. NH, s/o Lloyd G. Hanson (NH) and Natalie Wyatt (NH); W - 18, at home, b. NH, d/o Edward Genest (NH) and Phyllis Boyd (NH)

Ronald D. of Barnstead m. Beverly J. **Glover** of Penacook 6/25/1966; H - 23, meat cutter, b. Rochester, s/o Richard H. Hanson (NH) and Natalie L. Wyatt (NH); W - 19, balancer, b. Concord, d/o John W. Glover (NH) and Pauline V. Tardy (NH)

Ronald D. of Ctr. Barnstead m. Roberta A. **Plastridge** of Ctr. Barnstead 2/2/1973 in Chichester; H - b. 11/22/1942 in NH, s/o Richard H. Hanson (NH) and Natalie Wyatt (NH); W - b. 11/22/1942 in MA, d/o Charles Andrew (MA) and Catherine Spain (NH)

HARFORD,

Philip W. of Barnstead m. Marsha L. **Griffin** of Pittsfield 4/4/1970 in Ctr. Barnstead; H - b. 3/10/1953 in MA, s/o George P. Harford (ME) and Bertha L. Myers (MA); W - b. 9/29/1953 in NH, d/o Earl Griffin (MA) and Lena DeRoche (ME)

HARRIMAN,

Isaac E. of Barnstead m. Grace B. **Selman** of Hampton 2/9/1889 in Hampton; H – 27, shoemaker, b. Orland, ME, s/o Isaac H. Harriman (Orland, ME) and Sarah Tapley (N. Penobscot, ME); W – 31, shoe stitcher, b. Lynn, MA, d/o Archibald Selman and Fannie Selman

HARRINGTON,

John Edward of Barnstead m. Frances Naomi **Stevens** of Barnstead 9/4/1946 in Dover; H – 58, s/o John Harrington and Mary Jane MacDougal; W – 50, d/o Thomas Stevens and Jennie Atwell

Rodney E. of Barnstead m. Clara Jean **Thornton** of Woodsville 7/19/1969 in Woodsville; H - 25, b. ME, s/o Frank W. Harrington (Canada) and Beatrice Carpenter (ME); W - 23, b. NH, d/o Norman J. Thornton (NH) and Corabelle L. Clark (VT)

HARRIS,
Raymond A. of Barnstead m. Carolyn A. **Pocket** of Marlow 9/26/1981
Raymond A. of Barnstead m. Nelda A. **Fiske** of Barnstead 2/14/1986

HARTSHORN,
George M. m. Bertha Mae **Hill** 6/18/1930; H – 23, s/o George E. Hartshorn and Ina W. Main; W – 23, d/o James W. Hill and Margarett L. Gray

HATHAWAY,
Fred C. m. Elizabeth **McDonald** 6/20/1942 in Pittsfield; H – 60, s/o Lyman Hathaway and Julia D. Coombs; W – 50, d/o Mark McDonald and Ellen Cox
Michael J. of Barnstead m. Diane E. **Fraser** of Pittsfield 4/28/1979 in Pittsfield

HAWLEY,
George H. of Barnstead m. Ina G. **Powell** of Barnstead 10/10/1899; H – 41, physician, 2nd, b. Bath, ME, s/o George Hawley (ship builder, Canada) and Elizabeth Hawley; W – 23, housekeeper, b. Pittsfield, d/o Sylvester Powell and Ada Powell

HAZELTINE,
Kenneth A. of Ctr. Barnstead m. Sharon E. **Cassavanaugh** of Ctr. Barnstead 5/19/1989 in Epsom

HEALEY,
Dexter L. of NH m. Ellen C. **Bird** of NH 7/1/1972 in Pittsfield; H - b. 2/26/1947 in NH, s/o Frederick Healey (MA) and Marion Campbell (NH); W - b. 2/12/1952 in MA, d/o Martin C. Bird (MA) and Beatrice R. Grant (RI)

HEATH,
Carter Eldon of Barnstead m. Lori Jean **Freeman** of Pittsfield 5/1/1993 in Pittsfield
Donald E. of Barnstead m. Gloria A. **Gray** of Loudon 5/6/1995 in Loudon
Nathan T. of Barnstead m. Kristy M. **Pillsbury** of Grantham 8/9/1998 in Lebanon

HEINO,
William A., Jr. of Ctr. Barnstead m. Suzanne Dorise **Florand** of Ctr. Barnstead 2/15/1992

HEISER,
Frederick W., Jr. of Barnstead m. Jane Ellen **Fitzgibbons** of Barnstead 12/31/1993

HEINRICH,
Dieter W. H. of Ctr. Barnstead m. Michele S. **Brumet** of Ctr. Barnstead 9/16/1989 in Ctr. Barnstead

HEMINGWAY,
Jeffrey B. of Barnstead m. Rani J. **Majumder** of Chappaqua, NY 10/24/1981

HERNDON,
John A. of Barnstead m. Alma R. **Heywood** of Barnstead 11/17/1945 in Chichester; H – 18, s/o Alton Herndon and Agnes L. Galbraith; W – 18, d/o Warren H. Heywood and Rose A. Leduc

HERRING,
Neil Charles of Ctr. Barnstead m. Pamela S. **Brayden** of York Harbor, ME 3/15/1980 in Ctr. Barnstead

HERSEY,
Elmer P. of Dorchester, MA m. Irene E. **Huse** of Barnstead 7/8/1918 in Pittsfield; H – 33, b. Jamaica Plain, MA, s/o Charles S. Hersey and Clara A. Field; W – 33, b. Strafford, d/o George W. Huse and Addie M. Montgomery

HEYWOOD,
Fred L. of Barnstead m. Grace A. **Knowles** of Barnstead 11/1/1888; H – 22, cutter, b. Barnstead, s/o William Heywood (L'est'r, England) and Abbie M. Heywood (New Durham); W – 16, stitcher, b. Penacook, d/o Wyatt B. Knowles and Sarah E. Knowles

Lincoln Warren of Barnstead m. Ruth Hedwig **Locke** of Barnstead 1/7/1948; H – 24, clerk, b. Barnstead, s/o Harold Heywood and Rose Alma Leduc; W – 29, home, b. Barnstead, d/o Konrad Knirsch and Matilda Peltzl

HIGGINS,
Charles P. of Barnstead m. Virginia M. **Brown** of Barnstead 11/28/1952 in Belmont; H – 28, electro plater, b. NH, s/o William A. Higgins (NH) and Olive M. Corliss (NH); W – 21, louper, b. NH, d/o John P. Brown (NH) and Mabel L. Prescott (NH)

Michael L. of Barnstead m. Deanna L. **Millette** of Barnstead 7/4/1998 in Barrington

William A. m. Olive M. **Corliss** 9/3/1923 in Alton; H – 23, s/o Frank Higgins and Sadie Porter; W – 20, d/o Charles Corliss and Helen Tilton

HILL,
James W. of Barnstead m. Margaret L. **Gray** of Barnstead 8/23/1906 in Pittsfield; H – 18, steam mill emp., b. Strafford, s/o John S. Hill (steam mill emp., Strafford) and Laura Kimball (Alton); W – 17, housework, b. Barnstead, d/o Orris D. Gray (farmer, Barnstead) and Harriet A. Hannaford (housewife, Carlisle, MA)

HILLIS,
Michael Kenneth of Ctr. Barnstead m. Karen Louise **McDaniels** of Ctr. Barnstead 12/31/1992 in Wolfeboro

HILLSGROVE,
Casper Ewell m. Doris Katherine **Bixby** 6/26/1938 in Wilmot; H – 23, s/o Walter J. Hillsgrove and Myrtie O. Day; W – 20, d/o George H. Bixby and Margaret F. Smith

George C. of Barnstead m. Sandra J. **Publicover** of L. Gilmanton 10/2/1965 in Gilmanton; H - 21, saw operator, b. Wolfeboro, s/o Casper E. Hillsgrove (NH) and Doris K. Bixby (NH); W - 19, secretary, b. Concord, d/o Robert G. Publicover (NH) and Anna M. Shlaitas

George C. of Barnstead m. Diane M. **Murphy** of Barnstead 12/18/1999 in Pittsfield

James H. of Barnstead m. Louisa J. **Rose** of Barnstead 11/19/1887 in Pittsfield; H – machinist, b. Grafton, s/o Joseph Hillsgrove (shoemaker, Loudon) and Lydia Hillsgrove (housework); W – stitcher, b. NS, d/o James Rose (farmer, NS) and Addie Rose (housework, NS)

Joseph H. of Barnstead m. Lois F. **Partridge** of Barnstead 6/9/1951 in Pittsfield; H – 28, woodsman, b. NH, s/o Walter J. Hillsgrove (NH) and Myrtie O. Day (NH); W – 18, housekeeper, b. NH, d/o Horace F. Partridge (NH) and Florence J. Palmer (NH)

Robert H. m. Harriet **Maxfield** 2/25/1934 in Pittsfield; H – 20, s/o George E. Hillsgrove and Grace A. Pickering; W – 21, d/o Harry P. Maxfield and Martha Perkins

W. Merl m. Louise E. **Pike** 2/6/1933 in Pittsfield; H – 19, s/o Walter J. Hillsgrove and Myrtie O. Day; W – 20, d/o Philip G. Pike and Rosamond E. Piper

Walter J. of Barnstead m. Myrtie O. **Day** of Northwood 8/28/1907 in Pittsfield; H – 27, farmer, b. Wilmouth, s/o Joseph M. Hillsgrove (deceased) and Lydia M. Webster (housekeeper, Strafford); W – 21, housework, b. Northwood, d/o Henry Day (deceased, Northwood) and Elizza Randall (housekeeper, Barnstead)

Walter Merl m. Frances Luanna **Prescott** 10/14/1944 in Pittsfield; H – 30, s/o Walter J. Hillsgrove and Myrtie O. Day; W – 16, d/o Harold F. Prescott and Caroline H. Eastman

HILLTON,
Charles J. m. Caroline R. **Black** 10/30/1958 in Chichester

HINGSTON,
Mark R. of Ctr. Barnstead m. Leslie D. **O'Meara** of Ctr. Barnstead 11/5/1988 in Alton

HOAR,

Robert T. of UT m. Laura F. **Rennie** of UT 8/14/1999 in Moultonboro

HODGDON,

Charles A. of Barnstead m. Mary A. **Nutter** of Gilmanton 11/18/1900 in Gilmanton; H – 67, farmer, 2nd, b. Barnstead, s/o Timothy E. Hodgdon and Mary Hodgdon; W – 62, housework, 2nd, b. Epsom, d/o Greenleaf Allen and Fanny Langley

Maurice C., Jr. of Ctr. Barnstead m. Judith F. **Gardner** of Ctr. Barnstead 9/24/1988 in Northwood

Philip B. of Barnstead m. Sharen Renee **Rogers** of Barnstead 9/4/1994

HODGMAN,

Richard O. of Barnstead m. Doris L. **Prescott** of Barnstead 11/19/1960 in Pittsfield; H - 20, mechanic, b. MA, s/o Lander P. Hodgman (MA) and Alice Oliver (MA); W - 18, secretary, b. NH, d/o Leonard G. Prescott (NH) and Olive E. Burros (NH)

HOGENCAMP,

Harry, Jr. m. Katherine Anna **Wilson** 10/17/1931 in Manchester; H – 22, s/o Harry Hogencamp and Jennie R. Cornell; W – 19, d/o George Wilson and Sadie Sanford

John L. m. Florence M. **Newcomb** 1/7/1935; H – 28, s/o Harry Hogencamp and Jennie Cornell; W – 18, d/o George F. Newcomb and Florence L. Sweatland

William B. m. Blanche **Parsons** 11/6/1924; H – 30, s/o Harry Hogencamp and Jennie R. Cornell; W – 30, d/o Charles A. Parsons and Electa A. Ricker

HOLMES,

Charles A. of Barnstead m. Nellie F. **Hall** of Barnstead 8/30/1888 in Strafford; H – 28, farmer, b. Barnstead, s/o John F. Holmes (farmer, Barnstead) and Sarah A. Holmes (Barnstead); W – 21, teacher, b. Bridgewater, MA, d/o Jonathan L. Hall (farmer) and Mary M. Thayer (Bridgewater, MA)

David John of Barnstead m. Sally Jean **Ryder** of Concord 1/28/1978 in Ctr. Barnstead; H - b. 11/15/1957 in NH, s/o Herbert F. Holmes (NH) and Josephine Martell (VT); W - b.

10/14/1955 in NH, d/o Roy H. Ryder (NY) and Edith M. Towne (VT)

Donald E. of Barnstead m. Cynthia R. **Leighton** of Suncook 1/7/1967 in Manchester; H - 20, laborer, b. ME, s/o William E. Holmes (NH) and Pearl E. McEachern (ME); W - 23, waitress, b. NH, d/o Edwin O. Walker (NH) and Rose Marie Morono (NH)

Frank J. of Barnstead m. Hattie S. **McKennelly** of Barnstead 5/28/1893; H – 32, farmer, b. Barnstead, s/o John F. Holmes (farmer, Barnstead) and Sarah A. Jones (housewife, Barnstead); W – 26, stitcher, b. Springfield, NB, d/o Charles W. McKennelly (miller, Springfield, NB) and Louise A. (housewife, Springfield, NB)

Fred m. Elizabeth C. **Douglas** 11/22/1927 in Brookline, MA; H – 32, s/o Charles A. Holmes and Nellie F. Hall; W – 24, d/o David Douglas and Sarah MacLeod

Glenn O. of Ctr. Barnstead m. Annie R. **Tarbox** of Ctr. Barnstead 8/19/1967 in Pittsfield; H - 27, lineman, b. NH, s/o William Holmes (MA) and Marjorie Hanson (NH); W - 27, secretary, b. Gonic, d/o Fred O. Tarbox (NH) and Eleanor P. Chellis (NH)

Peter Dale of Ctr. Barnstead m. Brenda Elaine **DeVaney** of Ctr. Barnstead 12/31/1992 in Concord

William Donald of Ctr. Barnstead m. Hazel Mae **Emery** of Ctr. Barnstead 12/31/1991 in Concord

William E. m. Marjorie E. **Hanson** 9/2/1934 in Strafford; H – 20, s/o Frank J. Holmes and Harriet S. McKelly; W – 19, d/o Sidney E. Hanson and Lura M. Nutter

HOOKAILO,
Robert E. of MA m. Janet L. **Branagan** of MA 9/7/1969; H - 25, b. MA, s/o George Hookailo and Florence Riley (MA); W - 23, b. MA, d/o Walter R. Branagan and Alice D. Blomberg (RI)

HOPPS,
Elwin H., Jr. of Ctr. Barnstead m. Sharon Ann **Foss** of Ctr. Barnstead 11/6/1987 in Whitefield

HORLE,
Richard George m. Martha Edith **Philpott** 2/18/1940 in Pittsfield; H – 30, s/o Francis A. Horle and Louise Janse; W – 45, d/o Anthony J. Philpott and Georgianna Miles

HOSKINS,
Charles W. m. Lelia J. **Hill** 6/8/1936 in Pittsfield; H – 25, s/o J. Edward Hoskins and Daisy Chester; W – 20, d/o Sewall R. Hill and Annie J. White

HOULE,
Andrew A. of Barnstead m. Paula A. **Burbank** of Barnstead 6/3/1984 in Pittsfield
Reginald A. of Barnstead m. Lorraine G. **Cressy** of Barnstead 10/10/1996

HOWARD,
Timothy R. of Laconia m. Susan M. **Burden** of Barnstead 12/1/1978 in Laconia; H - b. 8/24/1953 in MA, s/o John R. Howard (MA) and Rita Y. Richard (MA); W - b. 9/12/1955 in MA, d/o Howard Rath (MA) and Ida Perrino (MA)

HOWE,
Edgar G. of Barnstead m. Cora F. **Davis** of Barnstead 7/14/1900 in Pittsfield; H – 30, carpenter, b. Concord, s/o F. H. Howe and Minerva A. Howe (housekeeper, Grantham); W – 19, housework, b. Barnstead, d/o J. A. Davis (farmer, Pittsfield) and Susan Davis (housewife, Barnstead)

HOWES,
Richard J. of Ctr. Barnstead m. Laurence L. **Marquenet** of Paris, France 10/21/1988

HOYT,
Randolph W. of Ctr. Barnstead m. Michele I. **Beauregard** of Ctr. Barnstead 9/12/1997

HROMIS,
Vladimir of Ctr. Barnstead m. Marianne C. **David** of Ctr. Barnstead 5/3/1998

HUFFSTUTLAR,
Vernon Eishmel m. Lucille Cordelia **Perreault** 10/28/1944 in Manchester; H – 21, s/o Eishmel Huffstutlar and Ruby Wilson; W – 23, d/o Conrad Perreault and Helen Killoran

HUNNEYMAN,
Lawrence J. of Concord m. Marie T. **Knirsch** of Barnstead 9/28/1957 in Concord; H - 21, salesman, b. NH, s/o William H. Hunneyman (NH) and Laura M. Dubois (NH); W - 20, hairdresser, b. NH, d/o Henry Knirsch (NH) and Velma J. Keniston (NH)

HUNT,
John F. of Barnstead m. Emma A. **Marsh** 3/28/1889; H – 35, shoemaker, b. Lynn, MA, s/o John K. Hunt and Lucy Hunt; W – 20, shoe stitcher, b. Barnstead, d/o Joseph W. Marsh and M. Marsh

HUNTLEY,
Mark Allen of Studio City, CA m. Sharon Lee **Beaupre** of Studio City, CA 9/1/1991

HURST,
Albert W., Jr. of Barnstead m. Kathi J. **Smith** of Barnstead 5/12/1984 in Ctr. Barnstead

HYSLOP,
Douglas W. of Barnstead m. Constance L. **Roberts** of Barnstead 5/31/1975 in Gilmanton; H - b. 4/11/1954 in NH, s/o Donald W. Nyslop (sic) (NH) and Rachel Straw (NH); W - b. 6/21/1955 in NH, d/o Chester E. Roberts (MA) and Alice T. Titcomb (NH)
Gerald Brian of Gilmanton m. Ruth Elaine **Braase** of Barnstead 2/23/1978; H - b. 12/18/1952 in NH, s/o Donald Hyslop (MA) and Rachel Straw (NH); W - b. 5/3/1951 in NH, d/o Randolph L. Boyd (NH) and Emma Gray (NH)

JACOBS,
C. M. of Barnstead m. Lettie A. **Hillsgrove** of Barnstead 11/24/1887 in Pittsfield; H – shoemaker, b. Barnstead, s/o David M. Jacobs (farmer, Barnstead) and Lizzie Jacobs

(Barnstead); W – stitcher, b. Grafton, d/o J. M. Hillsgrove (shoemaker, Portsmouth) and Lydia M. Hillsgrove

JACQUES,
Harold R. of Barnstead m. Dorothy A. **Goodwin** of Barnstead 2/1/1974; H - b. 5/29/1921 in MA, s/o Harold J. Jacques (MA) and Marion Mitchell (ME); W - b. 12/16/1940 in NH, d/o Dennis J. Corcoran (NH) and Dorothy E. Walker (NH)
Paul R. of Ctr. Barnstead m. Lisa D. **Dore** of Ctr. Barnstead 7/15/2000 in Sanbornton

JARELS,
Danny L. of Barnstead m. Debra M. **Keene** of Barnstead 6/20/1986

JAWORSKI,
Edward M. of Concord m. Althea J. **French** of Barnstead 10/10/1959; H - 23, s/o Joseph Jaworski and Margaret G. Moody; W - 24, d/o Ivo J. French and Althea M. Fulton

JEANSON,
Gregory Wayne of Alton m. Janet Lynn **Winterle** of Ctr. Barnstead 8/20/1994 in Gilford

JENISCH,
Alfred F. of Barnstead m. Margaret F. **Green** of Pittsfield 7/25/1945 in Pittsfield; H – 24, s/o Alois F. Jenisch and Matilda Pache; W – 24, d/o Charles E. Green and Florence M. Davis
Alois of Barnstead m. Mathilda **Pachl** of Barnstead 3/23/1909; H – 27, weaver, b. Moravia, Austria, s/o Franz Jenisch (weaver, Triebendorf, Austria) and Zecelia Heger (housewife, Triebendorf, Austria); W – 24, housework, b. Bohemia, Austria, d/o Johann Pachl (farmer, Koenigsfeld, Austria) and Emilie Suess (housewife, Koenigsfeld, Austria)
Alois of Barnstead m. Cora E. **Dodge** of Barnstead 10/13/1951 in Chichester; H – 34, weaver, b. NH, s/o Alois F. Jenisch (Austria) and Matilda Pabl (Austria); W – 39, inspector, b. MA, d/o Harry G. Clough (MA) and Edith E. Flagg (MA)
Douglas H. of Barnstead m. Anne B. **Orton** of Hanover 8/24/1963 in Hanover; H - 21, student, b. Concord, s/o William H. Jenisch (Barnstead) and Marion Park (Pittsfield); W - 22, teacher, b.

Newark, NJ, d/o Douglas B. Orton (Newark, NJ) and Adelane Y. Smith (Lock Haven, CT)

Frederick K. m. Odna G. **McIntosh** 10/30/1943; H – 32, s/o Alois Jenisch and Matilda Pachl; W – 24, d/o Howard W. McIntosh and Edith P. Sargent

Raymond Louis of Barnstead m. Eileen Rose **Lelko** of New York, NY 9/12/1948; H – 22, construction work, b. Barnstead, s/o Frank Jenisch and Metilda F. Schunk; W – 18, none, b. Long Island, NY, d/o John Lelko and Catherine Rice

Richard A. of Barnstead m. Margaret Ann **Veno** of Rochester 11/23/1968 in Rochester; H - 21, b. NH, s/o Richard R. Jenisch (NH) and Barbara Turner (MA); W - 19, b. NH, d/o Irving Veno (NH) and Madeline Long (MA)

William Henry m. Marion Louise **Moore** 6/24/1940 in Pittsfield; H – 30, s/o Alois F. Jenisch and Matilda Pachl; W – 33, d/o Edward H. Park and Alice L. Dickey

William P. of Barnstead m. Carole A. **Berkson** of Pittsfield 5/1/1965 in Chichester; H - 23, student, b. Concord, s/o William H. Jenisch (NH) and Marion Park (NH); W - 21, secretary, b. NH, d/o Leonard B. Berkson (MA) and Marguerite A. DeLacey (MA)

JENKINS,

Albert S. m. Elma I. **Armstrong** 9/13/1927; H – 50, s/o George W. Jenkins and Victoria Clark; W – 48, d/o Henry Shackford and Augusta Smart

Carroll E. of Barnstead m. Mary E. **Dow** of Barnstead 11/28/1917 in Pittsfield; H – 26, b. Barnstead, s/o Joseph E. Jenkins and Clara A. Carter; W – 21, b. Barnstead, d/o George W. Dow and Edith M. Shackford

Charles F. of Barnstead m. Christie A. **Maxfield** of Barnstead 5/9/1908 in Pittsfield; H – 24, morocco emp., b. Loudon, s/o E. J. Jenkins (morocco work, Barnstead) and Clara A. Carter (housewife, Loudon); W – 19, box maker, b. Pittsfield, d/o Austin C. Maxfield (farmer, Pittsfield) and S. Glady Hooper (Berwick, ME)

Charles W. of Barnstead m. Lillian D. **Foss** of Gilmanton 10/13/1898 in Tilton; H – 29, shoe cutter, b. Barnstead, s/o John R. Jenkins and Augusta H. Jenkins; W – 26, housekeeper, b. Gilmanton, d/o William J. Foss (farmer) and Jerusha Foss

Donald Warren of Barnstead m. Hilda Anne **Nichols** of Pittsfield 4/21/1946 in Pittsfield; H – 18, s/o John J. Jenkins and Marion S. Clapp; W – 22, d/o Ned A. Nichols and Grace E. Miller

Edgar of Barnstead m. Grace A. **Willey** of Barnstead 4/9/1891; H – 26, farmer, b. Barnstead, s/o Calvin (farmer, Barnstead) and Hannah M. (housekeeper, Barnstead); W – 22, teacher, b. Barnstead, d/o Horatio G. (farmer, Barnstead) and Mary A. (housekeeper, Barrington)

Edwin K. of Barnstead m. Eva J. **Fogg** of Barnstead 9/15/1897; H – 26, shoemaker, b. Barnstead, s/o G. W. Jenkins (farmer, Barnstead) and Victoria Clark (housework, Barnstead); W – 29, housekeeper, b. Belknap, d/o John F. Fogg and Jane H. Fogg

Ernest C. of Barnstead m. Bertha M. **Brown** of Pittsfield 2/16/1907 in Pittsfield; H – 18, morocco employee, b. Barnstead, s/o Joseph E. Jenkins (morocco employee, Barnstead) and Clara A. Carter (housewife, Loudon); W – 20, d/o Charlemagne Brown (shoemaker, Gilmanton) and Annie E. Brown (housewife)

Harry L. of Barnstead m. Ora M. **Tower** of Barnstead 11/30/1899; H – 25, butcher, b. Barnstead, s/o Charles F. Jenkins (farmer, Barnstead) and Mary Jenkins (housework, Barnstead); W – 24, housework, b. Boston, MA, d/o Mayhue Tower (carpenter, Boston, MA) and Minnie Tower (housewife, Boston, MA)

John J. of Barnstead m. M. Edith **Maxfield** of Barnstead 4/25/1898 in Gilmanton; H – 25, farmer, b. Barnstead, s/o John H. Jenkins (farmer, Barnstead) and Elvira R. Wilken (housewife, Ashburnham, MA); W – 19, music teacher, b. Lynn, MA, d/o H. Wheeler Maxfield (farmer, China, ME) and Harriett L. Mellen (housewife, Albion Vil., ME)

John J. m. Marion S. **Dahlquist** 5/11/1924; H – 51, s/o John H. Jenkins and Elvira Wilker; W – 28, d/o Frederick H. Clapp and Charlotte Sumners

Merton B. m. Bertha L. **Hillsgrove** 2/28/1931 in Pittsfield; H – 23, s/o Ernest C. Jenkins and Bertha Brown; W – 21, d/o Harry Pierce and Fannie French

Will A. of Barnstead m. Madge A. **Foss** of Barnstead 12/25/1889; H – 23, farmer, b. Barnstead, s/o John H. Jenkins (mechanic, Barnstead) and Elvira R. Jenkins (Ashburnham, MA); W – 27, teacher, b. Barnstead, d/o James L. Foss (farmer, Barnstead) and Eliza Foss (Barnstead)

JENNIS,
James S. of Ctr. Barnstead m. Joy A. **Mulcahy** of Ctr. Barnstead 2/18/1995 in Bow

JEWELL,
Carl A. of Barnstead m. Patricia L. **Elzea** of Barnstead 11/29/1985 in Greenland

Carl D. of Barnstead m. Anita J. **Doucette** of Kittery, ME 11/10/1983 in Greenland

JEWETT,
Mark David of Barnstead m. Cheryl Anne **Ashton** of Barnstead 8/19/1990 in Concord

JOHNSON,
David Gordon of NH m. Donna Jane **Palmer** of NH 8/19/1972 in Rye Beach; H - b. 4/29/1952 in NH, s/o Gordon Johnson (ME) and Carolyn Denison (ME); W - b. 11/28/1951 in NH, d/o Donald R. Palmer (NH) and Jane McGaw (MA)

John M. of Pittsfield m. Esther B. **Emerson** of Barnstead 7/14/1912 in Hooksett; H – 21, clerk, b. N. Derby, VT, s/o Michael Johnson (sec. foreman, Boston, MA) and Margaret Purtell (housewife, Canada); W – 18, domestic, b. Lynn, MA, d/o Andrew J. Emerson (fireman, Barnstead) and Isabelle Sullivan (housekeeper, Lynn, MA)

Peter A. of Pittsfield m. Susan E. **Morrissette** of Pittsfield 7/20/1983

Peter A. of Barnstead m. Crystal M. **McLeod** of Barnstead 8/27/1999

Peter Thoralf of Barnstead m. Sarah Margo **Matthewman** of MA 3/1/1969 in Goffstown; H - 27, b. MA, s/o Thoralf B. Johnson (Norway) and Lucy E. Norton (MA); W - 22, b. MA, d/o Rodger Matthewman (MA) and Alice Lund (MA)

Richard A. of Barnstead m. Rebecca J. **Elkins** of Barnstead 10/2/1982 in Concord

Wilbur A. m. Bertha J. **Parmenter** 6/30/1928 in Concord; H – 22, s/o Fred A. Johnson and Gladys E. Daniels; W – 22, d/o Will Parmenter and Clara Kingman

JOLLY,

Francis A., Jr. of Portsmouth m. Reta J. **MacPherson** of Barnstead 8/9/1963 in Chichester; H - 21, assem. elec., b. Stoddard, s/o Francis A. Jolly (NH) and Lettie V. Whitney (MA); W - 30, assem. elec., b. Barnstead, d/o Albert MacPherson (MA) and Ebha M. McDuffee (NH)

JONES,

Charles A. of Milton m. Nellie E. **Daniels** of Barnstead 6/7/1916 in Milton; H – 65, farmer, b. Milton, s/o George H. Jones and Lucy J. Varney; W – 40, housekeeper, b. Goffstown, d/o Louis Daniels and Adeline P. Gardner

Charles Henry of Alton m. Lois Marion **Straw** of Barnstead 11/19/1949; H – 33, carpenter, b. NH, s/o Albert W. Jones and Lillian S. Dale; W – 27, home, b. NH, d/o John H. Foss and Nina M. Higgins

Donald E. of Epsom m. Marguerite **Johnson** of Barnstead 10/18/1980 in Concord

JOY,

Alan D. of New Durham m. Nancy C. **Bondelvitch** of Barnstead 5/26/1973 in Swampscott, MA; H - b. 12/19/1954 in England, s/o Samuel O. Joy (NH) and Jean M. Norman (MA); W - b. 8/26/1953 in MA, d/o Stanley W. Bondelvitch (MA) and Dorothy Tierney (MA)

George E. m. Maud A. **Locke** 3/27/1937; H – 42, s/o Fred C. Joy and Mary F. Winkley; W – 22, d/o Sidney R. Locke and Mamie I. Hill

Kevin C. of Pittsfield m. Barbara M. **Gerlack** of Barnstead 2/24/1976; H - b. 12/17/1955 in NH, s/o Calvin C. Joy (NH) and Gladys Eloa Fifield (NH); W - b. 8/17/1958 in NH, d/o Henry C. Gerlack (VT) and Lorraine B. Berry (NH)

JUNK,

Kenneth W. of Iowa m. Annette L. **Latwesen** of Iowa 9/27/1999 in Rochester

JURSIK,

Robert F. of Ctr. Barnstead m. Lisa C. **Breton** of Concord 10/7/1995 in Concord

JUSSAUME,
Lucien B., Jr. of Barnstead m. Karen M. **Spaulding** of Barnstead
   4/17/1981
Lucien B., Jr. of Barnstead m. Peggy L. **Atwell** of Boscawen
   10/7/1989

KAIME,
Samuel F. of Barnstead m. Libbie E. **Smith** of Pittsfield 7/4/1900; H – 24, farmer, b. Barnstead, s/o J. F. Kaime (farmer, Barnstead) and Frances S. Kaime (Gilmanton); W – 28, housework, b. NS, d/o Stephen Smith (NS) and Amy Smith (NS)

KALLGREN,
James P. of Ctr. Barnstead m. Sally **Nelson** of Ctr. Barnstead
   6/25/1988

KANIA,
Stanley of Ctr. Barnstead m. Lila May **Sprague** of Ctr. Barnstead 6/8/1973 in Alton; H - b. 5/24/1918 in NJ, s/o Frank Kania (Poland) and Eleanor Zawistowski (Poland); W - b. 4/8/1926 in MA, d/o Robert A. Compston (Australia) and Georgina M. Christian (NS)

KARASEK,
Walter of Ctr. Barnstead m. Connie M. **Nadeau** of Ctr. Barnstead
   10/22/1988 in Concord

KASHULINES,
David Martin of Barnstead m. Dianna **Whitney** of Barnstead
   2/23/1992 in Hopkinton

KEATING,
Brian R. of Pittsfield m. Sylvia E. **Kimball** of Barnstead 11/25/1967 in Chichester; H - 21, salesman, b. NH, s/o Peter A. Keating (NH) and Elizabeth S. Gilmore (NH); W - 20, clerk, b. NH, d/o Edward C. Kimball (NH) and Reta B. Canfield (NH)
James Ralph of Barnstead m. Cynthia L. **Brewster** of Barnstead
   4/25/1992 in Wolfeboro

KEEFE,

Thomas C. of Ctr. Barnstead m. Helen L. **Engelsen** of MA 12/28/1968 in Ctr. Barnstead; H - 64, b. MA, s/o Thomas M. Keefe (MA) and Ellen Carroll (MA); W - 55, b. MA, d/o Olaf Engelsen (Norway) and Hilda M. Eckberg (Norway)

Thomas C., Jr. of Barnstead m. Monica M. **Vien** of Pittsfield 2/20/1965 in Pittsfield; H - 25, US Navy, b. W. Roxbury, MA, s/o Thomas C. Keefe (MA) and Margaret L. Hughes (MA); W - 18, at home, b. Germany, d/o Wilfred R. Vien and Emma Knauz (Hungary)

William J., Jr. of MA m. Loretta **Trudeau** of MA 2/15/1996

KEENE,

Kevin M. of Barnstead m. Katrina M. **Miller** of Barnstead 2/13/1984

Marshall G. of Barnstead m. Leone M. **Perkins** of Barnstead 10/13/1951 in Pittsfield; H – 23, US Army, b. MA, s/o Norman Keene (ME) and Eva Grenier (NH); W – 20, artistic web, b. NH, d/o David M. Perkins (NH) and Dora Foss (NH)

Richard M. of Livingston Manor, NY m. Roberta **Cotton** of Barnstead 3/4/1950; H – 18, construction, b. MA, s/o Norman Keene (NY) and Eva R. Grenier (NY); W – 19, quiller, b. MA, d/o Joseph H. Cotton (NH) and Ruth E. Hallett (NH)

Richard M. of Barnstead m. Martha T. **Yelle** of Barnstead 6/12/1992

KELLER,

Robert D. of Ctr. Barnstead m. Karen F. **Six** of Ctr. Barnstead 6/4/1996

Roger F. of Manchester m. Eileen Lydia **Emerson** of Barnstead 12/26/1921 in Gilmanton; H – 26, b. Manchester, s/o John H. Keller and Helma O. Anderson; W – 19, b. Barnstead, d/o Ansel Emerson and Alice J. Page

KELLEY,

Charles H. m. Bessie O. **Gray** 11/23/1924; H – 23, s/o Charles H. Kelley and Mary H. Sand; W – 17, d/o Albert B. Gray and Bessie O. Brown

David J. of Ctr. Barnstead m. Kathy R. **Deboer** of Ctr. Barnstead 9/6/1997

Edward Rodney of Barnstead m. Ilse Madeline **Frey** of Barnstead 6/18/1948; H – 18, lumberman, b. Barnstead, s/o Charles H.

Kelley and Bessie O. Gray; W – 18, shoeworker, b. New York City, d/o Leo Frey and Josephine Dopfer

Joseph of Barnstead m. Myra **Colburn** of Dorchester 6/9/1889 in Gilford; H – 29, shoemaker, b. Morie, NY, s/o Joel Kelley (farmer, Fort Car'ton) and Mary Leonard; W – 23, shoe stitcher, b. Dorchester, d/o Samuel Colburn and Mary Colburn (Dorchester)

Michael Scott of Ctr. Barnstead m. Hollie Helene **Eldridge** of Ctr. Barnstead 8/17/1996 in Gilford

Ray I. of Ctr. Barnstead m. Patricia **Rogers** of Ctr. Barnstead 8/16/1997

Richard A. of Barnstead m. Elizabeth **Whitehouse** of Barnstead 6/24/1973 in Gilmanton I.W.; H - b. 9/7/1951 in MA, s/o Edward R. Kelley (NH) and Ilse M. Frey (NY); W - b. 6/6/1955 in NH, d/o Richard Whitehouse (NH) and Mary E. Clark (MA)

KELLY,

Robert Anthony of Ctr. Barnstead m. Ruth Elizabeth **Chase** of So. Dartmouth, MA 5/29/1992 in Wolfeboro

Robert Anthony of Barnstead m. Maureen Glenda **Collum** of Barnstead 6/26/1993

KENDALL,

Richard A., Jr. of VT m. Dawn Marie **Holbrook** of VT 8/8/1993

KENISCH [see Kuirsch, Knirsch],

Konard of Barnstead m. Emma **Penka** of Austria 3/13/1921; H – 38, b. Austria, s/o Joseph Kenisch and Alvis Hagen; W – 31, b. Austria, d/o Fannie Penka and Marie Apple

KENISON,

Fred R. of Barnstead m. Gladys W. **Brady** of Barnstead 11/22/1914 in Pittsfield; H – 19, farmer, b. Sweden; W – 16, domestic, b. Barnstead, d/o John F. Brady (Lawrence, MA) and Alice E. Davis (Lynn, MA)

Herbert C. of Barnstead m. Blanche C. **Tuttle** of Barnstead 6/6/1896 in Alton; H – 21, farmer, b. Barnstead, s/o Owen M. Kenison (wheelwright, Barnstead) and Annie L. Kenison (housewife, Barnstead); W – 21, b. Barnstead, d/o Daniel E.

Tuttle (farmer, Barnstead) and Achsah K. Tuttle (housewife, Barnstead)

Terry L. of Barnstead m. Dale D. **Twitchell** of Pittsfield 7/8/1983 in New Durham

KENNEALLY,

Richard H. of Ctr. Barnstead m. Patricia M. **Cronan** of Chichester 12/30/1988 in Chichester

KENNEDY,

Gerald E. of Ctr. Barnstead m. Linda J. **Corson** of Ctr. Barnstead 5/28/1988 in Pittsfield

Thomas Francis, Jr. of Ctr. Barnstead m. Nancy Elizabeth **Boyd** of Pittsfield 5/21/1977 in Pittsfield; H - b. 11/18/1946 in MA, s/o Thomas F. Kennedy, Sr. (MA) and Rita M. Barron (MA); W - b. 3/33/1953 (sic) in NH, d/o Ogden Boyd, Jr. (NH) and Rowena Lank (RI)

KENNEY,

John L. of Loudon m. Marjorie L. **Brown** of Barnstead 6/14/1957; H - 20, mechanic, b. NH, s/o Charles L. Kenney (NH) and Viola I. Bailey (NH); W - 18, at home, b. NH, d/o John P. Brown (NH) and Mabel L. Griffin (NH)

KESSLER,

Marc J. of Cambridge, MA m. Susan E. **Osgood** of Cambridge, MA 10/8/1983

KIDDER,

Dana James of Barnstead m. Kristine Lynn **Hoadley** of Epsom 9/7/1996 in Epsom

James W. of Barnstead m. Patricia A. **Ford** of Pittsfield 4/27/1973 in Gilmanton I.W.; H - b. 10/14/1953 in NH, s/o Wilbur A. Kidder (NH) and Rachel Osborne (NH); W - b. 2/22/1954 in NH, d/o Myrl Ford (NH) and Florence Fox (NH)

Kenneth C. of Ctr. Barnstead m. Elva L. **Barton** of Pittsfield 7/30/1954 in Claremont; H - 20, clerk, b. NH, s/o Harold E. Kidder (NH) and Bernice E. Carswell (NH); W - 18, office, b. NH, d/o Clifford H. Barton (NH) and Shirley E. Fischer (NH)

Kenneth C. of Barnstead m. Elizabeth S. **Heath** of Pittsfield 5/30/1959 in Chichester; H - 25, s/o Harold E. Kidder and Bernice E. Caswell; W - 24, d/o John W. Small and Florence A. Arlin

Lloyd D. m. Abbie L. **Carson** 12/9/1941 in Chichester; H – 20, s/o Harold E. Kidder and Bernice E. Caswell; W – 19, d/o David L. Carson and Iva Z. Towle

Wilbur A. of Barnstead m. Rachel E. **Osborn** of Loudon 6/28/1952 in Pittsfield; H – 26, mechanic, b. NH, s/o Harold E. Kidder (NH) and Bernice E. Carswell (NH); W – 22, teacher, b. NH, d/o John F. Osborn (NH) and Rena A. Payne (NH)

KILEY,
Michael J. of Barnstead m. Rita J. **Doucette** of Pittsfield 7/28/1979 in Pittsfield

KIMBALL,
Edward C., II of Barnstead m. Debora S. **Daigle** of Gilmanton 11/6/1976 in Gilmanton; H - b. 10/19/1951 in NH, s/o Edward C. Kimball (NH) and Rita Canfield (NH); W - b. 5/23/1957 in MA, d/o Leo J. Daigle (MA) and Virginia M. Belcaster (MA)

Edward C., II of Barnstead m. Karen A. **Colby** of Loudon 11/4/1983 in Loudon

Edward C., II of Barnstead m. Lori E. **Newell** of Barnstead 5/10/1986 in Bradford

Edwin C. of Epsom m. Reta B. **Canfield** of Barnstead 11/22/1945; H – 25, s/o Myron B. Kimball and Lizzie E. Clark; W – 27, d/o Archie M. Canfield and Clara D. Mears

Lee L. of Barnstead m. Carrie L. **Riggle** of PA 6/24/1999 in Epping

Lloyd Elwin m. Ruth Helen **Yeaton** 7/1/1939 in Chichester; H – 22, s/o Myron B. Kimball and Lizzie E. Clark; W – 20, d/o William Yeaton and Ethel G. Gray

Michael Anthony of Derry m. Sheryl Ann **Fairburn** of Ctr. Barnstead 6/3/1990 in Alton

KING,
Robert C. m. Charlotte M. **Ball** 12/15/1934 in Colebrook; H – 25, s/o John King and Gladys Long; W – 24, d/o Grover C. Ball and Lillian M. Ball

Wayne J. of Barnstead m. Michaelene M. **Densmore** of Barnstead 8/2/1986 in Manchester

KINGSTON,
David J. of Manchester m. Heather Sue **McMahon** of Barnstead 9/4/1993 in Hooksett

KIRKLAND,
Frank L. of Roslindale, MA m. Mary E. **Quirk** of Billerica, MA 7/16/1988

KISSANE,
Robert of Oakland, CA m. Pamela J. **Mitchell** of Oakland, CA 6/28/1986

KNIGHT,
Alan L. of Strafford m. Beatrice E. **Pitman** of Barnstead 5/6/1951 in Strafford; H – 21, US Air Force, b. NH, s/o John M. Knight (NH) and Alberta F. Wheet (VT); W – 22, shoe worker, b. NH, d/o Fred T. Pitman (NH) and Harriet M. Lawrence (MA)

Burton W., II of Ctr. Barnstead m. Harriet Anne **Soriano** of Ctr. Barnstead 8/22/1991 in Concord

Jeffrey S. of Barnstead m. Heidi R. **Hussey** of Barnstead 10/3/1998 in Gilford

KNIRSCH [see Kenisch, Kuirsch],
Earl Frederick m. Mary Addie **Roberts** 11/30/1930; H – 21, s/o Conard Knirsch and Mathilda Pelzl; W – 20, d/o Fred W. Roberts and Jennie H. Foss

Henry m. Velma **Keniston** 6/28/1936; H – 18, s/o Conrad Knirsch and Matilda Belgel; W – 19, d/o Charles Keniston and Grace E. Watson

Reinhold B. of Barnstead m. Lorraine R. **Finnegan** of Pittsfield 1/21/1951 in Pittsfield; H – 25, weaver, b. NH, s/o Konrad Knirsch (Austria) and Emma Penka (Austria); W – 23, unemployed, b. NY, d/o James Finnegan (NY) and Ruth Hough (NY)

Robert K. of Barnstead m. Joanne M. **Senior** of Gilmanton I.W. 4/6/1974 in Gilmanton I.W.; H - b. 6/19/1953 in NH, s/o

Reinhold Knirsch (NH) and Lorraine Finnegan (NY); W - b. 6/9/1954 in NH, d/o Walter Senior (NH) and Eileen Luden (NY)

KNOWLES,
Russell of Barnstead m. Agnes B. **Thompson** of Barnstead 8/30/1913; H – 20, farmer, b. Nashua, s/o William H. Hall and Eugenia F. Blood (Nashua); W – 23, domestic, b. Barnstead, d/o Silas L. Thompson (painter, Gilmanton) and Josephine Babb (housewife, Barnstead)

KNOWLTON,
David Lee of Barnstead m. Lisa M. **Transue** of Barnstead 11/19/1983

KNOX,
Granville Shaw of Newington m. Shirley Johnson **Vogt** of Barnstead 10/6/1973 in Newington; H - b. 10/10/1913 in NH, s/o James H. Knox (NH) and Paulena A. Shaw (MA); W - b. 6/22/1922 in MA, d/o Clarence E. Johnson (NH) and Natalie E. Adams (NH)

KOEHLER,
Alford R. of Ctr. Barnstead m. Paula S. **Ingle** of Ctr. Barnstead 8/4/2000

KRAMER,
Daniel of Barnstead m. Mary Ellen **O'Brien** of Amherst 8/9/1986 in New Boston

KRAUSE,
George R. of Barnstead m. Emelyn F. **Ayer** of Sherburne, NY 2/28/1945 in Keene; H – 26, s/o George R. Krause and Catherine Sullivan; W – 24, d/o Andrew J. Ayer and Mary W. Roundy

George R., II of Barnstead m. Roxann M. **Tasker** of Barnstead 8/12/1978; H - b. 2/24/1951 in NH, s/o G. Russell Krause (NJ) and Emelyn A. Ayer (NH); W - b. 11/14/1953 in NH, d/o Roscoe W. Tasker (NH) and Janet A. Tuttle (NH)

KRAUSS,
Richard Russell of Barnstead m. Michelle C. **Waldron** of Barnstead 10/4/1971 in Ctr. Barnstead; H - b. 11/23/1945 in NJ, s/o George Krauss (IL) and Ruth E. Felts (VA); W - b. 12/2/1946 in NY, d/o Robert D. Waldron (PA) and Eileen Oberrieth (NY)

KRIETE,
Bill A. of Ctr. Barnstead m. Sharon B. **Prince** of Ctr. Barnstead 10/14/2000 in Strafford

KUIRSCH [see Kenisch, Knirsch],
Konrad of Barnstead m. Mathilda **Belyel** of Barnstead 3/23/1909; H – 26, weaver, b. Moravia, Austria, s/o Johann Kuirsch (weaver, Triebendorf, Austria) and Aloisia Heger (housewife, Triebendorf, Austria); W – 22, winder, b. Moravia, Austria, d/o Konrad Belyel (laborer, Pettersdorf, Austria) and Thresia Heger (housewife, Pettersdorf, Austria)

KYLLONEN,
Robert Royce of Ctr. Barnstead m. Kimberly Ann **Marchio** of Ctr. Barnstead 10/8/1994 in Alton

LABRECQUE,
David A. of Barnstead m. Wendy A. **Potter** of Barnstead 5/23/1981
Dennis J. of Barnstead m. Terry L. **Marsh** of Barnstead 9/21/1985 in Pembroke
Dennis Joseph of Ctr. Barnstead m. Dorothy Ann **Smith** of Laconia 10/10/1976; H - b. 5/4/1956 in NH, s/o Albert R. LaBrecque (NH) and Pauline M. Salice (NH); W - b. 8/10/1956 in CT, d/o Thomas J. Smith and Dorothy V. Greene (NH)
Donald L. of Barnstead m. Carolyn A. **Curley** of Barnstead 11/6/1976; H - b. 1/7/1954 in NH, s/o Albert R. LaBrecque (NH) and Pauline M. Salice (NH); W - b. 7/16/1957 in FL, d/o Walter W. Curley (MA) and Marie T. Sullivan (MA)
Roland V. of Barnstead m. Alice M. **Pitman** of Barnstead 2/8/1952; H – 26, leather worker, b. NH, s/o Arthur Z. LaBrecque (Canada) and Rosina Desmarais (Canada); W – 19, home, b. NH, d/o Fred L. Pitman (NH) and Harriet Lawrence (NH)
Roland V., Jr. of Ctr. Barnstead m. Deborah J. **Colpitt** of Farmington 11/19/1977; H - b. 8/24/1957 in NH, s/o Roland

LaBrecque (NH) and Alice Pitman (NH); W - b. 11/27/1954 in CO, d/o Robert M. Colpitt (NJ) and Vivian Mae Weston (ME)

LADD,
Eugene W., Jr. of Pittsfield m. Robyn **Keating** of Barnstead 11/15/1997 in Franklin

LAGRANGE,
Richard A. of Barnstead m. Barbara L. **Bryant** of Barnstead 4/27/1999

LALLIER,
Christopher M. of Ctr. Barnstead m. Tracey J. **VanBuskirk** of Ctr. Barnstead 10/17/1998 in Meredith
Thornton E., Jr. of Belmont, MA m. Karen **Theopold** of Salt Lake City, UT 6/30/1962; H - 30, lawyer, b. MA, s/o Thornton E. Lallier (NY) and Katherine E. Egan (MA); W - 26, teacher, b. MA, d/o Philip H. Theopold (MN) and Harriet E. Royce (MA)

LAMARRE,
Ryan David of Ctr. Barnstead m. Lisa J. **Beauchesne** of Ctr. Barnstead 8/31/1997 in Auburn

LAMB,
Robert Alan of E. Northport, NY m. Alison Town **Conrad** of Barnstead 6/6/1970; H - b. 11/9/1950 in ME, s/o Elliot E. Lamb (ME) and Martha Kenoyer (IA); W - b. 11/5/1950 in NY, d/o Harold Conrad, Jr. (PA) and Helena Davis (MA)

LAMERE,
Robert A. of Ctr. Barnstead m. Denise A. **Warren** of Ctr. Barnstead 6/27/1998 in Canterbury

LANCASTER,
David H. of Normal, IL m. Margaret A. **Johnson** of Normal, IL 8/7/1982

LANE,
Alan M. of Epsom m. Amy M. **Mackinnon** of Barnstead 2/6/1988

Alan Marshall of Barnstead m. Cynthia L. **Drouin** of Barnstead 9/29/1984 in Pittsfield

Henry C. of Barnstead m. Muriel A. **Osgood** of Woodstock, VT 1/8/1982 in Ctr. Barnstead

Stacy C. of Ctr. Barnstead m. Marjorie G. **Byers** of Ctr. Barnstead 2/25/1989

LANG,

Harry B. of Alton m. Ada **Powell** of Barnstead 5/2/1922; H – 43, b. Alton, s/o Alonzo B. Lang and Mary A. Stevens; W – 46, b. Pittsfield, d/o Sylvester Powell and Ada Munrey

LANGENDORFER,

Dwight P. of Holderness m. Linda L. **Blaisdell** of Barnstead 10/8/1983 in Holderness

LANGEVIN,

Edward m. Mildred **Foss** 3/8/1936 in Concord; H – 24, s/o Peter Langevin and Alphonsine Frenette; W – 21, d/o William Foss and Grace Drake

LANK,

Clinton L. of Gilmanton m. Carolyn R. **Locke** of Barnstead 10/16/1954 in Chichester; H - 23, lineman, b. RI, s/o Clinton L. Lank (Canada) and Ruth O. Butman (RI); W - 18, secretary, b. NH, d/o Elias W. Locke (NH) and Violet M. Gray (NH)

Clinton L. of Ctr. Barnstead m. Susan M. **Desjardins** of Ctr. Barnstead 12/22/1980 in Concord

Howard John of Barnstead m. Hazel Isabelle **Parker** of Gilmanton 2/28/1947; H – 20, plumbing, b. Providence, RI, s/o Clinton L. Lank and Ruth O. Butman; W – 19, home, b. Detroit, MI, d/o Leon D. Parker and Bella MacLeod

Howard Robert of Ctr. Barnstead m. Duska Joy **Murphy** of Pittsfield 4/27/1974 in Pittsfield; H - b. 10/16/1950 in NH, s/o Howard J. Lank (RI) and Hazel Parker (VT); W - b. 1/14/1957 in ME, d/o William A. Murphy (ME) and Anna M. Green (Canada)

Richard Royal of Barnstead m. Patricia Evelyn **Kenneally** of Pittsfield 7/2/1955 in Pittsfield; H - 20, lineman, b. NH, s/o Clinton L. Lank (Canada) and Ruth O. Lank (RI); W - 18, at home, b. NH, d/o Thomas J. Kenneally (Ireland) and Edith F. Medeiros (MA)

LAPOINTE,
Leopold G. m. Dorothy G. **Welch** 2/10/1935; H – 19, s/o Oliver Lapointe and Eva Michel; W – 23, d/o Frank W. Welch and Sadie E. Morrison

LAPRISE,
Herman Gerard m. Bernice E. **Jones** 5/13/1939 in Pittsfield; H – 21, s/o Philip Laprise and Juliette Beaudoin; W – 19, d/o Ernest E. Jones and Eva G. Smith

LARKIN,
John W. of Barnstead m. Kathleen M. **Sullivan** of MA 9/19/1998 in Wolfeboro

LARKINS,
Eric D. of Concord m. Debora L. **Dooley** of Ctr. Barnstead 6/26/1999 in Concord

LAROSE,
Christopher Richard of Ctr. Barnstead m. Diane Muriel **Demers** of Manchester 10/18/1996 in Manchester

LARSON,
Frederick Albert of Mansfield, MA m. Edith May **Corson** of Barnstead 5/4/1956 in Portsmouth; H - 22, Navy, b. RI, s/o Frederick N. Larson (RI) and Gertrude Capron (MA); W – 19, Navy, b. NH, d/o Jessie Corson (NH) and Barbara McKay (ME)

LAUDANI,
Mark of Ctr. Barnstead m. Shelby L. **Barrett** of Ctr. Barnstead 1/10/1999

LAVENTURE,
Gerard C. R. of Barnstead m. Irene **Dedascalou** of Barnstead 12/7/1996 in Concord

LAVOIE,
Ronald Wayne, Jr. of Ctr. Barnstead m. Donna Marie **Nassar** of Ctr. Barnstead 5/22/1992 in Manchester

LAWRENCE,
Christopher C. of Chichester m. Mary Elizabeth **Leonard** of Barnstead 1/19/1946 in Chichester; H – 22, s/o Irving I. Lawrence and Irene Perry; W – 26, d/o Chester Leonard and Pauline Ofstad

LEACH,
Harry L. of Barnstead m. Adelaide E. **Jenkins** of Barnstead 2/2/1901; H – 21, bookkeeper, b. Bucksport, ME, s/o Hudson Leach and Lizzie Leach; W – 18, housekeeper, b. Barnstead, d/o George W. Jenkins (farmer) and Victoria Jenkins (housewife, Barnstead)

LEE,
Michael R. of Pittsfield m. Roberta E. **Aversa** of Pittsfield 10/25/1975; H - b. 12/1/1957 in NH, s/o Jolen J. Lee (NH) and Marie McIntosh (NH); W - b. 6/4/1957 in FL, d/o Fred A. Aversa (NY) and Janet I. Walter (NY)

LENNON,
Murtha James of Barnstead m. Mildred Louise **Whittey** of Barnstead 11/17/1947; H – 48, retired, b. New York City, s/o Murtha Lennon and Mary Cusick; W – 38, home, b. New York City, d/o Arthur J. Whittey and Henrietta Quandt
Thomas J. of Nevada m. Amie F. **Blair** of Barnstead 5/24/1998 in Manchester

LESAGE,
Steven J. of Barnstead m. Stephanie C. **Tolken** of Barnstead 10/17/1998 in Epsom

LEVASSEUR,
Leo Joseph of Ctr. Barnstead m. Diana Glanton **Calder** of Ctr. Barnstead 12/22/1991

LEWIS,
Gregg M. of Barnstead m. Karen L. **Schacht** of Barnstead 8/29/1987 in Jackson
Richard A. of Barnstead m. Carol L. **Deveau** of Barnstead 12/31/1999

LEYLAND,
Joseph of Barnstead m. Carrie M. **Edgerly** of Gilmanton 3/30/1891 in Gilmanton; H – 28, shoemaker, b. England, s/o John (England) and Elizabeth (England); W – 28, teacher, b. Gilmanton, d/o Asa T. and Hannah T.

LICHTY,
John of Barnstead m. Bonnie R. **White** of Barnstead 4/8/1978 in Laconia; H - b. 10/28/1958 in MA, s/o John E. Lichty (IA) and Lois Bellows (RI); W - b. 1/29/1959 in MA, d/o James W. White (MA) and Nancy C. Allan (MA)

LINDAHL,
Arthur E. of Auburn, MA m. Mary C. **Demers** of Auburn, MA 10/21/1988

LINDBERG,
Bertile A. m. Mildred A. **Foss** 9/20/1933 in Center Harbor; H – 26, s/o Charles A. Lindberg and Emma Johnson; W – 19, d/o William B. Foss and Grace B. Drake

LIONSTONE,
Harry Emanuel of Chichester m. Angelina May **Boudrieau** of Barnstead 9/23/1969 in Chichester; H - 74, b. Sweden, s/o Alfred A. Lionstone (Sweden); W - 66, b. MA, d/o Thomas A. Coderre (Canada) and Rosanna Record (MA)

LITTLE,
Harry E. m. Della S. **Jeffers** 10/31/1934 in Pittsfield; H – 62, s/o Henry A. Little and Mary A. Ford; W – 63, d/o Ira Swain and Alma Glazier

LITTLEFIELD,

Abraham D. m. Marguerite A. **Deschanbault** 7/10/1935; H – 29, s/o William H. Littlefield and Jessie E. Andrews; W – 21, d/o Zetherim Deschanbault and Lea Leblanc

Chester W. of Barnstead m. Margaret **Williams** of Strafford 3/18/1916; H – 23, morocco, b. Woburn, MA, s/o Warren Littlefield and Catherine O'Brian; W – 20, b. New York, NY, d/o Fred J. Williams and Maggie Schultinger

Chester Warren of Barnstead m. Jennie L. **Glidden** of Alton 7/25/1920; H – 27, b. Woburn, MA, s/o Warren Littlefield and Katherine O'Brien; W – 18, b. Alton, d/o Earl Glidden and Flora Lamper

Stilson W. of Barnstead m. Agnes L. **Holmes** of Barnstead 7/19/1918 in Pittsfield; H – 22, b. Woburn, MA, s/o Warner Littlefield and Catherine O'Brien; W – 21, d/o Frank J. Holmes and Hattie McKinley

Wilmer L. m. Cyrena P. **Abbott** 6/20/1936 in Moultonville; H – 24, s/o George F. Littlefield and Susie E. Lyon; W – 32, d/o Arthur C. Paige and Mary A. Remick

LIVINGSTONE,

William E. m. Alice **Walker** 9/19/1934 in Epsom; H – 55, s/o Everett W. Livingstone and Annie M. Trow; W – 32, d/o Christopher Walker and Annie Barnes

LIZOTTE,

Thomas Joseph of Ctr. Barnstead m. Patricia Joan **Dodier** of Ctr. Barnstead 6/23/1990 in Laconia

LOCKE,

Bruce Paul of Barnstead m. Stacie Ann **Locke** of Barnstead 3/16/1996 in Chichester

Clayton W. of Ctr. Barnstead m. Mary E. **Blake** of Pittsfield 4/29/1972 in Concord; H - b. 12/1/1952 in NH, s/o Ernest E. Locke (NH) and Rachel Belville (MA); W - b. 4/9/1953 in NH, d/o Roland E. Blake (NH) and Bernice G. Connelly (Canada)

Dennis M. of Barnstead m. Bonnie S. **Durrell** of Pittsfield 9/11/1965 in Chichester; H - 17, helper, b. Concord, s/o Wallace W. Locke (NH) and Winifred M. Pollard (NH); W - 16, student, b.

Manchester, d/o Lynnwood A. Durrell (NH) and Margaret E. Thompson (NH)

E. Wesley m. Violet **Gray** 12/1/1934 in Manchester; H – 42, s/o E. Wesley Locke and Carrie Come; W – 25, d/o Albert B. Gray and Bessie Brown

Elias E. of Barnstead m. Susan M. **Danis** of Pittsfield 10/26/1963 in Pittsfield; H - 18, laborer, b. Portsmouth, s/o Wallace W. Locke (Barnstead) and Winifred M. Pollard (Marlow); W - 17, student, b. Manchester, d/o Kenneth M. Danis (Pittsfield) and Annette Cyr (Allenstown)

Ernest E. of Barnstead m. Brenda L. **Pratt** of Concord 9/30/1967 in Concord; H - 19, app. electrician, b. NH, s/o Ernest E. Locke, Sr. (NH) and Rachel Y. Belville (MA); W - 15, at home, b. NH, d/o Russell D. Pratt (NH) and Verna L. Tyrrell (NH)

Ernest E., Jr. of Barnstead m. Carol **Pletsch** of Alton 9/6/1975; H - b. 8/23/1948 in NH, s/o Ernest E. Locke, Sr. (NH) and Rachel Y. Bellidle (MA); W - b. 3/10/1950 in MA, d/o Alfred Pletsch (MA) and Ruth Scannell (MA)

Ernest Eugene of Barnstead m. Rachel Yvonne **Belville** of Medford, MA 10/10/1947; H – 23, lineman, b. Barnstead, s/o E. Wesley Locke and Elsie M. Garrick; W – 21, fancy packer, b. Sharron, MA, d/o Fred H. Belville and Flora A. Hannah

Frank A. of Barnstead m. Annie L. **Dixon** of Lebanon, ME 8/16/1893 in Farmington; H – 22, shoemaker, b. Barnstead, s/o William H. Locke (shoemaker, New Durham) and Lizzie S. Pickering (housewife, Barnstead); W – 22, b. Lebanon, ME, d/o Stephen Dixon and Alice

G. Malcolm m. Elva P. **Holland** 4/5/1931 in Durham; H – 26, s/o George E. Locke and Mabel Kelly; W – 25, d/o John E. Holland and Lottie M. Wilbury

George E. of Barnstead m. Mabel F. **Kelley** of Gilmanton 9/16/1897 in Alton; H – 24, farmer, b. Barnstead, s/o James Lock (farmer, Barnstead) and Mary E. Nutter (housewife, Roxbury, MA); W – 20, teacher, b. Gilmanton, d/o George F. Kelley (farmer, Gilmanton) and Francis H. Kelley (Gilmanton)

Harvey R., Jr. of Ctr. Barnstead m. Katherine M. **Corcoran** of Ctr. Barnstead 3/16/1980 in Ctr. Barnstead

Harvey R., Jr. of Barnstead m. Katherine M. M. **Corcoran** of Dover 3/15/1987 in Dover

Harvey Ray, Jr. of Ctr. Barnstead m. Pauline Estelle **Goudreau** of Manchester 9/1/1973 in Manchester; H - b. 5/8/1946 in NH, s/o

Harvey Locke, Sr. (NH) and Althea Perkins (NH); W - b. 2/16/1950 in NH, d/o Joseph Goudreau (NH) and Dora Prud'homme (NH)

Harvey Roy m. Althea Edna **Perkins** 2/5/1941; H – 18, s/o Elias W. Locke and Elsie Garrick; W – 17, d/o David M. Perkins and Dora Foss

James N. of Barnstead m. Natalie J. **Price** of Gilmanton 11/14/1959 in Gilmanton; H - 21, s/o Kent D. Locke and Margaret Johnston; W - 20, d/o W. Richard Price, Sr. and Pauline M. Richard

James N., II of Barnstead m. Tary L. **Deinhardt** of Epsom 6/6/1982 in Gilmanton

John M. of Barnstead m. Evelyn M. **Tasker** of Strafford 12/10/1950 in Chichester; H – 19, mason, b. NH, s/o C. Malcolm Locke (NH) and Elva P. Holland (NH); W – 20, housekeeper, b. NH, d/o Harold F. Tasker (NH) and Mary L. Wheeler (NH)

John M. of Barnstead m. Frances I. **Riel** of Barnstead 4/27/1984 in Chichester

John W. of Barnstead m. Maud P. **Green** of Pittsfield 5/12/1894 in Pittsfield; H – 18, shoemaker, b. Barnstead, s/o William H. Locke (shoemaker, New Durham) and Lizzie S. Locke (Barnstead); W – 18, b. Pittsfield, d/o Sherburn Green (farmer) and Celia Proctor (Barnstead)

Kent D. m. Margaret **Johnston** 4/9/1933 in Alton; H – 23, s/o George E. Locke and Mabel Kelly; W – 22, d/o John R. Johnston and Theresa Barnes

Kent D., Jr. m. Jean A. **Powers** 9/27/1958 in Farmington

Kerry of Barnstead m. Wendy **Paine** of Alton 12/27/1980 in Chichester

Nathan J. of Barnstead m. Nancy W. **Childress** of Pittsfield 9/8/1981

Nathan J. of Ctr. Barnstead m. Theresa A. **Webber** of Ctr. Barnstead 6/10/2000

Percival W. m. Ruth **Knirsch** 5/19/1935; H – 21, s/o Walter M. Locke and Effie Bryant; W – 16, d/o Konrad Knirsch and Mathilda Pelglo

Richard M. of Barnstead m. Carol N. **Smith** of Strafford 6/21/1975 in Strafford; H - b. 7/20/1952 in NH, s/o John M. Locke (NH) and Evelyn M. Tasker (NH); W - b. 7/9/1953 in NY, d/o Spencer C. Smith (NY) and Dorothy Duffield (NY)

Thomas G. of Barnstead m. Joanne D. **Meunier** of Great Neck, NY 10/15/1966; H - 26, teacher, b. Wolfeboro, s/o Kent D. Locke (NH) and Margaret Johnston (MA); W - 19, b. Mineola, NY, d/o Charles A. Meunier (CT) and Margaret E. Nangle (PA)

Wayland B. of Barnstead m. Bertha F. **Emerson** of Barnstead 2/3/1905 in Alton; H – 25, farmer, b. Barnstead, s/o William H. Locke (farmer, Barnstead) and Lizzie Pickering (housewife, Barnstead); W – 23, housework, b. Barnstead, d/o George H. Emerson (farmer, Barnstead) and Mary E. Pickering (housewife, Barnstead)

Wesley E. m. Mary E. **Garland** 8/26/1939; H – 25, s/o E. Wesley Locke and Elsie May Gerrish; W – 19, d/o Wilbur J. Garland and Hattie M. Cofran

LOPORCARO,
Joseph A., Jr. of Ctr. Barnstead m. Terri L. **Sullivan** of Ctr. Barnstead 7/5/1997

LOTHRIDGE,
Brian Lee of Ctr. Barnstead m. Jessica Lynn **Dennett** of Springvale, ME 8/15/1992 in Gilford

LOUGEE,
Arnold L. m. Nellie M. **Edmunds** 12/27/1927 in Pittsfield; H – 20, s/o Leslie Lougee and Emma J. Whitehouse; W – 17, d/o Charles Edmunds and Abbie Rogers

Leslie J. of Barnstead m. Emma J. **Whitehouse** of Laconia 5/23/1894 in Laconia; H – 27, farmer, b. Barnstead, s/o David Lougee and Betsy Lougee (Alton); W – 22, housekeeper, b. Canada, d/o Charles Whitehouse (stone mason, Canada) and Lucy J. Whitehouse (Troy, VT)

Richard William of W. Lebanon m. Carrie Lynn **Bickford** of Barnstead 5/22/1993 in Pittsfield

LOUIS,
Francois of Dallas, TX m. Sandra Rene **Skelton** of Dallas, TX 6/7/1980

LYONS,
Thomas F. of Ctr. Barnstead m. Karen L. **Cloonen** of Ctr. Barnstead 9/6/1997

MACDONALD,
Albert Edward m. Lena **Whiting** 6/1/1940 in Pittsfield; H – 30, s/o Frederick MacDonald and Jennie Scott; W – 55, d/o Joseph St. Pierre and Adell Rennie

John L., II of Barnstead m. Linda M. **Greenwood** of Barnstead 6/29/1985 in Manchester

MACKNIGHT,
Steven R. of Orange, MA m. Barbara S. **Hinds** of Orange, MA 2/25/1984 in Ctr. Barnstead

MACPHERSON,
Albert of Boston, MA m. Edna May **McDuffee** 7/13/1920 in Pittsfield; H – 21, b. Roxbury, MA, s/o Albert Macpherson and Kate McLean; W – 24, b. Barnstead, d/o David Leroy McDuffee and Mary Emma Besse

MAGOON,
Kevin C. of Barnstead m. Judith Ann **Fox** of Barnstead 10/16/1993 in Epsom

MALONEY,
Michael Frederick of Ctr. Barnstead m. Diane Marie **Lennon** of Ctr. Barnstead 8/1/1992

MALVEY,
Peter James of Concord m. Susan Helene **Patterson** of Barnstead 8/3/1991 in Concord

MANCINI,
David E. of Barnstead m. Lori J. **Irmick** of Barnstead 4/5/1981 in Concord

MANKIEWICZ,
Keith W. of Ctr. Barnstead m. Michelle A. **Davis** of Pittsfield 9/27/1986 in Pittsfield

MARDIN,
Eddie A. of Barnstead m. Helen C. **Janisch** of Barnstead
   9/23/1950; H – 45, woodsman, b. NH, s/o William Davis
   (unknown) and Ada N. Davis (NH); W – 31, weaver, b. NH, d/o
   Frank Jenisch (Austria) and Matilda F. Schunk (NJ)

MARRIOTT,
Bruce Alan of Barnstead m. Teresa Louise **Taylor** of Barnstead
   2/14/1993 in Strafford

MARSAL,
Thomas of Barnstead m. Virginia **Holmes** of Barnstead 6/6/1953 in
   Chichester; H – 25, US Army, b. IL, s/o Charles Marsal
   (Czechoslovakia) and Bessie Slanina (Czechoslovakia); W –
   19, home, b. NH, d/o William Holmes (MA) and Marjorie
   Hanson (NH)

MARSH,
Luther E. m. Doris A. **Bunker** 6/14/1935; H – 27, s/o Joseph H. L.
   Marsh and Alice C. Preble; W – 26, d/o Joseph S. Bunker and
   Nellie M. Aiken

MARSTON,
Lenard M. of Epsom m. Nancy A. G. **Sylvain** of Ctr. Barnstead
   6/28/1966 in Chichester; H – 20, mach. operator, b. Concord,
   s/o Gilbert J. Marston (NH) and Ellen Zinn (NH); W – 20,
   secretary, b. Wolfeboro, d/o Antonio J. Sylvain (NH) and Ethel
   L. Emerson (NH)
William H. of Barnstead m. Nancy L. **Haney** of Barnstead
   8/22/1981 in Concord

MARTEL,
Zoel of Barnstead m. Carrie **Locke** of Barnstead 9/6/1908 in
   Manchester; H – 45, laborer, 2nd, b. Canada, s/o Zef Martel
   and Nellie Valet; W – 46, shoemaker, 2nd, b. Canada, d/o Peter
   Come (farmer)

MARTIN,
Alfred George of Ctr. Barnstead m. Jane Helen **Stockman** of Ctr.
   Barnstead 12/24/1996 in New Durham

Gordon K. of Ctr. Barnstead m. Patricia M. **Ford** of Boscawen 10/23/1965 in Boscawen; H - 26, tel. co., b. Wolfeboro, s/o Lee Rowland Martin (NH) and Doris A. Kenison (NH); W - 18, at home, b. Concord, d/o Stanley Merle Ford (NH) and Virginia E. Houston (NH)

Gregory Keith of Barnstead m. Jennifer B. **Clement** of Barnstead 7/24/1993

James L. of Barnstead m. Dorinda L. **Snow** of Barnstead 4/28/1978; H - b. 11/14/1952 in RI, s/o Roger Martin (RI) and Constance Henault (RI); W - b. 4/4/1950 in NH, d/o Harry E. McKenzie, Sr. (NH) and Eleanor Come (VT)

Jonathan W. of Barnstead m. Maryanne H. **Gardner** of Barnstead 11/19/1983 in Alton

Lee Roland m. Doris Alice **Chagnon** 8/30/1941 in Farmington; H – 28, s/o Elisha H. Martin and Marie J. Dubois; W – 25, d/o Fred R. Kenison and Gladys W. Brady

Ronald E. of Ctr. Barnstead m. Loretta A. **Brown** of Boscawen 2/1/1964 in Boscawen; H - 27, mechanic, b. Wolfeboro, s/o Maurice Martin (NH) and Doris Keniston (NH); W - 16, clerk, b. Concord, d/o Forrest Brown (NH) and Rebecca Swain (NH)

MATLOCK,
Jeffrey J. of Barnstead m. Nancy A. **Carr** of Barnstead 3/28/1981

MAXFIELD,
Austin C. of Barnstead m. Maggie **Dickey** of Barnstead 10/28/1893 in Pittsfield; H – 28, farmer, 2nd, b. Pittsfield, s/o John H. Maxfield (Starksborough, VT) and Julia A. (Loudon); W – 19, housekeeper, b. NB, d/o Adam Dickey (NS)

John A., III of Barnstead m. Debra Ellen **Eastman** of Concord 3/19/1971 in Chichester; H - b. 7/12/1945 in NH, s/o John A. Maxfield, Jr. (WI) and Gertrude Swain (NH); W - b. 10/4/1953 in NY, d/o Clifford Eastman (VT) and Ruth Weeks (NH)

John Austin of Barnstead m. Irene **Ayotte** of Barnstead 6/18/1984

MAY,
Sylvester L. of Barnstead m. Georgiana **Young** of Barrington 1/7/1903 in Barrington; H – 34, sawyer, b. Burlington, VT, s/o Samuel M. May (carpenter, Burlington, VT) and Lucy Whittier (domestic, Orange); W – 28, housework, 2nd, b. Worcester,

MA, d/o George T. Brown (Northwood) and Julia Waterhouse (Barrington)

McALLISTER,
Robert Willis m. Shirley Annette **Avery** 6/23/1940 in Hanover; H – 27, s/o Arthur McAllister and Mytie Willis; W – 24, d/o Leon Avery and Gladys Blood

McCAIN,
William H. of Barnstead m. Peggy S. **Houlne** of Barnstead 3/27/1999

McCORMACK,
Bernard P. of Pembroke m. Marjorie Ann **Atwell** of Barnstead 10/1/1946 in Concord; H – 23, d/o James B. McCormack and Eva O. Clark; W – 20, d/o Ralph B. Atwell and Louise H. Wilhelm
David Anthony of Barnstead m. Donna Marie **Kling** of Barnstead 6/27/1992

McCREADY,
Alan W. of Ctr. Barnstead m. Ronda D. **Gagne** of Ctr. Barnstead 2/14/1987 in Manchester

McDONOUGH,
Richard Kevin of Barnstead m. Patricia Ann **Duggan** of MA 10/17/1993

McDOWELL,
Lance E. of Dover m. Carol A. **Pike** of Barnstead 12/24/1965 in Dover; H - 22, student, b. Lafayette, IN, s/o Floyd E. McDowell (IN) and Phyllis J. Herod (IN); W - 22, teacher, b. Rochester, d/o Charles N. Pike (NY) and Barbara Lothrop (NY)

McDUFFEE,
David L. of Barnstead m. Mary E. **Bessir** of Foxcroft, ME 11/30/1887 in Pittsfield; H – 37, farmer, b. Alton, s/o Jonathan McDuffee; W – 28, b. Foxcroft, ME, d/o Wellington Bessir

McGLAME,
Thomas R. of Boston, MA m. Ellen T. **McCarthy** of Boston, MA 11/26/1983

McGONAGLE,
Matthew J. of Gilford m. Amy **Papaioanou** of Barnstead 8/21/1993 in Concord

McKENNA,
James P., Jr. of Ctr. Barnstead m. Donna M. **Ashton** of Ctr. Barnstead 10/7/1989 in Chichester

McKENZIE,
Kenneth R., Jr. of Loudon m. Sandra J. **Cotton** of Barnstead 4/1/1960 in Pittsfield; H - 20, laborer, b. Pittsfield, s/o Kenneth R. McKenzie (NH) and Helen L. Riel (NH); W - 20, lab. tech., b. Barnstead, d/o Joseph H. Cotton (MA) and Ruth E. Hallett (MA)
Russell W. of Ctr. Barnstead m. Nicole **Esburnett** of Ctr. Barnstead 3/1/1997 in Dixville

McLEAN,
Kenneth Alan of Barnstead m. Mona B. **Gustafson** of Barnstead 3/20/1981 in New Durham

MEDEIROS,
Bryan J. of Barnstead m. Maureen R. **Jones** of Barnstead 9/26/1999 in Chichester

MELANSON,
Charles W., Jr. of Barnstead m. Karen **D'Ambrosio** of Barnstead 8/24/1996

MELLO,
Edward Joseph of Ctr. Barnstead m. Susan Eileen **Costa** of Ctr. Barnstead 9/22/1992 in Pittsfield

MERRILL,
Bruce K. of Ctr. Barnstead m. Helen F. **Neville** of Hudson 5/4/1957 in Ctr. Barnstead; H - 22, elec. tech., b. NH, s/o Fred J. Merrill

(NH) and Elizabeth E. Bolt (MA); W - 22, secretary, b. MA, d/o Henry A. Basil (MA) and Ann F. Alukonia (NH)

George E. of Barnstead m. Lottie M. **Randall** of Barnstead 5/18/1903; H – 37, farmer, b. Hampton, s/o John B. Merrill (Hampton) and Sarah J. Shaw; W – 17, housework, b. Loudon, d/o George H. Randall (laborer) and Julia F. Twombly (domestic)

Herbert H. of Lynn, MA m. Gertrude M. **Webster** of Barnstead 10/10/1914; H – 39, bookkeeper, b. Lynn, MA, s/o Henry Merrill and Laura E. Lewis; W – 34, teacher, b. Stratham, d/o George Webster and Elizabeth Rogers

James Edwin of Gonic m. Margaret Ina **Gray** of Barnstead 9/3/1946 in Rochester; H – 31, s/o Otis Merrill and Myra B. Rhine; W – 23, d/o Albert B. Gray and Bessie J. Brown

Otis of Pittsfield m. Myra B. **Rines** of Barnstead 3/17/1897; H – 25, farmer, b. Loudon, s/o Bela Merrill (farmer, Loudon) and Eliza Young (housewife); W – 16, b. Pittsfield, d/o G. W. Rines (RR emp.) and Ida B. Brock

Stuart B. of Barnstead m. Grace A. **Higgins** of Barnstead 6/25/1959 in Chichester; H - 26, s/o Harvey S. Merrill and Helen Hutchinson; W - 19, d/o William Higgins and Olive Corliss

METZGER,

Jeffrey Lynn of Toccoa Falls, GA m. Janice Carolyn **Storey** of Barnstead 5/27/1978; H - b. 8/2/1948 in PA, s/o Frederick L. Metzger (FL) and Laura Womer (PA); W - b. 4/12/1956 in MA, d/o Robert I. Storey (MA) and Winifred Lavash (MA)

MEYER,

Randolph A. of Barnstead m. Janice G. **Gomes** of Barnstead 11/9/1985

MICHAUD,

Curtis J., Jr. of Barnstead m. Nadine A. **McMillan** of Barnstead 9/9/1987 in Chichester

MILES,

John B. of Nashua m. Ann M. **Bunker** of Barnstead 11/24/1999 in Pittsfield

MILLER,
Richard James of Ctr. Barnstead m. Karlene Ann **Normandin** of Ctr. Barnstead 8/8/1992
Thomas J. of Barnstead m. Deborah Ann **Cove** of Barnstead 3/26/1983

MILLIGAN,
Roy L. of Ctr. Ossipee m. Dorothy A. **Abbott** of Wolfeboro 7/4/1952; H – 27, barber, b. GA, s/o W. H. Milligan (GA) and May Bradford (GA); W – 18, home, b. NH, d/o W. L. Abbott (NH) and Gladys Sprague (NH)

MILLS,
Lowell J. m. Dora E. **Lougee** 6/14/1928; H – 33, s/o Fred W. Mills and Belle Brown; W – 18, d/o Leslie Lougee and Emma Whitehouse

MILNE,
William R. C., Jr. of Barnstead m. Norma M. **Place** of Barnstead 8/29/1975; H - b. 12/3/1946 in CT, s/o William R. C. Milne, Sr. (CT) and Marjorie Eddy (CT); W - b. 10/31/1950 in NH, d/o Francis R. Mooney (VT) and Mildred A. Peasley (NH)

MINER,
David A. of Barnstead m. Julie L. **Luckert** of Barnstead 3/24/1979 in Chichester
David Ashley of Barnstead m. Marina Ruth **Hewett** of Barnstead 9/18/1993 in Rochester
Dennis A. of Barnstead m. Patricia M. **Richardson** of Barnstead 9/14/1974; H - b. 9/30/1956 in NH, s/o Harold A. Miner (NH) and Marjorie M. Wade (NH); W - b. 12/4/1956 in MA, d/o James W. Richardson (MA) and Ruth Whoriskey (MA)
Dennis A. of Barnstead m. Brigitte M. **Pratt** of Ctr. Barnstead 8/23/1980 in Chichester
Dennis A. of Barnstead m. Lynn **Carey** of Gilmanton I.W. 9/9/1995 in Woodstock

MITCHELL,
Albert Carl of Ctr. Barnstead m. Diane Marie **Vokes** of Ctr. Barnstead 9/27/1992 in Pittsfield

Joseph J. of Barnstead m. Judith R. **Nelson** of Barnstead 1/31/1976; H - b. 10/13/1953 in NH, s/o Richard Mitchell (NH) and Pearl Joyce (NH); W - b. 3/9/1947 in NH, d/o Warren J. Riel (NH) and Evelyn Stevens (NH)

Richard L. of Pittsfield m. Irene A. **Wheet** of Barnstead 7/11/1951 in Plymouth; H – 21, US Navy, b. NH, s/o Herbert R. Mitchell (MA) and Gladys M. Rogers (NH); W – 18, home, b. NH, d/o Rexford E. Wheet (NH) and Bessie McDuffy (NH)

Robert Alan of Ctr. Barnstead m. Amy Jo **Donnelly** of Ctr. Barnstead 2/20/1991 in Pittsfield

Robert B. of Ctr. Barnstead m. Kathleen **Greer** of Ctr. Barnstead 5/12/1989 in Chichester

Roderick Ernest of Barnstead m. Fay Allison **Towle** of Belmont 10/21/1978 in Belmont; H - b. 4/28/1940 in NH, s/o John A. Mitchell (NY) and Rita M. Santy (NH); W - b. 3/15/1937 in CT, d/o Russell Hinman (CT) and Helen Sugrue (CT)

Stephen Robert of Pittsfield m. Deborah Fate **Sylvain** of Barnstead 6/28/1969 in Concord; H - 24, b. NH, s/o Donald M. Mitchell (NH) and Edith M. Jenkins (NH); W - 20, b. NH, d/o Antonia J. Sylvain (NH) and Ethel L. Emerson (NH)

Wallace W. of Pittsfield m. Virginia L. **Wells** of Barnstead 6/22/1951 in Northwood; H – 43, garment cutter, b. MA, s/o Winfield S. Mitchell (MA) and Eva M. Clerke (MA); W – 28, garment stitcher, b. NH, d/o Walter B. Wells (NH) and Sophrona M. Yeaton (NH)

Walter J. of Barnstead m. Annie T. **Place** of Barnstead 2/22/1908 in Pittsfield; H – 18, laborer, b. Worcester, MA, s/o Julius Mitchell (farmer, Canada) and P. Brown (housewife, Canada); W – 24, aitress, b. England, d/o John Place (farmer, England) and Annie Towrey (housewife, England)

MIZO,
Harold A., Jr. of Keene m. Evelyn M. **Zecha** of Barnstead 7/7/1951 in Winchester; H – 19, truck driver, b. MA, s/o Harold A. Mizo (NH) and Hazel A. Makin (NH); W – 22, home, b. NH, d/o Ferdinand Zecha (MA) and Gertrude M. Barnes (NH)

MONTGOMERY,
Rickie Glenn of Ctr. Barnstead m. Karen Marie **Labrecque** of Ctr. Barnstead 7/28/1990 in No. Barnstead

MOODY,
Terry Lee of Pittsfield m. Denice Francine **Bartlett** of Ctr. Barnstead 8/1/1992
Theodore Joseph m. Ruth Blanche **Golden** 6/25/1943; H – 23, s/o Joseph Moody and Nettie Williams; W – 18, d/o John E. Golden and Blanche N. Locke

MOORE,
Alfred E. of Barnstead m. Lucille E. **Cass** of Laconia 6/15/1945 in Laconia; H – 29, s/o John H. Moore and Lettie H. Harriman; W – 25, d/o Frank H. Cass and Eleanor N. Davis
Frank H. of Barnstead m. Sadie F. **Hillsgrove** of Barnstead 4/18/1891 in Pittsfield; H – 30, shoemaker, b. Loudon, s/o John B. (news agent, Loudon) and Lucy M. (housekeeper, Loudon); W – 20, shoe stitcher, b. Grafton, d/o Joseph M. (shoemaker, Portsmouth) and Lydia (housekeeper)

MORRIS,
Colin Tallman of Belmont m. Deborah Ann **Kiley** of Barnstead 5/5/1990
David Edward of Barnstead m. Robin Lynn **Stock** of Barnstead 5/30/1992 in Pittsfield

MORRISSETTE,
Dennis A. of Barnstead m. Estelle M. **Rollins** of Barnstead 8/26/1983 in Chichester
Raymond A. of Nashua m. Ginette **Gagnon** of Nashua 7/12/1969; H - 32, b. NH, s/o Arthur Morrissette (NH) and Lena Cote (NH); W - 24, b. Canada, d/o Arthur Gagnon (Canada) and Ann A. Rioux (Canada)

MORSE,
Kevin M. of Barnstead m. Lynne C. **Schlottmann** of Barnstead 12/9/1990 in Ctr. Barnstead

MOSHER,
Burr B. of Brooklyn m. Harriet D. **Piper** of Barnstead 10/5/1892 in Gilmanton; H – 27, physician, b. Union Springs, s/o E. D. Mosher (Auburn); W – 24, b. Barnstead, d/o John L. (farmer)

MOSTOVOY,
Gregory of DeSoto, TX m. Donna E. **Ericson** of DeSoto, TX 6/30/1984 in Ctr. Barnstead

MOULTON,
Harold Earl of Pittsfield m. Velna Virginia **Gray** of Barnstead 2/8/1947; H – 26, carpenter, b. Pittsfield, s/o Edward P. Moulton and Addie F. Cram; W – 25, home, b. Barnstead, s/o Leslie M. Gray and Virginia Shouys

MOUNTAIN,
Henry D. of Ctr. Barnstead m. Karen **MacKnight** of Alton 8/2/1975 in Alton; H - b. 4/10/1946 in MA, s/o Henry Mountain (Canada) and Rachel Anderson (MA); W - b. 6/11/1951 in MA, d/o Sheldon MacKnight (MA) and Audrey F. Strange (MA)

Henry Joseph of Ctr. Barnstead m. Freda Alberta **Boyd** of Ctr. Barnstead 4/25/1954; H - 41, merchant, b. NS, s/o Thomas W. Mountain (Canada) and Mary Martell (Canada); W - 43, clerk, b. NH, d/o Fred S. Gilman (NH) and Etta Belle Coffin (NH)

MOUSSEAU,
Sherman P. of Pittsfield m. Tami J. **Bessaw** of Barnstead 10/18/1975 in Chichester; H - b. 3/2/1957 in NH, s/o Roland Mousseau (NH) and Ann H. Smith (MI); W - b. 7/18/1958 in NH, d/o Wallace Brasaw (sic) (MA) and Mary Sullivan (NH)

MULCAHY,
Robert E., Jr. of Barnstead m. Margaret M. **Hoyt** of Concord 10/14/1978 in Pittsfield; H - b. 4/1/1923 in MA, s/o Robert E. Mulcahy, Sr. (MA) and Maude Dahey (MA); W - b. 10/7/1924 in NH, d/o George F. Fox (NH) and Florence O. Corson (NH)

Robert E., III of Ctr. Barnstead m. Diane M. **LaBrecque** of Rochester 6/21/1975; H - b. 6/17/1950 in MA, s/o Robert E. Mulcahy, Jr. (MA) and Dorothy A. Doran (MA); W - b. 8/1/1951 in NH, d/o Albert R. LaBrecque (NH) and Pauline M. Salice (NH)

Shawn Adrian of Ctr. Barnstead m. Stacy Luann **Shaw** of Ctr. Barnstead 10/31/1992

MUNROE,
Dale K. of Ctr. Barnstead m. Lori J. **Gray** of Ctr. Barnstead 9/24/1988 in Suncook

Donald S. of Epsom m. Patricia A. **Brown** of Barnstead 4/22/1960 in Pittsfield; H - 31, mechanic, b. Epsom, s/o Norman S. Munroe (NH) and Mary H. Brown (NH); W - 19, belt insp., b. Pittsfield, d/o Philip W. Brown (MA) and Marjorie E. Crossett (NH)

MUNSEY,
George M. of Barnstead m. Kattie M. **Nelson** of Dover 3/6/1889; H – 27, shoemaker, b. Barnstead, s/o Henry J. Munsey (Barnstead) and Annie Munsey (Barnstead); W – 23, 2nd, b. Lynn, MA, d/o Henry Welds (Haverhill) and Emma Welds (Haverhill)

Linwood B. m. Cecil May **Prince** 9/1/1923; H – 27, s/o George M. Munsey and Kate Weld; W – 17, d/o George H. Prince and Mary E. Moore

Steven Alan of Ctr. Barnstead m. Ellena Annette **Watson** of Ctr. Barnstead 7/21/1990 in Northwood

MURLEY,
David Freeman of Barnstead m. Eileen Elizabeth **Conley** of Nashua 6/23/1990 in Nashua

MURPHREE,
Stephen Eugene of Ctr. Barnstead m. Priscilla Ann **Smith** of Ctr. Barnstead 10/20/1990 in Ctr. Barnstead

MURRAY,
Richard Charles of Concord m. Debora Lea **Dooley** of Ctr. Barnstead 12/7/1996 in Concord

MURZIN,
Donald W. of Barnstead m. Rebecca R. **Evans** of Barnstead 6/27/1998

MYATT,
Ronald F., Jr. of Ctr. Barnstead m. Candice E. **Gosse** of Ctr. Barnstead 12/16/2000

MYERS,
Dennis Richard of Pittsfield m. Judith Grace **Sylvain** of Ctr. Barnstead 6/28/1969 in Pittsfield; H - 20, b. NH, s/o William Myers (MA) and Theresa Bishop (NH); W - 19, b. NH, d/o Antonia J. Sylvain (NH) and Ethel L. Emerson (NH)

NELSON,
Jerry of Barnstead m. Judith A. **Riel** of Barnstead 9/3/1965 in Chichester; H - 22, leather worker, b. Pittsfield, s/o Ralph H. Keyser (NH) and Dorothy M. Nelson (NH); W - 18, secretary, b. Pittsfield, d/o Warren J. Riel (NH) and Evelyn A. Stevens (NH)

John E. m. Sarah M. **Lorris** 12/3/1934 in Hudson; H – 47, s/o John A. Nelson and Hannah I. Anderson; W – 36, d/o Frank Lorris and May Smith

John S. of Barnstead m. Gail M. **Webster** of Rochester 4/20/1985 in Meredith

Todd E. of Ctr. Barnstead m. Tammy L. **Locke** of Ctr. Barnstead 8/5/2000

Troy J. of Ctr. Barnstead m. Vicki L. **Silva** of Newton 9/30/1995 in Newton

NERO,
John L. of Providence, RI m. Andrea L. **Scarpo** of Stoneham, MA 8/10/1985

NEWHOUSE,
David Roy of Ctr. Barnstead m. Debra Jeanne **Kelton** of Ctr. Barnstead 12/8/1990 in Ctr. Barnstead

NEWTON,
Bruce E. of Ctr. Barnstead m. Sharon J. **LaPorte** of Ctr. Barnstead 8/8/1998

NICHOLS,
Howard F. of Barnstead m. Margery Claire **Pyne** of Medford, MA 8/3/1991 in Amherst

NIGHELLI,
Benjamin R. of Barnstead m. Jeston M. **Doughty** of Barnstead 5/11/1984

NOBLE,
William J. of Barnstead m. Crystal **Pouliot** of Barnstead 6/13/1998

NOYES,
Charles R., Jr. of Alton m. Cindy L. **Clement** of Barnstead 8/3/1985 in Alton

NUTTER,
- Carl C. of Pittsfield m. Lillian M. **Richardson** of Barnstead 6/15/1910; H – 27, teacher, b. Pittsfield, s/o Matthew H. Nutter (plumber, Pittsfield) and Minerva J. Merrill (housewife, Deerfield); W – 25, housework, b. Barnstead, d/o Walter Richardson (merchant, Boston, MA) and Hattie B. Brown (housewife, Barrington)
- Carl N. m. Mary A. **Richardson** 9/2/1923; H – 40, s/o Mathy H. Nutter and Meninia J. Merrill; W – 32, d/o Walter Richardson and Hattie B. Brown
- Everett W. of Barnstead m. Edith M. **Locke** of Barnstead 6/6/1906 in Farmington; H – 21, laborer, b. Gilmanton, s/o Isaac B. Nutter (steam mill eme., Gilmanton) and Cora F. Clough (Gilmanton); W – 20, shoemaker, b. Pittsfield, d/o Elias Locke (Boston, MA) and Caroline M. Come (shoemaker, Canada)
- Frank C. of Barnstead m. Ina P. **Berry** of Barnstead 12/10/1904 in Pittsfield; H – 23, teacher, b. Barnstead, s/o Frank S. Nutter (farmer, Barnstead) and Sarah Caswell (Strafford); W – 16, b. Barnstead, d/o Joel S. Berry (farmer, Barnstead) and Emma Webster (Danbury)
- George A. of Barnstead m. Ella B. **Whitehouse** of Barnstead 6/20/1901; H – 44, farmer, b. Barnstead, s/o Josiah K. Nutter and Mary A. Nutter (housekeeper, Pittsfield); W – 24, housework, b. Canada, d/o Charles Whitehouse (stone mason, Canada) and Lucy J. Whitehouse (housewife, Troy, VT)
- George H. of Lynn, MA m. Maggie **Murry** of Lynn, MA 10/15/1898; H – 41, clerk, 2nd, b. Barnstead, s/o Samuel D. Nutter and Ruth M. Nutter; W – 27, housekeeper, b. Ireland, d/o Patrick Murry (farmer) and Julia Murry

Joseph S. of Pittsfield m. May **Nuttall** of Barnstead 1/12/1921 in Pittsfield; H – 21, b. Woodsville, s/o Nathan H. Nutter and Althe Thayer; W – 21, b. Lynn, MA, d/o James Nuttall and Annie Peabody

Malcolm H. m. Grace E. **Gray** 10/2/1940 in Milton; H – 25, s/o Addis S. Nutter and Marion G. Rand; W – 18, d/o Unknown and Bessie O. Gray

Ralph Edward of Windsor, VT m. Mildred M. **Starbird** of Barnstead 9/30/1916 in Pittsfield; H – 22, stock clerk, b. Pittsfield, s/o Nathan Harvey Nutter and Miniora Jane Merrill; W – 21, at home, b. Lynn, MA, d/o George W. Starbird and Eva Maud Knowles

O'BRIEN,
James E. of NH m. Alice C. **Blakmer** of Ctr. Barnstead 3/28/1969 in Ctr. Barnstead; H - 27, b. NH, s/o Joseph A. O'Brien (MA) and Alice Mooney (MA); W - 27, b. MA, d/o Paul Blakmer (NH) and Catherine Hogan (Ireland)

O'HALLORAN,
Michael J. of Melrose, MA m. Kristin **Ellis** of Melrose, MA 7/23/1995

O'MEARA,
Stephen H. of Barnstead m. Dary A. **Deinhardt** of Barnstead 5/3/1981

O'NEIL,
Charles Allen m. Phyllis Elvira **Dodge** 3/19/1938; H – 23, s/o Thomas F. O'Neil and Phoebe Herbert; W – 23, d/o James W. Dodge and Emma Chatterton

O'TOOLE,
Kevin Dennis of Dorchester, MA m. Joyce Margaret **Roddy** of Boston, MA 8/22/1973 in Ctr. Barnstead; H - b. 3/9/1951 in MA, s/o William O'Toole (MA) and Margaret O'Neil (MA); W - b. 2/13/1948 in MA, d/o George Roddy (MA) and Katherine Halligan (MA)

OBARTON [see Aubertin, Bartin],
Edward of Barnstead m. Jennie **Daily** of Strafford 7/16/1903 in Manchester; H – 26, laborer, b. Canada, s/o Ezra Obarton (Canada); W – 19, factory, b. Gilmanton, d/o John Daily (Canada) and Mary Daily (Canada)

OGDEN,
David K. of Barnstead m. Sharon L. **Conary** of Barnstead 8/11/1984 in Alton

OLSON,
Mark D. of Ctr. Barnstead m. Kristine A. **Fuller** of Ctr. Barnstead 8/26/2000 in Laconia

ONUFRY,
Richard A. of Ctr. Barnstead m. Lynn A. **Peterson** of Ctr. Barnstead 7/29/2000 in Alton

OSBORNE,
Richard K. of Ctr. Barnstead m. Julia S. **Jochums** of Ctr. Barnstead 4/24/1987 in Sunapee

OSGOOD,
Charles H. of Barnstead m. Ora G. **Parsons** of West Concord 5/6/1895 in Epsom; H – 22, b. Barnstead, s/o James Y. Osgood (shoemaker) and Angie M. Elliott (Barnstead); W – 19, teacher, b. Barnstead, d/o Charles R. Parsons (conductor) and Caroline Kelley (housewife)

OTIS,
Arthur D. of Barnstead m. Etta M. **Hanson** of Barnstead 2/7/1892; H – 23, carriage maker, b. Strafford, s/o Dyer L. (farmer) and Mary M.; W – 19, housekeeper, b. Barnstead, d/o Levi H. (farmer, Barnstead) and Abbie (Barnstead)
Lewis L. m. Marjorie **Rowe** 12/14/1941 in Winchester; H – 41, s/o Arthur D. Otis and Etta M. Hanson; W – 30, d/o George A. Rowe and Annie Shepard
Lewis W. of Barnstead m. Gladys W. **Kenison** of Barnstead 6/4/1921; H – 21, b. Barnstead, s/o Arthur D. Otis and Etta M.

Hanson; W – 22, b. Barnstead, d/o James Brady and Alice E. Davis

OTTERSON,
Thomas J. of Barnstead m. Hannah S. **Bickford** of Hooksett 9/5/1899 in Hooksett; H – 28, RR employee, b. Hooksett, s/o Martin L. Otterson (farmer, Hooksett) and Mary E. Whitehouse (housewife, Hooksett); W – 28, domestic, b. Epsom, d/o Samuel T. Bickford (RR foreman, Allenstown) and Sarah M. Foss (housewife, Strafford)

OUELLETTE,
Alberic, III of Alton Bay m. Suzanne Marie **Barrett** of Barnstead 6/26/1993

OUMARHOUGH,
Mohammed of Ctr. Barnstead m. Stephanie **Aparicio** of Ctr. Barnstead 6/17/2000 in Salem

OWEN,
Ryan J. of Pittsfield m. Jeri **Thompson** of Ctr. Barnstead 3/10/1999 in Bow

PACKARD,
Jay Leyland of New York, NY m. Minnie L. **Reynolds** of Barnstead 6/27/1904; H – 31, manager, 2nd, b. Harrisonburg, LA, s/o James B. Packard (hotel, NY) and Clara Bishop (New Orleans, LA); W – 23, professional, 2nd, b. Barnstead, d/o John H. Ellsworth (editor, Calcutta, India) and Ida G. Babb (Calcutta, India)
Roger H. of Barnstead m. Katie J. **Hood** of Barnstead 1/18/1951; H – 57, farmer, b. NH, s/o Horace U. Packard (VT) and Lidia Billings (NH); W – 43, housekeeper, b. VT, d/o Henry H. Hood (VT) and Minnie Flanders (VT)

PAGE,
Jesse H. of Concord m. Susan M. **Smith** of Ctr. Barnstead 3/7/1986 in Pembroke
Walter D. of Barnstead m. Alice **Foss** of Barnstead 5/19/1899 in Gilmanton; H – 25, farmer, b. Gilmanton, s/o Albert R. Page

(farmer, Gilmanton) and Addie C. Page (housekeeper, New Durham); W – 18, housework, b. Barnstead, d/o Charles A. Foss (shoemaker, Barnstead) and Emma F. Foss (housewife, Barnstead)

PAIGE,
John A. of Pittsfield m. Kathleen **Soulia** of Barnstead 6/27/1970 in Ctr. Barnstead; H - b. 3/21/1950 in NH, s/o Courtland Paige (NH) and Olive Elkins (NH); W - b. 11/3/1950 in NH, d/o John Soulia (VT) and Helen Lyons (NH)

PAJANEN,
David John of Ctr. Barnstead m. Corliss Jane **Mitchell** of Ctr. Barnstead 7/20/1994 in Nottingham

PALMER,
Charles E. of Barnstead m. Saddie M. **Carr** of Barnstead 12/31/1890 in Newmarket; H – 36, mechanic, 2nd, b. Barnstead, s/o Ranscom C. Palmer (Sutton) and Alice Palmer; W – 35, 3rd, b. Gilmanton, d/o Henry T. Carr and J. J. Carr
Christopher Douglas of Ctr. Barnstead m. Jo-Anne Gail **Bean** of Ctr. Barnstead 9/27/1991 in Loudon
Donald S. m. Madeline O. **Merrill** 3/3/1934 in Bristol; H – 21, s/o Wendell S. Palmer and Amelia Fowler; W – 20, d/o Lyman Merrill and Fannie Fifield

PAPPAS,
Leonard Charles, Jr. of Manchester m. Jennifer Sue **Hart** of Barnstead 4/9/1994 in Peterborough

PAQUETTE,
Paul Owen of Barnstead m. Bridget **Swain** of Barnstead 9/14/1996 in Pittsfield

PAQUIN,
Joseph E. of Ctr. Barnstead m. Ellen C. **McManus** of Ctr. Barnstead 4/1/1988 in Pittsfield
Steven J. of Barnstead m. Lauraine G. **Isaksen** of Barnstead 1/1/2000 in Hudson

PARKEY,
Peter J. of Barnstead m. Theresa A. **Blanchette** of Manchester 1/25/1964 in Manchester; H - 32, pipefitter, b. N. Haverhill, NH, s/o Peter J. Parkey (MO) and Mary L. Bailey (MA); W - 34, office clerk, b. Methuen, MA, d/o Jules Blanchette (MA) and Ada Levasseur (Canada)

PARKINGTON,
Leon of Ctr. Barnstead m. Joyce M. **Stannard** of Ctr. Barnstead 6/29/1988

PARSHLEY,
Levi C. of Barnstead m. Alvira F. **Adams** of Francestown 4/30/1903 in Gilmanton; H – 25, farmer, b. Barnstead, s/o Frank P. Parshley (shoemaker) and Mary E. Aikens; W – 21, housework, b. Fitchburg, MA, d/o David H. Adams and Etta N. Whitefield

PARSON [see Parsons],
C. A. of Barnstead m. E. S. **Ricker** of S. Dover, ME 3/30/1887 in Pittsfield; H – 29, farmer, b. Lawrence, MA, s/o Philaman Parson (mechanic, ME) and Miranda E. Parson (Barnstead); W – 28, housework, b. Dover, ME, d/o Moses Ricker (farmer, ME) and Susan H. Lambert (Milo, ME)

PARSONS [see Parson],
Scott D. m. Sadie F. **Hoyt** 10/1/1927; H – 39, s/o Charles Parsons and Electa S. Ricker; W – 32, d/o Reuben S. Hoyt and Mabel F. Hoyt

PARTRIDGE,
Brian L. of Barnstead m. Roberta E. **Lee** of Barnstead 10/23/1982

PASSANO,
Joseph V. of RI m. Esther L. **Duarte** of Barnstead 8/1/1999

PATTERSON,
David M. of Barnstead m. Sandra D. **Anderson** of Barnstead 9/25/1999 in Hudson

PEAVEY,
Ray A. of Barnstead m. Jennie S. **Knapp** of Manchester 8/12/1918 in Manchester; H – 28, b. Derby, VT, s/o Thomas L. Peavey and Emma Kenney; W – 27, b. Piermont, d/o Frederick Knapp and Ella S. -----

PENNEY,
Richard D. of Barnstead m. Paula S. **Smith** of Barnstead 8/2/1986 in Concord

PEPE,
Joseph F., III of Ctr. Barnstead m. Lisa M. **Weston** of Salem 4/29/2000 in Laconia

PEREZ,
Alfred J., Sr. of Barnstead m. May L. **Trusten** of Barnstead 8/12/1995

PERKINS,
Brian K. of Ctr. Barnstead m. Stacy D. **Miller** of Concord 1/3/1998 in Concord

David M. of Barnstead m. Dora E. **Foss** of Strafford 10/8/1922; H – 21, b. Strafford, s/o Harry D. Perkins and Mabel F. Rower; W – 18, b. Strafford, d/o George T. Foss and Edna Caswell

David M., II of Ctr. Barnstead m. Sherry Lee **Constant** of Laconia 4/16/1972 in New Hampton; H - b. 3/23/1949 in NH, s/o Maynard H. Perkins (NH) and Dorothy E. Belville (MA); W - b. 9/1/1950 in NH, d/o Leander Constant (NH) and Ruth Thompson (NH)

Noel E. of Northwood m. Grace L. **Parsons** of Barnstead 6/13/1987 in Northwood

Randy Jay of Barrington m. Mary Ellen **Welch** of Ctr. Barnstead 10/26/1974 in Somersworth; H - b. 9/1/1954 in NH, s/o Fenelon Jay Perkins (ME) and Hazel Louise Cross (NH); W - b. 2/4/1956 in NH, d/o Ashton W. Welch (NH) and Wilma F. Hanson (NH)

William C. of Barnstead m. Gloria H. **Wade** of Chichester 10/19/1945; H – 18, s/o David M. Perkins and Dora Foss; W – 18, d/o Nathan Wade and Hazel B. Edmunds

PERRY,
Albert C. m. Edna R. **Locke** 7/14/1928 in Nashua; H – 37, s/o Charles H. Perry and Annie B. Perkins; W – 21, d/o Wayland B. Locke and Bertha Emerson

PERVERE,
Dwight L. of Lynn, MA m. Eleanor N. **Hastings** of Barnstead 2/11/1950; H – 66, retired, b. MA, s/o Willie O. Pervere (NH) and Katie R. Downs (ME); W – 59, housewife, b. Newfoundland, d/o John C. Newhook (Newfoundland) and Elizabeth Wilcox (England)

PESTANA,
Lui M. of Hawaii m. Linda-Marie **Horton** of Ctr. Barnstead 5/2/1999

PETERSON,
Mark Evert of Barnstead m. Sally Louanne **Decota** of Barnstead 7/19/1992 in Concord

PETHIC,
Wayne of Pittsfield m. Ann E. **Riel** of Barnstead 12/12/1964 in Concord; H - 20, salesman, b. Meredith, s/o Everett L. Pethic (NH) and Helen Morris (NH); W - 18, student, b. Concord, d/o Arthur Riel (NH) and Mary E. Clark (MA)

PETIX,
Robert Gilbert of Barnstead m. Laura L. **Moroney** of Barnstead 8/21/1993 in Salem

PHILBRICK,
Eugene Holden of Pittsfield m. Wanda **Perkins** of Ctr. Barnstead 8/11/1973 in Ctr. Barnstead; H - b. 10/6/1947 in NH, s/o Eugene H. Philbrick (MA) and Ruth Garland (NH); W - b. 4/11/1954 in NH, d/o Maynard H. Perkins (NH) and Dorothy E. Belville (MA)
Gary L. m. Dorothy L. **Lank** 7/12/1958 in Chichester

PHILLIPPS,
Paul J. of Ctr. Barnstead m. Lori A. **Ross** of Ctr. Barnstead 10/11/1987 in Manchester

PHILLIPS,

Ceiland A. of Barnstead m. Pamela A. **Pollard** of Barnstead 6/19/1987

Michael of Londonderry m. Paula L. **Hennigan** of Londonderry 5/19/1984

Shirley N. of Barnstead m. Wendy P. **Smith** of Barnstead 11/8/1959; H - 24, s/o Jesse F. Phillips and Josephine M. Young; W - 18, d/o Gordon M. Smith and Virginia T. Baker

PHILPOT,

Jeffrey T. of Barnstead m. Donna A. **Pearce** of Barnstead 6/13/1981

PIASECZNY,

James Daniel of Ctr. Barnstead m. Cheryl Ann **Vincent** of Ctr. Barnstead 2/14/1996 in Epsom

Steven R. of Pittsfield m. Debra J. **Locke** of Barnstead 8/23/1986 in Pittsfield

PICKARD,

Richard D. of Barnstead m. Frieda L. **Marston** of Chichester 10/28/1961 in Newport; H - 34, lineman, b. MA, s/o Arthur G. Pickard (NH) and Irene R. Surette (MA); W - 23, clerk-steno., b. NH, d/o Gilbert J. Marston (NH) and Ellen Zinn (NH)

Robert A., Jr. of Chichester m. Dorothy A. **Tasker** of Ctr. Barnstead 7/16/1966 in Alton; H - 21, US Army, b. Salem, MA, s/o Robert A. Packard, Sr. (sic) (NH) and Dorothy LaBonte (MA); W - 19, clerk-typist, b. Manchester, d/o Harry W. Tasker (NH) and Helen M. Owens (MA)

PICKERING,

Albert C. of Barnstead m. Nettie **Gray** of Strafford 10/1/1892 in Pittsfield; H – 23, farmer, b. Barnstead, s/o Joshua C. (farmer, Barnstead) and Ellen G. (Barnstead); W – 19, stitcher, b. Strafford, d/o Wilson (carpenter, ME) and Nancy L. (Strafford)

Charles H. of Barnstead m. Liberty W. **Wentworth** of Barnstead 11/4/1895 in Northwood; H – 68, farmer, 2nd, b. Barnstead, s/o Jonathan Pickering and Eliza Foster; W – 54, housework, 2nd, b. Farmington

Fred C. of Barnstead m. Fannie H. **Chadwick** of Barnstead 12/26/1907 in Dover; H – 45, clerk, 3rd, b. Barnstead, s/o Charles Pickering (Barnstead) and Martha A. Williams; W – 33, housekeeper, b. Farmington, d/o William N. Chadwick (salesman, Farmington) and Abbie F. Horne (housewife, New Durham)

Ralph E. of Pittsfield m. Margaret J. **Hogencamp** of Barnstead 1/5/1918 in Pittsfield; H – 20, b. Barnstead, s/o Albert C. Pickering and Nettie Gray; W – 19, b. Philadelphia, PA, d/o Harry E. Hogencamp and Jennie R. Cornell

PICKETT,
Fredrick W. of Barnstead m. Sandra J. **Boisvert** of Southington, CT 2/24/1978 in Pittsfield; H - b. 1/1/1957 in MA, s/o Kenneth E. Pickett (MI) and Ethel Gianotis (MA); W - b. 8/16/1957 in CT, d/o Lawrence E. Boisvert (CT) and Jean Frenette (NH)

PIERCE,
Keith R. of Ctr. Barnstead m. Linda A. **Smith** of Ctr. Barnstead 11/15/1997 in Bow

Wilbert M. of Concord m. Doris A. **Boyd** of Barnstead 7/26/1969; H - 29, b. NH, s/o Kenneth Pierce (MA) and Esther Dixon (MA); W - 20, b. NH, d/o Randolph L. Boyd (NH) and Emma J. Boyd (NH)

PIERCEY,
Harold J. of Ctr. Barnstead m. Louise A. **McElwain** of Parsonsfield, ME 1/8/2000 in Concord

PINKHAM,
Philip J. of Barnstead m. Sally A. **Brown** of Derry 8/16/1975; H - b. 8/18/1949 in NH, s/o John H. Pinkham (MA) and Esther L. McAllister (ME); W - b. 8/26/1951 in NH, d/o James L. Sutton (NH) and Doris Ramadell (NH)

PINTO,
Robert of Ctr. Barnstead m. Christine L. **Clement** of Ctr. Barnstead 7/8/1989 in Pittsfield

PITMAN,
Albert G. of Barnstead m. Nellie F. **Clough** of Barnstead 7/12/1891 in Pittsfield; H – 21, mechanic, b. Alexandria, s/o George T. (farmer) and Aurilla M. (housekeeper, Alexandria); W – 23, stitcher, b. Belmont, d/o George F. (farmer) and Jane S. (housekeeper)

Albert G. of Barnstead m. Ellen R. **Kittredge** of Auburn 11/11/1915 in Auburn, ME; H – 45, farmer, b. Alexandria, s/o George F. Pitman (farming, Alexandria) and Aurilla M. Brock (housewife, Alexandria); W – 40, housekeeper, b. Brownville, ME, d/o Stephen A. Thomas (farmer, Brownville, ME) and Mary E. Rodgers (housewife, Brownville, ME)

Arthur J. of Barnstead m. Ida M. **Bunker** of Barnstead 4/25/1892; H – 24, physician, b. Alexandria, s/o George T. (farmer) and Aurilla M. (Alexandria); W – 20, teacher, b. IL, d/o Milo (station agent)

Arthur William of Barnstead m. Carol Isabel **Atwell** of Barnstead 10/17/1949; H – 19, laborer, b. Barnstead, s/o Fred T. Pitman and Harriet M. Lawrence; W – 18, factory worker, b. Barnstead, d/o Ralph B. Atwell and Louise H. Wilhelm

Fred T. m. Harrietta M. **Lawrence** 5/28/1925 in Pittsfield; H – 23, s/o Oscar E. Pitman and Laurena B. Spooner; W – 26, d/o Horace A. Lawrence and Elizabeth Bassett

George Albert m. Alma Louisa **Lakeman** 6/14/1938 in Pittsfield; H – 29, s/o Albert G. Pitman and Nellie F. Clough; W – 25, d/o Carlton H. Lakeman and Lottie A. McFadden

Oscar E. of Barre, VT m. Lurena B. **Spooner** of Barnstead 8/13/1899; H – 34, farmer, b. Barnstead, s/o Hiram T. Pitman (farmer, Barnstead) and Sophronia J. Pitman (housewife, Gilford); W – 20, housework, b. Barre, VT, d/o Thomas D. Spooner (lumberman, Colchester, VT) and H'p'bth M. Spooner (housewife, Plattsburg, NY)

PLACE,
George E. of Barnstead m. Mary E. W. **Chesley** of Alton 10/2/1912 in Alton; H – 75, farmer, b. Gilmanton, s/o Smith Place (millman, Gilmanton) and Nancy Dicey (housekeeper, Gilmanton); W – 69, tailoress, b. Tewksbury, MA, d/o Loring Loker (farmer, Chelmsford, MA) and Hannah Smith (housekeeper, Needham, MA)

PLATT,
Lawrence Harold of Barnstead m. Judy Mae **Fife** of Pittsfield 10/5/1973 in Pittsfield; H - b. 9/11/1942 in CT, s/o Coley A. Platt (NY) and Dorothy May Whaley (CT); W - b. 3/5/1949 in NH, d/o Clifford A. Fife (NH) and Alice Ernestine Moses (NH)

PODMORE,
Kerry Shane of Ctr. Barnstead m. Carol Lynn **Young** of Ctr. Barnstead 4/20/1996 in Pittsfield

PONTELL,
Ernest E. of Ctr. Barnstead m. Susan J. **McMillen** of Ctr. Barnstead 9/25/1987 in Chichester

POOLE,
Daniel J. of Ctr. Barnstead m. Bethany Ann **Colling** of Ctr. Barnstead 6/8/1991 in Ctr. Barnstead

POPE,
David M. of CA m. Kimberly A. **Butcher** of CA 8/7/1999 in Tilton

POST,
Chester of Barnstead m. Winnie B. **Littlefield** of Barnstead 4/21/1912; H – 26, laborer, b. Rockland, ME, s/o William Post (farmer, Rockland, ME) and Adiline Hall (housewife, Rockland, ME); W – 20, domestic, b. Ashland, ME, d/o Orrin Littlefield (farmer, Conway) and Laura P. Botting (housewife, Oxbow, ME)

POTTER,
Gary Wayne of Ctr. Barnstead m. Jennifer Louise **McGarrigle** of Ctr. Barnstead 1/5/1991 in Northfield

POWELL,
Harry L. of Barnstead m. Alice M. **Shackford** of Barnstead 10/27/1894 in Northwood; H – 21, shoemaker, b. Pittsfield, s/o Sylvester Powell (painter, Concord) and Ada Munsey (Barnstead); W – 21, stitcher, b. Barnstead, d/o William H. Shackford (hotel keeper, Barnstead) and Augusta M. Smart (housewife, Barnstead)

Harry L. m. May E. **Huckins** 8/28/1930; H – 57, s/o Sylvester Powell and Ada Munsey; W – 57, d/o Harvey A. Emery and Lydia E. Robinson

Sylvester of Barnstead m. Marietta C. **Shannon** of Barnstead 3/13/1896 in Pittsfield; H – 49, painter, 2nd, b. Concord, s/o Amasa P. Powell and Sarah Price; W – 29, stitcher, 2nd, b. Barnstead, d/o James R. Berry and Sarah Berry

PRECIADO,

Edgard M. of MA m. Clara Ines **Mora** of MA 10/23/1993

PRESCOTT,

Alan G. of Ctr. Barnstead m. RoseAnn **Greenwood** of Ctr. Barnstead 6/17/1989 in Penacook

Gordon H. of Barnstead m. Mary E. **Wheet** of Barnstead 6/10/1950 in Gilmanton Iron Works; H – 23, carpenter, b. NH, s/o Harold F. Franklin (sic) (NH) and Caroline H. Eastman (NH); W – 21, housekeeper, b. NH, d/o Rexford E. Wheet (NH) and Bessie McDuffee (NH)

Harold F. of Barnstead m. Caroline H. **Eastman** of Barnstead 12/25/1921 in Gilmanton; H – 25, b. Barnstead, s/o Frank A. Prescott and Louenna Hurd; W – 20, b. Chelsea, MA, d/o Hiram B. Eastman and Caroline Sherman

PRESTON,

Howard Robert, Jr. of Ctr. Barnstead m. Kathleen Susan **Patchen** of Ctr. Barnstead 5/14/1994 in Londonderry

PRICE,

David S. of Barnstead m. Jolene M. **Newell** of Barnstead 4/4/1998 in Pembroke

PRINCE,

Charles R. m. Dorothy I. **Davis** 11/5/1928; H – 34, s/o George H. Prince and Mary E. Morse; W – 18, d/o Myrtie M. Davis

PROCTOR,

Leigh V. m. Florence May **Fuller** 2/14/1942 in Rochester; H – 47, s/o Leigh V. Proctor and Lottie Lynn; W – 47, d/o Alphonse Hodsdon and Georgia Carter

PRUITT,
Billy A. of Barnstead m. Teresa Anne **Lawrence** of Barnstead 10/9/1982 in Alton

PSZONOWSKY,
Michael G. of Barnstead m. Beatrice K. **Davis** of Pittsfield 8/18/1984 in Pittsfield

Roger D. of MA m. Violet Nadine **Bateman** of MA 8/26/1972; H - b. 8/25/1948 in RI, s/o Joseph G. Pszonowsky (RI) and Dorothy W. Dennett (NH); W - b. 5/8/1950 in HI, d/o Clarence R. Bateman (OK) and Violet N. Riddle (OK)

PUBLICOVER,
Kenneth G. of Pittsfield m. Pamela L. **Ayer** of Ctr. Barnstead 11/3/1973; H - b. 10/24/1950 in NH, s/o Robert Publicover (Truro, NS) and Annie Shaitas (NH); W - b. 1/25/1955 in NH, d/o Charles Ayer (NH) and Barbara Clark (NH)

PUDE,
William B. of Middlesex, MA m. Christine G. **Murray** of Middlesex, MA 5/3/1980 in Ctr. Barnstead (see following entry)

William B. of Dracut, MA m. Christine G. **Murray** of Westford, MA 5/5/1980 in Ctr. Barnstead (see preceding entry)

PUGH,
Ralph m. Rachel M. **Doe** 5/18/1935 in Manchester; H – 27, s/o Charles Pugh and Amelia Rockwood; W – 29, d/o James F. Doe and Etta F. Martin

PUGLIA,
Robert V. of Ctr. Barnstead m. Geraldine B. **Steeves** of Ctr. Barnstead 1/14/1995 in Ctr. Barnstead

RAICHE,
Alvah F. of Framingham, MA m. Helen M. **Moore** of Framingham, MA 10/22/1949; H – 49, clerk, b. MA, s/o Felix Raiche and Josephine M. Gaudette; W – 46, clerk, b. Chicago, IL, d/o William Pascher and Christine Vondrach

RAINVILLE,
Alan Joseph of Barnstead m. Brenda Lee **MacDonald** of Barnstead 1/19/1991

RAMSELL,
Barry Myles of Ctr. Barnstead m. Diana Claire **Cantara** of Ctr. Barnstead 7/27/1991 in Epsom

RANDALL,
Daniel Clifford of Chichester m. Nancy Ann **Tasker** of Barnstead 11/27/1994

RANEY,
Steven M. of Pittsfield m. Karen L. **Drolet** of Barnstead 8/6/1983 in Pittsfield

RATTEE,
Matthew Steven of Loudon m. Tina Maureen **Richardson** of Barnstead 8/14/1993

RAYMOND,
Donald Andre of Barnstead m. Renee Leslie **Bonenfant** of Pembroke 7/22/1977 in Pembroke; H - b. 10/29/1950 in NH, s/o Andre Raymond (NH) and Vargee Malatras (NH); W - b. 11/5/1955 in NH, d/o Norman Bonenfant (NH) and Patricia Browning (NH)

REDMOND,
Richard D. of Ctr. Barnstead m. Robin A. **Howe** of Ctr. Barnstead 8/16/1997

REED,
Herbert A., Jr. of Barnstead m. Michelle L. **Nation** of Barnstead 3/6/1999 in Pittsfield
Ronald N. of Pittsfield m. Patricia L. **Riley** of Ctr. Barnstead 7/31/1965 in Chichester; H - 18, truck driver, b. NH, s/o Herbert A. Reed (NH) and Rowena M. Clark (NH); W - 17, shoe shop, b. NH, d/o Warren E. Riley (MA) and Charlotte L. Baldwin (MA)

Terry A. of Barnstead m. Sharyn D. **Drolet** of Pittsfield 3/30/1968 in Pittsfield; H - 21, b. NH, s/o Warren G. Reed (NH) and Dorothy P. Canfield (NH); W - 20, b. NH, d/o Lionel D. Drolet (NH) and Katherine C. Riel (NH)

Thomas Robertson of Gilmanton I.W. m. Barbara Diane **Halla** of Barnstead 5/24/1992 in Pittsfield

Warren Grant m. Dorothy Pearl **Canfield** 11/10/1938; H – 22, s/o Fred W. Reed and Gladys May Cheney; W – 21, d/o Archie Canfield and Clara D. Meara

REID,
Wilmot P. of Hartford, CT m. Patricia A. **Plaisted** of Hartford, CT 4/18/1959; H - 25, s/o David P. Reid and Eleanor W. Wilmot; W - 27, d/o Frank H. Plaisted and Winifred M. Miller

RENAUD,
Mark A. of Barnstead m. Patricia C. **Peterson** of Barnstead 6/6/1992 in Manchester

REYNOLDS,
Francis J. of NY m. Susan E. **Riordan** of Alton 6/15/1968 in Ctr. Barnstead; H - 26, b. NY, s/o John E. Reynolds (NY) and Florence Costello (NY); W - 25, b. MA, d/o John D. Riordan (MA) and Elizabeth A. Kelley (MA)

Leon H. of Barnstead m. Minnie P. **Murray** of Barnstead 1/2/1892 in Derry; H – 23, shoe cutter, b. Barnstead, s/o Charles H. (farmer, Barnstead) and Lydia J. (Strafford); W – 15, b. Rochester, d/o James (shoemaker, Portsmouth) and Ida G. (Dover)

RICHARDSON,
Christopher M. of Barnstead m. Jacquelyn M. **Flibbert** of Kennebec, ME 2/14/1981 in Pittsfield

James W. of Barnstead m. Mildred Ellen **Iacono** of MA 6/1/1996 in Laconia

Robert of Dover m. Margaret G. **Tudor** of Barnstead 9/27/1975 in Alton; H - b. 2/8/1951 in ME, s/o Leslie M. Richardson (CT) and Mary Conroy (ME); W - b. 10/8/1952 in NH, d/o Andrew Tudor (MA) and Charlotte Tafer (MA)

William H. of Campton m. Angeline H. **Sanborn** of Barnstead 5/6/1895; H – 43, farmer, 2nd, b. Lowell, MA, s/o C. W. Richardson and Phebe Moses; W – 48, housekeeper, 2nd, b. Bethlehem, d/o Horatio Eaton (farmer)

RICHEY,
Robert H. of Ctr. Barnstead m. D'Arcy A. **Fontaine** of Ctr. Barnstead 9/20/1980
William S., Jr. of Barnstead m. Jean Mary **Thyng** of Barnstead 4/25/1970; H - b. 10/13/1947 in MA, s/o William S. Richey (MA) and Frances M. Pearson (TX); W - b. 7/20/1947 in ME, d/o Harrison R. Thyng (NH) and Mary Rogers (NH)
William S., Jr. of Barnstead m. Judith Lee **Bryan** of New Durham 6/11/1975 in Concord; H - b. 10/13/1947 in MA, s/o William S. Richey (MA) and Frances Pearson (TX); W - b. 1/23/1943 in NH, d/o Harrison R. Thyng (NH) and Mary Rogers (NH)

RICKEY,
Denis G. of Ctr. Barnstead m. Katharine M. **Coolidge** of Barnstead 2/26/2000

RIEL,
Arnold J. of Barnstead m. Patricia W. **Nyhan** of Concord 10/13/1959 in Concord; H - 20, s/o Maurice Riel and Berkie Sharp; W - 20, d/o Daniel E. Nyhan and Alice Valliere
Arthur Donald m. Mary Elizabeth **Clark** 5/9/1942; H – 22, s/o Wilfred E. Riel and Alice Trembley; W – 20, d/o Guy E. Clark and Dora M. MacKenzie
Daniel P. of NH m. Judith Ann **Richardson** of NH 7/1/1972 in Pittsfield; H - b. 1/29/1954 in NH, s/o Arthur D. Riel (NH) and Melizzie Lord (NH); W - b. 7/26/1954 in MA, d/o James W. Richardson (MA) and Ruth W. Whorisky (MA)
Donald Cleon, Jr. of NH m. Diane Lee **Pyne** of NH 10/4/1969 in Pittsfield; H - 24, b. NH, s/o Donald C. Riel (NH) and Eleanor Twombly (NH); W - 21, b. NH, d/o Ralph E. Pyne (MA) and Priscilla Curran (MA)
George W. of Ctr. Barnstead m. Cynthia A. **Paige** of Pittsfield 11/10/1966 in Pittsfield; H - 18, student, b. Pittsfield, s/o Warren J. Riel (NH) and Evelyn Stevens (NH); W - 17, b. Concord, d/o Gilbert S. Paige (NH) and June Remington (RI)

George W. of Ctr. Barnstead m. Glenna C. **Purtell** of Barnstead 5/1/1976 in Ctr. Barnstead; H - b. 8/28/1948 in NH, s/o Warren J. Riel (NH) and Evelyn Stevens (NH); W - b. 2/22/1953 in NH, d/o Arnold J. Purtell (NH) and Ruth Geddes (NH)

Kevin J. of Barnstead m. Andrea K. **Lodestein** of Barnstead 8/7/1981 in Strafford

Leonard E. of Barnstead m. Ruth J. **Bousquet** of Barnstead 6/2/1956 in Chichester; H - 29, drilling, b. NH, s/o Jerry H. Riel (NH) and Evelyn M. Moulton (RI); W - 26, stitcher, b. RI, d/o Clinton L. Lank (Canada) and Ruth O. Butman (RI)

Michael David of Barnstead m. Kathryn **Holbrook** of Barnstead 3/17/1990 in Alton

Steven Ellwood of Pittsfield m. Grace Marjorie **Murphy** of Pittsfield 7/2/1977; H - b. 10/14/1954 in NH, s/o Leonard J. Riel (NH) and Joan H. Trace (NH); W - b. 3/7/1958 in NH, d/o Charles W. Murphy (NH) and Gertrude M. Dyke (MA)

Thomas A. of Pittsfield m. Frances I. **Tarbox** of Ctr. Barnstead 10/26/1963 in Chichester; H - 19, lumber, b. Gilmanton, s/o Allen I. Riel (NH) and Martha P. French (NH); W - 19, secretary, b. Concord, d/o Fred O. Tarbox (NH) and Elanor P. Chellis (NH)

Timothy E. of Pittsfield m. Theresa A. **Lopez** of Barnstead 10/27/1984 in Pittsfield

Timothy M. of Barnstead m. Rosemary J. **Kelly** of Barnstead 9/9/1978; H - b. 4/14/1956 in NH, s/o Leonard E. Riel (NH) and Ruth J. Lank (RI); W - b. 9/21/1958 in NH, d/o Edward R. Kelly (NH) and Ilse M. Frey (NY)

Timothy M. of Barnstead m. Joan B. **Potter** of Gilmanton 12/1/1984 in Gilmanton

RIENDEAU,
Dana H. of Barnstead m. Mary L. **Giguere** of Barnstead 9/21/1985 in Laconia

RINES,
George H. of Alton m. Priscilla M. **Cotton** of Barnstead 10/28/1961; H - 25, carpenter, b. NH, s/o Charles P. Rines (NH) and Elsie Londo (NH); W - 22, clerk, b. NH, d/o John L. Cotton (MA) and Dorothy Buckle (MA)

George H. of Barnstead m. Nancy B. **Nichols** of Barnstead 5/27/1978 in Chichester; H - b. 6/4/1936 in NH, s/o Charles P. Rines, Sr. (NH) and Elsie Londo (NH); W - b. 11/4/1939 in WV, d/o Dale S. Scott (WV) and Mildred Foutty (WV)

George Henry of Barnstead m. Carolyn Frances **Caldwell** of Barnstead 5/10/1990 in Ctr. Barnstead

RIPLEY,
Richard A., Jr. of Ctr. Barnstead m. Joni P. **Pariseau** of Ctr. Barnstead 2/9/1980 in Chichester

ROBB,
Ernest E., Jr. of Pittsfield m. Susan E. **Lichty** of Barnstead 9/1/1978; H - b. 2/4/1954 in MA, s/o Ernest E. Robb, Sr. (IN) and Joan B. Steele (NH); W - b. 2/22/1956 in MA, d/o John E. Lichty (IA) and Lois Bellows (RI)

ROBBINS,
Jon W. of Barnstead m. Linda D. **Therrien** of Barnstead 2/14/2000 in Northwood

ROBERGE,
Roger Wilfred of Barnstead m. Cheryl Ann **Fauteux** of Barnstead 7/11/1992

ROBERTS,
James A. of Barnstead m. Bonnie L. **Kidder** of Rumney 8/8/1981

Scott A. of Ctr. Barnstead m. Cindy A. **Picard** of Ctr. Barnstead 9/25/1999

ROBIE,
Dwight A. of Ctr. Barnstead m. Deborah A. **Minette** of Cornish Flat 6/19/1988 in Piermont

ROBINSON,
Dennis Allen of Barnstead m. Helen Louise **Baldi** of Barnstead 7/27/1979 in Pembroke

Gregory L. of Barnstead m. Paula A. **Inman** of Barnstead 11/18/1978 in Pittsfield; H - b. 2/7/1947 in MA, s/o Ellen Rice

(NH); W - b. 3/21/1954 in ME, d/o Francis Inman (Canada) and Eva Wilson (Scotland)

Henry R. of Barnstead m. Agnes G. **Whitten** of Barnstead 10/12/1888 in Pittsfield; H – 24, shoe cutter, b. Montreal, PQ, s/o David Robinson (England) and Mary A. Gillespie (Ireland); W – 22, stitcher, b. Lynn, MA, d/o Augustus Whitten (Lynn, MA) and Adelaide G. Porter (Scotland)

Jack S. of Pittsfield m. Prudence G. **Magoon** of Barnstead 8/18/1979

John A. of Barnstead m. Rosemary J. **Riel** of Barnstead 4/20/1985

ROFFO,
Charles William of Barnstead m. Barbara Joy **McKinnon** of Concord 8/7/1993

ROGERS,
Albert Edward of Pittsfield m. Lucille Edna **Davis** of Barnstead 3/22/1947; H – 20, shoeworker, b. Pittsfield, s/o George A. Rogers and Beatrice T. Caughlin; W – 20, hairdresser, b. Barnstead, d/o Albert C. Davis and Helen Brown

Clarence Lewis of Barnstead m. Felicia Louise **Littlefield** of Barnstead 10/28/1920; H – 32, b. Johnson, VT, s/o Benton H. Rogers and Ida E. Levene; W – 21, b. Masardis, ME, d/o Orrin Littlefield and Louisa Bootling

George A. of Pittsfield m. Agnes L. **Herndon** of Barnstead 9/6/1951 in Pittsfield; H – 54, electrician, b. NH, s/o Albert E. Rogers (NH) and Carrie Munsey (NH); W – 50, assembler, b. IN, d/o John T. Galbreath (IN) and Ura Frain (IN)

Harvey L. of Portsmouth m. Ethel B. **Witham** of Barnstead 10/13/1959 in Portsmouth; H - 26, s/o Harvey C. Rogers and Leona M. Ricker; W - 57, d/o John A. Brown and Alice M. Tibbetts

Harvey L. of New Castle m. Barbara L. **Yeaton** of Barnstead 12/29/1962 in Portsmouth; H - 29, laborer, b. NH, s/o Harvey E. Rogers (ME) and Leona M. Ricker (NH); W - 19, tel. oper., b. NH, d/o Earle M. Yeaton (NH) and Phyllis L. McIntosh (NH)

Paul E. of Barnstead m. Sandra L. **Brunk** of Barnstead 10/2/1982 in Ctr. Barnstead

ROLLINS,
Leon S. of Ctr. Barnstead m. Alicia R. **Mahon** of Ctr. Barnstead 11/27/1992 in Ctr. Barnstead

Leon Selden of Ctr. Barnstead m. Joyce Ann **McDonnell** of Concord 9/26/1969 in Concord; H - 19, b. NH, s/o Selden Rollins (NH) and Belle J. Parker (MA); W - 18, b. NH, d/o Kenneth McDonnell (NH) and Mary Blanchard (MA)

ROMANOS,
Seth D. of Ctr. Barnstead m. Nancy **Perez** of Concord 8/26/2000 in Concord

ROMANSKY,
Richard of Barnstead m. Martha L. **Thorpe** of Pittsfield 2/19/1972 in Ctr. Barnstead; H - b. 8/27/1952 in NH, s/o Alexander Romansky (NY) and Gertrude F. Barney (MA); W - b. 3/14/1954 in NH, d/o James H. Thorpe (NH) and Patricia Dumont (VT)

ROMERO,
Eleazer of Honduras m. Linda **Meredith** of NH 6/24/1972 in So. Barnstead; H - b. 1/17/1946 in Honduras, s/o Eleazer Romero (Honduras) and Carmen Mendoza (Honduras); W - b. 6/1/1949 in MA, d/o Robert K. Meredith (TX) and Mary Martin (MS)

ROSADO,
Gerald of Medford, NY m. Michelle M. **Smith** of Ctr. Barnstead 10/22/1989 in Bedford

ROSINQUIST,
Bror A. of Barnstead m. Annie L. **Pettersen** of Seattle, WA 9/2/1950 in Concord; H – 67, retired eng., b. Sweden, s/o Enoch Johanson (Sweden) and Maria Johanson (Sweden); W – 29, nurse, R.N., b. Norway, d/o Iver O. Pettersen (Norway) and Eline M. Eriksen (Norway)

ROSS,
Frank I. of Barnstead m. Hildred E. **Merrifield** of Derry 9/23/1903; H – 24, shoemaker, b. Ossipee, s/o Charles I. Ross (shoemaker, Ossipee) and Hattie Smart (housewife,

Barnstead); W – 17, b. Manchester, d/o Frank Merrifield (dealer in stock, ME) and Etta L. Williams (domestic)
Frank I. of Barnstead m. Flossie B. **Edison** of Pittsfield 1/12/1911; H – 31, shoemaker, 2nd, b. Ossipee, s/o Charles F. Ross (painter, Ossipee) and Hattie A. Pray (housework, Barnstead); W – 23, shoemaker, 2nd, b. Pittsfield, d/o Lorenzo Welch (laborer, Gilmanton) and Florence Mathers (shoemaker, Bridgeport, CT)

ROTT,
Daniel A. of Virginia Beach, VA m. Carol L. **Hoffman** of Virginia Beach, VA 6/26/1987 in Ctr. Barnstead
Nicholas Christopher of Barnstead m. Linda Gertrude **Houle** of Barnstead 6/19/1992

ROWE,
George R. of Barnstead m. Linda J. **Rooney** of Barnstead 6/20/1981 in Pittsfield

ROWELL,
Charles A. of Manchester m. Henrietta A. **Whitney** of Barnstead 9/30/1945; H – 49, s/o Fred A. Rowell and Jennie Walsh; W – 56, d/o Andrew Quandt and Mary E. Kessler
Kenneth Paul of VT m. Nancy Lee **Rowell** of Ctr. Barnstead 9/10/1994 in Ctr. Barnstead

ROY,
James R. of Meriden, CT m. Erna **Atmannsdottir** of Meriden, CT 2/18/1989 in Ctr. Barnstead

RUEDIGER,
Bunt E. of Durham m. Eline M. **Rosenguist** of Barnstead 5/31/1975; H - b. 3/12/1953 in NY, s/o Bunt A. Ruediger (Germany) and Dolores Lucis (NE); W - b. 9/29/1953 in NH, d/o Bior A. Rasenguist (Sweden) and Annie Pettersen (Norway)

RUGGIERI,
Daniel K. of Barnstead m. Christine M. **Diperri** of Barnstead 10/23/1999

RUSSELL,

Joseph C. of Barnstead m. Mary A. **Larkin** of Concord 11/25/1903 in Manchester; H – 67, merchant, 2nd, b. Franconia, s/o Joseph Russell and Abigail S. Pinkham (Durham); W – 47, 2nd

Kevin C. of Ctr. Barnstead m. Terri L. **Maher** of Ctr. Barnstead 6/13/1998 in Alton

RYAN,

John J. of Passaic, NJ m. Janice L. **Clayton** of Clifton, NJ 7/31/1954 in No. Barnstead; H – 45, self employed, b. NJ, s/o John E. Ryan (NJ) and Nellie F. Caulfield (Ireland); W - 33, home, b. NY, d/o Paul L. Clayton (MO) and Anne L. Felter (NY)

RYDER,

Lorrine Endicott of Barnstead m. Arline M. **Thompson** of Barnstead 6/24/1915; H – 21, instructor of art, b. Melrose, MA, s/o Henry A. Ryder (floor walker, Sierra Leone) and Mabelle W. Thyng (housewife, Salem, MA); W – 20, b. Barnstead, d/o Silas L. Thompson (painter, Barnstead) and Josephine Babb (housewife, Barnstead)

Warren A. of Barnstead m. Alma M. **Heywood** of Pittsfield 8/27/1913 in Pittsfield; H – 21, weaver, b. Salem, s/o Henry A. A. Ryder (clergyman, Africa) and Mabel Thyng (housewife, Salem); W – 18, domestic, b. Barnstead, d/o Fred L. Heywood (shoemaker, Barnstead) and Grace A. Knowles (housewife, Penacook)

ST. CLAIR,

David Paul of Barnstead m. Leslie Susan **Crane** of Barnstead 9/21/1991 in Strafford

ST. GEORGE,

David A. of Pittsfield m. Edith E. **Yeaton** of Barnstead 7/31/1959 in Chichester; H - 22, s/o Alban St. George and Antoinette Ouelette; W - 20, d/o Earle M. Yeaton and Phyllis L. McIntosh

SAARI,

Larry A. of Barnstead m. Linda **Laskey** of Barnstead 8/11/1979 in Gilmanton

SAINSBURY,
Sean E. of Ctr. Barnstead m. Christal L. **Gilliam** of Havana, FL 3/25/2000

SALEY,
Earl D., Jr. of Barnstead m. Ellen M. **Giovanucci** of Alton 8/28/1982 in Alton
Edwin N. of Barnstead m. Roseanna E. **Hillsgrove** of Barnstead 6/30/1979 in Gilmanton

SANBORN,
Paul Gilbert of NH m. Susan Miller **Grindle** of NH 7/9/1972 in Conway; H - b. 7/9/1951 in NH, s/o Stanley G. Sanborn (ME) and Patricia Samper (NH); W - b. 5/17/1952 in NH, d/o Ralph L. Grindle (NH) and Alice Gordon (NH)

SANDERS,
Gordon R. of Alton m. Nancy A. **LaCroix** of Ctr. Barnstead 6/28/1975; H - b. 4/21/1949 in NH, s/o Robert D. Sanders (NH) and Gladys I. Emerson (NH); W - b. 12/5/1954 in NH, d/o Joseph L. LeCroix (sic) (VT) and Ida V. Thompson (VT)

SANFORD,
Alan C. of Gilmanton m. Linda C. **Smith** of Ctr. Barnstead 6/4/1988

SANSOM,
Robert John of Ctr. Barnstead m. Brenda **Doherty** of Ctr. Barnstead 8/27/1994 in Ctr. Barnstead

SARGENT,
Roy A. of Pittsfield m. Janice M. **Corliss** of Barnstead 10/6/1956; H - 20, lumber, b. NH, s/o Charles Sargent (NH) and Selma Moody (NH); W - 20, tannery, b. NH, d/o Earl Corliss (NH) and Mildred Hill (NH)
Roy A. of Barnstead m. Barbara R. **Ehlen** of Pittsfield 12/10/1977; H - b. 6/13/1957 in NH, s/o Roy A. Sargent (NH) and Janice M. Corliss (NH); W - b. 10/13/1955 in NY, d/o Henry A. Ehlen (NY) and Hattie Morris (NJ)
Roy A. of Barnstead m. Martha S. **Canfield** of Barnstead 7/7/1979

SAUNDERS,
Jonathan F., Jr. of Barnstead m. Donna M. **Hodgdon** of Barnstead 9/8/1990

SAVELO,
Peter P. of Concord m. Faith Lindberg **Strout** of Barnstead 5/28/1977 in Gilmanton; H - b. 9/17/1946 in MA, s/o Peter Savelo (MA) and Elizabeth Famo (MA); W - b. 4/2/1953 in NH, d/o George M. Strout (ME) and Nadine Lindberg (ME)

SCAHILL,
Michael T. of Barnstead m. Teresa L. **Flanders** of Barnstead 5/18/1996 in Epsom

SCARPA,
Daniel William of MA m. Maria **Lebel** of MA 7/13/1996

SCHNOUDT,
Otto of Barnstead m. Emmy **Loeffler** of Barnstead 10/12/1912 in Manchester; H – 26, weaver, b. Germany, s/o William Schnoudt (weaver, Germany); W – 21, domestic, b. Germany, d/o Paul Loeffler (weaver, Germany)

SCHWAB,
Dennis Michael of Ctr. Barnstead m. Robin Renee **Morse** of Ctr. Barnstead 9/12/1992 in Chichester

SCOVILL,
Lawrence S. m. Virginia A. **Prescott** 12/10/1940 in Laconia; H – 25, s/o Sorensen L. Scovill and Lenna Crosby; W – 18, d/o Harold F. Prescott and Caroline Eastman

SCRUTON,
Thomas J. of Barnstead m. Lucy J. **Davis** of Barnstead 4/5/1908 in Pittsfield; H – 21, morocco emp., b. Haverhill, s/o Walter G. Scruton (mail carrier, Barnstead) and Annie B. Smith; W – 20, lace worker, b. Barnstead, d/o Joseph A. Davis (farmer, Barnstead) and Susan Pendergast (housewife, Barnstead)
Walter G. of Barnstead m. Annie L. **Welch** of Barnstead 11/21/1908 in Pittsfield; H – 52, mail carrier, 2nd, b. Barnstead, s/o Levi C.

Scruton and Dorothy H. Foss; W – 30, housework, 2nd, b. Tunbridge, VT, d/o Eugene Lyman (carpenter) and Emma J. DeWolfe

SEARLE,
Charles M. of Somerville, MA m. Bessie F. **Fletcher** of Barnstead 7/1/1908 in Manchester; H – 30, railroad man, 2nd, b. Fairfax, VT, s/o Edgar Searle and Annie M. Gregger (housewife); W – 19, lace worker, b. Manchester, d/o Austin G. Fletcher (farmer) and Helen A. Fletcher (housewife)

SEVERANCE,
Randy Roland of Concord m. Jamie Louisa **Brickner** of Ctr. Barnstead 7/28/1990 in Pittsfield

SEWARD,
Harry F. of Barnstead m. Mabel J. **Marsh** of Barnstead 7/4/1896 in N. Hampton; H – 22, lumber dealer, b. Barnstead, s/o T. F. Seward (lumber dealer, Haverhill, MA) and Mary A. Seward (housewife, Barnstead); W – 19, teacher, b. Barnstead, d/o David K. Marsh (liveryman, Barnstead) and Sarah M. Palmer (housewife, Pittsfield)
Harry Frank m. Hattie May **Garland** 4/4/1940 in Laconia; H – 65, s/o Thomas F. Seward and Mary A. Chesley; W – 41, d/o Edward A. Cofran and Millie E. Hartford
Thomas F. of Barnstead m. Carrie A. **Varney** of Alton 12/22/1917 in Alton; H – 67, b. Haverhill, MA, s/o George H. Seward and Emmeline Williams; W – 51, b. Alton, d/o John J. Lang and Eliza J. Locke

SHAPIRO,
Rob of Ctr. Barnstead m. Karin A. **Wisniewski** of Ctr. Barnstead 10/4/1980 in Alton

SHAW,
Barry W. of Colrain, MA m. Willa **Breslaw** of Colrain, MA 9/25/1982

SHERBURNE,
Albert E. of Barnstead m. Edith L. **Deach** of Barnstead 3/28/1970 in Ctr. Barnstead; H - b. 3/13/1943 in NH, s/o Albert Sherburne (NH) and Florence McCarthy (NH); W - b. 10/19/1936 in NY, d/o Frederick K. Rippel (NY) and Harriette Tyson (NY)

SHIELDS,
Hartley J. m. Louise A. **Gilman** 1/12/1936 in Chichester; H – 21, s/o Sinclair Shields and Mary Tucker; W – 19, d/o Fred S. Gilman and Etta A. Coffin

SHUMAN,
Scott Elwin of Barnstead m. Sandra Lynn **Mooney** of Barnstead 8/14/1993 in Belmont

SICKMUND,
Gordon Boyd m. Constance Sceva **Chandler** 4/24/1944; H – 29, s/o Edward C. Sickmund and Florence E. Slack; W – 28, d/o Chester W. Chandler and Olive E. Main

SILVA,
Christopher M. of Ctr. Barnstead m. Rebecca K. **Dunne** of Ctr. Barnstead 10/24/1991 in Ctr. Barnstead

SIMONDS,
Malcolm Frank of Alton m. Freida Jean **Tarbox** of Ctr. Barnstead 4/4/1970 in Ctr. Barnstead; H - b. 8/10/1938 in NH, s/o Frank Simonds (NH) and Eleanor Higgins (NH); W - b. 7/22/1945 in NH, d/o Fred Tarbox (NH) and Eleanor Chellis (NH)

SIMPSON,
David Richard of Barnstead m. Susan Chesterton **Jameson** of ME 1/29/1969 in Exeter; H - 23, b. MA, s/o Sidney J. Simpson (England) and Gertrude M. McGovern (MA); W - 22, b. NH, d/o Arthur C. Jameson (MA) and Mary E. Loddy (Finland)
Mark R. of Barnstead m. Lisa M. **Silva** of Barnstead 9/5/1999 in Henniker
Mark Reinhardt of Ctr. Barnstead m. Kathy Dawn **Harriman** of Alton 3/18/1990 in Rochester

Robert Seagrave of Ctr. Barnstead m. Susan Janet **Pitman** of Ctr. Barnstead 5/26/1990 in Pembroke

Russell E. of Ctr. Barnstead m. Lorraine T. **Fifield** of Londonderry 6/2/1986 in Weare

SINOTTE,

Richard L. of Concord m. Carol A. **Riley** of Barnstead 5/7/1966 in Pittsfield; H - 27, technician, b. Concord, s/o Eli Sinotte (Canada) and Rose Maltais (MA); W - 19, tel. operator, b. MA, d/o Warren E. Riley (MA) and Charlotte Baldwin (MA)

SIRRELL,

Verne Harold m. Harriett Mae **Perkins** 6/3/1942; H – 24, s/o Edward F. Sirrell and Marion York; W – 22, d/o Sadie Perkins

SLATER,

Keith A. of Ctr. Barnstead m. Marilyn J. **LaPointe** of Ctr. Barnstead 9/6/1997 in Epsom

SLEEPER,

Fred W. of Barnstead m. Amy T. **Maxfield** of Pittsfield 4/4/1908 in Pittsfield; H – 23, morocco emp., b. Alton, s/o Eben G. Sleeper (carpenter, Alton) and Annie E. Glidden (Gilford); W – 16, shoemaker, b. Pittsfield, d/o Austin C. Maxfield (shoemaker, Pittsfield) and S. Glady Hooper (Berwick, ME)

Paul D. m. Hazel M. **Gray** 1/1/1925 in Concord; H – 21, s/o George A. Sleeper and Mildred Chesley; W – 18, d/o Herbert A. Gray and Myrtie S. Cate

SMALL,

Charles F. of Barnstead m. Blanche L. **Ellis** of Barnstead 12/24/1910; H – 20, farmer, b. Boston, MA, s/o James D. Small (carpenter, Boston, MA) and Josephine Dosson (dressmaker, Boston, MA); W – 24, housework, 2nd, b. Gilmanton, d/o James H. Beck (farmer, Gilmanton) and Martha Lougee (housewife, Gilmanton)

Warren Linnell of Barnstead m. Patricia Marie **Johnson** of Barnstead 9/30/1990 in Chichester

SMITH,
David Hugh of Ctr. Barnstead m. Kristie **Hunter** of Ctr. Barnstead 8/3/1996 in Melvin Village

Frederick D. of Weston, MA m. Holly J. **Davis** of Barnstead 8/15/1970; H - b. 3/29/1950 in MA, s/o Shaw B. Smith (MA) and Donna Derbyshire (MA); W - b. 12/2/1950 in NH, d/o Ernest Davis (NH) and Virginia Kelley (NH)

Gary of Barnstead m. Sandra Joan **Steele** of Barnstead 5/18/1969; H - b. 11/15/1949 in MA, s/o Gordon Smith (MA) and Virginia Baker (MA); W - b. 10/8/1950 in NY, d/o Leonard Steele (NY) and Letty Burdick (NY)

Gilbert H. of Pittsburgh, PA m. Emily E. **Corson** of Barnstead 9/13/1953 in Chichester; H - 25, b. NH, s/o Harry M. Smith (NH) and Eva A. Beauchenac (MA); W - 20, b. NH

Gordon M. of Barnstead m. Roberta C. **Keene** of Barnstead 2/8/1974 in Ctr. Barnstead; H - b. 2/19/1914, s/o Thomas Gordon (sic) (MA) and Esther Whittredge (MA); W - b. 2/21/1930 in MA, d/o Joseph Cotton (MA) and Ruth E. Hallett (MA)

Harold A. of Barnstead m. Ella Francis **Clark** of Barnstead 12/25/1922; H – 28, b. Keene, s/o Albert W. Smith and Mary Carmichael; W – 27, b. Barnstead, d/o Jonathan Clark and Ida M. Hanson

Jack D. of Barnstead m. Mary **Beauchine** of Barnstead 3/6/1972; H - b. 9/19/1949 in FL, s/o Perley Stoddard (NH) and Josie Johnson (FL); W - b. 8/10/1953 in NH, d/o John Beauchine (NH) and Jennie St. Pierre (VT)

James D. of Barnstead m. Sandra E. **Hartford** of Allenstown 6/26/1970 in Allenstown; H - b. 5/22/1948 in FL, s/o Donald Smith and Josie Johnson (FL); W - b. 12/15/1950 in NH, d/o Edgar C. Hartford (NH) and Madeleine Raymond (NH)

Keith L. of Barnstead m. Carol J. **Sillars** of Pittsfield 11/6/1982 in Chichester

Keith Leonard of Barnstead m. Cherie Ellen **Day** of Barnstead 12/27/1992 in Chichester

Larry R. of Barnstead m. Alisha E. **Dumond** of Barnstead 9/2/2000

Leonard H. of Barnstead m. Earlene H. **Merrill** of Barnstead 8/25/1945; H – 21, s/o Harold A. Smith and Ella F. Clark; W – 18, d/o Harvey S. Merrill and Helen Hutchinson

Leonard H. of Barnstead m. Madlyn F. **Brown** of Barnstead 8/21/1954 in Chichester; H - 30, truck driver, b. NH, s/o Harold A. Smith (NH) and Ella F. Clark (NH); W - 24, factory, b. NH, d/o John P. Brown (NH) and Mabel Prescott (NH)

Louis R. of Rochester m. Mary L. **Stoddard** of Barnstead 4/28/1973 in Ctr. Barnstead; H - b. 1/13/1950 in MA, s/o William Smith (RI) and Mildred Noonan (MA); W - b. 9/14/1954 in VA, d/o Perley Stoddard (NH) and Josie Johnson (FL)

Paul S. of Barnstead m. Arlene J. **Locke** of Barnstead 5/10/1963 in Chichester; H - 40, machinist, b. MI, s/o Randolph Smith (Denmark) and Hette F. Woodward (MI); W - 24, shoe shop, b. Barnstead, d/o Elias W. Locke (Haverhill, MA) and Violet M. Gray (Barnstead)

Stephen Jay of Ctr. Barnstead m. Roberta Lee **Mantegani** of Ctr. Barnstead 8/20/1994 in Wolfeboro

William Ross of Barnstead m. Penny Sue **Nyberg** of Barnstead 8/13/1983 in Chichester

SOUCY,
Steven P. of Barnstead m. Tanya L. **Philbrick** of Barnstead 7/1/1995

SOULE,
Brian G. of Epsom m. Rebecca J. **Pickett** of Ctr. Barnstead 10/14/1989 in Concord

SOUTHER,
Abram of Barnstead m. Nancy E. **Brown** of Alton 7/3/1970; H - b. 5/3/1947 in MA, s/o Abram Souther (NH) and Patricia Frank (MA); W - b. 3/7/1943 in NH, d/o Richard Brown (NH) and Florence Wells (NH)

SPEIKERS,
John C. of Barnstead m. Sheri L. **Chandler** of Barnstead 10/15/1994 in Franklin

SPENCER,
George Albert of ME m. Sharon Ruth **Curtis** of NH 10/12/1968; H - 26, b. ME, s/o George A. Spencer (ME) and Amy L. Carter

(ME); W - 22, b. NH, d/o Maurice Curtis (NH) and Evelyn Pickard (MA)

SPRINCE,
Jeremy J. of Ctr. Barnstead m. Julie M. **Hansell** of Ctr. Barnstead 10/14/2000 in Conway

SROCZYNSKI,
Thomas J. of Barnstead m. Barbara Jean **Pataki** of Barnstead 5/28/1978; H - b. 12/4/1944 in MA, s/o Stanley Sroczynski (MA) and Jennie Tokarz (MA); W - b. 4/4/1948 in NY, d/o Joseph Pataki (Hungary) and Doris Lewis (NY)

STANLEY,
Robert F. of Rochester m. Linda I. **Dow** of Barnstead 4/6/1968; H - 20, b. MA, s/o Morris Stanley (USA) and Mabel Barlow (USA); W - 19, b. NH, d/o Alvah H. Dow (USA) and Barbara Gray (NH)

STANTON,
Charles Nelson of Ctr. Barnstead m. Susan Mary **Beaudet** of Ctr. Barnstead 8/1/1992

STAPLETON,
Timothy J. of Pittsfield m. Sandra J. **St. Cyr** of Pittsfield 7/23/1977; H - b. 1/16/1952 in NH, s/o John D. Stapleton (NH) and Mae E. Geddes (NH); W - b. 9/17/1952 in NH, d/o Lionel D. Drolet (NH) and Katherine E. Riel (NH)

STARKEY,
John M. of Ctr. Barnstead m. Rebecca F. **Johnson** of Merrimack 12/17/1986 in Ctr. Barnstead

John McMahon of Ctr. Barnstead m. Susan Lynne **Paige** of Pittsfield 8/28/1976 in Pittsfield; H - b. 12/17/1953 in CT, s/o Lowell G. Starkey (PA) and Julia J. Semsel (CT); W - b. 11/2/1956 in NH, d/o Gilbert S. Paige (NH) and June W. Remington (RI)

STEDMAN,
Herbert David of Medford, MA m. Helen May **Ingalls** of Barnstead 9/29/1917; H – 33, b. Halifax, NS, s/o Alfred G. Stedman and Sarah L. Ingel; W – 18, b. Bradford, d/o George Ingalls and Juba Ann Weeks

STEVENS,
James K. of Barnstead m. Mary A. **Clark** of Barnstead 11/29/1889; H – 63, farmer, 2nd, b. Manchester, s/o Roger Stevens (mechanic, Manchester) and Sarah Stevens (Goffstown); W – 57, 2nd, b. Barnstead, d/o Aaron Snell (farmer) and Mary Snell (Barnstead)

William D. of Concord m. Marilyn **Bickford** of Barnstead 9/3/1960 in Concord; H - 20, ex. contractor, b. Concord, s/o Richard E. Stevens (NH) and Cora F. Chamberlin (VT); W - 20, account clerk, b. Pittsfield, d/o Herbert S. Bickford (NH) and Lillian M. Smith (NH)

William D., III of Barnstead m. Beth A. **Brown** of Barnstead 10/15/1994

STEWART,
Carl E. of Barnstead m. Donna L. **Hanson** of Barnstead 11/18/1995 in Pittsfield

Leroy of Barnstead m. Penny J. **Lorden** of Barnstead 12/28/1987 in Chichester

Phillip N., Jr. of Ctr. Barnstead m. Cindy J. **Button** of Ctr. Barnstead 10/21/1989 in Hampstead

STIMMELL,
Jean Leighton of Northwood m. Judy Juanita **Buzzell** of Barnstead 1/28/1977 in Northwood; H - b. 10/1/1945 in NH, s/o John H. Stimmell (MA) and Elizabeth Leighton (NH); W - b. 1/4/1948 in CA, d/o Donald Jenkins (NH) and Hilda Ann Nichols (NH)

STOCK,
Arnold C. of Barnstead m. Beatrice T. **Chagnon** of Pittsfield 7/5/1952 in Pittsfield; H – 24, parts clerk, b. NH, s/o Arthur H. Stock (MA) and Martha C. Henry (NH); W – 23, shoe worker, b. NH, d/o Lewis Chagnon (Canada) and Laura Barron (Canada)

Hamilton Henry of Barnstead m. Judith A. **Breen** of Barnstead 1/7/1972; H - b. 2/5/1939 in NH, s/o Arthur H. Stock (MA) and Martha G. Henry (NH); W - b. 10/23/1938 in MA, d/o Edward F. Breen (MA) and Alice Needham (MA)

Richard H. of Barnstead m. Constance Elizabeth **Harper** of Pittsfield 4/16/1949; H – 23, farming, b. Manchester, s/o Arthur H. Stock and Martha C. Henry; W – 22, home, b. Waltham, MA, d/o Ernest Harper and Constance E. Hill

Robert P. m. Annie L. **Pettersen** 12/21/1958 in Pittsfield

STOCKMAN,

Everett Lee m. Marion Edna **Gray** 2/28/1942 in Pittsfield; H – 20, s/o Everett F. Stockman and Josephine Dennett; W – 17, d/o Albert Wellington and Violet M. Gray

Jack L. of Barnstead m. Gail J. **Turnpaugh** of Barnstead 9/22/1984 on Lake Winnipesaukee

Larry L. of Barnstead m. Patricia A. **Daley** of Pittsfield 1/4/1964 in Pittsfield; H - 21, side laster, b. Barnstead, s/o Everett L. Stockman (Pittsfield) and Marion E. Gray (Barnstead); W - 19, beautician, b. Pittsfield, d/o Clarence Daley (Pittsfield) and Jeanette M. J. Perry (Pittsfield)

Michael L. of Barnstead m. Pamela J. **Benson** of Pittsfield 11/5/1977; H - b. 12/28/1956 in NH, s/o Everett L. Stockman (NH) and Marion Gray (NH); W - b. 3/24/1958 in MA, d/o Alton W. Benson (MA) and Gladys Doten (CT)

Michael L. of Barnstead m. Theresa A. **Jennings** of Barnstead 5/1/1992 in Epsom

Ronald H. of Ctr. Barnstead m. Jane H. **Main** of York, ME 1/22/1988

Ronald Lee of Ctr. Barnstead m. Donna Ilene **Locke** of Pittsfield 2/6/1970 in Chichester; H - b. 8/11/1945 in NH, s/o Everett Lee Stockman (NH) and Marion Gray (NH); W - b. 10/2/1951 in NH, d/o Harold Ozro Locke (NH) and Grace J. Magoon (VT)

STOCKWELL,

F. A. of Barnstead m. Gertrude **Clark** of Barnstead 10/6/1888 in Pittsfield; H – 21, shoemaker, b. Bennington, VT, s/o John A. Stockwell (England) and Nettie A. Stockwell (Peabody, MA); W – 21, b. North Weare, d/o Henry Clark and Mary E. Hull

STONE,
Michael J. of Barnstead m. Angela W. **Talley** of Chichester 12/23/1979 in Chichester
Michael J. of Ctr. Barnstead m. Judy J. **Stimmell** of Ctr. Barnstead 9/10/1988
Thomas Jefferson m. Erma Ruth **Burnbrier** 10/13/1943 in New London, CT; H – 32, s/o Charles E. Stone and Mary Jane Marling; W – 26, d/o Carl J. Burnbrier and Maud Dennison

STOREY,
Charles Sidney of Barnstead m. Theresa Lynn **Potter** of Loudon 10/12/1974 in Rochester; H - b. 1/3/1955 in MA, s/o Robert L. Storey (MA) and Winifred Kelley (MA); W - b. 5/1/1955 in NH, d/o Lester F. Potter (MA) and Alberta Staples (NH)

STOWELL,
Andrew J. of Rochester m. Judith F. **Aversa** of Barnstead 8/8/1986 in Alton

STRACHAN,
Guy R. m. Maud T. **Corson** 6/8/1929 in Pittsfield; H – 22, s/o Charles Strachan and Addie Garland; W – 21, d/o Harry O. Corson and Stella F. Carr

STRAIGHT,
Terrence W. of Ctr. Barnstead m. Nancy A. **Tasker** of Northwood 8/30/1986

STRANG,
Keith R. of MA m. Colleen R. **Carmen** of Barnstead 6/27/1998

STRAW,
Alba C. of Barnstead m. Cilla **Tibbetts** of Barnstead 4/20/1902 in Alton; H – 40, farmer, b. Barnstead, s/o Thomas S. Straw (farmer, Alton) and Lavina Hill (housework, Barnstead); W – 20, housework, b. New Durham, d/o George Tibbetts (farmer, Farmington) and Clara Chesley (housework, Alton)
Cecil Thomas m. Lois Marion **Foss** 1/1/1941; H- 31, s/o Alba C. Straw and Cila Tibbetts; W – 18, d/o John F. Foss and Nina M. Higgins

STREETER,
Raymond of Barnstead m. Christina V. **Grant** of Barnstead 12/23/1974 in Chichester; H - b. 4/26/1952 in NH, s/o Clifford Streeter (VT) and Lorraine Evans (NH); W - b. 1/19/1956 in MD, d/o Richard Grant (NH) and Evelyn Love (MD)

STRESE,
Robin L. of Ctr. Barnstead m. Cheryl A. **Roberts** of Ctr. Barnstead 3/20/1987 in Ctr. Barnstead

STRICKLAND,
Robert B. of Barnstead m. Sharon B. **Briscoe** of Gilmanton 8/9/1980 in Greenfield

STRONG,
James A. of Barnstead m. Dianne L. **Moore** of Barnstead 2/20/1993 in Penacook

SULLIVAN,
Thomas W., Jr. of Ctr. Barnstead m. Virginia A. **Doten** of Alton 5/5/1962 in Alton; H - 26, const., b. NH, s/o Thomas W. Sullivan (NH) and Gladys T. Wilkes (NH); W - 20, at home, b. MA, d/o Edward W. Doten (MA) and Maude A. Ellis (MA)

SUPRY,
Daniel Patrick of Ctr. Barnstead m. Roberta Rae **Green** of Concord 8/27/1994 in Concord

SUTCLIFFE,
Warren P. of MA m. Brenda A. **Belloise** of MA 8/20/1994
Warren Paul of Ctr. Barnstead m. Debra M. **Bostrom** of Ctr. Barnstead 3/1/1980 in Salem

SWAIN,
Dennis H. of Barnstead m. Martha J. **Munsey** of Barnstead 8/17/1991

SWANSON,
Arnold V. of Barnstead m. Christie P. **Miner** of Concord 10/17/1959 in Pembroke; H - 21, s/o Victor Swanson and Ebba Yngve; W - 18, d/o Henry Simpson and Mary H. Riddell

SYSYN,
James of Barnstead m. April R. **Greene** of Barnstead 8/7/1983

TARBOX,
Clarence Earl of Barnstead m. Audrey Lee **Aubertin** of Pittsfield 3/31/1973 in Pittsfield; H - b. 8/17/1941 in NH, s/o Fred O. Tarbox (NH) and Eleanor P. Chellis (NH); W - b. 4/20/1947 in NH, d/o Leo A. Aubertin (NH) and Marjorie E. Stockman (NH)

TASKER,
Arthur W. of Barnstead m. Helen L. **Merrill** of Barnstead 3/16/1909 in Pittsfield; H – 18, motorman, b. Barnstead, s/o Andrew B. Tasker (shoemaker, Strafford) and Jane George (housekeeper, Barnstead); W – 18, housework, b. Haverhill, MA, d/o John Leighton (manufacturer, Strafford) and Kathine Bean (housewife, Haverhill, MA)

Arthur W., II of Enumclaw, WA m. Helen W. **Jacobs** of Barnstead 12/26/1988

Edward Arthur of Barnstead m. Christina **Van Horn** of Pittsfield 9/8/1973 in Pittsfield; H - b. 6/1/1947 in TX, s/o Leonard G. Tasker (NH) and Jessie F. Hickey (ME); W - b. 4/17/1951 in NY, d/o Ralph C. Van Horn (MA) and Mureen Fletcher (England)

Eric M. of Barnstead m. Michele A. **Zube** of Derry 5/30/1998 in Bedford

Francis H. of Strafford m. Evelyn R. **Corliss** of Barnstead 11/12/1950; H – 24, farm, b. NH, s/o Harold F. Tasker (NH) and Mary Wheeler (NH); W – 18, carpenter, b. NH, d/o Earl S. Corliss (NH) and Mildred Hill (NH)

Leighton E. m. Beulah M. **Jesseman** 6/28/1933; H – 22, s/o Arthur W. Tasker and Helen Merrill; W – 24, d/o Fred H. Jesseman and Florence H. Dexter

Leonard G. of Barnstead m. Evelyn M. **Corson** of Barnstead 7/22/1988 in Chichester

Michael F. of Barnstead m. Linda S. **Kelley** of Barnstead
    10/11/1975; H - b. 7/20/1954 in NH, s/o Francis H. Tasker (NH)
    and Evelyn R. Corliss (NH); W - b. 1/6/1956 in NH, d/o Edward
    R. Kelley (NH) and Ilse M. Frey (NY)
Michael F. of Barnstead m. Nancy A. **Wilson** of Northwood
    8/11/1979 in Northwood
Milton S. of Concord m. Nancy R. **Cotton** of Barnstead 9/3/1950; H
    – 25, mechanic, b. NH, s/o Everette Tasker (NH) and Mary
    Stone (NH); W – 18, at home, b. MA, d/o Joseph H. Cotton
    (MA) and Ruth Hallett (MA)
Paul E. of Barnstead m. Barbara E. **Robinson** of Pittsfield
    10/6/1945; H – 23, s/o Arthur W. Tasker and Helen L. Merrill;
    W – 23, d/o Kenneth J. Robinson and Georgiana M. Brown
Paul E. of Alton m. Paulette E. **Griffin** of Barnstead 6/25/1975 in
    Amherst; H - b. 6/10/1922 in NH, s/o Arthur W. Tasker (NH)
    and Helen Merrill (NH); W - b. 9/29/1946 in NH, d/o Albert
    Emerson (NH) and Madelyn Jenkins (NH)
Paul E., Jr. of Barnstead m. Sherry A. **Ashley** of Barnstead
    5/4/1996 in Chichester
Philip G. of Barnstead m. Ivy Rose **Troughton** of Barnstead
    10/1/1977 in Pittsfield; H - b. 2/21/1952 in NH, s/o Leonard J.
    Tasker (CT) and Jessie F. Hickey (ME); W - b. 1/20/1958 in
    CT, d/o Theodore M. Troughton (CT) and Edith Minery (CT)
Roscoe of Barnstead m. Janet **Tuttle** of Barnstead 5/31/1953; H -
    24, farmer, b. NH, s/o Harold Tasker (NH) and Mary Wheeler
    (NH); W - 20, home, b. NH, d/o George Tuttle (NH) and Lillian
    Buzzell (NH)
Roscoe W., Jr. of Barnstead m. Gail J. **Bunnell** of Pittsfield
    9/6/1980 in Pittsfield

TAYLOR,
Adam C. of ME m. Megan L. **Davis** of Barnstead 7/4/1998
Carl of Barnstead m. Gayle Louise **Brescia** of Barnstead
    11/24/1990
James P. of Barnstead m. Anne M. **Keach** of Pittsfield 2/4/1996
Leon L. of Barnstead m. Bertha F. **Bancroft** of Somerville, MA
    2/7/1910 in Somerville, MA; H – 27, fireman, b. Woburn, MA,
    s/o W. E. Taylor (currier, Wilmington) and Hattie A. Bancroft
    (Wilmington); W – 17, housework, b. Wilmington, MA, d/o
    Harrison Bancroft (conductor, Wilmington)

Robert G. of Ctr. Barnstead m. Deanna L. **Klinefelter** of Allenstown 4/10/1999 in Pembroke

TEBBITTS,
George F. of Barnstead m. Nancy A. **Watson** of Pittsfield 1/27/1903 in Pittsfield; H – 48, farmer, 2nd, b. Farmington, s/o Joshua A. Tebbitts (farmer, Farmington) and Mary A. Wentworth (domestic, Milton); W – 55, dressmaker, 3rd, b. Londonderry, d/o Rebecca Goodwin (domestic, Londonderry)

TEDCASTLE,
Douglas Coe of Barnstead m. Elaine Marcia **Dame** of Ctr. Barnstead 4/27/1968; H - 24, b. NY, s/o Arthur T. Tedcastle (England) and Ethel L. Coe (USA); W - 21, b. NH, d/o Herman P. Dame and Edna M. Banks (Canada)

TERRY,
Richard D. of Concord m. Marjorie J. **Eastman** of Barnstead 10/17/1970; H - b. 9/18/1943 in NY, s/o Richard C. Terry (NY) and Sara Hill (NY); W - b. 12/17/1946 in MA, d/o James I. Eastman (MA) and Frances J. Banks (MA)

THERRIAN,
Mark A. of Ctr. Barnstead m. Tracey A. **Morse** of Ctr. Barnstead 9/10/1994 in Chichester

THIBODEAU,
Paul L. of Barnstead m. Beverly I. **Curtis** of Barnstead 8/6/1960 in Pittsfield; H - 20, US Navy, b. RI, s/o Lucien J. Thibodeau (MA) and Virginia A. Bishop (RI); W - 16, at home, b. NH, d/o Morris Curtis (NH) and Evelyn M. Picard (NH)

THOMPSON,
Gordon S. of Gilmanton I.W. m. Mary A. **Dame** of Barnstead 3/31/1979

Mellard H. of Barnstead m. Carolyn **Hogencamp** of Barnstead 6/9/1917; H – 19, b. Barnstead, s/o Silas L. Thompson and Josephine Babb; W – 21, b. Philadelphia, PA, d/o Harry Hogencamp and Jennie Cornell

Thomas M. of Barnstead m. Mary Jane **Clay** of Plymouth 10/5/1968 in Plymouth; H - 22, b. NH, s/o Vernol M. Thompson (NH) and Louise Fisher (MA); W - 21, b. NH, d/o John G. Clay (NH) and Jessie A. Hicken (Canada)

Vernol Millard m. Louise **Fischer** 5/22/1943 in Pittsfield; H – 24, s/o Millard H. Thompson and Carolyn Hogencamp; W – 26, d/o Louis Fischer and Shirley W. Spurr

THOROUGHGOOD,

Kenneth J. of Barnstead m. Dawn M. **Stillings** of Tilton 7/29/1978; H - b. 10/27/1958 in NH, s/o Ralph H. Thoroughgood (NH) and Phyllis A. Young (NH); W - b. 11/12/1960 in NH, d/o Leroy C. Stillings (NH) and Deanna Sue Leary (NH)

Kenneth J. of Barnstead m. Pamela M. **LaPlante** of Barnstead 5/24/1985 in Chichester

Ralph H. of Alton m. Phyllis A. **Young** of Ctr. Barnstead 8/26/1955; H - 18, shoe shop, b. NH, s/o George W. Thoroughgood (NH) and Erma Witham (ME); W - 18, stitcher, b. NH, d/o Benjamin Young (NH) and Edna Lakeman (NH)

Richard J. of Ctr. Barnstead m. Diana L. **Purtell** of Gilmanton I.W. 11/17/1977; H - b. 8/18/1957 in NH, s/o Ralph H. Thoroughgood (NH) and Phyllis Young (NH); W - b. 2/5/1961 in NH, d/o Stanley P. Purtell (NH) and Barbara J. Parker (NH)

Richard J. of Barnstead m. Diana L. **Thoroughgood** of Gilmanton I.W. 11/17/1981

Richard J. of Barnstead m. Prudence G. **Robinson** of Barnstead 5/7/1994

THURSTON,

Karl O. of Barnstead m. Eva M. **Reeck** of Germany 8/7/1998

THYNG,

Charles E. m. Addie S. **Sanborn** 1/11/1930; H – 73, s/o John S. Thyng and Ann M. Mooney; W – 66, d/o Charles H. Tebbetts and Hannah S. Thurston

Charles Herbert m. Beryle Marguerite **Thompson** 6/7/1941 in Winchester; H – 24, s/o Herbert M. Thyng and Elizabeth A. Thyng; W – 24, d/o Grover C. Thompson and Rose Northrop

Herbert M. of Laconia m. Elizabeth A. **Thyng** of Barnstead 8/12/1916; H – 43, real estate agent, b. New Hampton, s/o

Charles D. Thyng and Caroline Bowker; W – 21, clerk, b. Barnstead, d/o Charles E. Thyng and Ora Fletcher

James E. of Barnstead m. Ann Elizabeth **Connell** of Medford, MA 7/26/1917 in Medford, MA; H – 33, b. Barnstead, s/o Charles E. Thyng and Ora A. Fletcher; W – 34, b. Leeds, Yorkshire, England, d/o Thomas Connell and Anna B. High

James E. of Barnstead m. Marietta **Cory** of Barnstead 8/26/1918; H – 34, b. Barnstead, s/o Charles E. Thyng and Ora A. Fletcher; W – 30, b. Ireland, d/o William Henry Burk and Helen M. Carroll

John C. of Barnstead m. Grace A. **Downs** of Barnstead 6/18/1910 in Gilmanton Iron Works; H – 21, farmer, b. Barnstead, s/o Charles E. Thyng (farmer, Alton) and Ora A. Fletcher (housewife, Dover); W – 19, housework, b. Barnstead, d/o Herbert O. Downs (farmer, Barnstead) and Calista McKeen (housewife, Strafford)

TIEDE,

Alan R. of Barnstead m. Lynn M. **Pethic** of Pittsfield 9/15/1979 in Pittsfield

Brett H. of Barnstead m. Donna M. **Doucette** of Pittsfield 10/23/1992

Brett Hamilton of Barnstead m. Robin Annette **Bouchard** of Pittsfield 6/18/1977 in Pittsfield; H - b. 3/12/1959 in NH, s/o Ernst Tiede (MA) and Carol Stock (NH); W - b. 10/30/1959 in NH, d/o Robert A. Bouchard (NH) and H. Kathryn Bucknam (FL)

David E. of Barnstead m. Susan A. **Bachelder** of Barnstead 12/22/1984

Ernie of Barnstead m. Renee L. **Oberg** of Barnstead 5/7/1999 in Alton

Ernst Emil Herman, Jr. of Ctr. Barnstead m. Laurel **Troughton** of Pittsfield 11/25/1973; H - b. 12/12/1940 in MA, s/o Ernst E. Tiede (MA) and Carol Stock (NH); W - b. 3/3/1955 in CT, d/o Theodore M. Troughton (CT) and Edith Rose Minery (CT)

Kurt F. of Barnstead m. Terry Jean **Rollins** of Barnstead 1/20/1979

Robert A. of Barnstead m. Priscilla B. **Kirby** of Pittsfield 4/8/1978; H - b. 12/10/1952 in NH, s/o Ernst E. Tiede (MA) and Carol A. Stock (NH); W - b. 5/18/1955 in NY, d/o William C. Kirby (NY) and Theresa Curran (PA)

TILTON,

Frank S. of Barnstead m. Nettie J. **Reynolds** of Barnstead 8/3/1899; H – 24, farmer, b. Pittsfield, s/o Ransom S. Tilton and Almeda Tilton; W –18, housekeeper, b. Boston, MA, d/o George Robinson and Hannah Robinson

George Everett m. Lillian Velna **Hill** 3/19/1943 in Chichester; H – 41, s/o George C. Tilton and Hattie E. Call; W – 31, d/o James W. Hill and Margaret Gray

TODARO,

Joseph G. of Monessen, PA m. Mary G. **Carson** of Ctr. Barnstead 10/2/1954 in Pittsfield; H - 25, Navy, b. PA, s/o Cosimo Todaro (N. O.) and Harriett Ditta (N. O.); W - 21, nurse, b. MI, d/o Floyd O. Carson (NH) and Helen Durkin (Ireland)

TODD,

Richard m. Maud **Moncrieff** 6/11/1935; H – 20, s/o Leroy Todd and Jennie B. Davis; W – 18, d/o James Moncrieff and Annie Green

TOPHAM,

James H. of Barnstead m. Laurie A. **Miner** of Barnstead 5/29/1999 in Concord

TOTHILL,

Joel S. of Barnstead m. Dori B. **Hartman** of Penacook 8/14/1999

TOWLE,

Bradley James of Barnstead m. Susan Carol **Bruemmer** of Pembroke 12/27/1993 in Epsom

Ronald G. of Ctr. Barnstead m. Rebecca Lee **Loomis** of Ctr. Barnstead 5/1/1976 in Concord; H - b. 9/12/1953 in NH, s/o Robert Towle (NH) and Ruby Avery (NH); W - b. 11/16/1954 in NH, d/o Robert Loomis (NH) and Carolyn Colburn (NH)

TRAINER,

William Perry of VA m. Mary Eileen **Green** of VA 8/15/1970; H - b. 2/13/1947 in TN, s/o Perry F. Trainer (TN) and Margery J. Pleasants (TN); W - b. 9/28/1945 in NJ, d/o Harold L. Marden (WI) and Helen R. Smith (NJ)

TREADWELL,
Gordon L. of Ctr. Barnstead m. Linda P. **Parent** of Ctr. Barnstead 6/29/1996

TREFREY,
Michael Joseph of Ctr. Barnstead m. Karen Ann **Trefrey** of Ctr. Barnstead 12/28/1996

TREMBLAY,
Leo P. of Ctr. Barnstead m. Amy L. **Griffin** of Ctr. Barnstead 8/25/1990 in Farmington
Roger A. of Jaffrey m. Sharon K. **Locke** of Barnstead 2/1/1964; H - 21, student, b. MA, s/o Louis C. Tremblay (Jaffrey) and Dorothy A. Haskens (Jaffrey); W - 19, bookkeeper, b. Rochester, d/o George M. Locke (Barnstead) and Elva P. Holland (Barnstead)

TROTTER,
Gary H. of Barnstead m. Patricia J. **Johnson** of Dover 10/3/1981 in Durham

TROVATO,
James M. of Barnstead m. Michelle L. **Poulin** of Barnstead 10/7/2000 in Belmont

TRUE,
David L. of Ctr. Barnstead m. Brenda Joyce **Brown** of Greenland 2/11/1995 in Deerfield

TURBAVILLE,
Herbert T. of Barnstead m. Christine M. **Towle** of Barnstead 8/14/1981 in Union (Wakefield)

TURNER,
Greg A. of Barnstead m. Veronica A. **Turner** of Barnstead 2/7/1998 in Epsom
Jason L. of Barnstead m. Courtne L. **Parker** of Barnstead 9/23/2000

TUTTLE,
Charles of Barnstead m. Anna H. **Alm** of Alton 12/25/1906 in
 Nottingham; H – 30, farmer, b. Barnstead, s/o George Tuttle
 (farmer, Barnstead) and Isabella Davis (housewife,
 Barnstead); W – 31, housework, 2nd, divorced, b. Sweden, d/o
 Jons Noren (lumber surveyor, Sweden) and Birggeta Kamppe
 (Sweden)
Clarence E., Jr. of Alton m. Ann S. **Bickford** of Ctr. Barnstead
 9/27/1957 in Chichester; H - 33, carpenter, b. NH, s/o Clarence
 E. Tuttle (NH) and Mary M. Patch (NH); W - 18, at home, b.
 NH, d/o Lawrence F. Bickford (NH) and Florence R. Kitteridge
 (NH)
George S. m. Lillian G. **Buzzell** 7/15/1932; H – 22, s/o Charles
 Tuttle and Anna H. Norin; W – 24, d/o Charles E. Buzzell and
 Maybelle M. Gray
Norman N. of Barnstead m. Mary E. **Howe** of Pittsfield 3/6/1965 in
 Pittsfield; H - 24, mechanic, b. Barnstead, s/o George S. Tuttle
 (NH) and Lillian G. Buzzell (NH); W - 18, office worker, b.
 Pittsfield, d/o Darwin F. Howe (NH) and Barbara F. Hill (NH)
Osom M. of Barnstead m. Nettie F. **Foss** of Strafford 3/15/1888 in
 Strafford; H – 23, farmer, b. Barnstead, s/o James C. Tuttle
 (farmer, Barnstead) and Alice J. Tuttle (Middleton); W – 24,
 teacher, b. Strafford, d/o Mark F. Foss (farmer, Strafford) and
 Linavia E. Foss (Strafford)

TWOMBLY,
George F. of Barnstead m. Anna **Ricker** of Barnstead 8/31/1888; H
 – 32, mail carrier, b. Barnstead, s/o Paul H. Twombly and
 Nancy Twombly; W – 32, housework, 2nd, b. Barnstead, d/o T.
 G. Burroughs and Emily Burroughs

UNDERHILL,
Frank of Barnstead m. Inez E. **Parshley** of Barnstead 2/25/1912; H
 – 31, clerk, b. Springfield, s/o Frank T. Underhill (farmer,
 Orange) and Susan A. Burnham (Hanover); W – 31, domestic,
 b. Barnstead, d/o Horace M. Parshley (farmer, Barnstead) and
 Abbie Bickford (housework, Barnstead)
Frank T. of Barnstead m. Nellie F. **Underwood** of Lisbon
 1/28/1902; H – 57, farmer, 2nd, b. Orange, s/o Robert Underhill
 (farmer, Grantham) and Betsey Underhill (housekeeper,

Chelsea, VT); W – 57, housekeeper, 2nd, b. Haverhill, MA, d/o William Woodcock and Adeline Woodcock

VACHON,
David R. of Ctr. Barnstead m. Stacey G. **Stevens** of Ctr. Barnstead 6/24/1995 in Northfield

VAIL,
Steven L. of Barnstead m. Lisa D. **Toscano** of Barnstead 7/5/1985 in Concord

VALENTI,
Michael of Ctr. Barnstead m. Susan A. **Leighton** of Ctr. Barnstead 12/15/1988

VAN DYKE,
Douglas A. of Ossipee m. Dorothy P. **Van Dyke** of Barnstead 12/24/1999 in Ossipee

VARNEY,
John B. of Barnstead m. Hattie E. **Harrington** of Cornish 6/30/1946 in Cornish; H – 22, s/o John C. Varney and Ruth Berry; W – 23, d/o Elbert R. Harrington and Mabel A. Cheever
John C. of Barnstead m. Ruth M. **Berry** of Belmont 9/30/1917 in Belmont; H – 22, b. Barnstead, s/o John H. Varney and Ida A. Chesley; W – 19, b. Middleton, MA, d/o Marshall A. Berry and Maud A. Perkins

VEILLETTE,
Joseph R. of Pittsfield m. Joan M. **Ashton** of Barnstead 3/5/1990 in Chichester

VENO,
Gerald Ansel m. Barbara Ruth **Finlayson** 9/5/1942 in Pittsfield; H – 22, s/o Frank P. Veno and Georgia LaFountain; W – 24, d/o Willard R. Finlayson and Emlie P. Dole

VERNAL,
Steven Edward of Alton m. Diane Lynn **Petschauer** of Barnstead 12/19/1992 in New Durham

VICKERS,
Jerry D. of Ctr. Barnstead m. Jeanne M. **Hoar** of Ctr. Barnstead 9/23/1966; H - 23, technician, b. Memphis, TX, s/o Dewey L. Vickers (OK) and Addie L. Norton (OK); W - 21, b. Boston, MA, d/o John J. Hoar (MA) and Mary S. Mountain (Canada)

VIEN,
Roland A. of Pittsfield m. Eleanor H. **Scott** of Barnstead 3/12/1966 in Chichester; H - 19, clerk, b. Pittsfield, s/o Alpha R. Vien (NH) and Jeanette M. Rollins (NH); W - 15, at home, b. Nashua, d/o Willard F. Scott (NH) and Luella E. Chick (NH)

VINSON,
James W. of Wrentham, MA m. Carolyn Y. **Sinclair** of Barnstead 4/13/1991 in No. Barnstead

VINTINNER,
John Frederick of Ctr. Barnstead m. Brenda Lynn **Moses** of Chichester 11/17/1973 in Pembroke; H - b. 10/13/1954 in NH, s/o Parker Mitchell Vintinner (NH) and Helena N. Holbrook (NH); W - b. 6/15/1954 in NH, d/o Fred Arthur Moses (NH) and Lorraine Edna LaRose (MA)

VONFRICKEN,
Henry A. of Pittsfield m. Dorothy M. **Thurston** of Barnstead 11/14/1992 in Milton

VULNER,
Glen Durwood of Barnstead m. Caroline E. **Wheeler** of Epsom 6/7/1980 in Pittsfield
Glen Durwood of Barnstead m. Kristine Barbara **Adams** of Barnstead 7/30/1993

WADE,
Allan W. of Barnstead m. Gail A. **Goodell** of Barnstead 12/12/1981 in Rochester
Charles H. of Loudon m. Izora J. **Darling** of Barnstead 6/10/1906 in Loudon; H – 38, carpenter, b. Sandwich, s/o Symon M. Wade (farmer, Moultonborough) and Martha A. Blackey (housekeeper, Center Harbor); W – 26, housekeeper, 2nd,

widow, b. Pittsfield, d/o John Chase (shoemaker, Deerfield) and Lucy Moody (housewife, Pittsfield)

WAKEFIELD,
Clyde F. of Barnstead m. Ida May **Davis** of Epsom 12/11/1919 in Pittsfield; H – 22, b. Rochester, s/o Frank Wakefield and Nettie G. Chamberlin; W – 18, b. Epsom, d/o Charles Woodman Davis and Sarah Francis -----

WALCH,
Fred H. of Barnstead m. Nora **Galivan** of Suncook 5/13/1897 in Pittsfield; H – 25, RR employee, 2nd, b. Poughkeepsie, NY, s/o John Walch and Nellie Walch; W – 23, d/o John Galivan and Mary Galivan

WALKER,
Albert D. of Barnstead m. Mary L. **Nutter** of Barnstead 6/9/1893; H – 44, farmer, 2nd, b. Strafford, s/o Edward Walker and Paulina Caswell; W – 25, housekeeper, 2nd, b. Barnstead, d/o Samuel D. Caswell (farmer, Barnstead) and Laura A. Young (housekeeper, Barnstead)

Frederick J. of Ctr. Barnstead m. Margaret J. **Dale** of Northwood 4/12/1988 in Northwood

Horace of Barnstead m. Mary A. **Elkins** of Barnstead 1/1/1896 in New Durham; H – 59, farmer, b. Barnstead, s/o Joseph Walker (Barnstead) and Mary Tasker (Strafford); W – 60, housekeeper, 2nd, b. Strafford, d/o Joseph Gray and Hannah Gray

James W. of Barnstead m. Debra M. **Keene** of Barnstead 2/14/1976 in Chichester; H - b. 5/9/1952 in NH, s/o George F. Walker (NH) and Phyllis Boushway (NH); W - b. 12/18/1950 in NY, d/o Richard M. Keene (MA) and Roberta Cotton (MA)

WARBURTON,
John F. of Gilmanton m. Muriel R. **Emerson** of Barnstead 11/12/1955 in Alton; H - 29, farmer, b. NH, s/o John H. Warburton (England) and Clara H. Elkins (NH); W - 22, home, b. NH, d/o Ralph A. Emerson (NH) and Ruth E. Emerson (NH)

WATERMAN,
Bruce R. of Alton Bay m. Sharon S. **Finethy** of Alton Bay 7/21/1984 in Alton

William R. of Barnstead m. Maryann **Forsyth** of Barnstead 8/4/1984

WATKINS,
Robert Thomas of Pittsfield m. Debra Marlene **Keene** of Barnstead 6/5/1971 in Pittsfield; H - b. 10/22/1947 in NH, s/o Robert F. Watkins (NH) and Eleanor B. Erickson (NH); W - b. 12/18/1950 in NY, d/o Richard M. Keene (MA) and Roberta Cotton (MA)

WATSON,
Curtis D. of Barnstead m. Phyllis A. **Potter** of Pittsfield 11/12/1977; H - b. 2/13/1943 in MA, s/o Ernest A. Watson, Sr. (NH) and Alice French (FL); W - b. 11/11/1941 in ME, d/o Wilburn H. Sargent (ME) and Emma Newbegin (ME)

Curtis D. of Barnstead m. Linda S. **Tasker** of Barnstead 10/19/1984

Eddie Allen of Barnstead m. Cathy Lynn **Locke** of Barnstead 8/11/1990 in Pittsfield

Ernest Arthur, Sr. of Barnstead m. Wilma Christine **LaBranche** of Barnstead 12/25/1978 in Chichester; H - b. 12/16/1914 in NH, s/o Everett A. Watson (MA) and Lena Kearney (Canada); W - b. 10/12/1924 in MA, d/o Arvid H. Nelson (MA) and Maybelle S. Wilson (Scotland)

WEARING,
Michael D. of Barnstead m. Mary Anne S. **Quinn** of Barnstead 12/20/1979

WEAVER,
Gerald Byron, II of Barnstead m. Tina Yvette **Bouffard** of Barnstead 10/19/1996 in Allenstown

WEBBER,
Parker, Jr. of Barnstead m. Iva R. **Weeks** of Barnstead 3/31/1900 in New Durham; H – 19, laborer, b. No. Shapleigh, ME, s/o Parker G. Webber (carpenter, No. Shapleigh, ME) and Mary S. Webber (housekeeper, Milton Mills); W – 18, housework, b.

Gilmanton, d/o Charles T. Weeks (farmer, Alton) and Alice R. Weeks (housewife, Peabody, MA)

WEBSTER,
Otis of Manchester m. Bessie **Ober** of No. Barnstead 11/5/1902; H – 25, teamster, b. Manchester, s/o John S. Webster (teamster) and Anna Moody (housework); W – 16, housework, b. Unity, d/o Frank Ober (laborer) and Mary Small (housekeeper)

WEEKS,
Alfred H. of Barnstead m. Betty A. **Rainaod** of Rochester 10/6/1953 in Rochester; H - 24, b. NH, s/o Henry P. Weeks (NH) and Myrtle E. Hanson (NH); W - 18, b. NH, d/o Warren C. Rainaod and Evelyn M. Garhard
Calvin H. of Barnstead m. Alice E. **Therrien** of Farmington 5/26/1951 in Farmington; H – 23, farmer, b. NH, s/o Henry P. Weeks (NH) and Myrtle Hanson (NH); W – 18, factory, b. NH, d/o Edward N. Therrien (NH) and Edith N. Armstrong (NH)
Henry P. of Barnstead m. Myrtie E. **Hanson** of Barnstead 6/15/1913; H – 28, mail carrier, b. Barnstead, s/o Charles T. Weeks (farmer, Gilmanton) and Alice A. Berry (housewife, Peabody); W – 24, domestic, b. Barnstead, d/o Levi Hanson (farmer, Barnstead) and Abbie Clark (housewife, Barnstead)
Satchell of Wakefield m. Susie M. **Proctor** of Barnstead 6/5/1888 in Wakefield; H – 59, farmer, 2nd, b. Wakefield, s/o Nathan Weeks (Wakefield) and Sally Weeks (Wakefield); W – 40, b. Barnstead, d/o Joseph D. Proctor (farmer, Barnstead) and Sarah L. Proctor (Gilmanton)

WEIS,
Maximilian Karl m. Pearl Cecil **Webster** 1/10/1941 in Concord; H – 46, s/o Maximilian W. Weis and Annie F. Wilson; W – 44, d/o Frank Ketcham and Matie Burlingame

WEISS,
Harold F. m. Beverly P. **Merrill** 9/27/1958 in Sullivan

WELCH,
Charles Ham of Barnstead m. Florence Adeline **Potter** of Gilmanton 12/25/1948; H – 35, farmer, b. Barnstead, s/o Frank

W. Welch and Sadie E. Morrison; W – 22, shoeworker, b. Gilmanton, d/o George D. Potter and Mildred E. Page

Frank W. of Barnstead m. Sadie E. **Morrison** of Rochester 11/30/1905; H – 21, farmer, b. Pittsfield, s/o John W. Welch (farmer, Barnstead) and Josephine Clark (housewife, Barnstead); W – 19, b. Rochester, d/o James Morrison (shoemaker, Newburyport) and Fannie Morrison (Talmouth)

Fred T. m. Rena L. **Wells** 11/25/1929; H – 20, s/o Frank W. Welch and Sadie Morrison; W – 19, d/o Ernest Wells and Laura Jones

Richard O. of Bow m. Marjorie M. **Cotton** of Barnstead 8/19/1967 in Chichester; H - 32, mechanic, b. Concord, s/o Clarence O. Welch (NH) and Mildred W. Wilhelmson (NH); W - 31, typist, b. Woburn, MA, d/o George R. Cotton (MA) and Marjorie H. Hallett (MA)

Richard W. of Manchester m. Leora G. **Williams** of Barnstead 9/8/1951; H – 22, USAF, b. IL, s/o Jason Welch (IL) and Addie E. Snider (IL); W – 18, home, b. ME, d/o Walter W. Clark (ME) and Ruth E. McEachern (ME)

Walter Ray of Ctr. Barnstead m. Cassie Lynn **Robbins** of Concord 12/4/1976 in Ctr. Barnstead; H - b. 10/21/1955 in ME, s/o Paul Welch (NH) and Ruth Loring (NH); W - b. 1/29/1958 in NH, d/o Albin Robbins (NH) and Elaine Smith (NH)

WELCOME,
Richard F. of Ctr. Barnstead m. Barbara J. **Hubert** of Ctr. Barnstead 3/25/2000 in Colebrook

WELDON,
Smith G. of Pittsfield m. Jan Marie **Prescott** of Barnstead 9/29/1978 in Gilmanton; H - b. 4/14/1954 in NH, s/o Gordon R. Weldon (NH) and Peggy J. Smith (MI); W - b. 1/24/1954 in NH, d/o Gordon H. Prescott (NH) and Mary E. Wheet (NH)

WELLS,
Eugene Y. of Barnstead m. Joan **Carr** of Barnstead 3/31/1951; H – 34, state highway, b. NH, s/o Walter B. Wells (NH) and Sophronia M. Yeaton (NH); W – 21, home, b. NH, d/o George S. Carr (NH) and E. May Powell (NH)

Gary Flint of Ctr. Barnstead m. Darlene Marie **Clay** of Barnstead 1/6/1996

Kevin W. of Barnstead m. Tina M. **Locke** of Barnstead 2/19/1982 in Chichester

Oscar A. of Rochester m. Della M. **Gerlack** of Ctr. Barnstead 8/8/1964 in Chichester; H - 21, woodsman, b. Rochester, s/o Chester E. Wells (Northwood) and Elizabeth E. Brown (Barrington); W - 17, home, b. Antrim, d/o Henry A. Gerlack (Elizabeth, NJ) and Dorinda I. Come (Websterville, VT)

WELMAN,
Peter Anthony of Pittsfield m. Paula Ann **Golden** of Ctr. Barnstead 8/25/1973 in Concord; H - b. 10/26/1943 in ME, s/o Elwin Weeman (sic) (ME) and Velma G. Wales (ME); W - b. 2/18/1950 in NH, d/o Paul A. Golden (NH) and Leona C. Parker (NC)

WENBLAD,
Anders Jouhan of Ctr. Barnstead m. Darlene Imelda **Green** of Auburn 9/29/1990 in Hooksett

WHEELER,
Barry J. of Fairfield, CT m. Christine A. **Pinkham** of Ctr. Barnstead 9/24/1966 in Manchester; H - 23, US Navy, b. NY, s/o Kenneth Wheeler (NH) and Elizabeth Pfeifer (NY); W - 22, med. tech., b. Portsmouth, d/o John H. Pinkham (MA) and Ethel L. McAllister (ME)

Charles R. of Manchester m. Priscilla E. **Soulia** of Barnstead 8/24/1968 in Ctr. Barnstead; H - 21, b. ME, s/o Robert S. Wheeler (ME) and Leona Mariner (ME); W - 20, b. NH, d/o John L. Soulia (NY) and Helen Lyons (NH)

Frank A. of Barnstead m. Goldie **Bunker** of Barnstead 1/7/1917 in Loudon; H – 33, b. Pittsfield, s/o Lorine A. Wheeler and Abbie Griffin; W – 32, b. Loudon, d/o Harry Bunker and Nellie Green

George L. of Barnstead m. Violet I. **Nickerson** of Strafford 9/19/1919 in Pittsfield; H – 39, b. Pittsfield, s/o Loran A. Wheeler and Abbie Griffin; W – 23, b. Lynn, MA, d/o Roger W. Nickerson and S. Caroline Gray

Larry D. of Barnstead m. Madeline A. **Stephens** of Barnstead 6/30/1990

WHEET,
Rexford Elwin m. Bessie Wellington **McDuffee** 11/10/1923; H – 26, s/o Joshia Wheet and Abbie Anne McCluer; W – 29, d/o David Leroy McDuffee and Mary Emma Besse

WHITE,
Brian A. of Barnstead m. Vera L. **Wessely** of Pittsfield 6/21/1981
Brian A. of Barnstead m. Evelyn D. **Langevin** of Pittsfield 5/29/1987
Kenneth H. of Barnstead m. Linda A. **Tuttle** of Barnstead 11/10/1991

WHITNEY,
John W. of Syracuse, NY m. Lucy A. **Berry** of Barnstead 9/7/1887 in Gilmanton; H – 37, physician, b. Macomb, NY, s/o John Whitney (farmer, Canada) and Mary A. Whitney (NY); W – 27, teacher, b. Barnstead, d/o Ira L. Berry (farmer, Barnstead) and Lavina Berry (Barnstead)
Maurice T. of Barnstead m. Martha J. **Caswell** of Barnstead 7/10/1959 in Lexington, MA; H - 76, s/o Warren Whiting (sic) and Nellie Muzzey; W - 72, d/o Franz Dretzel and Marie Ludwig

WHITTAKER,
Fred R. m. S. Anna **French** 2/18/1928 in Pittsfield; H – 47, s/o George E. Whittaker and Mary E. Randall; W – 44, d/o John Van Dusen and Amelia Braley

WHITTIER,
Alton John of Alton Bay m. Maria **DePerri** of Barnstead 10/3/1992 in Pittsfield
Dean Elthan m. Myrtle Justine **Leavitt** 8/26/1940 in Wells, ME; H – 21, s/o Ronello J. Whittier and Lena M. White; W – 18, d/o Harry E. Leavitt and Grace E. Sargent
Keith A. of Pittsfield m. Teri A. **Brassaw** of Barnstead 8/18/1979 in Pittsfield
Keith A. of Pittsfield m. Patti A. **Rollins** of Barnstead 9/25/1993 in Pittsfield

WHITTINGTON,
Glen Dale of Ctr. Barnstead m. Ruth Elaine **Boyd** of Ctr. Barnstead 8/15/1970; H - b. 7/7/1947 in AR, s/o Dillard M. Whittington (AR) and Evelyne Shaw (AR); W - b. 5/3/1951 in NH, d/o Randolph L. Boyd (NH) and Emma J. Gray (NH)

WIGGIN,
George E. of Salem, MA m. Lizzie M. **Nutter** of Salem, MA 6/6/1901; H – 56, carpenter, 2nd, b. Quincy, MA, s/o Jacob B. Wiggin (carpenter, Newmarket) and Caroline Wiggin (housewife, Newmarket); W – 29, housework, b. Barnstead, d/o Samuel L. Nutter (farmer) and Lydia Nutter (shoe factory)

WILEY,
John W., II of Barnstead m. Dawna C. **Dame** of Strafford 12/7/1985

WILLETT,
Charles J. of Ctr. Barnstead m. Melva E. **Clark** of Ctr. Barnstead 9/30/1989

WILLIAMS,
Stephen Charles of Ctr. Barnstead m. Nancy Ellen **Coe** of Arbovale, WV 8/8/1992 in Laconia

WILSON,
Thomas of Scotland m. Dorothy A. **Twaddle** of Barnstead 4/21/1999

WING,
Samuel G. of Fairfield m. Carrie M. **Manning** of Barnstead 7/21/1913; H – 31, lumberman, b. Bar Mill, s/o Franklin P. Wing (fum. m'f'g, No. Anson) and Hortense Gilman (Fairfield); W – 26, domestic, b. Perry Sound, d/o Dexter A. Manning (engineer, Canada) and Alice Beck (housekeeper, VT)

WIRTH,
Raymond P. of Derry m. Lisa M. **Bailey** of Ctr. Barnstead 8/20/1989 in Durham

WITHAM,
Allen G. of Barnstead m. Maureen E. **Dame** of Barnstead 9/27/1969 in Ctr. Barnstead; H - 25, b. MA, s/o Alden W. Witham (MA) and Doreth Thomas (MA); W - 18, b. NH, d/o Herman Dame (NH) and Edna Banks (Canada)

WITHAN,
Roy Wesley of Northwood m. Ethel May **Brown** of Barnstead 5/30/1922 in Northwood; H – 23, b. Northwood, s/o Fred Harvey and Stella B. Withan; W – 21, b. Barnstead, d/o John A. Brown and Alice Tibbetts

WOOD,
Almon G. of Barnstead m. Chloe B. **Young** of Barnstead 1/1/1952; H – 64, retired engineer, b. NH, s/o Elmer J. Wood (NH) and Emma E. Tourtelett (ME); W – 62, housekeeper, b. NH, d/o Levi Brooks (NH) and Matilda A. Terrill (NH)

WOODWARD,
William of Gilmanton m. Barbara J. **Stock** of Barnstead 9/13/1959; H - 22, s/o Richard M. Woodward and Iris R. Ford; W - 18, d/o Arthur H. Stock and Martha C. Henry

WORDON,
W. A. of Barnstead m. Theda A. **Genest** of Pittsfield 10/3/1999 in Pittsfield

YANNIZZE,
Joseph J. of Ctr. Barnstead m. Jennifer A. **Koehler** of Ctr. Barnstead 4/7/1998

YANSKI,
Michael S. of Barnstead m. Barbara E. **Mulligan** of Barnstead 11/18/1983 in Laconia

YEATON,
Douglas W. m. Gloria G. **Drolet** 11/15/1958 in Pittsfield
Earle M. m. Phyllis L. **McIntosh** 9/27/1938 in Pittsfield; H – 21, s/o William H. Yeaton and Ethel G. Gray; W – 17, d/o Howard McIntosh and Pearl E. Sargent

William H. of Northwood m. Ethel G. **Gray** of Barnstead 7/10/1915 in Pittsfield; H – 25, teamster, b. Northwood, s/o Alvah L. Yeaton (farmer, Epsom) and Etta Bartlett (housewife, Northwood); W – 26, b. Barnstead, d/o Herbert A. Gray (farmer, Barnstead) and Mertie S. Cate (housewife, Barnstead)

YOUNG,
Adam L. of Ctr. Barnstead m. Jennifer A. **Emeney** of Ctr. Barnstead 6/21/1997

Alfred C. m. Jessie E. **Phillip** 6/11/1923 in Portsmouth; H – 69, s/o Joseph Young and Julia Kendall; W – 55, d/o Charles H. Lewis and Mary A. Tibbetts

Burt of Barnstead m. Alice **Palmer** of Concord 1/20/1902 in Gilmanton Iron Works; H – 23, railroad, b. Barnstead, s/o Hanson H. Young (wheelwright, Barnstead) and Priscilla Sackett (housekeeper, Barnstead); W – 21, milliner, b. Barnstead, d/o Frank E. Palmer (carpenter, Barnstead) and Ida J. Shackford (housekeeper, Barnstead)

Forrest B. of Ctr. Barnstead m. Jacquelyn L. **Myers** of Concord 10/28/1965; H - 19, electronics, b. Barnstead, s/o Benjamin N. Young (NH) and Edna P. Lakeman (NH); W - 21, electronics, b. Concord, d/o John J. Lee (Canada) and Orissa M. Armstrong (NH)

Percy C. of Barnstead m. Clara **Hillsgrove** of Barnstead 3/19/1892 in Pittsfield; H – 18, packer, b. Belmont; W – 18, stitcher, b. Loudon, d/o Joseph M. (laborer, Loudon) and Lydia (Strafford)

Samuel Fletcher of Concord m. Verna H. **MacNeil** of Barnstead 12/29/1971 in Lebanon; H - b. 3/28/1930 in NH, s/o Charles E. Young (ME) and Marjorie L. Parris (NH); W - b. 8/1/1939 in NH, d/o John Brewster (NH) and Gladys Call (NH)

ZAVIDNIAK,
James J. of Ctr. Barnstead m. Barbara R. **Brellis** of Trumbull, CT 7/22/1982

ZECHA,
Ernest A. of Barnstead m. Alice A. **Whitcher** of Strafford 10/12/1910 in Strafford; H – 21, weaver, b. Chelsea, MA, s/o Ferdinand Zecha (superintendent, Triebendorf, Germany) and Helena Vogt (housewife, Seiferts, Germany); W – 20, teacher,

b. Strafford, d/o Joseph E. Whitcher (Strafford) and Abbie D. Perkins (housework, Strafford)

Ferdinand, Jr. of Barnstead m. Arlene T. **Naylor** of Pittsfield 5/12/1950 in Keene; H – 25, weaver, b. NH, s/o Ferdinand Zecha, Sr. (NH) and Gertrude M. Barnes (MA); W – 22, waitress, b. NH, d/o Harold H. Whitcomb (ME) and Mamie Mettevia (NH)

Ferdinand, Sr. of Barnstead m. Katherine N. **Vincent** of Keene 5/4/1974; H - b. 2/20/1899 in MA, s/o Florian Zecha (Austria) and Lena Hart (Germany); W - b. 8/2/1907 in NH, d/o Oscar Nelson (Finland) and Samnra Heltamaki (Finland)

ZIELSKI,

Dennis H. of Salem, MA m. Kathleen A. **Hogan** of Peabody, MA 8/3/1986 in Ctr. Barnstead

BRIDES' NAMES

Abbott, Cyrena P. (Paige) - Littlefield, Wilmer L.
Abbott, Dorothy A. - Milligan, Roy L.
Adams, Alvira F. - Parshley, Levi C.
Adams, Beverly F. - Beesmer, Richard R.
Adams, Kristine Barbara - Vulner, Glen Durwood
Aikens, Nellie M. - Bunker, Joseph S.
Aikins, Addie F. - Bunker, George M.
Albrecht, Linda J. - Fraser, Mark T.
Allen-Serell, Lori - Allen, Michael R.
Alm, Anna H. (Noren) - Tuttle, Charles
Alm, Clara E. - Griffin, Charles E.
Anderson, Sandra D. - Patterson, David M.
Anderson, Valerie S. - Blanchette, Gene R.
Antonelli, Tara L. - Abbott, Joshua O.
Aparicio, Stephanie - Oumarhough, Mohammed
Armansdottir, Erna - Roy, James R.
Armstrong, Elma I. (Shackford) - Jenkins, Albert S.
Ashley, Sherry A. - Tasker, Paul E., Jr.
Ashton, Cheryl Anne - Jewett, Mark David
Ashton, Donna M. - McKenna, James P., Jr.
Ashton, Joan M. - Veillette, Joseph R.
Ashton, Vickie J. - Frost, Theodore W., III
Atwell, Carol Isabel - Pitman, Arthur William
Atwell, Marjorie Ann - McCormack, Bernard P.
Atwell, Peggy L. - Jussaume, Lucien B., Jr.
Aubertin, Audrey Lee - Tarbox, Clarence Earl
Aubertin, Lucille E. (Gwinn) - Golden, Richard L.
Auger, Clara - Boudreault, Albert
Aversa, Judith F. - Stowell, Andrew J.
Aversa, Roberta E. - Lee, Michael R.
Avery, Sallie L. - Avery, Daniel H.
Avery, Shirley Annette - McAllister, Robert Willis
Axinger, Ellamarie N. (Nourse) - Carr, Robert B.
Ayer, Cynthia L. - Foss, Dan H.
Ayer, Emelyn F. - Krause, George R.
Ayer, Pamela L. - Publicover, Kenneth G.
Ayers, Annie E. - Chesley, Herbert L.
Ayotte, Irene - Maxfield, John Austin
Azar, Lynda S. - Dickinson, Charles A., Jr.

Bachelder, Susan A. - Tiede, David E.

Bailey, Lisa M. - Wirth, Raymond P.
Baker, Beth H. - Hall, George F.
Baldi, Helen Louise - Robinson, Dennis Allen
Ball, Charlotte M. - King, Robert C.
Bamford, Ann Marie - Foote, Michael Armand
Bancroft, Bertha F. - Taylor, Leon L.
Banks, Edna M. - Bickford, George A.
Banks, Edna Myrtle - Dame, Herman Perley
Banks, Frances Jeannette - Eastman, James Irving
Barnett, Sally Ann - Delollis, Joseph B.
Barrett, Shelby L. - Laudani, Mark
Barrett, Suzanne Marie - Ouellette, Alberic, III
Barron, Lena - Brooks, Fred
Bartlett, Angie Mae - Gray, Frank Clarence
Bartlett, Denice Francine - Moody, Terry Lee
Bartlett, Velma L. - Gilman, Gary E.
Barton, Elva L. - Kidder, Kenneth C.
Barton, Marguerite - Clark, Eugene F.
Bassett, Pauline F. (Fay) - French, John D.
Bateman, Violet Nadine - Pszonowsky, Roger D.
Bean, Jo-Anne Gail - Palmer, Christopher Douglas
Beauchesne, Lisa J. - Lamarre, Ryan David
Beauchine, Mary - Smith, Jack D.
Beaudet, Susan Mary - Stanton, Charles Nelson
Beaupre, Sharon Lee - Huntley, Mark Allen
Beauregard, Michele I. - Hoyt, Randolph W.
Bedell, Dawn M. - Foss, David L.
Bedore, Adrith L. - Bicchieri, Joseph W.
Beede, Mary E. - Gray, George H.
Belanger, Diane M. - Cloutier, Laurent A.
Belleville, Susan J. - Carter, Scott A.
Belloise, Brenda A. - Sutcliffe, Warren P.
Belville, Rachel Yvonne - Locke, Ernest Eugene
Belyel, Mathilda - Kuirsch, Konrad
Bennett, Irene V. - Carswell, William H.
Benson, Pamela J. - Stockman, Michael J.
Berg, Patty Ellen - Gustafson, Michael Eric
Bergeron, Dawn Mae - Farnham, Donald Burton
Berkson, Carole A. - Jenisch, William P.
Berry, Alma M. - Emerson, Harold B.
Berry, Ina P. - Nutter, Frank C.

Berry, Jodi L. - Glines, Jonathan A.
Berry, Lorraine Blanche - Gerlack, Henry Charles
Berry, Lucy A. - Whitney, John W.
Berry, Ruth M. - Varney, John C.
Berwick, Kristine - Girard, David M.
Bessaw, Tami J. - Mousseau, Sherman P.
Bessir, Mary E. - McDuffee, David L.
Bianchi, Norma V. - Golotto, Robert M.
Bickford, Alison P. - Fleury, Ronald G.
Bickford, Ann S. - Tuttle, Clarence E., Jr.
Bickford, Betty J. - Bousquet, John A.
Bickford, Carrie Lynn - Lougee, Richard William
Bickford, Hannah S. - Otterson, Thomas J.
Bickford, Marilyn - Stevens, William D.
Biddle, Amy S. - Dickinson, Gary E.
Bird, Ellen C. - Healey, Dexter L.
Bisson, Lorraine Y. - Brewster, John M.
Bixby, Doris Katherine - Hillsgrove, Casper Ewell
Blachsl, Auguste - Doelz, Adolf
Black, Caroline R. - Hillton, Charles J.
Blackey, Jessica L. - Bell, Eric S.
Blair, Amie F. - Lennon, Thomas J.
Blair, Amy E. - Dall, Gary P.
Blaisdell, Linda L. - Langendorfer, Dwight P.
Blake, Mary E. - Locke, Clayton W.
Blakmer, Alice C. - O'Brien, James E.
Blanchette, Theresa A. - Parkey, Peter J.
Bodge, Ethel G. - Clark, Frank H.
Boisvert, Sandra J. - Pickett, Fredrick W.
Boland, Nancy Marie - Gray, Richard Malcolm
Bond, Joanne L. - Cotton, John Patrick
Bond, Ruth L. - Feinn, Maurice H.
Bondelvitch, Nancy C. - Joy, Alan D.
Bonenfant, Renee Leslie - Raymond, Donald Andre
Bostrom, Debra M. - Sutcliffe, Warren Paul
Bouchard, Robin Annette - Tiede, Brett Hamilton
Boudreau, Leslie Jean - Follansbee, Calvin A.
Boudrieau, Angelina May (Coderre) - Lionstone, Harry Emanuel
Bouffard, Tina Yvette - Weaver, Gerald Byron, II
Bouley, Denise Germaine - Christiansen, Kevin Lee
Bousquet, Amy B. - Burley, Richard O.

Bousquet, Ruth J. - Riel, Leonard E.
Bousquet, Theresa Irene (Couch) - Abbott, John Emerson
Bowen, Cheryl L. - Clements, Michael P.
Boyd, Arline Marjorie - Crossett, William Wilbur
Boyd, Doris A. - Pierce, Wilbert M.
Boyd, Freda Alberta (Gilman) - Mountain, Henry Joseph
Boyd, Nancy Elizabeth - Kennedy, Thomas Francis, Jr.
Boyd, Ruth Elaine - Whittington, Glen Dale
Braase, Ruth Elaine (Boyd) - Hyslop, Gerald Brian
Brady, Gladys W. - Kenison, Fred R.
Branagan, Janet L. - Hookailo, Robert E.
Brassaw, Teri A. - Whittier, Keith A.
Brayden, Pamela S. - Herring, Neil Charles
Breen, Judith A. - Stock, Hamilton Henry
Brellis, Barbara R. - Zavidniak, James J.
Brescia, Gayle Louise - Taylor, Carl
Breslaw, Willa - Shaw, Barry W.
Breton, Lisa C. - Jursik, Robert F.
Brewster, Cynthia L. - Keating, James Ralph
Brewster, Nellie Mira - Emerson, Harry
Brickner, Jamie Louisa - Severance, Randy Roland
Briggs, Sharon M. - Adams, Michael C.
Brigham, Sarah Louise - Bickford, Howard James
Briscoe, Sharon B. - Strickland, Robert B.
Brock, Anita M. - Golden, Scott L.
Brock, Doris Esther (Chapman) - Brock, Burley Barton
Brodie, Lizzie E. - Dickey, Charles B.
Brousseau, L. Aldea - Black, Norman Emerson
Brown, Adela - Emerson, Charles
Brown, Bertha M. - Jenkins, Ernest C.
Brown, Bessie J. - Gray, Albert B.
Brown, Beth A. - Stevens, William D., III
Brown, Brenda Joyce - True, David L.
Brown, Denise M. - Alexander, Paul Stephen
Brown, Ethel May - Withan, Roy Wesley
Brown, Georgia B. - Emerson, Albert F.
Brown, Gladys M. - Evans, Arva
Brown, Helen E. - Davis, Albert C.
Brown, Leslie Ann - Forsyth, Ralph Gordon
Brown, Lillian E. - Garland, Wilbur J.
Brown, Loretta A. - Martin, Ronald E.

Brown, Madgeline E. (Gerlack) - Brown, Roland E.
Brown, Madlyn F. - Smith, Leonard H.
Brown, Marjorie L. - Kenney, John L.
Brown, Nancy E. - Souther, Abram
Brown, Patricia A. - Munroe, Donald S.
Brown, Sally A. (Sutton) - Pinkham, Philip J.
Broxy, Paula M. - Armer, James H.
Brown, Virginia M. - Higgins, Charles P.
Bruemmer, Susan Carol - Towle, Bradley James
Brumet, Michele S. - Heinrich, Dieter W. H.
Brunk, Sandra L. - Rogers, Paul E.
Bryan, Judith Lee (Thyng) - Richey, William S., Jr.
Bryant, Barbara L. - Lagrange, Richard A.
Bunker, Ann M. - Miles, John B.
Bunker, Debra A. - Ashley, George M.
Bunker, Doris A. - Marsh, Luther E.
Bunker, Goldie - Wheeler, Frank A.
Bunker, Ida M. - Pitman, Arthur J.
Bunnell, Gail J. - Tasker, Roscoe W., Jr.
Burbank, Paula A. - Houle, Andrew A.
Burden, Susan M. (Rath) - Howard, Timothy R.
Burley, Deborah Sue - Collins, Joseph Martin
Burnbrier, Erma Ruth - Stone, Thomas Jefferson
Burritt, Allison Jean - Gosse, Thomas Arthur
Burtt, Sara J. - Kimball, Steven A.
Butcher, Kimberly A. - Pope, David M.
Button, Cindy J. - Stewart, Philip N., Jr.
Buzzell, Judy Juanita (Jenkins) - Stimmell, Jean Leighton
Buzzell, Lillian G. - Tuttle, George S.
Byers, Marjorie G. - Lane, Stacy C.

Calder, Diana Glanton - Levasseur, Leo Joseph
Caldwell, Carolyn Frances - Rines, George Henry
Caldwell, Cheryl-Ann - Charette, Paul J.
Call, Lura Gladys - Brewster, John Merrill
Campbell, Christie Anna - Gosse, Robert Alan
Canfield, Dorothy Pearl - Reed, Warren Grant
Canfield, Martha S. - Sargent, Roy A.
Canfield, Reta B. - Kimball, Edwin C.
Canfield, Tracy L. - Garland, Gary R.
Cantara, Diane Claire - Ramsell, Barry Myles

Carey, Lynn - Miner, Dennis A.
Carlson, Norma J. - Fitzpatrick, Ronald S., Jr.
Carmen, Colleen R. - Strang, Keith R.
Carney, Gladys - Gelinas, William M.
Carpenter, Beatrice V. - Eastman, Ralph W.
Carr, Joan - Wells, Eugene Y.
Carr, Nancy A. - Matlock, Jeffrey J.
Carr, Saddie M. - Palmer, Charles E.
Carson, Abbie L. - Kidder, Lloyd D.
Carson, Deborah L. - Cofferen, Arthur F., Jr.
Carson, Lillian Smart - Garland, Robert Minot
Carson, Mary G. - Todaro, Joseph G.
Carson, Stella F. - Bergerin, Donald A.
Carter, Gail Ruth - Brown, Allan P.
Cass, Lucille E. - Moore, Alfred E.
Cassavanaugh, Sharon E. - Hazeltine, Kenneth A.
Caswell, Martha J. (Dretzel) - Whitney, Maurice T.
Cate, Charlotte - Bunker, Roland E., Jr.
Cate, Mabel Idella - Cameron, Daniel R.
Cate, Patricia L. - Gerlack, Alfred F.
Chadwick, Fannie H. - Pickering, Fred C.
Chagnon, Beatrice T. - Stock, Arnold T.
Chagnon, Doris Alice (Kenison) - Martin, Lee Roland
Chagnon, Gail M. - Duhaime, Daniel A.
Chagnon, Laura A. - Caruso, Robert C.
Chandler, Constance Sceva - Sickmund, Gordon Boyd
Chandler, Sheri L. - Speikers, John C.
Chapman, Margaret L. (Coburn) - Foss, Lindy E.
Chase, Ruth Elizabeth - Kelly, Robert Anthony
Chatham, Jeanne M. - Gottlieb, Sheldon L.
Chesley, Alice L. - Bunker, Lewis W.
Chesley, Mary E. W. (Loker) - Place, George E.
Childress, Nancy W. - Locke, Nathan J.
Chirchill, Freedith - Davis, Leroy A.
Chown, Deborah A. - Fransway, John D.
Clark, Ella Francis - Smith, Harold A.
Clark, Florence M. - Curtin, Michael J.
Clark, Gertrude - Stockwell, F. A.
Clark, Josie - Emerson, Elmer J.
Clark, Mary A. (Snell) - Stevens, James K.
Clark, Mary Elizabeth - Riel, Arthur Donald

Clark, Melva E. - Willett, Charles J.
Clark, Patricia A. - Cunningham, Thomas
Clark, Staci L. - Bousquet, Jeffrey J.
Clay, Darlene Marie - Wells, Gary Flint
Clay, Mary Jane - Thompson, Thomas M.
Clayton, Janice L. - Ryan, John J.
Clement, Anita Linda - Bousquet, Paul Judson
Clement, Christine L. - Pinto, Robert
Clement, Cindy L. - Noyes, Charles R., Jr.
Clement, Deborah Lynn - Fair, Timmie Robert
Clement, Jennifer B. - Martin, Gregory Keith
Cleveland, Beatrice M. - Dow, John H.
Clifford, Terese Lee - Beaudry, Gene Edward
Cloonen, Karen L. - Lyons, Thomas F.
Clough, Cora B. - Dodge, Walter S.
Clough, Essel - Emerson, Arthur C.
Clough, Nellie F. - Pitman, Albert G.
Coe, Nancy Ellen - Williams, Stephen Charles
Coffan, Hattie M. - Garland, Wilbur J.
Coffin, Dora A. (Young) - Clough, George T.
Colburn, Myra - Kelley, Joseph
Colby, Karen A. - Kimball, Edward C., II
Colling, Bethany Ann - Poole, Daniel J.
Collum, Maureen Glenda - Kelly, Robert Anthony
Colpitt, Deborah J. - LaBrecque, Roland V., Jr.
Conary, Sharon L. - Ogden, David K.
Conley, Eileen Elizabeth - Murley, David Freeman
Connell, Ann Elizabeth - Thyng, James E.
Connell, Margaret O. - Brown, Bradbury P.
Connelly, Patricia N. (Murphy) - Atton, Arthur
Conrad, Alison Town - Lamb, Robert Alan
Conrad, Jennifer L. - Brand, Thomas E.
Constant, Jennifer L. - Gray, Steven E.
Constant, Sherry Lee - Perkins, David M., II
Coolidge, Katharine M. - Rickey, Denis G.
Corcoran, Katherine M. - Locke, Harvey R., Jr.
Corcoran, Katherine M. M. - Locke, Harvey R., Jr.
Corliss, Evelyn R. - Tasker, Francis H.
Corliss, Janice M. - Sargent, Roy A.
Corliss, Olive M. - Higgins, William A.
Cornell, Ada P. B. (Manning) - Derby, Francis C.

Corrow, Shirley M. - Chappelle, John E.
Corson, Edith May - Larson, Frederick Albert
Corson, Emily E. - Smith, Gilbert H.
Corson, Evelyn M. - Tasker, Leonard G.
Corson, Flora I. - Collins, Ralph M.
Corson, Geraldine F. - Bowen, Burton M.
Corson, Linda J. - Kennedy, Gerald E,
Corson, Maud T. - Strachan, Guy R.
Corson, Sybel Madeline - Elkins, John Hollis
Corson, Sylvia Ann - Doucette, Donald David
Cory, Marietta (Burk) - Thyng, James E.
Costa, Susan Eileen - Mello, Edward Joseph
Cotton, Marjorie M. - Welch, Richard O.
Cotton, Nancy R. - Tasker, Milton S.
Cotton, Priscilla M. - Rines, George H.
Cotton, Roberta - Keene, Richard M.
Cotton, Sandra J. - McKenzie, Kenneth R., Jr.
Courchene, Brenda M. - Bergeron, Herve R.
Cove, Deborah Ann - Miller, Thomas J.
Cram, Marguerite - Carr, Archie B.
Cramp, Ruth E. (McEacheon) - Green, Elwin G.
Crane, Leslie Susan - St. Clair, David Paul
Cressy, Lorraine G. - Houle, Reginald A.
Cronan, Patricia M. - Kenneally, Richard H.
Crosby, Gladys M. - Eastman, Robert W.
Crossett, Marjorie E. - Brown, Philip W.
Cummings, Virginia - Cotton, Joseph H., Jr.
Cunniff, Susan Marie - Fortier, David Laurent
Curley, Carolyn A. - LaBrecque, Donald L.
Curtis, Beverly I. - Thibodeau, Paul L.
Curtis, Sandra E. - Gardner, Kenneth A.
Curtis, Sharon Ruth - Spencer, George Albert
Czerwienska, Jane - Ames, Harold

D'Ambrosio, Karen - Melanson, Charles W., Jr.
Dahlquist, Marion S. (Clapp) - Jenkins, John J.
Daigle, Debora S. (Welch) - Kimball, Edward C., II
Daily, Jennie - Obarton, Edward
Dale, Margaret J. - Walker, Frederick J.
Daley, Patricia A. - Stockman, Larry L.
Dame, Dawna C. - Wiley, John W., II

Dame, Elaine Marcia - Tedcastle, Douglas Coe
Dame, Mary A. - Thompson, Gordon S.
Dame, Maureen E. - Witham, Allen G.
Dame, Thelma Stevens - Eastman, Ralph Waldo
Daneault, Leona D. (Locke) - Abbott, Richard G.
Daniels, Nellie E. - Jones, Charles A.
Danis, Susan M. - Locke, Elias E.
Dansereau, Amy L. - Barnet, Paul A.
Darling, Izora J. (Chase) - Wade, Charles H.
David, Marianne C. - Hromis, Vladimir
Davis, Beatrice K. - Pszonowsky, Michael G.
Davis, Cora F. - Howe, Edgar G.
Davis, Dana M. - Burke, Andrew S.
Davis, Dorothy I. - Prince, Charles R.
Davis, Ella H. - Clark, Sewell J.
Davis, Holly J. - Smith, Frederick D.
Davis, Ida May - Wakefield, Clyde F.
Davis, Lucille Edna - Rogers, Albert Edward
Davis, Lucy J. - Scruton, Thomas J.
Davis, Margaret L. - Emerson, Harold B.
Davis, Megan L. - Taylor, Adam C.
Davis, Michelle A. - Mankiewicz, Keith W.
Davis, Ruth - Gray, William C.
Davis, Sandra A. - Collins, Richard K.
Davis, Sheryl Ann - Chagnon, David Wayne
Day, Cherie Ellen - Smith, Keith Leonard
Day, Myrtie O. - Hillsgrove, Walter J.
Deach, Edith L. (Rippel) - Sherburne, Albert E.
Deboer, Kathy R. - Kelley, David J.
Decota, Sally Louanne - Peterson, Mark Evert
Dedascalou, Irene - Laventure, Gerard C. R.
Degan, Diana M. - Abbott, John E.
Deinhardt, Dary A. - O'Meara, Stephen H.
Deinhardt, Tary L. - Locke, James N., II
Delaney, Susan G. - Glashow, David J.
Demers, Diane Muriel - Larose, Christopher Richard
Demers, Mary C. - Lindahl, Arthur E.
Dennett, Jessica Lynn - Lothridge, Brian Lee
Densmore, Michaelene M. - King, Wayne J.
Derosier, Ardith Grace (Shea) - Davis, Howard Everett
Deschanbault, Marguerite A. - Littlefield, Abraham D.

Desjardins, Susan M. - Lank, Clinton L.
deSousa, April L. - Coyman, Terrence J., Jr.
DeVaney, Brenda Elaine - Holmes, Peter Dale
Deveau, Carol L. - Lewis, Richard A.
Devino, Clover V. - Gehrig, August
Dickey, Maggie - Maxfield, Austin C.
Dickinson, Eunice Edwina (Minery) - Bunker, Robert John
DiPerri, Christine M. - Ashcroft, Mitchell D.
DiPerri, Christine M. - Ruggieri, Daniel K.
DiPerri, Maria - Whittier, Alton John
Dixon, Annie L. - Locke, Frank A.
Dodge, Carole J. - Greene, Daniel J.
Dodge, Cora E. (Clough) - Jenisch, Alois
Dodge, Phyllis Elvira - O'Neil, Charles Allen
Dodier, Patricia Joan - Lizotte, Thomas Joseph
Doe, Rachel M. - Pugh, Ralph
Doherty, Brenda - Sansom, Robert John
Donnelly, Amy Jo - Mitchell, Robert Alan
Dooley, Debora L. - Larkins, Eric D.
Dooley, Debora Lee - Murray, Richard Charles
Dore, Lisa D. - Jacques, Paul R.
Dorsey, Jane A. - Byers, Steven C.
Doten, Virginia A. - Sullivan, Thomas W., Jr.
Doub, Pamela Jean - Drew, Brian Everette
Doucette, Anita J. - Jewell, Carl D.
Doucette, Donna M. - Tiede, Brett H.
Doucette, Rita J. - Kiley, Michael J.
Doughty, Jeston M. - Nighelli, Benjamin R.
Douglas, Elizabeth C. - Holmes, Fred
Dow, Linda I. - Stanley, Robert F.
Dow, Mary E. - Jenkins, Carroll E.
Dow, Mildred - Crossett, Ernest Wm.
Dow, Zelma K. - Gault, Roland W.
Downes, Bessie A. - Call, Horace C.
Downs, Addie M. - Barrett, Daniel L.
Downs, Grace A. - Thyng, John C.
Drake, Grace - Foss, William B.
Drake, Evelyn - Corson, Raymond
Drew, Cora M. - Ham, Charles L.
Drolet, Gloria G. - Yeaton, Douglas W.
Drolet, Karen L. - Raney, Steven M.

Drolet, Sharyn D. - Reed, Terry A.
Drouin, Cynthia L. - Lane, Alan Marshall
Drouin, Dorothy Loretta - Chagnon, Leon Oscar
Duarte, Esther L. - Passano, Joseph V.
Dudley, Whanitta P. (Parry) - Dillon, John Matthew
Duggan, Patricia Ann - McDonough, Richard Kevin
Duhamme, Lumma (Gamelin) - Bourdreau, Nestor
Dumond, Alisha E. - Smith, Larry R.
Dunleavey, Kathleen L. - Buckman, George S., III
Dunne, Rebecca K. - Sliva, Christopher M.
Duquette, Mary L. - Glidden, Albert E.
Durham, Shirley M. - Brown, Floyd J.
Durrell, Bonnie S. - Locke, Dennis M.

Eastman, Caroline H. - Prescott, Harold F.
Eastman, Debra Ellen - Maxfield, John A., III
Eastman, Judith L. - Forsyth, George S.
Eastman, Marjorie J. - Terry, Richard D.
Eaton, Amy G. - Davis, Charles B.
Eckert, Janet E. - Eckert, John F.
Edgerly, Carrie M. - Leyland, Joseph
Edgerly, Helena M. - Dickerman, Irving M.
Edison, Flossie B. (Welch) - Ross, Frank I.
Edmunds, Nellie M. - Lougee, Arnold L.
Ehlen, Barbara R. - Sargent, Roy A.
Eldridge, Hollie Helene - Kelley, Michael Scott
Elkins, Agnes Jean (Herndon) - Eckhardt, Ralph Frank
Elkins, Mary A. (Gray) - Walker, Horace
Elkins, Rebecca J. - Johnson, Richard A.
Ellis, Blanche L. (Beck) - Small, Charles F.
Ellis, Kristin - O'Halloran, Michael J.
Elzea, Patricia L. - Jewell, Carl A.
Emeney, Jennifer A. - Young, Adam L.
Emerson, Amy Rose - Eastman, Michael Paul
Emerson, Bertha F. - Locke, Wayland B.
Emerson, Eileen Lydia - Keller, Roger F.
Emerson, Esther B. - Johnson, John M.
Emerson, Florence I. - Gault, Rowland W.
Emerson, Georgia D. - Drake, Edwin B.
Emerson, Glendle - Ashley, George M., III
Emerson, Jody L. - Clark, Robert T.

Emerson, Linda Lee - Fitzmorris, Bernard P.
Emerson, Marguerite A. - Black, Herbert F.
Emerson, Muriel R. - Warburton, John F.
Emerson, Ruth - Emerson, Ralph A.
Emerson, Velma E. - Ashley, Jack E.
Emery, Hazel Mae - Holmes, William Donald
Engel, Diane E. - Ford, Michael T.
Engelsen, Helen L. - Keefe, Thomas C.
Enright, Donna K. - Gosse, William A.
Erff, Cheryl Zannah - Bergeron, James A. Osgood
Ericson, Donna E. - Mostovoy, Gregory
Ernest, Carole A. - Gadomski, Robert S.
Erwin, Edith J. (Thompson) - Andrews, Leonard E.
Esburnett, Nicole - McKenzie, Russell W.
Evans, Alice A. - Cameron, Donald E.
Evans, Rebecca R. - Murzin, Donald W.
Evans, Ruth A. - Bunker, Roland E.

Fairburn, Sheryl Ann - Kimball, Michael Anthony
Farrell, Ruth Margaret - Carson, Charles Louis
Fauteux, Cheryl Anne - Roberge, Roger Wilfred
Fickett, Valeria M. - Glines, Joseph A.
Fife, Judy Mae - Platt, Lawrence Harold
Fifield, Lorraine T. - Simpson, Russell E.
Finethy, Sharon S. - Waterman, Bruce R.
Finlayson, Barbara Ruth - Veno, Gerald Ansel
Finnegan, Lorraine R. - Knirsch, Reinhold B.
Fischer, Louise - Thompson, Vernol Millard
Fiske, Nelda A. - Harris, Raymond A.
Fitzgibbons, Jane Ellen - Heiser, Frederick W., Jr.
Flanders, Teresa L. - Scahill, Michael T.
Fletcher, Bessie D. - Searle, Charles M.
Fletcher, Elizabeth Emma - Forbes, Lewis Augustus, Jr.
Flibbert, Jacquelyn M. - Richardson, Christopher M.
Florand, Suzanne Dorise - Heino, William A., Jr.
Florie, Lillian M. - Boudreau, Nestor
Fogg, Eva J. - Jenkins, Edwin K.
Fontaine, D'Arcy A. - Richey, Robert H.
Fontaine, Mary M. - Bronnenberg, Jackie R.
Forbes, Doris Louise - Aubertin, Ezra, Jr.
Ford, Patricia A. - Kidder, James W.

Ford, Patricia M. - Martin, Gordon K.
Forsyth, Maryann - Waterman, William R.
Fortier, Eva A. - Frey, Eric C.
Fortunata, Leanne B. - Florence, David J.
Foss, Alice - Page, Walter D.
Foss, Dora E. - Perkins, David M.
Foss, Estella G. - Colbath, George F.
Foss, Jennie M. - Curtis, Asa A.
Foss, Joan A. - Hall, David E.
Foss, Lilian D. - Jenkins, Charles W.
Foss, Lois Marion - Straw, Cecil Thomas
Foss, Madge A. - Jenkins, Will A.
Foss, Mildred - Langevin, Edward
Foss, Mildred A. - Lindberg, Bertile A.
Foss, Nettie F. - Tuttle, Osom M.
Foss, Sharon Ann - Hopps, Elwin H., Jr.
Foss, Stella M. - Colbath, Ernest
Foster, Shanah Lynn - Gross, Dennis B.
Fothergill, Mildred - Green, Wesley W.
Fox, Florence (Corson) - Barnard, William A., Jr.
Fox, Judith Ann - Magoon, Kevin C.
Fraedrich, Beatrice A. - Emerson, Wilbur A.
Fraser, Diane E. - Hathaway, Michael J.
Fraser, Jane - Aldrich, Paul Richard
Freeman, Lori Jean - Heath, Carter Eldon
French, Althea J. - Jaworski, Edward M.
French, Barbara J. - Corson, Clyde C., Jr.
French, Marie S. (Sumner) - Clark, Sewell J.
French, Marjorie P. - Byers, Steven C.
French, S. Anna (Van Dusen) - Whittaker, Fred R.
Frenette, Alphonsine - Berry, John
Frennette, Katherine C. (Curtis) - Carr, George S.
Frey, Ilse Madeline - Kelley, Edward Rodney
Fuller, Florence May (Hodsdon) - Proctor, Leigh V.
Fuller, Kristine A. - Olson, Mark D.

Gagne, Muriel T. - Aubertin, Donald Everett
Gagne, Ronda D. - McCready, Alan W.
Gagne, Stacey A. - Abbott, John E., Jr.
Gagnon, Ginette - Morrissette, Raymond A.
Gallivan, Nora - Walch, Fred H.

Gardner, Judith F. - Hodgdon, Maurice C., Jr.
Gardner, Maryanne H. - Martin, Jonathan W.
Garland, Hattie May (Cofran) - Seward, Harry Frank
Garland, Mary E. - Locke, Wesley E.
Gaudreault, Lucille A. - Hackett, Patrick Charles
Gelinas, Elaine C. - Duford, Robert
Genest, Jean M. - Hanson, Ronald D.
Genest, Karen Lynn - Fung, Pak Kuen
Genest, Lisa J. - Gagnon, William D.
Genest, Theda A. - Wordon, W. A.
Gennest, Elizabeth B. (Stone) - Gullage, J. Russell
George, Florence H. - Gustin, Walter S.
George, Myra S. - Boocock, John
Gerlack, Barbara M. - Joy, Kevin C.
Gerlack, Cecelia C. - Brown, David M.
Gerlack, Della M. - Wells, Oscar A.
Gerlack, Madgeline E. - Brown, Roland E.
Giddis, Sherry Ann - Ashley, Brad Scott
Giguere, Mary L. - Riendeau, Dana H.
Gillespie, Frances Conwell - Barnes, John Squarey
Gilliam, Christal L. - Sainsbury, Sean E.
Gilman, Freda A. - Boyd, Howard M.
Gilman, Louise A. - Shields, Hartley J.
Giovanucci, Ellen M. - Saley, Earl D., Jr.
Glidden, Jennie L. - Littlefield, Chester Warren
Glover, Beverly J. - Hanson, Ronald D.
Golden, Paula Ann - Welman, Peter Anthony
Golden, Ruth Blanche - Moody, Theodore Joseph
Golubinski, Diana - Brennan, Richard Sheffield
Gomes, Janice G. - Meyer, Randolph A.
Goodell, Gail A. - Wade, Allan W.
Goodwin, Dorothy A. (Corcoran) - Jacques, Harold R.
Gorden, Edith L. - Downs, Archer L.
Gosse, Candice E. - Myatt, Ronald F., Jr.
Gosse, Tania E. - Doucette, Paul E., Jr.
Goudreau, Pauline Estelle - Locke, Harvey Ray, Jr.
Grant, Christina V. - Streeter, Raymond
Grau, Alice H. C. - Adjutant, Dennis W.
Gray, Beatrice May - Cameron, Donald E.
Gray, Beaulah Gertrude - Gagne, David Joseph
Gray, Bessie O. - Kelley, Charles H.

Gray, Emma J. - Davis, Percy A.
Gray, Emma Jane - Boyd, Randolph Leslie, Jr.
Gray, Ethel G. - Yeaton, William H.
Gray, Gloria A. - Heath, Donald E.
Gray, Grace E. - Nutter, Malcolm H.
Gray, Harriett E. - Bebo, Philix
Gray, Hazel M. - Sleeper, Paul D.
Gray, Jeanne T. - Clement, George E., III
Gray, Laura A. - Grattage, Wanton A.
Gray, Lori J. - Munroe, Dale K.
Gray, Margaret Ina - Merrill, James Edwin
Gray, Margaret L. - Hill, James W.
Gray, Marion Edna - Stockman, Everett Lee
Gray, Nettie - Pickering, Albert C.
Gray, Sadie F. - Cate, Willie
Gray, Shirley H. (McIntosh) - Benson, Ronald K.
Gray, Velna Virginia - Moulton, Harold Earl
Gray, Violet - Locke, E. Wesley
Green, Darlene Imelda - Wenblad, Anders Jouhan
Green, Grace Kathryn - Chase, Jackson E.
Green, Margaret F. - Jenisch, Alfred F.
Green, Mary E. - Eaton, Lewis F.
Green, Mary Eileen (Marden) - Trainer, William Perry
Green, Maud P. - Locke, John W.
Green, Roberta Rae - Supry, Daniel Patrick
Greene, April R. - Sysyn, James
Greenwood, Linda M. - MacDonald, John L., II
Greenwood, RoseAnn - Prescott, Alan G.
Greer, Kathleen - Mitchell, Robert B.
Griffin, Amy L. - Tremblay, Leo P.
Griffin, Georgie Mae - Davis, Jose L.
Griffin, Marsha L. - Harford, Philip W.
Griffin, Paulette E. (Emerson) - Tasker, Paul E.
Grindle, Susan Miller - Sanborn, Paul Gilbert
Gustafson, Cynthia A. - Freehling, Joseph M.
Gustafson, Mona B. - McLean, Kenneth Alan

Hall, Nettie F. - Holmes, Charles A.
Hall, Olive (Merrill) - Blake, George F.
Hall, Sarah E. - Drew, David
Halla, Barbara Diane - Reed, Thomas Robertson

Hallee, Manon T. - Beetz, Robert P.
Ham, Carole J. - Duane, Richard D., Jr.
Ham, Marion Elizabeth - Clark, Eugene Fremont
Hanchett, Suzanne Jean - Almeida, Steven Leo
Haney, Nancy L. - Marston, William H.
Hannaford, Karen J. - Eastman, Roger L.
Hanscom, Patricia F. - Fournier, Edgar G.
Hansell, Julie M. - Sprince, Jeremy J.
Hanson, Annie R. - Emerson, James C.
Hanson, Catherine M. - Everett, Joseph E.
Hanson, Donna L. - Stewart, Carl E.
Hanson, Etta M. - Otis, Arthur D.
Hanson, Mariana J. - Campbell, Donald C.
Hanson, Marjorie E. - Holmes, William E.
Hanson, Myrtie E. - Weeks, Henry P.
Hanson, Natalie L. (Wyatt) - Hanson, Lloyd G.
Harlow, Mildred E. (Caswell) - Currier, John W.
Harmon, Carrie E. - Drake, Edwin B.
Harper, Constance Elizabeth - Stock, Richard H.
Harriman, Kathy Dawn - Simpson, Mark Reinhardt
Harrington, Angela R. - Edge, Charles K.
Harrington, Hattie E. - Varney, John B.
Harris, Catherine - Glidden, Herbert
Hart, Jennifer Sue - Pappas, Leonard Charles, Jr.
Hartford, Sandra E. - Smith, James D.
Hartman, Dori B. - Tothill, Joel S.
Hast, Hulda Ann - Bickford, Richard O.
Hastings, Eleanor N. (Newhook) - Pervere, Dwight L.
Hastings, Nicole M. - Carter, Mark A.
Hayes, Constance Marie - Allard, Robert Wallie
Hayes, Mychelle Lynn - Brown, Michael Philip
Heath, Elizabeth S. (Small) - Kidder, Kenneth C.
Heath, Elsie C. - Derosia, Joseph E.
Hennigan, Paula L. - Phillips, Michael
Herbert, Margaret L. (Newell) - Gray, Edwin A.
Herbert, Renie A. - Foote, James O.
Herndon, Agnes L. (Galbreath) - Rogers, George A.
Hersey, Irene Elizabeth - Goodwin, Ray Fuller
Herzog, Barbara A. - Dalpe, Dean A.
Hewett, Marina Ruth - Miner, David Ashley
Heywood, Alma M. - Ryder, Warren A.

Heywood, Alma R. - Herndon, John A.
Heywood, Grace Frances - Burnell, Fred Arthur
Higgins, Grace A. - Merrill, Stuart B.
Higgins, Jeri-Anne - Brown, Gordon J.
Higgins, Nina M. - Foss, John Henry
Hildreth, Dorothy May - Goodwin, Harold S.
Hill, Bertha Mae - Hartshorn, George M.
Hill, Elsie M. - Clough, Walter L.
Hill, Lelia J. - Hoskins, Charles W.
Hill, Lilian Velna - Tilton, George Everett
Hill, Margaret C. - Alden, Arthur W.
Hill, Mildred - Corliss, Earl S.
Hillard, Florence L. - Bunker, Daniel
Hillsgrove, Bertha L. (Pierce) - Jenkins, Merton B.
Hillsgrove, Clara - Young, Percy C.
Hillsgrove, Eunice J. - Gerlack, Frank R.
Hillsgrove, Lena M. - Emerson, Henry W.
Hillsgrove, Lettie A. - Jacobs, C. M.
Hillsgrove, Marla M. - Brown, Russell D.
Hillsgrove, May E. (Jarvis) - Greenleaf, Milton
Hillsgrove, Roseanna E. - Saley, Edwin N.
Hillsgrove, Sadie D. - Moore, Frank H.
Hinds, Barbara S. - MacKnight, Steven R.
Hoadley, Kristine Lynn - Kidder, Dana James
Hoar, Jeanne M. - Vickers, Jerry D.
Hodgdon, Donna M. - Saunders, Jonathan F., Jr.
Hoffman, Carol L. - Rott, Daniel A.
Hogan, Kathleen A. - Zielski, Dennis H.
Hogencamp, Carolyn - Thompson, Mellard H.
Hogencamp, Margaret J. - Pickering, Ralph E.
Holbrook, Dawn Marie - Kendall, Richard A., Jr.
Holbrook, Kathryn - Riel, Michael David
Holland, Elva P. - Locke, G. Malcolm
Holmes, Agnes L. - Littlefield, Stilson W.
Holmes, Marjorie (Hanson) - Carr, Fred
Holmes, Virginia - Marsal, Thomas
Hood, Katie J. - Packard, Roger H.
Hopkins, Tina M. - Cowdrey, John H., Jr.
Horton, Linda-Marie - Pestana, Lui M.
Houle, Linda Gertrude - Rott, Nicholas Christopher
Houle, Susan Janet - Burke, William Albert

Houlne, Peggy S. - McCain, William H.
Howe, Mary E. - Tuttle, Norman N.
Howe, Robin A. - Redmond, Richard D.
Hoyt, Candice E. - Gosse, William A.
Hoyt, Margaret M. (Fox) - Mulcahy, Robert E., Jr.
Hoyt, Sadie F. - Parsons, Scott D.
Hubbell, Linda S. - Gorman, George L., Jr.
Hubert, Barbara J. - Welcome, Richard F.
Huckins, Helen Mary (Brown) - Campbell, Clyde Foster
Huckins, May E. (Emery) - Powell, Harry L.
Hunt, Barbara A. - Conant, Frank A.
Hunt, Karen H. - Baas, John C., III
Hunter, Kristie - Smith, David Hugh
Huntress, May Pierce - Connolly, Carl Bartlett
Hurst, Devere D. - Groleau, James P.
Huse, Carlotta M. - Engle, Tracy R.
Huse, Irene E. - Hersey, Elmer P.
Hussey, Heidi R. - Knight, Jeffrey S.
Huston, Maud S. - Ackerman, Royal I.
Hutchins, Ruth L. - Emerson, Daniel E., Jr.

Iacono, Mildred Ellen - Richardson, James W.
Ingalls, Elaine Lee - Hanson, Lloyd George, Jr.
Ingalls, Helen May - Stedman, Herbert David
Ingle, Paula S. - Koehler, Alford R.
Inman, Paula A. - Robinson, Gregory L.
Irmick, Lori J. - Mancini, David E.
Isaksen, Lauraine G. - Paquin, Steven J.

Jacobs, Helen W. - Tasker, Arthur W., II
Jacques, Carol I. - Chapman, David A.
Jameson, Susan Chesterton - Simpson, David Richard
Janisch, Helen C. - Mardin, Eddie A.
Jeffers, Della S. (Swain) - Little, Harry E.
Jenisch, Kristine Barbara - Adams, James Henry
Jenkins, Adelaide E. - Leach, Harry L.
Jenkins, Florence L. - Colbath, Frank J.
Jenkins, Grace D. - Emerson, Llewellyn H.
Jenkins, Madeline A. - Emerson, Albert L.
Jenkins, Mary A. - Emerson, Llewellyn H.
Jenkins, Mirie A. - Frame, Frederick P.

Jenkins, Nellie M. - Ayers, Charles F.
Jennings, Linda L. - Gilman, Leonard G., Jr.
Jennings, Theresa A. - Clement, George E., III
Jennings, Theresa A. - Stockman, Michael L.
Jensen, Patricia I. - Costa, Steven D.
Jesseman, Beulah M. - Tasker, Leighton E.
Jessop, Maryann M. - Davis, Paul Howard
Jochums, Julia S. - Osborne, Richard K.
Johnson, Cathryn M. - Buiel, Richard S.
Johnson, Eliza B. - Brady, Kim D.
Johnson, Gretchen A. - Guinard, Scott M.
Johnson, Margaret A. - Lancaster, David H.
Johnson, Marguerite - Jones, Donald E.
Johnson, Patricia J. - Trotter, Gary H.
Johnson, Patricia M. - Darling, Philip S.
Johnson, Patricia Marie - Small, Warren Linnell
Johnson, Rebecca F. - Starkey, John M.
Johnston, Margaret - Locke, Kent
Jones, Anna V. - Dicey, Harold
Jones, Annie - Clark, Solomon
Jones, Bernice E. - Laprise, Herman Gerard
Jones, Ella R. - Fletcher, Fred P.
Jones, Maureen R. - Medeiros, Bryan J.
Jordan, Diane M. - Beijer, Alexander F.
Joy, Doris C. - Gerlack, Clarence G.

Karsch, Judith L. - Elliott, Charles L.
Katz, Joan E. - Deyette, Ronald A.
Keach, Anne M. - Taylor, James P.
Keating, Robyn - Ladd, Eugene W., Jr.
Keefe, Marilyn L. - Eckhardt, Ralph F.
Keene, Debra M. - Walker, James W.
Keene, Debra M. - Jarels, Danny L.
Keene, Debra Marlene - Watkins, Robert Thomas
Keene, Roberta C. (Cotton) - Smith, Gordon M.
Kelley, Linda S. - Tasker, Michael F.
Kelley, Mabel F. - Locke, George E.
Kelley, Virginia Charlotte - Davis, Ernest Albert
Kelly, Rosemary J. - Riel, Timothy M.
Kelton, Debra Jeanne - Newhouse, David Roy
Kenison, Altha - Emerson, Woodrow W.

Kenison, Doris A. - Chagnon, Maurice L.
Kenison, Gladys W. (Brady) - Otis, Lewis E.
Kenison, Sandra Faye - Farnsworth, Dana Francis
Keniston, Velma - Knirsch, Henry
Kenneally, Patricia Evelyn - Lank, Richard Royal
Kenney, Bettie A. - Foss, Lindy E.
Kenney, Janice M. - Fortado, Stephen M.
Kidder, Bonnie L. - Roberts, James A.
Kidder, Elizabeth S. (Smart) - Cameron, Daniel R.
Kidder, Virginia May - Dore, Rawland Edwin
Kiley, Deborah Ann - Morris, Colin Tallman
Kimball, Patricia R. - Carson, Floyd J.
Kimball, Sylvia E. - Keating, Brian R.
Kimborowicz, Tracy Lynn - Carter, Marc Donald
Kirby, Pamela Catherine - Carr, John Kenneth
Kirby, Priscilla B. - Tiede, Robert A.
Kittridge, Ellen R. (Thomas) - Pitman, Albert G.
Klesse, Sylvia - Denton, Stuart P.
Klinefelter, Deanna L. - Taylor, Robert G.
Kling, Donna Marie - McCormack, David Anthony
Knapp, Jennie S. - Peavey, Ray A.
Knirsch, Marie T. - Hunneyman, Lawrence J.
Knirsch, Ruth - Locke, Percival W.
Knowles, Annie M. - Glines, Joseph A.
Knowles, Grace A. - Heywood, Fred L.
Knowlton, Lisa Marie - Dawson, Richard Thomas, Jr.
Koehler, Jennifer A. - Yannizze, Joseph J.
Komisarek, Susan M. - Drolet, Robert L.
Kremser, Patricia B. - Calder, John W.
Kyllonen, Elizabeth M. - Armer, James H.

LaBranche, Wilma Christine (Nelson) - Watson, Ernest Arthur, Sr.
Labrecque, Bette Anne - Forst, Barry John
LaBrecque, Diane M. - Mulcahy, Robert E., III
Labrecque, Karen Marie - Montgomery, Ricky Glenn
LaCroix, Nancy A. - Sanders, Gordon R.
Lakeman, Alma Louise - Pitman, George Albert
Lane, Margaret A. (Desjadon) - Bryant, Harry E.
Langevin, Dorothy Ann - Byers, Patrick Timothy
Langevin, Evelyn D. - White, Brian A.

Lank, Dorothy L. - Philbrick, Gary L.
Lank, Elinor N. - Boyd, Richard P.
Lank, Ruth J. - Bousquet, Alfred J.
Laplante, Nancy Lee - Fair, Timmie R.
LaPlante, Pamela M. - Thoroughgood, Kenneth J.
LaPointe, Marilyn J. - Slater, Keith A.
LaPorte, Sharon J. - Newton, Bruce E.
Larabee, Carrie M. - Ackerman, Peter P.
Larkin, Mary A. - Russell, Joseph C.
Laro, Ada Mae - Gray, Edward A.
Laskey, Linda - Saari, Larry A.
Latwesen, Annette L. - Junk, Kenneth W.
Lawrence, Harrietta M. - Pitman, Fred T.
Lawrence, Teresa Anne - Pruitt, Billy A.
Leavitt, Ida J. - Christopher, Elmwood
Leavitt, Myrtle Justine - Whittier, Dean Elthan
Leavitt, Wendy L. - Goralski, Stephen T.
Lebel, Maria - Scarpa, Daniel William
Leblanc, Karen Ella - Hammond, David Edward, Jr.
Lee, Roberta E. - Partridge, Brian L.
Leighton, Cynthia R. (Walker) - Holmes, Donald E.
Leighton, Susan A. - Valenti, Michael
Leithead, Phyllis E. - Brooks, Wayne P.
Lelko, Eileen Rose - Jenisch, Raymond Louis
Lennon, Diane Marie - Maloney, Michael Frederick
Leonard, Mary Elizabeth - Lawrence, Christopher C.
LeRoux, Velvet L. - Artesi, John S.
Levasseur, Patricia A. - Gerlack, Arthur L.
Lichty, Susan E. - Robb, Ernest E., Jr.
Linehan, Christine J. - Barriere, Laurian
Little, Nellie Ruth - Cobb, Warren James
Little, Sylbie Elizabeth - Eldridge, John Owen
Littlefield, Felicia Louise - Rogers, Clarence Lewis
Littlefield, Vida - Carr, Fred M.
Littlefield, Winnie B. - Post, Chester
Locke, Arlene J. - Smith, Paul S.
Locke, Blanche N. - Golden, John E.
Locke, Carolyn R. - Lank, Clinton L.
Locke, Carrie (Come) - Martel, Zoel
Locke, Cathy Lynn - Watson, Eddie Allen
Locke, Debra J. - Piaseczny, Steven R.

Locke, Donna Ilene - Stockman, Ronald Lee
Locke, Edith M. - Nutter, Everett W.
Locke, Edna R. - Perry, Albert C.
Locke, Judith D. - Dumont, Robert J.
Locke, Leona D. - Daneault, Andre J.
Locke, Lillian - Dias, Alden
Locke, Lillian M. - Dias, Aldin
Locke, Lydia A. - Chesley, Orrin F.
Locke, Margaret Jean - Emerson, Roger Burke
Locke, Maud A. - Joy, George E.
Locke, Ruth Hedwig (Knirsch) - Heywood, Lincoln Warren
Locke, Sharon K. - Tremblay, Roger A.
Locke, Stacie Ann - Locke, Bruce Paul
Locke, Tammy L. - Nelson, Todd E.
Locke, Tina M. - Wells, Kevin W.
Lodestein, Andrea K. - Riel, Kevin J.
Loeffler, Emmy - Schnoudt, Otto
Longval, Sonya Ann - Butterworth, William M.
Loomis, Rebecca Lee - Towle, Ronald G.
Lopez, Theresa A. - Riel, Timothy E.
Lord, Mary - Arnett, Gregory Arlen
Lorden, Penny J. - Stewart, Leroy
Lorris, Sarah M. - Melson, John E.
Lougee, Celia R. - Downs, Herbert L.
Lougee, Dora E. - Mills, Lowell J.
Luckert, Julie L. - Miner, David A.
Lund, Edna A. (Bullard) - Brooks, Glenn P.
Lynch, Eleanor Rae (Finlayson) - Fletcher, James

MacDonald, Brenda Lee - Rainville, Alan Joseph
MacKenzie, Eleanor L. (Compo) - Gray, Robert A.
Mackinnon, Amy M. - Lane, Alan M.
MacKnight, Karen - Mountain, Henry D.
MacNeill, Verna H. (Brewster) - Young, Samuel Fletcher
MacPherson, Reta J. - Jolly, Francis A., Jr.
Magoon, Prudence G. - Robinson, Jack S.
Mahar, Eleanor Margret - Deegan, Thomas John
Maher, Terri L. - Russell, Kevin C.
Mahon, Alicia R. - Rollins, Leon S.
Majumder, Rani J. - Hemingway, Jeffrey B.
Malin, Jane H. - Stockman, Ronald H.

Manning, Carrie M. - Wing, Samuel G.
Manning, Janina M. - Anderson, William G.
Manson, Mary J. - Davis, Clarence N.
Manson, Sarah A. (Cummings) - Emerson, Carleton E.
Mantegani, Roberta Lee - Smith, Stephen Jay
Marchio, Kimberly Ann - Kyllonen, Robert Royce
Marquenet, Laurence L. - Howes, Richard J.
Marsal, Charlotte - Dotson, William Marvin
Marsh, Emma A. - Hunt, John F.
Marsh, Mabel J. - Seward, Harry F.
Marsh, Terry L. - Labrecque, Dennis J.
Marston, Frieda L. - Pickard, Richard D.
Martel, Arlene E. - Forsyth, Richard W.
Martin, Cynthia J. - Brunk, Michael D.
Martin, Dorinda Louise - Garland, Charles Leroy
Martin, Frances M. (Wells) - Fisher, Thomas P.
Martin, Pamela J. - Bourassa, Andrew Gerard
Matthewman, Sarah Margo - Johnson, Peter Thoralf
Maxfield, Amy T. - Sleeper, Fred W.
Maxfield, Christie A. - Jenkins, Charles F.
Maxfield, Harriet - Hillsgrove, Robert H.
Maxfield, M. Edith - Jenkins, John J.
Mayhew, Estella M. - Foss, John H.
McAuley, Regina M. - Downing, Russell F.
McCarron, Juddy H. - Grimes, Steven P.
McCarthy, Ellen T. - McGlame, Thomas R.
McClary, Jean L. - Frost, Maurice A.
McConaghy, Ethel Webb - Allen, David Ormes
McDaniels, Karen Louise - Hillis, Michael Kenneth
McDonald, Elizabeth - Hathaway, Fred C.
McDonnell, Joyce Ann - Rollins, Leon Selden
McDuffee, Bessie Wellington - Wheet, Rexford Elwin
McDuffee, Edna May - Macpherson, Albert
McElwain, Louise A. - Piercey, Harold J.
McGarrigle, Jennifer Louise - Potter, Gary Wayne
McIntosh, Odna G. - Jenisch, Frederick K.
McIntosh, Phyllis L. - Yeaton, Earle M.
McKennelley, Mary - Aikens, Edwin J.
McKennelly, Hattie B. - Holmes, Frank J.
McKinnon, Barbara Joy - Roffo, Charles William
McLeod, Crystal M. - Johnson, Peter A.

McMahon, Heather Sue - Kingston, David J.
McManus, Ellen C. - Paquin, Joseph E.
McMillan, Nadine A. - Michaud, Curtis J., Jr.
McMillen, Susan J. - Pontell, Ernest E.
McWilliams, Kelly A. - Guo, Fan
Meredith, Jane - Carpenter, Glenn S.
Meredith, Linda - Romero, Eleazer
Meredith, Susan - Drescher, Robert W.
Merrifield, Hildred E. - Ross, Frank I.
Merrill, Beverly P. - Weiss, Harold F.
Merrill, Earlene H. - Smith, Leonard H.
Merrill, Helen L. - Tasker, Arthur W.
Merrill, Madeline O. - Palmer, Donald S.
Messier, Lynn M. - Fortin, Raymond J.
Meunier, Joanne D. - Locke, Thomas G.
Michie, Marjorie E. - Gourley, Chester
Miller, Annie - Davis, Burt N.
Miller, Katrina M. - Keene, Kevin M.
Miller, Stacy D. - Perkins, Brian K.
Millette, Deanna L. - Higgins, Michael L.
Milne, Tara F. - Brassaw, Ricky Allen
Miner, Christie P. (Simpson) - Swanson, Arnold V.
Miner, Dolores Ann - Emerson, Roland C., Jr.
Miner, Laurie A. - Topham, James H.
Minery, Kathleen M. - Emerson, Keith M.
Minette, Deborah A. - Robie, Dwight A.
Mitchell, Corliss Jane - Pajanen, David John
Mitchell, Pamela J. - Kissane, Robert
Mitrano, Susan E. - Bourassa, Steven H.
Moncrieff, Maud - Todd, Richard
Montague, Cheryl Jean - Gannon, Shawn Gregory
Mooney, Sandra Lynn - Shuman, Scott Elwin
Moore, Dianne L. - Strong, James A.
Moore, Helen M. (Pascher) - Raiche, Alvah F.
Moore, Marion Louise (Park) - Jenisch, William Henry
Mora, Clara Ines - Preciado, Edgard M.
Morasse, Carol A. - Conley, James E.
Morgan, Sandra A. - Congdon, William P.
Moroney, Laura L. - Petix, Robert Gilbert
Morren, Cindy J. - Guilbert, Brian P.
Morrison, Sadie E. - Welch, Frank W.

Morrissette, Susan E. - Johnson, Peter A.
Morse, Robin Renee - Schwab, Dennis Michael
Morse, Tracey A. - Therrien, Mark A.
Mortell, Susan L. - Donovan, Keith J.
Moses, Brenda Lynn - Vintinner, John Frederick
Mulcahy, Joy A. - Jennis, James S.
Mulligan, Barbara E. - Yanski, Michael S.
Munsey, Lizzie B. - Garland, Edward C.
Munsey, Martha J. - Swain, Dennis H.
Munsey, Myria M. - Evans, Austin H.
Murphy, Diane M. - Hillsgrove, George C.
Murphy, Duska Joy - Lank, Howard Robert
Murphy, Grace Marjorie - Riel, Steven Ellwood
Murray, Carrie A. (Harvey) - Decrow, Delbert S.
Murray, Christine G. - Pude, William B.
Murray, Minnie P. - Reynolds, Leon H.
Murry, Maggie - Nutter, George H.
Myers, Jacquelyn L. (Lee) - Young, Forrest B.
Myers, Priscilla W. (Wells) - French, Walter

Nadeau, Connie M. - Karasek, Walter
Nassar, Donna Marie - Lavoie, Ronald Wayne, Jr.
Nation, Michelle L. - Reed, Herbert A., Jr.
Naylor, Arlene T. (Whitcomb) - Zecha, Ferdinand, Jr.
Neal, Catherine E. - Clark, Dennis E.
Nelson, Judith R. (Riel) - Mitchell, Joseph J.
Nelson, Kattie M. (Welds) - Munsey, George M.
Nelson, Sally - Kallgren, James P.
Neville, Helen F. (Basil) - Merrill, Bruce K.
Newcomb, Florence (Sweatland) - Emerson, Carleton E.
Newcomb, Florence M. - Hogencamp, John L.
Newell, Jolene M. - Price, David S.
Newell, Lori E. - Kimball, Edward C., II
Nichols, Hilda Anne - Jenkins, Donald Warren
Nichols, Nancy B. (Scott) - Rines, George H.
Nichols, Ruby M. - French, Walter E.
Nickerson, Paula - Driscoll, Richard J., Jr.
Nickerson, Violet I. - Wheeler, George L.
Nilges, Debbie A. - Gilman, William E.
Normandin, Karlene Ann - Miller, Richard James
Nuttall, May - Nutter, Joseph S.

Nutter, Augusta G. - Aikins, George L.
Nutter, Effie - Emerson, Herbert O.
Nutter, Lizzie M. - Wiggin, George E.
Nutter, Mary A. (Allen) - Hodgdon, Charles A.
Nutter, Mary L. (Caswell) - Walker, Albert D.
Nutter, Sarah E. - Hanson, Carl N.
Nyberg, Penny Sue - Smith, William Ross
Nyhan, Patricia W. - Riel, Arnold J.

O'Brien, Alice Maud - Bittues, Armo Alex.
O'Brien, Mary Ellen - Kramer, Daniel
O'Meara, Leslie D. - Hingston, Mark R.
O'Neill, Julieann - Dubois, Paul R.
O'Rourke, Mary E. - Hanson, Alvin G.
Ober, Bessie - Webster, Otis
Oberg, Renee L. - Tiede, Ernie
Oberg, Renee Lynn - Dempsey, Chadd James
Oelcher, Virginia - Finlayson, Donald R.
Ohlson, Ann C. - Genest, John E.
Ordway, Velna Emma - Foss, Fred
Orton, Anne B. - Jenisch, Douglas H.
Osborn, Rachel E. - Kidder, Wilbur A.
Osgood, Muriel A. - Lane, Henry C.
Osgood, Susan E. - Kessler, Marc J.
Ossoff, Karen I. - Danaher, Michael D.
Otis, Erlma Jane - Davis, William Charles
Otis, Nettie - Clark, Robert L.
Otis, Shirley Mae - Berry, John Melvin

Pachl, Mathilda - Jenisch, Alois
Paige, Cynthia A. - Riel, George W.
Paige, Susan Lynn - Starkey, John McMahon
Paine, Wendy - Locke, Kerry
Palmer, Alice - Young, Burt
Palmer, Donna Jane - Johnson, David Gordon
Papaioanou, Amy - McGonagle, Matthew J.
Parelius, Carol Ann - Gray, William Frank
Parent, Linda P. - Treadwell, Gordon L.
Pariseau, Joni P. - Ripley, Richard A., Jr.
Parker, Courtne L. - Turner, Jason L.
Parker, Hazel Isabelle - Lank, Howard John

Parker, Leona Christine - Golden, Paul Anthony
Parmenter, Bertha J. - Johnson, Willard A.
Parshley, Inez E. - Underhill, Frank
Parsons, Blanche - Hogencamp, William B.
Parsons, Grace L. - Perkins, Noel E.
Parsons, Joan - Driscoll, Harry P.
Parsons, Ora G. - Osgood, Charles H.
Parsons, Priscilla J. - Dustin, Robert E.
Partridge, Lois F. - Hillsgrove, Joseph H.
Pataki, Barbara Jean - Sroczynski, Thomas J.
Patchen, Kathleen Susan - Preston, Howard Robert, Jr.
Patten, Lucinda (Ballard) - Foss, John H.
Patterson, Heather M. - Corriveau, Troy T.
Patterson, Susan Helene - Malvey, Peter James
Pearce, Donna A. - Philpot, Jeffrey T.
Penka, Emma - Kenisch, Konard
Penley, Mary E. (Drew) - Cook, Hervey A.
Perez, Nancy - Romanos, Seth D.
Perkins, Althea Edna - Locke, Harvey Roy
Perkins, Harriett Mae - Sirrell, Verne Harold
Perkins, Leone M. - Keene, Marshall G.
Perkins, Nilda A. (Anderson) - Goodwin, Ray F.
Perkins, Tamika Laura - Carter, Benjamin Joshua
Perkins, Wanda - Philbrick, Eugene Holden
Perreault, Lucille Cordelia - Huffstutlar, Vernon Eishmel
Perry, Edna R. (Locke) - Bickford, Herbert S.
Perry, Linda F. - Corriveau, Edward C.
Pervere, Donna Marie - Dickerman, Lester D.
Peterson, Lynn A. - Onufry, Richard A.
Peterson, Patricia C. - Renaud, Mark A.
Pethic, Lynn M. - Tiede, Alan R.
Petschauer, Diane Lynn - Vernal, Steven Edward
Pettersen, Annie L. - Rosinquist, Bror A.
Pettersen, Annie L. - Stock, Robert P.
Phelps, Rose Opland - Chase, Lester Henry
Philbrick, Tanya L. - Soucy, Steven P.
Phillip, Jessie E. (Lowe) - Young, Alfred C.
Phillips, Lori-Anne - Dupont, Robert D.
Philpott, Martha Edith - Horle, Richard George
Piaseczny, Deborah A. - Caldwell, William D.
Picard, Cindy A. - Roberts, Scott A.

Pichette, Cathy S. - Gaffney, John F.
Pickering, Libbertie W. (Ham) - Clark, Charles A. W.
Pickett, Rebecca J. - Soule, Brian G.
Pierce, Sandra J. - Briggs, Russell M.
Pike, Carol A. - McDowell, Lance E.
Pike, Louise E. - Hillsgrove, W. Merl
Pillsbury, Kristy M. - Heath, Nathan T.
Pinet, Huguette L. - Forsythe, James Edward
Pinkham, Christine A. - Wheeler, Barry J.
Piper, Harriet D. - Mosher, Burr B.
Pitman, Abbie J. - Bridge, John W.
Pitman, Alice M. - LaBrecque, Roland V.
Pitman, Beatrice E. - Knight, Alan L.
Pitman, Ethel M. - Black, William Osburn
Pitman, Grace Aurilla - Greene, Clarence Elmer
Pitman, Susan Janet - Simpson, Robert Seagrave
Place, Annie T. - Mitchell, Walter J.
Place, Norma M. (Mooney) - Milne, William R. C., Jr.
Plaisted, Patricia A. - Reid, Wilmot P.
Plante, Cricket Lee - Aguilar, Carlos Edward
Plastridge, Roberta A. (Andrew) - Hanson, Ronald D.
Pletsch, Carol - Locke, Ernest E., Jr.
Plumer, Jenipher S. - Bishop, Jerry L.
Pocket, Carolyn A. - Harris, Raymond A.
Podmore, Gail L. - Glidden, Robert L.
Poirier, Jennifer Anne - Beck, William H.
Pollard, Pamela A. - Phillips, Ceiland A.
Pomerleau, Andrea Lee - Gray, Dennis Robert
Ponusky, Carole A. - Anderson, Clarence E.
Poole, Bethany A. - Drew, John L., Jr.
Potito, Kathleen Ann - Butterfield, William Albert
Potter, Florence Adeline - Welch, Charles Ham
Potter, Joan B. - Riel, Timothy M.
Potter, Phyllis A. (Sargent) - Watson, Curtis D.
Potter, Theresa Lynn - Storey, Charles Sidney
Potter, Wendy A. - LaBrecque, David A.
Poulin, Michelle L. - Trovato, James M.
Pouliot, Crystal - Noble, William J.
Powell, Ada - Lang, Harry B.
Powell, Ina G. - Hawley, George H.
Powers, Jean A. - Locke, Kent D., Jr.

Pratt, Brenda L. - Locke, Ernest E.
Pratt, Brigitte M. - Miner, Dennis A.
Prescott, Doris L. - Hodgman, Richard O.
Prescott, Frances Luanna - Hillsgrove, Walter Merl
Prescott, Jan Marie - Weldon, Smith G.
Prescott, Virginia A. - Scovill, Lawrence S.
Price, Natalie J. - Locke, James N.
Prince, Annie J. - Drake, Harvey W.
Prince, Cecil May - Munsey, Linwood B.
Prince, Hattie Viola - Gray, Myron Earl
Prince, Sharon B. - Kriete, Bill A.
Proctor, Susie M. - Weeks, Satchell
Provencal, Debra L. - Bennet, Michael Scott
Publicover, Sandra J. - Hillsgrove, George C.
Pugh, Milda P. - Dahlquist, Theodore G.
Purtell, Diane L. - Thoroughgood, Richard J.
Purtell, Glenna C. - Riel, George W.
Pyne, Diane Lee - Riel, Donald Cleon, Jr.
Pyne, Margery Claire - Nichols, Howard F.

Quinn, Mary Anne S. - Wearing, Michael D.
Quirk, Mary E. - Kirkland, Frank L.

Rainoad, Betty A. - Weeks, Alfred H.
Randall, Lottie M. - Merrill, George E.
Ranger, Lillia F. - Chamberlain, George C.
Raymond, Gail Ann - French, John David, II
Reeck, Eva M. - Thurston, Karl O.
Reed, Maxine J. - Genest, Roger E.
Reid, Patricia L. (Riley) - Evans, John Joseph
Reil, Gladys E. - Corson, Harry M.
Reiman, Liisa - Archibald, Peter Ellis, Jr.
Rennie, Laura F. - Hoar, Robert T.
Reynolds, Minnie L. (Ellsworth) - Packard, Jay Leyland
Reynolds, Nettie J. - Tilton, Frank S.
Reynolds, Sherri L. - Corliss, Eric R.
Richards, Abbie - Furgerson, Arthur W.
Richards, Lena Rita - Golden, Robert F.
Richardson, Harriet - Ames, Irving M.
Richardson, Judith Ann - Riel, Daniel P.
Richardson, Lillian M. - Nutter, Carl C.

Richardson, Mary A. - Nutter, Carl N.
Richardson, Patricia M. - Miner, Dennis A.
Richardson, Patricia M. - Byers, Steven C.
Richardson, Tina Maureen - Rattee, Matthew Steven
Richey, Ruth F. (Crosby) - Eastman, Ralph W.
Ricker, Anna - Twombly, George F.
Ricker, E. S. - Parson, C. A.
Ricker, Laura E. - Caswell, Samuel D.
Ricker, Victoria A. - Doucette, Paul E., Jr.
Riel, Ann E. - Pethic, Wayne
Riel, Brenda J. - Boyd, Rodney T., Jr.
Riel, Dorothy A. - Chappelle, John E., Jr.
Riel, Edna Irene - Gray, Clifford F.
Riel, Frances I. - Locke, John M.
Riel, Judith A. - Nelson, Jerry
Riel, Pamela J. - Dalhaus, Richard W.
Riel, Patricia N. - Cotton, John G.
Riel, Robin L. - Gibbons, Paul K.
Riel, Rosemary J. - Robinson, John A.
Riel, Sally A. - Burkhalter, Joe Rayne
Riel, Tammy Marie - Flanders, Alan Joseph
Riggle, Carrie L. - Kimball, Lee L.
Riley, Carol A. - Sinotte, Richard L.
Riley, Patricia L. - Reed, Ronald N.
Rines, Elsie (Londo) - Eastman, Ralph W.
Rines, Myra B. - Merrill, Otis
Riordan, Susan E. - Reynolds, Francis J.
Ritchie, Jacquelyn P. - Gardiner, Craig T.
Robbins, Cassie Lynn - Welch, Walter Roy
Roberts, Cheryl A. - Strese, Robin L.
Roberts, Clara (Pickering) - Bartlett, J. O. D.
Roberts, Constance L. - Hyslop, Douglas W.
Roberts, Lauri A. - Boyd, Allan R.
Roberts, Mary Addie - Knirsch, Earl Frederick
Robinson, Barbara E. - Tasker, Paul E.
Robinson, Maude Kent - Burleigh, Eugene Fred
Robinson, Prudence G. - Thoroughgood, Richard J.
Roddy, Joyce Margaret - O'Toole, Kevin Dennis
Rog, Kniertje A. - Antonucci, Anthony S.
Rogers, Elizabeth M. - Collins, Ralph K.
Rogers, Mary Ellen - Gosse, Harvey Willis

Rogers, Patricia - Kelley, Ray I.
Rogers, Sharen Renee - Hodgdon, Philip B.
Rollins, Estelle M. - Morrissette, Dennis A.
Rollins, Patti A. - Whittier, Keith A.
Rollins, Terry Jean - Tiede, Kurt F.
Rooney, Linda J. - Rowe, George R.
Rose, Louisa J. - Hillsgrove, James H.
Rose, Norma L. - Delois, Jeffrey J.
Rosenguist, Eline M. - Ruediger, Bunt E.
Ross, Lori A. - Phillipps, Paul J.
Ross, Ruth H. - Golden, James E.
Ross, Tammy Jean - Bousquet, Paul Judson, Jr.
Rothwell, Sandra J. - Clough, Leonard W.
Rowe, Marjorie - Otis, Lewis L.
Rowe, Myra A. (Bunker) - Blaisdell, Joseph P.
Rowell, Nancy Lee - Rowell, Kenneth Paul
Russell, Alicia E. - Foss, Russell J.
Ryder, Sally Jean - Holmes, David John

St. Cyr, Sandra J. (Drolet) - Stapleton, Timothy J.
St. Louis, Rose A. - Albee, G. Paige
Sanborn, Addie S. (Tebbetts) - Thyng, Charles E.
Sanborn, Angeline H. (Eaton) - Richardson, William H.
Sanborn, Meretta - Berchner, William H.
Sanders, Ann L. (Pendergast) - Clark, Isaac H.
Sargent, Clara Jane (Smith) - Cotton, John G.
Sargent, Elizabeth A. - Golden, Richard L.
Sargent, Madeline - Emerson, Harold Brown
Scalese, Joan E. - Folsom, Richard B.
Scarpa, Andrea L. - Nero, John L.
Schacht, Karen L. - Lewis, Gregg M.
Schaffer, Ruth E. - Black, Harland P.
Schlottmann, Lynne C. - Morse, Kevin M.
Scott, Eleanor H. - Vien, Roland A.
Scott, Patricia A. - Bowen, Dale M.
Seavey, Marie L. (Halfman) - Blanchard, John E.
Selman, Grace B. - Harriman, Isaac E.
Senior, Joanne M. - Knirsch, Robert K.
Shackford, Alice M. - Powell, Harry L.
Shackford, Alma I. - Armstrong, James W.
Shackford, Augusta I. (Smart) - Gould, Daniel A.

Shackford, Edith M. - Dow, George W.
Shackford, Maud E. - Gray, Frank W.
Shannon, Marietta C. (Berry) - Powell, Sylvester
Shaw, Stacy Luann - Mulcahy, Shawn Adrian
Sherman, Mary Beth - Chase, Ricky L.
Sherman, Rebecca Jeannine - Bousquet, Peter Judson
Shonyo, Virginia E. - Gray, Leslie M.
Sillars, Carol J. - Smith, Keith L.
Silva, Lisa M. - Simpson, Mark R.
Silva, Vicki L. - Nelson, Troy J.
Sinclair, Carolyn Y. - Vinson, James W.
Six, Karen F. - Keller, Robert D.
Skelton, Sandra Rene - Louis, Francois
Slaney, Viola M. - Ehrstein, Barry N.
Smith, Carol N. - Locke, Richard M.
Smith, Charna L. - Aversa, Michael S.
Smith, Dorothy Ann - LaBrecque, Dennis Joseph
Smith, Etta M. - Gaskell, Harry C.
Smith, Joyce M. - Golden, Scott L.
Smith, Kathi J. - Hurst, Albert W., Jr.
Smith, Libbie E. - Kaime, Samuel F.
Smith, Linda A. - Pierce, Keith R.
Smith, Linda C. - Sanford, Alan C.
Smith, Marjorie E. (Robicheau) - Barry, John J.
Smith, Michelle M. - Rosado, Gerald
Smith, Patricia J. - Berubee, Douglas
Smith, Paula S. - Penney, Richard D.
Smith, Priscilla Ann - Murphree, Stephen Eugene
Smith, Stacey Ellen - Beapure, Douglas Herve
Smith, Susan M. - Page, Jesse H.
Smith, Wendy P. - Phillips, Shirley N.
Snow, Dorinda L. (McKenzie) - Martin, James L.
Sohnes, Celia A. - Manning, Edward M.
Soles, Sandra Jean - Barton, Kevin Albert
Soriano, Harriet Anne - Knight, Burton W., II
Soulia, Kathleen - Paige, John A.
Soulia, Priscilla E. - Wheeler, Charles R.
Southard, Bonita G. - Brannigan, Eugene
Spargo, Lila May (Compston) - Kania, Stanley
Spataro, Christina Marie - Blutt, Stephen Richard
Spaulding, Karen M. - Jussaume, Lucien B., Jr.

Spooner, Lurena B. - Pitman, Oscar E.
Springfield, Jairetta E. (Main) - Albee, G. Paige
Stanley, Andrea Jeanette - Drouin, Serge Yvan
Stannard, Joyce M. - Parkington, Leon
Stapleton, Sandra J. - Croteau, Peter J.
Starbird, Mildred M. - Nutter, Ralph Edward
Steele, Sandra Joan - Smith, Gary
Steeves, Geraldine B. - Puglia, Robert V.
Stephens, Madeline A. - Wheeler, Larry D.
Sterken, Antonia Maria - Brown, Kent Lewis
Stevens, Frances Naomi - Harrington, John Edward
Stevens, Stacey G. - Vachon, David R.
Stillings, Dawn M. - Thoroughgood, Kenneth J.
Stimmell, Judy J. - Stone, Michael J.
Stock, Barbara J. - Woodward, William
Stock, Robin Lynn - Morris, David Edward
Stockman, Jane Helen - Martin, Alfred George
Stockman, Pamela Jean - Ducey, Richard James
Stoddard, Mary L. - Smith, Louis R.
Stone, Bertha E. - Genest, Henry
Storey, Janice Caroline - Metzger, Jeffrey Lynn
Straw, Lois Marion (Foss) - Jones, Charles Henry
Strout, Faith Lindberg - Savelo, Peter P.
Sullivan, Kathleen M. - Larkin, John W.
Sullivan, Marie T. - Curley, Walter W.
Sullivan, Maureen L. - Foss, Donald Clyde
Sullivan, Terri L. - Loporcaro, Joseph A., Jr.
Sumner, Marie P. - French, Herbert C.
Swain, Bridget - Paquette, Paul Owen
Swain, Esther E. - Corson, Clyde E.
Swain, Rebekah M. - Brown, Forrest P.
Sylvain, Deborah Fate - Mitchell, Stephen Robert
Sylvain, Judith Grace - Myers, Dennis Richard
Sylvain, Nancy A. G. - Marston, Lenard M.

Talley, Angela W. - Stone, Michael J.
Tarbox, Annie R. - Holmes, Glenn O.
Tarbox, Frances I. - Riel, Thomas A.
Tarbox, Freida Jean - Simonds, Malcolm Frank
Tarbox, Patricia A. - Elliott, Eugene W.
Tasker, Dorothy A. - Pickard, Robert A., Jr.

Tasker, Evelyn M. - Locke, John M.
Tasker, Ivy R. - Cimon, Peter N.
Tasker, Lillian E. - Clark, Herbert E.
Tasker, Linda S. - Watson, Curtis D.
Tasker, Melanie Jean - Fife, Stephen Allen
Tasker, Nancy A. - Straight, Terrence W.
Tasker, Nancy Ann - Randall, Daniel Clifford
Tasker, Roxann M. - Krause, George R., II
Taylor, Teresa L. - Ellis, Robert B.
Taylor, Teresa Louise - Marriott, Bruce Alan
Terry, Hattie A. - Foss, George G.
Theopold, Karen - Lallier, Thornton E., Jr.
Therrien, Alice E. - Weeks, Calvin H.
Therrien, Linda D. - Robbins, Jon W.
Thompson, Agnes B. - Knowles, Russell
Thompson, Arline M. - Ryder, Lorrine Endicott
Thompson, Beryle Marguerite - Thyng, Charles Herbert
Thompson, Jeri - Owen, Ryan J.
Thompson, Melissa M. - Byers, Steven I.
Thornton, Clara Jean - Harrington, Rodney E.
Thorpe, Martha L. - Romansky, Richard
Thoroughgood, Diana L. - Thoroughgood, Richard J.
Thoroughgood, Susan M. - Comeau, Fred L.
Thurston, Dorothy M. - Vonfricken, Henry A.
Thurston, Susan L. - Corson, William H.
Thyng, Elizabeth A. - Thyng, Herbert M.
Thyng, Jean Mary - Richey, William S., Jr.
Tibbetts, Cilla - Straw, Alba C.
Tiede, Carol Louise - Gates, Robert Kenneth
Tiede, Jennifer R. - Driscoll, David A.
Tillinghast, Carla A. - Bickford, Alfred L.
Tilton, Margaret Ann - Chagnon, Jerry Martin
Tilton, Mary Elmerta - Bunker, Roland E.
Tolken, Stephanie C. - LeSage, Steven J.
Toscano, Lisa D. - Vail, Steven L.
Toutloff, Edith J. - Chagnon, Norman D.
Tower, Ora M. - Jenkins, Harry L.
Towle, Christine M. - Turbaville, Herbert T.
Towle, Fay Allison (Hinman) - Mitchell, Roderick Ernest
Towle, Kelly J. - Conrad, Gregory S.
Towle, Susan L. - Conrad, Harold, III

Transue, Lisa M. - Knowlton, David Lee
Trefrey, Karen Ann - Trefrey, Michael Joseph
Troegel, Cheryl J. - Guilbert, Scott R.
Troughton, Ivy Rose - Tasker, Philip G.
Troughton, Laurel - Tiede, Ernst Emil Herman, Jr.
Trudeau, Loretta - Keefe, William J.
Trusten, May L. - Perez, Alfred J., Sr.
Tudor, Charlotte M. - Berry, Kenneth A.
Tudor, Margaret G. - Richardson, Robert
Turner, Veronica A. - Turner, Greg A.
Turnpaugh, Gail J. - Stockman, Jack L.
Tuttle, Annie F. - Davis, Coran K.
Tuttle, Blanche C. - Kenison, Herbert C.
Tuttle, Janet - Tasker, Roscoe
Tuttle, Linda A. - White, Kenneth H.
Twaddle, Dorothy A. - Wilson, Thomas
Twitchell, Dale D. - Kenison, Terry L.

Underwood, Nellie F. (Woodcock) - Underhill, Frank T.

Van Buskirk, Tracey J. - Lallier, Christopher M.
Van Dyke, Dorothy P. - Van Dyke, Douglas A.
Van Horn, Christina - Tasker, Edward Arthur
Varney, Carrie A. (Lang) - Seward, Thomas F.
Varney, Hattie C. - Foss, Haven B.
Varney, LeeAnne M. - Connors, Stephen A.
Varney, Lisa A. - Clements, David L.
Veno, Margaret Ann - Jenisch, Richard A.
Veno, Sandra Lee - Boudreau, William A.
Vernal, Patricia A. - Gerlack, Rolla D.
Veroneau, Jane Marie - Dupont, David G.
Vien, Monica M. - Keefe, Thomas C., Jr.
Vincent, Cheryl Ann - Piaseczny, James Daniel
Vincent, Katherine N. (Nelson) - Zecha, Ferdinand, Sr.
Vogt, Shirley (Johnson) - Knox, Granville Shaw
Vokes, Diane Marie - Mitchell, Albert Carl

Wade, Gloria H. - Perkins, William C.
Wakefield, Ada Belle - Foss, Richard Colby
Waldron, Michelle C. - Krauss, Richard Russell
Walker, Alice - Livingstone, William E.

Walker, Kathleen E. - Carpenter, William T.
Ward, Grace M. - Dennett, Linn M.
Warren, Denise A. - Lamere, Robert A.
Watson, Ellena Annette - Munsey, Steven Alan
Watson, Nancy A. (Goodwin) - Tebbitts, George F.
Watson, Pamela J. - Bergevin, Ernest A.
Watts, Donna M. - Fair, Lawrence E., Jr.
Webber, Iva (Weeks) - Downing, Henry C.
Webber, Theresa A. - Locke, Nathan J.
Webster, Emma A. - Berry, S. J.
Webster, Gail M. - Nelson, John S.
Webster, Gertrude M. - Merrill, Herbert H.
Webster, Margaret H. - Griffin, James J.
Webster, Pearl Cecil (Ketcham) - Weis, Maximilian Karl
Weeks, Iva R. - Webber, Parker G., Jr.
Welch, Annie L. (Lyman) - Scruton, Walter G.
Welch, Diane M. - Brady, Robert M.
Welch, Dorothy G. - Lapointe, Leopold G.
Welch, Frances J. - Clough, Charles H.
Welch, Mary Ellen - Perkins, Randy Jay
Welch, Maud E. - Downs, Arthur L.
Weldon, Faith A. - Debold, Richard W.
Wells, Minnie B. - Emerson, John O.
Wells, Rena L. - Welch, Fred T.
Wells, Virginia L. - Mitchell, Wallace W.
Wentworth, Liberty W. - Pickering, Charles H.
Wessely, Vera L. - White, Brian A.
Weston, Lida M. - Pepe, Joseph F., III
Wheeler, Caroline E. - Vulner, Glen Durwood
Wheet, Irene A. - Mitchell, Richard L.
Wheet, Lee E. - Dawson, Robert W.
Wheet, Mary E. - Prescott, Gordon H.
Wheet, Vera B. - Brown, Ralph A.
Whitcher, Alice A. - Zecha, Ernest A.
White, Bonnie R. - Lichty, John
White, Jennie M. - Chesley, Charles W.
White, Martha B. - Drouin, John F.
White, Vera L. - Flanders, Henry J.
Whitehouse, Elizabeth - Kelley, Richard A.
Whitehouse, Ella B. - Nutter, George A.
Whitehouse, Emma J. - Lougee, Leslie J.

Whiten, Agnes G. - Robinson, Henry R.
Whithan, Laura - Barton, David E.
Whiting, Lena (St. Pierre) - MacDonald, Albert Edward
Whitney, Dianna - Kashulines, David Martin
Whittey, Henrietta A. (Quandt) - Rowell, Charles A.
Whittey, Mildred Louise - Lennon, Murtha James
Whittington, Ruth E. (Boyd) - Brasse, Peter A.
Wiggins, Annie M. - Drescher, Robert W.
Wilkins, Lulu E. - Emerson, Carlton E.
Willey, Grace A. - Jenkins, Edgar
Williams, Leora G. (Clark) - Welch, Richard W.
Williams, Margaret - Littlefield, Chester W.
Wilson, Dorohy E. - Bebo, Nelson F.
Wilson, Katherine Anna - Hogencamp, Harry, Jr.
Wilson, Nancy A. - Tasker, Michael F.
Winch, Kristen L. - Brown, Willie W.
Winkley, Clara J. (Straw) - Ayers, Lyman J.
Winterle, Janet Lynn - Jeanson, Gregory Wayne
Wisniewski, Karin A. - Shapiro, Rob
Witham, Ethel B. (Brown) - Rogers, Harvey L.
Wolcott, Mona E. - Churchill, Ralph K.
Wolfgang, Terri Lee - Hanson, Leonard D.
Wood, Hazel Miriam - Call, Will H., Jr.
Woods, Mary Ann - Boston, Robert Alan
Wright, Lillian P. - Fernald, Charles W.
Wyatt, Marion - Golden, William

Yeaton, Barbara L. - Rogers, Harvey L.
Yeaton, Edith E. - St. George, David
Yeaton, Ruth Helen - Kimball, Lloyd Elwin
Yelle, Allison M. - Buttafuoco, James
Yelle, Martha T. - Keene, Richard M.
Young, Addie F. (Aikins) - Bunker, George M.
Young, Carol Lynn - Podmore, Kerry Shane
Young, Chloe B. (Brooks) - Wood, Almon G.
Young, Georgiana (Brown) - May, Sylvester L.
Young, Harriet A. - Boston, Stuart L.
Young, Phyllis A. - Thoroughgood, Ralph H.
Zecha, Evelyn M. - Mizo, Harold A., Jr.
Zetto, Angela Marie - Bardwell, Thomas Stevens
Zube, Michele A. - Tasker, Eric M.

DEATHS

ABBOTT,
Lewis R., d. 6/9/1907 at 43/6/4; apoplexy; dining room; married; b. Tunbridge, VT; W. S. Abbott (Pomfret, VT) and Mary Houghton (Winchester, VT)

ACKERMAN,
Arthur, d. 8/24/1953 at 91 in Manchester; b. NH; Peter T. Ackerman and Emily Berry
Ava M., d. 2/27/1960 at 66 in Manchester; shoeworker; single; b. Alexandria; Arthur Ackerman and Clara E. Berry
Clara E., d. 2/27/1938 at 77; b. Barnstead; James R. Berry and Sarah Berry

ADAIR,
Robert John, d. 7/19/1994 at 64 in Barnstead; William Adair and Jennie Madlaine McAllister

ADAMAITIS,
Keith R., d. 1/2/1984 at 18 in Barnstead; Theodore Adamaitis and Jacqueline Lagasse

ADAMS,
Bruce E., d. 3/28/1999 in Concord; J. Adams and Bessie Wilson
Charles W., d. 5/27/1895 at 70; mortification; farmer; widower; b. Barnstead; James Adams
Ebenezer (Capt.), d. 1820 at 35**
Ebenezer, d. 1832 at 79**
George A., d. 9/15/1896 at 77; cancer of liver
James, d. 1868 at 72**
Joseph (Dr.), d. 1799 at 78**
Nancy, d. 1/5/1892 at 67; la grippe; housewife; married
Nathaniel, d. 1853 at 82**; son of Dr. Joseph

AGAR,
Beulah C., d. 1/14/1987 at 88 in Rochester; Arthur Clark and Emma Kendall
John G., d. 3/5/1992 at 91 in Rochester; Frederick William Agar and Clara P. Whitcher

AIKEN,
Levi, d. 11/30/1920 at 88/5/18*; b. Barnstead

AIKENS,
Abbie L., d. 11/19/1900 at 74; rheumatism; married; b. Alton; David Langley and ----- Chamberlain

AIKIN,
George, d. 1863 at 22** (soldier)
Hannah, d. 1843 at 84**; wife of John
Jacob, d. 5/15/1905 at 87/2/18; Bright's disease; farmer; widower; b. Barnstead; John Aikin (Strafford) and Rebecca Berry (Strafford)
John, d. 1847 at 93**
John (Col.), d. 1868 at 77**

ALLEN,
H. Raymond, d. 9/3/1969 at 75 in Wolfeboro; manufacturer, leather; b. NH; Horace E. Allen and Sarah Lee
Mary, d. 1867 at 62**; wife of Rev. Levi
Robert (Rev.), d. 1847 at 55**

ANDERSON,
Flora, d. 11/16/1920 at 61/0/12; b. NS; Duncan McKenzie (NS) and Mary Cory (NS)

ANDREWS,
Leonard E., d. 4/9/1979 at 72 in Manchester; Thomas Andrews and Harriet E. Brown
Louis J., d. 5/10/1995 at 78 in Concord; Louis A. Andrews and Margaret Pisani

APPLEBY,
Avis Pearl, d. 5/15/1994 at 96 in Wolfeboro; Clarence Golding and Lois Cavenaugh

ARLIN,
William H., d. 1/29/1887 at 33/8; shoemaker; married

ARMER,
Linda J., d. 2/21/1984 at 36 in Barnstead; Ralph Barkhouse and Irene Moore

ARMSTRONG,
Darrell, d. 2/15/1906 at 0/4/21; marasmus; b. Barnstead; James Armstrong (Portsmouth) and Alma Shackford (Barnstead)
Tom, d. 9/14/1910 at 0/1/18; unknown; b. Barnstead; J. W. Armstrong (Portsmouth) and Alma Shackford (Barnstead)

ARSENAULT,
Jacqueline C., d. 8/30/1971 at 46 in Pittsfield; machine stitcher; b. Rumford, ME; Arthur Beaudet and Marie -----

ARTESI,
Velvet L., d. 9/30/1995 at 30 in Concord; Armand Leroux and Carol Hart

ASH,
Leslie Earl, d. 2/13/1968 at 39 in Pittsfield; floorman; b. NH; Edgar A. Ash and Blanche E. Lane

ASHCROFT,
Maria P., d. 9/19/1899 at 42/7/2; cancer; married; b. Barnstead; William Roberts and Clara Pickering

ASHLEY,
George M., d. 7/27/1969 at 73 in Concord; farmer-carpenter; b. NH; George M. Ashley and Anna B. White

AVERY,
Celia, d. 12/14/1935 at 15; b. Pittsfield; Reuben Avery and Hattie Scruton
Daniel E., d. 4/9/1887 at 26/5/7; farmer; single; b. Barnstead
Daniel H., d. 11/24/1927 at 83*; b. Barnstead; Samuel Avery and Lucinda Holmes
Edward, d. 1838 at 58**
Elizabeth V., d. 2/3/1919 at 69/3/22*
George P., d. 9/8/1973 at 84 in Concord; retired; b. NH; John Avery and Mary Staples
Hattie H., d. 3/26/1967 at 73 in Rochester; housewife; b. Strafford; Herbert Scruton and Laura M. Yeaton
John, d. 10/10/1893 at 50; softening of brain; farmer; married; b. Barnstead; Stephen Avery (Barnstead) and Ann Avery (Epsom)

Mary J., d. 8/12/1931 at 73*; b. Strafford; David Avery and Mary Chick

Noah H., d. 12/27/1890 at 53/0/13; farmer; single; b. Barnstead; Samuel Avery (Barnstead) and Lucinda Holmes (Barnstead)

Reuben, d. 12/9/1963 at 75 in Strafford; head sawyer; b. Strafford; Daniel H. Avery and Sally L. Avery

Sallie L., d. 6/22/1930 at 63; b. Strafford; John W. Avery and Hannah S. Libbey

Samuel, d. 1795 at 76**

Samuel, d. 1/15/1890 at 84/10/24

Samuel J., d. 4/29/1911 at 79/10/29; unknown; farmer; married; b. Barnstead; Samuel Avery (VT) and Lucinda Holmes (Barnstead)

Stanton C., d. 10/15/1918 at 18/4/3; b. Laconia; Chester Avery and Mannie Helliged

AYER,
John M., d. 7/4/1985 at 74 in Nashua; Willis E. Ayer and Myrtle Sawyer

AYERS,
Abigail M., d. 1854 at 68**

Charles F., d. 7/26/1944 at 77/9/9 in Rochester*; b. Barnstead; George Ayers and Mary Jenkins

Charles W., d. 12/30/1915 at 59; farmer; divorced; b. Barnstead

Clara Jane, d. 9/14/1949 at 87/7/9 in Center Harbor*; b. Barnstead; Thomas S. Straw and Louisa A. Hill

Clarisa J., d. 1/19/1921 at 77; b. Worcester, MA; Charles Worcester (Ellsworth, ME) and Sarah Munsey (Barnstead)

Enos G., d. 2/18/1931 at 88; b. Barnstead; Joseph Ayers and Nancy Lougee

France E., d. 5/20/1912 at 28/5/21; suicide by hanging; housekeeper; single; b. Alton; Charles W. Ayers (Barnstead) and Clara I. Ross (Gilmanton)

George W., d. 2/20/1910 at 70/0/3; heart disease, paralysis; farmer; widower; b. Barnstead; Joshua Ayers and Sally Raymond

John K., d. 3/5/1888 at 64/5/23; farmer; married; b. Barnstead; Samuel Ayers (Greenland) and Sarah Lang (Greenland)

John P., d. 2/25/1911 at 70/8/16; pneumonia; farmer; single; b. Barnstead; Joseph Ayers (Greenland) and Susan Piper (Tuftonboro)

Joseph, d. 1872 at 71**
Joseph S., d. 1851 at 49**
Mary J., d. 3/9/1887 at 43; housework; married; b. Barnstead; Joseph Jenkins
Nellie M., d. 1/11/1938 at 69*; b. Barnstead; George W. Jenkins and Victoria Clark
Perkins, d. 1856 at 72**
Phebe, d. 2/16/1902 at 64/11/16; tuberculosis
Ruth, d. 1855 at 91**; widow of Winthrop
Samuel, d. 1842 at 80**
Samuel, d. 1871 at 83**
Samuel J., d. 2/2/1926 at 83
Susan M., d. 11/20/1896 at 90; old age; widow
Winthrop, d. 1849 at 86**

BABB,
Adelaide, d. 7/28/1937 at 69; b. Enfield; Leander H. Talbert and Jane P. Butman
Edwin O., d. 10/26/1927 at 65*
Elmera, d. 2/24/1909 at 84/6/28; pneumonia; housewife; widow; b. Strafford; Samuel Evans (Strafford) and Lizzie Willey (Barnstead)
Elvin, d. 2/8/1913 at 83/6/15; chro. nephritis; widower; b. Strafford; Dennis Babb and Judith Willey
Ezekiel, d. 10/18/1908 at 85/6/26; chronic nephritis; farmer; married; b. Barnstead; Ralph Babb (Strafford) and Delilar Hayes (Rochester)
Mary Ellen, d. 10/7/1916 at 48/0/26; housewife; married; b. Acton, ME; Fred Furlong (ME) and Mary ----- (NS)
Mildred E., d. 3/27/1920 at 51/8/20*; George A. Nichols (Dixmont, ME)
Sampson, d. 1849 at 86**
Sampson H., d. 12/7/1910 at 89/11/7; organic disease of heart; farmer; widower; b. Barnstead; Ralph Babb (Barnstead) and Delilah Hayes (Rochester)
William A., d. 3/8/1936 at 70 in Barnstead; Dyer Babb and Melvina Doe

BABCOCK,
Panthea P., d. 1/15/1898 at 82/1/7; organic disease of heart; widow; b. Barnstead

BACHELDER,
Lydia, d. 1841 at 88**

BADGER,
Frank, d. 4/22/1942 at 69 in Barnstead; b. Gaysville, VT; Daniel M. Badger and Miranda Lull

BAINBRIDGE,
Mary E., d. 5/23/1999 in Concord; Donald McKenna and Monica Ryan

BAKER,
Edward I., d. 4/24/1970 at 81 in Concord; laborer; b. NY; Carrie Wade

BALDNER,
Mary B., d. 6/3/1979 at 61 in Concord; Eugene O'Leacy and Margaret Kehoe

BANKS,
Elbourn N., d. 4/28/1960 at 72 in Barnstead; plumber; married; b. Middleton, NS; Adoniram Banks and Nettie Neily
Mary Jeannette, d. 6/12/1972 at 85 in Manchester; housewife; b. NS; Alexander G. Musgrave and Katherine Daley

BARBOUR,
Lois, d. 1855 at 80**

BARKER,
Cora E., d. 7/18/1912 at 51/8/29 in Concord*; heart failure; married; b. Jersey City, NJ; John Neville

BARNEY,
Charles, d. 5/6/1963 at 79 in Hillsborough; laborer
Nellie M., d. 7/17/1889 at 22/11; mach. op.; single; Jesse Barney and Eliza Hall

BARRAFORD,
Daniel Justin McPhearson, d. 12/15/1991 at 18 in Barnstead; Daniel M. Barraford, III and Stephanie K. Crafton

BARRELLI,
Frank X., d. 12/13/1973 at 65 in Concord; floral designer; b. NY; Cono V. Barrelli and Rose Marie Tuoti

BARTLETT,
John H., d. 2/27/1926 at 81; b. Canada; Thomas Bartlett and Ann Goodhard
Mary Hannah, d. 10/27/1940 at 85*; b. Barnstead; James P. Foss and Eliza Blake

BARTON [see O'Barton, Obarton],
Georgina, d. 9/18/1899 at 0/6/2; dysentery; b. Pittsfield; Ezra Barton and Virginia Dupry

BATCHELDER,
Della H., d. 1/21/1974 at 81 in Pittsfield; housewife; b. Orford; Alvah B. Heath and Mary Hawland

BATES,
Eleanor W., d. 9/27/1983 at 64 in Hanover; Ralph Raymond and Marjorie Munroe

BAXENDALE,
George E., d. 7/12/1991 at 72 in Manchester; Walter Baxendale and Betsy Mason

BEBO,
Harriet E., d. 1/2/1965 at 73 in Pittsfield; housewife; b. Chichester; Oris Gray and Harriet Hannaford
John F., d. 8/6/1959 at 81 in Concord

BEESMER,
Beverly F., d. 3/29/1982 at 57 in Concord; James H. Adams and Bessie Wilson
Richard, d. 9/24/1984 at 62 in Manchester; Roy R. Beesmer and Lucy Moore

BELL,
Virginia, d. 6/18/1998 in Barnstead; Warren Hartshorn and Edith Herstrom

BELLOWS,
John F., d. 6/13/1986 at 86 in Manchester
Myrtie R., d. 2/15/1979 at 79 in Epsom; James A. Hastings and Annie Belle Riggs

BELONGA,
Edwin, d. 1/23/1908 at 38/0/28; tuberculosis; shoemaker; widower; b. Skowhegan; Paul Belonga and Mary Booth

BELVILLE,
Flora A., d. 4/2/1965 at 78 in Concord; housewife; b. Laconia; Charles Hannah and Agnes Armstrong

BEMIS,
George F., d. 3/1/1934 at 59 in Concord*
Maria Kerr, d. 3/18/1955 at 96 in Plymouth; b. Brudnell, PEI; Ephraim Stewart and Mary Sutherland
Sena M., d. 12/15/1925 at 54; b. Strafford; Charles H. Avery and Pauline Hartford

BENKA,
Mary Tilton, d. 10/16/1918 at 31/1/9*; b. Deerfield; George C. Tilton (Pittsfield) and Hattie E. Call (Chichester)

BENNETT,
Cheryl E., d. 6/30/1983 at 17 in Barnstead; Roland Bennett and Barbara Fox
Minnie L., d. 4/23/1956 at 88 in Barnstead; b. Bridgeport, CT; John Cosier and Sarah Blackman

BENSON,
Ronald Keith, d. 4/3/1996 at 76 in Wolfeboro; Charles D. Benson and Alzada Littlefield

BERCEANN,
John, d. 8/6/1996 at 71 in Barnstead; John Berceann and Bessie Walker

BERCHEN,
Jill C., d. 12/4/1998 in Barnstead; William Tothill and Dorothy Altieri

BERKSON,
Leonard B., d. 1/7/1976 at 63 in Concord; clothier; b. MA; Barnett Berkson and Anna Rosenthal

BERRY,
Abbie M., d. 9/2/1914 at 92/3/6; cerebral hemorrhage; widow; b. Barnstead; Daniel Parshley (NH) and H. Pickering (NH)
Alberton Herman, d. 1/15/1974 at 57 in Manchester; truck driver; b. NH; Guy Berry and Eva Weymouth
Cecelia M., d. 1/3/1997 at 79 in Concord; Anthony J. Foster and Martha Surrette
Charles H., d. 4/1/1897 at 60/3/8; apoplexy; farmer; married; b. Barnstead
Edith A., d. 8/31/1995 at 92 in Wolfeboro; Carl S. Anderson and Hilda Larson
Eliphalet, d. 1859 at 61**
Eliza, d. 9/15/1904 at 84/3/15; old age; b. Strafford; Paul Brewster and Lizzie Brewster
Ella, d. 4/21/1935 at 65; b. Barnstead; James Berry and Sarah Berry
Emma A., d. 8/10/1920 at 56/1/17; b. Danbury; Joseph Webster and Sarah Otis (Strafford)
Ethel G., d. 11/3/1969 at 81 in Concord; housewife; b. NH; Albion N. Foss and Josephine M. Clough
Fred E., d. 1/27/1929 at 72; b. Barnstead; Ira L. Berry and Leonia Drew
Hannah, d. 1864 at 88**; widow of John
Helen J., d. 9/20/1987 at 96 in Wolfeboro; Fred E. Berry and Edith M. Tarbox
Ira L., d. 2/28/1892 at 62; heart disease; farmer; married
James R., d. 5/16/1924 at 90; b. Strafford
Jane M., d. 7/4/1915 at 76/4/6; housewife; widow; b. Barnstead; Aaron Snell (Pittsfield) and May Nutter (Barnstead)
John, d. 1837 at 59**
John, d. 8/7/1887 at 72/7/13; farmer; married
Margarita E., d. 7/24/1943 at 72 in Barnstead; b. Christiana, Norway; Oscar Olson and Natalie Olson
Marjorie E., d. 3/25/1974 at 55 in Rochester; housewife; Frank Wilkenson and Lucy Roles
Mary, d. 1872 at 72**; wife of Samuel B., Esq.

Philip R., d. 4/17/1965 at 79 in Keene; machinist; b. Alton; William H. Berry and Martha A. Garland

Rebecca, d. 9/17/1896 at 76; apoplexy; widow

Sarah F., d. 5/30/1902 at 71/10; Bright's disease; housekeeper; married; b. Barnstead; William Berry

Stephen B., d. 5/2/1906 at 81/1/20; old age; widower; b. Strafford; Peter Berry (Strafford) and Susan Babb (Barnstead)

Stephen J., d. 6/27/1914 at 59/0/22; cerebral hemorrhage; farmer; married; b. Barnstead; Stephen Berry (Barnstead) and Eliza Berry (Strafford)

Tamson, d. 1872 at 69**; widow of William

Warren C., d. 6/27/1896 at 35/1; bronchitis; single; b. Barnstead; Stephen Berry

William, d. 1857 at 57**

William H., d. 1863 at 24** (soldier)

BERUBEE,
Rodney A., d. 3/13/1990 at 66 in Concord; Fred Berubee and Daisy Powers

BESSON,
Charles L., d. 3/5/1910 at 20/7/27; typhoid fever; P.O. sub clerk; single; b. Lynn, MA; Charles E. Besson (Lynn, MA) and Ida E. Nutter (Gilmanton)

BETTENCOURT,
John, d. 2/22/1982 at 72 in Concord; John Bettencourt and Emily Cortez

BICKFORD,
Abigail, d. 1834 at 70**; wife of Moses

Alice Wakefield, d. 11/8/1932 at 64*; b. Pittsford, VT; Charles Martin and Marilla Carpenter

Charles P., d. 8/2/1899 at 75; pneumonia; single; b. Barnstead; Arthur Bickford

Clarence H., d. 3/19/1998 in Barnstead; Arthur Bickford and Ida Brewster

Edna B., d. 1/2/1990 at 69 in Concord; Albion Banks and Mary Musgrave

George A., d. 10/10/1997 at 77 in Barnstead; Arthur Bickford and Ida Brewster

John, d. 1851 at 83**
John P., d. 4/7/1919 at 78/11/1; b. Barnstead; Daniel Bickford (Barnstead) and Abigail Peavey (Barnstead)
Lillian May, d. 11/29/1952 at 42 in Barnstead; b. Rochester; Harry S. Smith and Hazel Hussey
Moses, d. 1859 at 93**
Moses, d. 6/8/1902 at 66/1/19; pneumonia; farmer; single; b. Barnstead; Samuel Bickford (Lee) and Betsey Bickford (Barnstead)
Nancy, d. 1860 at 84**; wife of John
Vera Hill, d. 1/12/1996 at 92 in Barnstead; Elwood Hill and Mercedas Mae Dame
William S., d. 5/29/1964 at 54 in Concord; woodsman; b. Tamworth; John Bickford and Carrie Fifield

BILLINGS,
Donald C., d. 7/13/1994 at 68 in Manchester; Theodore Billings and Ruth Rand
Mildred A., d. 7/31/1994 at 76 in Concord; Benjamin Simmons and Amelia Williams

BIXBY,
Mary E., d. 7/27/1925 at 73; b. Strafford; Joseph Webster and Sarah Otis

BLACK,
William O., d. 12/30/1979 at 83 in Manchester; Alexander Black and Henrietta Osborne

BLAHSL,
August, d. 6/23/1907 at 28/5/5; accidental drowning; weaver; single; b. Austria; August Blahsl (Austria) and Mary Glmoch (Austria)

BLAIKIE,
Eva, d. 11/20/1966 at 90 in Brentwood; shoe shop; b. Alexandria; George T. Pitman and Aurilla Brook

BLAIR,
Herbert F., d. 6/15/1956 at 70 in Laconia; b. Boston, MA; Harry Blair and Amelia Foster

BLAISDELL,
Joseph P., d. 3/22/1916 at 93/3/22*; carpenter; married; b.
    Campton; Nathaniel Blaisdell (Campton)
Mary B., d. 8/12/1889 at 39/5; single; b. Pittsfield; Joseph P.
    Blaisdell (Campton) and ----- (Gilmanton)
Nathan, d. 1859 at 62**
Nathaniel, d. 1867 at 27**
Soph. W., d. 9/29/1895 at 75/2; heart disease; housewife; married;
    b. Deerfield
Sophia, d. 1867 at 28**; wife of Nathaniel

BLAKE,
George F., d. 10/2/1917 at 69/9/8; b. Barnstead; John Blake and
    Mary Buzzell
John, d. 12/22/1899 at 77/0/15; acute heart failure; cooper; married;
    b. Epsom; Timothy Blake
Joseph, d. 3/8/1893 at 73/10/25; pneumonia, following la grippe;
    farmer; married; b. Epsom; Timothy Blake and ----- Emerson
Mary J., d. 6/4/1903 at 77/2/24; cancer; domestic; widow; b.
    Barnstead; Aaron Buzzell (Gilford) and Rachael Buzzel
Olive A., d. 2/8/1943 at 91 in Barnstead; b. Barnstead; John J.
    Merrill and Mary E. Jenness
Timothy, d. 11/6/1887 at 52; musician; married; b. Barnstead;
    Timothy Blake

BLANCHARD,
Cyrus W., d. 12/12/1899 at 81/2; cystitis; merchant; married; b.
    Windham; Emery C. Blanchard and Dolly Wheeler
John E., d. 4/30/1917 at 54/1/3*; b. Barnstead; Cyrus W. Blanchard
    (Methuen, MA) and Abbie Chesley (Barnstead)
Lovey N., d. 1/28/1906 at 79/10/20; carcinoma; housework; widow;
    b. Barnstead; Eliphalet Nutter (Barnstead) and Lovey Locke
    (Barnstead)

BLOOD,
Mrs. Amauller, d. 9/29/1909 at 86/11/14; la grippe; widow; b. VT

BLUESTONE,
Miriam, d. 9/26/1996 at 88 in Barnstead; Morris Sussman and
    Rebecca Makover

Naomi R., d. 11/13/1999 in Barnstead; Harry Bluestone and Mirium Sussman

BLY,
Caroline Anna, d. 7/30/1941 at 0/2/14 in Presque Isle, ME*; b. Presque Isle, ME; Rufus W. Bly and Elsie A. Tuttle
Robert Willis, d. 12/17/1943 at 0 in Strafford*; b. Rochester; Rufus W. Bly and Elsie A. Tuttle
Sabina P., d. 3/28/2000 in Concord; Rupert Poechl and Rosina -----

BODEN,
Gertrude Royal, d. 7/18/1949 at 74 in Concord*; b. Ellsworth, ME; Charles Geery and Ruby Hamilton

BODGE,
Elwin A., d. 1/12/1942 at 71 in Barnstead; b. Barnstead; Jeremiah Bodge and Helen Stockbridge
Helen M., d. 4/13/1934 at 93 in Barnstead; Shedric Stockbridge and Abagail Clough
James, d. 1/22/1943 at 89 in Gilford*; b. Barnstead; ----- Bodge and Lavina Durgin
Jeremiah, d. 1866 at 76**
John, d. 1846 at 81**
Martha, d. 1/22/1901 at 82/2/; septicemia; housekeeper; widow; b. Gilmanton; John Thurston (Gilmanton) and Hannah Nutter (Barnstead)
Mary, d. 1851 at 90**; widow of John
William, d. 7/1/1890 at 74/4/27; minister; married; b. Barnstead; Jeremiah Bodge (Barnstead) and Mary Ayers (Barnstead)

BOISVERT,
Rene Leo, d. 11/12/1993 at 68 in Barnstead; Oscar Boisvert and Delima Crevier

BOLDUC,
Charles E., d. 2/20/1973 at 75 in Laconia; lumberman; b. Salisbury; Joseph Bolduc and Hattie Fleury

BOOCOCK,
John, d. 9/8/1922 at --

Myra, d. 10/30/1940 at 73*; b. Barnstead; Charles George and Myra Waldron

BOUDREAU,
George H., d. 8/16/1991 at 74 in Barnstead; David Boudreau and Flora Adams
Lillian F., d. 5/30/1912 at 28 in Boston, MA*; general peritonitis; married
Margaret, d. 1/21/1972 at 80 in Concord; housewife; b. NS; Henry Mountain and Honorah Campbell
Michael D., d. 5/24/1981 at 24 in Barnstead; Rene L. Boudreau and June E. Courtemanche

BOWEN,
Burton M., d. 10/4/1985 at 49 in Concord; ----- Bowen and Lena Johnson
C. Kenneth, d. 2/24/1924 at 9
Thomas R., d. 4/13/1941 at 68 in Gilmanton*

BOYD,
Dolly M., d. 10/16/1966 at 78 in Barnstead; housewife; b. Brooklyn, NY; Thomas F. Price and Margaret E. Byron
Grace E., d. 3/18/1930 at 36*; b. Barnstead; Fred B. Berry and Edith Tarbon
Rodney W., d. 4/30/1991 at 75 in Oklahoma City, OK; Thomas Edmund Boyd and Dolly Price
Thomas E., d. 12/22/1958 at 72 in Barnstead

BRADY,
Albert S., Sr., d. 7/19/1963 at 61 in Manchester; maint., shoe; b. Barnstead; Alice Davis
Alice E., d. 6/15/1958 at 83 in Manchester

BRALEY,
Israel S., d. 4/23/1934 at 64 in Barnstead; Cornelius Braley and Philora Vodney

BRANDT,
Fannie, d. 9/20/1956 at 90 in Concord; b. Sweden; John Larson and ----- Anderson

BREWSTER,
Annie E., d. 3/1/1946 at 83/1/3 in Barnstead; b. Barnstead; John L. Merrill and Mary E. Jenness
Elise M., d. 2/1/1929 at 26; b. Barnstead; Mark W. Brewster and Anna E. Merrill
John M., d. 12/13/1956 at 64 in Barnstead; b. Barnstead; Mark W. Brewster and Annie E. Merrill
Judith, d. 11/5/1891 at 85/1/7; single
Mark W., d. 3/8/1918 at 57/8/14; b. Barnstead; Nathaniel Brewster (Strafford) and Sarah J. Babb (Strafford)
Sarah J., d. 5/17/1895 at 78/7/13; anemia; widow

BRICKETT,
Sarah, d. 1/8/1902 at 57; heart disease; housekeeper; married

BRIDGE,
Abbie P., d. 5/1/1919 at 22/1/5; b. Barnstead; Albert G. Pitman (Alexandria) and Nellie F. Clough (Belmont)
John W., d. 3/27/1948 at 30/11/5 in Concord*; b. Rochester; John W. Bridge and Abbie Pitman

BRIGGS,
Paul W., Sr., d. 9/1/1978 at 70 in Concord; laborer; b. NH; Clarence Briggs and Florence Bartlett

BROCK,
Helen P., d. 4/2/1906 at 66/9/12; hemiphlegia; seamstress; single; b. Madbury; John P. Brock and Lucy W. Young
John, d. 10/28/1895 at 75/11; heart disease; farmer; widower; b. Strafford; John Brock
Miriam H., d. 1/13/1910 at 85/9/5; pneumonia; widow; b. Strafford; Nathaniel Berry (Strafford) and Sally Tuttle (Strafford)

BROWN,
child, d. 6/26/1921 at --; b. Barnstead; Scott Parsons and Ethel Brown (Farmington)
Abigail, d. 1/18/1897 at 70/5; organic disease of heart; housework; widow; b. Barnstead; Arthur Bickford (Barnstead) and Jane Pendergast (Barnstead)
Agnes M., d. 2/4/1922 at 17/9/4; b. Farmington; John A. Brown (Alton) and Alice Tibbetts (Berwick, ME)

Alice M., d. 9/14/1957 at 73 in Barnstead; b. Berwick, ME; John H. Tebbetts and Eliza J. Hadley

Annie C., d. 6/23/1938 at 72; b. Gilmanton; George Griffin and Mary Hill

Charles R., d. 1/22/1979 at 79 in Concord; Aubrey F. Brown and Mabel L. Pratt

Clara Belle, d. 7/9/1938 at 83*; b. Northwood; Edward Brown and Abigail Bickford

Eunice A., d. 11/18/1930 at 89; b. Kingston; Timothy Rowe and Emmiline Bagley

Evelyn M., d. 9/22/1986 at 82 in Concord; Robert Watson and Effie Stewart

Forrest P., d. 11/10/1963 at 53 in Boscawen; truck driver; b. Northwood; Ivory Brown and Gertrude Pender

George H., d. 10/30/1896 at 63/8/28; organic disease of heart; farmer; married

Hannah C., d. 4/3/1891 at 87; widow; b. Barnstead; James Nutter (Portsmouth)

James (Lieut.), d. 1814 at 50**

John, d. 1850 at 49**

John A., d. 4/21/1939 at 62; b. Alton; Henry A. Brown and Angelina Rand

Lilla, d. 10/10/1933 at 68*; b. Barnstead; John Welch and Josephine Clark

Lois, d. 1838 at 69**; wife of Robert

Lorenzo A., d. 5/31/1922 at 87/0/30; b. Barnstead; Elizabeth Brown (Barrington)

Mabel, d. 11/10/1958 at 85 in Concord

Marjorie E., d. 6/4/1992 at 73 in Concord; Ernest Crossett and Mildred Dow

Mary A., d. 9/20/1923 at 89; b. Barrington; Ezra Berry and Mary Pearl

Mary L., d. 10/31/1899 at 31/2/4; pernicious anemia; housewife; married; b. Halifax, NS; Robert Stuart and Mary L. McDonald

Nathaniel G., d. 1871 at 45**

Patience, d. 1828 at 52**; widow of Lieut. James

Philip W., d. 2/13/1983 at 70 in Concord; Aubrey F. Brown and Mabel L. Pratt

Ralph A., d. 11/13/1998 in Barnstead; Charles Brown and Evelyn Watson

Raymond R., d. 7/15/1985 at 31 in Hinckley, ME; Ralph A. Brown and Vera Wheet

BRYAN,
Clara Florence, d. 8/17/1990 at 91 in Concord; Herbert Kennedy and Clara Styles

BRYANT,
Lester Earl, d. 8/3/1934 at 34 in Wiscasset, ME*; Alphonzo Bryant and Grace Peasley

BUCHANAN,
Myra L., d. 9/17/1971 at 83 in Rochester; housewife; b. ME; Warren Littlefield and Catherine O'Brien
William A., d. 4/20/1916 at 8/10/20; b. Malden, MA; Herbert H. Buchanan (Waterford, NB) and Elurira Littlefield (ME)

BUCKLE,
Marie C., d. 5/9/1962 at 88 in Barnstead; housewife; b. ON; Alfred Crowhurst and Ruth Earl

BULGER,
Albion Francis, d. 5/29/1970 at 62 in Barnstead; supervisor; b. Rumford, ME; Augustin P. Bulger and Gertrude Sharkey

BUNKER,
Abram, d. 1860 at 75**
Abram, d. 3/22/1903 at 76/3; heart disease; farmer; married; b. Barnstead; Joseph Bunker (Barnstead) and Olive Otis (Strafford)
Alfred, d. 1/20/1891 at 82/1/8; farmer; married; b. Barnstead; Daniel Bunker (Pittsfield) and Lovey Edgerly (Barnstead)
Ammon, d. 7/19/1903 at 81/1/12; carcinoma; farmer; married; b. Barnstead; Timothy Bunker (Barnstead) and Margaret Rogers
Andrew, d. 1851 at 67**
Anna, d. 1842 at 79**; wife of Eli
Charles F., d. 1858 at 29**
Daniel (Capt.), d. 1842 at 69**
Daniel, d. 11/25/1945 at 72/10 in Gilmanton*; b. Barnstead; Daniel Bunker and Hannah Tilton
Deborah, d. 1824 at 91**; wife of Thomas

Eli, d. 1842 at 82**
Eliza N., d. 1/3/1890 at 80/7/10; widow; b. Barnstead; Eliphalet Nutter (Barnstead) and Lucy Lock (Barnstead)
Florence, d. 6/19/1967 at 85 in Concord; housewife; b. Loudon; Hiram A. B. Hilliard and Virginia Osgood
Florence M., d. 12/31/1923 at 50*; b. Austin, IL; Milo Bunker and Mary E. Pendergast
George R., d. 12/16/1931 at 68*; b. Barnstead; Amon R. Bunker and Hannah Webster
Hannah B., d. 9/30/1911 at 79/8/24; apoplexy; housewife; widow; b. Danville, VT; Jonathan G. Webster and Betsey Sanborn
Hannah T., d. 12/30/1923 at 75*; b. Pittsfield; John Tilton and Sally Chesley
Hollis, d. 11/21/1889 at 76/0/12; farmer; married
John, d. 1841 at 80**
John E., d. 1872 at 65**
John M., d. 11/16/1925 at 76; b. Barnstead; John E. Bunker and Eliza Miller
Jonathan, d. 1796 at 67**
Joseph, d. 1830 at 47**
Joseph, d. 1832 at 38**
Joseph S., d. 10/5/1923 at 54; b. Barnstead; Joseph Bunker and Hannah Tilton
Lemuel, d. 1858 at 85**
Leon, d. 1/17/1895 at 0/1/15; peritonitis; b. Barnstead; Joseph Bunker and Nellie Aikins
Lovey, d. 1860 at 83**; widow of Capt. Daniel
Margaret, d. 1864 at 66**; widow of Timothy
Mary, d. 2/24/1892 at 79/6; la grippe; widow; b. Barnstead; Thomas Tuttle
Mary A., d. 1/23/1914 at 80/8/27; pneumonia; widow; b. Lee; Hiram Leathers (Lee) and Mary A. Elliott (Lee)
Mary A., d. 2/26/1917 at 63/10/15; Nathaniel Ellsworth (US)
Mary Amanda, d. 11/24/1940 at 91*; b. Barnstead; Alfred Bunker and Polly Hodgdon
Mary L., d. 6/30/1947 at 73/5/12 in Newton, MA*; b. Barnstead; Ammon R. Bunker and Hannah B. Webster
Moses, d. 1848 at 35**
Mrs., d. 1815 at 106**; mother of Joseph (see following entry)
Mrs. Joseph, d. 1817 at 107** (see preceding entry)

Muriel L., d. 2/24/1921 at 4/11/22*; Daniel Bunker (Barnstead) and Florence Hilliard (Loudon)
Nellie E., d. 9/29/1947 at 85/9/10 in Concord*; b. Barnstead
Nellie M., d. 9/1/1938 at 65; b. Concord; David Aiken and Annie Shaw
Olive, d. 1830 at 46**; wife of Joseph
Polly, d. 1844 at 84**; widow of John
Polly, d. 1870 at 81**; widow of Abram
Polly, d. 4/26/1900 at 87/4/30; heart failure; widow; b. Barnstead; Benjamin Hodgdon and Mary Emerson
Rebecca, d. 1853 at 67**; widow of Andrew
Ruth E., d. 9/27/1979 at 78 in Concord; Austin Evans and Myra Munsey
Sally, d. 1857 at 82**; wife of Lemuel
Sarah, d. 1825 at 96**; widow of Jonathan (see following entry)
Sarah, d. 1826 at 96** (see preceding entry)
Thomas, d. 1826 at 95**
Timothy, d. 1840 at 41**
Unis, d. 1/20/1889 at 75; widow; James Avery (Barnstead)

BUORO,
Joel F., d. 11/7/1926 at 81; b. ME; Edward Buoro and May McDonald

BURNHAM,
Edward M., d. 4/2/1999 in Barnstead; Emmett Burnham and Ida Gerry-King

BURNS,
Elizabeth C., d. 11/3/1993 at 88 in Barnstead; Edgar Clifton and Frances Callahan
Hectorine G., d. 4/13/1999 in Concord; Joseph Arel and Emma Dauphanais

BURRELL,
Charles J., d. 5/1/1946 at 72/8/24 in Barnstead; b. Dedham, ME; John B. Burrill and Ella A. Dunn

BURROUGH,
Frederick C., d. 2/14/1939 at 49*

BURROUGHS,
Celia, d. 1/1/1930 at 79*; b. Barnstead; John Green and Martha Brown
George F., d. 1/15/1919 at 70/4/29*; b. Barnstead; Thomas C. Burroughs and Emily J. Spokefield

BURT,
Karl K., d. 6/4/2000 in Concord; Kenneth Burt and Sandy Esty

BUSHINSKI,
Anthony, d. 7/6/1993 at 54 in Concord; John R. Bushinski and Theresa Marsh

BUZZELL,
Aaron, d. 6/27/1889 at 88; farmer
Charles E., d. 10/3/1943 at 62 in Pittsfield*; b. Gilmanton; Charles E. Emerson and Anna Buzzell
Elizabeth, d. 9/6/1892 at 79/3/2; old age; widow; b. Strafford
Maybelle M., d. 12/13/1929 at 56*; b. Barnstead; William P. Gray and Margaret E. Foss

BYERS,
Agnes M., d. 2/5/1991 at 68 in Manchester; Michael Joseph Duffy and Mary Agnes Travers

CACICIO,
Leo Anthony, d. 7/27/1996 at 74 in Barnstead; Nathan Cacicio and Rose D'Augla

CALDWELL,
Sarah G., d. 7/5/1989 at 42 in Ctr. Barnstead; Harry Goodhead and Elizabeth Cattanack

CALL,
Bessie, d. 8/1/1900 at 18/6/19; septecaemia; housewife; married; b. Barnstead; Herbert O. Downes and Calista McKeen
George M., d. 5/21/1937 at 80; b. Louisville, NY; William Call and Ann Dow
Mattie G., d. 4/20/1943 at 86 in Laconia; b. Louisville, KY; Hiland J. Clark and Sophronia Howard

CALLUM,
Dorris E., d. 6/13/1905 at 2/3/27; diphtheria; b. Derry; Oscar L. Callum (Portsmouth) and Addie L. Gannett (Haverhill)

CALWELL,
Emma J., d. 12/9/1913 at 61/2/13; chronic nephritis; b. Barnstead; Moses Canney

CAMERON,
Mabel C., d. 3/9/1974 at 58 in Concord; shoe worker; b. NH; William S. Cate and Sadie Gray

CAMPBELL,
Dorothy K., d. 6/12/1965 at 67 in Dover; retired; b. Rollinsford; Walter Frost and Emma B. Gould

CANFIELD,
Archie Merton, d. 7/12/1951 at 64 in Barnstead; b. Guildhall, VT; --- Canfield and Annette Bailey

CANNEY,
Betsey, d. 9/18/1889 at 79/4; married; b. Rochester; Moses Jenness
George H., d. 4/2/1887 at 34/5/26; farmer; single; b. Barnstead; M. J. Canney (Barnstead) and Sarah Ham
Jacob, d. 1855 at 82**
Joseph, d. 7/1/1891 at 79/3/13; farmer; widower; b. Barnstead
Moses J., d. 5/10/1900 at 85/1/10; old age; widower; b. Madbury; Jacob Canney and Susan Jenness
Paul J., d. 2/23/1888 at 79/5/11; farmer; married; b. Madbury; Jacob Canney (Madbury) and Susan Jenness (Madbury)
Paul J., d. 4/6/1935 at 84; b. Barnstead; Moses Canney and Sarah Ham
Ruth H., d. 12/30/1905 at 68/0/13; heart disease; single; Joseph Canney and Betsy Jenness

CAREY,
daughter, d. 5/14/1894 at 0/0/11; peritonitis; b. Barnstead; Thomas Carey (Exeter) and Euphe'a Parshley (Barnstead)

CARMAN,
Grace I., d. 11/30/1999 in Ctr. Barnstead; Frank Schlueter and Carrie Knieling

CARMEL,
Michael P., d. 7/6/1999 in Alton; Leo Carmel and Judith Lupi

CARPENTER,
George J., d. 3/28/1994 at 85 in Barnstead; Wesley Carpenter and Anne Sargent
Nicholas G., d. 8/24/1992 at 12 in Concord; Glen S. Carpenter and Jane Meredith

CARR,
Archie B., d. 7/13/1959 at 71 in Barnstead
Ella May, d. 3/22/1933 at 36; b. Barnstead; Sylvesta Powell and Etta Berry
George Sylvester, d. 9/18/1973 at 80 in Manchester; fireman; b. NH; Sylvester W. Carr and Martha Perkins
Gertrude, d. 11/5/1967 at 77 in Concord; housekeeper; b. Barnstead; Sylvester Carr and Martha Perkins
Louis E., d. 12/16/1966 at 70 in Wolfeboro; b. Barnstead; Fred E. Berry and Edith M. Tarbox
Marjorie E., d. 1/1/1988 at 72 in Epsom; Sidney Hanson and Lura Nutter
Martha A., d. 9/20/1932 at 77; b. Pittsfield; Ezra Greenwood and ---- Elliott
Mary Marguerite, d. 8/16/1980 at 85 in Concord; Harry Cram and Mary Tucker
Sylvestus W., d. 6/17/1918 at 77/5/17; b. Pawtucket, RI; Sylvester W. Carr and Sarah Lennard

CARRY,
Katherine E., d. 1/9/1916 at 76*; housework; single; b. Boston, MA

CARSON [see Corson],
Bertha D., d. 7/10/1909 at 0/0/14; hemorrhage of brain; b. Barnstead; Harry O. Carson (Pittsfield) and Stella Carr (Epsom)
Floyd O., d. 11/26/1992 at 86 in Concord; Harry Carson and Stella Carr

Leonard H., d. 5/17/1902 at 0/0/12; b. No. Barnstead; Harry Carson (Pittsfield) and Stella Carr (Epsom)
Stella, d. 1/24/1941 at 54 in Concord*; b. Epsom; Sylvester Carr and Martha Perkins

CARSWELL,
Laura Ethel, d. 12/23/1917 at 56; ----- Ricker and ----- Ham

CASAVANT [see Cassavant],
Ina M., d. 3/28/1962 at 72 in Concord; weaver; b. Barnstead; Herbert L. Casavant and Hannah J. Berry
J. M., d. 2/3/1914 at 73/9/28; heart disease; farmer; widower; b. Westford, VT; Joseph Casavant

CASSAVANT [see Casavant],
Herbert L., d. 1/24/1961 at 86 in Barnstead; sta. steam eng.; b. Nashua; John Cassavant and Amelia Redman

CASWELL,
Clara L., d. 9/10/1920 at 63/8/20; b. Barnstead; Aaron Snell (NH) and Mary Nutter (Barnstead)
Elwin, d. 8/17/1948 at 87/0/17 in Pittsfield*; b. Barnstead; Diah Caswell and Laura Caswell
Enoch, d. 4/28/1889 at 87; farmer; widower; b. Barnstead; Samuel Caswell
George B., d. 1/9/1908 at 56/3/17; leukemia; shoemaker; married; b. Barnstead; Richard Caswell (Northwood) and Martha Willey (Barnstead)
Jennie, d. 5/19/1934 at 80 in Westborough, MA*; Oliver Greenleaf Caswell and Wealthy Ann Clark
Martha T., d. 6/13/1907 at 84/4/14; apoplexy; housewife; widow; Caleb Willey and Mary Chase (Pittsfield)
Mrs. Samuel, d. 1866 at 93**
Preston, d. 1/17/1914 at 59/9/6; pneumonia; farmer; married; b. Barnstead; Richard Caswell (Barnstead) and Martha Willey (Barnstead)
Samuel, d. 1865 at 107** (see following entry)
Samuel, d. 1866 at 103** (see preceding entry)
Samuel D., d. 4/1/1913 at 77/3/16; cancer; farmer; married; b. Barnstead; Enoch Caswell (Barnstead) and Judith Flanders (Alton)

Sarah C., d. 8/31/1925 at 87; b. Strafford; John Caoarus and Sarah Davie

CATE,
Robert Miller, d. 5/9/1984 at 86 in Manchester; George Washington Cate and Anna Elizabeth Mueller
Sadie F., d. 9/16/1957 at 72 in Pittsfield; b. Barnstead; Oris Gray and Harriet Hannaford
William, d. 12/30/1960 at 91 in Concord; farmer; b. Alton; Joseph A. Cate and Margaret Hurd

CHAMBERLAIN,
Sophia, d. 2/8/1923 at 81; b. Alton; John Jones and Lydia Drew

CHAMBERLIN,
Frank J., d. 7/3/1927 at 79; b. Dover; Joseph Chamberlin and Lydia Tibbetts

CHANDLER,
Chester W., d. 4/9/1951 at 76 in Concord*; b. MA; Scera Chandler and Alma Lowe
Kathleen O., d. 2/23/1999 in Concord; Chester Chandler and Olive Main
Lizzie G., d. 7/21/1911 at 47/1/16; typhoid fever; housewife; married; b. Barnstead; Nathaniel Blaisdell and Sophia Hodgdon (Barnstead)
Olive M., d. 9/21/1959 at 82 in Pittsfield

CHAPMAN,
Alice B., d. 8/30/1974 at 81 in Epsom; factory worker; b. NH; Frank Sewall and Sarah Evans
Clarence A., d. 11/8/1992 at 72 in Concord; William F. Chapman and Cecilia McPherson
Patience, d. 1845 at 70**; widow of Valentine
Valentine, d. 1844 at 86**
William F., d. 1/14/1968 at 85 in Concord; retired; b. MA

CHAPPELLE,
Florence L., d. 9/29/1998 in Concord; Joseph Pastina and Margaret Vitali

CHARBONNEAU,
James J., d. 5/7/1952 at 69 in Concord; b. NY; Francis Charbonneau and Margaret Lafayette

CHASE,
Dorothy M., d. 1/6/1966 at 45 in Laconia; housewife; b. Stoneham, MA; Ernest F. Riley and Lavina Kelly
Elbridge Gerry, d. 10/2/1917 at 80/10/16; b. Sebec, ME; Owen Chase (Sebec, ME) and ----- Burrill (Sebec, ME)
James A., d. 4/29/1970 at 50 in Laconia; chef; b. Medford, MA; James Chase and Ann Norton
Levi, d. 1852 at 82**
Lydia, d. 1845 at 71**; wife of Levi

CHAULK,
Allen James, d. 10/12/1993 at 64 in Concord; Archibald Chaulk and Amelia Simmonds

CHENEY,
Winslow, d. 8/12/1968 at 65 in Barnstead; concert organist; b. UT; William Cheney and Agnes Anderson

CHESLEY,
Aaron, d. 1823 at 69**
Aaron, d. 1825 at 40**
Aaron, d. 1864 at 36**
Benjamin, d. 1854 at 64**
C. L., d. 6/24/1907 at 68/7/27; angina pectoris; farmer; widower; b. Barnstead; Jefferson Chesley (Barnstead) and Irene Hussy (Barnstead)
Calvin C., d. 9/29/1889 at 47/3/28; dentist; married; b. Barnstead; Benjamin Chesley (Barnstead) and Sally Bodge (Barnstead)
Comfort, d. 1847 at 86**
Daniel, d. 3/16/1895 at 64/7/12; disease of heart; farmer; divorced; b. Barnstead; Benjamin Chesley and Sallie Bodge
David G., d. 9/20/1906 at 82/1/8; dysentery; farmer; widower; b. Barnstead; Henry Chesley and Mary Goodwin
George (Capt.), d. 1833 at 51**
Grover H., d. 8/29/1968 at 45 in Kittery, ME; helper woodworker; b. NH; Grover Chesley and Mary Holmes

Isaac, d. 4/22/1892 at 64/6; marasmus; farmer; single; b. Barnstead; Henry Chesley

John, d. 1825 at 83**

John B., d. 3/3/1919 at 84/6/1; b. Barnstead; Benjamin Chesley (Barnstead) and Sally Bodge (Barnstead)

Jonathan, d. 1826 at 90**

Lydia A., d. 8/19/1906 at 70/10/5; Bright's disease of kidney; married; b. Barnstead; Sampson Locke (Barnstead) and Esther Nutter (Barnstead)

Mariah, d. 6/30/1905 at 84/6/27; dilation of heart; widow; b. Alton; John Hanson (Strafford) and ----- Hall (Strafford)

Martha J., d. 3/28/1896 at 54/6/6; apoplexy; housewifre; married; b. Barnstead; William Bodge and Martha Thurston

Mary, d. 1854 at 56**; wife of Henry

Mary Esther, d. 3/28/1938 at 85; b. Barnstead; John Blake and Mary Blake

Mary H., d. 11/12/1925 at 80; b. Barnstead; Daniel Moore and Mary Sargent

Moses, d. 1862 at 86**

Nancy T., d. 3/19/1906 at 74/1/24; heart disease; housewife; married; b. Farmington; Peter Twombly (Farmington) and Anna Evans (Farmington)

Orin F., d. 4/19/1907 at 72/1/26; enlargement of prostate gland; shoemaker; widower; b. Barnstead; Jefferson Chesley and Irene Hussy

Polly H., d. 5/18/1901 at 86/4/15; apoplexy; housekeeper; widow; b. Alton; John McDuffee (Alton) and Margaret Hayes (Rochester)

Ruth, d. 1818 at 63**; wife of Aaron

Samuel, d. 1847 at 39**

William A., d. 2/13/1920 at 77/2/17; b. Pittsfield; John M. Chesley (Barrington) and Sarah Jenkins (Lee)

CHILD,
N. Susan, d. 6/12/1933 at 54; b. Farmington; Prisham H. Fletcher and Emily F. Bensa

CHITTIM,
Harold D., d. 6/26/1963 at 65 in New Boston; ret. opt. analyst; b. Easthampton, MA; Harry Chittim and Lulu Hodges

CILLEY,
James M., d. 1865 at 31**

CLAPP,
Charles M., d. 7/16/1937 at 49; b. Auburndale, MA; Frederick H. Clapp and Charlotte Sumner
Charlotte Jane, d. 6/17/1925 at 63; b. Milton, MA; Edmon Scunness and Jane Davenport
Frederich H., d. 7/11/1941 at 82 in Barnstead; b. Dorchester, MA
Philip H., d. 5/20/1962 at 69 in Gardiner, ME; carpenter; b. Auburndale, MA; Frederick H. Clapp and Charlotte Sumner

CLARK,
Abbie A., d. 4/4/1895 at 54/5/2; Bright's disease; housework; married; b. Barnstead; Richard Chesley and Sarah Davis
Ada E., d. 10/15/1917 at 56/5/19*; b. Barnstead; Jefferson Emerson (Barnstead) and Vienna Cilley (Barnstead)
Alonzo, d. 1/8/1908 at 48/0/28; diabetes; farmer; single; b. Barnstead; John D. Clark (Barnstead) and Elizabeth Adams (Barnstead)
Ann L., d. 11/2/1910 at 72/7/6; organic disease of heart; housewife; married; b. Barnstead
Annie T., d. 8/17/1950 at 80 in Nashua*; b. Barnstead; John Tasker and Sarah C. Johnson
Asa, d. 1867 at 43**
Betsey, d. 1857 at 78**; wife of Levi
Calvin D., d. 7/27/1930 at 77*
Charles A. W., d. 5/2/1916 at 76/1/2*; retired; widower; b. Barnstead; William Clark (Barnstead) and Olive Monsey (Barnstead)
Daniel, d. 1845 at 45**
Daniel, d. 1845 at 44**
David, d. 12/5/1894 at 85/11/5; paresis; farmer; widower; b. Barnstead
Dora M., d. 6/23/1964 at 75 in Concord; housewife; b. NS; William McKenzie and Christy Ann -----
Elizabeth, d. 1870 at 53**; wife of John D.
Elizabeth A., d. 5/14/1893 at 26/1; convulsions; housewife; married; b. NB; Charles McKenelly (NB) and Louise Clark (NB)
Ella H., d. 12/30/1958 at 37 in So. Barnstead
Enoch, d. 1825 at 57**

Ethel Grace, d. 4/18/1952 at 78 in Barnstead; b. Barnstead; Jeremiah Bodge and Helen Stockbridge

Eunice Ida, d. 2/23/1919 at 0/0/1; b. Barnstead; Guy E. Clark (Barnstead) and Dora MacKenzie (E. Boston, MA)

Ezekiel, d. 10/27/1889 at 77; farmer; widower; Jonathan Clark and Temperance Bickford

Frank H., d. 10/19/1931 at 68; b. Barnstead; Charles Clark and Mary Snell

Guy E., d. 12/13/1978 at 89 in Concord; farming; b. NH; Johnathan Clark and Ida Hanson

Hannah, d. 1863 at 44**; wife of Asa

Hannah, d. 7/2/1897 at 88/5/12; gastritis; housewife; widow

Harold T., d. 5/6/1954 at 56 in Portland, ME; b. Center Barnstead; Herbert E. Clark and Lillian Tasker

Hazel Estella, d. 12/24/1972 at 79 in Barnstead; school teacher; b. Lynn, MA; Henry Clark and Mabel Fowler

Henry, d. 10/1/1925 at 65

Herbert, d. 12/23/1936 at 69 in Concord*; John Clark and Lucy Thompson

Ida M., d. 5/2/1948 at 83/8/19 in Barnstead; b. Barnstead; Levi Hanson and Abbie E. Clark

Isaac H., d. 1/6/1920 at 86/6/6; b. Barnstead; Isaac Clark (Barnstead) and Rebecca Hovey

Jeremiah, d. 1855 at 85**

Joel, d. 3/12/1893 at 75; apoplexy; farmer; single; b. Barnstead; Jonathan Clark and Temperance Bickford

John, d. 1799 at —**

John, d. 1842 at 76**

John, d. 1867 at 48**

John A., d. 11/9/1920 at 79/2/12*; b. Barnstead; Solomon Clark (Barnstead) and Louisa P. Adams

John D., d. 1/16/1904 at 83/11/20; old age; farmer; married; b. Barnstead; Solomon Clark (Barnstead) and Sarah Daniels

Jonathan, d. 1854 at 90**

Jonathan, Jr., d. 1826 at 29**

Joseph, d. 1871 at 57**

Judith, d. 1865 at 60**; wife of William S.

Leonard, d. 1857 at 28**

Leonard Frank, d. 1/30/1941 at 89 in Concord*; b. Barnstead; Leonard Clark and Jane G. Clark

Levi, d. 1862 at 89**

Levi, d. 4/16/1918 at 65/5/14*; b. Barnstead; John D. Clark (Barnstead) and Elizabeth A. Adams (Barnstead)
Levi, Jr., d. 1853 at 44**
Lewis, d. 12/10/1917 at 59/2/26*; b. Barnstead; Joseph Clark and Jane Clark
Lillian E., d. 5/5/1967 at 94 in Manchester; housewife; b. Barnstead; Albert Tasker and Georgia Scruton
Louisa A., d. 7/11/1893 at 65/7; cancer; housekeeper; married; b. Strafford; Peter Berry (Strafford) and Susan Babb (Barnstead)
Louise N., d. 9/17/1906 at 64/1; paresis; housewife; married; David B. Davis (Barnstead) and Hannah Perkins (Barnstead)
Louise Wood, d. 10/7/1967 at 77 in Manchester; housewife; b. So. Rawdon, NS; Alfred Wood and Rebecca Hamilton
Lucy A., d. 10/7/1900 at 51/11/22; carcinoma; housewife; married; b. Barrington; Isaac Thompson and Lucy Brock
Marie, d. 2/17/1985 at 90 in Concord; Howard Sumner and Anna Joyce
Mary, d. 1/31/1900 at 86; paresis; widow
Nancy, d. 1837 at 40**; wife of Daniel
Olive E., d. 3/9/1887 at 20/11; stitcher; single; C. A. W. Clark (Barnstead) and Sarah Canney
Sabrina T., d. 1/8/1889 at 89/4/14
Sally, d. 1857 at 78**; widow of Jeremiah
Samuel, d. 1777 at –**
Samuel, d. 1826 at 32**
Samuel, d. 9/22/1898 at 87/2; old age; farmer; widower
Samuel B., d. 1866 at 53**
Samuel H., d. 2/6/1912 at 70/4/23; cancer of bowels; farmer; widower; b. Barnstead; Joseph Clark (Barnstead) and Jane Clark (Barnstead)
Sarah, d. 1868 at 75**; widow of Solomon
Sewell J., d. 3/11/1983 at 90 in Concord; Jonathan Clark and Ida Hanson
Solomon, d. 1859 at 76**
Solomon, d. 2/1/1901 at 83/8/30; Bright's disease; merchant; married; b. Barnstead; Solomon Clark (Barnstead) and Sarah Daniels (Barnstead)
Susannah, d. 1811 at 39**; wife of Enoch
Temperance, d. 1826 at 56**; wife of Jonathan
Theodore H., d. 7/14/1909 at 0/8/17; tumor of bowels; b. Barnstead; Jonathan Clark (Barnstead) and Iva Hanson (Barnstead)

CLEMENT,
Betty Ann, d. 3/14/1986 at 21 in Concord; George Clement and Barbara Clark
Elizabeth, d. 4/13/1905 at 5/9/26; meningitis; b. Berwick; John Clement (Rollinsford) and Mary Kerrigan (Glasgow)
George E., Jr., d. 11/18/1992 at 60 in Concord; George E. Clement, Sr. and Bertha Norman
Matthew G., d. 5/7/1978 at – in Hanover; Cindy Lee Clement

CLOUGH,
Charles, d. 5/1/1896 at 74/9/1; apoplexy; farmer; widower; b. Barnstead; Caleb Clough and Sally Clark
Dorothy G., d. 5/20/1916 at 0/2/6; b. Barnstead; Harry G. Clough (Lynn, MA) and Edith E. Flagg (Conway, MA)
Edith E., d. 7/11/1967 at 91 in Concord; housewife; b. Conway, MA; C. Chandler Flagg and Mary Brown
Ella I., d. 5/13/1924 at 68; b. Haverhill, MA; Thomas Grives and Almia Foss
George C., d. 11/7/1913 at 79/0/25; paresis; married; b. Gilmanton; Isiah Clough (Gilmanton) and Nancy Kimball
Nancy L., d. 1/16/1915 at 76/11/29; housewife; married; b. Strafford; Daniel Bobb (Strafford) and Mehitabel Lyford (Pittsfield)
Sarah, d. 1869 at 77**; wife of Caleb
Sarah A., d. 5/30/1891 at 48/0/6; housekeeper; married; b. Barnstead; Daniel Bickford (Barnstead) and Abigail Peavey (Barnstead)
Walter L., d. 2/14/1969 at 59 in Concord; weaver; b. MA; Harry Clough and Edith Flagg
William, d. 6/12/1922 at 90/3/22; b. Barnstead; Sarah Clark (Barnstead)

CLOUGHERTY,
Jolen Joseph, d. 6/19/1975 at 23 in Barnstead; typesetter; b. England; Michael Clougherty and Ann Folan

COBOURN,
William D., d. 10/19/1997 at 78 in Rochester; William Cobourn, Sr. and Mary Fears

COCHRAN,
Euphema, d. 9/17/1921 at 74/5/18; b. Scotland; Stephen Rowan (Scotland) and Agnes Maties (Scotland)
Lewis W., d. 3/24/1900 at 74/1/11; pneumonia; farmer; married

COCKRAN,
John N., d. 2/10/1924 at 75; b. Scotland

COGGSWELL,
M. D., d. 12/30/1908 at 56/9/26; tumor of brain; housewife; married; b. St. John, NB

COLBATH,
Ann, d. 7/2/1897 at 87/6/6; gangrene; housewife; widow; b. Barnstead
Dependence, d. 1838 at 90**
Eleanor, d. 1831 at 81**; wife of Dependence
Florence J., d. 2/27/1940 at 62*; b. Barnstead; Charles F. Jenkins and Mary Reynolds
Frank J., d. 8/18/1956 at 80 in Berlin; b. Barnstead; James H. Colbath and ----- Nutter
George, d. 1/17/1894 at 89/5/23; la grippe; married; b. Barnstead; John Colbath (Newington) and Lettice Colbath (Newington)
George H., d. 8/29/1943 at 78 in Wolfeboro*; b. Barnstead; James H. Colbath and Mary E. Nutter
Horace N., d. 1/25/1917 at 82/3/12; b. Barnstead; George Colbath (Barnstead) and Ann Nutter (Barnstead)
John, d. 1861 at 95**
John, d. 4/7/1915 at 86/3/12; shoemaker; widower; b. Barnstead; George Colbath (Barnstead)
Lettice, d. 1852 at 85**; wife of John
Lucinda I., d. 4/1/1906 at 62/0/25; pernicious anemia; housewife; married; b. Barnstead; John L. Nutter (Barnstead) and Hannah W. French (New Durham)
Mary E., d. 6/28/1896 at 23/2; consumption; single; b. Barnstead; James H. Colbath and Nellie Nutter
Nellie H., d. 2/15/1924 at 73; b. Barnstead; John L. Nutter and Hannah M. French

COLBURNE,
Jack W., d. 3/14/1981 at 56 in Concord; Walter Colburne and Robene Moore

COLE,
Benjamin, d. 5/5/1905 at 89/9/23; organic disease of heart; blacksmith; widower; b. Gloucester; Weeden Cole and Emma Herrick
David F., d. 2/23/1909 at 74/6/12; uremico intoxicate; clerk; widower; b. Milton, MA; ----- Cole (Gloucester, MA) and Nancy Fudge (Sanbornton)

COLELLA,
Dominic A., d. 8/23/1994 at 70 in Laconia; Pellegrino Colella and Philomenia Silvatella

COLLINS,
Martin R., d. 3/23/1935 at 0/0/21; b. Pittsfield; Ralph M. Collins and Flora Corson
Nathan, d. 1868 at 82**
Patience, d. 1845 at 70**; wife of Richard
Phebe, d. 1868 at 75**
Ralph M., d. 2/21/1970 at 66 in Wolfeboro; Pittsfield gas; b. Canada; Martin W. Collins and Grace B. Hall
Richard, d. 1848 at 79**
Ruth, d. 1871 at 82**; widow of Nathan

COLLYER,
James Almon, d. 5/15/1936 at 59 in Barnstead; James Collyer

COLWELL,
Lucinda P., d. 6/29/1899 at 67/2/1; apoplexy; housework; widow; b. Woodstock; Russell S. Davis and Percis Dunn

COME,
Peter, d. 6/29/1911 at 84/2/14; organic disease of heart; farmer; married; b. Canada
Peter, d. 6/29/1925 at 78; b. Canada; Peter Come and Elsie Lomondy

COMEAU,
Joseph R., d. 10/11/1983 at 82 in Concord; Ambrose Comeau and Mary M. Deaveau

CONANT,
Archer L., d. 11/20/1966 at 52 in Barnstead; salesman; b. Dedham, MA; Roger Conant and Hilda Landan
Frank A., d. 11/15/1932 at 73; b. Boston, MA; Fredrick Conant and Rachel Rogers

CONNOLLY,
May H., d. 11/4/1919 at 49/8/17*; Henry O. Huntress (Barnstead) and Julia A. Pierce (Barnstead)

CONNOR,
Josephine Woodley, d. 1/7/1941 at 85 in Pittsfield*; b. Boston, MA; Jesse O. Winkley and Frances Nutter

CONRAD,
Harold, Jr., d. 4/27/1979 at 55 in Laconia; Harold Conrad and Elizabeth P. Hill

COOK,
Eri, d. 10/21/1905 at 82/4; organic disease of heart; farmer; married; b. Milton; James Cook (Milton) and Mercy Wentworth (Milton)
Freelove S., d. 5/22/1909 at 68/11/28; asstrenia; housewife; married; Royal Downing (Holderness) and Fannie Prescott (Holderness)
George L., d. 5/10/1893 at 1/1; pneumonia; b. Barnstead
L. D. S., d. 10/22/1887 at 27/0/25; shoemaker; single; Eri Cook
Lavina, d. 10/18/1906 at 86/4; dysentery; housework; widow; b. Canada; Ezra Hill (Strafford) and Hannah Howard (Strafford)
Moses, d. 7/8/1890 at 53/10/19; shoemaker; b. Milton; Isaac Cook (Milton) and Elizabeth Peavey (Milton)
Natt Parker, d. 7/2/1922 at --; b. Barnstead; George W. Cook (Milton) and Lillian B. Cook (Barnstead)
Richard L., d. 9/30/1941 at 0/8/12 in Rochester*; b. Rochester; Herbert Cook and Ruth D. Pickering

COOMBS,
Fred H., d. 5/171/932 at 57; b. Lewiston, ME

COPP,
Betsey J., d. 2/23/1889 at 51/3/1; married; ----- (Barnstead) and ----- (Alton)
Isaac, d. 1/22/1888 at 86/11/22; carpenter; widower; b. Lebanon, ME; Reuben Copp (Lebanon) and Eleanor Rugg (Newcastle)
Reuben R., d. 11/26/1960 at 73 in Wolfeboro; engineer; b. Strafford; Isaac Copp and Edna Bickford

CORLISS,
Charles S., d. 5/16/1937 at 55; b. Topsham, VT; Samuel Corliss and Helen Willey
Earl S., d. 1/25/1978 at 69 in Concord; maintenance; b. NH; Charles S. Corliss and Helen Tilton
George Edward, d. 7/3/1976 at 68 in Tilton; clothing industry; b. NH; William H. Corliss and Cora Ordway
Helen G., d. 10/15/1964 at 82 in Concord; housewife; b. Chichester; George Tilton and Hattie Call
Mildred, d. 10/3/1974 at 61 in Concord; textile worker; b. NH; James W. Hill and Margaret Gray
Robert C., d. 12/14/1940 at 0*; b. Concord; Charles C. Corliss and Luella Frost

CORMIER,
Mary E., d. 3/5/1960 at 51 in Concord; reg. nurse; single; b. St. Johnsbury, VT; Napoleon P. Cormier and Catherine Provencal
Napoleon P., d. 4/5/1948 at 73/1/29 in Barnstead; b. Canada; Louis Cormier and Eliza Gilbert

CORSON [see Carson],
infant, d. 2/11/1937 at 0; b. Barnstead; Floyd O. Corson and Helen Durkin
Clyde E., d. 9/16/1985 at 77 in Manchester; Harry Corson and Gertrude Carr
Esther E., d. 1/1/1997 at 78 in Concord; Henry Swain and Florence Gray
Frank, d. 7/23/1943 at 12 in Concord*; b. Detroit, MI; Floyd Carson
Thelma, d. 9/5/1907 at 2/6/29; cholera morbus; b. Barnstead; Harry O. Corsons (Pittsfield) and Stella Carr

COSTINE,
Clifford, d. 9/29/1962 at 81 in Pittsfield; mill supt.; b. Pittsfield, MA; David Costine and Mary Ann Robertson
Rosa C., d. 12/5/1962 at 77 in Concord; housewife; b. Pittsfield, MA; John Kuhnlee and Dora Brundage

COTE,
Joseph B., d. 7/9/1991 at 46 in Concord; Joseph Jean Cote and Genevieve V. Fernandes

COTTON,
Dorothy B., d. 12/23/1966 at 63 in Concord; teacher; b. Reading, MA; Thomas Buckle and Marie Crowhurst
George R., d. 4/18/1982 at 73 in Barnstead; Joseph Cotton and May Peavey
John L., d. 5/29/1990 at 84 in Concord; Joseph Cotton and May Pavey
Ruth Emily, d. 7/20/1996 at 88 in Barnstead; Fred Hallett and Maude Ames

COUGHLAN,
Anita C., d. 5/11/1999 in Concord; Ralph Pratt and Anita Snow

COUTURE,
Cynthia H., d. 12/20/1958 at 92 in Barnstead
George W., d. 4/20/1948 at 78/8/19 in Barnstead; b. Canada; Jean Couture

CRAIG,
Mabel F., d. 2/14/1971 at 83 in Concord; housewife; b. MA; John Walsh and Honora Flynn

CRAN,
Chorlotte, d. 1/1/1967 at 85 in Dover; b. Charlottetown, PEI; Malcolm MacLeod and Margaret MacLean

CRAVARITIS,
Alma K., d. 11/19/1991 at 86 in Barnstead; Juho A. Wallius and Eeva K. Voutilainen

CRONIN,
Marion L., d. 12/11/1986 at 85 in Rochester; James A. MacKnight and Litica Bustard

CROSSETT,
Arline M., d. 11/9/1991 at 75 in Lebanon; William S. Boyd and Angie Nelson
Ernest William, d. 10/18/1977 at 84 in Concord; weaver; b. VT; William S. Crossett and Agnes Gamash
Mildred D., d. 10/4/1984 at 86 in Concord; George W. Dow and Edith M. Shackford
William W., Sr., d. 7/15/1995 at 78 in Concord; Ernest Crossett and Mildred Dow

CUNNIFF,
Rita C., d. 8/4/1995 at 78 in Concord; Joseph Ferrara and Rose Peluso

CURRIER,
Fred Roscoe, d. 1/10/1952 at 78 in Manchester*; b. NH; John W. Currier and Catharine Doten

CURTIS,
Albion A., d. 6/4/1945 at 39/1/21 in Newington*; b. Barnstead; Asa Curtis and Jennie Foss
Asa Augustus, d. 7/29/1970 at 91 in Pittsfield; shoe worker; b. Milton; Moses Curtis and ----- Cook
Chester F., d. 4/28/1974 at 69 in Concord; shoe worker; b. NH; Fred Curtis and Carrie -----
Ethel H., d. 4/18/1913 at 0/0/6; heart; b. Barnstead; Asa Curtis (Milton) and Jennie Foss (Barnstead)
Jennie M., d. 6/5/1958 at 73 in Pittsfield
Jesse L., d. 7/19/1975 at 83 in Epsom; shoe worker; b. NH; ----- Ward and Harriet Wynn

CURTISS,
Eldon G., d. 8/21/1981 at 53 in Concord; Frederick H. Johnson and Esther Bullerman

CUTLER,
Albert Frank, d. 9/29/1916 at 0/11/22*; b. Hooksett; Frank R. Cutler (Brighton, MA) and Lucille B. Varney (Strafford)

CUTRER,
Mary L., d. 8/21/2000 in Concord; Roland Dionne and Beatrice Morel

D'ORAZIO,
Vincent, d. 8/1/1979 at 86 in Barnstead; Michael D'Orazio and Maria -----

DAHL,
Edith, d. 11/6/1983 at 86 in Barnstead; Albert E. B. Garlick and Annie Cowle

DAME,
Herman P., d. 10/5/1964 at 54 in Hartford, VT; leather worker; b. Gilmanton; Perley C. Dame and Eva M. Straw
Perley C., d. 5/13/1950 at 66 in Concord; b. NH; Alonzo Dame and Etta French

DAMOUR,
Napoleon F., d. 8/7/1968 at 58 in Barnstead; traffic policeman; b. NH; Joseph Damour and Exilda Daperron

DANATO,
daughter, d. 8/28/1916 at 00; b. Barnstead; Angelo Danato (Italy) and Zena Siras (Italy)

DANIELS,
Abbie D., d. 10/14/1947 at 79/10/21 in Pittsfield*; b. Strafford; Paul Perkins and Mary Perkins
Hollis G., d. 9/16/1943 at 77 in Pittsfield*; b. Nottingham; Nathan Daniels and Rachel Daniels
John (Capt.), d. 1830 at 35**
Mary A., d. 1854 at 28**
Pelatiah, d. 1833 at 63**

DANIS,
Hatty J., d. 11/22/1984 at 68 in Concord; Asa A. Curtis and Jennie Foss
Henry J., d. 11/11/1992 at 76 in Concord; Joseph Danis and Arline Constant
Marie A., d. 8/20/1956 at 81 in Barnstead; b. Canada; Leon Constant and Georgina Descoteaux

DAVIE,
Edward, d. 2/18/1948 at 76/11/8 in Laconia*; b. Auburn, NY

DAVIS,
Abby D., d. 2/7/1906 at 79/3/5; organic disease of heart; widow; b. Barnstead; William Walker (Portsmouth) and Betsey Drew (Barnstead)
Albert C., d. 10/3/1967 at 64 in Hanover; weaver; b. Auburn; Daniel Davis and Anna Cate
Annie, d. 1866 at 96**; "first child born in B."
Annie Tuttle, d. 2/7/1939 at 65; b. Barnstead; James C. Tuttle and Alice J. Hill
Charles F., d. 5/24/1900 at 58/8/7; pneumonia; farmer; married; b. Barnstead; Samuel Davis and Susan Yeaton
Coran K., d. 1/1/1965 at 95 in Rochester; retired teacher; b. N. Barnstead; John K. Davis and Abbie Walker
Daniel C., d. 8/19/1910 at 49/0/6; tuberculosis of lungs; farmer; married; b. Candia; Daniel C. Davis (Thetford, VT) and Louisa Quimby (Hooksett)
Elbra R., d. 7/9/1925 at 73
Ephraim H., d. 8/16/1954 at 56 in Concord; b. Wentworth; Ephraim Davis and Elizabeth Barker
Frank, d. 3/13/1915 at 64/11/17
George Edward, Jr., d. 11/9/1987 at 42 in Barnstead; George Edward Davis, Sr. and Alice C. Moynihan
Hattie M., d. 7/11/1950 at 87/3/14 in Barnstead; b. Lyme; Thomas Downer and Myra -----
Helen E., d. 3/7/1993 at 88 in Concord; John Brown and Alice Tibbetts
Jacob (Rev.), d. 1854 at 68**
James R. C., d. 5/13/1921 at 86/0/7*; b. Barnstead
Jeremiah, d. 1854 at 91**
John, d. 1836 at 56**

John K., d. 12/16/1904 at 83/7/3; organic heart disease; farmer; married; b. Alton; Rev. Jacob Davis (Alton) and Lois Kelley (Gilmanton)
Levi, d. 1844 at 87**
Lois, d. 1849 at 79**; wife of Josiah
Louise, d. 1839 at 48**; wife of Rev. Jacob
Mabel A., d. 9/28/1930 at 40; b. Hooksett; Daniel C. Davis and Clara D. Cate
Mary, d. 2/12/1938 at 78; b. Landaff; Samuel Howland and Lucinda Bowles
Mrs. Jeremiah, d. 1852 at 86**
Sarah L., d. 5/12/1907 at 63/2/19; angiara pectoris; housewife; widow; John J. Tuttle and Betsey Jacobs
Susan, d. 7/18/1916 at 68/7/29; divorced; b. Barnstead; Thomas Pendegast and Lucy Pendegast

DAWSON,
Joseph C., d. 6/22/1958 at 63 in Manchester

DAY,
Jessie Amelia, d. 8/22/1996 at 71 in Barnstead; Albion L. Richards and Bertha F. Dyer

DEAN,
Addie, d. 7/12/1936 at 56 in Brooklyn, NY*; Sylvester Powell and Ada Munsey

DEASEY,
Richard E., d. 4/13/1932 at 73*; b. Pittsfield

DECROW,
Harriett I., d. 5/4/1911 at 58/2/19; pneumonia; housewife; married; b. Hebron, ME; Abel Taylor (Hebron, ME) and Harriett I. Merrill

DEEGAN,
John, d. 10/8/1981 at 62 in Barnstead; John Deegan and Mary Clarity

DEMERITT,
Abbie, d. 1/27/1903 at 16/9/7; meningitis; single; b. Strafford; John J. Demeritt (Strafford) and Caroline Plympton (Medfield, MA)

DEMPSEY,
Patricia M., d. 6/13/1991 at 67 in Manchester; Clare K. Madden and Ruth Gilhams

DENNETT,
Betsey, d. 1852 at 90**; widow of Moses
Eunice, d. 1/28/1890 at 92/11/11; housework; widow; b. VT; George Sewards and ----- Huckins
Frank B., d. 10/16/1962 at 88 in Concord; real & ins. agt.; b. Barnstead; Oliver A. Dennett and Frances E. Hopson
Freeman, d. 7/30/1907 at 31/0/23; sercona of jaw; machinist; married; Alvin A. Dennett and Fannie Hopson (Norwich, VT)
Moses, d. 1811 at 57**
Oliver, d. 1866 at 75**
Oliver A., d. 5/25/1915 at 78/2/18; farmer; married; b. Barnstead; Oliver Dennett (Barnstead) and Eunice Whitny (VT)
Ruth S., d. 2/13/1968 at 84 in Concord; teacher; b. NH; Oliver A. Dennett and Frances E. Hopson

DESJARLAIS,
Frances A., d. 1/9/1991 at 70 in Wolfeboro; Percy Fairbanks and Frances Alexander

DESMULIER,
Edmond Alphonse, d. 7/18/1974 at 79 in Manchester; mule spinning; b. France; Louis J. Desmulier and Adele A. Masure

DESROSIERS,
Robert A., Sr., d. 5/24/1986 at 66 in Barnstead; Eugene Desrosiers and Julienne Barbeau

DEVOL,
Elizabeth P., d. 11/30/1888 at 78/0/24

DICKERMAN,
Irene B., d. 10/21/1981 at 60 in Concord; John Carreaux and Mildred Smith

DICKEY,
Minnie E., d. 4/28/1893 at 21/3/11; phthisis; mill operative; single; b. NB

DIXON,
Evard, d. 10/24/1940 at 69*

DOCKHAM,
Angela, d. 9/20/1891 at 0/9; b. Barnstead; Orrin A. Dockham (Gilmanton)
Anna, d. 1835 at 82**

DODGE,
Frances E., d. 9/4/1941 at 95 in Barnstead; b. Barnstead; Swith Webster and Betsy Parshley
Marion E., d. 6/7/1950 at 19 in Hanover*; b. Barnstead; Walter S. Dodge and Cora E. Clough

DOHMS,
Herman W., d. 7/15/1985 at 61 in Concord; Walter Dohms and Augusta Banern

DOLBIER,
Doris M., d. 2/6/1987 at 69 in Hanover; Walter Langell and Mary J. Noonan

DONATI,
Lillian Y., d. 6/1/2000 in Nashua; Leopold Dewyngaert and Lucienne Picot

DOUGLASS,
Cora, d. 4/10/1942 at 70 in Concord*; b. Waterville, Canada; Edwin Webster and Elizabeth Hammond

DOW,
Abigail, d. 1820 at 55**; wife of Simon
Beatrice C., d. 8/30/1970 at 60 in Wolfeboro; housewife; b. NH; George Cleveland and Delia Demers
Charles H., d. 3/29/1903 at 80/8/10; la grippe; farmer; married; b. Barnstead; Timothy Dow and Mary Hodgdon
Charles W., d. 1862 at 22**
Edith M., d. 11/22/1954 at 83 in Concord; b. Barnstead; George H. Emerson and Mary Ellen Pickering
Emma, d. 2/20/1919 at 79/10/3; b. Quincy, MA; Salathiel Cole (Gloucester, MA) and Nancy F. Cole (Sanbornton)

George W., d. 9/4/1935 at 68; b. Barnstead; John Dow and Mary J. Lang
Harold Fred, d. 3/25/1972 at 85 in Manchester; painter; b. IL; Fred Dow and Georgiana Davis
John, d. 3/1/1911 at 85/7/20; enlarged prostate gland; farmer; married; b. Barnstead; Timothy Dow and Mary P. Hodgdon
John Harold, d. 2/5/1975 at 73 in Concord; line foreman; b. NH; George W. Dow and Edith M. Shackford
John O., d. 4/5/1895 at 89; old age; widower
Lydia A., d. 8/4/1923 at 86; b. Barnstead; Seth Shackford and Harriett Hill
Mary, d. 1871 at 76**; widow of Gen. Timothy
Mary C., d. 1/22/1893 at 80/6/4; heart disease; housewife; married; b. Barnstead; Joseph Nutter (Seabrook) and Mary Clough (Gilmanton)
Mary Jane, d. 7/22/1917 at 87/9/20; b. Alton; John Lang (NH) and Mary J. Webb (NH)
Ruth, d. 1829 at 59**; second wife of Simon
Sarah, d. 1864 at 69**; wife of Jacob
Simon, d. 1839 at 77**
Timothy (Gen.), d. 1861 at 64**
William H., d. 2/13/1895 at 2/5/24; tuberculous meningitis; b. Barnstead; George W. Dow and Edith Shackford

DOWNES,
Karenhappuch, d. 5/13/1963 at 86 in Pittsfield; housewife; b. Ludlow, England; John Webster and Kezia Porterfield

DOWNING,
Ada N., d. 9/28/1941 at 74 in Barnstead; b. Barnstead; Daniel Bunker and Hannah Tilton
James, d. 5/31/1941 at 79 in Barnstead; b. Newcastle, PA

DOWNS,
Adaline B., d. 4/10/1892 at 73/6/27; heart disease; housekeeper; widow; b. Barnstead; ----- Locke
Albert, d. 3/1/1921 at 68; b. Barnstead; Jesse Downs and Adeline --
Archer L., d. 1/8/1950 at 61 in Laconia*; b. NH; Herbert Downs and Calista McKean
Calista M., d. 1/26/1920 at 71/1/12; b. Strafford; James McKeen (ME) and ----- (Strafford)

Herbert L., d. 1/1/1906 at 32/8/25; organic disease of heart; laborer; married; b. Barnstead; Herbert Downs (Barnstead) and Calista McKeene (Strafford)

Herbert Oriso, d. 10/18/1918 at 68/8/3; b. Barnstead; Jesse Downs (Berwick, ME) and Adline Locke (Strafford)

John E., d. 5/26/1946 at 76/2/20 in Barnstead; b. Gilmanton; Isaac A. Downs and Agusta Smith

Laura A., d. 0/29/1906 at 58/9/20; dysentery; single; Jesse Downs (Berwick, ME) and Adeline B. Locke (Strafford)

Maud Welch, d. 10/7/1918 at 22/0/25; b. Tunbridge, VT; Fred Welch (Barnstead) and Annie Lyman (Tunbridge, VT)

William H., d. 1/10/1927 at 71; b. Gilmanton; Isaac Downs and Augusta Smith

DRAKE,

Annie J., d. 5/27/1976 at 71 in Concord; housewife; b. NH; George H. Prince and Mary E. Moore

Arthur W., d. 2/27/1921 at 51/0/3; b. Pittsfield; Walter B. Drake (Center Harbor) and Sarah J. Batchelder

Carrie E., d. 1/10/1893 at 19/7/6; consumption; housewife; married; b. Portsmouth

Edwin B., d. 3/21/1926 at 63; b. Pittsfield; Walter B. Drake and Sarah Batchelder

Frank J., d. 8/20/1891 at 48/9/17; merchant; married; b. Pittsfield; James Drake (Pittsfield) and Betsey Seavey (Chichester)

Hannah W., d. 11/27/1910 at 78/11/10; apoplexy cerebral; housekeeper; single; b. Center Harbor; Simon Drake (Pittsfield) and Sarah Biny (Pittsfield)

Howard, d. 6/22/1974 at 79 in Franklin; b. NH; Edwin B. Drake and Gurgia D. Emerson

Norman H., d. 9/14/1931 at --; b. Barnstead; Harvey W. Drake and Annie J. Prince

Sarah J., d. 4/22/1906 at 75/4; paresis; housewife; married; b. Pittsfield; Samuel Batchelder (Pittsfield) and Mary A. Lane (Hampton Falls)

Walter B., d. 6/5/1907 at 73/8/16; cerebral hyperanoxia; lumber mfgr.; widower; b. Center Harbor; Simon Drake (Pittsfield) and Sarah Berry (Pittsfield)

DRECHSLER,
Henry G., Jr., d. 6/11/1990 at 59 in Manchester; Henry G. Drechsler, Sr. and Ethel C. Howard

DREW,
Aaron, d. 1864 at 71**
Abbie Idell, d. 1/15/1938 at 85*; b. Pittsfield; ----- Tilton and Bettsy Cram
Abigail Hall, d. 1872 at 62**; widow of Joseph
Albert Russell, d. 6/18/1939 at 86*; b. Strafford; John P. Drew and Mary Willey
Alice M., d. 11/2/1965 at 75 in E. Rochester; housewife; b. Barrington; Frank Brown and Eliza A. Allen
Betty, d. 1871 at 92**; wife of Jacob
Daniel, d. 1863 at 67**
David, d. 1814 at 30**
David, d. 1842 at 84**
David, d. 12/7/1888 at 58; farmer; married; Aaron Drew (Barrington) and Eliza Gilman (VT)
Dollie, d. 1843 at 51**
E. Clarke, d. 1864 at 45**
Elizabeth, d. 1856 at 68**; wife of Aaron
Elizabeth, d. 10/11/1942 at 59 in Pembroke*; b. Charlestown, MA; Florence Donahue and Annie Kelley
George M., d. 4/1/1945 at 70/11/18 in Barrington*; b. Pittsfield; Albert R. Drew and Abbie Tilton
Hannah, d. 1855 at 43**; wife of James
John L., d. 3/6/1998 in Laconia; Wendell Drew and Grace Lawlor
Joseph, d. 1848 at 46**
Lucy, d. 1859 at 66**; second wife of James
Martha W., d. 1855 at 95**; widow of David
Mrs., d. 1862 at 90**
Theophelus, d. 1/22/1913 at 84/6/9; pneumonia; shoemaker; married
Wendell Franklin, d. 10/29/1972 at 79 in Manchester; maintenance, resort hotel; b. NH; Charles Jackson Drew and Elizabeth Haselton

DRISCOLL,
Frederick J., d. 7/22/1946 at 72/10/25 in Barnstead; b. PEI; George Driscoll and Annie Bevin

DROLET,
Lionel D., d. 11/9/1987 at 64 in Concord; Fernando Drolet and Annette Nerbonne

DUBUQUE,
infant of Camille Dubuque, d. 9/12/1930 at --*; b. Manchester; Camille Dubuque and Dorothy Haywood

DUDLEY,
Harriett, d. 5/2/1896 at 85/2/10; pneumonia; housekeeper; widow; Gilman Dudley and Polly Haynes
Jeannette Blanche, d. 7/29/1996 at 84 in Concord; Eugene Desrosiers and Julienne Bourbeau
Joseph, d. 1833 at 65**
Smith G., d. 6/22/1887 at 74/5/1; farmer; married; b. Barnstead

DUFFY,
Michael William, d. 10/12/1967 at 46 in Ctr. Barnstead; dispatcher; b. Concord; Michael J. Duffy and Mary Travers

DUHAIME,
Georgianna G., d. 2/5/1982 at 73 in Concord; Napoleon Duhaime and Delias Brochu

DURGIN,
Esther, d. 1866 at 99**
Jonathan, d. 1841 at 69**
Mrs. Sarah, d. 1847 at 78**
Nellie T., d. 8/24/1891 at 28/11/18; housekeeper; married; b. No. Groton; A. A. Hall
Samuel, d. 1867 at 70**
Susan, d. 1855 at 82**; widow of Jonathan

DUTCH,
Marshall, d. 9/8/1913 at 68/9/29; angina pectoris; broker; married; b. Bro'field; Darins Dutch and Lydia Storer

DUTTON,
Fred W., d. 6/7/1969 at 85 in Concord; mechanical draftsman; b. MA; Alvin P. Dutton and Ella J. Wentworth

DWYER,
John F., d. 11/24/1990 at 78 in Dover; John Dwyer and Maude Mace

EARNEST,
Norman A., d. 4/14/1990 at 61 in Concord; Norman L. Earnest and Edith Kohler

EASTMAN,
Caroline, d. 4/22/1927 at 60; b. Chelsea, MA; Charles Schuman and Charlotte Bartlett
Charles I., d. 11/11/1983 at 89 in Concord; Hiram Eastman and Caroline Schumann
Cora, d. 4/23/1988 at 93 in Barnstead; James Nutall and Addie Peabody
George Warren, d. 6/5/1990 at 86 in Concord; Harry Eastman and Caroline Schuman
Grace M., d. 3/12/1990 at 82 in Concord; Harold Tibbetts and Glider -----
Hiram B., d. 2/3/1941 at 77 in Portland, ME*; b. Belfast, ME
James I., d. 2/27/1984 at 59 in Concord; Charles E. Eastman and Cora Nutall
Mrs. Ezekiel, d. 1827 at 91**
Paul R., d. 7/28/1993 at 58 in Barnstead; Charles Eastman and Cora Nutall

EATON,
Abbie F., d. 2/5/1922 at 69/5/17*; b. Barnstead; Timothy Emerson and Sarah Foster
David F., d. 1855 at 49**
Eleanor, d. 1827 at 32**; wife of David F.
Etta, d. 8/16/1905 at 52/10/20; paralysis; widow; b. Barnstead; Alfred Willey and ----- Clark (Barnstead)
Frank S., d. 4/9/1946 at 74/11/20 in Laconia*; b. Barnstead; John C. Eaton and Abbie F. Emerson
Samuel, d. 1848 at 71**

ECKHARDT,
Frieda Edith, d. 12/17/1992 at 87 in Pittsfield; Joseph Knaus and Louise Schaier

George Henry, d. 8/10/1992 at 88 in Concord; Karl Eckhardt and Louise Baldoff

EDDY,
Laura M., d. 9/10/1960 at 81 in Wolfeboro; housewife; widow; b. NS; William H. McFadden and Minna L. Wicker

EDGERLY,
Betsey, d. 1847 at 87**; widow of Samuel
Charles E., d. 12/7/1910 at 69/8/4; cancer of face; farmer; married; b. Barnstead; Nicholas Edgerly and Elinor Twombly
Datharuah, d. 1808 at 78**; wife of Thomas
Dorothy, d. 1798 at 26**; wife of Samuel
Ezekiel (Dea.), d. 1836 at 72**
Mrs. Paul, d. 1852 at 87**
Paul, d. 1841 at 82**
Peter, d. 1784 at 21**
Samuel, d. 1839 at 71**
Thomas, d. 1814 at 85**
True, d. 4/10/1889 at 82; farmer; married; b. Barnstead

EDMONDS,
Robert J., d. 6/15/1948 at 61/8/16 in Barnstead; b. Hazelton, PA; Robert Edmonds and Matilda Biscombe

ELLIOTT,
Francis, d. 1855 at —**
John W., d. 6/27/1896 at 80/7; old age; farmer; married; Zachariah Elliott and Dorcas Walker
William H., d. 1859 at 52**

ELLIS,
Colin Taylor, d. 3/10/1986 at — in Hanover; Robert B. Ellis and Teresa Taylor

ELLISON,
Raymond, d. 11/7/1922 at 0/1/14; b. Barnstead; Walter Ellison (Nottingham) and Alta Glover (Nottingham)

EMENEY,
Victor L., d. 1/4/1978 at 48 in Concord; Walter Emeney and Beatrice Gray

EMERSON,
infant, d. 3/22/1939; b. Concord; Albert L. Emerson and Madeline Jenkins
Adella B., d. 7/1/1934 at 74 in Lynn, MA*
Albert Frank, d. 10/27/1952 at 78 in Barnstead; b. Barnstead; Frank Emerson and Electa Nutter
Albert L., d. 4/9/1983 at 78 in Concord; Carlton Emerson and Lula Wilkins
Alice J., d. 7/27/1930 at 61; b. Gilmanton; Harlan Paige and Lydia Sleeper
Anna H., d. 1/10/1899 at 27; phthisis; housewife; married; b. Barnstead; Eben Hanson and Jane Hodgdon
Benjamin, d. 1822 at 77**
Bessie O., d. 11/4/1898 at 14; diabetes; b. Barnstead; Herman Emerson and ----- Kenney
Carleton E., d. 10/4/1942 at 60 in Barnstead; b. Barnstead; Simeon E. Emerson and Eldora Lougee
Charles, d. 11/14/1925 at 66; b. Barnstead; Thimothy Emerson and Sarah Foster
Charles B., d. 5/10/1924 at 63; b. Etna, ME; Luke Emerson
Charles F., d. 3/9/1899 at 65; apoplexy; farmer; married; b. Barnstead; Moses P. Emerson and Sally Caswell
David M., d. 2/5/1907 at 73/10/4; heart disease; shoemaker; married; b. Pittsfield
Deborah, d. 1843 at 58**; wife of Solomon
Earl L., d. 7/27/1934 at 32 in Barnstead; Albert F. Emerson and Georgia B. Brown
Eldora M., d. 5/13/1936 at 79 in Barnstead; David Lougee and Laura Jones
Elijah, d. 1866 at 83**
Elmer J., d. 8/29/1948 at 78/10/11 in Barnstead; b. Barnstead; Jefferson Emerson and Viana Cilley
Ernest H., d. 9/26/1904 at 5/7/9; gastritis; b. Ctr. Barnstead; Albert Emerson (Barnstead) and Georgie B. Brown (Northwood)
Florence, d. 10/10/1905 at 5/1/10; dysentery; A. Emerson (Rollinsford) and Flora B. Hurd (Farmington)

Florence, d. 2/24/1913 at 18/5/25; pneumonia; single; b. Alton; James Emerson (Barnstead) and Annie R. Hanson (Barnstead)

Frank, d. 6/22/1921 at 69/2/10; b. Barnstead; Timothy Emerson (Barnstead) and Sarah Foster (Barnstead)

G. H., d. 8/19/1914 at 73/7/7; carcinoma of abdomen; farmer; married; b. Barnstead; M. P. Emerson (Barnstead) and Salley M. Caswell (Barnstead)

George W., d. 2/26/1902 at 79/3/27; heart disease; dentist; single; b. Barnstead; Solomon Emerson

Georgia, d. 12/13/1955 at 79 in Concord; b. Northwood; Henry Brown and Abbie Lane

Grace D., d. 5/14/1892 at 22/1/12; pyemia; housewife; married; b. Barnstead; John H. Jenkins (Barnstead) and Elvira Marble

Hannah, d. 11/27/1896 at 82/0/9; pneumonia; widow; b. Barnstead; Jonathan Clark and Temperance Bickford

Harold, d. 5/30/1979 at 73 in Wolfeboro; Albert F. Emerson and Georgia B. Brown

Harriett E., d. 2/3/1965 at 70 in Strafford; housewife; b. Bridgewater; David L. Barrett and Lavinia Smith

Harry, d. 12/10/1958 at 79 in Barnstead

Herbert O., d. 6/20/1946 at 82/5/8 in Pittsfield*; b. Pittsfield; David Emerson and Isabelle Emerson

Jefferson, d. 8/27/1898 at 75/10/2; paralysis; farmer; widower; b. Barnstead; Solomon Emerson and Deborah Young

John J., d. 1868 at 53**

John Oscar, d. 10/21/1971 at 87 in Barnstead; dairy farming; b. Barnstead; Simeon E. Emerson and Eldora M. Lougee

Jonathan, d. 1825 at 76**

Josie Clark, d. 1/12/1949 at 80/0/5 in Barnstead; b. Deerfield; Daniel G. Clark and Sarah Meserve

Kenneth, d. 5/29/1913 at 0/1/10; whooping cough; b. Barnstead; Herbert Burnap (MA) and Marg'iti Emerson (Barnstead)

Kristen Lee, d. 10/15/1980 at – in Concord; Catherine A. Emerson

L. H., d. 2/26/1922 at 6/10/29*; b. Burlington, VT; Ray Emerson (Barnstead) and Harriet Barrett

Lucie J., d. 7/2/1980 at 76 in Concord; Peter Tuttle and Esther Bush

Madeline, d. 3/17/1995 at 89 in Epsom; Charles Jenkins and Lilla Foss

Mahala J., d. 8/7/1901 at 74; angina pectoris; housewife; married; b. Barnstead

Mary A., d. 12/21/1932 at 71*; b. Newmarket; John H. Jenkins and Elvira R. Wilker

Mary E., d. 11/7/1918 at 73/1/4; b. Dover; John F. Pickering and Phebe C. Trethering (Kittery, ME)

Mary E., d. 3/30/1935 at 77; b. Barnstead; Richard Caswell and Martha Willey

Minnie B., d. 5/4/1963 at 80 in Barnstead; housewife; b. Alton; Horace Wells and Ida Hill

Nabby, d. 1864 at 83**; wife of Elijah

Nellie M., d. 11/12/1967 at 73 in Barnstead; housewife; b. Barnstead; Mark Brewster and Annie Merrill

Olive W., d. 1/15/1900 at 75/6/17; pneumonia; housewife; widow; --- --- Kenison

Oscar, d. 3/22/1907 at 0/2/25; marasmus; b. Barnstead; C. E. Emerson (Barnstead) and Lula Wilkins

Paul, d. 1842 at 21**

Pauline L., d. 3/11/1935 at 1; b. Barnstead; Albert L. Emerson and Madeline A. Jenkins

Polly, d. 1871 at 68**; wife of Moses

Prudence, d. 1844 at 53**; wife of Eliphalet

Ralph A., d. 9/7/1985 at 76 in Barnstead; Albert F. Emerson and Georgia Brown

Ralph J., d. 11/11/1915 at 80/6/28; retired; widower; b. Northwood; Richard J. Emerson (Northwood) and Delia Goss (Pittsfield)

Ray J., d. 5/24/1965 at 70 in Plymouth; retired; b. Ctr. Barnstead; Llewellyn Emerson and Mary A. Jenkins

Raymond F., d. 11/24/1910 at 0/11/14; acute indigestion; b. Chichester; A. C. Emerson (Barnstead) and Essel A. Clough (Pittsfield)

Samuel H., d. 3/26/1893 at 69/6/10; pneumonia; farmer; married; b. Barnstead

Sarah, d. 1810 at 68**; wife of Jonathan

Sarah A., d. 2/16/1931 at 46; b. Warren; Calvin W. Cummings and Emogene P. Brown

Sarah E., d. 5/18/1896 at 71/10/26; organic disease of stomach; housewife; married; b. Barnstead

Sarah E., d. 6/20/1908 at 65/5/2; catarrh bile ducts; housewife; married; b. Barnstead; Samuel D. Nutter (Barnstead) and Ruth Knowles (Epsom)

Simeon, d. 11/16/1910 at 90/1; organic disease of heart; farmer; widower; Moses Emerson and Sally M. Caswell

Simeon E., d. 1/29/1944 at 86/1/4 in Barnstead; b. Barnstead; Simeon Emerson and Mahala J. Adams
Solomon, d. 1841 at 24**
Solomon, d. 1868 at 89**
Thomas, d. 1811 at 37**
Thomas, d. 1855 at 40**
Timothy, d. 1/5/1905 at 79/6/13; gangrene; blacksmith; widower; b. Barnstead; Elijah Emerson (Madbury) and Abigail Jones (Lee)
Vienna, d. 10/31/1892 at 65/8/17; heart disease; housewife; married; b. Northfield; Sewell Cilley (Northfield) and Rebecca Mears (Tewksbury)
William S., d. 8/28/1916 at 49/0/23; single; b. Barnstead; David M. Emerson (Pittsfield) and Isabel Emerson (Northwood)
Woodrow Wilson, d. 12/16/1996 at 84 in Concord; Albert Emerson and Georgie B. Brown

ESTEY,
Marion C., d. 10/20/1961 at 74 in Concord; housewife; b. Chelsea, MA; John Conner and Josephine Winkley

EVANS,
Arva, d. 8/9/1972 at 67 in Manchester; cook; b. NH; Austin Evans and Myra Munsey
Austin H., d. 6/27/1944 at 79/2/1 in Barnstead; b. Strafford; Enoch Evans and Harriett Tuttle
Carrie Hill, d. 1/2/1949 at 88/9/21 in Barnstead; b. Barnstead; David H. Evans and Catherine Hill
Catherine, d. 10/30/1908 at 76/5/2; gastric disease; housekeeper; widow; b. Northwood; John Hill (Northwood) and Fannie Hall (Strafford)
Clarence, d. 6/8/1933 at 39; b. Barnstead; Austin Evans and Myra Munsey
Fannie L., d. 3/27/1920 at 58/11/19*; David Evans
Florence, d. 3/10/1897 at 0/0/27; marasmus; b. Barnstead; Austin Evans (Strafford) and Myra Munsey (Barnstead)
Fred W., d. 9/29/1955 at 89 in Pittsfield; b. Barnstead; David H. Evans and Catherine Hill
George Irving, d. 9/29/1934 at 71 in Boston, MA*
Jacob W., d. 9/24/1903 at 82/3/28; carcinoma; farmer; married; b. Strafford; Lemuel Evans (Strafford) and Eliza Willey (Barnstead)

Mabel C., d. 11/3/1972 at 91 in Loudon; housewife; b. Gilmanton; Isaac D. Nutter and Cora F. Clough

Mary E., d. 12/25/1911 at 87/9/21; enteritis; housekeeper; widow; b. Wolfeboro

Mary E., d. 8/4/1937 at 65; b. Rochester; Charles R. Parsons and Caroline J. Kelly

Myra M., d. 5/14/1942 at 73 in Barnstead; b. Barnstead; Henry J. Munsey and Annie M. Young

Oliver, d. 7/25/1898 at 65; farmer; married

Sarah, d. 2/14/1909 at 76; pneumonia; housework; widow; b. Barnstead; Ralph Babb (Barnstead) and Delilah Hayes (Barrington)

FALLER,
Inga, d. 1/8/1965 at 71 in Barnstead; housewife; b. Norway; Abraham Dybvik and Severine Dibvik

Marcel, d. 2/18/1980 at 85 in Barnstead; Florent Faller and Lucy Saaf

FALLON,
William J., d. 6/4/1987 at 79 in Concord; William P. Fallon and Elizabeth Costello

FARREN,
Richard, d. 2/3/1903 at 1/10/7; unknown; b. Pittsfield; James Farren (Boston) and Grace Gilman (Northwood)

FAY,
Dolly, d. 12/16/1979 at – in Rochester
Joseph, d. 1837 at 63**
Olive, d. 1854 at 87**; widow of Joseph

FEINN,
Maurice H., d. 6/1/1985 at 57 in Concord; Benjamin Feinn and Lena Port

FESSENDEN,
Louise, d. 2/7/1914 at 72/11/1; cere. thrombosis; clerk; single; b. Portland, ME; N. Fessenden (ME) and Mary Fessenden (ME)

FIFIELD,
Effie M., d. 11/9/1961 at 77 in Barnstead; housewife; b. Plymouth; Alba B. Heath and Mary Howland
Joseph, d. 1/24/1962 at 60 in Concord; lumberjack; b. Warren; Melvin Fifield and Effie May

FINLAYSON,
Roy W., d. 11/5/1947 at 72/11/12 in Wolfeboro*; b. PEI; Kenneth Finlayson and Frances Scheurman

FISHER,
Edna, d. 1/20/1933 at 0/10; b. Haverhill; Ira Fischer (sic) and Annie Powell

FISKE,
Carmelia Arlene, d. 2/28/1987 at 11 in Boston, MA; Charles William Fiske and Janice Audrey Wicks

FITTS,
George J., d. 10/--/1916 at 17/5; b. New Boston; Joseph F. Fitts (Francestown) and Annie G. Lash (New Boston)

FLANDERS,
Henrietta M., d. 11/20/1943 at 73 in Concord*; b. Sutton, PQ; Amable Lafleur and Mary Mativier
James A., d. 2/3/1932 at 71; b. Danbury

FLETCHER,
Ardella, d. 11/22/1942 at 63 in Quincy, MA*
Nellie M., d. 2/9/1890 at 36/7/10; housework; married; b. Alton; John Jones (Lebanon) and Lydia Drew (Alton)

FOLEY,
Thomas J., d. 3/13/1936 at 75 in Barnstead; Michael Foley and Bridget Cooley

FOLLANSBEE,
Joy R., d. 1/16/1989 at 51 in Laconia; Noah Killam and Lillian -----

FOLSOM,
Marsha Ann, d. 7/20/1994 at 13 in Barnstead; Brian Carroll Folsom and Catherine Ann Charron

FORD,
Ardis Louise, d. 7/15/1975 at 51 in Rochester; weaver; b. ME; Percy J. Nelson and Rena Tuttle
William A., d. 6/10/1990 at 57 in Concord; Arthur Ford and Emma Glover

FORNIER,
Harriet E., d. 12/12/1905 at 15/2/21; diabetes mellitus; single; b. Barnstead; Joseph A. Fournier (Canada) and Harriet A. Jones (Barnstead)

FORTIER,
daughter, d. 10/7/1984 at – in Hanover; Richard Fortier and Diane Meuse

FOSHER,
Clarence H., d. 6/28/1947 at 55/8/29 in Barnstead; b. Bedford; Herbert N. Fosher and Mary Adams

FOSS,
child, d. 4/14/1902 at 0/0/13; bronchitis; b. Barnstead; Oliver M. Foss (Strafford) and Abbie F. Avery (Barnstead)
child, d. 5/10/1922 at 1 hr; b. Barnstead; William B. Foss (Strafford) and Grace Drake (Barnstead)
Albion N., d. 5/20/1941 at 80 in Barnstead; b. Gilmanton; Samuel G. Foss and Mary Nutter
Alice, d. 1863 at 72**; wife of Jonathan
Alice B., d. 5/8/1895 at 92/1/5; apoplexy; widow; b. Strafford; Samuel Foss and Betsy Babb
Bessie H., d. 7/9/1942 at 69 in Pembroke*; b. Strafford; John F. Hall and Eliza Scranton
Bettie A., d. [unknown]/1965 at 27 in Pittsfield; housewife; b. Loudon; C. Langdon Kenney and Viola Bailey
Charles A., d. 6/18/1921 at 68/10/28*; b. Barnstead; James L. Foss (Barnstead) and Eliza Blake
Charles M., d. 6/8/1953 at 81 in Concord; b. Strafford; William Foss and Abbie Winkley

Charles W., d. 2/1/1927 at 77*; b. Alton; William J. Foss and Jerusha S. Pettingill

Dorothy, d. 1871 at 55**; wife of Simon

Edwin Rufus, d. 11/9/1915 at 38/3/9; electrician; married; b. Barnstead; Rufus S. Foss (Alton) and Mary E. Tasker (Strafford)

Eli H., d. 6/29/1908 at 88/11/13; biliary calculi; blacksmith; widower; b. Barnstead; Jonathan Foss (Newington) and Alice Nutter

Eliza J., d. 1/31/1916 at 88/6/16*; widow; b. Epsom; Timothy E. Blake (Epsom) and Sally Emerson (Epsom)

Elmira E., d. 7/14/1931 at 59*; b. Strafford; Charles P. Foss and Hannah E. Swain

Florence A., d. 6/30/1948 at 59/4/22 in Pittsfield*; b. Strafford; Henry R. Foss and Adie Tripp

Frank G., d. 12/1/1947 at 83/8/4 in Pembroke*; b. Strafford; Gorham T. Foss and Lucretia Williams

George Gerrish, d. 4/4/1973 at 82 in Barnstead; maintenance tel. co.; b. Barnstead; Albion N. Foss and Josephine M. Clough

Gorham T., d. 1/26/1906 at 73/9/17; atrophy of liver; farmer; married; b. Strafford; Jeremiah Foss (Barrington) and Eliza Tenney

Grace D., d. 2/22/1934 at 38 in Barnstead; Edwin B. Drake and Georgia D. Emerson

Hannah E., d. 1/13/1946 at 85/1/14 in Nashua*

Hattie E., d. 3/14/1892 at 0/0/9; b. Barnstead; Haven B. Foss (Strafford) and Hattie C. Varney (Farmington)

Haven B., d. 9/1/1900 at 52/11/18; peritonitis; farmer; married; b. Strafford; George S. Foss and Elizabeth Foss

James, d. 1870 at 77**

James L., d. 2/14/1899 at 76/10/14; heart failure; farmer; married; b. Barnstead; Jonathan Foss and Alice Nutter

Jennie B., d. 11/26/1945 at 93/2/24 in Franklin*; b. Barnstead; Nathaniel Hanson and Margery Evans

Josephine M., d. 3/2/1953 at 86 in Keene; b. NH; George Clough and Mary Clough

Levonia, d. 1/17/1922 at 81/1/17; b. Durham; Jonathan Berry (Strafford) and Hannah Brewster (Barrington)

Lucretia, d. 12/30/1913 at 80/3/16*; chronic bronchitis; widow; b. Strafford; Moses Williams (MA) and Salley Yeaton (Epsom)

Margaret C., d. 10/8/1982 at – in Concord

Mary A., d. 10/26/1888 at 71; married; b. Alton

Nellie C., d. 2/26/1908 at 23/8/26; gastritis; housewife; married; b. Canada; Charles Whitehouse (Canada) and Lucie Fifield (VT)

Oscar, d. 7/6/1913 at 67/7/30*; cancer; lumber; married; b. Barnstead

Robert S., d. 1/8/1925 at 0/0/4; b. Barnstead; William B. Foss and Grace Drake

Rufus, d. 10/17/1926 at 85; b. Alton; Simon Foss and Dorothy Hayes

Ruth, d. 10/31/1918 at 0/2/2; b. Barnstead; William B. Foss (Strafford) and Grace Drake (Barnstead)

Sally, d. 1871 at 65**; wife of Solomon

Sarah A., d. 1/24/1888 at 60/2

Sarah Ursula, d. 4/6/1923 at 71*; b. Barnstead; Oliver P. H. Young and Emily J. Tuttle

Solomon, d. 3/12/1896 at 85/10/24; neuralgia of the heart; farmer; widower

Susan, d. 6/23/1892 at 67/6; dropsy; single

Wilbur R., d. 1/22/1995 at 78 in Barnstead; William Foss and Grace Drake

William B., d. 6/16/1959 at 67 in Concord

FOSTER,
Abigail, d. 1868 at 78**; widow of Charles

C. W., d. 9/17/1907 at 77/7/18; enlarged prostate gland; farmer; widower; Charles Foster (Barnstead) and Abagail Nutter (Barnstead)

Charles, d. 1846 at 48**

Charles E., d. 3/11/1898 at 34 in Boston; pneumonia; dentist; single; b. Barnstead; Charles W. Foster and Olive Greenleaf

Olive M., d. 5/3/1895 at 64/3/12; cancer of liver; widow; b. Barnstead; John Greenleaf and Mary Davis

William P., d. 3/7/1887 at –; mechanic; married; b. Barnstead

FOURNIER,
Joseph A., d. 12/21/1919 at 64/6/6*; b. Troispoistles, Canada; Ausustas Faunier (France) and Juluth Bernier

FOWLE,
Barbara S., d. 10/15/1977 at 65 in Ctr. Barnstead; senior clerk interviewer (ret.); b. MA; Joseph T. Unwin and Elizabeth Pickthall

FOWLER,
Clarence D., d. 11/19/1965 at 76 in Barnstead; woodsman; b. Strafford; Arthur Fowler
Mary, d. 5/21/1890 at 29

FRAME,
Frederick P., d. 10/20/1917 at 47/3/17; b. Lynn, MA; Henry L. Frame (Halifax, NS) and Ellen M. Alley (Lynn, MA)

FRASER,
Warren G., d. 7/5/1991 at 78 in Manchester; Warren F. Fraser and Ella Mitton

FRENCH,
Clyde, d. 2/21/1915 at 18/8/17; student; single; b. Benton; Lewis E. French (Warren) and Gertrude A. Little (Warren)
Gertrude L., d. 3/29/1935 at 68; b. Warren; Henry A. Little and Mary L. Ford
Herbert C., d. 2/5/1951 at 61 in Concord*; b. Benton; Louis E. French and Gertrude Little
Ivo P., d. 1/28/1995 at 89 in Epsom; John French and Mary Pearl
Lewis E., d. 9/3/1945 at 81/5/19 in Concord*; b. Warren; Alonzo French and Rhuhamia Fifield
Pauline Jeanette, d. 9/9/1994 at 65 in Concord; Edward Fay and Dolly Clanton
Walter F., d. 7/17/1961 at 57 in Lebanon; laborer; b. Colebrook; Asa French

FREUND,
Henry Edward, d. 7/6/1991 at 69 in Barnstead; Henry Richard Freund and Gertrude Elizabeth Freidmann

FREY,
Josephine Ann, d. 2/9/1968 at 65 in Barnstead; housewife; b. Germany; George Dopfer
Leo, d. 7/29/1978 at 78 in Ctr. Barnstead; carpenter; b. Germany; Eduard Frey and Genovia -----

FROST,
Arthur L., d. 5/22/1989 at 64 in Manchester; Ira S. Frost and Emma Newton

Betty J., d. 3/2/1986 at 58 in Wolfeboro; Arthur Frenette and Katherine Curtis

FRYE,
Lance L., d. 11/22/1964 at 53 in Barnstead; shaving bailer; b. Kingston; Lance L. Frye and Vera Cilley

FURLONG,
Louis J., d. 11/18/1997 at 73 in Barnstead

GAGNE,
Gerald S., d. 6/29/1995 at 70 in Ctr. Barnstead; Louis Gagne and Antoinette Boisvert

GALLAGHER,
Jane, d. 8/11/1984 at 34 in Concord; Burnell Gallagher and Forence Munson

GARDNER,
Doris C., d. 1/15/1979 at 72 in Concord; Frank Byron
Dorothy M., d. 12/19/2000 in Concord; Walter Pattern and Lolita Benjamin
James J., d. 7/24/1997 at 76 in Barnstead; Peter Gardner and Helen Conroy
Julius, d. 10/1/1921 at 72/5/9; b. Pittsfield; Nelson Gardner (VT) and Nancy ----- (VT)
Olive T., d. 5/16/1932 at 78*; b. Barnstead; Samuel T. Knowles and Olive Bunker

GARLAND,
Abigail, d. 1839 at 74**; widow of Samuel
Abigail, d. 1850 at 58**; wife of Rev. David
Abigail, d. 4/19/1899 at 79; la grippe; housewife; married; b. Pittsfield; Smith Shaw
Cyrus F., d. 1846 at 29**
David (Rev.), d. 1863 at 71**
Eliza V., d. 12/17/1938 at 80*; b. New Perch, PEI; James McVean
Elsie M., d. 4/4/1910 at 18/6/30; anemia; single; b. Barnstead; Melvin Garland (Barnstead) and Nellie J. Green (Loudon)
Emily, d. 1850 at 27**; widow of Cyrus F.

Herbert A., d. 3/23/1930 at 72*; b. Barnstead; John F. Garland and Susan Hall
Ida May, d. 8/25/1940 at 80*; b. Portsmouth; Walter Scott and Ann E. Garland
Isaac, d. 1867 at 92**
John, d. 1861 at 56**
John Babb, d. 4/12/1896 at 85/4/23; apoplexy; farmer; single; b. Barnstead; Isaac Garland and Lydia Babb
John F., d. 3/13/1913 at 80/3/26; bronchitis; farmer; widower; b. Barnstead; John Garland (Barnstead) and Soppa Adams (Rochester)
Lavinia W., d. 1/18/1895 at 76/6/3; dropsy; housework; single; b. Gilmanton; Joseph Garland and Mehitable B. Kimball
Lizzie E., d. 12/11/1910 at 52/0/13; peritonitis after operation; housework; single; b. NH; Calvin Garland (NH) and Betsey G. Drew (NH)
Lois, d. 1864 at 64**; wife of Samuel
Lydia, d. 1865 at 89**; wife of Isaac
Mary O., d. 4/2/1898 at 94/7 in Portland; pneumonia
Mary S., d. 4/22/1911 at 73/4/17; epitheliona of face; housewife; married; b. Barnstead; Joseph Hall (Barnstead) and Betsy Drew (Alton)
Melvin H., d. 12/4/1940 at 76; b. Barnstead; Calvin D. Garland and Betsy Drew
Nellie J., d. 3/28/1948 at 82/2/7 in Concord*; b. Loudon; Cyrus B. Green and Eliza J. Clark
Oscar J., d. 3/22/1936 at 74 in Barnstead; John F. Garland and Mary S. Hall
Richard, d. 1868 at 68**
Ronald F., d. 11/15/1980 at 33 in Concord; Wilbur J. Garland and Lillian E. Brown
Samuel, d. 1829 at 62**
Shirley, d. 12/28/1986 at 47 in Barnstead; Wilber Garland and Lillian Brown
Wilbur J., d. 6/9/1972 at 84 in Barnstead; lumbering teamster; b. NH; Oscar J. Garland and Eliza McVean
William, d. 1838 at 42**

GARNEY,
Agnes M., d. 6/25/1957 at 78 in Wolfeboro; b. Norwich, CT; John Cochrane and Sophronia -----

J. Russell, d. 2/28/1933 at 55; b. Lynn, MA; John Garney and Mary Jane Cole

GATES,
Eleanor, d. 3/18/1906 at 64/11/18; pneumonia; housewife; married; b. Goffstown; Dr. Burnham
Kenneth G., d. 10/8/1979 at 78 in Concord; James E. Gates and Dora Steadman

GATTO,
Mary E., d. 5/17/1985 at 71 in Ctr. Barnstead; Archie Osborne and Mabel Flanders
Vincent, d. 7/13/1991 at 78 in Franklin; Barttlo Gatto and Rose Aveni

GAULT,
Zelma D., d. 2/10/1928 at 25; b. Barnstead; George W. Dow and Edith Shackford

GAW,
Norman W., Sr., d. 4/16/1954 at 49 in Barnstead; b. Kansas; William Gaw and Annie Nielson
William Bowden, d. 10/14/1950 at 82 in Concord; b. Ireland

GEDDES,
Alan Taylor, d. 11/24/1997 at 65 in Concord; Leland Geddes and Edna Pickard

GEISER,
Emma C., d. 9/22/1977 at 82 in Epsom; housewife; b. NH; Alfonso F. Bryant and Grace Parshley

GENEST,
Mary Lou, d. 7/24/1987 at 39 in Concord; Ernest Riel and Edith Kenneally

GEORGE,
Alice W., d. 10/25/1936 at 81 in Barnstead; Charles S. George and Elmira Waldron
Almira, d. 4/9/1893 at 67/6/14; organic disease of liver; housewife; married; b. Barrington

Charles S., d. 6/22/1896 at 79/4/7; organic disease of heart; farmer; widower; b. Barnstead; Enos George and ----- Chesley

Enos (Rev.), d. 1859 at 78**

Enos, d. 4/15/1914 at 64/1/22; tuberculosis; farmer; single; b. Barnstead; Charles S. George (Barnstead) and H. Waldron (Strafford)

Henry W., d. 6/10/1938 at 87; b. Barnstead; Charles S. George and Almyra Waldron

John, d. 3/10/1924 at 76; b. Warner; Charles George and Margaret Warren

Lizzie E., d. 9/19/1946 at 93/9/6 in Nashua*

Myra A., d. 5/1/1936 at 78 in Barnstead; Joseph Whitney and Ann Hale

Noah J. T. (Dr.), d. 1845 at 50**

Sophia, d. 1858 at 76**; wife of Rev. Enos

GERLACH,

Henry A., Sr., d. 8/4/1996 at 81 in Epsom; Henry Gerlach and Madaline Brandt

GIBSON,

Jennie P., d. 2/15/1957 at 88 in Pittsfield; b. Sunapee; Charles A. Rowell and Susan F. Quimby

GIESER,

Don R., d. 1/19/1961 at 72 in Dunedin, FL; mortician; b. Marion, OH; Peter Gieser and Nettie Slapp

GILES,

Benjamin Curtis, d. 4/16/1917 at 81/1/16; b. Deerfield; Benjamin Giles (NH) and Lucendia Hoitt (NH)

GILLESPIE,

Robert Ellis, d. 12/31/1950 at 34 in Concord; b. FL; Horace Gillespie and May Henderson

GILMAN,

Abbie H., d. 4/3/1933 at 82; b. Barnstead; Asa C. Hurd and Mary J. Goodwin

Amasa K., d. 11/1/1907 at 91/9/23; heart disease; b. Gilmanton; John Gilman and Mary Kelley

Charles H., d. 6/28/1953 at 79 in Pittsfield; b. NH; Horatio A.
    Gilman and Maria M. Stevens
Ellen S., d. 1/21/1954 at 79 in Pittsfield; b. West Canaan; Frank T.
    Underhill and Susan A. Burnham
Mehitable F., d. 3/6/1902 at 82; valvular disease of heart; married;
    Mehitable Hill
Samuel, d. 1819 at 89**

GILSON,
Myra, d. 3/22/1943 at 62 in Goffstown*; b. Barnstead; John H.
    Jenkins and Elvira Wilkes

GINGRAS,
Keith, d. 4/14/1993 at 0 in Lebanon; Scott Gingras and Wendy
    Gingras

GIROUARD,
Eva L., d. 1/18/1989 at 94 in Concord; Phillip Girouard and Athle
    Roux

GLIDDEN,
Adeline, d. 5/6/1893 at 75; heart disease; housekeeper; widow; b.
    Barnstead
Herbert, d. 7/30/1931 at 82; b. Alton; Daniel F. Glidden and Adeline
    E. Glidden
John E., d. 10/25/1904 at 46/3/14; fracture of skull; laborer; single;
    b. Alton; Levi B. Glidden (Effingham) and Lavina Dore (Alton)

GLOVER,
William Robert, d. 9/15/1967 at 67 in Ctr. Barnstead; electrician; b.
    Rockwall, TX; Lewis Glover and Emily K. Wooding

GOLDEN,
Elizabeth, d. 11/2/1982 at 80 in Barnstead; Guilford Gray and
    Minnie Shaw
John E., d. 10/14/1972 at 92 in Wolfeboro; railroad fireman; b. NY;
    John Golden and Bridget Thornton
Kenneth J., d. 5/14/1959 at 18 in Concord
Leona C., d. 7/16/1997 at 71 in Concord; Leon Parker and Bella
    McLeod
Paul A., d. 11/8/1999 in Concord; John Golden and Blanche Locke

Richard M., d. 2/21/1927 at 0/0/12; b. Barnstead; John E. Golden and N. Blanche Locke

GOODALE,
Anne-Marie, d. 6/30/1983 at 42 in Barnstead; Dennis O'Neill and ----- Sullivan

GOODRICH,
John A., d. 8/6/1934 at 80 in Barnstead; Lewis Goodrich and Mary Baker
Robert M., d. 11/10/1974 at 79 in Barnstead; executive secretary; b. NH; Robert V. Goodrich and Jessie A. Lang
Ruth W., d. 9/23/1976 at 92 in Epsom; housewife; b. NH; George R. Drake and Jennie C. Clarke

GOODWIN,
Abigail, d. 1829 at 32**; wife of David
Byron C., d. 11/15/1925 at 3; b. Barnstead; Clifton Goodwin and Ethel Dame
Charles, d. 6/29/1947 at 70 in Rochester*; b. Franklin; William Goodwin and Mary Collins
Edward L., d. 6/22/1925 at 7; b. Gilmanton; Clifton Goodwin and Ethel Dame
Ethan L., d. 10/21/1966 at 11 mins. in Peterborough; b. Peterborough; Gressy Goodwin and Jeanne E. Pike
Inez A., d. 2/5/1954 at 87 in Barnstead; b. Bow; Rufus Fuller and Sarah Noyes
Irene E., d. 7/25/1959 at 74 in Barnstead
Nilda A., d. 7/20/1982 at 82 in Concord; William E. Anderson and Nellie Carpenter
Ray Fuller, d. 6/12/1988 at 92 in Barnstead; Walter N. Goodwin and Inez A. Fuller
Walter, d. 12/16/1918 at 3/0/6; b. Gilmanton; Clifton Goodwin (Gilmanton) and Ethel Dame (New Durham)

GORDON,
Arthur E., d. 11/9/1948 at 80/0/2 in Barnstead; b. Natick, MA; James Gordon and Eleanor E. Glidden
Carrie D., d. 11/8/1967 at 88 in Concord; secretary; b. Barnstead; Oliver F. Dennett and Frances Hopson

Mary E., d. 1/9/1965 at 77 in Ctr. Barnstead; house keeper; b. Groveton; John Gordon and Ida Phillips

Susan E. (Porter), d. 2/22/1949 at 82 in Worcester, MA; b. Holbrook, MA; John F. Porter and Mary J. Wright

GOSSE,
Willis, d. 10/14/1950 at 79/9/9 in Barnstead; b. Newfoundland; Nathaniel R. Gosse and Mary A. Shepard

GOVE,
Frances May, d. 4/19/1995 at 92 in Epsom; Fred Hankin and Betty Valliere

Grace E., d. 11/30/1981 at 72 in Wolfeboro; Clarence Potter and Nellie Norwood

GRACE,
Ella Russ, d. 1/14/1941 at 91 in Newburyport, MA*

Eunice S., d. 12/5/1927 at 71*; b. Barnstead; Moses Grace and Jane Proctor

Moses L., d. 1869 at 64**

GRATTAGE,
Wanton A., d. 5/6/1996 at 72 in Concord; William Grattage and Clara St. Germaine

GRAU,
Ellen M., d. 9/9/1990 at 91 in Wolfeboro; Andrew Christensen and Caroline -----

Henry, d. 10/28/1972 at 71 in Concord; hotel work - farmer; b. Germany; Ernest Grau and Hedwig Collerbusch

GRAVEMAN,
Dietrick W., d. 1/30/1965 at 66 in Concord; accountant; b. Germany; Frederick Graveman and Sophie Strackman

GRAY,
Albert B., d. 7/12/1957 at 76 in Barnstead; b. Strafford; George A. Gray and Hannah F. Tuttle

Angie M., d. 8/25/1984 at 61 in Concord; William E. Bartlett and Alice G. Garland

Bessie J., d. 2/2/1963 at 80 in Pittsfield; housewife; b. Durham; Charles E. Brown and Emma Amazeen

Blanche L., d. 6/4/1928 at 2; b. Barnstead; William C. Gray and Ruth Davis

Cahin G., d. 5/6/1913 at 0/6/11; pertussis; b. Barnstead; Albert S. Gray (Barnstead) and Bessie Brown (Barnstead)

Carol Ann, d. 10/31/1970 at 15 in Concord; student; b. Concord; Frank C. Gray and Angie M. Bartlett

Clarence L., d. 2/27/1951 at 87/8/27 in Pittsfield*; b. Barnstead; William P. Gray and Margaret Foss

Donald N., d. 1/6/1993 at 55 in Concord; William C. Gray and Ruth Davis

Edgar Frank, d. 2/1/1952 at 81 in Barnstead; b. Barnstead; William P. Gray and Margaret Foss

Edward A., d. 7/30/1982 at 80 in Barnstead; Albert B. Gray and Bessie J. Brown

Edwin Albert, d. 12/30/1973 at 60 in Manchester; shoe cutter; b. MA; Edward Albert Gray and Sadie Hatstat

Fidelia P., d. 1/9/1914 at 78/10/8; pneumonia; widow; b. Strafford; W. M. Foss and Eliza Foss

Frank C., d. 6/3/1981 at 61 in Hanover; William Gray and Ruth Davis

Fred W., d. 9/28/1897 at 0/3/22; meningitis; b. Barnstead; Herbert Gray (Barnstead)

George, Jr., d. 4/2/1898 at 0/0/14; b. Barnstead; George Gray and Emma J. Cole

George A., d. 3/20/1932 at 74; b. Barnstead; William P. Gray and Margaret Foss

Harriett A., d. 6/8/1921 at 65/7/27; b. Carlisle, MA; Frank Hanaford

Herbert A., d. 4/14/1946 at 81/10/5 in Barnstead; b. Strafford; William P. Gray and Margaret E. Foss

Lavina, d. 2/3/1902 at 87/2/22; heart disease; widow; b. Barnstead; Moses Clough and Betsey Durgin (Barnstead)

Leslie Morton, d. 10/29/1969 at 74 in Manchester; machinist; b. NH; Horace Gray and Harriette Hannaford

Margaret E., d. 3/19/1919 at 89/9/7*; b. Strafford; Woodbury Foss and Eliza -----

Myrtie S., d. 5/16/1943 at 72 in Barnstead; b. Allenstown; Edwin Cote and Hannah Wheeler

Myron E., d. 9/21/1972 at 73 in Portsmouth; shoeworker; b. NH; Herbert A. Gray and Mertie S. Cate

Oliver J., d. 7/11/1893 at --; fracture of cervical vertebra; farmer; married; Joseph P. Gray (Strafford) and Hannah Gray (Strafford)

Orris D., d. 3/29/1914 at 54/4/17; pneumonia; farmer; married; William P. Gray (Strafford) and Margaret E. Foss (Strafford)

Ralph H., d. 2/13/1987 at 56 in Manchester; William Gray and Ruth Davis

Reginald W., d. 11/2/1938 at 9; b. Barnstead; Violet Gray

Robert Leslie, d. 6/13/1975 at 50 in Barnstead; painter; b. NH; Leslie M. Gray and Virginia Chagnon

Ruth D., d. 1/31/1979 at 81 in Concord; Daniel Davis and Anna Cate

Stephen H., d. 8/8/1895 at 75/9/18; heart disease; farmer; married

Virginia E., d. 3/23/1958 at 57 in Barnstead

William Clarence, d. 6/18/1973 at 85 in Concord; farmer; b. Barnstead; Orris Gray and Hattie Hammerford

William P., d. 8/14/1910 at 82/10/18; cystitis; farmer; married; b. Strafford; William Gray and Polly Gray

GREEN,
Albert N., d. 5/9/1917 at 0/11/28*; b. Rochester; Clarence E. Green (Moultonboro) and Grace A. Pitman (Barnstead)

Annie H., d. 5/25/1916 at 45/9/13; housewife; married; b. Auburn, ME; Liberty H. Hutchinson (Milan) and Mary W. Emery (W. Newbury, MA)

GREENFIELD,
Mary F., d. 10/10/1939 at 59; b. Norfolk, MA; Frederick H. Clapp and Charlotte J. Sumner

Oswald J., d. 8/23/1941 at 58 in California*; b. MA

GREENLEAF,
Benjamin F., d. 7/27/1944 at 74/10/0 in Laconia*; b. Stark, ME; Benjamin L. Greenleaf and Emily Laemain

Milton, d. 6/10/1941 at 82 in Gilmanton*; b. Northwood; George Greenleaf and Elizabeth Winslow

Molly, d. 1868 at 75**

GREENSHIELDS,
James M., d. 12/14/1937 at 73; b. Montreal, Canada; James M. Greenshields

GRIEVES,
Almira, d. 1/25/1925 at 96; b. Alton; Simon Foss and Sarah Wakefield
Thomas, d. 7/21/1910 at 84/7/7; senile decay; blacksmith; married; b. Scotland; James Grieves (Scotland)

GRIFFIN,
George W., d. 4/26/1910 at 78/1/26; disease of heart, liver; farmer; married; b. Gilmanton; Richard Griffin (Sandown) and Linda Hutchinson (Gilmanton)
Nancy H, d. 8/16/1919 at 82/3/21; b. New Durham; Jonathan Hill (Gilmanton) and Eliza Chesley (New Durham)

GRINDLE,
Jackalyn Leonne, d. 7/7/1952 at 12 in Barnstead; b. Freeport, ME; Richard W. Grindle and Ruth Liscord

GROVER,
William, M.D., d. 1853 at 50**

GUSTIN,
Florence, d. 9/9/1912 at 36/5/17 in Enfield*; carcinoma of liver; married; b. Barnstead; John Clark (Barnstead) and Alice George (Barnstead)

HALL,
Abigail, d. 1859 at 54**; wife of Eben
Betsy, d. 6/13/1896 at 91/1/1; old age; widow; b. Alton; Joseph Drew and Leah Jones
Daniel, d. 1819 at 17**
George A., d. 1869 at 30**
George L., d. 3/1/1917 at 71/11/22; b. Barnstead; George Hall (Barnstead) and Sallie Drew (Alton)
Jeshoba, d. 1/10/1892 at 85; heart disease; widow; b. Barnstead
Joseph, d. 1844 at 76**
Joseph, d. 1864 at 18**
Lorenzo, d. 1864 at 36**
Lydia, d. 1845 at 71**; wife of Solomon
Mary, d. 1845 at 71**; widow of Joseph
Mary Ann, d. 1852 at 37**; wife of Alfred

Mary E., d. 11/16/1910 at 48/11/6; dilitation of heart; housewife; married; b. Barnstead; John F. Holmes (Barnstead) and Sarah Jones (Barnstead)
Sally, d. 6/12/1890 at 77/10/3
Solomon, d. 1819 at 15**
Solomon, d. 1852 at 83**
Susan, d. 1824 at 21**; wife of Benjamin R.
Warren, d. 2/10/1898 at 61/6/20; organic disease of heart; farmer; married; b. Barnstead
William, d. 9/25/1889 at 83; farmer; married

HALLETT,
Fred Arnold, d. 10/2/1950 at 79/9/28 in Barnstead; b. Lexington, MA; Charles H. Hallett and Helen M. Horne

HAM,
infant, d. 3/25/1938 at --*; b. Wolfeboro; Charles L. Ham and Elizabeth Pedigo
Charles E., d. 9/27/1898 at 50/1/12; diabetes; farmer; married; b. Strafford
Cora May, d. 2/3/1941 at 58 in Rochester*; b. Dover; Albert R. Drew and Abbie I. Tilton
George W., d. 2/9/1894 at 75; paralysis; widower; b. Barrington
Mary E., d. 9/8/1910 at 80/11/10; cancer of liver; housekeeper; widow; b. Rochester; Jonathan Ham (Farmington) and Mary Coffin (Dover)

HAMEL,
Delia, d. 7/7/1934 at 86 in Laconia*
Philip, d. 1/27/1934 at 82 in Pittsfield*

HANSCAM,
Sarah, d. 1/19/1891 at 78/11; housekeeper; widow; b. Strafford; Richard Foss and Mary Daniels

HANSCOM,
Aaron W., d. 7/11/1890 at --; farmer
Gary J., d. 11/17/1998 in Barnstead; Elmer Hanscom and Jean McCloskey
Hannah, d. 1852 at 68**; widow of John
John, d. 1842 at 57**

Kenneth N., d. 8/18/1987 at 48 in Barnstead; Colin Hanscom and Alice MacDonald

Nellie, d. 12/31/1919 at 69; b. Dover; Warren Hanscom

HANSON,

Alice M., d. 10/4/1970 at 79 in Wolfeboro; at home; b. MA; Henry Pickernell and Carrie Lyons

Alvin G., d. 12/14/1942 at 73 in Concord*; b. Barnstead; Levi Hanson and Abbie Clark

Austin, d. 5/8/1974 at 70 in Concord; retired; b. MA; Sidney Hanson and Laura Nutter

Carl, d. 12/9/1939 at 11*; b. Barnstead; Vina Hanson

Carl N., d. 10/28/1980 at 74 in Concord; Sidney Hanson and Laura Nutter

Eben, d. 11/9/1917 at 76/7/18; b. Barnstead; Nathaniel Hanson (NH) and Margery Evans (NH)

Edward C., d. 10/1/1913 at 2/1/16; asphyxiation; b. Barnstead; Sidney Hanson (Barnstead) and Lura Nutter (Gilmanton)

Ellen, d. 10/2/1964 at 88 in Concord; at home; b. Hatley, PQ; John Carbe and Charlotte Kent

George G., d. 8/29/1938 at 57; b. Barnstead; Ebenezer Hanson and Martha J. Hodgdon

Levi H., d. 7/28/1928 at 92*; Nathaniel Hanson and Marjorie Evans

Lloyd G., Sr., d. 4/1/1997 at 77 in Barnstead; George Hanson and Alice Pickernell

Margaret, d. 3/9/1891 at 83; housekeeper; married; b. Barnstead

Martha J., d. 9/22/1920 at 79/5/21; b. Barnstead; Emerson Hodsdon (Barnstead) and Mary George (Barnstead)

Mary, d. 4/23/1901 at 30/3/23; Bright's disease; housekeeper; married; b. Boston

Natalie, d. 9/5/1996 at 73 in Epsom; Ralph Wyatt and Ellen Thompson

Nathaniel, d. 10/5/1891 at 84/4/26; farmer; widower

Sarah, d. 11/21/1976 at 71 in Laconia; housewife; b. NH; Frank C. Nutter and Iva Berry Nutter

Sidney E., d. 3/4/1943 at 67 in Strafford*; b. Barnstead; Levi Hanson and Abbie F. Clark

HARDWICK,

Violet C., d. 11/11/1988 at 68 in Concord; Clarence Crowder and Lillian Anderson

HARFORD,
Bertha L., d. 11/14/2000 in Ctr. Barnstead; Harold Myers and Molly McKean

HARLOW,
James P., d. 7/31/1919 at 75/11/1; b. Shelburne; Moses B. Harlow (Cornish) and Priscilla B. ----- (Shelburne)

HARNOLD,
Alfred G., d. 12/16/1927 at 11; b. Barnstead; Fred Harnold and May Powell
Frederick, d. 4/9/1918 at 33*; b. England

HARRIMAN,
Francis R., d. 8/27/1896 at --; stillborn; b. Barnstead; I. E. Harriman and Grace Sellman

HARRINGTON,
Rodney E., d. 3/4/1995 at 51 in Concord; Frank W. Harrington and Beatrice Carpenter

HARTSHORN,
George Main, d. 12/29/1988 at 81 in Barnstead; George Edgar Hartshorn and Ina Woodlawn Main

HARVEY,
Annette B., d. 4/30/1962 at 70 in Cambridge, MA; teacher; b. New York, NY; Thomas McKnight and Irene Smith
Bernice M., d. 8/2/1968 at 86 in Manchester; housewife; b. NH; Orrin Pitman and Mary Babb
Jonas H., d. 10/16/1949 at 74 in Manchester*; b. Auburn; Jonas H. Harvey and Mary Ann Nutt
Joseph H., d. 4/30/1967 at 54 in Concord; lineman; b. Warren; Henry Harvey and Nancy Houghton

HARVILLE,
Alice B., d. 8/1/1954 at 74 in Barnstead; b. Sherbrooke, Canada; Peter Betters and Charlotte Burns
Guy Lee, d. 1/31/1972 at 89 in Gossville (Epsom); farmer; b. ME

HATCH,
Mary, d. 1836 at 51**; wife of Hosea
Orilla, d. 4/1/1930 at 85; b. Patsham, NY

HATHAWAY,
Elizabeth, d. 7/30/1954 at 62 in Concord; b. Fall River, MA; ----- McDonald and Ellen Cox
Sarah Ruby, d. 7/27/1940 at 57*; b. Middleboro, MA; William Macomber and Etta Haskell

HAUSERMANN,
Olga, d. 4/30/1999 in Barnstead; Fritz Hausermann and Lina Bruder

HAWKINS,
Joseph, d. 1819 at 83**

HAWLEY,
Carrie A., d. 4/7/1897 at 37/6; meningitis; housewife; married; b. Barnstead; George Young (Barnstead) and Sarah A. Bickford (Barnstead)
George H., d. 7/11/1927 at 69; b. Bath, ME; George Hawley and Elizabeth Ferren
Ina G., d. 7/19/1942 at 64 in Pittsfield*; b. Pittsfield; Sylvester Powell and Ada Munsey

HAYES,
Annabella, d. 8/7/1944 at 82/2/19 in Barnstead; b. Strafford; Benjamin Hayes and Charlotte Hawkins
Ellen E., d. 5/23/1944 at 91/8/6 in Barnstead; b. West Milton; John W. Varney and Lydia Place
George W., d. 10/26/1957 at 70 in Barnstead; b. Milton; Charles Hayes and Nellie Parmenter
Ivory, d. 12/31/1908 at 82/6/18; organic disease of heart; farmer; married; b. Rochester; John Hayes (Rochester) and Elizabeth Plumer (Alton)
Veliria Olive, d. 4/4/1915 at 80/10/16; housewife; widow; b. Alton; Nehimiah Morrison and Mary French

HAYWARD,
Alonzo, d. 12/7/1939 at 82*

Ruth F., d. 12/15/1980 at 62 in Barnstead; Linn M. Dennett and Grace Ward

Walter Oliver, d. 9/4/1970 at 24 in Barnstead; none; b. Concord; Walter F. Hayward and Ruth F. Dennett

HAYWOOD,
William, d. 2/8/1917 at 70/3/27*; b. England; John Heywood (England) and Cecelia Burns (Ireland)

HEALD,
Laura T., d. 2/25/1936 at 77 in Barnstead; Asa E. Estes and Eunice B. Tracy

HEATH,
Janice B., d. 12/14/1992 at 66 in Concord; Arthur C. Staples and Hazel Whitney

Lewis B., d. 10/29/1927 at 10*; b. Derry; Bert Heath and Margaret Moorhouse

Margaret M., d. 1/23/1959 at 64 in Reeds Ferry

HEINDL,
Mary I., d. 6/25/1922 at 51/11/25; b. Newport, RI; John H. Irish (Newport, RI) and Mary E. McCarty (Boston, MA)

HELLUM,
James A., d. 10/7/1997 at 71 in Barnstead; Robert Hellum and Madeline -----

HENDERSON,
Elliott, d. 10/16/1986 at 92 in Barnstead; Gus A. Henderson and Mary Smith

HERBERT,
Joseph L., d. 12/12/1998 in Concord; Joseph Herbert and Mabel Baker

HERNDON,
Alton G., d. 2/23/1945 at 56 in Concord*; b. McMeuville, TN; Benjamin Herndon and America Whittock

Charles, d. 2/6/1946 at 17/4/24 in Pittsfield*; b. Winter Park, FL; Alton Herndon and Agnes Gailbrith

HERRING,
Annie R., d. 8/29/1899 at 17/4/5; neurasthenia; single; b. Farmington; James C. Herring and Addie Nutter

HEYWOOD,
Abbie M., d. 1/22/1911 at 63/2/1 in Pittsfield*; erysipelas; housewife; married; b. New Durham; John Chamberlain (Alton) and Emeline Elkins (New Durham)
Cecelia, d. 3/7/1900 at 67/6; brain disease; widow; b. Ireland
Etta, d. 4/15/1936 at 75 in Concord*; Thomas Peter and Margaret Burns
Evelyn, d. 2/16/1921 at --; b. Barnstead; Warren H. Heywood (Barnstead) and Rosalina LaDuc (Pittsfield)
Fred L., d. 12/15/1929 at 62*
Grace, d. 9/24/1937 at 64; b. Pembroke; Wyatt Knowles and Elizabeth Jon
John, d. 10/4/1890 at 76/11; married; b. England; Thomas Heywood (England) and Sarah Woolstenholm (England)
Warren Harold, d. 3/3/1952 at 62 in Barnstead; b. Barnstead; Fred Heywood and Grace Knowles

HIER,
Harry K., d. 12/9/1939 at 47*; b. Worcester, MA; Arthur A. Hier and Myrtie E. Knowles
Ruth J., d. 2/23/1961 at 65 in Exeter; b. Morrisville, VT; Ben Blake and Meta Buxton

HIGGINS,
child, d. 10/19/1928 at 0; b. Barnstead; William A. Higgins and Olive M. Corliss
Frank H., d. 5/8/1962 at 90 in Laconia; farmer; b. Eilie Mines, VT; Milo J. Higgins and Elila Hunt
Olive M., d. 5/10/1970 at 67 in Concord; shoe worker; b. Hooksett; Charles S. Corliss and Helen Tilton
Ray, d. 7/7/1944 at 12/10/12 in Canterbury*; b. Barnstead; William Higgins and Olive Corliss
Sadie E. P., d. 4/23/1923 at 44; b. Fairlee, VT; Hiram Porter and Francenia Stowell

HILDRETH,
Martha F., d. 6/26/1893 at 30/9; consumption; married; b. Barnstead; J. W. Randall and Louisa A. Twombly

HILL,
child, d. 9/21/1890 at –; Eugene Hill
Abbie, d. 8/27/1954 at 89 in Concord; b. Barnstead; Horatio Shackford and Mary Holmes
Abbie C., d. 4/29/1917 at 71*; b. Barnstead; Cyrus Chesley (Barnstead) and Abbie Chesley (Barnstead)
Abbie S., d. 11/4/1927 at 92; b. Northwood; John Hill and Fannie Hall
Alexis, d. 9/6/1902 at 64/8; tuberculosis of lung; farmer; b. Strafford; John Hill and Betsey Foss
Allie M., d. 2/5/1932 at 61*; b. Northwood; Alfred Hill and Mary Adams
Charles, d. 8/11/1902 at 76; farmer; widower
Clarissa, d. 4/30/1895 at 73; cirrhosis of liver; housewife; married; b. Barnstead; Solomon Munsey
George D., d. 1871 at 53**
Herbert M., d. 3/16/1956 at 94 in Concord; b. Barnstead; Alexis A. Hill and Abbie Chesley
James W., Jr., d. 2/19/1921 at 0/2/19*; b. Deerfield; James W. Hill (Strafford) and Margaret Gray (Barnstead)
John, d. 1845 at 59**
Joseph (Corp.), d. 1864 at 29**; "a soldier wounded at Cold Harbor"
Joseph, d. 11/9/1889 at 78/0/25; farmer; widower; b. Barnstead
Joseph, d. 5/17/1906 at 78/5; Bright's disease; farmer; widower; b. Gloucester, MA
Margaret L., d. 12/17/1941 at 52 in Wolfeboro*; b. Barnstead; Oris Gray and Hattie Hannaford
Mary M., d. 4/11/1977 at 50 in Concord; police woman - crossing guard; b. NH; Edward A. Gray and Ada M. Lord
Mercedas May, d. 12/12/1967 at 86 in Concord; b. Middleton; Alonzo Dame and Etta French
Raymond, d. 4/12/1974 at 79; b. NH; Sylvester Hill
Sally, d. 1857 at 62**; widow of John
Sally, d. 1867 at 72**; wife of Robert S.
Samuel, d. 1872 at 96**
Warren B., d. 5/28/1931 at 84*; b. Barnstead

HILLSGROVE,
Albert, d. 5/28/1904 at 64/3/21; organic disease of heart; married; b. Portsmouth; James Hillsgrove (Kuax, ME) and Sarah A. Night (Portland, ME)
Casper E., d. 12/24/1987 at 72 in Concord; J. Walter Hillsgrove and Myrtie O. Day
Charles F., d. 2/5/1962 at 85 in Concord; weaver; b. Wilmot; Joseph Hillsgrove and Lydia Webster
Doris K., d. 6/14/1986 at 68 in Concord; George Bixby and Margaret F. Smith
Fannie P., d. 4/15/1937 at 60; b. Barnstead; Joshua C. Pickering and Ellen M. Grace
George E., d. 3/21/1927 at 57*; Joseph M. Hillsgrove and Lydia Webster
Grace A., d. 4/29/1947 at 75/1/17 in Pittsfield*; b. Barnstead; Joshua Pickering and Ellen Grace
Joseph M., d. 10/2/1905 at 61/6; general paralysis; farmer; married; b. Portsmouth; J. H. Hillsgrove (England) and Sarah Knights (Portsmouth)
Leon E., d. 3/18/1946 at 45/9/11 in Concord*; b. Barnstead; George E. Hillsgrove and Grace Pickering
Lydia M., d. 6/2/1919 at 70/0/2*; b. Strafford; Joseph Webster (Enfield) and Sarah Ann Otis (Strafford)
Myrtie Ola, d. 4/6/1952 at 66 in Wolfeboro*; b. Northwood; Henry Day and Elizabeth Randall
Richard G., d. 3/23/1952 at 8 in Concord*; b. Pittsfield; Frank Hillsgrove and Virginia Boyd

HOBBS,
Betsy, d. 5/30/1916 at 77/6/3; widow; b. Barnstead; Charles Hodgdon (Barnstead) and Mirian York (Barnstead)

HODGDON,
Abigail, d. 1830 at 83**; widow of Charles
Addie O., d. 7/28/1899 at 55; housewife; married; b. Barnstead; William Pierce
Albert E., d. 1847 at 25**
Annie M., d. 5/13/1921 at 86/1/5*; b. Barrington; Elias Varney (Barrington) and Susan Clark (Durham)
Benjamin, Esq., d. 1849 at 82**
Betsey, d. 1825 at 42**; wife of Charles, Jr.

C. A., d. 6/12/1907 at 73/10/5; organic disease of heart; farmer; widower; b. Barnstead; T. E. Hodgdon (Barnstead) and Mary E. George (Barnstead)
Charles, d. 1817 at 75**
Charles, Jr., d. 1835 at 61**
Charles, Jr., d. 1853 at 89**
Charles, Jr., d. 1863 at 64**
Charles J., d. 1832 at 26**
Hannah, d. 1790 at 57**; wife of Charles
John, d. 1842 at 23**
Lyman, d. 1836 at 23**
Mary, d. 1851 at 24**; wife of William A.
Moses, d. 1861 at 83**
Mrs. Moses, d. 1863 at 91**
Polly, d. 1858 at 82**; widow of Benjamin, Esq.
Temperance, d. 1842 at 85**; widow of Charles, Jr.
Thomas P., d. 1860 at 60**
Timothy Emerson, d. 1864 at 56**

HOEY,
Henry M., d. 12/15/1933 at 47; b. Ireland; James Hoey and ----- Rachel ("registered ward, Center Barnstead")

HOGENCAMP,
Blanche P., d. 5/20/1982 at 88 in Concord; Charles Parsons and Electa Ricker
Grace L., d. 12/24/1947 at 67/3/20 in Boston, MA*; Frank Chamberlain and Sophia Chamberlain
Harry, d. 1/27/1944 at 68/3/29 in Franklin, MA*; b. Paterson, NJ; Martin Hogencamp and Margaret J. Zabriefkie
James C., d. 4/29/1939 at --*
Jennie R., d. 10/20/1952 at 79 in Center Harbor*; b. Philadelphia, PA; Charles R. Cornell and Caroline Rhodes
W. A., d. 10/8/1914 at 31/3/24; tuberculosis; farmer; married; b. Patterson, NJ; M. Hogencamp (NJ) and M. Zabriskia (NJ)
William R., d. 5/5/1933 at 0/0/5*; b. Lewiston, ME; William B. Hogencamp and Blanche Parsons

HOITT,
Benjamin, d. 1865 at 71**

Betsy, d. 12/4/1894 at 81/6/14; ulcer in the intestines; widow; b. Barnstead; Ebenezer Pitman and Abigail Montgomery

Fannie P., d. 12/27/1913 at 84/7/7; heart; widow; b. Barnstead; James Woodhouse

John S., d. 1/13/1905 at 83/11/23; organic disease of heart; manufacturer; married; b. Barnstead; Benjamin Hoitt (Hampstead) and Mehitable Babson (Dunbarton)

Lois, d. 1837 at 39**; wife of Col. James

Martha Ella, d. 10/13/1918 at 84/9/18; b. Saco, ME; Rufus Seavey (ME)

Mehitable, d. 1853 at 60**; wife of Benjamin

Thomas L., d. 1/31/1918 at 90/10/1; b. Barnstead

William A., d. 1858 at 27**

HOLDEN,
Frank Leslie, d. 8/11/1986 at 53 in Manchester; Willie J. Holden and Louis Chase

HOLLIS,
Herbert H., d. 9/8/1909 at 75/9/7; accidental burning; retired; widower; b. Lynn, MA; David Hollis (ME) and Sarah Newhall (Lynn, MA)

HOLMBERG,
Lucy Ethel, d. 8/22/1973 at 78 in Concord; none; b. Midville, NS; Oben Arenburg and Ethel Okile

HOLMES,
Azariah, d. 1869 at 58**

Barbara R., d. 12/5/1925 at 0/0/2; b. Concord; Harry F. Holmes and Bertha Smith

Bertha N., d. 8/27/1978 at 85 in Concord; homemaker; b. NH; Herbert Smith and Edith Nutter

Charles A., d. 10/17/1953 at 93 in Concord; b. Barnstead; John Holmes and Sarah Jones

Francis S., d. 11/16/1905 at 45/7/23; cancer; housewife; married; b. Farmington; Brewster Hayes (Farmington) and Sarah Berry (Strafford)

Frank J., d. 3/13/1963 at 96 in Barnstead; farmer; b. Barnstead; John F. Holmes and Sarah Jones

Harriett S., d. 10/7/1921 at 50/10/9*; b. NB; Charles McKenley (NB) and Louise Clark (NB)
John, d. 1851 at 62**
John F., d. 11/7/1909 at 72/4/7; cystitis; farmer; married; b. Barnstead; John Holmes (Strafford) and Priscilla Fisher (Strafford)
Lenora J., d. 9/4/1896 at 27/7/8; gastritis; nurse; single; b. Barnstead; John F. Holmes and Sarah Jones
Nellie F., d. 1/20/1938 at 90; b. Barnstead; Jonathan Welch and Nancy Durgin
Nellie F., d. 3/18/1950 at 83/3/9 in Center Harbor*; b. Bridgewater, MA; Jonathan Hall and Abbie Dunbar
Pearl E., d. 3/3/1995 at 65 in Barnstead; Donald E. McEachern and Sara G. McIntire
Sarah A., d. 1/26/1933 at 92; b. Barnstead; Ebenezer Jones and Hannah Foss
William E., d. 1/30/1980 at 65 in Concord; Frank J. Holmes and Hadie McKinley

HOPPS,
Barbara A., d. 7/1/1987 at 62 in Concord; John Peabody and Eva Nichols
Elwin H., Jr., d. 7/1/1999 in Barnstead; Elwin Hopps, Sr. and Barbara Peabody

HORNE,
Izah N., d. 4/20/1936 at 62 in Barnstead; Nathaniel Horne

HOTCHKISS,
Norton Royce, d. 1/11/1978 at 78 in Concord; silversmith; b. CT; Norton R. Hotchkiss, Sr. and Lucinda E. Belk

HOUK,
Rudolph J., III, d. 9/4/1999 in Barnstead; Rudolph Houk, II and Sally Horner

HOULE,
Delia, d. 8/16/1998 in Laconia; Napoleon Duhaime and Delias Brochu

HOWE,
Arthur J., d. 9/9/1942 at 74 in Penacook*; b. Barnstead; James M. Howe and Emma Clark
Cora F., d. 5/7/1960 at 79 in Boscawen; shoeworker; widow; b. Barnstead; Joseph A. Davis and Susan Pendergast
Warren H., d. 2/28/1951 at 44/3/3 in Pittsfield*; b. Gilmanton; Carl D. Howe and Grace Foss

HOYT,
Alonzo, d. 3/23/1938 at 91; b. Rochester

HUBBARD,
Mary Lou, d. 9/5/1991 at 53 in Barnstead; George S. Rust and Pauline G. Glover

HUGHES,
Mary E., d. 6/20/1988 at 71 in Concord; Denis McGillicuddy and Mary Briely

HUMPHREY,
William H., d. 9/5/1913 at 0/2/7; cholera infantum; b. Concord; William H. Humphy (sic) (H'dn, MA) and Florence Dissel (Trenton, NJ)

HUNT,
Agusta Belle, d. 7/16/1954 at 77 in Manchester; b. Alton; Sylvester B. Huckins and Georgianna L. Berry
Emma, d. 7/16/1905 at 36/5/16; tumor of bowels; married; b. Barnstead; Joseph Marsh (Derry) and Margery Stone (Charlotte T'n)
Frank S. K., d. 1/11/1919 at 25/9/27*; b. Nelson, BC; Frederick T. Hunt (England) and Ora V. Caverly (Strafford)
Fred T., d. 11/20/1923 at 56; b. England; Charles Hunt
John S., d. 6/11/1917 at 63/3/6; b. Lynn, MA; John R. Hunt (Halifax, NS) and Lucy P. Gage (Malden, MA)

HUNTEE,
Charles N., d. 1/5/1952 at 77 in Concord; b. Concord; William Huntee and Louella Manter

HUNTRESS,
Frank, d. 7/23/1914 at 65/9/23; farmer; single; b. Laconia; Noah Huntress and Salley Gowan
Guy F., d. 8/16/1933 at 53*; b. Barnstead; Henry O. Huntress and Julie Pierce
Henry O., d. 4/3/1897 at 56/11/11; farmer; married; b. Barnstead; Noah Huntress and Sally Gowen
John W., d. 5/7/1921 at 70/3/6; b. Barnstead; Noah C. Huntress and Sally Gowen (North Berwick)
Sally, d. 3/5/1894 at 79/10; senile gangrene; housewife; widow; b. Berwick, ME; Isaac Gowan and Mercy Chick

HURD,
Asa, d. 3/26/1918 at 95/5/19; b. Gilford; Ebenezer Hurd and Nancy Whitehouse
Ida, d. 3/1/1891 at --; gastritis; housework; single; b. Barnstead; Asa C. Hurd (Barnstead) (1892, see following entry)
Ida, d. 6/3/1891 at 30/0/22; housekeeper; single; b. Barnstead; Asa C. Hurd (Wolfeboro) and Mary J. Goodwin (Barnstead) (see preceding entry)
Mary H., d. 12/24/1909 at 81/10/3; fracture of femur; housewife; married; b. Gilmanton; David Goodwin and Abigail Chesley
Sophia J., d. 2/8/1910 at 67/1/13; cancer of stomach; widow; b. Strafford; Benjamin T. Foss (Strafford) and Sophia Jones (Strafford)

HUSE,
Addie Mary, d. 2/5/1940 at 73; b. Strafford; Charles Montgomery and Mary Locke
Elizabeth, d. 4/20/1911 at 94/7/28; senile decay; widow; b. Francestown; ----- Scoby and Jane E. Dickey
Jennie M., d. 11/6/1906 at 62/11/14; organic disease of heart; school teacher; single; b. Lowell, MA; Thomas M. Huse (VT) and Elizabeth Scoby (Francestown)

HUSSEY,
Stephen, d. 1857 at 79**

HUTCHINS,
Almira E., d. 9/29/1939 at 81*; b. Pittsfield; Lyman Parsons and Elizabeth King

HYDE,
Edith D., d. 10/11/1973 at 91 in Concord; housewife; b. Dover; Alvin P. Dutton and Ella J. Wentworth

HYMAN,
Robert L., d. 7/7/1995 at 77 in Manchester; David Hyman and Ida Brown

INGERSOLL,
Mary E., d. 1/27/1927 at 72*

INGERSON,
Dorothy L., d. 11/2/1993 at 68 in Concord; John William Stowers and Ollie Isobel Leffel
Howard R., d. 11/20/1979 at 60 in Concord; Ernest Ingerson and Minnie Banfill

JACOBS,
Albert J., d. 10/28/1917 at 70/11/4*; b. Barnstead; Daniel Jacobs (Barnstead) and Dorothy Tuttle (Barnstead)
Alfred, d. 11/5/1911 at 89/10/6; senile decay; farmer; widower; b. Barnstead; Jonathan Jacobs and Sarah Hodgdon
Betsey, d. 1868 at 81**; wife of David Wiggins
Coran M., d. 7/8/1928 at 61; b. Barnstead; David M. Jacobs and Mary Jacobs
Daniel, d. 1833 at 74**
David, d. 1804 at 48**
David Wiggins, d. 1872 at 81**
H. Mighill, d. 12/4/1910 at 17/4; pneumonia; shoemaker; single; b. Barnstead; Coran M. Jacobs (Barnstead) and Lettie Hillsgrove (Danbury)
John, d. 1833 at 55**
Lura B., d. 8/--/1932 (date "undecided by State") at 30*; b. Barnstead; Coran M. Jacobs and Lettie A. Hillsgrove
Margaret, d. 1819 at 57**; wife of Daniel
Mary E., d. 12/24/1899 at 68/0/16; pneumonia; housekeeper; widow; b. Barnstead; David Young
Molly, d. 1848 at 92**; widow of David
Samuel, d. 1831 at 43**
Sarah, d. 1823 at 21**; wife of Isaac

JAEGER,
Etta M., d. 11/22/1979 at 83 in Epsom; Willard C. Chase and Emelia Breed
William Wilson, d. 3/2/1974 at 75 in Manchester; machinist; b. ME; Robert Carl Jaeger and Louise Hoyt

JAMES,
Ellen F., d. 8/5/1938 at 88; b. Iowa; Oliver James and Mary Newhall
John, d. 2/27/1888 at 77/1/19; farmer; widower; b. Lebanon, ME

JENISCH,
child, d. 7/1/1941 at 0 in Concord*; b. Concord; William Jenisch and Marion Park
Alois, d. 10/4/1985 at 68 in Concord; Alois Jenisch and Matilda Packer
Alois F., d. 9/10/1966 at 84 in Pittsfield; weaver; b. Austria; Franz Jenisch and Cecilia Hager
Barbara E., d. 9/21/1980 at 55 in Concord; Harold Turner and Elsie Salisbury
Cora E., d. 2/19/1997 at 85 in Concord; Henry G. Clough and Edith E. Flagg
Frank, d. 5/12/1952 at 59 in Barnstead; b. Austria; Franz Jenisch and Cecelia -----
Frederick K., d. 2/3/1984 at 72 in Manchester; Alois Jenish and Metilda Packel
Mathilda, d. 12/5/1949 at 54 in Concord*; b. Hoboken, NJ; Louis Schunk and Mathilda Heiges
Matilda P., d. 3/30/1973 at 87 in Pittsfield; at home; b. Austria; Johann Pachl and ----- Suess
Richard R., d. 10/17/1999 in Barnstead; Alois Jenisch and Matilda Packer

JENKINS,
unnamed child, d. 2/2/1925 at --; b. Barnstead; John J. Jenkins and Marion Clapp
unnamed child, d. 2/2/1925 at --; b. Barnstead; John J. Jenkins and Marion Clapp
Abra H., d. 12/25/1890 at 83/4/20; housework; widow
Albert S., d. 5/6/1936 at 58 in Barnstead; George W. Jenkins and Victoria Clark

Carroll E., d. 6/30/1976 at 84 in Manchester; B&M railroad; b. NH; Erskine Jenkins and Clara Carter

Charles Franklin, d. 4/12/1949 at 67/8/8 in Barnstead; b. Barnstead; Joseph E. Jenkins and Clara A. Carter

Charles W., d. 6/28/1945 at 76/3/1 in Barnstead; b. Barnstead; John B. Jenkins and Agusta Huntress

Clara Anna, d. 11/27/1947 at 88/1/1 in Barnstead; b. Loudon; Clark Carter and Eunice Elliott

Clara E., d. 12/18/1936 at 72 in Barnstead; Peleg Perkins and Sarah E. Dow

Doris, d. 2/3/1903 at 0/6/2; bronchitis; b. Barnstead; Charles W. Jenkins (Barnstead) and Lilla Foss (Gilmanton)

Doris C., d. 12/7/1912 at 1/0/16; congestion of brain; b. Barnstead; Ernest C. Jenkins (Barnstead) and Bertha Brown (Gilmanton)

Edwin K., d. 2/15/1927 at --*; b. Barnstead; George W. Jenkins and Victoria Clark

Elizabeth M., d. 3/2/1916 at 65/8/22; housewife; married; b. Nashua; John Fife and Sarah Pollard

Elma Ida, d. 8/28/1936 at 57 in Barnstead; William Henry Shackford and Augusta M. Smart

Elvira R., d. 4/19/1910 at 73/1/18; pneumonia; housewife; widow; b. Ashburnham; Jacob Wilker (Ashburnham) and Emma Richardson

Emma A., d. 5/21/1935 at 67; b. Penacook; John H. Jenkins and Elvie R. Wilker

Ernest C., d. 4/24/1958 at 69 in Concord

Forrest Lee, d. 1/17/1944 at 83/5/18 in Laconia*; b. Barnstead; William A. Jenkins and Maria G. Berry

George F., d. 2/16/1943 at 81 in Laconia*; b. Barnstead; John W. Jenkins and Mary A. Ayers

George William, d. 9/14/1916 at 77/2/17; farmer; married; b. Barnstead; Stephen Jenkins (Barnstead) and Sarah Joy (New Durham)

Hannah, d. 7/3/1900 at 57/6; meningitis; housewife; married; b. Barnstead; Noble Sackett and Roxby Jacobs

John H., d. 3/14/1908 at 75/5/19; organic disease of heart; farmer; married; b. Barnstead; William Jenkins and Abra Hanscom

John J., d. 3/21/1943 at 70 in Wolfeboro*; b. Barnstead; John H. Jenkins and Elvira Wilkes

John R., d. 1869 at 27**

John W., d. 11/7/1905 at 79/11/; Bright's disease; farmer; widower; b. Barnstead; Joseph Jenkins (Lee) and ----- Walker (Barnstead)

Joseph E., d. 1/20/1927 at 66; b. Barnstead; Charles F. Jenkins and Lucy Young

Leon M., d. 9/2/1920 at 19/2/26*; b. Barnstead; Harry L. Jenkins (Barnstead) and Ora M. Tower (Boston, MA)

Liller D., d. 10/16/1957 at 87 in Barnstead; b. Gilmanton; William B. Foss and Jerusiah Pettingill

Lyman, d. 3/2/1935 at 89; b. Barnstead; Joseph Jenkins and Mary A. Shackford

Margaret A., d. 2/22/1942 at 80 in Payson, IL*; b. Barnstead; James L. Foss and Eliza J. Blake

Marion S., d. 3/15/1928 at 33; b. Auburndale, MA; Frederick H. Clapp and Charlotte J. Sumner

Mary Ann, d. 1/16/1931 at 78; b. Barnstead; Samuel C. Shakford and ----- Foss

Mary E., d. 10/9/1903 at 24/8/4; burn of trunk; domestic; married; b. Lynn, MA; Henry Maxfield and Harriet L. Mullen

Mary H., d. 11/9/1901 at 48/8/16; heart disease; housewife; married; John Reynolds and Cynthia Busiel

Miandia, d. 4/7/1918 at 87/0/5; b. Barnstead; Stephen Jenkins (Barnstead) and Sally Joy (New Durham)

Nancy, d. 1833 at 40**; wife of Joseph

Nina H., d. 8/20/1901 at 0/7/20; enteritis; b. Barnstead; John J. Jenkins (Barnstead) and Edith Maxfield (Lynn, MA)

Russell, d. 3/3/1913 at 0/11/14; bronchitis; b. Barnstead; Charles W. Jenkins (Barnstead) and Lilla B. Foss (Gilmanton)

Urban T., d. 5/19/1904 at 1/10/9; enteritis; b. Barnstead; Erskine Jenkins (Barnstead) and Clara Carter (Loudon)

Victoria, d. 12/12/1930 at 85*; b. Barnstead

William A., d. 9/11/1948 at 81/5/20 in Leominster, MA*; b. Barnstead; John H. Jenkins and Elvira Wilker

JENNESS,
Susan, d. 3/24/1897 at 86/9/11; old age; housework; b. Madbury; Jacob Canney (Madbury) and Sarah Jenness (Rochester)

JENNINGS,
Marie C., d. 6/1/1997 at 59 in Barnstead; Harry Rossi and Mary Defuria

JEWELL,
Margaret L., d. 6/28/1983 at 52 in Portsmouth; Clarence Rollins and Blanche Rollins
Patricia L., d. 5/1/1991 at 55 in Barnstead; Thomas Bledsoe and Pearl Young

JEWETT,
Jeremiah (Dr.), d. 1836 at 79**

JOHNSON,
Barbara A., d. 7/21/1969 at 55 in No. Barnstead; clerk; Charles P. LaViska and Katherine A. Gidney
Gordon L., d. 9/23/1998 in Concord; Merton Johnson and Mabelle Loring
Lucy E., d. 2/10/1990 at 85 in Wolfeboro; Frank L. Norton and Lucy R. -----
Marion C., d. 2/9/1997 at 62 in Concord; Gerald Larose and Magdeline Bilicki
Minnie M., d. 11/3/1947 at 68/10/2 in Barnstead
Ralph M., d. 10/19/1989 at 62 in Ctr. Barnstead; A. Alfred Johnson and Anna Berg

JONES,
Caroline D., d. 5/8/1936 at 90 in Manchester*; Edward Warren and ----- Towne
E. Frank, d. 3/12/1889 at 45/7/7; farmer; married; b. Barnstead; Ebenezer Jones (Durham) and Hannah Foss (Strafford)
Ebenezer, d. 10/16/1891 at 89/3/26; farmer; married
Goodwin C., d. 11/14/1904 at 64/10/14; probably heart disease; RR engineer; married; b. Thornton Ferry; Caleb Jones
Hannah H., d. 9/18/1900 at 88/3; apoplexy; housekeeper; widow; b. Strafford; Robert Foss and Hannah Hill
Harwood D., d. 10/21/1987 at 65 in Concord; Ernest Jones and Eva Smith
James A., d. 1/28/1956 at 27 in Laconia; b. Burlington, VT; James A. Jones and ----- Berbo

John, Sr., d. 5/20/1964 at 80 in Concord; auto mechanic; b.
   Brooklyn, NY; Thomas Jones and Catherine Petry
Jonathan P., d. 12/24/1921 at 88/8/11; b. Pittsfield; Jonathan P.
   Jones (Seabrook)
Martha Elizabeth, d. 2/22/1993 at 89 in Concord; Thomas Palmer
   and Bessie Weatherwax
Rebecca V., d. 4/22/1903 at 57/8; ovarian tumor; domestic;
   married; b. Barnstead; Joel Clark (Barnstead) and Sophronia
   Cille (Barnstead)
Stephen S., d. 12/19/1904 at 79/6/4; paralysis; farmer; widower; b.
   Strafford; Stephen Jones (Strafford) and Lois Foye (Strafford)

JORE,
David S., d. 7/20/2000 in Concord; Daniel Jore and Mary Sherack

JUDKINS,
Abigail, d. 1848 at 75**; widow of John
John, d. 1839 at 60**

KAIME,
Dodivah, d. 1866 at 62**
Frances, d. 11/27/1902 at 54/3/4; cancer; housewife; married; b.
   Gilmanton; William Swain (Gilmanton) and Mary Chamberlain
   (Gilmanton)
Hannah, d. 1795 at 29**; wife of James G.
James G., d. 1805 at 40**
Joanna, d. 1834 at 42**; wife of John
John K., d. 1846 at 30**
Joseph F., d. 1/5/1907 at 72/1/29; prostatris; farmer; married; b.
   Barnstead; Samuel Kaime (Madbury) and Nancy Nutter (Lee)
Permelia, d. 1851 at 49**; second wife of John
S. Frank, d. 10/8/1924 at 47; Joseph Kaime and Francis Swain

KAINE,
James, d. 2/2/1926 at 83

KAMINSKI,
Donald J., d. 6/18/1990 at 54 in Barnstead; Joseph Kaminski and
   Mary Stakiewicz

KANIA,
Lila M., d. 10/13/1981 at 55 in Portsmouth; Robert A. Compston and Georgina -----

KEARNS,
Addie M., d. 12/14/1948 at 82/4/19 in Barnstead; b. Barnstead; Joseph Osborne and Mary Griffin
Earl, d. 5/16/1899 at --; stillborn; b. Barnstead; Timothy Kearns and Addie Osborne
Timothy L., d. 3/11/1943 at 84 in Barnstead; b. Milwaukee, WI; Frederick Kearns and Mary E. Burns

KEEFE,
Thomas Carroll, d. 2/15/1972 at 67 in Ctr. Barnstead; salesman; b. MA; Thomas M. Keefe and Ellen Carroll

KEENE,
son, d. 12/30/1954 at 38 hrs., 25 min. in Concord; b. Concord; Richard Keene and Roberta Cotton
daughter, d. 12/30/1954 at 39 hrs., 44 min. in Concord; b. Concord; Richard Keene and Roberta Cotton
Orin Marcey, d. 7/25/1952 at 71 in Barnstead; b. Marlboro, MA; Edward Keene and Carrie Ricker

KELLEY [see Kelly],
Charles H., d. 2/18/1958 at 55 in Barnstead
Emma F., d. 4/20/1948 at 80/11/23 in Wolfeboro*; b. Portsmouth; William Harmon
Everett B., d. 8/16/1950 at 82 in Concord*; b. NH; Charles W. Kelley and Sarah Horne
Fern L., d. 4/24/1959 at 59 in Concord
Joseph L., d. 10/18/1925 at 67; b. NH; Joseph Kelley and Mary Leonard
Myra E., d. 6/6/1930 at 64*; b. Dorchester; ----- Colburn
Thelma M., d. 6/5/1925 at 0/3; b. Barnstead; Charles H. Kelley and Bessie Gray
Velna M., d. 6/17/1925 at 0/3; b. Barnstead; Charles H. Kelley and Bessie Gray
Virginia H., d. 8/30/1994 at 89 in Concord; Herbert Franklin Simonds and Charlotte Welch

KELLY [see Kelley],
Frank C., d. 10/19/1926 at 29; b. Barnstead; Joseph L. Kelley and Myra Colburn

KELSEY,
May W., d. 6/13/1922 at 53/10/6; b. Farmington, IA; John L. Woodhouse (Barnstead) and Lydia Rand (Barnstead)

KENISCH [see Knirsch, Kuirsch],
Helda, d. 8/3/1912 at 0/5/3; marasmus; b. Barnstead; Conrad Kenisch (Austria) and Mathilda Pachl (Austria)

KENISON,
Annie, d. 10/16/1928 at 80; b. Barnstead; Samuel Clark and Mercy Foss
Blanche Cynthia, d. 2/20/1955 at 80 in Concord; b. NH; Daniel Tuttle and Achsah Willey
Charles A., d. 5/5/1969 at 82 in Rochester; painter; b. NH; Joseph C. Kenison and Jennie A. Varney
Charles N., d. 11/3/1921 at 70/9/18*
Doris B., d. 10/31/1897 at 0/7/16; organic disease of heart; b. Barnstead; Herbert Kenison (Barnstead) and Blanche Tuttle (Barnstead)
Fred R., d. 10/2/1918 at 23/3/18; b. Sweden; Herbert C. Kenison (Barnstead) and Blanche C. Tuttle (Barnstead)
Hannah, d. 9/1/1907 at 95/10/2; old age; none; widow; b. Epsom; Timothy Blake (at sea) and Sally Emerson (Epsom)
Herbert C., d. 4/11/1947 at 72/7/9 in Concord*; b. Barnstead; Owen Kenison and Lydia A. Clark
John C., d. 3/20/1891 at 45/4; shoemaker; married; b. Pittsfield; Newell B. Kenison and Martha Sargent
Newell B., d. 4/29/1888 at 75/11; shoemaker; widower; b. Pittsfield; Lemuel Kenison and Loisa Chesley
Owen M., d. 6/28/1929 at 81; b. Barnstead; John O. Kenison and Hannah P. Blake

KENISTON,
Adonijah, d. 1834 at 43**
Betsy, d. 12/12/1892 at 80/10; valvular affection; housewife; married; b. Barnstead; Solomon Pendergast (Durham) and Rebecca Sherburn (Strafford)

Furber, d. 2/2/1894 at 84/0/18; cystitis; farmer; widower; b. Newington; John Keniston (Newington) and Lydia Furber (Newington)

Grace A., d. 10/15/1968 at 71 in Concord; stitcher; b. NH; John W. Watson and Lucinda G. Meeks

John, d. 1825 at 21**

John O., d. 8/2/1894 at 81/10/19; mechanic; married; b. Barnstead; Adonijah Keniston and Olive Jacobs

Jonathan, d. 1854 at 83**

Olive, d. 1872 at 79**; widow of Adonijah

Sally, d. 1861 at 82**; widow of Jonathan

KENNEY,
Isaac, d. 1857 at 38**

KEYSER,
Ralph H., d. 7/5/1982 at 65 in Concord; Budd Keyser and Mabel Keniston

KIDDER,
Alonzo Weston, d. 1/2/1950 at 81 in Grasmere; b. Grasmere; Agustus Kidder and Joseph Koskey

Bernice Eva, d. 12/27/1976 at 82 in Ctr. Barnstead; housewife; b. NH; Luther Carswell and Eva Titus

Eva Jane, d. 11/24/1942 at 75 in Manchester*

Harold E., d. 2/10/1980 at 86 in Ctr. Barnstead; Alonzo W. Kidder and Myrtie J. Cleveland

John Henry, d. 11/27/1994 at 64 in Concord; Harold E. Kidder and Bernice Carswell

Kenneth C., Sr., d. 4/9/1990 at 56 in Barnstead; Harold Kidder and E. Bernice Carswell

Roger W., d. 3/5/1949 at 20 in Okinawa Shrine; b. Manchester; Harold E. Kidder and Bernice Carswell

Wilbur A., d. 8/29/1993 at 67 in Concord; Harold Kidder and Bernice Carswell

KIMBALL,
Edward Curtis, II, d. 6/8/1996 at 44 in Concord; Edward C. Kimball, I and Rita Canfield

Helen M., d. 3/19/1980 at 84 in Epsom; Seth A. Kimball and Mary Ellen Shaw

KING,
Gladys L., d. 10/19/1976 at 89 in Concord; housewife; b. Canada; Charles A. Long and Maria M. Milner
John, d. 10/6/1969 at 86 in Concord; rural mail carrier; b. NY; Alexander King and Cynthia Long
June E., d. 4/25/1966 at 47 in Allenstown; electronics; b. Saugus, MA; Robert C. King and Helen -----

KLEIN,
Michael A., d. 10/16/1999 in Rochester; Thomas Klein and Janet Hart

KNIRSCH [see Kenisch, Kuirsch],
Carl F., d. 9/2/1993 at 84 in Concord; Konrad Knirsch and Matilda Pelzer
Konrad, d. 1/7/1971 at 88 in Concord; weaver; b. Austria; Johann Knirsch and Alosie Heger
Reinhold Baylia, d. 8/21/1992 at 66 in Barnstead; Konrad Knirsch and Emma Penka

KNOWLES,
Etta O., d. 12/10/1909 at 62/3/24; organic disease of heart; housekeeper; divorced; b. Barnstead; Noah C. Huntress and Salley Gowen (Berwick, ME)
George Frank, d. 11/20/1918 at 70/9/25; b. Barnstead; Samuel Knowles (Chichester) and Olive Bunker (Barnstead)
John H., d. 1/22/1914 at 73/11/22; heart; farmer; married; b. Epsom; S. B. Knowles (Epsom) and Olive S. Bunker (Barnstead)
Olive, d. 9/23/1890 at 74; widow
Russell, d. 10/29/1971 at 78 in Goffstown; mechanic; b. NH; George Knowles and Elizabeth Blood

KNOWLTON,
Anne E., d. 2/1/1980 at 28 in Laconia; Richard Fitzpatrick and Marion -----

KNOX,
Alice, d. 9/10/1989 at 91 in Concord; Huntlie Gordon and Elvia Knapp

KRAFT,
Elizabeth T., d. 8/13/1995 at 75 in Concord; Owen F. Donovan and Anna C. Rooney
John J., d. 11/3/1995 at 75 in Barnstead; William Kraft and Louise Brooker

KRAUSE,
child, d. 8/14/1957 at 1 hr., 50 min. in Concord; b. Concord; George Krause and Emelyn Ayer
George R., d. 9/16/1953 at 63 in Concord; b. Germany; Reinhold Krause and Emma Wasche

KRYSTYNIAK,
Catherine B., d. 7/25/1959 at 53 in Barnstead
Felix, d. 7/25/1959 at – in Barnstead

KUHAR,
Michael, d. 8/22/1982 at 65 in Barnstead; John C. Kuhar, Sr. and Mary Hanuscsak

KUIRSCH [see Kenisch, Knirsch],
Emma, d. 6/7/1947 at 56/11/9 in Barnstead; b. Austria; Franz Penka

KYLE,
William J., d. 10/15/1964 at 80 in Concord; elevator constructor; b. Glasgow, Scotland; James Kyle and Rose Cameron

LABONTE,
Antonio Rodrick, d. 8/17/1975 at 69 in Concord; proprietor; b. NH; George Labonte and Alexina Cyr

LABRECQUE,
Albert R., d. 5/22/1989 at 69 in Manchester; Arthur Labrecque and Rosina Desmarais
Pauline, d. 12/26/1983 at 58 in Ctr. Barnstead; Frank Salice and Delphine Pare
Roland V., d. 4/13/2000 in Rochester; Arthur Labrecque and Rosina Desmarais

LAKE,
Marlyne W., d. 11/6/1979 at 52 in Concord; William Waddell and Edith Kane

LAKEMAN,
Carleton H., d. 11/24/1945 at 61/9/2 in Wolfeboro*; b. Jonesport, ME; Falmer Lakeman and Harriett A. Glidden
Lattie A., d. 7/10/1945 at 66/11/6 in Barnstead; b. Clementsport, NS; William H. MacFadden and Minnie L. Fiendel

LAMPER,
Maude Elizabeth, d. 6/13/1987 at 79 in Ossipee; William Malsbury and Minnie Bickford

LANDRY,
Leo J., d. 1/11/1999 in Barnstead; Leo Landry and Laura Jean
Leon N., d. 8/14/1996 at 81 in Barnstead; Major Landry and Helen Hachez

LANE,
Lyntha M., d. 10/15/1930 at 98*
Mary K., d. 10/2/1980 at 68 in Portsmouth; George Locke and Mabel Kelley

LANGLEY,
Abigail, d. 1852 at 69**; wife of Henry
Eliza J., d. 1/31/1921 at 68/8/27; b. Bridgton, NS; Andrew Chums (Bridgton, NS)
James, d. 1848 at 47**
Mary, d. 1844 at 79**; wife of Joseph
Samuel N., d. 1/8/1889 at 72/1/30; farmer; married; b. Barnstead; Henry Langley (Strafford) and Abigail Tasker
Susan, d. 1866 at 74**; widow of James

LANK,
Clinton L., d. 10/17/1947 at 43/0/5 in Barnstead; b. Campobello, NB; Gordon Arthur and Sarah Brown
Howard John, d. 3/16/1991 at 64 in Barnstead; Clinton L. Lank and Ruth O. Butman

LANZEY,
Alvinia S., d. 11/17/1935 at 62; b. NS

LAPALME,
Mary E., d. 6/27/1903 at 21/7; menorrhagia; single

LAPRISE,
Julia K., d. 7/12/1999 in Ctr. Barnstead; William Karcher and Martha Wilfert

LARY,
Alfred R., d. 5/24/1954 at 70 in Barnstead; b. Pelham; George Lary and Ellen Jennings

LAVENTURE,
Gerald C. Russell, d. 12/1/1997 at 63 in Concord; Wilfred Laventure and Alice Guilmette
June Rose, d. 2/26/1994 at 64 in Barnstead; Victor Edison McLaughlin and Rose Alma Arquin

LAVIN,
Wesley, d. 3/11/1967 at 53 in Manchester; assembler; b. Methuen, MA; John Lavin and Jane Harris

LEATHERS,
Mrs. Aaron, d. 1842 at 83**

LEAVITT,
Minnie, d. 4/22/1968 at 80 in Concord; housewife; b. NH; John Avery and Mary Staples

LECLAIR,
Edward Z., Sr., d. 9/8/1970 at 67 in Concord; transport truck driver; b. NH; Cyriac LeClair and Mellvina St. Onge

LECLAIRE,
Angeline, d. 11/3/1887 at 85; housework; married

LEDUC,
Sophronia, d. 7/1/1950 at 77 in Concord; b. Bristol, RI; Alexander Langlois and Azila Pelitier

LEIGHTON,
Jane, d. 6/3/1895 at 78; old age; housework; widow; b. Barnstead
Rodney B., Jr., d. 6/15/1989 at 66 in Ctr. Barnstead; Rodney B. Leighton, Sr. and Nellie W. Allen

LEMAIRE,
Henry, d. 8/13/1996 at 86 in Manchester; Ernest Lemaire

LEMIRE,
Leta J., d. 12/16/1936 at 54 in Barnstead; William E. Jenkins and Emma Moore

LEON,
Janet, d. 12/10/1975 at 33 in Concord; teamster; b. IA; Harry McRoberts and Elma Novak

LESLIE,
Frederick J., d. 1/3/1953 at 84 in Concord; b. England; John Leslie and Mary A. Hurry
Mollie Bowen, d. 6/22/1949 at 72/11/14 in Barnstead; b. Warren, RI; Charles Hoar and Betsy Burr Bliss

LEWIS,
John N., d. 10/21/1914 at 76/10/16; cerebral hemorrhage; farmer; married; b. MA; John M. Lewis (MA) and May J. Todd (MA)

LIBBY,
Richard, d. 1846 at 28**

LIONSTONE,
Angelina Mae, d. 11/26/1982 at 79 in Keene; Thomas Coderre and Roseanne Record

LITTLE,
Bertha E., d. 9/9/1933 at 63; b. Campton, PQ; Alonzo Crosby and Mary J. Eliott
Della G., d. 12/2/1946 at 75/3/29 in Barnstead; b. Suncook; Ira C. Swain and Alma J. Glazier
Harry E., d. 6/9/1953 at 80 in Epping; b. MO; Henry A. Little
Marshall, d. 11/30/1972 at 63 in Brentwood; none; b. Meredith; Irving Harry Little and Bertha Crosby

LITTLEFIELD,
Catherine, d. 9/24/1946 at 92/7/26 in Alton*; b. Pugwash, NS; Warren O'Brine
Freeman, d. 1/25/1917 at 89/10/5; b. Albany; Samuel Littlefield (Sanford, ME) and Mary Chase (NH)
George F., d. 11/16/1965 at 84 in Rochester; farmer; b. Mapleton, ME; Warren Littlefield and Cathrine O'Brien
Louise P., d. 4/6/1933 at 62; b. Oxborough, ME; Fielder Betting and Mary McKee
Margaret, d. 9/9/1918 at 23/1/22; b. New York, NY; Fred J. Williams (New York, NY) and Margaret Schultinger (New York, NY)
Orin, d. 9/2/1938 at 78*; b. Albany; Freeman Littlefield and Belinda Allard
Susie E., d. 5/29/1954 at 73 in Rochester; b. NS; Leonard Lyon and Theresa DeWolfe
Warren, d. 4/3/1926 at 74

LOCK,
Enoch, d. 6/11/1896 at 84; bronchitis; farmer; widower; b. Barnstead; Nabby Nutter
Martha B., d. 10/20/1895 at 82; old age; housewife; married; b. Hampton; David Lane and Sally Brown

LOCKE,
Abigail, d. 1869 at 82**; widow of James
Bertha F., d. 11/2/1954 at 72 in Barnstead; b. Barnstead; Jefferson Chesley and Irene Hussey
Betsy, d. 3/4/1918 at 78/0/13; b. Strafford; William Saunders (Strafford) and Abigail Mills (VT)
Dennis M., d. 9/22/1969 at 21 in Concord; mason's helper; b. Concord; Wallace W. Locke and Winifred M. Pollard
Douglas W., d. 10/30/1952 at 2 in Concord; b. Barnstead; Ernest Locke and Rachel Belville
Electa A., d. 1/23/1907 at 62/5/12; tuberculosis; housewife; married; Jefferson Chesley (Barnstead) and Irene Hussey (Barnstead)
Elias Wesley, d. 2/12/1977 at 84 in Ctr. Barnstead; lumberman; b. MA; Elias W. Locke and Carrie Come
Eliphalet, d. 1871 at 69**
Ellen S., d. 2/7/1913 at 70/5/29; bronchitis; single; b. Barnstead; Jacob B. Locke (Barnstead) and Permelia Dow (Barnstead)

Elsie M., d. 4/14/1925 at 32; b. Boston, MA; Nathan Garrick and Henriette Burgess

Elva P., d. 2/2/1971 at 64 in Barnstead; housewife; b. ME; John Holland and Lottie Blackwood

Emma R., d. 8/20/1904 at 58/6/2; Bright's disease; housekeeper; married; William Rogers (Bath, England) and Katharine Barret (Wells, England)

Enoch, d. 1872 at 79**

Frank Alonzo, d. 3/2/1924 at 52; b. Barnstead; William H. Locke and Sarah E. Pickering

George E., d. 10/8/1936 at 64 in Barnstead; James Locke and Mary E. Nutter

George M., d. 6/2/2000 in Nashua; George Locke and Mabel Kelly

George Malcolm, II, d. 4/6/1991 at 24 in Concord; John Locke and Evelyn Tasker

Jacob B., d. 1840 at 40**

James, d. 1822 at 38**

James, d. 1832 at 80**

James, d. 11/22/1905 at 67/10/28; atrophy of liver; farmer; married; Sampson Locke (Barnstead) and Esther Nutter (Barnstead)

James C., d. 10/15/1932 at 86; b. Barnstead; Jacob Locke and Pamelia Dow

James E., d. 7/30/1908 at 76/3/7; organic disease of heart; farmer; married; b. New Durham; Phineas Locke (Barnstead) and Marion Pinkham (New Durham)

James S., d. 3/22/1957 at 58 in Barnstead; b. Barnstead; George M. Locke and Mabel Kelley

Jethro N., d. 2/28/1916 at 75/10/28; farmer; widower; b. Barnstead; Sampson B. Locke (Barnstead) and Ester Nutter (Barnstead)

Kent D., Sr., d. 5/2/2000 in Wolfeboro; George Locke and Mabel Kelly

Lucy C., d. 3/17/1889 at 73/6/6; housekeeper; single; b. Barnstead; Enoch B. Locke (Barnstead) and Sarah Berry (Strafford)

Mabel K., d. 12/26/1935 at 58; b. Gilmanton; George Kelley and Frances Maxfield

Margaret J., d. 11/9/1997 at 86 in Wolfeboro; John R. Johnston and Theresa Barnes

Marguerite, d. 7/16/1901 at 1/1; inflammation of bowels; b. Barnstead; George Locke (Barnstead) and Mabel Kelley (Gilmanton)

Marjorie, d. 5/27/1901 at 0/11/15; acute indigestion; b. Barnstead; George Locke (Barnstead) and Mabel Kelley (Gilmanton)

Mary, d. 1844 at 86**; wife of James

Mary, d. 1/18/1892 at 80/8/16; la grippe; housekeeper; widow; b. Barnstead

Mary E., d. 9/6/1929 at 83; b. Roxbury, MA; Joseph Nutter and Sophrona Drew

Mary G., d. 5/27/1987 at 67 in Concord; Wilbur J. Garland and Hattie Cofran

Sarah E., d. 6/30/1920 at 72/6/24; b. Barnstead; Cabel Pickering (Barnstead) and Elizabeth Roberts (Barnstead)

Smith W., d. 12/12/1906 at 54/1/7; sarcoma; farmer; single; b. Barnstead; Phineas Locke (Barnstead) and Mary Pinkham (New Durham)

Susan, d. 2/12/1888 at 87 in Laconia; widow

Violet M., d. 6/18/1995 at 86 in Wolfeboro; Albert Gray and Bessie Brown

Wallace G., d. 12/11/1981 at 34 in Barnstead; Wallace W. Locke and Winifred M. Pollard

Wayland B., d. 2/20/1962 at 82 in Barnstead; lumberman; b. Barnstead; William H. Locke and Sarah E. Pickering

Wesley E., d. 2/9/1999 in Concord; Elias Locke and Elsie Garrick

William H., d. 8/2/1915 at 68/6/21; farmer; married; b. New Durham; ----- (Barnstead) and Mary Pinkham (New Durham)

Winifred M., d. 2/25/1989 at 64 in Manchester; Louis Pollard and Sylvia LaPage

LODGE,

James T., d. 7/11/1950 at 71 in Concord; b. Buffalo, NY; James T. Lodge and Elizabeth Thornton

LOUGEE,

Bernard A., d. 8/13/1936 at 49 in Barnstead; Sewall M. Lougee and Sarah A. Smith

Betsey M., d. 4/1/1897 at 69; housework; widow; b. Alton; Jesse Sumner (Boston, MA) and Martha McDuffee (Alton)

David E., d. 5/6/1894 at 77/10; cirrhosis of liver; farmer; married; Simeon Lougee (Gilmanton) and Mary Edgerly

Emma J., d. 12/29/1936 at 68 in Barnstead; Charles Whitehouse and Lucy Fifield

Gilman, d. 1842 at 27**

Harold S., d. 3/5/1902 at 0/7; bronchitis; b. Barnstead; Leslie G. Lougee
Leslie G., d. 12/24/1936 at 70 in Barnstead; David Lougee and Mary Edgerly
Mary, d. 1811 at 38**; wife of Simeon
Mary E., d. 1850 at 72**; second wife of Simeon
Robert A., d. 5/21/1930 at --; b. Pittsfield; Arnold L. Lougee and Nellie M. Edmonds
Simeon, d. 1855 at 88**

LOWDEN,
Ronald Douglas, d. 9/23/1969 at 71 in Barnstead; arborist; b. NS; Harry Lowden and Almira Gordon

LULL,
Charles P., d. 5/28/1925 at 61

LUNDVALL,
Carl F., d. 4/23/1947 at 51/0/29 in Pittsfield*; b. New Sweden, ME; Carl O. Lundvall and Emma Leugrist

LYFORD,
Mrs. Anna, d. 1833 at 75**
Eunice, d. 1852 at 26**; wife of Rev. Frank H.

MACCAUSLAND,
Geraldine Frances, d. 11/15/1993 at 66 in Laconia; William J. Lynch and Bernadette A. Brennan

MACPHERSON,
infant, d. 3/13/1937 at 5 hrs.; b. Barnstead; Albert MacPherson and Edna McDuffee
Albert, d. 4/15/1954 at 55 in Barnstead; b. Roxbury, MA; Albert MacPherson and Katherine McLane
Albert Leroy, d. 10/6/1984 at 62 in Manchester; Albert MacPherson and Edna McDuffee
Donald E., d. 11/11/1947 at 17/9/17 in Barnstead; b. Barnstead; Albert MacPherson and Edna McDuffy
Edna M., d. 6/10/1974 at 78 in Concord; housewife; b. NH; David L. McDuffee and Mary E. Besse

MAESTRANZI,
Ernest Joseph, d. 10/26/1994 at 76 in Concord; Giovanni Maestranzi and Adelina Maganzini
Iginio, d. 7/25/1976 at 67 in Scituate, MA; electrician; b. Austria; John Maestranzi and Adaline Maganzini

MAGOON,
John, d. 6/30/1906 at 61/8/20; cystitis; minister gospel; married; b. Stanstead, PQ; Stewart Magoon (Stanstead, PQ) and Caroline Miller (Stanstead, PQ)

MAHAN,
Mary A., d. 7/31/1963 at 69 in Somerville, MA; housewife; b. Cambridge, MA; John F. McMinamin and Harriett E. Bird

MANNING,
Robert C., d. 1/10/1919 at 34/10/12; b. Canada; Dexter A. Manning (Canada) and Alie S. Qurke (Canada)

MARCH,
June M., d. 6/13/1978 at 74 in Barnstead; receptionist; b. NY; Sanford J. McWilliams and Helen Hill
Robert P., d. 12/27/1984 at 81 in Milford, MA; Francis A. March and Alice Youngman

MARCOU,
Henry R., d. 1/14/1946 at 36/4/15 in Barnstead; b. No. Walden, VT; Fred Marcou and Lila Ainsworth

MARDEN,
Eddie A., d. 5/14/1968 at 62 in Concord; laborer; b. NH; William Marden and Ada Davis
James, d. 1842 at 89**

MARDIN,
Barbara, d. 5/14/1944 at 12/2/14 in Wolfeboro*
Nancy A., d. 2/23/1930 at 64*; b. Barnstead; Horace Davis and Martha Bridges

MARSH,
George F., d. 2/28/1929 at 83; b. Barnstead; Aaron Marsh and Sarah Marden
Joseph, d. 11/25/1909 at 67/10/28; diabetes mellitus; farmer; married; b. Derry; Aaron Marsh and Sarah Warden
Margerey, d. 2/25/1915 at 75/0/15; housekeeper; widow; b. Charlottetown, PEI; Lepton Stone (PEI) and Margaret Bradshaw (PEI)
Mary A., d. 2/17/1931 at 84*
Sarah A., d. 12/20/1894 at 79/10; la grippe; widow; b. Sutton; Samuel Meader (Epsom) and Sarah Meader (Epsom)
Sherman, d. 1/12/1903 at 29/4/15; embolism of heart; laborer; single; b. Barnstead; Joseph Marsh (Derry) and Margery Stowell (PEI)

MARSHALL,
John, d. 7/27/1899 at 72/6; apoplexy; farmer; single; b. Barnstead; Andrew Marshall and Mary Merrill
Josiah D., d. 8/13/1890 at 56/9/9; farmer; married; b. Barnstead; Andrew Marshall (Portsmouth) and Mary Morrill (Brentwood)
Mary, d. 1864 at 68**; wife of Andrew

MARSTON,
Charles D., d. 5/17/1925 at 67; b. Holderness; Benjamin P. Marston and Rebecca Winkley

MARTELL,
Carrie, d. 11/13/1952 at 90 in Concord; b. NY; Peter Conne and Elin -----

MARTIN,
Doris A., d. 11/22/1972 at 55 in Hanover; purchasing agent; b. NH; Fred R. Kenison and Gladys W. Brady
Ruth H., d. 1/24/1999 in Concord; Robert Harrison and Lottie Green

MATHEWS,
Rose, d. 2/4/1942 at 70 in Barnstead; b. Ireland; John McDonald and Mary Agnew

MAXFIELD,
child, d. 11/27/1890 at –; b. Barnstead; Frank A. Maxfield and Emma E. Winkley
Doris E., d. 9/22/1940 at 36; b. Alton; Edgar F. Seward and Jennie F. Shepardson
Frank, d. 11/15/1898 at 34/5/15; diabetes mellitus; farmer; married; b. Loudon; Oliver Maxfield and Ann Towle
Gertrude F., d. 4/3/1980 at 57 in Concord; Henry B. Swain and Florence M. Gray
Harriette, d. 4/2/1918 at 75/9/8; b. Brooks, ME; Emery Miller (NH) and Mary Anna Huxford (Brooks, ME)
Henry E., d. 8/22/1969 at 17 in Alton; student; b. NH; John A. Maxfield and Gertrude Swain
Henry Wheeler, d. 4/16/1918 at 79/5/28; b. China, ME; William Maxfield (US) and Mary Parkman (US)
John A., d. 6/15/2000 in Concord; John Maxfield and Doris Seward
John H., d. 4/26/1901 at 76/8/19; chronic prostatitis; farmer; divorced; Ezra Maxfield and Abigail Philbrick

MAXWELL,
Maynard Warren, d. 11/9/1977 at 73 in Laconia; school teacher; b. MA; Randall Maxwell and Fannie Bragg

MAZE,
Josephine, d. 6/15/1977 at 77 in Barnstead; housekeeper; b. SC; James E. Boyd and Jeanette Kershaw

McALLISTER,
Arthur H., d. 1/19/1985 at 96 in Concord; Hiram McAllister and Mary Wellman
Mertie Lunette, d. 11/4/1968 at 82 in Ctr. Barnstead; postmaster; b. ME; Ernest Willis and Gertrude Brown

McCONNELL,
stillborn son, d. 6/6/1906 at --; b. Barnstead; William A. McConnel (Canada) and Annie Oberton (Canada)

McCORMICK,
Charles, d. 7/20/1992 at 82 in Dover; Thomas McCormick and Frances Mooers

Virginia O., d. 12/31/1991 at 79 in Rochester; William Orcutt and Margaret McClatchie

McCREADY,
Crystal Marie, d. 1/27/1987 at – in Manchester; Alan W. McCready and Ronda Dee Gagne

McDUFFEE,
David LeRoy, d. 11/14/1938 at 88; b. Alton; Jonathan McDuffee and Betsey Sumner
Frank S., d. 11/7/1942 at 54 in NY*; b. Barnstead; Leroy McDuffee and Emma Bessie
Margaret H., d. 12/5/1901 at 10/11/17; abscess abdominal cavity; b. Barnstead; David L. McDuffee (Alton) and Mary E. Besse (Foxcroft, ME)
Mary Emma, d. 2/7/1934 at 78 in Barnstead; Wellington Besse and Susan Parsons

McGUIRE,
T. H., d. 6/17/1914 at 20/6; accidental drowning; single; b. CT

McKEAN,
Betsy, d. 5/13/1894 at 81/8; heart disease; housewife; widow

McLATCHEY,
Millicent, d. 4/29/1972 at 74 in Concord; housewife; b. NS; William A. Hope and Sophia Robinson

McLAUGHLIN,
Helen I., d. 11/17/1992 at 61 in Concord; Harry McLaughlin, Sr. and Tillie Smith
Tillie M., d. 10/31/1992 at 83 in Epsom; Michael Szemeta and Anna -----

McLELLAN,
Amy H., d. 1/24/1999 in Barnstead; Erich Nilges and Ruth Billings
Frederic Austin, d. 11/8/1993 at 66 in Barnstead; John Clarke McLellan and Bertha McFadden

McNEAL,
Albion J., d. 5/28/1936 at 81 in Barnstead; Jonathan McNeal and Sarah J. Garland
Cecil, d. 12/29/1919 at 39/3/23; b. Barnstead; Albion McNeal (Barnstead) and Ida J. Copp (Farmington)
Sarah, d. 2/6/1901 at 78/11/2; apoplexy; married; b. Barnstead; David Garland (Barnstead) and Abigail Daniels (Barnstead)

MEADER,
Betsey (Miss), d. 1836 at 76**

MEARA,
Almira Jane, d. 6/20/1955 at 66 in Pittsfield; b. Chichester; John Meara and Belle Paige
Belle A., d. 6/17/1928 at 71; b. Pittsfield; Samuel T. Paige

MEEKINS,
Betty Ann, d. 4/3/1950 at 0/8 in Gilmanton*; b. Concord; Ruth M. Meekins

MEIKLE,
Ethel M., d. 8/22/1995 at 87 in Barnstead; George Livesley and Ethel Webb

MELVIN,
Arthur L., d. 3/23/1983 at 86 in Loudon; Louis Melvin and Clara Adams
Charlotte H., d. 2/20/1964 at 60 in Concord; housewife; b. Philadelphia, PA; Harry Hogencamp and Jennie Cornell

MERRILL,
Aaron, d. 1837 at 62**
Abigail, d. 1841 at 55**; widow of Aaron
Charles, d. 9/25/1915 at 68/10/28; farmer; married; b. Gilmanton; Joseph A. Merrill (Gilmanton) and Margaret Osborn (Loudon)
Charles F., d. 11/28/1935 at 82; b. Barnstead
George J., d. 1/9/1933 at 71; b. Barnstead; John J. Merrill and Mary E. Jenness
Harvey S., d. 3/20/1980 at 80 in Concord; Fred J. Merrill and Lizzie B. Cummings

John, d. 12/6/1909 at 90/5/24; old age; farmer; widower; b. Barnstead; Aaron Merrill (Salisbury, MA) and Abagail Genness (Strafford)

Lyman George, d. 10/28/1968 at 81 in Barnstead; teamster; b. NH; Fred H. Merrill and Lizzie Cummings

Marion (Evans), d. 11/21/1973 at 65 in Northwood; waitress; b. MA; Edson James Evans and Mabel Cora Nutter

Myrtle B., d. 10/28/1966 at 75 in Barnstead; housewife; b. Piermont; Alba B. Heath and Mary Howland

Sarah, d. 6/24/1921 at 70/5/20; b. Strafford; Ezekiel Babb and Almira -----

MESERVE,
son, d. 4/26/1888 at –; b. Barnstead; Albert Meserve (Pittsfield) and ----- (Boston)

MEUNIER,
Charles A., d. 12/13/1966 at 78 in Concord; retired; b. Egry, France

Lillian A. (Brorstrom), d. 9/7/1965 at 74 in Brookline, MA; housewife; b. Jersey City, NJ; Paul Brorstrom and Berhardine Wenstrom

MICHIE,
Mertie E., d. 6/30/1931 at 50*; b. Center Barnstead; George Jenkins and Victoria Clark

William Pickard, d. 5/14/1971 at 64 in Manchester; truck driver; b. NH; William Michie and Mertie Jenkins

MILLER,
Alice E., d. 6/21/1926 at 63; b. Macon, GA; ----- Smith

Clementine H., d. 1/30/1951 at 92/1/8 in Barnstead; b. Boston, MA; John C. Miller and Henrietta Vogel

Mellissa A., d. 1/6/1932 at 86; b. Alton; John Lang and Mary J. Welch

MILLS,
Betsey, d. 7/31/1895 at 89/8; inflammation of bowels; widow; b. Strafford

George R., d. 5/7/1936 at 3 in Pittsfield*; Lowell Mills and Dora Lougee

MILOT,
Omar C., d. 11/30/1965 at 57 in Barnstead; plumber; b. Canada; Charles Milot and Valeda Lajoie

MINER,
Dennis A., d. 7/2/1998 in Alton; Harold Miner and Marjorie Wade

MINOR,
James P., d. 7/1/1999 in Concord; Thomas Minor and Margaret Murphy

MITCHELL,
Eva Mabel, d. 3/14/1969 at 87 in Ctr. Barnstead; housewife; William J. Clerke and Olive Compton
Virginia L., d. 2/10/1990 at 67 in Barnstead; Walter Wells and Sophronia Yeaton

MOLLOY,
Thomas W., d. 9/3/1999 in Manchester; John Molloy and Catherine Thornton

MONTGOMERY,
Rickie Glenn, II, d. 3/25/1992 at 0 in Lebanon; Ricky Glenn Montgomery and Karen M. Labrecque

MOONEY,
Lizzie, d. 10/20/1914 at 48/8/8; tuberculosis; housekeeper; single; b. Barnstead; H. P. Mooney (Alton)
Mildred P., d. 3/7/1976 at 57 in Concord; sch. librarian; b. NH; Frank Peasley and Alice Douglas

MOORE,
Charlotte, d. 1856 at 54**; wife of Jonathan
Edward William, d. 9/1/1951 at 24 in Barnstead; b. Boston, MA; Lawrence A. Moore and Kathryn White
Frank H., d. 12/31/1948 at 89/3/10 in Barnstead; b. Loudon; John B. Moore and Lucy Diamond
Frank L., d. 4/5/1891 at 25; dentist; single; Thomas Moore (Barnstead) and Mary Greene (Pittsfield)
Jonathan, d. 1856 at 58**

Lettie H., d. 12/8/1968 at 74 in Concord; at home; b. MA; Charles Harriman and Anna Phipps
Lyle Kenneth, d. 11/12/1967 at 77 in Barnstead; laborer, retired; b. Milton; William E. Moore and Sarah Downe
Mary P., d. 2/7/1912 at 75/1/29 in Pittsfield*; apoplexy; housekeeper; widow; b. Pittsfield; William Green (Pittsfield) and Harriett C. Drake (Pittsfield)
Sarah F., d. 1/30/1948 at 75/6/3 in Barnstead; b. Tilton; Joseph M. Hillsgrove and Lydia Webster
Thomas, d. 11/6/1907 at 81/0/25; urena; married; b. Dover; Jonathan Moore (Stratham) and Charlott M. Chick

MOORHOUSE,
Jane E., d. 4/19/1930 at 62; b. Canada; Thomas Graham and Emerline McKee

MORGAN,
Mary, d. 1856 at 71**; wife of Reuben

MORRIS,
Ethel Dolloff, d. 5/12/1971 at 79 in Concord; housewife; b. Meredith; Phileas Dolloff and Emma Blake
Nelson L., d. 8/30/1998 in Barnstead; Uzeb Morris and Jane Dolloff

MORRISON,
Charles H., d. 9/10/1920 at 63/8/20*; b. Alton; James N. Morrison (Alton) and Mary C. Walker (Barnstead)
Dorothy G., d. 3/7/1974 at 71 in Concord; stenographer; b. MA; Harry W. Gordon and Blanche -----
Frederick J., d. 5/13/1976 at 73 in Barnstead; draftsman; b. MA; Matthew Morrison and Lucy Graham
Helen M., d. 5/7/1946 at 82/6/13 in Pittsfield*; b. Barnstead; Horace N. Colbath and Lucinda Nutter

MORRISSETTE,
Raymond A., d. 5/28/1997 in Barnstead; Arthur Morrissette and Lena Cote

MORSE,
Charles W., d. 8/18/1961 at 68 in Barnstead; yarn twister; b. Voluntown, CT; Noia Morse

Doris M., d. 4/9/1959 at 33 in Concord

MOUNTAIN,
Freda A., d. 5/29/1974 at 63 in Wolfeboro; store keeper; b. NH; Fred S. Gilman and Ettabelle Coffin
Henry J., d. 3/31/1980 at 67 in Wolfeboro; Thomas Mountain and Mary Martell
Thomas, d. 12/26/1966 at 80 in Laconia; painter; b. Canada; Henry Mountain and Hanorah Burke

MOUSSEAU,
Sherman P., d. 5/17/1980 at 23 in Barnstead; Roland E. Mousseau and Ann L. Smith

MUNCY,
Mary, d. 1853 at 70**
Molly, d. 1839 at 89**
Timothy, d. 1848 at 24**
William, d. 1831 at 86**

MUNROE,
Mark P., d. 9/17/1982 at 21 in Concord; Donald S. Munroe and Patricia Brown

MUNSEY,
Annie M., d. 2/5/1917 at 79/4/7*; b. Barnstead; David Young (Barnstead) and Eliza Hartford (Strafford)
Clyde, d. 4/6/1932 at 58*; b. Barnstead; John Munsey and ----- Young
Eben, d. 1853 at 80**
Ebenezer, d. 1858 at 80**
George F., d. 1863 at 24**
George M., d. 12/4/1941 at 79 in Barnstead; b. Barnstead; Henry J. Munsey and Melvina A. Young
Henry, d. 1811 at 75**
Henry, d. 1868 at 70**
Henry J., d. 12/14/1895 at 63/1/23; heart disease; carpenter; married; b. Barnstead; Henry Munsey
Horace T., d. 1863 at 27**
Jenny, d. 1857 at 82**
Mary, d. 1830 at 80**; wife of Timothy

Mary, d. 1858 at 69**; wife of Ebenezer
Minnie J., d. 1/7/1919 at 45/1; b. Barnstead; Woodbury Munsey (Alton) and Josephine Worcester (Barnstead)
Mrs. Solomon, d. 1827 at 80**
Solomon, d. 1827 at 82**
Solomon, Jr., d. 1850 at 49**
Sophia C., d. 2/8/1904 at 65/4/18; organic disease of heart; widow; b. Barnstead; John J. Tuttle (Barnstead) and Betsey Jacobs (Barnstead)
Timothy, d. 1832 at 83**
William, d. 1835 at 85**

MURPHY,
Gilbert J., d. 1/29/1986 at 82 in Barnstead; John Murphy and Mary Hanson
Mary M., d. 12/30/1893 at 81/7; heart disease; widow; b. Alton; Joseph Meader and Elizabeth Leighton
Mary P., d. 9/23/2000 in Barnstead; Patrick Burke and Mary Craven

MYATT,
Ronald F., Sr., d. 7/21/1997 at 72 in Barnstead; Leo Myatt and Ethel F. Frasier

MYERS,
Harold Carter, d. 7/10/1969 at 76 in Concord; bookkeeper; b. VT; James E. Myers and Louise B. Carter
Mollie M., d. 7/18/1987 at 90 in Concord; Walter N. McKean and Bertha Litchfield
William, d. 7/19/1948 at 47/1/10 in Concord*; b. Sayerville, NY; William Henry Myers and Pauline Beaverlock

NEALAND,
Patrick, d. 12/25/1933 at 67; b. Rochester; Patrick Nealand and Mary Allen

NELSON,
Ameth R., d. 1/28/1925 at 77; b. NS; John Hicks and Rebecca Charlton
Carleton E., d. 2/9/1988 at 61 in Concord; Arvid Nelson and Mabel Wilson
Charles, d. 1/18/1951 at 79 in Barnstead; b. Switzerland

Dorothy M., d. 1/18/1997 at 74 in Concord; Percy S. Nelson and Rena M. Tuttle
Ellen Grace, d. 7/16/1932 at 68; b. Groton; George Hazelton and Martha Hunkins
John L., d. 1/30/1943 at 66 in Laconia*
Samuel, d. 1811 at 73**
Samuel, Jr., d. 1812 at 24**

NEWCOMB,
Helen F., d. 5/19/1984 at 73 in Concord; Frederick Smith and Leora Webster
Irving S., d. 10/24/1987 at 80 in Concord; William I. Newcomb and Cora Smith

NEWELL,
Mrs. Netsey, d. 1853 at 89**

NICHOLS,
George A., d. 6/11/1920 at 77/6*; b. Dixmont, ME; Abner Nichols (Reading, MA) and Harriet Fowler (Salem, MA)
Nancy L., d. 1/11/1911 at 64/2/3; heart disease; housewife; married; Messic Clark (VT) and Mary I. Siders (VT)

NICOLS,
James, d. 12/7/1994 at 64 in Concord; George Nicoloudis and Angela Rallis

NIMMRICHTER,
Franz, d. 8/14/1916 at 32/1/28*; weaver; married; b. Austria; Johana Nimmrichter (Austria)

NOBLE,
Breieta, d. 11/4/1918 at 0/2/20; b. Roxbury, MA
Hazen L., d. 4/27/1958 at 44 in Barnstead
Marion A., d. 9/17/1960 at 52 in Manchester; housewife; widow; b. Pittsfield; Joseph H. Danis and Arline Constant

NOLIN,
Dorothy E., d. 7/18/1982 at 66 in Barnstead; Harley Goss and Ella -
----

NORRIS,
Hannah, d. 1852 at 87**; widow of Joseph
Joseph, d. 1848 at 80**

NOYES,
Warren P., d. 11/1/1908 at 60/3/10; peritonitis; farmer; single; b. Haverhill, MA; Folinsby Noyes and Clarissa Noyes

NUTTALL,
Addie F., d. 9/16/1954 at 81 in Concord; b. MA; John Cross and Mary Ramsdell
James, d. 2/1/1926 at 70; b. Lancashire, England; Lawrence Nuttall and Hannah Chadwick

NUTTER,
daughter, d. 11/24/1897 at 0/0/11; b. Barnstead; Ralph Nutter (Barnstead) and Addie Powell (Barnstead)
baby boy, d. 4/23/1951 at 0/0/1 in Concord*; b. Concord; Malcolm Nutter and Grace Gray
Abbie F., d. 12/17/1892 at 47; heart disease; single; b. Barnstead; William P. Nutter (Barnstead) and Hannah Chesley (Barnstead)
Abbie J., d. 2/27/1891 at 73; dressmaker; single; b. Barnstead; James Nutter (Barnstead) and Mary Jenkins (Barnstead)
Abbie Maude, d. 4/19/1974 at 87 in Concord; housewife; b. Epsom; Mark Nutter and Mary E. Weeks
Albion P., d. 1/16/1899 at 74; la grippe; farmer; single; b. Barnstead; George Nutter
Anna, d. 1813 at 53**; widow of William
Annie, d. 1844 at 86**; widow of Anthony
Anthony, d. 1843 at 79**
Benjamin, d. 1832 at 88**
Betty, d. 1817 at 62**; wife of Major John
Carl N., d. 7/24/1971 at 88 in Concord; school teacher; b. Pittsfield; Matthew H. Nutter and Minerva J. Merrill
Charles H., d. 4/3/1891 at 64/10/7; farmer; single; b. Barnstead; George Nutter (Barnstead) and Sally Hodgdon (Newington)
Chester H., d. 1853 at 26 in Cal.**
Deborah B., d. 8/26/1946 at 56/3/4 in So. Berwick, ME*
Dolly, d. 1872 at 90**; widow of Nathaniel
Dorothy, d. 1855 at 89**; widow of Nathaniel

Ebenezer (Dea.), d. 1843 at 87**
Ebenezer, d. 5/29/1913 at 81/8/15; apoplexy; widower; b. Barnstead; George Nutter (Barnstead) and Sally Hodgdon (Barnstead)
Eleanor, d. 1871 at 81**; widow of William
Eliphalet, d. 1855 at 70**
Elizabeth A., d. 7/4/1927 at 75*; b. Nottingham; William H. Tibbetts and Mary Powers
Ella B., d. 10/1/1936 at 60 in Barnstead; Charles Whitehouse and Lucy Fifield
Esther, d. 1829 at 77**; wife of Hatevil
Frank C., d. 5/28/1954 at 72 in Franklin; b. Barnstead; Frank S. Nutter and Sarah E. Caswell
Frank J., d. 5/29/1909 at 0/3/20; marasmus; b. Barnstead; Frank C. Nutter (Barnstead) and Ira P. Berry (Barnstead)
Frank S., d. 3/4/1939 at 83; William S. Nutter and Mary E. Collins
George, d. 1861 at 63**
George A., d. 6/12/1939 at 82; b. Barnstead; Josiah K. Nutter and Mary Hill
George F., d. 3/14/1903 at 64/1; pneumonia; farmer; single; b. Barnstead; George Nutter (Barnstead) and Sally Hodgdon (Barnstead)
George Hop, d. 1836 at 35**
George W., d. 10/25/1920 at 31/3/27; b. Concord; Charles C. Nutter (Barnstead) and Elizabeth Tibbetts (Nottingham)
Hannah, d. 1869 at 75**; widow of Capt. William
Hannah, d. 1872 at 60**; wife of William P.
Hannah I., d. 3/4/1927 at 75*; b. Barnstead; William Nutter
Henry, d. 1857 at 75**
Ida F., d. 2/11/1932 at 70; b. Alton
Iva, d. 4/28/1962 at 73 in Concord; nurse; b. Barnstead; Joel Berry and Emma Webster
James A., d. 5/31/1891 at 38/8/10; gun maker; married; b. Barnstead; William S. Nutter (Barnstead) and Mary E. Collins (Barnstead)
Jethro, d. 1855 at 91**
John (Major), d. 1840 at 83**
John, d. 1847 at 42**
John (Ensign), d. 1869 at 74**
John H. (Rev.), d. 1872 at 83**
John L., d. 8/8/1889 at 77/1/8; farmer; married; b. Barnstead

John M., d. 1861 at 62**
John Matt., d. 1845 at 26**
Joseph, d. 2/10/1896 at 81/7/6; apoplexy; farmer; widower; b. Farmington; John H. Nutter and Hannah Hall
Joseph E., d. 1851 at 44**
Joseph P., Jr., d. 1844 at 28**
Laura M., d. 3/25/1889 at 30/5/27; housekeeper; married; b. Barnstead; Perley C. Place (Alton)
Lavina, d. 3/17/1894 at 86/8; old age; widow; b. Barnstead
Lillian M., d. 4/14/1922 at 37/7/14; b. Barnstead; Walter Richardson (Boston, MA) and Hattie Brown (Barnstead)
Lovey, d. 1861 at 75**; widow of Eliphalet
Margaret, d. 5/5/1894 at 75/1/9; pneumonia; housekeeper; widow; b. Barnstead; John Tuttle (Barnstead) and ----- Jacobs (Barnstead)
Martha, d. 1869 at 20**
Martin T. B., d. 3/13/1905 at 70/6/5; angina pectoris; farmer; single; b. Barnstead; George Nutter (Barnstead) and Sally Hodgdon (Barnstead)
Mary, d. 1866 at 81**; widow of Jethro
Mary A., d. 3/16/1903 at 69/11/21; senicidal; widow; b. Pittsfield; Robert S. Hill and Sally Bunker
Mary E., d. 1/2/1892 at 65/2/21; heart disease; housewife; married; b. Barnstead; John H. Collins (Barnstead) and Phebe Hanson (Dover)
Mary M., d. 6/12/1971 at 50 in Strafford; assembler; b. Strafford; Sidney Hanson and Lura Nutter
Mercy, d. 1830 at 81**; wife of Benjamin
Nathaniel, d. 1849 at 91**
Nathaniel, d. 1871 at 89**
Nathaniel, d. 9/18/1891 at 74/6/9; farmer; married; b. Barnstead; Nathaniel Nutter (Barnstead) and Dorothy Nutter
Polly, d. 1862 at 81**
Ralph L., d. 7/20/1931 at 49*; b. Barnstead; John D. Nutter and Sarah A. Emerson
Robert Carroll, d. 1/8/1917 at 0/2/8; b. Barnstead; Frank C. Nutter (Barnstead) and Iva P. Berry (Barnstead)
Ruth M. K., d. 8/7/1896 at 77/8/23; chronic inflammation of stomach; housewife; widow; b. Epsom; Jonathan Knowles and Ruth M. Philbrick
Sally (Mrs.), d. 1854 at 76**

Samuel D., d. 12/30/1889 at 84/3/3; farmer; married; b. Barnstead; ----- (Barnstead) and ----- (Barnstead)
Samuel L., d. 5/21/1909 at 64/1/1*; atrophy of liver; farmer; married; b. Barnstead; Samuel D. Nutter (Barnstead) and Ruth M. Philbrick (Epsom)
Sarah, d. 1853 at 73**; wife of Henry
Sarah A., d. 2/24/1900 at 56/8/5; disease of heart; housewife; married; b. Barnstead; George W. Emerson and Hannah Clark
Sarah O., d. 12/18/1894 at 65/11; heart disease; housekeeper; widow; b. Northwood
Susan H., d. 1/4/1937 at 62; b. S. Brewer, ME; Foster A. Parker and Martha Burton
Temperance, d. 1829 at 70**; wife of Dea. Ebenezer
William, d. 1811 at 55**
William (Capt.), d. 1867 at 78**
William, d. 1869 at 71**
William, d. 1869 at 76**
William P., d. 3/27/1900 at 85; hemiplegia; farmer; widower; b. Barnstead
William S., d. 4/25/1898 at 77/4/5; paresis; farmer; married; b. Barnstead; Eleanor Nutter

O'BARTON [see Barton, Obarton],
Edward, d. 1/14/1964 at 86 in Concord; woodsman; b. Canada; Azarie Aubertin and Philomene Dobois
George, d. 6/6/1913 at 9/3/15; convulsions; b. Barnstead; Edward O'Barton (Canada) and Jennie Daly (Gilmanton)
Rosa, d. 7/10/1949 at 40 in Laconia; b. Barnstead; Edward O'Barton and Jennie B. Daily

O'BRIEN,
James Edward, d. 4/13/1996 at 54 in Concord; Joseph A. O'Brien and Alice Mooney

O'CONNOR,
Doris L., d. 6/1/1990 at 73 in Concord; Seldon L. Drisko and Gertrude LaPurl

O'LEARY,
Francis, d. 6/21/2000 in Concord; John O'Leary and Gertrude Meyer

O'MEARA,
Richard J., Sr., d. 12/26/1984 at 58 in Concord; Rudolph O'Meara and Cecelia Southwell

O'ROURKE,
Edward F., Jr., d. 11/20/1992 at 62 in Concord; Edward F. O'Rourke, Sr. and France McGoldrick

OBARTON [see Barton, O'Barton],
Jennie B., d. 10/14/1918 at 33/7; b. Gilmanton; John Daily (Canada) and May Vein (Canada)

ORDWAY,
Eunice, d. 1/18/1924 at 57; b. Barnstead; Frank Ordway and ----- Barnard

OSBORN,
Ellen M., d. 12/11/1935 at 83; b. Sherbrooke, PQ
Emma, d. 1/17/1895 at 37; typhoid pneumonia; stitcher; single; b. Barnstead; Joseph Osborn and Mary E. Griffin
J. C., d. 3/20/1907 at 83/1/16; apoplexy; farmer; married; b. Loudon; Joshua Osborn (Loudon) and Hannah Clough
Mary E., d. 1/25/1895 at 65/7; typhoid pneumonia; housework; married; b. Gilmanton; Richard Griffin and Filinda Huckins

OSBORNE-TERRY,
Nancy J., d. 1/25/1985 at 31 in Concord; Norman H. Osborne and Elizabeth MacLean

OSGOOD,
Angeline, d. 3/14/1889 at 44; housekeeper; married; b. Barnstead; Eli Elliott (Barnstead) and Mary Ham (Alton)
James G., d. 2/28/1925 at 81; b. Madbury; John Osgood

OSHIER,
Eva, d. 10/30/1897 at 0/3/25; b. Barnstead
Phebe, d. 4/11/1900 at 38; pneumonia; housewife; married; b. Canada

OSIS,
Elizabeth, d. 6/26/1991 at 80 in Barnstead; Waldemars Osis and Elizabeth -----

OSTROWSKI,
Anthony, d. 8/1/1992 at 74 in Barnstead; Anthony A. Ostrowski and Annie Kozluwski

OTIS,
Arthur, d. 1/31/1938 at 69*; b. Barnstead; Dyer Otis and Margaret Howe
Dyer L., d. 3/30/1914 at 80/3; pneumonia; farmer; married; b. Strafford; Nicholas Otis (Strafford) and B. Leighton (Ossipee)
Ernest G., d. 7/25/1979 at 72 in Manchester; Arthur Otis and Etta Hanson
Etta M., d. 9/5/1923 at 50; b. Barnstead; Levi H. Hanson and Abbie F. Clark
Gladys, d. 11/21/1977 at 79 in Boscawen; nurse assistant; b. NH; John F. Brady and Alice Davis
Harrison G., d. 4/29/1902 at 70/4/24; acute bronchitis; farmer; married; b. Strafford; Nicholas Otis and Linda Young
Martha, d. 3/4/1920 at 74/3/29; b. Barnstead; Asa Otis (Strafford)
Nancy, d. 4/17/1914 at 73/3/26; chronic nephritis; housekeeper; widow; b. Barnstead; John Merrill (Pittsfield) and Lavina Caswell (Barnstead)
Nellie B., d. 5/19/1913 at 19/4/22; tuberculosis of lungs; b. Barnstead; Arthur D. Otis (Strafford) and Etta Hanson (Barnstead)

OTTERSON,
Thomas J., d. 12/21/1918 at 46/5/1; b. Hooksett; Martin L. Otterson (Hooksett) and Mary E. Whitemore (Nashua)

OULTON,
Mary E., d. 7/6/1965 at 104 in Barnstead; housewife; b. Mt. Whatley, NB; Silas Robinson and Caroline Lowerison

PACKARD,
Kate E., d. 6/17/1971 at 65 in Concord; housewife; b. Corinth, VT; Henry Hood and Minnie Flanders
Roger, d. 4/17/1974 at 81 in Laconia; laborer; b. NH

PACKER,
George William, Jr., d. 6/12/1993 at 51 in Concord; George William Packer, Sr. and Mary Davidson

PAGE,
daughter, d. 11/4/1892 at 0/0/3; flatulence and colic; b. Barnstead; William Page (Woburn) and Katherine Kearns (Canada)
Effie M., d. 6/18/1905 at 18/2/19; peritonitis; housewife; married; b. Henniker; Jessie W. Browne (Deering) and Leora Vollins (W. Springfield)
Jessie F., d. 9/20/1924 at 75; b. Gilmanton; Jessie L. Page and Betsey F. Marsh
Lura A., d. 2/25/1920 at 78/1/19; b. Gilmanton; Joseph Page (Gilmanton) and Betsey Marsh (Loudon)

PALMER,
Frank E., d. 10/2/1916 at 66/5/27*; carpenter; married; b. Barnstead; Ranson C. Palmer (Sutton) and Alice Foss (Sutton)
Hattie C., d. 12/24/1889 at –; b. Barnstead. Thomas Moore (Barnstead) and Mary P. Green (Pittsfield)
Lawrence, d. 4/20/1891 at 0/2/10; b. Barnstead; Frank E. Palmer (Barnstead) and Ida J. Shackford (Barnstead)
Leonard S., d. 11/9/1956 at 74 in Concord; b. Barnstead; Frank Palmer and Ida Shackford
Lulu L., d. 12/21/1953 at 71 in Concord; b. Kansas; Joseph Boucher and Mina Thompson
Pearl S., d. 5/5/1956 at 73 in Concord; b. Manchester; George Smith and Alice Perkins
Sarah M., d. 1/6/1929 at 73*
Warren F., d. 11/15/1954 at 76 in Barnstead; b. Barnstead; Frank Palmer and Ida Shackford

PARENT,
Emma F., d. 5/10/1977 at 54 in Ctr. Barnstead; housewife; b. Italy; Pasquale Fasciano and Maria Miale
Maxine Rose, d. 5/28/1992 at 59 in Wolfeboro; Jacob Rizinck and Sarah -----

PARK,
Irwin J., d. 8/21/1959 at 66 in Concord

PARKER,
Clyde Robert, d. 4/1/1970 at 63 in Concord; Sheriff, Merrimack Co.; b. W. Warren, MA; Horace F. Parker and Janet Carey
Minnie D., d. 7/20/1905 at 21/5/27; burned by kerosene; married; b. Casco, ME; Anson J. Winslow (Casco, ME) and Addie Tenney (Casco, ME)

PARKEY,
Mary L., d. 11/20/1965 at 82 in Exeter; housewife; b. N. Pepperell, MA; John Bailey and Hattie Mason
Peter J., d. 7/1/1954 at 72 in Hartford, VT; b. Chillicothe, MO; Peter Parkey and Sarah Herring

PARO,
Peter, d. 5/1/1918 at 76; b. Mecalett, Canada; Trerre Duparron and Mary Laporte

PARSHLEY,
Abbie, d. 4/8/1917 at 74/11/25*; b. Barnstead; Samuel Bickford and ----- Bickford
Frances A., d. 3/25/1913 at 30/5/2; heart failure; housewife; married; b. Fitchburg; Harry Adams and Etta N. Whitfield (Fra'town)
Frank L., d. 2/19/1921 at 59*; b. Barnstead; Horace M. Parshley (Barnstead) and Abbie Bickford (Barnstead)
Horace M., d. 3/3/1909 at 78/9/21; organic disease of heart; laborer; married; b. Barnstead; Joshua Parshley (Barnstead) and Patience Keniston (New Durham)
John B., d. 1827 at 84**
Patience, d. 1869 at 77**; wife of Joshua
Sarah, d. 1823 at 77**; wife of John B.

PARSONS,
Alberta W., d. 8/21/1902 at 32/2/5; eclampsia; married
Charles A., d. 7/19/1933 at 74; b. Lawrence, MA; Philimon Parsons and Miranda Dennett
Charles R., d. 3/20/1918 at 69/8/5*
Clarence Edgar, d. 9/4/1934 at 71 in Concord*; Lyman Parsons and Elizabeth King
Electa, d. 1/22/1925 at 68; b. Lee, ME; ----- Ricker
Elizabeth, d. 2/12/1912 at 82/5/10 in Dover*; cerebral hemorrhage

Lyman, d. 6/8/1891 at 73/11/8; farmer; married; b. Northwood

Myranda D., d. 11/30/1924 at 94; b. Barnstead; Oliver A. Dennett and Eunice Seward

Ralph A., d. 12/6/1908 at 18/4/2; drowning; farmer; single; b. Barnstead; Charles A. Parsons (Lawrence, MA) and Electa S. Ricker (Dover, ME)

Sadie H., d. 2/22/1979 at 84 in Epsom; Rueben H. Hoyt and Mabel F. -----

Scott D., d. 5/5/1957 at 69 in Concord; b. Barnstead; Charles Parsons and Electa Ricker

PATCH,
George A., d. 7/6/1913 at 65/0/3; epilepsy; single; b. Boston

PEABODY,
Grace E., d. 4/13/1963 at 79 in Concord; housewife; b. Gilmanton; Warren Foss and Lucy Marsh

Lulu B., d. 7/7/1891 at 23; housekeeper; married; b. Laconia; William Aikins (Barnstead)

PEASE,
Effie R., d. 7/15/1904 at 26/11/26; pulmonary tuberculosis; housekeeper; b. Canada; Charles Whitehouse (Canada) and Lucy J. Fifield (VT)

PEAVEY,
Deborah, d. 1864 at 87**; widow of John, Esq.
John, Esq., d. 1856 at 80**

PEAVY,
Hannah, d. 1855 at 71**; widow of James B.
James B., d. 1852 at 74**

PENDERGAST,
Abiah, d. 4/26/1930 at 95*
Ann, d. 1855 at 61**; wife of Stephen
Arthur T., d. 9/26/1943 at 77 in Haverhill, MA*; b. Barnstead
Betsey, d. 1836 at 99**; widow of Stephen
Christine, d. 11/13/1905 at 69/3/27; aenemia; housework; widow; b. Barnstead; Thomas Pendergast (Barnstead) and Lucy Ayers (Greenland)

Dennis, d. 1840 at 76**
Hannah, d. 1840 at 69**; wife of Dennis
John, d. 1796 at 15**
Joseph, d. 1860 at 86**
Joseph, d. 1863 at 37** (soldier)
Lydia, d. 1850 at 20**; wife of Joseph
Mary Nelson, d. 1865 at 86**; widow of Thomas
Nancy, d. 1851 at 84**
Nancy, d. 1866 at 58**; wife of Dea. John
Phebe, d. 1869 at 64**; widow of Stephen
Rebecca, d. 1856 at 86**; wife of Dea. Solomon
Samuel G., d. 5/31/1910 at 75/10/4; organic disease of heart; farmer; single; b. Barnstead; Thomas Pendergast (Barnstead) and Lucy Ayers (Greenland)
Sarah, d. 1858 at 90**
Solomon (Dea.), d. 1865 at 84**
Stephen, d. 1797 at 68**
Stephen, d. 1827 at 57**
Stephen, d. 1864 at 65**
Stephen, d. 4/25/1893 at 60/10/13; heart disease; farmer; married; b. Barnstead; Thomas Pendergast and Lucy Ayers
T. Irving, d. 2/24/1924 at 62; b. Barnstead; Joseph Pendergast and Christina J. Pendergast
Thomas, d. 1862 at 78**

PENDERGENT,
Abbie, d. 8/9/1913 at 69/4/9*; tuberculosis; b. Barnstead; Isaac Kenney (Barnstead) and Clarrina Nurry (Barnstead)

PENHUNE,
Paul, d. 4/10/1976 at 75 in Clearwater, FL; civil engineer; b. England; John Penhune and Marie Burdet

PENN,
Malcolm Kenneth Ira, d. 1/25/1990 at 73 in Concord; Ira Penn and Bessie Caroline Way

PENNELL,
John W., d. 3/9/1946 at 17/0/5 in Barnstead; b. Milton; Edwin A. Pennell and Dora Williams

PENNY,
Mary, d. 1840 at 81**; wife of Peletiah
Peletiah, d. 1842 at 85**
Thomas, d. 1828 at 29**

PEPELIS,
Peter P., d. 1/8/1980 at 54 in Concord; Matthew Pepelis and Julia --

PERKINS,
Charles E., d. 6/18/1928 at 77; b. Strafford; Asa Perkins and
   Deborah Young
David M., d. 12/13/1977 at 76 in Wolfeboro; taxidermist; b. NH;
   Harry D. Perkins and Mabel Rowe
Dora F., d. 1/12/1978 at 73 in Epsom; housewife; b. NH; George P.
   Foss and Edna Caswell
Harry D., d. 1/21/1945 at 71/2/17 in Barnstead; b. Lowell, MA;
   David M. Perkins and Clara Winkley
Maynard H., d. 10/16/1992 at 66 in Rochester; David Perkins and
   Dora Foss

PERRY,
Albert Charles, d. 6/25/1949 at 57/10/7 in Barnstead; b. Strafford;
   Charles Perry and Annie Perkins
Annie B., d. 3/9/1944 at 83/7/7 in Barnstead; b. Lowell, MA; David
   M. Perkins and Clara Winkley
Charles H., d. 7/14/1937 at 78; b. Strafford; Samuel Perry and
   Judith Leighton
Elizabeth E., d. 4/19/1958 at 69 in Barnstead
John A., d. 3/16/1982 at 84 in Concord; Alfred Perry and Mary
   Packard
Mabel C., d. 9/28/1953 at 63 in Barnstead; b. Strafford; Charles
   Perry and Annie Perkins
Vina H., d. 2/9/1966 at 61 in Concord; practical nurse; b. Barnstead;
   Sidney E. Hanson and Lura M. Nutter

PERVERE,
Dwight L., d. 1/18/1964 at 80 in Pittsfield; draftsman; b. Lynn, MA;
   Willie O. Pervere and Katie R. Downs
Katie R., d. 7/10/1959 at 92 in Wolfeboro

PETERSON,
Robert W., d. 7/9/1966 at 44 in Barnstead; lineman; b. Boston, MA; Hadar Peterson and Grace Whitehill

PETHIC,
Everett L., d. 12/6/1970 at 59 in Concord; Rich Plan of NH; b. NH; Willis Pethic and Gladys Lovejoy

PHILBRICK,
Jenness Wallace, d. 12/22/1952 at 70 in Barnstead; b. Chicopee, MA; Nelson Philbrick and Ella Irish

PHILBROOK,
Barbara M., d. 7/31/1966 at 34 in Derry; home; b. Manchester; Arthur Philbrook and Nellie Waterfield

PHILLIPS,
Ken L., Jr., d. 4/5/1985 at 62 in Barnstead; Ken L. Phillips, Sr. and Cordilia Williamson
Lona J., d. 8/11/1958 at 24 in Wolfeboro
Muriel V., d. 1/16/1965 at 6 hrs. in Concord; b. Concord; Ceiland A. Phillips and Kathleen Holly

PICKERING,
Abigail, d. 1839 at 72**
Ada R., d. 5/7/1922 at 67/4/27; b. Strafford; David Evans (Strafford) and Emily Hanscom (Strafford)
Andrew, d. 1851 at 76**
Betsey J., d. 5/7/1941 at 66 in Concord*; b. Barnstead; Joshua C. Pickering and Mary Ellen Grace
Caleb S., d. 1/4/1894 at 81/1/25; dropsy from heart disease; farmer; widower; b. Barnstead; Samuel Pickering (Barnstead) and Polly Avery (Barnstead)
Daniel, d. 1849 at 75**
Elizabeth, d. 10/12/1890 at –; housework; b. Strafford; Jonathan Roberts (Strafford) and Elizabeth Foss (Strafford)
Elizabeth Mae, d. 4/15/1956 at 62 in Chichester; b. Barnstead; Tobias Pickering and Ada R. Evans
Emily E., d. 1/20/1938 at 54; b. Barnstead; Tobias Pickering and Ada Evans

Hazel A., d. 8/28/1927 at 2*; b. Pittsfield; Ralph E. Pickering and Margaret Hogencamp
Hettie, d. 1811 at 71**; wife of Stephen
Jacob, d. 1852 at 87**
Joseph, d. 1864 at 77**
Joshua, d. 1852 at 35**
Joshua Chase, d. 6/15/1918 at 75/3/2; b. Barnstead; Caleb S. Pickering (Barnstead) and Betsy Roberts (NH)
Martha, d. 3/17/1895 at 73; paraletis; housework; married; b. Barnstead; Thomas Williams and Hannah Lane
Mary Ellen, d. 9/24/1918 at 74/6/19; b. Barnstead; Moses L. Grace (Kittery, ME) and Jane D. Proctor (Barnstead)
Nathaniel, d. 1856 at 63**
Phoebe, d. 8/5/1913 at 89/10/4; pneumonia; b. Barnstead; Daniel Treffethen (Kittery, ME) and Sally Card (Kittery, ME)
Polly, d. 1856 at 44**; wife of Nathaniel
Polly L., d. 1844 at 57**; wife of Joseph
Sally (Miss), d. 1849 at 73**
Samuel, d. 1868 at 78**
Stephen, d. 1825 at 85**
Tobias R., d. 10/6/1923 at 82; b. Barnstead; Cabel Pickering and Elizabeth Roberts

PICKETT,
Carl Fredrick, d. 1/26/1988 at – in MA; Fredrick W. Pickett and Sandra J. Boisvert
Ethel A., d. 12/28/1991 at 68 in Concord; Paul Gianotis and Constance -----

PIERCE,
Donald F., d. 7/27/1937 at 0/6/21; b. Barnstead; Kenneth L. Pierce and Esther H. Dixon
Mary E., d. 1861 at 35**
Polly G., d. 1859 at 53**; wife of Harvey
Shirley J., d. 11/6/1976 at 41 in Pembroke; b. NH; Kenneth Pierce and Esther Dixon
Thomas J., d. 1863 at 24** (soldier)
William, d. 4/5/1901 at 87/8; old age; farmer; widower; b. Barnstead

PIERCEY,
Constance J., d. 8/27/1998 in Manchester; John Kustra and Joan Sopel

PINSONNEAULT,
Joseph E., d. 8/19/1957 at 65 in Concord; b. Manchester; Joseph Pinsonneault and Olive Vallee

PIPER,
John L., d. 7/21/1903 at 67/4/6; valvular disease of heart; farmer; married; b. Gilmanton

PITMAN,
Abigail, d. 1856 at 61**; widow of Eben
Albert G., d. 9/7/1935 at 65; b. Alexandria; George T. Pitman and Aurilla Brock
Annie T., d. 9/19/1923 at 23; b. Deerfield; Adolphus Lindquist and Emma Jolson
Armilla M., d. 10/3/1925 at 82
Charles W., d. 3/7/1916 at 56/6/25; dentist; married; b. Barnstead; Samuel J. Pitman (Barnstead) and Mary A. Nutter (Portsmouth)
Dorothy, d. 11/26/1892 at 86; pneumonia; widow; b. Strafford; Miss Daniels
Drusilla, d. 1/16/1895 at 81; softening of the brain; widow; b. Barnstead
Eben, d. 1845 at 58**
Edward, d. 1865 at 57**
Eugene F., d. 8/19/1890 at 1/6/3; b. Barnstead; Charles Pitman (Barnstead) and Nettie Stevens
Fred T., d. 10/12/1987 at 86 in Rochester; Oscar Pitman and Lurena Spooner
George Albert, d. 2/22/1994 at 84 in Manchester; Albert G. Pitman and Nellie F. Clough
George F., d. 7/1/1905 at 1/9/6; diabetes mellitus; b. Barnstead; Oscar E. Pitman (Barnstead) and Lurena Spooner (Barre, VT)
George T., d. 2/27/1895 at 60/6 in Manchester; melcontic sarcoma; farmer; married; b. Alexandria; John Pitman and Fannie Miles
Hannah, d. 4/27/1907 at 69/6/27; organic disease of heart; none; widow; b. Walpole

Hiram T., d.1/5/1923 at 90; b. Barnstead; Daniel Pitman and Betsey Straw
Jane S., d. 2/23/1915 at 84/11/10; housewife; married; b. Gilford; Ezekiel Collins (Gilford) and Charlotte Crosby
John, d. 1834 at 102**
John, d. 1856 at 86**
Jonathan, d. 1860 at 44**
Josiah, d. 1858 at 83**
Lurena Belle, d. 6/16/1967 at 88 in Rockingham; housewife; b. Barre, VT; Thomas Spooner and Hepsebeth Fielders
Mary A., d. 1/7/1908 at 80/4/13; organic disease of heart; widow; b. Portsmouth; William Nutter (Barnstead) and Hannah Norris
Nellie F., d. 12/29/1913 at 45/9/11; tuberculosis; married; b. Belmont; George Clough (Belmont) and Sophia J. Nutter (Portsmouth)
Nettie Frances, d. 10/8/1934 at 78 in Barnstead; James K. Stevens and Mary Thurston
Noah, d. 1828 at 23**
Noah T., d. 9/23/1895 at 62/4/18; heart disease; farmer; married; b. Barnstead; David Pitman and Sally Avery
Orrin C., d. 4/25/1923 at 69*; b. Barnstead; David Pitman and Sally Chick
Oscar E., d. 7/18/1934 at 68 in Barnstead; Hiram Pitman and Jane Collins
Roger C., d. 6/15/1946 at 0/0/4 in Concord*; b. Concord; George A. Pitman and Alma Lakeman
Sally, d. 11/28/1900 at 87/0/12; disease of heart; widow; Thomas Chick and Mercy Holmes
Samuel, d. 1825 at 89**
Samuel J., d. 10/26/1900 at 76/10/28; cancer of liver; farmer; married; b. Barnstead; Ebenezer Pitman and Abigail Montgomery
Sarah, d. 1825 at 88**; widow of Samuel
Shuah, d. 1850 at 79**; wife of John
Susan, d. 1858 at 82**; wife of Josiah
Susanna, d. 1835 at 95**; widow of John
Thomas C., d. 8/4/1888 at 76/10/27; farmer; married; b. Pittsfield
Veonie F., d. 9/9/1933 at 46; b. NS; Min H. Chute and Fannie A. Savoy

PLACE,
Anna, d. 1871 at 102**; wife of Joseph
Dorothy, d. 1870 at 67**; widow of John
John, d. 1867 at 75**
Joseph, d. 1829 at 75**

PLAISTED,
Emma B., d. 11/11/1900 at 29/6/3; carcinoma; housewife; married; b. Sutton
Leon A., d. 6/1/1898 at 4/7/18; drowning; b. Barnstead; George G. Plaisted
Madeline, d. 10/28/1895 at 0/1/18; gastritis; b. Barnstead; George G. Plaisted and Emma B. Hunt

POIRIER,
Louis J., d. 1/25/1962 at 74 in Barnstead; shoe worker; b. Lynn, MA; Joseph Poirier and Mary Hebert

PORTER,
Albert M., d. 5/2/1982 at 82 in Manchester; Edward Porter and Esther Embree

POST,
Norman, d. 5/1/1912 at --; lack of vitality; b. Barnstead; Chester Post (Rockland, ME) and Winnie B. Littlefield (Ashland, ME)

POTTER,
Frank A., d. 10/15/1943 at 66 in Barnstead; b. Providence, RI; Frank A. Potter and Leonora A. Barnes

POWELL,
Alice M., d. 6/28/1905 at 32/4/14; organic disease of heart; married; b. Barnstead; William H. Shackford (Barnstead) and Agusta Smart (Barnstead)
Harry L., d. 1/13/1948 at 74/5/4 in Barnstead; b. Pittsfield; Sylvester Powell and Ada Munsey
Mary Etta, d. 1/25/1910 at 43/6/17; pneumonia; laborer; widow; b. Barnstead; James R. Berry (Strafford) and Sarah F. Berry (Strafford)
May E., d. 5/23/1944 at 71/8/23 in Barnstead; b. Manchester; Harvey A. Emerson and Lydia E. Robinson

Sylvester, d. 6/11/1899 at 62; angina pectoris; painter; married; b. Concord

PRATT,
Frank H., d. 3/20/1918 at 44/9/9*; b. Everett, MA; Silas H. Pratt (NS) and Lydia Dodge
Hannah, d. 12/21/1914 at 88/5/5; pneumonia; widow; b. Barnstead; Dodah Kaine and Lavina Foye
Oscar Boynton, d. 12/9/1974 at 77 in Concord; greenhouse grower; b. NH; Frank Pratt and Abbie M. -----

PRAY,
Hattie A., d. 4/27/1927 at 68*; b. Barnstead; Nathaniel Smart and Harriet Daggett
Levi B., d. 5/19/1899 at 47/19/26; gastric hemorrhage; laborer; married; b. Effingham; Levi Pray and Rhoda Hodgdon

PREBLE,
Allan C., d. 5/24/1976 at 71 in Concord; asst. credit mgr.; b. MA; Harry Preble and Mary Curtis

PRIME,
Henry C., d. 1867 at 28**
Joseph, d. 10/14/1911 at 96/11/20; pernicious anemia; farmer; married; b. Dover; Joseph Prime (Dover) and Mahala Vickiry (Wakefield)

PRINCE,
George William, d. 1/20/1974 at 75 in Barnstead; shoe worker; b. Milton; George H. Prince and Mary Moore
Mary E., d. 11/19/1962 at 87 in Pittsfield; housewife; b. West Milton; William E. Moore and Sarah E. Downs

PROCTOR,
Clara A., d. 2/5/1916 at 66/4/23; single; b. Barnstead; Joseph D. Proctor (Barnstead) and Sarah Ayers (Gilmanton)
Comfort, d. 1847 at 66**; second wife of Thomas
Eda J., d. 7/6/1933 at 77*; b. Barnstead; Joseph Proctor and Sarah Ayers
Ida Josephine, d. 10/14/1939 at 83*; b. Barnstead; Joseph Proctor and Sarah Ayers

M. Francis, d. 11/7/1894 at 55/2/26; disease of heart; housekeeper; single; b. Barnstead; Thomas K. Procter (Barnstead) and Mary J. Chesley (Barnstead)
Martha, d. 1825 at 41**; wife of Thomas
Mary J., d. 1/24/1892 at 80/10; la grippe; housewife; married; b. Barnstead; Moses Chesley and Miss Nelson (Barnstead)
Samuel B., d. 1852 at 30**
Thomas, d. 1856 at 77**

PUBLICOVER,
Robert G., d. 2/27/1954 at 35 in Barnstead; b. Canada; Robert Publicover and Mary Chisholm

PUGH,
Charles, d. 5/16/1946 at 77/7/12 in Barnstead; b. Hearts Content, NF; Eveu Pugh and Harriet Hopkins

RAND,
David, d. 1814 at 70**
Hannah, d. 1844 at 80**; second wife of Moses
Harriett N., d. 2/15/1900 at 74/9/19; heart and liver; housewife; married; Benjamin Hoitt and Mehitable Babson
Hiram, d. 6/22/1903 at 76/2/17; uremia; farmer; widower
Mary, d. 1852 at 78**; widow of Samuel
Moses, d. 1810 at 70**
Samuel, d. 1836 at 60**

RANDALL,
George H., d. 4/3/1930 at 77*; b. Barnstead; Jeremiah Randall and Louisa Trombley

RANDELL,
Jeremiah W., d. 1/23/1890 at 63/11/5; farmer; b. Middleton; William Randell (New Durham) and Patima Keniston (Wolfeboro)

RAPOZA,
Alfred D., d. 10/10/1990 at 76 in Concord; ----- Rapoza

RAYMOND,
Armand D., d. 12/1/1968 at 63 in Hanover; retired; b. NH; George Raymond and Emestine S. Laurant

Desneiges D., d. 11/25/1981 at 72 in Concord; Napoleon Duhaime and Delias Brochu

Ella, d. 11/10/1960 at 79 in Concord; housewife; widow; b. East Washington; Alvah Davis

REARDON,
Amy L., d. 7/2/1936 at 59 in Barnstead; Michael Reardon and ----- Cushing

REDD,
William, d. 12/15/1995 at 69 in Ctr. Barnstead; Herbert Redd and Elizabeth Weems

REDFIELD,
Leona Madaline, d. 1/21/1994 at 78 in Barnstead; George B. Ricker and Seddie E. White

REED,
Dorothy P., d. 4/1/2000 in Concord; Archie Canfield and Clara Meara

Frank H., d. 1/29/1943 at 79 in Hopkinton*; b. Boston, MA; Robert H. Reed and Mattie Fosgate

Helen G., d. 10/20/1924 at 50; Harry W. George and Elizabeth Thompson

Orrin C., d. 3/17/1977 at 41 in Ctr. Barnstead; utility lineman; b. NH; Ivan Reed and Mary Marshall

Warren G., d. 11/15/1984 at 68 in Pittsfield; Fred W. Reed and Gladys M. Cheney

REIL,
Fred J., d. 7/4/1953 at 57 in Barnstead; b. Pittsfield; John J. Reil and Melinda Laro

REMICK,
Mathilda, d. 5/24/1920 at 32*; b. Austria; Konard Belgel (Austria) and Theresa Hegar (Austria)

RENARD,
Philip, d. 9/8/1922 at 47/1/29; b. Canada; Enchrist Renard (Canada) and Louise Deffour (Canada)

RENAULD,
Fred, d. 12/27/1949 at 81/10/6 in Wolfeboro*; b. Quebec, Canada; Amerime Raymond and Mary -----

RENEW,
Mary E., d. 11/22/1925 at 63; b. Lynn, MA; Richard H. Renew and Elizabeth Kimball

REYNOLDS,
Betty A., d. 7/1/1987 at 58 in Barnstead; John Tribou and Katherine Burgess
Charles H., d. 9/26/1895 at 65; apoplexy; farmer; married
Leon B., d. 7/14/1949 at 82/5/8 in Barnstead; b. Barnstead; Charles Reynolds and Lydia Jones
Lydia Jane, d. 6/26/1921 at 74/10/17; b. Strafford; Stephen S. Jones (Strafford) and Harriet Holmes
Stella B., d. 6/1/1965 at 82 in Deerfield; housewife; b. Northwood; Lorenzo G. Witham and Mary S. Pender

RHEAULT,
Eva M., d. 8/16/1974 at 68 in Ctr. Barnstead; photographer; b. NH; Joseph Beaulieu and Lucia Lafreniere

RICHARDSON,
Hattie, d. 7/31/1945 at 80/9/14 in Concord*; b. Barrington; Lorenzo Brown and Mary Berry
Ruth Marie, d. 5/2/1994 at 63 in Laconia; Gordon Whorisky and Adel Gutoski
Walter, d. 8/19/1936 at 76 in Barnstead; William H. Richardson and Abbie B. Gove

RICHEY,
William S., d. 5/6/1983 at 66 in Barnstead; William B. Richey and May E. Goff

RIDER,
Donald N., d. 4/23/1989 at 63 in Concord; Isaac Rider and Ines Parsons

RIEL,
Arnold James, d. 12/9/1978 at 39 in Ctr. Barnstead; insurance adjuster; b. NH; Maurice E. Riel and Birgitta Skarp
Daniel P., d. 4/23/1974 at 20 in Barnstead; offset press operator; b. Concord; Arthur D. Riel and Melissa Lord
Evelyn A., d. 7/16/1996 at 76 in Barnstead; George Stevens and Flossie French
Warren J., d. 4/9/1959 at 20 in Concord

RILEY,
Lavina M., d. 7/29/1962 at 61 in Rochester; housewife; b. NS; Howard McKay

RIPEAULT,
Florence, d. 1/17/1902 at 18/2/6; epilepsia; single; b. Canada; David Ripeault (Canada) and Hermi'e Lefebvre (Canada)

RIPLEY,
Merle, d. 7/12/1969 at 33 in Barnstead; laborer; Clair Ripley and Rena Collins

ROBERGE,
Joseph, d. 5/19/1984 at 88 in Concord; Pierre Roberge

ROBERTS,
Elizabeth, d. 1854 at 87**
Jennie Hill, d. 12/7/1970 at 87 in Barnstead; housewife; b. Strafford; Henry R. Foss and Addie R. Tripp
Jonathan, d. 1824 at 55**

ROBINSON,
Mrs. Noah, d. 1840 at 65**

ROCKWELL,
Frederick W., d. 9/23/1941 at 74 in Pittsfield*; b. NS; Timothy Rockwell and Rebecca Dickie
John A., d. 2/7/1937 at 56; b. Town Plot, NS; Timothy Rockwell and Rebecca Dukie

RODGERS,
Burton H., d. 11/14/1911 at 60/2/23; heart disease; blacksmith; married; b. VT; Lewis D. Rodgers (VT) and Rhoda Tatten (VT)

ROGERS,
Ida L., d. 8/6/1936 at 74 in Leominster, MA*; John E. Lavene and Emily J. Ladoo
Maureen, d. 1/25/1982 at 47 in Concord; John McCarthy and Nellie McDuff

ROKES,
Loren Wendell, d. 5/31/1994 at 71 in Concord; Ralph H. Rokes and Ida M. Jones

ROLLINS,
Abigail, d. 1847 at 58**; wife of Samuel
Deborah, d. 1857 at 52**; widow of Samuel
Mary Jane, d. 2/8/1961 at – in Rochester; b. Rochester; Selden B. Rollins and Belle Joan Parker
Samuel, d. 1845 at 75**
Samuel, d. 1866 at 73**

ROMANSKY,
Alexander, d. 8/13/1997 at 85 in Laconia

ROOP,
son, d. 6/28/1898 at 0/0/1; lack of development; b. Barnstead; C. G. Roop and Mazie Spencer
son, d. 6/28/1898 at 0/0/1; undeveloped; b. Barnstead; C. G. Roop and Mazie Spencer

ROSENQUIST [see Rosinquist],
Bror A. E., d. 2/6/1956 at 72 in Barnstead; b. Sweden; Enok Johanson and Maria Johanson

ROSINQUIST [see Rosenquist],
Helene, d. 3/22/1950 at 60/2/11 in Barnstead; b. Norway; Abraham Dybrik and Severene Dybrick

ROSS,
daughter, d. 1/31/1904 at 0/0/4; undeveloped; b. Barnstead; Frank I. Ross (Ossipee) and Hildred Merryfield (Manchester)
Frank I., d. 6/9/1938 at 59; b. Ossipee; Charles Ross and Hattie Smart

ROSTRUM,
Carl F., d. 7/17/1979 at 68 in Concord; Gustave Rostrum and Annie Adler

ROWE,
Clara Thestah, d. 1/27/1978 at 97 in Concord; housewife; b. NH; Charles Henry Avery and Pauline Hatfield
Emma F., d. 2/2/1937 at 76; b. Barnstead; Isaac H. Clark and Abbie Chesley
Forrest Clark, d. 7/5/1933 at 54*; b. Barnstead; James M. Rowe and Emma S. Clark
Frank H., d. 11/16/1946 at 76/1/27 in Concord*; b. Barnstead; James M. Rowe and Emma S. Clark
George N., d. 1/21/1933 at 67; b. Haverhill, MA; George W. Rowe and Sarah Cochrane
Ia May, d. 9/9/1950 at 82 in Concord*; b. Strafford; Charles H. Avery and Pauline Hatfield
James M., d. 6/18/1896 at 62/5; cancer of liver; dentist; married; b. Strafford

ROWELL,
Edwin, d. 3/14/1993 at 52 in Concord; Clayton Rowell and Thelma Ricker

ROY,
Kenny Arnold, d. 12/8/1967 at 12 mins. in Concord; b. Concord; Lennis Arnold Roy and Diane May Schmalke

ROYAL,
Charles G., d. 12/3/1945 at 81/0/13 in Barnstead; b. Ellsworth, ME; Sewell L. Royal and Martha Hoogs
Charles G., Jr., d. 8/26/1949 at 44/1/27 in Lynn, MA*; b. Ellsworth, ME; Charles Royal and Gertrude G.

RUDER,
Gabriella, d. 8/5/1995 at 86 in Barnstead; Theodore Botzok and Julia Cimean

RUNNELS,
Lillis, d. 1857 at 62**; wife of Israel

RUSSELL,
Arthur T., d. 3/18/1998 in Florida; Robert Russell and Grace Thomas
Jennie B., d. 5/24/1902 at 63/0/5; tuberculosis of lung; housekeeper; married; b. Barnstead; John Hoitt and Betsey Pitman
Joseph C., d. 2/10/1920 at 83/8/20*; b. Franconia; Joseph Russell (Meredith) and Abigail Pinkham

RYAN,
Charlotte J., d. 12/2/1969 at 83 in Wolfeboro; housewife; b. MI; Edwin Pink and Josephine Payment

ST. GEORGE,
Alban R., d. 4/1/1979 at 71 in Concord; Ovila St. George and Elise Martin

ST. ONGE,
Richard N., d. 12/27/1975 at 39 in Exeter; nuclear physicist; b. MA; Lionel St. Onge and Genieve Lukasiewicz

SACKETT,
Austin H., d. 3/27/1904 at 19/2/29; pneumonia; shoemaker; single; b. Barnstead; George Sackett (Barnstead) and Alice Huckins (Alton)
Carroll A., d. 1/3/1906 at 18/10/15; acute meningitis; RR employee; single; b. Barnstead; George A. Sackett (Barnstead) and Alice Huckins (Alton)
George A., d. 7/26/1929 at 67; b. Barnstead; Noble Sackett and Rooxbe Jacobs
Hiram N., d. 2/22/1887 at 37; salesman; married; b. Barnstead; Noble Sackett and Roxie Jacobs (Barnstead)
Lois, d. 8/29/1889 at 1/0/22; b. Barnstead; George Sackett (Barnstead) and Alice Huckins (Alton)

May, d. 10/22/1948 at 91/0/8 in Wolfeboro*; b. Barnstead
Nellie E., d. 11/15/1897 at 27/7/15; milliner; single; b. Barnstead;
    David N. Sackett (Barnstead) and Sarah Young (Laconia)
Rooxbe, d. 6/13/1894 at 77/3; heart disease; widow; b. Barnstead;
    David Jacobs (Barnstead) and Hannah Tuttle (Barnstead)

SALEY,
Norma H., d. 4/27/1988 at 67 in Barnstead; Earl MacDonald and
    Sadie MacRury

SALICE,
Delphine, d. 3/16/1977 at 94 in Manchester; retired; b. NH;
    Abraham Parselin and Julienne Gosselin

SALTER,
Mrs. Thomas, d. 1819 at –**
Thomas, d. 1819 at –**

SAMPSON,
Garland, d. 10/1/1968 at 92 in Derry; lumber yard; b.
    Newfoundland; ----- Sampson

SAMSON,
Myrtie A., d. 9/7/1936 at 51 in Derry*; James Webster and Mary
    Clark

SANBORN,
Ann W., d. 10/8/1914 at 85/5/20; chronic disease of heart; widow; b.
    Franklin; Simeon B. Hale (Grafton) and Jean Williams
    (Grafton)
Charlotte, d. 1/14/1898 at 78; Bright's disease; widow; b. Barnstead
John, d. 1859 at 82**
Marion E., d. 12/19/1995 at 84 in North Conway; Forrest Perkins
    and Hazel Bootby
Reuben, d. 1836 at 63**

SANBORNE,
Nathan, d. 6/11/1903 at 62/11/10; heart disease; painter; widower;
    b. Alexandria

SANDERS,
stillborn child, d. 5/28/1923; b. Barnstead; William B. Sanders and Lena B. Hamilton
Russell A., d. 2/16/1911 at 63/4/30; senile gangrene; hostler; widower; b. Barnstead; Samuel Sanders and Lydia Sawyer

SANDERSON,
Judson, d. 1/20/1995 at 88 in Ctr. Barnstead; Lynn J. Sanderson and Myria McKay

SANFORD,
Alan C., d. 6/23/1993 at 33 in Barnstead; Charles H. Sanford and Dorothy B. Blaisdell

SANSONSE,
Napoleon, d. 5/5/1910 at 45; drowning; mill hand; single

SAUNDERS,
George F., d. 5/12/1891 at 57/2/19; farmer; married; b. Strafford; William F. Saunders (Strafford) and Abigail Niles (Sheffield)
Jacob, d. 1852 at 62**
Laban M. (Dr.), d. 1867 at 34**

SAVAGE,
Henry W., d. 11/29/1927 at 68*; b. Barnstead; Moses H. Savage and Betsey Woodhouse

SAYWARD,
Nettie M., d. 7/31/1945 at 78/3/1 in Rochester*; J. H. F. Varney

SCHACHT,
Gerard John, d. 8/2/1994 at 54 in Barnstead; Rudolph Max Schacht and Margaret Mary McKeon

SCHROEDER,
Eliza, d. 8/21/1934 at 87 in Danvers, MA*
John H., d. 9/15/1910 at 67/11/2; hemiplegia; farmer; married; b. Germany

SCOTT,
Allen B., d. 8/24/1968 at 15 in Pittsfield; student; b. NH; Willard Scott and Luella E. Chick
Willard F., Sr., d. 10/28/1977 at 57 in Concord; truck driver; b. NH; Clarence Scott and Helen Hazard

SCRIGGINS,
Sally, d. 1811 at 41**; wife of William
William, d. 1838 at 72**

SCRUTON,
Alphonso C., d. 11/3/1925 at 29; b. Plaistow; Walter G. Scruton and Belle Smith
Annie L., d. 9/6/1938 at 60*; b. Chelsea, VT
Thomas J., d. 6/11/1961 at 73 in Concord; weaver; b. Haverhill, MA; Walter Scruton and Belle Smith
Walter G., d. 12/20/1933 ay 77*; b. Barnstead; Levi Scruton

SEAVEY,
Nathan L., d. 5/--/1921 at 92/1/15

SEAVY,
Joanna M., d. 12/30/1907 at 74/0/5; Bright's disease; none; married; b. Ireland; Thomas Berry (Ireland)

SELMAN,
Frances, d. 11/15/1891 at 72/1/6; widow; b. Cape Breton; Seth Brown (NJ) and Lydia Proctor (Cape Breton)

SEWARD,
Carrie A., d. 12/19/1936 at 70 in Barnstead; John J. Lang and Eliza J. Locke
Harry Frank, d. 9/21/1955 at 81 in Barnstead; b. Barnstead; Thomas F. Seward and Mary A. Chesley
Hattie May, d. 10/3/1974 at 76 in Barnstead; practical nurse; b. NH; Edward A. Cofran and Millie E. Hardford
Mabel J., d. 2/12/1936 at 59 in Barnstead; David K. Marsh and Sarah M. Carr
Mary Ann, d. 12/10/1916 at 62/1/3; home; married; b. Barnstead; Orrin Chesley (Barnstead) and Lydia Ann Lang (Barnstead)

Thomas F., d. 9/21/1933 at 83; b. Haverhill, MA; George H. Seward and Emmaline Williams

SEYMOUR,
Ellen P., d. 7/9/1930 at 84*; b. Barnstead; Joseph Proctor and Sarah Ayers

SHACKFORD,
Albert F., d. 12/5/1927 at 81; b. Barnstead; Samuel Shackford and Margaret Foss
Augusta H., d. 5/4/1889 at 39/0/14; housekeeper; married; b. Barnstead; N. C. Huntress (Strafford) and Sally Gowen (Berwick, ME)
Augusta M., d. 10/23/1911 at 63/11/20 in Pittsfield*; organic heart disease; housekeeper; divorced; b. Barnstead; Nathaniel Smart (Durham) and Mariett Daggett (NH)
Esta L., d. 7/19/1921 at 88/6/19; b. Mt. Desert, ME; ----- Higgins
Eugene F., d. 12/29/1941 at 68 in Lynn, MA*; b. Barnstead; Frank Shackford
Harriett, d. 1864 at 51**; wife of Seth
Harry A., d. 1/18/1928 at 53; b. Barnstead; Albert F. Shackford and Augusta Huntress
Horatio, d. 12/5/1901 at 69/9; paresis; shoemaker; widower; Seth Shackford and Harriett Hill
Josiah, d. 1843 at 77**
Lydia, d. 1859 at 86**; widow of Josiah
Mary, d. 1867 at 71**; wife of Josiah, Jr.
Mary A., d. 7/14/1887 at 44/10/15; housework; married; b. Barnstead; E. Holmes (Barnstead)
Seth, d. 12/6/1888 at 71; farmer; married; b. Barnstead; Josiah Shackford (Newington) and Lydia Dennett (Portsmouth)
William H., d. 6/3/1899 at 50/1/18; uremia; hotel; married; b. Barnstead; Samuel G. Shackford and Marguerite A. Foss

SHALLOW,
Brian P., d. 11/24/1991 at 18 in Concord; John Shallow and Linda Silveira

SHAW,
Herbert J., d. 10/23/1921 at 46/1/3; b. Victory, VT; Albert John Shaw (Peacham, VT) and Frances M. Damon (Curly, VT)

Nancy, d. 1872 at 80**; wife of William
William, d. 1861 at 71**

SHEPHERD,
Robert, d. 3/30/1899 at 90/10/16; old age; farmer; widower; b. Amherst; James Shepherd and Hannah Glover

SHINO,
Johnny, d. 10/29/1903 at 0/5; enteritis; ----- (Canada)

SIDEBOTHAM,
Eleanor L., d. 3/22/1980 at 63 in Concord; Charles L. Work and Myrtle L. Berringer

SIEGEL,
Mabel D., d. 3/13/1975 at 83 in Concord; housewife; b. IN; Moses Alexander and Rosalie Baruch

SILVER,
Stephen, d. 9/25/1986 at 17 in Ctr. Barnstead; Thomas Silver and Sharon Silver

SINCLAIR,
Betsey Hodgdon, d. 1840 at 78**; wife of Lieut. Richard
Charles G., d. 1834 at 41**

SKELTON,
Horace C., d. 7/20/1982 at – in MA

SKINNER,
Charles G., d. 4/25/1986 at 47 in Concord; Charles G. Skinner and Gladys Doran
Hope B., d. 3/23/1999 in Concord; John Skinner and Tracy Enos

SLOCOMB,
Richard E., d. 2/11/1985 at 65 in Rochester; Ingalls Slocomb and Ella Sandler

SMALL,
Arthur C., d. 8/28/1959 at 70 in Concord
Charles E., d. 4/25/1926 at 48

Harold E., d. 10/28/1950 at 53 in Barnstead; b. Charlestown; -----
Small and Caroline Kimball

Roxanna W., d. 6/17/1891 at 84/11; housekeeper; married; b. New
Boston; Benjamin Small and Sarah Patch

Warren A., d. 9/9/1935 at 82; b. Northwood; Warren Small and
Dorothy Gray

Warren L., d. 10/18/1991 at 56 in Laconia; Arthur G. Small and
Ethel M. Gates

SMART,
infant, d. 3/16/1939; b. Wolfeboro; Fred T. Smart and Lyra A.
Davis; buried in Hooksett

SMITH,
Adelbert E., d. 2/26/1980 at 92 in Barnstead

Athol Everard, d. 7/19/1974 at 78 in Concord; engineer; b. ME;
Norman A. Smith and Nellie F. Bragdon

Benjamin F., d. 5/31/1907 at 56/10/4; angina pectoris; contractor;
married; b. Sandwich; C. G. Smith (Newmarket) and Betsey
Jones (Durham)

Betsy, d. 4/25/1905 at 90/11/22; old age; widow; b. Newmarket;
Jonathan Jones and Lydia Smith

David A., d. 9/28/1984 at 21 in Concord; David D. Smith and Lois
A. Arnold

Edith N., d. 4/10/1952 at 77 in Concord*; b. Concord; Charles C.
Nutter and Elizabeth Tibbetts

Ella Frances, d. 3/19/1949 at 53 in Manchester*; b. Barnstead;
Jonathan Clark and Ida Hanson

Frank Ira, d. 8/1/1929 at 83; b. New Ipswich; Ira Smith and Hannah
Maxwell

Gary Roberts, d. 12/29/1971 at 22 in Concord; college; b. MA;
Gordon M. Smith and Virginia T. Baker

George L., d. 7/22/1999 in Ctr. Barnstead; Charles Smith and Hattie
Stockbridge

Harold A., d. 8/14/1987 at 93 in Barnstead; Albert Smith and Mary
Emerson

Harriet P., d. 9/23/1970 at 82 in Pittsfield; housewife; b. Durham,
CT; Arnold Spencer and Lillian Baldin

Herbert, d. 3/3/1923 at 51; b. Manchester; John B. Smith and Annie
Bazter

Herbert W., d. 6/21/1928 at 73*; b. Concord; Alfred C. Smith and Sarah J. Dowlin

James R., d. 11/20/1971 at 19 in Barnstead; shoe worker; b. MA; William R. Smith and Mildred R. Noonan

Joseph Henry, d. 12/18/1985 at 49 in Manchester; Joseph H. Smith and Estelle Monette

Joseph M., d. 7/18/1981 at 49 in Concord; Herbert C. Smith, Jr. and Grace E. Frye

Kenneth L., d. 12/2/1957 at 52 in Strafford; b. New Haven, CT; Howard P. Smith and Harriet P. Spencer

Lucille L., d. 6/10/1996 at 90 in Barnstead; Arthur Look and Emma Brehm

Martha J., d. 6/18/1943 at 94 in Gilmanton*; b. Barnstead; Timothy Emerson and Sarah E. Foster

Mary F., d. 1/25/1960 at 97 in Pittsfield; housewife; widow; b. Bradford; David D. Butman and Lucy A. Hadley

Mary L., d. 2/13/1927 at 68; b. Margree, Cape Breton; John Carmichael and Sarah Ethridge

Michael C., d. 5/26/1994 at 44 in Concord; George L. Smith and Ellen Davis

Miron O., d. 11/10/1937 at 72; b. Pittsfield; J. Gerney Smith and Cedelia S. Sackett

Paul S., d. 10/3/2000 in Laconia; Rudolph Smith and Hetty Woodward

Samuel R., d. 2/13/1966 at 0/11/22 in Rochester; b. Rochester; William R. Smith and Mildred Noonan

Vera M., d. 12/4/1964 at 72 in Boscawen; housewife; b. Georgetown, MA; Samuel Cilley

Virginia T., d. 6/1/1973 at 59 in Concord; antique dealer; b. MA; Alfred T. Baker and Ruth Whitten

Walter I., d. 5/19/1972 at 69 in Concord; watchmaker; b. MA; Walter I. Smith and Rose Gately

William Ross, d. 9/8/1973 at 60 in Manchester; boilerman; b. RI; William Ross Smith and Elizabeth Plum

SNELL,
Aaron, d. 1871 at 69**
Joanna, d. 1848 at 68**
Josiah, d. 1835 at 75**
Thomas, d. 1855 at 82**

SNOW,
Kenneth D., d. 7/31/1985 at 32 in Concord; Gerald P. Snow and Josephine Spencer

SNYDER,
Walter E., d. 4/12/1997 at 83 in Concord; John Snyder and Marie Krieger

SOLIMANTO,
Lillian, d. 7/6/1994 at 73 in Concord; George Welch and Lauretta Statutto

SOULE,
Deane C., d. 12/7/1995 at 58 in Ctr. Barnstead; Herman Soule and Doris Jeffery

SOULIA,
John L., d. 7/5/1976 at 71 in Concord; plumber, steam fitter; b. NY; Zeb Saulia (sic) and Bertha LaBrecque

SOUTHARD,
Edna M., d. 3/16/1998 in Concord; John King and Gladys Long
Reginald W., d. 5/22/1993 at 83 in Concord; William B. Southard and Lizziebelle Wells

SPALDING,
Harriet Hall, d. 4/12/1923 at 56*

SPRAGUE,
Juliet, d. 2/14/1966 at 77 in Pittsfield; housewife; b. Philadelphia, PA; ----- Dougherty and Mary Henderson

STALKNER,
Florence R., d. 3/18/1970 at 74 in Concord; housewife; b. ME; Edward Ramsey and Catherine Robinson

STANTON,
W. W., d. 9/6/1913 at 65/0/21*; circulation; labor; widower; b. Alton; Hiram G. Laihers (Lee) and Ana N. Williams (Durham)

STAPLETON,
John David, d. 5/6/1994 at 67 in Concord; Edmond J. Stapleton, Jr. and Helen C. Odell
Timothy J., d. 4/19/1999 in Concord; John Stapleton and Mae Geddes

STARKEY,
Lowell G., Sr., d. 3/29/1984 at 73 in Barnstead; Don C. Starkey and Mary McMahon

STEARNS,
Hannah S., d. 4/10/1913 at 89/4/6; pneumonia; housekeeper; widow; b. Gilmanton; John Marston (Gilmanton) and Hannah Nutter (Barnstead)
Irving W., d. 3/25/1931 at 71; b. Manchester; Ezra B. Stearns and Hannah S. Thurston

STEVENS,
Edith F., d. 8/3/1963 at 85 in Concord; housewife; b. Barnstead; Jethro Locke and Electra Chesley
Ethel May, d. 7/18/1949 at 64/9/20 in Franklin*; b. Lyndonville, VT; Frederick E. Stevens and Mary Annie Shonyo
Fred E., d. 12/25/1935 at 73; b. Quebec; Edmund Stevens and Sarah Caswell
Gertrude H., d. 9/19/1906 at 22/6/29; acute Bright's disease; married; b. Manchester; Orin D. Sawyer (Hill) and Ellen M. Rogers (Manchester)
James K., d. 6/5/1893 at 66/8/6; organic disease of liver; farmer; married
Mary A., d. 8/7/1911 at 78/9/16; apoplexy; widow; b. Barnstead; Aaron Snell (Pittsfield) and Mary Nutter
Mary F., d. 11/22/1887 at 67; housework; married; b. Barnstead; ---- Thurston
May A., d. 6/7/1926 at 64; b. North Cumberland, NY; Joseph Hovey and May Sharp
Olive, d. 1843 at 60**
Thur. B., d. 8/31/1906 at 0/0/1; premature birth; b. Barnstead; Timothy Stevens (Bedford) and Gertrude Sawyer (Manchester)

STEVENSON,
Gordon L., d. 1/1/1999 in Ctr. Barnstead; ----- Stevenson and Ida Crawford
James C., d. 3/27/1988 at 74 in Barnstead; George Stevenson and Utiville Campbell
Lester Edwin, d. 4/10/1968 at 76 in Barnstead; salesman; b. MA; Robert E. Stevenson and Emma -----

STEWART,
James E., d. 11/5/1943 at 80 in Barnstead; b. Scotland; James Stewart

STILES,
William J., d. 1850 at 23**

STIMPSON,
Maggie, d. 3/22/1922 at 40*; b. Boston, MA

STOCK,
Annie Rosenquist, d. 3/13/1993 at 71 in Barnstead; Iver O. Pettersen and Eline M. Eriksen
Arthur Henry, d. 6/24/1975 at 71 in Barnstead; fireman & steam eng.; b. MA; Herbert G. Stack (sic) and Annie M. Henry
Hamilton Henry, d. 12/14/1992 at 53 in Barnstead; Arthur Henry Stock and Martha C. Henry
Herbert A., d. 4/16/1963 at 54 in Hartford, VT; truck driver; b. Reading, MA; Herbert Stock and Annie Henry
Martha C., d. 4/13/1995 at 92 in Ctr. Barnstead; Hamilton M. Henry and Cora C. Russell
Richard Hamilton, d. 5/4/1971 at 45 in Ctr. Barnstead; carpenter; b. Manchester; Arthur H. Stock and Martha Henry
Robert Perry, d. 8/7/1993 at 64 in Barnstead; Arthur H. Stock and Martha C. Henry

STOCKBRIDGE,
Abigail, d. 3/23/1889 at 74/2; housekeeper; widow; b. Barnstead; Stephen Clough (Gilmanton) and Mercy Sanborn (ME)
Edgar P., d. 11/21/1916 at 69/6/14; farmer; widower; b. Alton; William G. Stockbridge (Alton) and Adeline Stockbridge (Alton)

Nancy S., d. 3/2/1913 at 68/10; la grippe; housewife; married; b. Barnstead; Nathaniel Nutter (Barnstead) and Margaret Tuttle (Barnstead)

STOCKMAN,
Everett L., d. 7/6/1992 at 71 in Conocrd; Everett L. Stockman and Josephine Dennett

STONE,
John W., d. 6/19/1937 at 58; b. Brookfield, MA; John Stone and Rose Filleon
Mary Jane, d. 4/16/1938 at 66; b. Tilton Ville, OH; William E. Ellis and Mary E. West

STRACHAN,
Anna Davis, d. 3/24/1949 at 78/3/6 in Barnstead; b. Hooksett; Jesse Cate and Cynthia Davis
George Edgar, d. 8/13/1933 at 1*; b. Concord; Guy R. Strachan and Maud T. Corson
Guy R., d. 9/14/1953 at 46 in Concord; b. NH; Charles E. Strachan and Addie Arlin

STRAW,
Alba Chase, d. 7/23/1940 at 80*; b. Barnstead; Thomas S. Straw and Louisa A. Hill
Cecil T., d. 3/13/1966 at 50 in Barnstead; floorman; b. Barnstead; Alba Straw and Celia Tibbetts
Celia M., d. 9/28/1909 at 27/2/11; maemia; housewife; married; b. New Durham; George F. Tibbitts (Farmington) and Clara E. Chesley (New Durham)
Charles H., d. 2/15/1911 at 79/5/8; old age; farmer; single; b. Barnstead; Samuel Straw and Lizzie Eastman
Louisa A., d. 7/16/1901 at 74; heart disease; married
Mary E., d. 7/27/1897 at 77; housewife; widow; b. Barnstead

STREETER,
Charles, d. 6/10/1960 at 80 in Manchester; painter; married; b. Whitefield; Arnold Streeter and Olive Whiting

SULLIVAN,
Edward, d. 1/19/1985 at 62 in Concord; Ernest Sullivan and Yolande Duhamel
Ellen, d. 10/28/1892 at 54; dropsy; housewife; married; b. Ireland
George W., d. 5/24/1973 at 30 in Barnstead; plumber; b. Boston, MA; James F. Sullivan and Madeline Ladrook
Joanne Marie, d. 5/24/1973 at 4 in Barnstead; b. Boston, MA; George W. Sullivan and Eileen Harrison
John E., d. 1/27/1910 at 54/1/24; tumor; engineer; single; b. Lynn, MA; George Sullivan (Ireland) and Eileen Murphy (Ireland)
John F., d. 4/2/1959 at 64 in Barnstead
John L., d. 10/7/1962 at 17 in Barnstead; b. Farmington; Thomas W. Sullivan and Gladys T. Wilkes
Linda Marie, d. 5/24/1973 at 5 in Barnstead; b. Boston, MA; George W. Sullivan and Eileen Harrison
Suzanne Carol, d. 5/24/1973 at 2 in Barnstead; b. Boston, MA; George W. Sullivan and Eileen Harrison
T. G., d. 4/3/1888 at 28/1/10; shoemaker; married; b. Lynn, MA; Mark Sullivan (Ireland) and Margaret Hingston (Ireland)
Thomas W., d. 7/30/1980 at 76 in Barnstead; Cornelius M. Sullivan and Annie Keaney
Timothy Joseph, d. 8/12/1967 at 78 in Barnstead; blacksmith; b. Lynn, MA; Timothy D. Sullivan and Nora O'Meara

SWAIN,
Florence, d. 8/13/1964 at 71 in Concord; housewife; b. Barnstead; Herbert Gray and Murty Cate
Henry B., d. 2/28/1939 at 46*; b. Northwood; Walter L. Swain and Etta Bartlett

SWAINE,
William N., d. 3/8/1893 at 78/3/24; prostate gland enlargement and inflammation; farmer; widower; Stephen Swaine and Sarah Sweet

SWANSON,
Victor, d. 4/13/1977 at 81 in Ctr. Barnstead; cabinet maker - carpenter; b. Sweden; Sven Swanson

SWEENEY,
Margaret M., d. 3/6/1986 at 64 in Concord; Thomas McGrath and Margaret Brennan

SYLVAIN,
Antonio Joseph, d. 1/13/1974 at 72 in Manchester; ret. maintenance; b. NH; Francoise Sylvain and Alphonsine Lessard
Ethel L., d. 4/30/1979 at 60 in Concord; Arthur C. Emerson and Essel M. Clough

SYLVIA,
Priscilla, d. 9/2/1932 at 5*; b. Farmington; John Sylvia and Gladys Wilkes

TARBOX,
Charles L., d. 9/1/1932 at 91; Andrew Tarbox and Phoebol Holt
Julia A., d. 8/16/1930 at 87; James A. Tuck and Abigail Huntress

TASKER,
Albert F., d. 2/11/1922 at 74*; b. Barnstead; Seth Tasker (Barnstead)
Alice, d. 1/5/1988 at 104 in Concord; T. Frank Seward and Mary Chesley
Alma M., d. 8/23/1964 at 55 in Ctr. Barnstead; housewife; b. Pittsfield; John Berry and Alphonsine Frenette
Arthur L., d. 6/13/1910 at 0/1/24; marasmus; b. Barnstead; Arthur W. Tasker (Barnstead) and Helen L. Merrill (Haverhill, MA)
Arthur W., d. 2/27/1954 at 70 in Laconia; b. NH; Albert F. Tasker and Georgia Scruton
Arthur William, d. 8/15/1971 at 80 in Barnstead; auto mechanic; b. Barnstead; Andrew Tasker and Jane George
Betsey M., d. 9/26/1914 at 82/8/5; organic disease of heart; housekeeper; widow; b. Barnstead; Arthur Bickford (Barnstead) and Jane Pendergast (Barnstead)
Charles G., d. 10/13/1937 at 71; b. Barnstead; John Tasker and Sarah C. Johnson
Emery Arthur, d. 5/22/1945 at 19 in Germany*; b. Barnstead; Arthur Tasher (sic) and Helen L. Merrill
Frank, d. 12/21/1925 at 71

Georgia A., d. 11/24/1915 at 62/2/7; none; divorced; b. Pittsfield; Levi C. Scruton (Strafford) and Dorothy H. Foss (Barnstead)
Harry W., d. 11/22/1977 at 74 in Concord; bus driver; b. NH; Arthur W. Tasker and Alice M. Seward
Helen L., d. 4/16/1964 at 72 in Barnstead; housewife; b. Haverhill, MA; John F. Leighton and Catherine Bean
Herbert E., d. 5/28/1927 at 68*; b. Strafford; Paul Tasker and Polly Hill
Horace, d. 12/14/1926 at 70; b. Strafford; Paul Tasker and May Hill
Ira, d. 1836 at 37**
Jane, d. 7/25/1927 at 64; b. Barnstead; Smith George and Elmira Waldron
Jessie F., d. 8/16/1986 at 72 in Manchester; Edward Hickey and Nellie Sargent
John, d. 1797 at –**
John, d. 9/11/1934 at 96 in Milford*
Joseph, d. 1833 at 77**
Leonard G., d. 1/30/1993 at 73 in Barnstead; Arthur Tasker and Ellen Merrill
Malcolm, d. 11/13/1924 at 20; b. Barnstead; Arthur W. Tasker and Alice M. Seward
Mary A., d. 1/21/1943 at 79 in Strafford*; b. Strafford; Richard W. Foss and Emily Place
Mary J., d. 2/22/1922 at 71/4/3*; b. Barnstead; Seth Tasker
Mary L., d. 8/28/1965 at 67 in Concord; housewife; b. Epsom; Frank Wheeler and Lillian Hilliard
Nathaniel, d. 1817 at 53**
Philip G., d. 6/21/1990 at 38 in Manchester; Leonard Tasker and Jessie Hickey
Richard, d. 11/17/1936 at 23 in Wolfeboro*; Arthur Tasker and Helen Merrill
Sally, d. 1837 at 56**; widow of Nathaniel
Sally, d. 1834 at 78**; widow of Joseph
Sarah, d. 4/25/1921 at 82/8/14; b. Chichester; James J. Johnson (Pittsfield) and Eleanor Prescott (Chichester)

TAYLOR,
Arline, d. 4/16/1990 at 70 in Barnstead; Edwin Taylor and Emily Garlic

TEBBETS,
Mrs. Robert, Esq., d. 1845 at 88**
Robert, Esq., d. 1842 at 83**

TEBBETTS,
Clara, d. 3/24/1899 at 52; disease of brain; housewife; married
Cyntha, d. 1/10/1894 at 71/2; asthma; housework; widow
Dorothy, d. 1832 at 68**; wife of John
Ephraim, d. 1840 at 86**
Eunice, d. 1867 at 82**; widow of Josiah
John, d. 1854 at 89**
John F., d. 5/12/1889 at 63; housekeeper (sic); married; b. Barnstead; Robert Tibbetts (sic) (Barnstead) and Hannah Mooney (Alton)
Josiah, d. 1840 at 56**
Nancy A., d. 1/20/1910 at 62/8/2; apoplexy; housewife; married; b. Londonderry; Tilly H. Wheeler and Rebecca Goodwin

TEDCASTLE,
Elaine, d. 4/5/2000 in Concord; Herman Dame and Edna Banks

THATCHER,
Ethel Maude, d. 5/25/1967 at 77 in Barnstead; housewife; b. England; Albert Morton and Amy Iliff
John, d. 2/16/1942 at 80 in Marlboro*; b. Shepard, PQ; James Thatcher and Julia A. Williams
Lettie A., d. 4/5/1957 at 86 in Chesterfield; b. Danbury; Joseph Hillsgrove and Lydia M. Webster

THAYER,
Owen M., d. 11/29/1928 at 79*; b. Providence, RI
Ruby E., d. 3/6/1945 at 48/9/22 in Concord*; b. Barnstead; Owen H. Tuttle and Nettie Foss

THING,
John S., d. 1/1/1890 at 59/8/16; farmer; widower; b. Alton; Mark P. Thing (Gilford)

THOMAS,
Frederick G., d. 1/8/1955 at 68 in Nashua; b. England
Rosie M., d. 11/12/1959 at 85 in Barnstead

THOMPSON,
Audrey S., d. 2/14/1959 at 66 in Barnstead
Betsey J., d. 7/17/1913 at 88/1/22; tumor; widow; b. Tuftonboro; Silas Bunker (Barnstead) and Sarah Nerrow (Milton)
Carolyn, d. 2/1/1944 at 48/2/16 in Barnstead; b. Philadelphia, PA; Harry Hogancamp and Jean Cornell
Hattie M., d. 12/25/1958 at 95 in Concord
Henry P., d. 4/2/1912 at 87/7/5; pleuro pneumonia; farmer; married; b. Gilmanton; Seni Thompson (Gilmanton) and Mathilda Jacobs (Barnstead)
Josephine, d. 2/22/1943 at 81 in Pittsfield*; b. Barnstead; Ezekiel Babb and Almira Babb
Louis F., d. 4/17/1986 at 69 in Concord; Louis Fischer and Shirley Spurr
Millard H., d. 9/20/1945 at 47/7/25 in Barnstead; b. Barnstead; Silas Thompson and Jane Babb
Ray Charles, d. 60/10/4 in Barnstead; b. Farmington; Herman Thompson and Hattie Dow
Silas L., d. 4/2/1939 at 76*; b. Barnstead
Vernol M., d. 8/10/1984 at 65 in Manchester; Millard Thompson and Carolyn Hogencamp

THOROUGHGOOD,
Ralph H., d. 12/18/1990 at 54 in Concord; Wesley Thoroughgood and Erma Whitham
Timothy Scott, d. 10/25/1967 at 0/0/0 in Concord; b. Concord; Ralph H. Thoroughgood and Phillis Alma Young

THURSTON,
Daniel W., d. 1852 at 26**
Hannah, d. 1868 at 75**; widow of John
John, d. 1859 at 66**

THYNG,
Addie S., d. 7/30/1945 at 82/1/13 in Newmarket*; b. Gilmanton; Charles Tibbetts
Charles E., d. 1/17/1931 at 74; b. Alton; John S. Thyng and Anne Mooney
Ora A., d. 12/28/1927 at 64; b. Dover; James A. Fletcher and Elizabeth Miller

TIBBETTS,
Flora Belle, d. 4/15/1932 at 0/8; b. Haverhill; Charles Tibbetts and Elsie Tibbetts
Hattie E., d. 2/17/1941 at 74 in Concord*; b. Portsmouth; John H. Chase and Mary M. Chase
Hiram P., d. 12/6/1908 at 69; organic disease of heart; farmer; widower; b. Barnstead; John Tibbetts (Barnstead) and Annie Felton (Barnstead)
John W., d. 11/29/1952 at 77 in Concord*; b. NH; Hiram P. Tibbetts and Jennie Hanson

TIEDE,
Elfrieda G., d. 3/27/1999 in Barnstead; Ernst Tiede and Louise Solger
Ernst E., Sr., d. 2/4/1991 at 64 in Concord; Ernst Tiede and Louise Solger
Louise J., d. 8/28/1990 at 92 in Barnstead; Johan Solger

TILTON,
Frank E., d. 4/30/1908 at 45/6/19; shock sev. thigh; brakeman; divorced; b. Pittsfield; John S. Tilton (Pittsfield) and Betsy J. Cram (Pittsfield)
George E., d. 10/1/1965 at 63 in Manchester; textile mill; b. Pembroke; George Tilton and Hattie E. Call

TOBINE,
Leona M., d. 5/26/1958 at 87 in Concord

TOMASZEWSKI,
Mabel H., d. 12/6/1983 at 60 in Manchester; William Reece and Angeline Pedro

TOMLINSON,
Dallas T., d. 12/4/1961 at 49 in Barnstead; custodian; b. Buena Vista, VA; Cyrus T. Tomlinson and Annie B. Tyree

TOWLE,
Abigail, d. 1844 at 33**; wife of Roby
Alan Scott, d. 9/3/1968 at 80 in Concord; executive secretary; b. NH; George W. Towle and Addie M. Abbatt
Betsey, d. 1832 at 68**

Christine D., d. 3/12/1974 at 79 in Concord; housewife; b. MA; Philip S. Deane and Mary Kennard

TRASK,
son, d. 1/10/1910 at --; stillborn; b. Barnstead; Alvin Trask (Mt. Vernon, ME) and Nellie E. Foss (Strafford)

TRICKEY,
Benjamin, d. 1869 at 83**
Thomas, d. 1867 at 37**

TROSKY,
Rosalin, d. 3/11/1976 at 58 in Laconia; housewife; b. NY; Max Adelstein and Bessie Bassin

TRUETT,
Kimberly Ann, d. 10/13/1990 at 0/4 in Hanover; Kenneth D. Truett and Shelli B. Kearsley

TUDOR,
Andrew, d. 7/16/1996 at 83 in Concord; John T. Tudor and Mary Williams
John T., d. 10/18/1953 at 79 in Barnstead; b. England; Nathan W. Tudor and Elizabeth Whittle
Margaret, d. 8/20/1992 at 85 in Barnstead; John Tudor and Mary Williams

TURCOTTE,
baby boy, d. 12/1/1935 at 0; b. Barnstead; Homer Turcotte and Leona Marcou

TUTTLE,
Achsah K., d. 2/1/1913 at 72/4/25; car. of bowels; housekeeper; widow; Stephen P. Willey and Sarah J. Babb (Strafford)
Alice J., d. 10/8/1934 at 93 in Manchester*; John Hill and Betsy Foss
Anna H., d. 4/28/1954 at 78 in Wolfeboro; b. Soderholm, Sweden; John Norin and Brekhen Kappa
Bertha, d. 9/9/1930 at 18; b. Barnstead; Charles Tuttle and Anna Norin
Betsey, d. 1872 at 69**; wife of John J.

Charles, d. 2/8/1950 at 73/6/17 in Barnstead; b. Northwood; George Tuttle and Isabel Davis
Charles H., d. 1871 at 50** "of great tumors"
Curtis C., d. 1872 at 57**
Daniel, d. 7/24/1887 at 69/11/9; farmer; married; b. Barnstead
Daniel E., d. 4/29/1899 at 66/11/12; heart disease; farmer; married; b. Barnstead; John J. Tuttle and Betsey Jacobs
Dolly, d. 1825 at 73**; wife of John
Enos G., d. 1/23/1914 at 89; cardir vas'lar dis; farmer; widower; b. Barnstead; Isaac Tuttle (Barnstead) and Sophia Jacobs (Barnstead)
George, d. 1/4/1918 at 77/10/29; b. Barnstead; Hanson Tuttle (NH)
George S., d. 4/19/1999 in Barnstead; Charles Tuttle and Anna Norin
Gordon A., d. 7/7/1944 at 10/3/10 in Canterbury*; b. Barnstead; George S. Tuttle and Lillian Buzzell
Isabelle, d. 1/18/1929 at 84; b. Barnstead; David Davis and Nancy Collin
James C., d. 11/1/1903 at 66/3/16; organic disease of heart; farmer; married; b. Barnstead; Hanson Tuttle (Strafford) and Sally Willey (Strafford)
John, d. 1827 at 75**
John (Col.), d. 1854 at 70**
Joseph, d. 1851 at 77**
Lillian G., d. 12/31/1994 at 86 in Barnstead; Charles Buzzell and Maybelle Gray
Linthia E., d. 9/18/1913 at 71/0/6; paresis; b. Pittsfield; John O. Kenison (Epsom) and Hannah Blake (Barnstead)
Nettie L., d. 11/29/1945 at 83/5/5 in Rochester*; b. Rochester; Mark Foss and Livonia Berry
Owen H., d. 12/27/1946 at 82/2/17 in Rochester*; b. Barnstead; Cyrus Tuttle and Alice Hill
Peter W., d. 7/6/1943 at 72 in Concord*; b. Athens, ME
Phebe, d. 1848 at 67**; wife of Joseph
Ruth, d. 3/6/1897 at 49/10; cancer; housework; widow
Sally, d. 1825 at 39**; wife of Col. John
Sally, d. 1848 at 70**; wife of Thomas
Sarah J., d. 11/6/1892 at 49/0/9; insanity; b. Barnstead; Hanson Tuttle (Strafford) and Sally G. Mills (Strafford)
Sophia J., d. 10/10/1888 at – in Lynn, MA; widow; b. Barnstead

TWOMBLY,
Addie, d. 10/18/1927 at 60*; b. Center Stratford
Albert H., d. 8/27/1897 at 38/3/27; pleuritis; shoemaker; married; b. Strafford; Paul Twombly
Arthur G., d. 7/20/1894 at 1/9; meningitis; b. Barnstead; Charles H. Twombly (Barnstead) and Lizzie Riggs (Kittery, ME)
Charles H., d. 6/28/1938 at 81*; b. Barnstead; Paul Twombly and Nancy Davis
Ellen, d. 9/17/1888 at 3/9; b. Strafford; Irving Twombly (Barnstead) and Elizabeth Hall (Strafford)
Emeline, d. 6/29/1892 at 53/8; heart failure; housekeeper; widow; b. Epsom; Aaron Marsh and Sarah Marden
Ernest F., d. 7/27/1891 at 5/1/4; b. Barnstead; Charles H. Twombly (Barnstead) and Lizzie Twombly (Kittery, ME)
Leroy E., d. 1/27/1948 at 73/9/3 in Newington*; b. Pittsfield; Elbridge A. Twombly and Emily Marsh

UNDERHILL,
Anabella, d. 7/23/1948 at 76/6/16 in Concord*; b. Manchester; Theophilus Blake and Rebecca Richards
Florence A., d. 2/15/1920 at 14/8/6; b. Barnstead; Arden Underhill (Orange) and Annabelle Blake (Manchester)
Frank T., d. 3/9/1913 at 68/6/25; chronic nephritis; farmer; married; b. Orange; Robert Underhill and Elmina Thompson

VAN DER ZEE,
Jacob, d. 10/22/1960 at 76 in Barnstead; professor; married; b. The Netherlands; Bouke Van der Zee and Janna Van der Weg

VARNEY,
Dorothy E., d. 12/25/1909 at 90/10/16; organic disease of heart; widow; b. Barnstead; Simeon Lougee and Mary Edgerly
Fred O., d. 2/15/1935 at 79; b. Farmington; J. H. F. H. Varney and Julia Downing
Ida A., d. 10/14/1954 at 96 in Ctr. Barnstead; b. Swampscott, MA; Torrey Peabody and Margaret Bryant
Ira, d. 1871 at 70**
John C., d. 7/10/1979 at 84 in Epsom; John Henry Varney and Ida A. Chesley
John Henry, d. 6/24/1936 at 85 in Barnstead
Mary, d. 1871 at 70**; wife of Ira

Ruth B., d. 10/16/1980 at 82 in Concord; Marshall A. Berry and Maud A. Perkins
Susanna H., d. 6/1/1939 at 80*

VENO,
Francis P., d. 9/9/1975 at 84 in Ctr. Barnstead; moulder; b. Canada; Daniel Veno and Christina Gould
Georgiana M., d. 3/11/1973 at 79 in Concord; housewife; b. ME; Felix LaFontaine and Mary Poulin

VIEN,
Alfred H., Jr., d. 11/15/1993 at 53 in Concord; Alfred H. Vien, Sr. and Blanche E. Durrell

VOLKMANN,
Theodore R., d. 8/31/1969 at 83 in Concord; sign painter; b. Germany; Robert G. Volkmann and Henriette Evers

VROMAN,
Fred, d. 2/22/1971 at 86 in Dover; b. Copuskill, NY; Roy Vroman and Cynthia Carl
Mabel, d. 10/30/1962 at 75 in Concord; b. Dover; Plummer Smith and Izetta Wiggin

WAKEFIELD,
Carrie Belle, d. 5/18/1950 at 81/1/21 in Barnstead; b. Belchertown, MA; Horace White and Susan -----
Josephine M., d. 10/26/1969 at 75 in Concord; inspector; b. NH; William Davis and Ada -----

WALDO,
Sarah A., d. 2/18/1905 at 65/10; cancer of breast; housewife; widow; b. Deerfield; Ephraim Wilson (Nottingham) and Sally Green (Pittsfield)

WALDRON,
Herbert, d. 12/12/1888 at 3; b. Barnstead; Samuel Waldron (Strafford) and Clara M. Church (Enfield)
Martha B., d. 6/16/1988 at 66 in Concord; Robert Busse and Helen Bowman

WALKER,
Abigail, d. 1856 at 58**; wife of Joseph A.
Albert D., d. 3/17/1901 at 51/6/10; heart disease; farmer; married; b. Strafford; Edward Walker (Strafford) and Paulina Walker (Strafford)
Augusta W., d. 5/12/1898 at 68/4/10; carcinoma; housewife; widow; b. Barnstead; Samuel Webster
Betsey, d. 1851 at 64**; widow of William, Jr.
Betsy, d. 1/11/1892 at 78/11/9; pneumonia; housewife; widow; b. Barnstead; Joseph Bunker and Olive Otis
Charles E., d. 12/11/1918 at 79/6/4; b. Barnstead; John Walker (Barnstead) and Betsy Bunker (VT)
Elizabeth, d. 1843 at 82**; widow of William
Hannah, d. 5/1/1895 at 84/8; hamplegia; widow; b. Barnstead; Samuel York and Ruth Hall
Jane, d. 2/2/1920 at 80/6/9*; b. E. Kingston; Charles Titcome (Newburyport, MA) and Sara Smith (E. Kingston)
John, d. 1/11/1892 at 80/6; old age; farmer; married; b. Barnstead; William Walker (Newington) and Betsy Dow
Joseph A., d. 1864 at 63**
Kenneth L., d. 10/5/2000 in Ctr. Barnstead; ----- and Minnie Banfield
Mark, d. 1826 at 21**
Mary, d. 5/9/1890 at 91/3/27
Ruth, d. 1852 at 49**; widow of Samuel
Samuel, d. 1843 at 43**
Seth (Capt.), d. 1843 at 28**
William (Dr.), d. 1828 at 27**
William, d. 1832 at 73**
William, M.D., d. 1855 at 27**
William, Jr., d. 1844 at 58**

WALLACE,
Glenn C., d. 5/17/1945 at 32/2/11 in Concord*; b. Concord; Norman M. Wallace and Ivy M. Palmer
Ivy, d. 6/8/1963 at 77 in Concord; laundress; b. Barnstead; Frank Palmer and Ida J. Shackford
Margaret, d. 1848 at 45**; wife of Capt. William

WARD,
Augustus S., d. 9/9/1941 at 79 in Alton*; b. St. John, NB; George Hamilton and Margaret Hamilton

Beulah M., d. 9/13/1962 at 77 in Manchester; housewife; b.
    Barnstead; John H. Bartlett and Mary Foss

Joseph F., d. 6/10/1924 at 83; b. Orleans, MA; Ithmer Ward and
    Mercey Rogers

Ralph J., d. 4/15/1966 at 80 in Manchester; ret., police dept.; b.
    Manchester; James S. Ward and Janet Reid

William, d. 7/21/1936 at 78 in Barnstead

WAR'ND,
Henrietta, d. 11/18/1902 at 78; abscess of liver; widow; b.
    Barnstead; Benjamin Hoitt (Hampstead) and Mahitable Rab'sn
    (Hopkinton)

WARREN,
Florence M., d. 11/13/1894 at --; died at birth; b. Barnstead; John H.
    Warren (Chichester) and Florence M. Shackford (Barnstead)

Florence M., d. 11/11/1947 at 73 in Lynn, MA*; b. Barnstead

WATSON,
Hattie F., d. 9/20/1945 at 35/4 in Somerville, MA*

J. T., d. 5/28/1907 at 83/10/19; senile gangreen; farmer; widower;
    b. Alton; Joseph Watson (Farmington) and Mary Peterson
    (Strafford)

Phyllis A., d. 5/4/1981 at 39 in Concord; Wilburn H. Sargent and
    Emma E. Newbegin

Sarah E., d. 9/25/1896 at 75/2/12; pneumonia; housewife; married;
    b. Strafford; Simon Foss and Sarah Blake

WATTS,
Robert Allen, Sr., d. 3/7/1993 at 64 in Barnstead; Harry Watts and
    Emma Voight

WEAVER,
Gerald Byron, d. 9/26/1996 at 69 in Manchester; Charles Weaver
    and Unice Hillsgrove

WEBSTER,
Allen G., d. 4/20/1933 at 49*; b. Grafton; Emma Webster

Betsey, d. 1857 at 36**; wife of Robert

Caroline, d. 1871 at 46**; second wife of Caleb

Edwin H., d. 1/25/1947 at 83/3/14 in Concord*; b. Barnstead; Robert S. Webster

Eliza, d. 1858 at 43**; wife of Caleb

George N., d. 6/3/1892 at 65/2/12; anemia; shoemaker; married; b. Gilmanton; Benjamin Webster (Kingston) and Sally Prescott (Hampton Falls)

Ina T., d. 9/4/1970 at 91 in Lancaster; teacher; b. NH; James C. Tuttle and Alice Hill

Joseph, d. 4/9/1901 at 75/2/7; pneumonia; minister; married; b. Springfield; Reuben Webster (Springfield) and Lydia Fifield (Salisbury)

Lois, d. 1852 at 69**; wife of Nathaniel

Lois, d. 8/27/1889 at 91/5/1; widow

Mary A., d. 11/10/1932 at 72*; b. Strafford; Abram S. Clark and Sarah E. Limball

Samuel, Esq., d. 1855 at 62**

Samuel F., d. 1/4/1937 at 80; b. Danbury; Jewell Webster

Sarah A., d. 5/28/1910 at 82/8/8; chronic nephritis; housewife; widow; b. Strafford; Samuel Otis (Strafford) and Lydia Smith (Strafford)

WEDEMEYER,

Karl Heinz, d. 5/30/1991 at 71 in Barnstead; Karl Wedemeyer and Charlotte Volkmann

WEEKS,

Alfred H., d. 12/26/1980 at 52 in Rochester; Henry P. Weeks and Myrtie Hanson

Alice E., d. 4/28/1935 at 77; b. Peabody, MA; Albert Berry and Melissa McNeal

Charles T., d. 2/3/1931 at 76; b. Alton; Noah Weeks and Sarah McNeil

Jesse Fremont, d. 12/17/1949 at 92 in Laconia*; b. Gilmanton; Mathias Weeks and Laurinda Hilliard

Minnie O., d. 9/9/1932 at 62; b. Laconia; George W. Woodhouse and Eliza F. Tebbetts

Myrtie E., d. 4/6/1963 at 73 in Concord; housewife; b. Barnstead; Levi Hanson and Abbie Clark

Susie M., d. 12/14/1919 at 72/1*; b. Barnstead; Joseph D. Proctor (Barnstead) and Sarah Ayers (Gilmanton)

WELCH,
Alonzo J., d. 6/13/1934 at 64 in Barnstead; John W. Welch and Josephine Clark
Euclid P., d. 10/2/1918 at 19/0/29; b. Tunbridge, VT; Fred Welch (Barnstead) and Annie Lyman (Tunbridge, VT)
Frank Warren, d. 12/26/1969 at 85 in Barnstead; farmer; b. Pittsfield; John Welch and Josephine Clark
Fred T., d. 9/15/1983 at 74 in Concord; Frank W. Welch and Sarah Morrison
John W., d. 12/31/1919 at 87/8/25; b. Barnstead; Jonathan Welch (Barnstead) and Nancy Durgin (Barnstead)
Josephine A., d. 8/24/1917 at 73/11/13; b. Barnstead; Ezekiel Clark (Barnstead) and Hannah Littlefield (S. Brunswick, ME)
Mary (Mrs.), d. 1852 at 97**
Rena E., d. 7/15/1992 at 82 in Concord; Ernest Wells and Laura Jones
Sadie E., d. 12/21/1940 at 54; b. Rochester; James Morrison and Fanny Atkins

WELLS,
Edgar S., Jr., d. 7/21/1908 at 0/3/24; marasmus; b. Barnstead; Edgar S. Wells (England) and Gertrude O'Driscoll (Boston, MA)
Ernest Lesley, d. 6/10/1951 at 73 in Barnstead; b. Alton; Horace Wells and Ida E. Hill
Eugene Y., d. 8/31/1978 at 62 in Concord; foreman ordinance man; b. NH; Walter B. Wells and Sophronia M. Yeaton
Evelyn, d. /7/1915 at 0/7/14; b. Barnstead; Edgar Stanley Wells (England) and Gertrude F. O'Driscoll (Boston, MA)
Frank, d. 6/14/1911 at 0/0/0; stillborn; b. Barnstead; Edgar S. Wells (England) and Gertrude Driscoll (Boston, MA)
Ida E., d. 2/1/1941 at 84 in Barnstead; b. Alton; Samuel D. Hill and Samson Wallingford
Joan G., d. 2/14/1977 at 47 in Concord; housewife; b. NH; George S. Carr and Ella May Powell
Walter B., d. 1/24/1972 at 80 in Concord; equipment operator; b. Epsom; Edgar E. Wells and Laura H. Flint

WENTWORTH,
Anna, d. 1867 at 72**; widow of William B.

Harriett P., d. 12/31/1921 at 81/6/28; b. Barnstead; John Gerry (Hillsboro) and Lucy A. Sturtevant (Croftsburg, VT)
Irving, d. 8/31/1948 at 77/8/29 in Ossipee*; b. Wolfeboro; Mark Wentworth and Harriet Geiry
William B., d. 1851 at 50**

WEST,
Mrs. Samuel, d. 1868 at 70**

WESTERBERG,
Paul J., d. 11/19/1993 at 57 in Barnstead; A. John Westerberg and Elizabeth Swenson

WEYDEMANN,
Marjorie M., d. 9/21/2000 in Concord; Raymond Adams and Mildred Blake

WHEAT,
Harvey A., d. 8/23/1953 at 76 in Barnstead; b. Groton; Josiah Wheat and Hannah Southwick

WHEELER,
Abbie M., d. 6/2/1930 at 70; b. Gilmanton; George W. Griffin and Mary H. Hill
Frank A., d. 7/31/1968 at 85 in Concord; saw mill operator; b. NH; Loren A. Wheeler and Abbie Griffin
George Leon, d. 9/5/1923 at 43; b. Pittsfield; Loren A. Wheeler and Abbie M. Griffin
Goldie M., d. 10/28/1959 at 75 in Concord
Jane J., d. 5/2/1892 at 94/1/3; influenza; widow; b. Barnstead; Jeremiah Jewett (Rowley) and Temperance Dodge (Rowley)
Loren A., d. 1/3/1943 at 90 in Barnstead; b. Canterbury; Joseph C. Wheeler and Arvilla Gould
Louis M., d. 2/8/1895 at 0/9; scrofula; b. Barnstead; Loren Wheeler and Abbie Griffin
Mabel P., d. 3/16/1953 at 71 in Barnstead; b. Pittsfield; Loren A. Wheeler and Abbie Griffin
Mary H., d. 4/26/1921 at 83/9/11; b. Barnstead; William Garland (Barnstead) and Mary J. Hall (Strafford)

WHEET,
Abbie A., d. 12/21/1927 at 68; b. Groton; Andrew J. McClure and Abbie C. Heath
Bessie W., d. 12/31/1970 at 76 in Barnstead; housewife; b. NH; David Leroy McDuffee and Emma Besse
David J., d. 2/17/1994 at 62 in Concord; Rexford E. Wheet and Bessie McDuffee
Rexford E., d. 12/28/1973 at 76 in Barnstead; carpenter & farmer; b. Groton; Josiah Wheet and Abbie G. McClure

WHITCHER,
Alice G., d. 3/6/1937 at 46; b. Everett, MA; Alfred Stedman and Louise Ingals
Harold P., d. 2/15/1952 at 64 in Concord*; b. Strafford; Joseph E. Whitcher and Abigail Perkins

WHITE,
James W., d. 5/1/1990 at 49 in Concord; Arthur White and Linda Arey

WHITEHOUSE,
Charles, d. 8/26/1919 at 73/5/15; b. Canada; Daniel Whitehouse (Alton) and Belinda Tufts (Middleton)
Olive B., d. 9/6/1935 at 53; b. New Haven, VT; ----- St. John and ----- Marquet

WHITING,
Joan M., d. 12/15/1967 at 82 in Concord; b. Germany; Frank Dietzel and Marie -----
Maurice T., d. 8/22/1972 at 89 in Epsom; businessman; b. ME; Warren T. Whiting and Ellen E. Muzzey
Randall K., d. 11/16/1971 at 14 in Strafford; student; b. MD; Clinton T. Whiting and Eleanor Culliford

WHITNEY,
George J., d. 10/21/1937 at 76; b. Barnstead; Joseph Whitney and Ann Hale

WHITTAKER,
Emma J., d. 5/8/1927 at 53; Alexander Barnaby

WHITTEN,
Charles E., d. 10/20/1905 at 43/10/19; pulmonary tuberculosis; shoemaker; single; b. Meredith; G. V. Whitten (Holderness) and Madeline Porter (Scotland)

WHITTIER,
Adelbert J., d. 6/4/1916 at 67/4/4; optician; married; b. Canaan; Abner Whittier (Canaan, VT) and Sarah Hoyt (VT)
Linda H., d. 8/1/1936 at 80 in Concord*; Charles Hodgdon and Miriam York
Sarah, d. 5/14/1889 at 71; housekeeper; widow; Moses Hoyt (Canaan) and ----- (Meredith)

WHITTING,
Ferdinand E., d. 5/29/1939 at 63*; b. VA

WIGGIN,
George E., d. 6/4/1909 at 65/11/5; apoplexy; on railroad; married; Jacob Wiggin (Lee) and Caroline Smart (Newmarket)
Lizzie M., d. 9/19/1927 at 55*; b. Pittsfield; Samuel Nutter and Lydia Hinds

WIGGINS,
Mercy Jacobs, d. 1833 at 40**; wife of D.

WILD,
infant, d. 6/19/1887 at –; William Wild (Boston) and ----- (Bath)

WILE,
Rupert F., d. 7/5/1910 at 0/0/2; undeveloped; b. Barnstead; Lawrence Wile (NS) and Mary E. Linscott (Pittsfield)

WILHELM,
Caroline W., d. 3/7/1946 at 83/6/15 in Barnstead; b. Steinback, Germany; Christoph Holland-Cunz and Maria Holland Cunz

WILKES,
George T., d. 5/6/1937 at 72; b. Thompson, CT

WILLET,
Lillian, d. 1/16/1932 at 67*; b. Barnstead; Jerthro Locke and Electa Chesley

WILLEY [see Willy],
Eliza, d. 2/9/1894 at 79/3; heart disease; housewife; widow
Isaac, d. 1856 at 79**
Jacob, d. 1853 at 85**
Mary A., d. 4/25/1906 at 72/9/15; heart disease; housewife; married; b. Barnstead; Levi Evans (Strafford) and Abigail Caswell (Barrington)
Sally, d. 1855 at 89**; widow of Jacob
Theodore, d. 1834 at 70**

WILLIAMS,
Elberton G., d. 7/3/1974 at 66 in Barnstead; rate clerk; b. MA; Thomas E. Williams and Alice E. Leishman
Irving W., d. 3/9/1946 at 19/4/3 in Barnstead; b. Milton; Ralph J. Williams and Lillian J. McCartan
Mary A., d. 4/18/1897 at 82/0/26; pneumonia; single; Thomas Williams and Hannah Lane

WILLIAMSON,
Edith C., d. 1/7/1925 at 69; b. Barnstead; Oliver G. Caswell and Wealth Ann Clark

WILLY [see Willey],
John C., d. 4/13/1925 at 82; b. Barnstead; Jacob Willy and Eliza Priest

WILSEY,
John D., d. 5/30/1979 at 81 in Concord; Philip Wilsey and Flora Gurnsey
Margery Maud, d. 8/2/1970 at 81 in Ctr. Barnstead; housewife; b. NH; Herbert House and Adelaide Davies

WILSON,
Esther, d. 6/19/1986 at 91 in Laconia; Richard H. Bond and Lillian Wilson

Lydia M., d. 5/7/1908 at 60/6/29; myelitis; superintendent; married; b. Lynn, MA; Archibald Selman (Marblehead) and Fanny Brown (Pt. Hawksbury)

WINGARD,
Bowman C., d. –/–/1981 in MA

WINKLEY,
Benjamin, d. 1851 at 79**
Betsey, d. 1863 at 85**; widow of Benjamin
Elizabeth, d. 1841 at 66**; wife of Benjamin
Elizabeth W., d. 3/17/1928 at 67*; b. Parsonsfield, ME; Jere O. Winkley and Frances Nutter
Herman P., d. 2/9/1961 at 86 in Concord; farmer; b. Stratford; Paul H. Winkley and Jennie Holmes
Lurie F., d. 12/25/1937 at 74; b. Parsonsfield, ME; Jess O. Winkley and Frances Nutter
Paul H., d. 2/16/1920 at 86/0/1*; b. Barnstead; Paul Winkley (Strafford) and Lydia Jones (Strafford)
William, d. 6/15/1974 at 57 in Concord; farmer; b. NH; Herman P. Winkley and Winnifred Chesley
Winifred E., d. 8/10/1920 at 41/3/17; b. Barnstead; Charles L. Chesley (Barnstead) and Martha J. Bodge (Barnstead)

WITHAM,
Martha J., d. 10/12/1961 at 78 in Concord; housewife; b. Northwood; Walter Pender and Anna Trombley
Roy W., d. 3/8/1958 at 58 in Pittsfield

WOOD,
Almon G., d. 2/28/1961 at 73 in Barnstead; laborer; b. Thornton; Elmer Wood and Emma Tourtelot
Chloe B., d. 8/27/1965 at 76 in Concord; housewife; b. Colebrook; Levi Brooks and Ann Terrill

WOODHOUSE,
E. F., d. 4/1/1907 at 70/1/18; paralysis; widow; Esrel Tibbetts

WORCESTER,
Charles, d. 5/11/1905 at 86/6; organic disease of heart; farmer; widower; b. Thornton; Noah Worcester and Elizabeth Brown

Sarah, d. 12/4/1903 at 86/7/20; uremia; domestic; married; b. Barnstead; Solomon Munsey and Olive Beck

WORDEN,
Jean A., d. 4/26/1999 in Concord; Frederick Archambo and Jennie Weller
Mary K., d. 6/19/1989 at 66 in Concord; Albert LaCroix and Rosetta Benoit

WORK,
Charles Ludwig, d. 2/19/1976 at 85 in Concord; gasoline station manager; b. Germany

WRIGHT,
Daniel, d. 8/11/1890 at 53
George W., d. 11/1/1997 at 58 in Concord; Mark Rupercht and Helen Horn
Harold M., d. 2/24/1998 in Hawaii; Stanley Wright and Grachea Fike

YEATON,
Earle M., d. 3/15/1986 at 68 in Concord; William H. Yeaton and Ethel G. Gray
William H., d. 9/18/1958 at 68 in Concord

YORK,
Betsey, d. 1845 at 72**; wife of Samuel
Samuel, d. 1854 at 82**
Samuel, Jr., d. 1863 at 65**

YOUNG,
child of Percy C. Young, d. 3/12/1893 at --; premature; b. Barnstead; Percy C. Young (Belmont) and Clara B. Young (Wilmot)
Alice, d. 2/28/1937 at 56; b. Barnstead; Frank E. Palmer and Ida J. Shackford
Benjamin N., d. 9/11/1980 at 73 in Concord; Orrin B. Young and Chloe B. Brooks
Bivet, d. 8/18/1947 at 69/6/23 in Concord*; b. Barnstead; Hanson H. Young and Priscilla A. Sackett

Charles E., d. 5/20/1933 at 72; b. Barnstead; John H. Young and Elizabeth Caswell

Claribel, d. 11/8/1949 at 75 in Laconia*; b. Wilmot; Joseph Hillsgrove and Lydia Margaret Webster

Cora Josephine, d. 10/10/1916 at 49/6/21; single; b. Laconia; Lemeral D. Young (MA) and Mary Ellen Somers (Laconia)

Dolly, d. 1862 at 80**; widow of Phineas

Edna P., d. 1/31/1982 at 75 in Concord; Carl Lakeman and Lottie MacFadden

Elizabeth A., d. 4/3/1891 at 58/8; housekeeper; married; b. Barnstead; Enoch Caswell and Judith Flanders (Alton)

Emily J., d. 4/10/1899 at 70/11/19; heart disease; housekeeper; married; b. Barnstead; John J. Tuttle and Betsey Jacobs

Hanson H., d. 12/14/1923 at 80; b. Barnstead; Samuel P. Young and Betsey A. Merrill

Harley, d. 4/30/1923 at --; b. NH; John S. Young

John H., d. 3/9/1905 at 77/8/9; anemia; farmer; widower; b. Dover; David Young (Barnstead) and Eliza Hartford (Strafford)

John M., d. 3/15/1920 at 89/6/10; b. Barnstead; David Loring (Strafford) and Eleanor M. Nutter (Barnstead)

Jonathan, d. 1861 at 62**

Leonard E., d. 2/9/1974 at 73 in Concord; motorman & starter; b. Medford, MA; Leonard Young and Esther Drew

Mary Ellen, d. 2/9/1915 at 76/4/5; widow; b. Laconia

Mary Jane, d. 9/22/1921 at 72/5/9; b. Barnstead; David Young (Strafford) and Eleanor Nutter (Barnstead)

Matilda, d. 8/27/1904 at 71; dysentery; housekeeper; married

Norman C., d. 8/4/1938 at 25; b. Stewartstown; Orrin B. Young and Chloe B. Brooks

Orin Benjamin, d. 1/28/1950 at 75/3/12 in Barnstead; b. Stewartstown; Benjamin Young and Miranda Covell

Percy C., d. 11/11/1949 at 75/10/17 in Laconia*; b. Belmont; John Young and Mehitable Cole

Phineas, d. 1848 at 72**

Priscilla A., d. 6/15/1935 at 86; b. Barnstead; Noble Sackett and ---- Jacobs

Robert, d. 8/7/1947 at 0/0/1 in Concord*; b. Concord; Benjamin Young and Edna Lakeman

Willis E., d. 12/12/1946 at 80/0/21 in Barnstead; b. Clarksville; Edmund Young and Ruth A. Cass

ZANES,
son, d. 8/26/1891 at –; b. Barnstead; Noah M. Zanes (Pembroke) and Nellie E. Blake (Gilmanton)

ZECHA,
Anna, d. 3/23/1940 at 38*; b. Jamaica Plains, MA; Henry Zecha and Bertha Zecha
Bertha, d. 1/19/1935 at 57; b. Germany; Frederick Kiefer
Gertrude M., d. 8/4/1970 at 67 in Alton; housewife; b. Keene; George W. Barnes and Grace M. Rowe
Henry, d. 11/9/1945 at 72/4/4 in Barnstead; b. Austria; Ferdinand Zecha and Anna Hager

Other Heritage Books by Richard P. Roberts:

Alton, New Hampshire Vital Records, 1890-1997

Barnstead, New Hampshire Vital Records, 1887-2000

Barrington, New Hampshire Vital Records

Dover, New Hampshire Death Records, 1887-1937

Gilmanton, New Hampshire Vital Records, 1887-2001

Marriage Records of Dover, New Hampshire, 1835-1909

Marriage Records of Dover, New Hampshire, 1910-1937

Milton, New Hampshire Vital Records, 1888-1999

Moultonborough, New Hampshire Vital Records

New Castle, New Hampshire Vital Records, 1891-1997

New Hampshire Name Changes, 1768-1923

New Hampshire Name Changes, 1923-1947

Ossipee, New Hampshire Vital Records, 1887-2001

Rochester, New Hampshire Death Records, 1887-1951

Vital Records of Durham, New Hampshire, 1887-2002

Vital Records of Effingham and Freedom, New Hampshire, 1888-2001

Vital Records of Farmington, New Hampshire, 1887-1938

Vital Records of Lyme and Dorchester, New Hampshire, 1887-2004

Vital Records of New Durham and Middleton, New Hampshire, 1887-1998

Vital Records of North Berwick, Maine, 1892-2002

Vital Records of Orford and Piermont, New Hampshire, 1887-2004

Vital Records of Tamworth and Albany, New Hampshire, 1887-2003

Vital Records of Tuftonboro and Brookfield, New Hampshire, 1888-2005

Vital Records of Wakefield, New Hampshire, 1887-1998

Vital Records of Warren, New Hampshire, 1887-2005

Wolfeboro, New Hampshire Vital Records, 1887-1999

www.ingramcontent.com/pod-product-compliance
Lightning Source LLC
Chambersburg PA
CBHW060909300426
44112CB00011B/1395